MW01054701

Analysis of Evidence

This is an enjoyable and rigorous introduction to the construction and criticism of arguments about questions of fact, and to the marshalling and evaluation of evidence at all stages of litigation. It covers the principles underlying the logic of proof; the uses and dangers of story-telling; standards for decision and the relationship between probabilities and proof; the chart method and other methods of analyzing and ordering evidence in fact-investigation, in preparing for trial, and in connection with other important decisions in legal processes and in criminal investigation and intelligence analysis. Most of the chapters in this new edition have been rewritten; the treatment of fact investigation, probabilities and narrative has been extended; and new examples and exercises have been added. Designed as a flexible tool for undergraduate and postgraduate courses on evidence and proof, students, practitioners and teachers alike will find this book challenging but rewarding.

Terence Anderson is Professor of Law at the University of Miami. He is an experienced litigator and teacher of courses on methods of analysis, evidence and trial practice. His writings include articles developing and illustrating topics covered in this book.

David Schum is Professor of Law and of Systems Engineering at George Mason University and Honorary Professor of Evidence Science, University College London.

William Twining is Quain Professor of Jurisprudence Emeritus, University College London, and a regular Visiting Professor at the University of Miami School of Law. His writings on evidence include *Rethinking Evidence* (2nd edn., Cambridge University Press).

Law in Context

The series is a vehicle for the publication of innovative scholarly books that treat law and legal phenomena critically in their social, political and economic contexts from a variety of perspectives. The series particularly aims to publish scholarly legal writings that bring fresh perspectives to bear on new and existing areas of law taught in universities. A contextual approach involves treating legal subjects broadly, using materials from other social sciences, and from any other discipline that helps to explain the operation in practice of the subject under discussion. It is hoped that this orientation is at once more stimulating and more realistic than the bare exposition of legal rules. The series includes original books that have a different emphasis from traditional legal textbooks, while maintaining the same high standards of scholarship. They are written primarily for students of law and of other disciplines, but most also appeal to a wider readership. Recent publications include books on globalization, transnational legal processes, and comparative law. In the past, most authors have come from, or been based in, Europe or the Commonwealth. In the future, we also expect to publish authors from, or based in, the United States or Canada, particularly those who adopt a clear transatlantic perspective. The books will include subject areas that have a transnational significance, drawing on European as well as North American scholarship.

Series Editors
William Twining, University College London
Christopher J. McCrudden, University of Oxford

Books in the series
Anderson, Schum & Twining: *Analysis of Evidence*
Ashworth: *Sentencing and Criminal Justice*
Barton & Douglas: *Law and Parenthood*
Bell: *French Legal Cultures*
Bercusson: *European Labour Law*
Birkinshaw: *European Public Law*
Birkinshaw: *Freedom of Information: The Law, the Practice and the Ideal*
Cane: *Atiyah's Accidents, Compensation and the Law*
Clarke & Kohler: *Property Law: Commentary and Materials*
Collins: *The Law of Contract*
Davies: *Perspectives on Labour Law*
de Sousa Santos: *Toward a New Legal Common Sense*
Diduck: *Law's Families*
Elworthy & Holder: *Environmental Protection: Text and Materials*
Fortin: *Children's Rights and the Developing Law*
Glover-Thomas: *Reconstructing Mental Health Law and Policy*
Gobert & Punch: *Rethinking Corporate Crime*
Harlow & Rawlings: *Law and Administration: Text and Materials*
Harris: *An Introduction to Law*
Harris: *Remedies in Contract and Tort*

Harvey: *Seeking Asylum in the UK: Problems and Prospects*
Hervey & McHale: *Health Law and the European Union*
Lacey & Wells: *Reconstructing Criminal Law*
Lewis: *Choice and the Legal Order: Rising above Politics*
Likosky: *Transnational Legal Processes*
Maughan & Webb: *Lawyering Skills and the Legal Process*
Moffat: *Trusts Law: Text and Materials*
Norrie: *Crime, Reason and History*
O'Dair: *Legal Ethics*
Oliver: *Common Values and the Public-Private Divide*
Oliver & Drewry: *The Law and Parliament*
Picciotto: *International Business Taxation*
Reed: *Internet Law: Text and Materials*
Richardson: *Law, Process and Custody*
Roberts & Palmer: *Dispute Processes-ADR and the Primary Forms of Decision Making*
Scott & Black: *Cranston's Consumers and the Law*
Seneviratne: *Ombudsmen: Public Services and Administrative Justice*
Stapleton: *Product Liability*
Turpin: *British Government and the Constitution: Text, Cases and Materials*
Twining: *Globalisation and Legal Theory*
Twining & Miers: *How to do Things with Rules*
Ward: *A Critical Introduction to European Law*
Ward: *Shakespeare and Legal Imagination*
Zander: *Cases and Materials on the English Legal System*
Zander: *The Law-Making Process*

Analysis of Evidence

Second edition

Terence Anderson
Professor of Law, University of Miami

David Schum
Professor of Systems Engineering and Law, George Mason University

William Twining
Quain Professor of Jurisprudence Emeritus, University College London

with online appendices at
www.cambridge.org/9780521673167
by Philip Dawid, University College London

CAMBRIDGE UNIVERSITY PRESS
Cambridge, New York, Melbourne, Madrid, Cape Town, Singapore, São Paulo

Cambridge University Press
The Edinburgh Building, Cambridge CB2 2RU, UK

Published in the United States of America by Cambridge University Press, New York

www.cambridge.org
Information on this title: www.cambridge.org/9780521673167

First published 1991 by Little, Brown & Co., Boston and by Little, Brown & Co. (Canada) Ltd.,
Toronto.

Re-issued 1998 by Northwestern University Press.

This edition published in 2005 by Cambridge University Press.

Printed in the United States of America

A catalogue record for this book is available from the British Library

ISBN-13 978-0-521-67316-7 paperback
ISBN-10 0-521-67316-X paperback

To our children and grandchildren
To Anne, Carolyn, and Penelope

Contents: summary

Contents

Preface
The why, what, and how of this book

The why

Inferential reasoning, analyzing and weighing evidence, forming judgments about what has happened in the past or what is likely to happen in the future are a necessary part of coping with the problems of everyday living. They are basic human skills that form part of ordinary practical reasoning. Historians, detectives, doctors, engineers, and intelligence analysts have to develop and apply these skills with rigor and precision in specialized professional contexts. So do lawyers.

These skills have not traditionally formed part of professional training. Perhaps this is because they are perceived to be "mere common sense"; or because it has been felt that they can only be learned by practical experience "on the job"; or because of a belief that these are matters of "intuition" or that great lawyers or historians or detectives or diagnosticians are "born and not made."[1]

This book starts from a different premise. Building on the work of the American legal scholar John Henry Wigmore (1863–1943), we believe that skills in analyzing and marshaling evidence and in constructing, criticizing and evaluating arguments about disputed questions of fact are intellectual skills that can and should be taught effectively and efficiently in law schools. They are as essential a part of "legal method" as legal analysis and reasoning about questions of law. Common sense, intuition, and practical experience all have a part to play in exercising these skills, but they are not adequate substitutes for a systematic grounding in what Wigmore called "the principles of proof." This book is designed to enable students to lay a foundation and to develop the basic skills to a high degree before they enter practice as lawyers or in other spheres of activity that involve practical reasoning.

Between us we have accumulated more than fifty years of experience in teaching analysis of evidence in a variety of courses in several different countries. This book builds on that experience. It is designed as a flexible tool to lay a foundation for mastering a necessary set of basic intellectual and professional skills in fact analysis. They include techniques for structuring a problem and organizing a mass of data (macroscopic analysis) and techniques for detailed analysis and evaluation of

1 For a detailed account see *Rethinking* Ch. 2.

particular data and phases of complex arguments (microscopic analysis). Our main purpose is to present a vehicle for learning certain usable basic skills of analysis, argument, and practical problem-solving. The primary audience is law students, especially in courses on evidence and trial practice, but the early chapters and many of the examples can be used to learn about and develop skills of inferential reasoning in other contexts.

The what

Chapter 1, "Evidence and inference: some food for thought," is a series of materials, cases, questions, and exercises. These are designed to achieve three objectives. First, to engage the interest of students and other readers, we have included some familiar and not so familiar examples illustrating the range of contexts in which inferential reasoning is necessary or useful. Second, we have provided examples that introduce concepts and issues that are developed in the remainder of the book so that readers can actively think about them from the outset. Third, these materials include concrete examples and exercises that are used as the basis for explaining and illustrating materials presented in later chapters. We have deliberately presented a wide variety of materials so that teachers can select which examples to use to introduce the subject and which can be studied later or omitted altogether. All of these examples have been used in the classroom, none of the authors use them all in one course, and each has his favorites. This is not a reading chapter; rather the idea is to encourage readers to engage actively with some concrete examples before moving on to the more abstract material that follows. Some teachers have used selected examples to illustrate concepts in subsequent chapters that students have been assigned to read later. Others may choose to recommend that their students begin by reading Chapters 2 and 3, referring back to particular examples as they appear in the text.

Chapter 2, "Fact investigation and the nature of evidence," introduces basic concepts and considerations that apply to evidence and inference across many contexts, with particular reference to the generation and testing of hypotheses in the process of any kind of factual investigation. This is illustrated vividly by the problem of "connecting the dots" in intelligence analysis. It deals specifically with the idea of "a substance-blind approach," which considers the basic inferential characteristics or credentials of evidence (relevance, credibility, and probative force) without regard to the substance or content of the evidence or to the context of the inquiry. This classification of evidence allows us to say general things about evidence regardless of its substance.

Chapter 3, "Principles of proof," develops these ideas in a legal context. It describes the "Rationalist Tradition" that has been the foundation of Anglo-American evidence scholarship and explains why it is relevant to contemporary legal practice. It identifies the forms of logic that must be used in analyzing evidence or in justifying conclusions based upon evidence and demonstrates how they can be applied to legal disputes, using the final exercise in Chapter 1, "An investigation."

Chapter 4, "Methods of analysis," introduces the main methods of analysis used in preparation for trial and their relations to each other: chronologies, the outline method, narrative, and the chart method. It presents a general seven-step protocol that fits all of them, using the material from the *O. J. Simpson* case from Chapter 1 to illustrate its application. We have included this generalized account as a separate chapter for two reasons: first, some teachers may wish to provide an overview of approaches without going into detail about the chart method. Second, in our experience we have found this an effective way of easing students into the rigors of the chart method.

Chapter 5, "The chart method," is the heart of the book for those who wish to master the most rigorous method of analysis. It is a substantially revised version of the method that Wigmore developed for the analysis of mixed masses of evidence early in the last century. It is an intellectual procedure for analyzing and organizing a complex body of evidential data and demonstrating precisely how the inferences from that data can be marshaled in support of and in opposition to the ultimate proposition that must be proved. It also makes it possible to subject selected phases of a complex argument to rigorous microscopic analysis. Such analysis can be used to identify and construct arguments about whether evidence should be admitted or its use restricted, as well as to evaluate the strengths and weaknesses of the particular phase of the argument based upon that data. Each step of the method is illustrated using *United States v. Able* and the *O. J. Simpson* example from Chapter 1.

Chapter 6, "Outline, chronologies, and narratives," considers other methods of analysis in the context of litigation. The outline method is a familiar device. Variations of it are common. It is, on its face, less difficult to grasp and easier to use than the chart method. Chronologies and narratives are other devices commonly used in practice to organize the available evidence and to develop and test arguments based on that evidence. Part C of that chapter, "The litigation context," describes which of the methods is best suited to the various stages of a case.

Chapter 7 uses an edited version of the record of *R. v. Bywaters and Thompson* to illustrate how the chart method can be applied to a complex decided case. The questions at the end have been organized to reflect the seven-step protocol. In our experience, if students immerse themselves in the detail and then are guided through the case using these questions step by step they readily grasp the basics of Wigmorean analysis. However, other cases involving mixed masses of evidence about which there is scope for reasoned disagreement, such as Sacco and Vanzetti, or O. J. Simpson, or the Lindbergh Baby (Bruno Hauptman), or any other complex case, can also be used for this purpose, provided that a detailed record is available and there is a historical doubt about the event.

Wigmore's presentation of the principles of reasoning and methods of analysis falls squarely within the mainstream of Anglo-American scholarship, but he did not satisfactorily address a class of problems that are important for lawyers and that have emerged in recent debates as central issues for scholars. How is the strength of an inference to be determined? How is the net persuasive value of a mass of evidence to be assessed? How are judgments about the probative force of different items of evidence to be combined? How can the lawyer (or the trier of fact) determine whether a mass of evidence, which logically supports the truth of the proposition ultimately to be proved, satisfies the applicable standard of proof? What do we mean when we say a proposition has been proven to be "more probable than not," proven by "clear and convincing evidence," or proven "beyond a reasonable doubt"? We confront these problems in Chapters 8 and 9.

Chapter 8, "Evaluating evidence," first presents the traditional vocabularies that lawyers and others use in arguing about these issues in court. The next part, "Standards for decision," introduces the distinction between standards intended to guide the decision-makers' exercise of discretion, such as the standards defining the burden of proof, and standards designed to define the limits of discretion, such as the standards that appellate courts apply in deciding whether the decision below exceeded those limits. That part moves beyond the familiar standards of proof to consider standards for other decisions that are involved in the total process of litigation from the first interview of a client to pre-trial decisions, through the trial process and beyond, including standards for lawyers' decisions, decisions to prosecute, and other standards for decision in litigation and adjudication.

Chapter 9, "Probabilities, weight, and probative force," provides a basic introduction to probability theory. It outlines the debates about the application of different theories of probability in legal contexts and elucidates some basic concepts. These debates mainly focus upon whether probability theory should be used in evaluating evidence for cases-as-a-whole – i.e. arguments to a judge or jury. As a practical matter, practitioners, judges, and most legal academics have rejected the use of Bayes's Theorem and other axioms of probability for these purposes, but have recognized that they should play a role in specific contexts – for example, in paternity suits, or disparate impact cases, as the basis for many scientific or expert opinions, or in wrongful death or total disability cases. There are further reasons why lawyers should be familiar with these concepts. Probability assessments have an important role as an aid to making many pre-trial decisions. The decision to prosecute or to contest a case requires analysis of the probability that liability or guilt will be established and, in a civil case, an estimate of the probable quantum of damages. Negotiations to settle a case or to reach a plea agreement are often argued in terms of probability assessments made by each of the parties.[2] Lawyers also need to be equipped to recognize fallacies and misuses of statistics that may be made by their opponents.

Chapter 9 provides the theoretical background to the separate appendix on Probabilities and Proof by Philip Dawid, which is included on the website for this book.[3] The appendix is a basic practical introduction to statistical method applied to

2 A simple formula for negotiating a settlement is discussed in Ch. 8 with an exercise based on *Sargent v. General Accident Co.*, a case presented for other purposes in Ch. 1.
3 Appendix I at www.cambridge.org/9780521673167. There is a second Website for the book at http://analysisofevidence.law.miami.edu/.

legal examples. It explores the theoretical and practical problems posed by the use of mathematical probabilities in evaluating evidence. It introduces some basic axioms of probabilistic analysis and, through a series of problems and exercises, illustrates their application in contexts such as DNA, paternity suits, discrimination cases, and actuarial analysis.

Chapter 10, "Necessary but dangerous," explores at greater length the roles of generalizations and stories in argumentation about questions of fact and the relations between them. This is mainly a theoretical chapter, but it includes two simple protocols that a lawyer might use in testing key generalizations or potential stories in preparing for trial.

Chapter 11, "The principles of proof and the law of evidence," explores the intimate relationship between the principles of proof and the law of evidence, recapping on points where the connections have been touched on previously, especially in relation to basic concepts and exploring these in more detail in relation to hearsay.

Chapter 12, "The trial lawyer's standpoint," integrates the materials and methods introduced in Chapters 2 to 11 into the practical context of preparation for trial. This chapter includes two simple traffic cases that have been adapted from exercises used at the Inns of Court School of Law in London and two more complex problems drawn from the oldest National Trial Competition in the United States. We have found that these cases work well either as a basis for class discussion or as problems for simulated mini-trials on either side of the Atlantic.

Changes in this edition

First, David Schum has joined us as a co-author. Trained in probability and psychology, he has in recent years been concerned with evidence as a multi-disciplinary subject. In *Evidential Foundations of Probabilistic Reasoning* (1994) he argued that other disciplines had a lot to learn about evidence from law, but that lawyers could also benefit by considering those features of evidence that cross all or most disciplines. This "substance-blind" approach to relevance, credibility, and probative force is introduced in Chapter 2, with particular reference to investigation and inquiry in both legal and non-legal contexts.

Second, scientific evidence, such as DNA, and the bearing of probability theory and practical statistics on evidence in legal contexts have increased in importance in recent years. Chapter 9 contains a brief introduction to probability theory; the Appendix provides a practical introduction to the application of statistical methods to legal issues as an optional extra. Placing this on the website has made it possible to shorten the hard copy of the book, while substantially expanding the treatment of statistics.

Third, Wigmorean analysis has become much better known outside legal circles as well as within law. Specialists in decision theory, artificial intelligence, and in other areas have taken great interest in assisting intelligence analysts in "connecting the dots" or trying to make sense out of masses of evidence. Wigmore's methods are now being routinely applied in such efforts. They have also been applied to investigation of multiple crimes and insurance fraud (Schum (1987), Leary (2003), Twining (2003)). We have expanded the scope of this edition to take account of such developments, especially in relation to intelligence analysis post 9/11.

Fourth, there have been many developments in the law of evidence, civil and criminal procedure, and in scientific evidence.[4] Evidence scholarship has continued to be a lively and pluralistic field. It is now a well-established area in comparative law. Evidence is becoming increasingly recognized as an exciting multidisciplinary subject of great importance in many spheres of practical activity (Schum (1994); Twining and Hampsher-Monk (2003); Twining (2003)). The first edition did not deal in detail with how the principles of proof and the law of evidence interact. We have added Chapter 11 in order to make this relationship clear and to facilitate the integration of the logic of proof and the rules of evidence in teaching.[5]

All of these developments have been taken into account in revising this edition. However, the principles of inferential reasoning, the basic concepts, and the skills involved in analyzing and marshaling mixed masses of evidence are quite stable. We have retained examples that we have found work well in teaching, even though some of them are quite old. We have dropped others and streamlined the presentation. We have tried to make the book more flexible and accessible to a variety of users, by giving clearer signposts.

Throughout this period the authors have continued to think, write, and teach in this area. Our ideas have continued to develop and we have learned from the experience of using the first edition in teaching and from the critical feedback of hundreds of students and some colleagues. Almost all our students have found the process of learning the method challenging and hard work (the motto of our courses has been "tough, but fun"); nevertheless, the vast majority have succeeded in mastering the basic techniques and many have produced work of outstanding quality. Interestingly, the subject has worked best with first year law students in Miami, where it is a popular elective in the second semester. Many of our students have reported that they have found the approach very helpful in practice, some claiming that it was the most useful course that they had in law school. Of course, they

---

4 For England these developments are surveyed in Zander (2003), Dennis (2004), and Roberts and Zuckerman (2004).

5 Throughout this edition we indicate important points of contact between the principles of proof and the law of evidence. For this purpose, we have used the Federal Rules of Evidence (as amended up to Dec. 1, 2002). This is a coherent, accessible, and important code that falls four-square within the Rationalist Tradition. In respect of English law we make regular reference to Ian Dennis, *The Law of Evidence* (2nd edn, 2002), especially Chs. 1–4, which is generally in tune with our approach. So is Roberts and Zuckerman, *Criminal Evidence* (2004). Michael Zander's *Cases and Materials on the English Legal System* (9th edn, 2003) contains useful discussions of debates and reforms concerning evidence and procedure in recent years. The main points of direct connection between the principles of proof and the law of evidence concern matters such as the basic concepts, relevance, standards of proof, and judicial notice, topics in respect of which there are not great differences between common law jurisdictions.

do not spend time drawing elaborate charts in straightforward cases, but the basic techniques of evidence marshaling and argument construction can become habits of mind that are invaluable and efficient in handling both simple and complex cases. This is hardly surprising because Wigmore's method is essentially a systematization of the "best practice" of good lawyers.

Most of our students and some colleagues are converts. Moreover, the type of analysis involved in the chart method has in recent years attracted interest in a number of fields, including police investigation, intelligence analysis, and various other spheres of practical decision-making (Schum (1987); Leary (2003), Twining (2003)). There are, however, still some skeptics, not least among teachers of the law of evidence (Roberts (2002), Murphy (2001); response by Twining (2005)). We have tried to address their central criticism that the first edition was too substantial and complex to use in an ordinary law of evidence course, and we hope that this edition is more accessible and user friendly.

How to use this book

Our main purpose is to present a vehicle for learning certain usable basic skills of analysis, argument, and practical problem-solving; hence this book can be used as core or supplemental material in a variety of ways and in a variety of courses. Chapter 1 contains a number of concrete examples and exercises that can be used selectively for different purposes.

First, the book can be used as the basis for a self-standing course on analysis of evidence. All three authors have used it in this way for over a decade in a postgraduate course in London, in first degree courses for lawyers and non-lawyers at George Mason University, and, most successfully, as a popular first year elective at the University of Miami Law School.

Second, this edition has been designed so that it can also be used as part of orthodox evidence courses. Anderson has regularly used it during the first three weeks of a standard four-credit course on the Law of Evidence in Miami; Twining teaches it as the first third of the year-long course on Evidence and Proof in the London LLM, the second half of which is devoted to selected topics in the Law of Evidence, the remainder being devoted to a brief introduction to statistical analysis. Other law teachers who have tried to introduce this approach at the start of their courses on evidence have tended to find the first edition too substantial and too dense to use in three to four weeks. With this in mind we have reorganized the book, shortened several chapters, and indicated more clearly how the principles of proof underpin and are integrated into evidence doctrine. We have also provided some guidance to teachers who wish to take some short cuts in order to fit this subject into a few weeks.

We would emphasize, however, that there are no short cuts to learning the basic skills involved. If the learning objectives include mastering the basic techniques of evidence marshaling and the construction and criticism of rigorous arguments about disputed questions of fact, these can only be acquired by repeated practice involving exercises that are inevitably time consuming for students. However, it is our experience that a student who has acquired these skills can much more rapidly and efficiently understand the law of evidence and its practical applications. In short, studying analysis of evidence takes time, but it also saves time. In our view, the basic approach can be taught in a minimum of eight to ten contact hours together with at least two written exercises.

Third, while the obvious and tested uses are in basic or advanced courses in evidence and trial or pre-trial advocacy, we believe that some chapters can also be usefully employed in any skills course that seeks to develop the intellectual component of practical lawyering skills (and indeed in pre-law and other undergraduate courses concerned with rigorous reasoning about disputed questions of fact). Handling evidence is a basic human skill and a neglected aspect of "thinking like a lawyer." Wigmorean analysis is beginning to feature in the training of intelligence analysts, police investigators, and others. It deserves to be a regular part of the curriculum of first degrees in law.

Acknowledgments

This book has been in gestation for over thirty years. During this period we have become indebted to so many people that it is impossible to name them all. In addition to those to whom inadequate acknowledgment was made in the first edition, we have since incurred many further debts. In preparing this edition, special thanks are due to colleagues, librarians, and deans in the law schools of George Mason University, the University of Miami and University College London; to Philip Dawid, who has prepared Appendix I on Probabilities and Proof for the website; to our students who have continued to be our most persistent critics and supporters; to Christopher Allen, Kola Abimbola, Ricardo Bacusas, Erica Becher-Monas, Philip Dawid, Ian Dennis, Jason Goldsmith, Michael Graham, Susan Haack, Richard Leary, Donald Nicolson, Mike Redmayne, Paul Roberts, Peter Tillers, and Bill Widen for many useful comments and suggestions; to Deborah Burns, Colette Hanna, Eileen Russell, Erna Stoddart, and, especially, Gloria Lastres, for unstinting assistance with word-processing, scanning, preparation of charts, and much else; to Noah Cox and Sisi Tran for research assistance; and, as ever, to our families, especially Anne, Carolyn, and Penelope for their tolerance, support, help, and love.

We are grateful to the sources identified below for permission to reprint or reproduce parts of the following works.

In Chapter 1, Harry Kemelman, *The Nine Mile Walk*, with copyright Harry Kemelman, is reproduced with permission of the author's agents. Extracts from *Morrison v. Jenkins*, 80 C.L.R. 626 (Aust. 1969) are reproduced with permission of The Law Book Company Ltd.

In Chapter 2, the cartoon at Figure 2.1 is reproduced with permission of both the artist John Trevor and the *Albuquerque Journal* in New Mexico.

In Chapter 7, the trial record extract from Filson Young, ed., *The Trial of Bywaters and Thompson* (2nd edn., 1951), is reproduced with permission of William Hodge and Company in Edinburgh.

In Chapter 12, the extract from Dart, *Is the Ford Motor Company Guilty of Killing Girls with a Pinto?* copyright 1980 by the Atlanta Constitution, is reproduced with permission. Exhibits and text *In the Matter of James Dale Warren (1981)* and the

United States v. Wainwright (1981) are reproduced with the permission of the Texas Young Lawyers Association and the National Trial Competition Committee.

Every effort has been made to secure necessary permissions to reproduce copyright material in this work, though in some cases it has proved impossible to trace copyright holders. If any omissions are brought to our notice, we will be happy to include appropriate acknowledgments on reprinting.

Table of cases

Causes célèbres[1]

Hypothetical cases

---

1 References to these *causes célèbres* are based upon materials in the trial record. Sources where
  additional information may be found are identified in the References. Additional sources can be
  found on the internet and at the websites for this book.

Table of legislation and rules

Abbreviations

Some of the points and themes in the text are treated at greater length in other writings by the authors. The following abbreviations for the most commonly cited works are used in the text and notes:[1]

Analysis	*Analysis of Evidence* (1st edn) by Terence Anderson and William Twining (1991)
Bazaar	*The Great Juristic Bazaar* by William Twining (2002)
Foundations	*Evidential Foundations of Probabilistic Reasoning* by David Schum (1994/2001)
Generalizations I	On Generalizations I: A Preliminary Exploration by Terence Anderson, 40 S. Texas. L. Rev. 455 (1999)
Rethinking	*Rethinking Evidence* by William Twining (1990/1994)
Sacco-Vanzetti	*A Probabilistic Analysis of the Sacco and Vanzetti Evidence* (1996)
Science	*The Science of Judicial Proof* by J. H. Wigmore (3rd edn, 1937)
Websites	www.cambridge.org/9780521673167; http://analysisofevidence.law.miami.edu

---

1 For full references see References at pages 388–95 below.

1

Evidence and inference: some food for thought

A. Introduction

> The field of evidence is no other than the field of knowledge. (Bentham, *An Introductory View,* Chapter 1)

> Evidence is the basis of justice: exclude evidence, you exclude justice. (Bentham, *Rationale of Judicial Evidence,* Part III, Chapter 1)

In this chapter we present some concrete examples and exercises that introduce the main questions and the basic concepts that are involved in analyzing evidence. The purpose of presenting them at this stage is partly to stimulate interest and puzzlement and partly to encourage you to start to think actively about some basic issues. We use many of the examples and exercises presented here to illustrate points developed later in the book.

The examples in part B raise questions about the similarities and differences involved in confronting problems of evidence and inference in different non-legal contexts, including bible stories, intelligence analysis, famous "analysts," and commonplace events. Each develops variations around the central theme that the kind of reasoning involved in all these different kinds of factual enquiries is based on the same underlying principles that apply differently as the contexts and standpoints vary.

The examples in part C illustrate the same central theme using examples from legal contexts. The first four examples introduce the process of imaginative reasoning and the roles that generalizations and stories play in arguments about disputed questions of fact. The remaining examples involve cases of increasing complexity that focus upon the kinds of analysis required at different stages of criminal and civil cases and raise issues about the relationship between law and fact, standards of proof, and inferential reasoning in both kinds of cases.

This book is concerned with techniques of analysis, but a central theme is that the logic of proof and the law of evidence are closely related and interdependent. *Sargent v Southern Accident Co.* and *United States v Able* were originally devised as examination questions in traditional evidence courses that had analysis of facts as a significant objective. Each item raises a number of interconnected issues dealing with the law of evidence and problems of proof within the context of a case as a whole. The final exercise, "An investigation," is intended as a vehicle for reviewing the basic concepts and for introducing a vocabulary for discourse about analysis and evaluation of evidence.

In our experience, all of these examples are good vehicles for use in teaching and reflection, but it is not necessary to introduce all of them at the start of a course. Several of the examples are used to illustrate important points in the text (principally, the cases involving Bywaters and Thompson, Sacco and Vanzetti, O. J. Simpson, the United States and Richard Able, Sargent and the Southern Accident Co., and An investigation). Readers and teachers may wish to postpone the detailed study of these until they come to the relevant topics.

B. Evidence and inference in non-legal contexts

1. Whose baby I? The judgment of Solomon

Then came there two women, that were harlots, unto the king, and stood before him. And the one woman said, O my lord, I and this woman dwell in one house; and I was delivered of a child with her in the house. And it came to pass the third day after that I was delivered, that this woman was delivered also: and we were together; there was no stranger with us in the house, save we two in the house. And this woman's child died in the night; because she overlaid it. And she arose at midnight, and took my son from beside me, while thine handmaid slept, and laid it in her bosom, and laid her dead child in my bosom. And when I rose in the morning to give my child suck, behold, it was dead: but when I had considered it in the morning, behold, it was not my son, which I did bear. And the other woman said, Nay; but the living is my son, and the dead is thy son. And this said, No; but the dead is thy son, and the living is my son. Thus they spake before the king.

Then said the king, The one saith, This is my son that liveth, and thy son is the dead: and the other saith, Nay; but thy son is the dead, and my son is the living. And the king said, Bring me a sword. And they brought a sword before the king. And the king said, Divide the living child in two, and give half to the one, and half to the other. Then spake the woman whose the living child was unto the king, for her bowels yearned upon her son, and she said, O my lord, give her the living child, and in no wise slay it. But the other said, Let it be neither mine nor thine, but divide it. Then the king answered and said, Give her the living child, and in no wise slay it: she is the mother thereof. And all Israel heard of the judgment which the king had judged; and they feared the king: for they saw that the wisdom of God was in him, to do judgment. (I Kings iii, 16–28)

Questions

1   Was this case concerned with
    a   the interpretation of a rule,
    b   a straightforward dispute about past facts,

   c solving a problem for the future, or

   d a combination of some or all of these?

2 Which of the following questions were pure questions of fact, and which were directly in issue in this case?

   a Who was the natural mother?

   b Who would look after the child better?

   c Who had a right to the child?

   d What disposition would be in the best interests of the child?

3 What general assumptions about the relations between mothers and children are implicit in this passage? Do you believe them to be universally or generally true today? What is the basis for your belief?

4 Do you think that (a) both women genuinely believed that the child was theirs? (b) both women believed that Solomon would carry out his threat?

5 Does this story suggest that Solomon's "wisdom" was founded on the notion that he was a clever investigator; a just judge; an enlightened problem-solver; or a potentially good poker-player?

6 There are different versions of the Bible. In the Revised Standard Edition of the Bible, the last sentence reads: "And all Israel heard the judgment which the king had rendered; and they stood in awe of the king, because they perceived that the wisdom of God was in him, to render justice." What evidence should a biblical scholar examine to determine which version is the most accurate? What standards should she apply? What evidence should a Justice of the United States Supreme Court examine to determine the meaning of a clause of the Constitution of the United States? What standards should the Justice apply?

2. The intelligence analyst: an intelligence scenario "from the top-down"

Investigations and inferences in intelligence analysis share many elements of such tasks that are performed in other areas such as law, medicine, history, and science. There are three disciplines in which persons performing analytic tasks must be prepared to encounter and evaluate every imaginable substantive kind of evidence; these disciplines are law, intelligence analysis, and history. Establishing the relevance, credibility, and inferential [probative] force of evidence is just as important in intelligence analysis as it is in law.

During fact investigation in law, as well as in intelligence investigations, hypotheses are generated as explanations for what is being observed. The generation of hypotheses requires imaginative reasoning mixed with critical reasoning. New hypotheses are put to use in generating new lines of inquiry and potential evidence. One criterion for assessing the merit of a new hypothesis concerns how well it assists the analyst in generating new and productive lines of inquiry that would not have been generated from other existing hypotheses. On occasion, the role of hypothesis generation is either downplayed or overlooked entirely. In some cases, new hypotheses come in the form of guesses about what has happened or what will happen. According to an old saying, hypotheses are like nets; only he who casts will catch. In every episode of fact investigation in law, intelligence analysis, or elsewhere, analysts have evidence in search of hypotheses at the same time as they have hypotheses in search of evidence. The following is an example from intelligence analysis in which a hypothesis is put to use in generating new observable evidence.

The generation of a new hypothesis from observations we make is frequently said to involve "bottom-up" reasoning; generation of new potential evidence from a hypothesis is said to involve "top-down" reasoning. In intelligence analysis, as in law, both forms of reasoning are necessary.

An important area of intelligence analysis is called "Indications and Warnings" (I & W). The purpose of I & W efforts is to alert decision-makers in our government and military organizations to the existence of possible immediate or near-term threats that are posed by hostile or potentially hostile forces or organizations. An obvious objective of I & W efforts today is to predict and prevent terrorist actions such as the destruction of the World Trade Center and parts of the Pentagon that we witnessed on September 11, 2001, during which more than 3,000 lives were lost. Those tragedies involved the hijacked domestic airliners used essentially as flying bombs. There is concern that such a method of destruction might be used again in the future. Unfortunately, there are other methods that terrorist organizations might employ in their efforts to cause loss of life, destruction, and widespread terror in our homeland.

You are a member of an I & W team. Based upon recent intelligence reports, your agency believes that there is a significant possibility that one or more terrorist groups are planning to commit a major terrorist action involving a "dirty bomb." Dirty bombs involve radioactive, but not fissionable, materials such as strontium, cobalt-60, and cesium 137. Such devices can be set off using conventional explosives such as TNT, Semtex, or C-4 plastic explosives. They are much less expensive to construct and require much less technical expertise.

A dirty bomb will simply have radioactive materials packed around a core of conventional explosives. Such devices can be triggered electronically from remote locations. When triggered, a dirty bomb can disperse radioactive material over a wide area. Though dirty bombs cause far less destruction and loss of life, they do produce serious consequences in any area where they are set off. Persons in the immediate vicinity will be subject to serious radiation and the surrounding area will be contaminated for long periods of time. A dirty bomb would certainly cause panic throughout any country in which it is set off.

Cesium 137 has already been employed in suspected terrorist activities. In March 1996 it was reported that certain Chechen leaders had threatened to expose the city of Moscow to radioactive devastation. Anonymous calls directed police officers to a park in Moscow where they would find a container of powdered cesium 137. Just a few ounces of this material could contaminate an entire city for decades. It is estimated that just one ounce of powdered cesium 137 released by a dirty bomb could spread radioactive fallout over 60 city blocks. Radioactive materials such as strontium, cobalt-60, and cesium 137 have been widely used for various medical and industrial purposes. For example, cesium 137 was used by the Soviets to bombard wheat and other seeds to see if radiated seeds would produce more abundant crops. It is also used in processing dental X-rays. Unfortunately, large numbers of canisters of cesium 137, and other radioactive wastes are known to be stored in facilities having little or no security. The Soviets appear to have left considerable stores of powdered cesium 137 in various places in Georgia. No one knows how much of this stored material has already been stolen or, possibly, sold.

Your I & W team has been assigned to the task evaluating the capabilities and intentions of a certain known terrorist organization codenamed X. Based on recent intelligence reports, your team has been asked to evaluate the hypothesis that group X may be planning one or more actions using dirty bombs. According to one report, a leader in group X was heard to boast that his group will have a very unpleasant surprise for an unnamed American city. According to another report, a person known to be a member of group X, codenamed "Ned," was dismissed in 2002 from a doctoral program in nuclear physics at a university in Germany.

The I & W team must identify and carefully state the hypothesis regarding terror-ist group X, taking into account the information it has. In any intelligence analysis regarding the actions of some actual or potential adversary, the analysts need to make inferences about an adversary's *capabilities* and *intentions*. Capability and intention must be distinguished: having capability does not entail intention, nor does having intention entail capability. At the moment, however, the I & W team is concerned with the capability of terrorist group X to develop a dirty bomb. Based upon information about group X, the agency considers it almost certain that group X has every intention of using any kind of weapon against the United States, given the appropriate opportunity. Group X, like other current terrorist organizations, seems to have an implacable hatred of American society and its values. Group X has already participated in terrorist activities in which the lives of innocent persons, including women and children, have been taken.

The team has identified the hypothesis as follows:

H: Group X now has the capability to assemble a dirty bomb containing cesium 137.

There is always an alternative hypothesis which, in this case, can be stated as:

not-H: Group X does not now have the capability to assemble a dirty bomb containing cesium 137.

The team's task is now to put hypothesis **H** to work in generating new evidence. The team deems it very unlikely that it could obtain any direct evidence on **H**. Group X maintains very strict control over the security of its operations and is known to have employed the most medieval means of punishing any member whom it suspects of divulging information about its activities. If they did have such direct evidence of **H**, this evidence would be termed a "nugget." Lacking any such nugget, they must be prepared to mine lots of lower-grade evidential ore.

If hypothesis **H** is true, one proposition can easily be deduced: that group X must have obtained, or will obtain, some powdered cesium 137. It is known that such materials seem to be available throughout Eastern Europe including Georgia and Poland. But we have no direct evidence that group X has in fact obtained any powdered cesium 137. But, if group X has obtained, or will obtain, some powdered cesium 137, we can deduce that some member of group X has had, or will have, contacts with potential suppliers of powdered cesium 137 in Eastern Europe. Finally, we deduce that the member of Group X who has had, or will have, contact with potential suppliers of cesium 137 has at least some knowledge of radioactive substances such as cesium 137. Figure 1.1 summarizes our top-down reasoning. At each stage of this top-down reasoning we have a proposition that may be true or false.

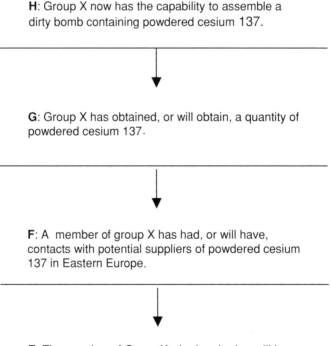

H: Group X now has the capability to assemble a dirty bomb containing powdered cesium 137.

G: Group X has obtained, or will obtain, a quantity of powdered cesium 137.

F: A member of group X has had, or will have, contacts with potential suppliers of powdered cesium 137 in Eastern Europe.

E: The member of Group X who has had or will have contacts with potential suppliers of powdered cesium 137 has knowledge of radioactive substances.

Figure 1.1 *Reasoning stages in the "top-down" intelligence example*

This chain of reasoning finally leads us to ask a question that can potentially be answered: Is there any evidence that any member of Group X has expertise regarding radioactive substances? According to the report the team has received, Ned, a known member of group X, failed to complete his PhD dissertation requirements in nuclear physics at a university in Germany. Though Ned may have failed to complete his PhD in nuclear physics, we can easily suppose that he knows enough about radioactive materials to be highly useful in obtaining such materials as powdered cesium 137 and in handling such materials during the construction of a dirty bomb. Here is a summary of what this top-down reasoning has enabled us to do.

From hypothesis **H** the team has generated a new line of inquiry involving the activities of group X. It is known that many members of known terrorist organizations have studied various areas of the sciences in Western universities. It is also known that not all of these persons have completed their degree requirements. So, just finding out that Ned left a university without finishing his degree is, by itself, quite uninformative. But the argument we have constructed links Ned with group X's efforts to develop one or more dirty weapons that could easily be used against us.

The top-down reasoning we have developed seems entirely plausible. If **H** is true, this suggests that **G** is true: Group X must have or will acquire some of this radioactive material to develop a dirty bomb using cesium 137. If **G** is true, this suggests that **F** is true: A member of group X has had or will have contact with potential suppliers of cesium 137. Finally, if **F** is true, this suggests that **E** may be true: Someone in group X is qualified to inspect the cesium 137, to see what kind of container it is in, and how it might best be made available for use by group X in constructing a dirty bomb.

Finally, we note that propositions or events at each stage of reasoning may or may not be true; in other words, each proposition represents a source of doubt. For a start, **H** might not be true; perhaps group X has other plans for our discomfort. Proposition **G** might not be true either. Perhaps the cost of obtaining a sufficient quantity of cesium 137 exceeds the present resources of group X (another hypothesis, **D**, to be explored). Or, perhaps the security of stores of radioactive materials in Eastern Europe has tightened in light of public knowledge about how weak such security has been in the past (another hypothesis, **C**, to be explored). Proposition **F** might not be true since obtaining materials like cesium 137 might not have to involve any member of group X itself (another hypothesis, **B**, to be explored). It is possible that group X might have obtained some of this material without exposing any of its members to the scrutiny of various intelligence agencies. Finally, it might not require an unusual degree of expertise in nuclear physics to negotiate for and obtain substances like cesium 137 (another hypothesis, **A**, to be explored).

Questions and a problem

1 Your I & W team has received evidence from an airline that Ned traveled to Warsaw last month and has booked another flight to Warsaw next week. The argument the team has constructed establishes the relevance of Ned's travel activities to hypothesis **H**. Ned is a member of group X who is qualified to inspect the cesium 137,

to see what kind of container it is in, and to work out how it might best be made available for use by group X in constructing a dirty bomb. In light of those facts, you have been asked to recommend steps that should be taken to confirm or negate a new hypothesis: Ned is traveling to Warsaw to arrange for or confirm the arrangements for the shipping and delivery of cesium 137 to group X. Will this require top-down or bottom-up reasoning or both? Identify plausible innocent explanations inconsistent with this new hypothesis. (There is a natural tendency to focus on finding evidence that will support a hypothesis, but a good analyst knows that it is equally important to seek evidence that would negate the hypothesis.)

2   How should the I & W team proceed to investigate hypotheses **A**, **B**, and **C**? Does your response with respect to each hypothesis involve top-down or bottom-up reasoning or both?

3   Top-down reasoning, as illustrated in the above fictitious example, is very common in fact investigation in law. Suppose your firm represents a client who claims that her arm was broken when she slipped and fell down the stairs in the building where her doctor has his office. You have determined that the firm must show that the owner or manager of the building breached a duty of care to warn persons who might use the stairs of any unusual conditions that might cause an injury. The senior partner has asked you to advise what steps the firm should take. Use the top-down method illustrated above in formulating your response.

3.   The doctor and the detective: Joseph Bell and Sherlock Holmes

Sir Arthur Conan Doyle frequently mentioned that a major source of inspiration for his development of the character of Sherlock Holmes was a professor he encountered when he was a student at the University of Edinburgh Medical School. Dr. Joseph Bell was then a noted professor of surgery who, in 1887, was president of the Royal College of Surgeons in Edinburgh. Dr. Bell was also personal surgeon to Queen Victoria whenever she was in Scotland. For a time when he was in medical school, Conan Doyle served as an assistant to Dr. Bell. As skilled as Dr. Bell was, it was his astonishingly acute inferential or diagnostic skills for which he is now best remembered, thanks, perhaps, to Sherlock Holmes. Over the years his students kept an account of examples of Dr. Bell's diagnostic feats, some of which are recorded in Britain's leading medical journals, such as the *Lancet*. Following is an example of his diagnostic skill that today we would say involves the same *abductive* reasoning illustrated in so many of the exploits of Sherlock Holmes and also illustrated in Kemelman's "The Nine Mile Walk."

a.   The doctor

The City of Edinburgh and its port city Leith lie on the Firth of Forth. Directly north across the Firth lies a town in Fife called Burntisland [pronounced "burnt island"]. In Bell's day, there was no Forth Road Bridge; travelers used any one of a number of ferries to cross from Fife to Edinburgh; the closest and most direct ferry left Fife from Burntisland. From Leith, a street called Inverleith Row leads in the direction of the University of Edinburgh. To the right of Inverleith Row, just past Leith, lie Edinburgh's Botanical Gardens. Dr. Bell frequently interviewed patients in an amphitheater and allowed his students to observe these interviews. Here is what his students observed on one occasion.

A woman, accompanied by a child, was shown into the amphitheater. Dr. Bell had never met nor seen this woman before. After greeting her, Dr. Bell first asked her if she had a good crossing from Burntisland; the woman replied "aye" [yes]. Bell then asked her if she had a good walk up Inverleith Row; the woman replied "aye." Then Bell asked her what she did with the other child; the woman replied that she had left the child with her sister in Leith. Finally, Dr. Bell asked the woman if she was still working at a linoleum factory; the woman replied "aye."

Dr. Bell's students were of course astonished by this encounter between Dr. Bell and the woman whom he had never seen before. In explanation, Dr. Bell first told his students that they must have noticed her Fife accent and that the closest ferry would have left from Burntisland. He then asked the students if they noticed the red clay on her shoes, which he explained was peculiar to areas around the Botanical Gardens. Then Bell asked his students if they noticed that a coat the woman was carrying over her shoulder was too large for the child who accompanied her; she very likely had another child with her when she crossed from Fife. Finally, Dr. Bell asked his students to observe the dermatitis on her hands, which he explained was peculiar to persons who worked in linoleum factories.

b. The detective

"Dr. Watson, Mr. Sherlock Holmes," said Stamford, introducing us.

"How are you?" he said cordially, gripping my hand with a strength for which I should hardly have given him credit. "You have been in Afghanistan, I perceive."

* * *

"Observation with me is second nature. You appeared to be surprised when I told you, on our first meeting, that you had come from Afghanistan."

"You were told, no doubt."

"Nothing of the sort. I knew you came from Afghanistan. From long habit the train of thoughts ran so swiftly through my mind that I arrived at the conclusion without being conscious of intermediate steps. There were such steps, however. The train of reasoning ran, 'Here is a gentleman of a medical type, but with the air of a military man. Clearly an army doctor, then. He has just come from the tropics, for his face is dark, and that is not the natural tint of his skin, for his wrists are fair. He has undergone hardship and sickness, as his haggard face says clearly. His left arm has been injured. He holds it in a stiff and unnatural manner. Where in the tropics could an English army doctor have seen much hardship and got his arm wounded? Clearly in Afghanistan.' The whole train of thought did not occupy a second. I then remarked that you came from Afghanistan, and you were astonished." (Conan Doyle, *A Study in Scarlet* (1887)).

Notes and a question

1   Sir Arthur Conan Doyle frequently mentioned that Dr. Joseph Bell was a major source of inspiration for his development of the character of Sherlock Holmes. For a time when he was in medical school Conan Doyle served as an assistant to Dr. Bell. If you have read any of the Sherlock Holmes stories, you will note the similarity between what happened in Dr. Bell's interview just described and so many instances in which Holmes amazed Dr. Watson with his acute observational and inferential abilities. Both were highly skilled in the use of what would today be called abductive logic. But abductive logic can only identify hypotheses to be tested.

2   In these anecdotes Bell's and Holmes's hypotheses were confirmed by the woman and Watson respectively. Suppose that they had not. Absent confirmation, would you accept Dr. Bell's or Holmes's conclusions? Can you construct a different scenario in each instance that would also be consistent with all of the observed details?

4. Generalizations and stories: Sam's party

Once upon a time, John went to Sam's party. Sam blew out the candles.[1]

Questions

1   Is this a story?
2   Can you infer from this passage:
   a   That there was a cake?
   b   What kind of party this was?
   c   Sam's age?
3   How would you justify such inferences?

C. Evidence and inference in legal contexts

1. Two murders

a. The murder of Y

Y was murdered in his home at approximately 4:30 p.m. on January 1. W states that she saw X enter Y's house at 4:15 p.m. on that day. Show how W's statement tends to support the conclusion that it was X who murdered Y.

b. Bywaters and Thompson

Edith Thompson was charged with the murder of her husband Percy in that she either conspired with or incited her lover, Frederick Bywaters, to murder Percy.

   i   In the trial it was assumed that the fact that Edith was 28 and Freddie was 20 was relevant to the charge. Is this a reasonable assumption? If so, why?

---

1 Adapted with grateful acknowledgment from Nancy Pennington, who uses it with great effect to illustrate the idea of confabulation.

ii Construct a chain of inferences from the fact that Edith was older than Freddie that supports the proposition that Edith incited him.

iii Can the same fact be used as part of an argument in defense of Edith?

2. Imaginative reasoning: The Nine Mile Walk (Kemelman (1947))

I had made an ass of myself in a speech I had given at the Good Government Association dinner, and Nicky Welt had cornered me at breakfast at the Blue Moon, where we both ate occasionally, for the pleasure of rubbing it in. I had made the mistake of departing from my prepared speech to criticize a statement my predecessor in the office of County Attorney had made to the press. I had drawn a number of inferences from his statement and had thus left myself open to a rebuttal which he had promptly made and which had the effect of making me appear intellectually dishonest. I was new to this political game, having but a few months before left the Law School faculty to become the Reform Party candidate for County Attorney. I said as much in extenuation, but Nicholas Welt, who could never drop his pedagogical manner (he was Snowdon Professor of English Language and Literature), replied in much the same tone that he would dismiss a request from a sophomore for an extension on a term paper, "That's no excuse."

Although he is only two or three years older than I, in his late forties, he always treats me like a schoolmaster hectoring a stupid pupil. And I, perhaps because he looks so much older with his white hair and lined, gnomelike face, suffer it.

"They were perfectly logical inferences," I pleaded.

"My dear boy," he purred, "although human intercourse is well-nigh impossible without inference, most inferences are usually wrong. The percentage of error is particularly high in the legal profession where the intention is not to discover what the speaker wishes to convey, but rather what he wishes to conceal."

I picked up my check and eased out from behind the table.

"I suppose you are referring to cross-examination of witnesses in court. Well, there's always an opposing counsel who will object if the inference is illogical."

"Who said anything about logic?" he retorted. "An inference can be logical and still not be true."

He followed me down the aisle to the cashier's booth. I paid my check and waited impatiently while he searched in an old-fashioned change purse, fishing out coins one by one and placing them on the counter beside his check, only to discover that the total was insufficient. He slid them back into his purse and with a tiny sigh extracted a bill from another compartment of the purse and handed it to the cashier.

"Give me any sentence of ten or twelve words," he said, "and I'll build you a logical chain of inferences that you never dreamed of when you framed the sentence."

Other customers were coming in, and since the space in front of the cashier's booth was small, I decided to wait outside until Nicky completed his transaction with the cashier. I remember being mildly amused at the idea that he probably thought I was still at his elbow and was going right ahead with his discourse.

When he joined me on the sidewalk I said, "A nine mile walk is no joke, especially in the rain."

"No, I shouldn't think it would be," he agreed absently. Then he stopped in his stride and looked at me sharply. "What the devil are you talking about?"

"It's a sentence and it has eleven words," I insisted. And I repeated the sentence, ticking off the words on my fingers.

"What about it?"

"You said that given a sentence of ten or twelve words – "

"Oh, yes." He looked at me suspiciously. "Where did you get it?"

"It just popped into my head. Come on now, build your inferences."

"You're serious about this?" he asked, his little blue eyes glittering with amusement. "You really want me to?"

It was just like him to issue a challenge and then to appear amused when I accepted it. And it made me angry.

"Put up or shut up," I said.

"All right," he said mildly. "No need to be huffy. I'll play. Hm-m, let me see, how did the sentence go? 'A nine mile walk is no joke, especially in the rain.' Not much to go on there."

"It's more than ten words," I rejoined.

"Very well." His voice became crisp as he mentally squared off to the problem. "First inference: the speaker is aggrieved."

"I'll grant that," I said, "although it hardly seems to be an inference. It's really implicit in the statement."

He nodded impatiently. "Next inference: the rain was unforeseen, otherwise he would have said, 'A nine mile walk in the rain is no joke,' instead of using the 'especially' phrase as an afterthought."

"I'll allow that," I said, "although it's pretty obvious."

"First inferences should be obvious," said Nicky tartly.

I let it go at that. He seemed to be floundering and I didn't want to rub it in.

"Next inference: the speaker is not an athlete or an outdoors man."

"You'll have to explain that one," I said.

"It's the 'especially' phrase again," he said. "The speaker does not say that a nine-mile walk in the rain is no joke, but merely the walk – just the distance, mind you – is no joke. Now, nine miles is not such a terribly long distance. You walk more than half that in eighteen holes of golf – and golf is an old man's game," he added slyly. *I* play golf.

"Well, that would be all right under ordinary circumstances," I said, "But there are other possibilities. The speaker might be a soldier in the jungle, in which case nine miles would be a pretty good hike, rain or no rain."

"Yes," and Nicky was sarcastic, "and the speaker might be one-legged. For that matter, the speaker might be a graduate student writing a Ph.D. thesis on humor and starting by listing all the things that are not funny. See here, I'll have to make a couple of assumptions before I continue."

"How do you mean?" I asked, suspiciously.

"Remember, I'm taking this sentence *in vacuo,* as it were. I don't know who said it or what the occasion was. Normally a sentence belongs in the framework of a situation."

"I see. What assumptions do you want to make?"

"For one thing, I want to assume that the intention was not frivolous, that the speaker is referring to a walk that was actually taken, and that the purpose of the walk was not to win a bet or something of that sort."

"That seems reasonable enough," I said.

"And I also want to assume that the locale of the walk is here."

"You mean here in Fairfield?"

"Not necessarily. I mean in this general section of the country."

"Fair enough."

"Then, if you grant those assumptions, you'll have to accept my last inference that the speaker is no athlete or outdoors man."

"Well, all right, go on."

"Then my next inference is that the walk was taken very late at night or very early in the morning – say, between midnight and five or six in the morning."

"How do you figure that one?" I asked.

"Consider the distance, nine miles. We're in a fairly well-populated section. Take any road and you'll find a community of some sort in less than nine miles. Hadley is five miles away, Hadley Falls is seven and a half, Goreton is eleven, but East Goreton is only eight and you strike East Goreton before you come to Goreton. There is local train service along the Goreton road and bus service along the others. All the highways are pretty well traveled. Would anyone have to walk nine miles in a rain unless it were late at night when no buses or trains were running and when the few automobiles that were out would hesitate to pick up a stranger on the highway?"

"He might not have wanted to be seen," I suggested.

Nicky smiled pityingly. "You think he would be less noticeable trudging along the highway than he would be riding in a public conveyance where everyone is usually absorbed in his newspaper?"

"Well, I won't press the point," I said brusquely.

"Then try this one: he was walking toward a town rather than away from one."

I nodded. "It is more likely, I suppose. If he were in a town, he could probably arrange for some sort of transportation. Is that the basis for your inference?"

"Partly that," said Nicky, "but there is also an inference to be drawn from the distance. Remember, it's a *nine* mile walk and nine is one of the exact numbers."

"I'm afraid I don't understand."

That exasperated schoolteacher-look appeared on Nicky's face again. "Suppose you say, 'I took a ten mile walk' or 'a hundred mile drive'; I would assume that you actually walked anywhere from eight to a dozen miles, or that you rode between ninety and a hundred and ten miles. In other words, *ten* and *hundred* are round numbers. You might have walked *exactly* ten miles or just as likely you might have walked *approximately* ten miles. But when you speak of walking *nine* miles, I have a right to assume that you have named an exact figure. Now, we are far more likely to know the distance of the city from a given point than we are to know the distance of a given point from the city. That is, ask anyone in the city how far out Farmer Brown lives, and if he knows him, he will say, 'Three or four miles.' But ask Farmer Brown how far he lives from the city and he will tell you, 'Three and six-tenths miles – measured it on my speedometer many a time.'"

"It's weak, Nicky," I said.

"But in conjunction with your own suggestion that he could have arranged transportation if he had been in a city – "

"Yes, that would do it," I said. "I'll pass it. Any more?"

"I've just begun to hit my stride," he boasted. "My next inference is that he was going to a definite destination and that he had to be there at a particular time. It was not a case of going off to get help because his car broke down or his wife was going to have a baby or somebody was trying to break into his house."

"Oh, come now," I said, "the car breaking down is really the most likely situation. He could have known the exact distance from having checked the mileage just as he was leaving the town."

Nicky shook his head. "Rather than walk nine miles in the rain, he would have curled up on the back seat and gone to sleep, or at least stayed by his car and tried to flag another motorist. Remember, it's nine miles. What would be the least it would take him to hike it?"

"Four hours," I offered.

He nodded. "Certainly no less, considering the rain. We've agreed that it happened very late at night or very early in the morning. Suppose he had his breakdown at one o'clock in the morning. It would be five o'clock before he would arrive. That's daybreak. You begin to see a lot of cars on the road. The buses start just a little later. In fact, the first buses hit Fairfield around five-thirty. Besides, if he were going for help, he would not have to go all the way to town – only as far as the nearest telephone. No, he had a definite appointment, and it was in a town, and it was for some time before five-thirty."

"Then why couldn't he have got there earlier and waited?" I asked. "He could have taken the last bus, arrived around one o'clock, and waited until his appointment. He walks nine miles in the rain instead, and you said he was no athlete."

We had arrived at the Municipal Building where my office is. Normally, any arguments begun at the Blue Moon ended at the entrance to the Municipal Building. But I was interested in Nicky's demonstration and I suggested that he come up for a few minutes.

When we were seated I said, "How about it, Nicky, why couldn't he have arrived early and waited?"

"He could have," Nicky retorted. "But since he did not, we must assume that he was either detained until after the last bus left, or that he had to wait where he was for a signal of some sort, perhaps a telephone call."

"Then according to you, he had an appointment some time between midnight and five-thirty –"

"We can draw it much finer than that. Remember, it takes him four hours to walk the distance. The last bus stops at twelve-thirty a.m. If he doesn't take that, but starts at the same time, he won't arrive at his destination until four-thirty. On the other hand, if he takes the first bus in the morning, he will arrive around five-thirty. That would mean that his appointment was for some time between four-thirty and five-thirty."

"You mean that if his appointment was earlier than four-thirty, he would have taken the last night bus, and if it was later than five-thirty, he would have taken the first morning bus?"

"Precisely. And another thing: if he was waiting for a signal or a phone call, it must have come not much later than one o'clock."

"Yes, I see that," I said. "If his appointment is around five o'clock and it takes him four hours to walk the distance, he'd have to start around one."

He nodded, silent and thoughtful. For some queer reason I could not explain, I did not feel like interrupting his thoughts. On the wall was a large map of the county and I walked over to it and began to study it.

"You're right, Nicky," I remarked over my shoulder, "there's no place as far as nine miles away from Fairfield that doesn't hit another town first, Fairfield is right in the middle of a bunch of smaller towns."

He joined me at the map. "It doesn't have to be Fairfield, you know," he said quietly. "It was probably one of the outlying towns he had to reach. Try Hadley."

"Why Hadley? What would anyone want in Hadley at five o'clock in the morning?"

"The Washington Flyer stops there to take on water about that time," he said quietly.

"That's right, too," I said. "I've heard that train many a night when I couldn't sleep. I'd hear it pulling in and then a minute or two later I'd hear the clock on the Methodist Church banging out five." I went back to my desk for a timetable. "The Flyer leaves Washington at twelve forty-seven a.m. and gets into Boston at eight a.m."

Nicky was still at the map measuring distances with a pencil.

"Exactly nine miles from Hadley is the Old Sumter Inn," he announced.

"Old Sumter Inn," I echoed. "But that upsets the whole theory. You can arrange for transportation there as easily as you can in a town."

He shook his head. "The cars are kept in an enclosure and you have to get an attendant to check you through the gate. The attendant would remember anyone taking out his car at a strange hour. It's a pretty conservative place. He could have waited in his room until he got a call from Washington about someone on the Flyer – maybe the number of the car and the berth. Then he could just slip out of the hotel and walk to Hadley."

I stared at him, hypnotized.

"It wouldn't be difficult to slip aboard while the train was taking on water, and then if he knew the car number and the berth –"

"Nicky," I said portentously, "as the Reform District Attorney who campaigned on an economy program, I am going to waste the taxpayers' money and call Boston long distance. It's ridiculous, it's insane – but I'm going to do it!"

His little blue eyes glittered and he moistened his lips with the tip of his tongue.

"Go ahead," he said hoarsely.

I replaced the telephone in its cradle.

"Nicky," I said, "this is probably the most remarkable coincidence in the history of criminal investigation: *a man was found murdered in his berth on last night's twelve-forty-seven from Washington!* He'd been dead about three hours, which would make it exactly right for Hadley."

"I thought it was something like that," said Nicky. "But you're wrong about its being a coincidence. It can't be. Where did you get that sentence?"

"It was just a sentence. It simply popped into my head."

"It couldn't have! It's not the sort of sentence that pops into one's head. If you had taught composition as long as I have, you'd know that when you ask someone for a sentence of ten words or so, you get an ordinary statement such as 'I like milk' – with the other words made up by a modifying clause like, 'because it is good for my health.' The sentence you offered related to a *particular situation.*"

"But I tell you I talked to no one this morning. And I was alone with you at the Blue Moon."

"You weren't with me all the time I paid my check," he said sharply. "Did you meet anyone while you were waiting on the sidewalk for me to come out of the Blue Moon?"

I shook my head. "I was outside for less than a minute before you joined me. You see, a couple of men came in while you were digging out your change and one of them bumped me, so I thought I'd wait –"

"Did you ever see them before?"

"Who?"

"The two men who came in," he said, the note of exasperation creeping into his voice again.

"Why, no – they weren't anyone I knew."

"Were they talking?"

"I guess so. Yes, they were. Quite absorbed in their conversation, as a matter of fact – otherwise, they would have noticed me and I would not have been bumped."

"Not many strangers come into the Blue Moon," he remarked.

"Do you think it was they?" I asked eagerly. "I think I'd know them again if I saw them."

Nicky's eyes narrowed. "It's possible. There had to be two – one to trail the victim in Washington and ascertain his berth number, the other to wait here and do the job. The Washington man would be likely to come down here afterwards. If there was theft as well as murder, it would be to divide the spoils. If it was just murder, he would probably have to come down to pay off his confederate."

I reached for the telephone.

"We've been gone less than half an hour," Nicky went on. "They were just coming in and service is slow at the Blue Moon. The one who walked all the way to Hadley must certainly be hungry and the other probably drove all night from Washington."

"Call me immediately if you make an arrest," I said into the phone and hung up.

Neither of us spoke a word while we waited. We paced the floor, avoiding each other almost as though we had done something we were ashamed of.

The telephone rang at last. I picked it up and listened. Then I said, "O.K." and turned to Nicky.

"One of them tried to escape through the kitchen but Winn had someone stationed at the back and they got him."

"That would seem to prove it," said Nicky with a frosty little smile.

I nodded agreement.

He glanced at his watch. "Gracious," he exclaimed, "I wanted to make an early start on my work this morning, and here I've already wasted all this time talking with you." I let him get to the door. "Oh, Nicky," I called, "what was it you set out to prove?" "That a chain of inferences could be logical and still not be true," he said. "Oh."

"What are you laughing at?" he asked snappishly. And then he laughed too.

Questions

1 "The Nine Mile Walk" is a nice example of imaginative reasoning leading to the construction of a hypothetical scenario of the events surrounding the murder on the Washington Flier. Assume that A and B are the men who have been arrested and that C was the victim. Restate Welt's conclusion in the form of a story starting at the New Sumter Inn and ending with the meeting at the Blue Moon Café. Is the story plausible? Given Kemelman's account, what odds might a rational betting person calculate as the likelihood that it was either A or B who murdered C?

2 Welt infers: "It is the man who said: 'A nine mile walk is no joke, especially in the rain' in the Blue Moon Café this morning who is the person who murdered C." For Kemelman, this may be critical.

   a How does Welt support the inference that the statement was made?

   b How does he support the inference that it was made in the Café that morning?

   c Assume that Kemelman's recollection does not improve. In most jurisdictions, the two men would be entitled to a preliminary hearing to determine whether the evidence shows that there was and is probable cause to believe that the two men are responsible for the murder of C sufficient to justify their (i) arrest and (ii) prosecution. Could the prosecution prove that either of the men arrested made the statement? Absent evidence that either of the men made the statement, could the prosecution show that the police had probable cause to arrest the two men?

3 Two men, A and B, have been arrested on suspicion of the murder of C. B is the one who left the Blue Moon by the rear. He was unarmed. Assume that one will be charged as principal; the other as accessory. Place yourself in Kemelman's position immediately after Welt has left the office. The time for playing Watson to Welt's Holmes is over; you are a prosecutor who must now seek evidence sufficient to prove that: It was A (or B) who murdered C.

   a The elements of the crime define the *conditions* that the *ultimate proposition* to be proved (the *ultimate probandum*) must satisfy. Connecticut statutes currently provide:

> A person is guilty of murder when, with intent to cause the death of another person, he causes the death of such person or of a third person or causes a suicide by force, duress or deception . . . (Conn. Gen. Stat. §53a–54a)

> A person, acting with the mental state required for commission of an offense, who solicits, requests, commands, importunes or intentionally aids another

person to engage in conduct which constitutes an offense shall be criminally liable for such conduct and may be prosecuted and punished as if he were the principal offender. (Conn. Gen. Stat. §53a–8)

What precisely must Kemelman seek to prove? Frame the ultimate proposition to be proved for the murderer and for the accessory. The standard of proof at trial will be "beyond reasonable doubt"; what standard should guide (a) the decision to arrest, (b) the decision to charge with murder? Are these standards met in the story?

3. Generalizations, stories, and arguments[2]

a. Brides in the bath: closing speech[3]

George Joseph Smith, who was married, had gone through a ceremony of marriage with three women in close succession – Bessie Mundy, Alice Burnham, and Margaret Lofty. He induced each of them to execute a will naming him as her beneficiary. Each of them drowned in a bathtub shortly thereafter. He was indicted and tried for the murder of Ms. Mundy. The prosecution was permitted to introduce evidence about the "marriages," wills, and circumstances of the death of the other two women. The following is an excerpt from the closing speech for the Crown.

The prisoner and the woman being alone in the house, he had the opportunity of committing the crime. The motive of the prisoner has been demonstrated, the opportunity admitted, and the exclusion of accident proved. You are entitled to look at the evidence as to the two other deaths to see whether the death of Miss Mundy was accident or designed, and, if designed, for the benefit of whom? You can also look at that evidence to see whether the death was part of a system or course of conduct – horrible as it is to think so – of deliberately causing people's deaths in order that monetary benefit might ensue to him.

The three cases are of such a character that such a large aggregation of resemblances cannot have occurred without design. In each case the prisoner went through the form of marriage; in each case the ready money of the woman was either realized or drawn out of whatever deposit bank it might have been in; in each case there was a will drawn in favour of the prisoner absolutely; in each case the will was drawn by a stranger to the testatrix; in each case the victim insured her life or was possessed of property which did not make it necessary to insure her life; in each case there was a visit to a doctor shortly before the death, which, we contend, was unnecessary from the physical condition of the patient; in each case the women wrote letters to relatives the night before, or on the night on which they died; in each case there was an inquiry as to a bathroom (or the provision of a bath); in each case the woman died from drowning, and the prisoner was the first to discover it; in each case the bathroom doors were unfastened and the water was not drawn off until after the doctor had been; and in each case the prisoner was putting demonstrably forward the purchase of either fish, or eggs, or tomatoes to show that he was absent from the house in which his wife was lying dead; and in each

2 These passages are discussed in *Rethinking* Ch. 7, *Bazaar* Chs. 12 and 14.
3 Eric Watson (1915) 261-62.

case there was the prisoner's subsequent disappearance and the monetary advantage resulting or attempted to be made to result.

Questions

This is the peroration of the famous closing speech by Archibald Bodkin QC in *R. v. George Joseph Smith.*

1   Is this a story or an argument or both?
2   To what extent does the persuasiveness of the passage depend on (i) logic (ii) rhetoric?
3   Can you summarize the argument in a single sentence?

b. *Huddleston v. United States,* 485 U.S. 681 (1988)

A federal grand jury indicted Gary Rufus Huddleston, charging that, in April 1985, he had sold (count one) and had possessed (count two) Memorex videocassette tapes (the "tapes") that had been stolen in interstate commerce. The tapes had been stolen, and Huddleston had sold and had possessed quantities of the tapes. The only issue in dispute was whether Huddleston knew that the tapes had been stolen at the time he had sold or possessed them. The issue was apparently a close one: After two days of deliberations, the jury acquitted Huddleston on the charge that he had knowingly sold stolen tapes, but convicted him on the charge that he had knowingly possessed stolen tapes.

According to Huddleston, Leroy Wesby had a large quantity of the tapes, had invited Huddleston to sell them on a commission basis, and had assured Huddleston that the tapes were legitimate. Huddleston offered and sold quantities of the tapes at prices that were below the cost of manufacturing the tapes. Huddleston acknowledged that he had possessed and sold substantial quantities of the tapes, but claimed that he had no knowledge that they were stolen.

The government introduced evidence that, in February 1985, Huddleston had arranged a sale of 38 new 12″ black and white television sets (the "TV sets"), also supplied by Wesby, to Paul Toney, a retailer, for $28 per set. Huddleston did not produce a bill of sale at trial and, according to Toney, he got the impression that Huddleston could obtain a lot more of these sets.

The government also offered evidence that in May 1985, Huddleston had offered to sell to an FBI undercover agent a large quantity of Amana appliances that also had been supplied by Wesby. It was undisputed that these appliances had been stolen. Huddleston testified that he had asked and Wesby had assured him that the TV sets and the appliances were legitimate.

Questions

1   In its opinion, the Supreme Court said:

> In assessing whether the evidence was sufficient to support a finding that the televisions were stolen, the court here was required to consider not only the direct

evidence on that point – the low price of the televisions, the large quantity offered for sale, and petitioner's inability to produce a bill of sale – *but also the evidence concerning petitioner's involvement in the sales of other stolen merchandise obtained from Wesby, such as the Memorex tapes and the Amana appliances.* Given this evidence, the jury reasonably could have concluded that the televisions were stolen, and the trial court therefore properly allowed the evidence to go to the jury. (Id. at 691 (emphasis added))

a   The Joint Appendix filed with the Court contained no evidence concerning the wholesale price of 12″ black and white TV sets. How did the Court conclude that $28 was a price so low as to excite suspicion that the sets were stolen?

b   Did the fact that the Memorex tapes Huddleston sold in April and the fact that the Amana appliances he offered for sale in May were stolen support an inference that the TV sets he stole in February were also stolen goods? If so, explain how.

c   For every step in an inferential argument, there must be a generalization that makes the step logical. What generalizations would justify the italicized portion of the Court's statement?

2   The government based its theory of relevance upon a generalization, which, according to the Supreme Court, was:

> . . . the televisions were stolen, and proof that petitioner [Huddleston] had engaged in a series of sales of stolen merchandise from the same suspicious source would be strong evidence that he was aware that each of these items, including the Memorex tapes, was stolen. (*Id.* at 686)

a   Do you find the generalization urged by the government persuasive? Are there any flaws that should be corrected?

b   How does the fact that the Amana appliances Huddleston offered for sale in May were stolen support an inference that Huddleston knew in April that the Memorex tapes were stolen?

c   Assuming that the sale of stolen tapes in April and the stolen appliances in May support an inference that the TV sets sold in February were stolen, did that fact support further inference that Huddleston knew that the Memorex tapes were stolen in February?

d   How would you argue that the improper prejudicial effects of introducing evidence about (i) Huddleston's sale of the TV sets and (ii) his offer to sell the Amana appliances substantially outweighed any legitimate probative value that evidence might have with respect to Huddleston's knowledge that the Memorex tapes were stolen? Examine each transaction separately and then in combination. Identify each improper prejudicial effect and then construct your argument.

c.   *Miller v. Jackson* (**Lord Denning MR**) **[1977] 3 All E. R. 340, 340–41 (CA)**

In a summer time village cricket is the delight of everyone. Nearly every village has its own cricket field where the young men play and the old men watch. In the village of Lintz in County Durham they have their own ground, where they have played these last 70 years. They tend it well. The wicket area is well rolled and mown. The outfield is kept short. It has a good club-house for the players and seats for the onlookers. The village team plays there on Saturdays and Sundays. They belong to a league, competing with the neighbouring villages. On other evenings after work they practice while the light lasts. Yet now after these 70 years a judge of the High Court has ordered that they must not play there any more. He has issued an injunction to stop them. He has done it at the instance of a newcomer who is no lover of cricket. This newcomer has built, or has had built for him, a house on the edge of the cricket ground which four years ago was a field where cattle grazed. The animals did not mind the cricket. But now this adjoining field has been turned into a housing estate. The newcomer bought one of the houses on the edge of the cricket ground. No doubt the open space was a selling point. Now he complains that, when a batsman hits a six, the ball has been known to land in his garden or on or near his house. His wife has got so upset about it that they always go out at weekends. They do not go into the garden when cricket is being played. They say that this is intolerable. So they asked the judge to stop the cricket being played. And the judge, much against his will, has felt that he must order the cricket to be stopped; with the consequences, I suppose, that the Lintz Cricket Club will disappear. The cricket ground will be turned to some other use. I expect for more houses or a factory. The young men will turn to other things instead of cricket. The whole village will be much the poorer. And all this because of a newcomer who has just bought a house there next to the cricket ground.

Questions

1 Is this a story?
2 Some people find this persuasive, but others consider it "unjudge-like." What reasons might be given in support of each view?
3 Can you show that in this passage, read on its own, Lord Denning (i) contradicted himself; (ii) invented some facts; (iii) introduced facts that are not relevant to a claim in nuisance?

4. Evidence from two *causes célèbres*

a. *Commonwealth v. Sacco and Vanzetti* (Mass. 1921)

Nicola Sacco and Bartolomeo Vanzetti emigrated from Italy to America in the early 1900s. They were regularly employed and were respected and well liked by everyone who had contact with them. In 1920 Sacco was employed as a shoe-edger and Vanzetti as a fish-peddler. But they were also implacable anarchists. Following World War I, there were many instances of what we would today call acts of terrorism. Members of anarchistic groups were associated with these acts of terrorism, and Sacco and Vanzetti were members of one of these groups. In 1920 they were charged with felony murder in a commonplace but ruthless crime. They were tried, convicted, and executed in 1927. Their trial is arguably the ranking cause célèbre in American legal history. Their case has been referred to as "the case that will not die." Arguments exist to this day about whether Sacco and Vanzetti were convicted for being murderers or for being anarchists. One major element of the argument that they were wrongly convicted concerns the authenticity of certain firearms evidence against Sacco.

On Thursday, April 15, 1920, two payroll guards, Alessandro Berardelli and Frederick Parmenter, were carrying two metal boxes containing $15,773.15 in bills and coin, which represented the week's payroll for employees of the Slater-Morrill Shoe Company in South Braintree, Massachusetts. As they headed down Pearl Street in the direction of this shoe company, Berardelli and Parmenter were attacked by two men whom witnesses said were loitering in the vicinity of the crime scene. Berardelli was shot four times and died instantly. Parmenter was shot twice and died the next day; he was not able to identify his assailants.

On May 5, 1920, Sacco and Vanzetti were arrested for reasons having nothing to do with this crime. Police officers Michael Connolly and Frank Vaughn arrested them. They had been told that they were suspicious persons and that they had stolen a car. At the time of their arrest, Sacco was carrying a 32-caliber Colt automatic pistol. On September 11, they were indicted and charged with first degree felony murder for the slaying of Berardelli and Parmenter.

At their trial, Officer Connolly testified: "Sacco attempted on several occasions to put his hand under his overcoat in spite of being warned [by Connolly] not to do so." Later in the trial, a forensic surgeon, Dr. Magrath, testified that he had extracted four 32-caliber bullets from the body of Berardelli and marked each one on its base with Roman numerals I, II, III, and IV. Magrath testified that Bullet III, admitted at trial as Exhibit 18, was the bullet that killed Berardelli. During the trial, the prosecution went to considerable lengths to show that Exhibit 18 had been fired through the 32-caliber Colt automatic that was alleged to belong to Sacco. The court allowed both the prosecution and defense to test-fire bullets through Sacco's 32-caliber Colt automatic to see if the markings on the test bullets matched those of Exhibit 18 shown at trial. Prosecution and defense ballistics experts disagreed about whether Exhibit 18 had been fired through Sacco's 32-caliber Colt automatic.

All witnesses to the shooting testified that one gunman fired four shots in succession into Berardelli's body. When the four bullets are examined together, however, it is obvious that the rifling pattern on Exhibit 18 does not match the patterns on Bullets I, II, and IV. Exhibit 18 cannot have been fired from the same weapon as the other three bullets. (The prosecution never showed the four bullets all together at trial and were never requested to do so by the defense.)

Questions

1   Did Connolly's testimony that: "Sacco attempted on several occasions to put his hand under his overcoat in spite of being warned [by Connolly] not to do so" make it any more probable that it was Sacco who shot Berardelli? Identify each inference that must be accepted in order to demonstrate that Connolly's testimony was relevant to the proposition it was Sacco who shot Berardelli.

2 What is the significance of the fact that the rifling pattern on Exhibit 18 does not match the patterns on Bullets I, II, and IV and the resulting inference that Exhibit 18 cannot have been fired from the same weapon as the other three bullets? What are the possible explanations for this discrepancy? Had the comparison been made at trial, how would you have explained the discrepancy if you were the prosecutor? If you were counsel for Sacco, what additional inferences would you argue that the jury should make based upon the comparison of the four bullets?

b. *People v. Simpson* (Cal. 1994)

In July, 1994, the state of California formally charged that Orenthal James Simpson (OJS) had murdered his former wife, Nicole Brown Simpson (NBS), and a bystander, Ronald L. Goldman (RLG), on June 12, 1994. The trial took place in 1995. One of the issues was whether OJS could have had an opportunity to commit the crimes. The only evidence presented at trial bearing upon that issue is summarized below.

Sometime between 10:15 and 10:20 p.m., on June 12, 1994, Pablo Fuentes heard the "plaintive wail" of a dog. Around 10:45 p.m., Steven Schwab found NBS's Akita with blood on its paws. At about the same time, Kato Kaelin, a guest in OJS's house, heard three thumps on the wall outside his bedroom that he thought might be an earthquake. He went out and walked along a path behind the house, but he did not see anything. Alan Park was a limousine driver scheduled to drive OJS to the Los Angeles Airport to catch an 11:45 p.m. flight to Chicago. He arrived at OJS's house early. He pressed the buzzer at the gate at 10:40 and again at 10:49 and got no answer. At 10:55, Park saw an African-American male dressed in dark clothes enter the house. At 10:56, he buzzed again and OJS answered. OJS said he had been in the shower and would be out in a few minutes. Kaelin opened the gate and Park drove the limo to the front door. There were two black duffel bags on the doorstep. At 11:00, OJS came out. He was wearing stone-washed blue jeans and a white polo shirt and was carrying a coat over his arm and a designer hanging bag. Park shook hands with him. He did not notice any cuts or blood on his hand or anything else unusual. According to Detective Vannatter, it took about five minutes to drive, observing the speed limit, from NBS's house at 875 Bundy Drive to OJS's house at 360 North Rockingham Avenue.

Problems

1 Construct a story that accounts for each event and observation reported above and that shows that OJS almost certainly could have murdered NBS and RLG.
2 Construct a story that accounts for each event and observation reported above and that shows that OJS almost certainly could not have murdered NBS and RLG.

5. *United States v. Richard Able*

Your firm represents Richard Able, the defendant in *United States v. Able*. The partner who has prepared the case is ill, and you have been assigned to try it. The following is an abstract of the materials in the firm's files.

The Case File

In January, the United States Attorney for the Middle District of New State filed an indictment alleging that Richard Able had knowingly filed a false federal income tax return for the year 2003 with intent to defraud the federal government of income tax due and owing. The indictment alleged that during 2003 Able had received income in an amount no less than $45,000 that had not been included on his income tax return for that year. The indictment is otherwise sufficient, and the court has denied the defendant's motion to dismiss.

Pursuant to the court's standing discovery order, the government has filed a list of prospective witnesses and copies of documents it may seek to introduce in evidence. The list of prospective witnesses include: (i) Samuel Baker, managing partner in a New York law firm (the "Law Firm"); (ii) Timothy Cooper, a certified public accountant in New City; (iii) Carol Able, Able's ex-wife; (iv) Linda Davis, a model and Able's ex-girlfriend; and (v) various bank officers, Internal Revenue Service officials, and others who can lay a proper foundation for certain of the documents listed. The documents produced include: (i) a cancelled check in the amount of $25,000 dated December 15, 2003, issued by the Law Firm payable to Able with endorsements showing that Able cashed it on December 20, 2003, at the Citibank branch in Las Vegas; (ii) a 2003 federal income tax return signed by Able and by Cooper as the preparer dated April 15, 2004, that reports Able's gross income from all sources for the year 2003 as $125,000; (iii)–(v) Able's federal income tax returns for prior years prepared by a New York accountant reporting gross income for 2000 as $375,000; for 2001 as $410,000; and for 2002 as $275,000; (vi)–(vii) cancelled checks from two law firms in New City showing payments to Able during 2003 aggregating $20,000 as consulting fees and bearing endorsements showing that they were deposited in Able's bank account during that year; (viii) a certified copy of a divorce decree entered by the Supreme Court of New York indicating that in 2000 Able agreed and the court ordered him to transfer assets with an aggregate value of $750,000 to his wife Carol in full settlement of all claims she might have arising from the marriage, for alimony or otherwise, and to pay the sum of $35,000 per year for the support of his two young children who remained in the custody of Carol; (ix) a xerox copy of a love letter from Linda Davis to Able dated December 1, 2003, that includes the statement, "Remember, darling, what we talked about in the disco – no risks, no me"; and (x) micro-film copies of Able's bank statements and cancelled checks for the years 1999 through 2003.

In response to Able's demand for discovery pursuant to constitutional and statutory requirements, the government has also produced a copy of reports submitted by FBI or IRS agents summarizing interviews with various witnesses. These include a three-page memorandum by FBI Agent Dawes stating that he had interviewed Timothy Cooper in August 2004 and that, among other things, Cooper had told him that Cooper had merged his accounting practice in July 2004 and that his secretary had lost or thrown out some materials, such as notes and work papers, contained in inactive client-files. According to the memorandum, Cooper told Dawes that Able was listed as an inactive client at the time because he had not consulted Cooper or returned Cooper's calls concerning preparation of Able's 2004 income tax return. Dawes's memorandum reported that Cooper could not tell from examining the file whether any materials from Able's file had been discarded, but said he thought it unlikely. Dawes's memorandum reported that Cooper had no recollection of how the signing of Able's return was handled, but Cooper said that he usually mailed two copies of a return to his clients with an envelope adressed to the Internal Revenue Service and a note instructing them to review, sign, and mail the completed returns by April 15. The memorandum reports that Cooper could not find a copy of such a note with the copy of Able's 2003 return in his files. Cooper reported that the file contains no information about any income other than Able's salary, and that Cooper did not recall Able informing him that he had received any other income.

Pursuant to the court's reciprocal discovery requirement, Able has listed the following possible witnesses: (i) Joan Evans, Able's present girlfriend; (ii) Karl Frank, dean of the New State University Law School; and (iii) various New State law professors and New York lawyers who have worked with Able during his professional career, as possible character witnesses. Able has also produced for the government a xerox copy of a handwritten note reading:

April 11, 2004

Dear Tim:

When we met last month, I gave you the information about my regular and summer school salary from the law school and my expenses last year. As promised, I have reviewed my bank records and notes and have determined that I received $25,000 from my former New York law firm as my share of a contingent fee they received on a case on which I had worked, and $20,000 for miscellaneous consulting work I did for firms here in New City. Because I will be out of town on the 15th, I have signed and enclosed a blank, undated 1040 form. I also enclose a signed check payable to the Internal Revenue Service with the amount to be filled in by you. Please complete, date, file, and send me a copy.

Regards,

Richard

The file also contains memoranda by your partner based upon various interviews. These include a memorandum based upon notes from interviews with Able. The principal points in that memorandum are as follows:

i Able spent 12 years with the Law Firm, seven as an associate, and five as a partner. The tax returns for 1999, 2000, and 2001 were prepared by a New York accounting firm that did the returns for all the Law Firm's partners. They are accurate insofar as Able knows.

ii Able left the firm in mid-2002 and joined the law faculty at New State University where he is presently employed. In 2003, his salary for the academic year was $105,000, and he was paid $20,000 for teaching in the summer quarter.

iii Able says he earned $20,000 for miscellaneous consulting work for New City firms. The $25,000 check represented his share of a court-awarded fee in a case on which he had worked while at the Law Firm.

iv Able says he retained Cooper in March 2004. He wrote the April letter just before he left for a one-week trip to attend a conference in Chicago. According to Able he gave the letter to his girlfriend, Joan Evans, and asked her to deliver it to Cooper after she dropped him at the airport. Able said that he did not like Cooper, and he has since done his own returns because they are rather simple.

v Able said that Baker disliked him because Able was one of the "young turk" partners who had led the Law Firm into plaintiff's litigation in which fees were contingent upon results. The practice was eventually successful, but Baker was an old-timer who thought that kind of practice was inconsistent with the Law Firm's reputation as an old-line corporate and banking firm.

vi Able acknowledged that he and his ex-wife Carol had been social cocaine users, and he suspects Baker may try to suggest that Able was asked to leave the Law Firm for this reason.

vii Able reported that as part of the settlement with Carol, she had waived any claim to his retirement account containing $600,000 and that, after transfering assets valued at $750,000 and paying his attorney's fees and costs, he had about $150,000 in cash, which he used to make a $100,000 down payment on a house he bought for $400,000 and to pay for moving expenses, for repairs and minor improvements to the house, and for furniture and other furnishings for the house. Able acknowledged that he made himself a promise when he entered practice that he would keep his pensions intact until he retired.

viii Able admitted that he went to Las Vegas with his ex-girlfriend, Linda Davis, in December 2003 in an effort to please her. He cashed the Law Firm check at a branch of his bank as convenience to be sure he had the cash before Christmas. Able said that he returned with more than $15,000 cash, he lent $6,000 to Linda as the down payment for a small Porsche, spent the $2,500 on Christmas gifts for Linda and his two children, and he used the balance for miscellaneous expenses in January and February.

ix Able said that shortly after their return from Las Vegas, he learned that Linda had a reputation as a heavy coke user and as a New City "call girl." He said they broke up when he asked her to sign a note for the $6,000 loan. According to Able, the breakup was bitter and Linda has since refused to discuss the loan. Able said he thinks Linda would say the $6,000 was a gift or would claim that he "blew" most of the $25,000 at the tables in Las Vegas.

x According to Able, he has not used cocaine even socially since he began dating Joan Evans because of her strong religious views. She works as a librarian and is still his girlfriend.

The file also contains memoranda and notes from telephone and personal interviews indicating that:

i Joan Evans confirms that she delivered the April 11 letter to Cooper's office and handed it to his secretary who identified herself as Mrs. Cooper. She says that Able is a brilliant lawyer and a good man and that he has never used cocaine in her presence;

ii Baker hung up the telephone after commenting that Able's taste for cocaine and fast women had finally brought him his just reward;

iii Carol Able said she bore her ex-husband no ill will and would be happy to testify if it would help; and

iv Cooper and Davis refused to discuss the matter.

Questions

1. *Provisional theories of the case*

a What do you anticipate will be the government's *theory of the case* in light of the available evidence and your analysis? What will be its principal *themes*? Its *story*?

b In light of that analysis and an analysis of the evidence available to you, what will be the defendant's *theory of the case*? The principal *themes*? The *story*?

2. *Admissibility of the evidence*

a *Trial preparation.* The government has identified four substantive witnesses and nine substantive documents through which it intends to prove its case.

i *The government's documents.* In light of the provisional theories, to what fact of consequence in the litigation will the government claim each document is relevant? Which documents will you seek to exclude and on what basis? How should counsel for the government respond, and what is the probable result?

ii *The government's witnesses.* Are you likely to be able to exclude any testimony concerning Able's use of cocaine? What will the government argue and how will you respond? How should the court rule? Are there other significant lines of testimony that the government is likely to seek to elicit that you would expect to be able to exclude? If so, which, and on what bases?

b *The trial.* The government has presented its case and rested. The court has denied your motion for a directed verdict.

i On cross-examination, Cooper testified that he did not recall seeing Able's April 11th letter; that had his office received it, it would have been in the client-file he maintained for Able, and it is not; that his files were perfectly maintained; that he does not recall discussing any papers being lost in his 2004 move; and that he has never seen Agent Dawes's memorandum and it does not refresh his recollection. How will you proceed to impeach his credibility in your case in chief? How will you respond to the government's hearsay objections? Are you likely to succeed?

ii Able has identified the April 11th letter and testified that he wrote and gave it to Joan Evans to deliver it to Cooper. The government has objected to the admission of the letter on the grounds that (1) its relevance has not been established; (2) it is not the best evidence; and (3) it is inadmissible hearsay. How do you respond?

iii Apart from Able's testimony concerning his conversations with Cooper and the April 11th letter and Evans's testimony concerning the delivery to Cooper's office, what additional testimony will you seek to introduce through these or other witnesses? Why? Does your answer depend upon whether you won or lost objections you made during the government's case? Explain.

3. *The Nature of Proof*

Would the application of the rules of evidence result in the exclusion of logically relevant evidence? Would the exclusion of such evidence enhance the likelihood that the jury would make a true determination? A just determination? Should the case of *United States v. Able* be submitted to the jury? What does it mean to say that a jury might find that the evidence established Able's guilt beyond and to the exclusion of every reasonable doubt?

6. *Sargent v. Southern Accident Co.*[4]

You are a lawyer in private practice. Southern Accident Company has retained you to defend it in an action by plaintiff Porter E. Sargent, beneficiary of a life insurance policy issued by the company and covering his son Upham Sargent. The plaintiff claims $500,000, the amount payable if the insured suffers an "accidental injury that is the sole cause of death resulting within 90 days after the accidental injury." The policy excludes suicide, but not recklessness or engaging in hazardous activities. The defendant company does not contend that the plaintiff's proof of loss was not timely or that the plaintiff failed to inform it in writing of all facts known or discovered by plaintiff. However, the policy requires "written proof covering the occurrence, character, and extent of the loss for which claim is made," and the company takes the position that the facts submitted to it fail to show that Upham Sargent died by "accidental injury" within the provisions of the policy.

Pre-trial discovery proceedings have been completed and the company's claims supervisor is considering making a final offer of settlement to plaintiff before trial. In order to make that decision he has asked your opinion whether the plaintiff's evidence is sufficient for the plaintiff to avoid a directed verdict in the defendant's favor, that is, whether there is sufficient evidence from which a reasonable jury could conclude that Upham Sargent suffered an "accidental injury that was the sole cause of death resulting within 90 days after the accidental injury."

Your answer will depend on your analysis of the evidence the plaintiff is likely to offer at the trial. The plaintiff's probable evidence, consisting of the testimony of five witnesses, is set forth on the following pages. Assume that all five witnesses will testify at the trial and that all will be credible. Assume the following standard for decision: Could a jury of reasonable persons find that the evidence presented satisfied the test on a "balance of probabilities"?

Plaintiff's Evidence

Testimony of Porter E. Sargent. The insured was my son, Upham Sargent. When he died he was 21 years old. He was financially comfortable, mentally well balanced, vigorous, athletic, resourceful, courageous, a good swimmer, and of some experience in living in wild country without provisions. For several years he had taken hazardous and adventurous journeys alone in this country and in Europe.

---

4   This exercise was devised by the late Professor Thomas R. Ewald and is based upon the facts reported in *Sargent v. Massachusetts Accident Company*, 307 Mass. 246, 29 N.E.2d 825 (1940).

Upham had finished his junior year in college in the spring of 2002. He lived with my wife and myself in our home in Boston until August, 2002, when he left to go on a kayak trip in northern Quebec. Before leaving he outlined to me the trip from Boston via Montreal to Senneterre. From Senneterre he planned to travel by kayak to Mattagami Lake at the head of the Nottaway River. His intention was to run down the river in his kayak in a northwesterly direction, into James Bay, and to go to a trading post of the Hudson's Bay Company on James Bay, called Rupert's House. He left Boston on a train for Montreal on August 1, 2002. He traveled with a green kayak. The boat was eighteen feet long and not as deep as a canoe. He transported the kayak in the baggage car of the train. The kayak had the name "Sargent" burned into the wood inside its stern. When he left Boston he also had with him a small repeating rifle with ammunition, a sleeping robe, matches, $800 in money, snares and fishing tackle, and a good supply of food. He had no clothes for winter weather. His mother and I said goodbye to him at North Station in Boston on August 1, 2002. We never saw him again.

Testimony of George Birdsong. I live on an Indian reservation at the northern reaches of the Nottaway River, near its mouth. We are friendly and hospitable Indians, who live by trapping and selling the skins at Rupert's House. The Indians who live at Mattagami Lake are equally friendly and hospitable. They trade at Senneterre, to the south. The Nottaway River varies from a fifth to a half-mile in width and consists of a series of dangerous rapids among large boulders. The river falls about seven hundred feet in its course. The only possible channel through rapids is usually near one bank or the other. In that river if one should not find the channel he could not cross to the other side. An upset in the river would probably mean death. Even the best canoeists would find that river very hazardous. Only three parties are known to have descended it safely. The customary route from Mattagami Lake to Rupert's House is much longer and avoids the Nottaway River. There are no portages, roads, trails, or paths in the country drained by the river. That country is flat, desolate, and unforested, with many swamps and with no elevations of consequence. Fish and blueberries are plentiful, and there are some ducks and rabbits.

I was visiting friends and working on the reservation at Mattagami Lake in August and September, 2002. I met Upham Sargent when he came there about September 1, 2002. He told me he was going down the Nottaway River in his kayak. I had never heard of anyone trying to go down the Nottaway River in a kayak. I warned him that the trip would be very dangerous. Sargent stayed in the Mattagami reservation until September 8. That day I saw him load his supplies and belongings into the kayak, get into the kayak and set off down the river. I never saw him again.

In October, 2002, I found his paddle on the bank of the Nottaway River, on the fringe of a whirlpool 50 or 60 miles from the mouth of the river.

Testimony of Henry Largetree. I live near the Nottaway River. I never met Upham Sargent. In May 2003 I found the bow section of a green kayak under some rocks in the Nottaway River. The place was about 40 miles from the river's mouth.

Testimony of Clarence Rockbound. I am a senior geologist in the service of the Canadian Government. Among my duties are preparing topographical surveys of various localities in Canada. I have surveyed the area of the Nottaway River. The length of the river from the head of the Nottaway River in Lake Mattagami to its mouth is 225 kilometers (140 miles). I prepared the "Nottaway Sheet" of the geological survey of Canada. I have never travelled through the rapids of the Nottaway River, but from my studies and work in the region I have acquired a general knowledge of the character of the river and the region through which it flows. I have descended the rapids of another river a little north of the Nottaway in a canoe. It is my opinion that an individual in a kayak loaded with supplies could not descend the Nottaway River without being drowned. In my opinion based upon my experience, a kayak managed by one person and carrying a load cannot stay afloat in the quick water of great power that flows among the boulders of the Nottaway River. I also have an opinion that it would be possible that in an upset the person would lose his kayak and all his equipment and, though he might reach the shore safely, he would eventually starve to death. At the same time I believe from my knowledge of the Nottaway River area that there were plenty of blueberries there in September and October, 2002, on which one could live for a month.

Testimony of Sergeant Horatio Renfrew. I am a sergeant in the Royal Canadian Mounted Police. I was in charge of coordinating the search efforts for Upham Sargent. Search parties were organized by the Royal Canadian Mounted Police, the Hudson's Bay Company, Revillon Freres Ltd., the Indians of the Nottaway River neighborhood, and other persons in the north country. The searches were made during the period from September 20, 2002 to February 28, 2003. I personally made an airplane flight in February 2003 over the northern reaches of the Nottaway River in the hope of sighting Upham Sargent or his body. I have never found him or his body. All of the other search parties reported to me that they had not found Sargent or his body. On March 1, 2003, I instructed them to discontinue the search.

Questions

1   What is the ultimate proposition of fact, the ultimate probandum, that the plaintiff must prove in order to prevail? State the proposition. How many conditions must be satisfied? State each condition as a simple proposition.
2   Analyze all of the plaintiff's evidence to determine whether it is sufficient to avoid a directed verdict in the defendant's favor. Prepare a concise outline identifying as a separate proposition each relevant fact that can be shown by the testimony. State as separate propositions the relevant inferences that can be drawn from these evidential propositions. Complete the analysis by organizing the data in a manner that compels the conclusion that the plaintiff does or does not have sufficient evidence to satisfy all of the conditions required by the ultimate proposition that he must prove, that is, to prove each of the material facts in issue.

3   Identify each testimonial proposition that you believe would not be admissible as
    evidence under the rules of evidence. State why that evidence is inadmissible and
    identify the rule of evidence that supports each conclusion. Identify only those
    propositions that you conclude are inadmissible. Would the exclusion of this evidence
    affect the result of your analysis under question 2? For each proposition excluded,
    would the exclusion promote the search for truth? If not what other policies are
    served by the exclusion?

7. Whose baby II? *Morrison v. Jenkins* 80 C.L.R. 626 (Aust. 1949)

[Melbourne, Oct. 13, 14, 17, 18; Dec. 22. Latham C.J., Rich, Dixon, McTiernan and
Webb JJ.]

[In proceedings to obtain the custody of a child, the applicants, Mr. and Mrs. M., alleged
that there had been a confusion of identity between their child and that of Mr. and Mrs.
J. at the hospital at which the two children were born at about the same time and that
each mother had been given the child of the other. They accordingly sought an order
for custody of the child which was – and had been for some four years – in the custody
of Mr. and Mrs. J. The primary judge found that the child was in fact that of Mr. and
Mrs. M., and he ordered that they have the custody of the child.

Held, by RICH, DIXON and WEBB JJ. (LATHAM C.J. and MCTIERNAN J. dis-
senting) that the order should be set aside because, per RICH and DIXON JJ., the
evidence left the parentage of the child so much in doubt that it would not be for the
child's welfare to remove it from its present custody: *per* WEBB J. (LATHAM C.J. and
MCTIERNAN J. *contra*), the evidence as a whole did not warrant the conclusion of the
primary judge that the child belonged to the appellants.]

Decision of the Supreme Court of Victoria (Full Court), (1949) V.L.R. 277
affirmed . . .

LATHAM C.J. On 22nd June 1945 a baby girl was born to Mrs. Alberta Gwen
Morrison in the labour ward at the Kyneton Hospital in Victoria. Within the preceding
five minutes a baby girl had been born in the same ward to Mrs. Jessie Jenkins. Mrs.
Morrison and her husband claim that the baby known as Nola Jenkins, who has lived
with the Jenkins family ever since Mrs. Jenkins left the hospital, is her (Mrs. Morrison's)
baby and that the girl known as Johanne Lee Morrison who was given to Mrs. Morrison
at the hospital as her baby is not in fact her child. Mr. and Mrs. Morrison took proceedings against Mr. and Mrs. Jenkins by way of habeas corpus, claiming the custody
of Nola . . .

The case for Mr. and Mrs. Morrison was supported by their own affidavits and by
affidavits of Mrs. Amelia Williams (Mrs. Morrison's mother), Dr. Douglas John Thomas
and Dr. Lucy Meredith Bryce – clinical pathologists highly skilled in the making of blood
tests, which is a very specialized form of medical practice. Mr. and Mrs. Jenkins made
affidavits in reply, as also did Sister Lockhart and Sister Cass of the Kyneton Hospital.
These two nurses attended upon the occasion of the confinement of the two ladies,
Mrs. Morrison and Mrs. Jenkins. The parties, the nurses and Dr. Lucy Bryce were cross-
examined upon their affidavits. An affidavit by Dr. Gerald Loughran, who delivered

both children, was also filed on behalf of Mr. and Mrs. Jenkins. Dr. Loughran at the time of the trial was absent in Singapore and was not available for cross-examination.

The learned trial judge examined the evidence in detail and approached the question of the parentage of Nola by asking four questions, which were as follows: – "1. Was the female child to which Mrs. Morrison gave birth on June 22, 1945, in the labour ward of the Kyneton District Hospital the offspring of the union between her and her husband William Henry Morrison? 2. Was the female child that was brought to Mrs. Morrison before she left the labour ward the female child to which she had given birth about half an hour earlier? 3. If the female child so brought to her was not the child to which she had given birth, was there an opportunity for a mistake to be made by which some other female child could have been substituted for the child to which she had given birth? 4. If there was such an opportunity, what other child could have been mistakenly substituted for the child to which Mrs. Morrison had given birth?"

The answers which his Honour gave to these questions were as follows: 1. Yes; 2. No; 3. Yes; 4. Johanne Lee. Bearing in mind the gravity of the issues before the Court, his Honour was thoroughly convinced that Nola was the daughter of Mr. and Mrs. Morrison and, after considering what course of action would be for the welfare of Nola, he made an order that Nola should be delivered up to Mr. and Mrs. Morrison, and that they should have custody of her.

As to some matters there is no room for doubt. In the first place, it is established beyond question that a female child was born to Mrs. Morrison in the Kyneton Hospital on 22nd June 1945.

In the second place, I regard it as also completely established that that child (whoever she was) was the issue of Mr. and Mrs. Morrison. Mrs. Morrison gave evidence that she had never had sexual intercourse with any person other than her husband. She was not cross-examined upon this matter. The learned trial judge believed her evidence. There is in my opinion no ground whatever for suggesting at this stage in the proceedings that Mrs. Morrison had been unchaste and that the child which was born to her was not the child of her husband.

The three separate sets of blood tests applied to Mr. and Mrs. Morrison and Johanne Lee show, according to the uncontradicted scientific evidence, that the child Johanne Lee, although she might be the child of Mrs. Morrison, cannot possibly be the child of Mr. and Mrs. Morrison. This proposition has not been challenged at any step of the case. The scientific evidence on this point is conclusive . . .

Mr. and Mrs. Jenkins submitted an affidavit by Dr. Loughran (who could not be cross-examined) to the effect that he made blood tests of them and of Nola and that according to his recollection the tests showed that Nola could be their child. They declined to have any further tests made by the highly-qualified experts who were available. No evidence was given by any witness to the effect that Dr. Loughran's evidence, even if completely accepted, showed or even tended to show that Nola actually was the child of Mr. and Mrs. Jenkins or that she could not be the child of Mr. and Mrs. Morrison. It is established that Johanne Lee is the child which was brought to Mrs. Morrison within not more than half an hour of the birth of her child and is the child which has been in her custody ever since. It is therefore clear that a mistake was made in the hospital and that Mrs. Morrison was given the wrong baby . . .

Sisters Cass and Lockhart gave evidence to the effect that before the two babies were born to Mrs. Jenkins and Mrs. Morrison either two cots containing clothes marked with the names of the mothers or one cot containing such garments was in the labour ward. The learned trial judge rejected this and other evidence of the nurses and accepted the evidence of Mrs. Morrison. He also accepted the evidence of Mrs. Morrison that the two babies were taken out of the labour ward at the same time in the arms of Sister Atkinson. I cannot see how a court of appeal could justify a reversal of the decision of the learned judge with reference to evidence of this character by believing evidence which the learned judge had rejected by reason of his opinion of the credibility of the witnesses. But, in any case, the evidence as to whether there were two cots or only one cot in the ward and where any cot was in the ward and as to whether Sister Atkinson took the babies out in her arms or otherwise is on the margin of the case.

The findings of the learned trial judge as to the credibility of the evidence of the various witnesses were hardly challenged. Upon appeal, though not at the trial, consid-erable attention was directed to evidence given by Mrs. Williams, the mother of Mrs. Morrison, that on the day when the children were born she was shown a baby by Sister Lockhart as being Mrs. Morrison's child and that that child had a fair complexion. Johanne Lee has a dark complexion. This evidence appears to me to be unimportant. Whether the evidence of Mrs. Williams is accepted or not, it leaves untouched the certain conclusion that Johanne Lee is not Mrs. Morrison's baby. Sister Lockhart may have shown Mrs. Williams the right baby, but even if the conclusion arose at a later time than that found by the learned trial judge, it still leaves for determination the problem of the identification of Mrs. Morrison's child . . .

Johanne Lee was substituted for the baby born to Mrs. Morrison. The question for determination is whether Nola was Mrs. Morrison's baby for whom Johanne Lee was substituted. The circumstances of the two births, which were practically simultaneous, the fact that Sister Atkinson had no midwifery experience as to tagging babies with some identifying label, that the two babies were taken out of the ward together by Sister Atkinson to be bathed by Sister Lockhart, wrapped up in some wrapper provided by the hospital, though possibly also with bunny rugs round them, that there was only one bath in which to bathe them, that the baby which was brought to Mrs. Morrison half an hour after birth as her baby was unclothed, wearing no identifying garments, that the learned trial judge did not accept the evidence of the nurses that there were cots in the ward tagged with the names Morrison and Jenkins, that there was every opportunity for confusion between the Morrison and Jenkins babies, and the most important fact that Johanne Lee is not the child of Mr. and Mrs. Morrison, so that Mrs. Morrison got the wrong baby, all go to support the conclusion that the Jenkins baby was by mistake given to Mrs. Morrison.

But it was argued that two other female children were born in the hospital at about the same time, namely to Mrs. Hayes on 19th June and to Mrs. Perry on 20th June, and that one of these babies might have been substituted for the baby born to Mrs. Morrison. Mrs. Morrison's baby was born on 22nd June. Sister Lockhart gave evidence that she did not think it was possible to mix up a newly-born baby with a baby who was even only twenty-four hours old. This evidence was apparently accepted at the trial by all parties as obviously true. No cross-examination was directed against it. The Hayes baby was about three days and the Perry baby about two days older than Mrs. Morrison's child. No evidence was given to support the speculation that Mrs. Morrison's baby was given to Mrs. Hayes or Mrs. Perry or that she was given one of their babies. In my opinion there was ample evidence to support the finding of the learned trial judge that Nola is the child of Mrs. Morrison . . .

RICH J. . . . Moreover, there is real doubt whether Nola is the child of the Morrisons and this is another factor to be taken into consideration in determining the issue of welfare. I am not satisfied that the scientific evidence is infallible. At most it goes to show that Johanne Lee is not the child of the Morrison union. But it neither shows nor purports to show that Nola Jenkins is the child of that union although it does show that Johanne Lee could be the child of Mrs. Morrison. On this issue the appellants must exclude every other reasonable hypothesis. Did a mistake in fact occur? The evidence of Mrs. Williams is inconsistent with that of her daughter, the female appellant, and is also inconsistent with the finding of the learned primary judge that the exchange of babies occurred shortly after birth. Moreover at the time of the alleged mistake two other recently born babies – the Perry and Hayes children – were born on the 19th and 20th June in the same nursery in the same hospital. The appellants had no evidence as to these children or their mothers or that either mother had ever seen her child before the morning of 22nd June. In these circumstances the possibility of a mistake with either of these children cannot be excluded. Thus the probability of a mistake with the Jenkins' child to the exclusion of any other is considerably lessened, if, indeed, a mistake did in fact occur. A decision as to parentage will not bind the child and at a later stage in other proceedings – for example under a will or settlement in which the child should be a party [to] a decision contrary to that in the instant case would be a grievous blow to the happiness and welfare of the child. Indeed in a proceeding to which the child is not a party the Court has no jurisdiction to decide a question of legitimacy . . .

DIXON J. . . . The inference that Nola is the child of the Morrisons rests of course wholly on circumstantial evidence. Notwithstanding the wealth of detail gone into, particularly as to the circumstances of the birth of the two children, the whole case depends upon a chain consisting of a very few evidentiary facts or circumstances and some steps in reasoning which together are relied upon as warranting the inference. The first of these facts or steps is the conclusion deposed to by scientific witnesses that Johanne Lee belongs to a blood group that is inconsistent with her being the child of Mr. Morrison. This conclusion the Jenkins are powerless to deny. The second step is the inference that she is therefore not the child of Mrs. Morrison. Any other inference would reflect upon Mrs. Morrison and the Jenkins make no such reflection. The third is the fact that from the time that Mrs. Morrison left the hospital with a girl child and until the scientists took the blood tests there has been no change in the identity of that child and she is Johanne Lee and was the child submitted to the blood tests. This fact is proved by the Morrisons. Nothing of course could be more probable and it may be accepted as possessing as much certainty as attaches to the proof of any fact in human affairs. But as it is an essential step in the reasoning it must not be omitted. The fourth step is proof that at the hospital where both women were confined there was a real chance of confusion between the female child which Mrs. Morrison bore and some other female child. The fifth step is the elimination of the possibility that any other child but Mrs. Jenkins' could have been attributed to Mrs. Morrison. The sixth step is the inference that correspondingly Mrs. Jenkins must have received Mrs. Morrison's child.

By this chain of reasoning the result that Nola is Mrs. Morrison's child is said to be established. To make good the last three steps a great deal of evidence was adduced at the hearing. The events of the morning of 22nd June 1945 when both women were delivered of female children within ten or fifteen minutes in the same labour ward were inquired into in great detail. I should have thought that neither nurses nor patients could be expected to observe or recall so much and that their attempts to reconstruct the incidents of the morning could not safely be relied upon. But two conclusions emerge which are clear enough. One is that there was no routine for identifying babies which excluded the possibility of mistake and the other is that because two women were delivered by the same doctor and nursing staff in the same ward within such a short time there was a greater liability to confusion.

But in my opinion the further inference or conclusions which have been drawn as to the precise manner in which the babies were handled and exactly by whom are doubtful and in some respects speculative and they are unsafe.

Two other recently born female children were in the hospital, one born on 20th and the other on 19th of June. It does not appear whether they were full-term children nor was the condition of the mothers or any other circumstances proved really relevant to the possibility or impossibility, likelihood or unlikelihood, of the confusion (if one took place) being with either of those children. The case for the Morrisons naturally was that their child was confused with the Jenkins' child immediately after the birth of the children. That was the view which Barry J. adopted and acted upon. But Mrs. Morrison's mother, who visited the hospital later on the same day, in the afternoon, said that she was shown a child as her daughter's which was not the child her daughter brought home from the hospital. The tendency of her evidence if it were correct was to show a confusion at some later time and not as a result of the birth of two children at nearly the same time in the same ward. There would therefore be little or no reason to suppose that the confusion was with Mrs. Jenkins' child rather than with one of the other two girl babies.

The only further fact I shall mention is that little or nothing is known concerning the blood grouping of the Jenkins and Nola. They submitted themselves to their medical adviser for a blood test and he reported that it disclosed that Nola might be their child, that is that their blood grouping was consistent with their being the parents of Nola. He made an affidavit to that effect but he was abroad and not available for cross-examination. The Jenkins declined to submit themselves and the child to further blood tests . . .

With any chain of circumstantial evidence the chances of error in the conclusion arise first from the chances of error in each fact or consideration forming the steps and second from the chance of error in reasoning to the conclusion from the whole of those facts and considerations. It is therefore wrong to take each fact or consideration separately, to assess the possibilities of error in finding it is established and then if you think it should be found afterwards to treat it as a certainty and pass to the next fact or consideration and so on to the conclusion. The possibilities of error at all points must be combined and assessed together.

In the present case I think that when all the possibilities are taken into account there is too much uncertainty in the inference that Nola is the child of Mr. and Mrs. Morrison to warrant an order taking her from Mr. and Mrs. Jenkins and placing her in the custody of Mr. and Mrs. Morrison. It was a sound exercise of the discretion of the Supreme Court to leave her in the custody of Mr. and Mrs. Jenkins . . .

McTIERNAN J. . . . The evidence proves that the child born to Mrs. Morrison on 22nd June 1945 in the labour ward of the Kyneton District Hospital was begotten by her husband. This fact is an irresistible inference from the evidence, given by Mrs. Morrison, that she never had sexual intercourse with any man other than her husband. Barry J. believed this evidence. There is no ground upon which an appeal court could properly decide that his Honour erred in believing this evidence or why the Court itself should disbelieve it or suspect that the child born to Mrs. Morrison was not begotten by her husband. The scientific evidence of the blood tests, the validity and the reliability of which are established by the evidence, proves that Johanne Lee, a child under the custody of the appellants, could be the child of Mrs. Morrison but not of her and her husband. The evidence further proves that Johanne Lee is the baby who was given to Mrs. Morrison after she had given birth to a child at the above-mentioned time and place, upon the supposition that it was the child to which she had given birth; she was the child whom Mrs. Morrison took with her from the hospital when she returned to her home.

These facts establish beyond any reasonable doubt that Mrs. Morrison was given a baby to which she did not give birth and the baby is Johanne Lee.

The next crucial question is when was the mistake made at the hospital which led to the substitution of Johanne Lee for the baby to which Mrs. Morrison gave birth. The answer to this question is that the mistake was made within half an hour of the birth of Mrs. Morrison's own child. This fact is proved by the following evidence elicited by the cross-examination of Mrs. Morrison: – Q. "May we take it that that was the baby that was brought back to you within half an hour at the outside of its birth and that you took away with you when you ultimately left the hospital? – Yes." Q. "So that, if any mistake was made, in the transposition of these babies, it was prior to that time? – Yes."

Barry J. accepted this evidence. It proved that the result of the mistake was complete before the afternoon of 22nd June. Mrs. Morrison's baby was then in the possession of some other woman.

In the light of this fact, Mrs. Williams' evidence, to which importance was attached in the Full Court, can have but small significance. It probably provides the reason why Barry J. paid no attention to Mrs. Williams' evidence (a fact noticed in the Full Court); she was not cross-examined. Mrs. Williams is Mrs. Morrison's mother; her evidence is in an affidavit filed in support of the appellant's application.

To whom was the baby born to Mrs. Morrison given?

The evidence proves that the parturitions of Mrs. Morrison and Mrs. Jenkins occurred at the same time and place and their babies were born within five to ten minutes of each other: their simultaneous parturitions created an emergency described in the evidence, arrangements had to be made quickly to cope with it.

The evidence further proves that in this hospital a female baby was born on 19th June 1945; and another female baby was born on 20th June 1945.

Assuming that each of these babies was born at the latest point of time to make those dates respectively their birthdays, then on the morning of 22nd June, when Mrs. Morrison and Mrs. Jenkins gave birth to their babies, the first of the two other babies would then be fifty-five hours old, and the second thirty-one hours old. If either was born at an earlier hour she would of course be older.

It is reasonably certain that before the morning of 22nd June these older babies would have been placed under the usual routine of a baby's life. They would have been more than once bathed, dressed, fed, and have been in the possession of their mother. It is hardly probable that either would at that stage of her life have been placed with a woman not her mother.

Sister Lockhart, a double-certificated nurse, said in the course of her evidence that she did not think it was possible to mix up a newly-born baby with a baby forty-eight hours old.

It is less probable that confusion could have taken place between Mrs. Morrison's baby and one of the older babies, than between her baby and Mrs. Jenkins' baby. The births of their babies were almost contemporaneous.

Barry J. found that a nurse carried them out, one on each arm, from the labour ward to the nursery to be bathed, and they were left unattended until Sister Lockhart bathed them.

The field within which the mistake could occur, upon any reasonable view, must be limited to the two mothers and the two babies who were all together in the comparatively small labour ward, receiving the attention of the doctor and nurses: these two mothers and babies were involved in the same set of circumstances . . .

There is no evidence which could raise a doubt that the members of the hospital staff did give each of the babies born on 19th June and 20th June respectively to her mother. It is not a probable hypothesis that Mrs. Morrison's baby was exchanged for one of those babies, upon a reasonable view of the circumstances . . .

Mrs. Morrison said that the child brought to her within half an hour of the birth was dark and unclad and was the child she took home with her. Mrs. Williams said the baby shown to her on that afternoon and which a member of the nursing staff told her was her daughter's baby was a fairskinned baby and resembled Mrs. Morrison's other children. This incident might possess significance only if Mrs. Morrison was present. She was not present . . .

WEBB J. . . . If there had been only two infants in the Kyneton District Hospital on 22nd June, 1945, namely those born on that day, this Court would, I think, be obliged to restore the judgment of Barry J. and give the custody of Nola to the Morrisons as their child. The onus of proof was on the Morrisons, but the credibility of witnesses was for the learned judge to determine. His Honour believed Mrs. Morrison when she said that the child born to her on 22nd June, 1945, was by her husband, and he naturally accepted the evidence of the blood tests that Johanne was not a child by Mr. Morrison. So he could properly have concluded that Nola was the child of the Morrisons, if there were only the two infants in the hospital on 22nd June, 1945. The same result would follow if it had been common ground that Mrs. Morrison and Mrs. Jenkins each received a newly-born baby on the morning of 22nd June, 1945. Mrs. Morrison and Mrs. Jenkins each claim to have received a newly-born infant that day. Mrs. Morrison contends that Mrs. Jenkins did receive a newly-born baby, because Mrs. Morrison is claiming Nola from Mrs. Jenkins. But the case for Mrs. Jenkins is that if Mrs. Morrison did not get her own baby, she got one of the older babies born on 19th and 20th June, 1945, and not the baby of Mrs. Jenkins. The conduct of the proceedings and the judgment indicate that there was no common ground that Mrs. Morrison and Mrs. Jenkins each received a newly-born baby. Sister Lockhart, who made an affidavit on behalf of Mr. and Mrs. Jenkins, was cross-examined with a view to showing that Mrs. Morrison's child was not given to one of the mothers of the two older infants born on 19th and 20th June, 1945, and the judgment gives ground for holding why Mrs. Morrison's child was not given to one of these two mothers, namely, an assumption by his Honour as to the ability of mothers generally to recognize their infants, and the evidence of Sister Lockhart as to the impossibility in ordinary circumstances of mixing up a newly-born baby with one twenty-four hours old.

Part of the cross-examination of Sister Lockhart was as follows: – "Is there much difference between a newly-born baby and a baby twenty-four hours old from the point of view of telling the difference to a nurse or a mother? . . . Sometimes there is. Are they any more likely, and better developed, any different characteristics? . . . Oh! the features settle a bit sometimes. Would you think it possible to mix up a newly-born baby with a baby twenty-four hours old? . . . I don't think so."

These questions suggest the possibility that the infant born on 20th June was born about midnight of that date. Of course the baby born on 20th June was at least thirty-one hours older than the babies born about 7 a.m. on 22nd June; but the older the baby is the less likely is it to be mistaken for a newly-born baby.

His Honour in his judgment under the heading "What other child could have been substituted for Mrs. Morrison's?" says: – "It appears that between the 19th June 1945 and 22nd June 1945, four female children were born at the Kyneton District Hospital. A female child was born on the 19th, another on the 20th and the two children, the circumstances of whose births have been examined, on the 22nd. It was submitted by Mr. Hudson that the evidence did not exclude the possibility that some baby other than Mrs. Jenkins' child may have been mistakenly exchanged for Mrs. Morrison's baby. I do not think there is any substance in this submission. It appears to me most unlikely that a mother of a child born on the 19th or 20th would fail to detect a mistake if a child born on the 22nd were brought to her. Moreover, Sister Lockhart was asked: 'Would you think it possible to mix up a newly-born baby with a baby twenty-four hours old?' and she answered, 'I don't think so.' If this be excluded as a possibility the findings of fact I have set forth earlier leave open only one conclusion, and it is that the only baby that could have been exchanged for Mrs. Morrison's baby was the baby born to Mrs. Jenkins."

Neither the cross-examination of Sister Lockhart nor the judgment of Barry J. deal with the actual condition of the two mothers of the older infants or the appearance of those infants. It is confined to mothers and infants generally. There was no evidence to show the actual condition of these two mothers on 22nd June. Neither may have been in a condition to receive or to recognize her infant. Further there was no evidence that neither of the two older infants could have been mistaken on 22nd June for a newly-born infant. Either or both could have been prematurely born. There was no evidence to the contrary. It is not a matter of common knowledge that under no circumstances could a baby two or three days old be mistaken for a newly-born infant. Sister Lockhart said twice that sometimes there is a noticeable difference before saying she did not think it possible to mix up a newly-born baby with a baby twenty-four hours old; that is, of course, if both mothers and both infants are normal at the time of the exchange, in which event no evidence is really necessary to show a mistake would not be likely to occur. I do not think that any presumption arose that the other two mothers and infants were normal, or that the Morrisons had given enough evidence, as a result of getting these obvious answers from Sister Lockhart, to shift the onus of proof to Mr. and Mrs. Jenkins that one of the two other mothers or one of the two older infants was not normal in condition or appearance on 22nd June, 1945. The onus of proof is not shifted by a mere statement of what is common knowledge. Although Mrs. Morrison had ether administered to her at the birth of her child on 22nd June she appears to have been in a normal condition when she received Johanne; but if Johanne was prematurely born on 20th June, or even on the 19th, she might have appeared newly-born on 22nd June...

Questions

1 Frame the ultimate proposition that the Morrisons would have had to have *proven* in order to satisfy the judges of the High Court. From the portions of their opinions included here, was each judge assessing the evidence and inferences against the same *ultimate probandum*? If not, how many different versions of the *ultimate probandum* were used? Was each judge applying the same standard of review?
2 In all, ten affidavits were submitted and seven witnesses were cross-examined on their affidavits. Which direct assertions by affidavit or on cross-examination were disputed or contradicted at trial? Which were undisputed and uncontradicted?
3 All judges (or all but one) agree that "It was a baby other than the baby known as Johanne Lee Morrison that was the baby borne by Mrs. Morrison." This is an inference critical to the case. What *evidential data* (here assertions by affidavit or by testimony) are *relevant* to this inference? Do these data directly support this inference, or are there intermediate inferences that must be made? How do the data and any intermediate inferences *combine* to support this inference? The judges agreed upon the conclusion that the evidence supported this inference, but is the reasoning by which each reached that conclusion the same?
4 Latham, C.J., and McTiernan, J., thought the evidence provided by Mrs. Williams "unimportant." Rich and Dixon, J.J., attached considerable significance to it. What is the inference that Mrs. Williams's assertions can be argued to have established that is relevant to the case? How does that inference undermine the argument that the evidence proved that "It was Nola who was the baby born to Mrs. Morrison"?
5 In light of the evidence, how confident are you that Nola was the natural child of Mr. and Mrs. Morrison? If we today had conclusive blood tests on all four children

and their parents analyzed by the leading experts in the field, how much would you bet that their conclusion would be that Nola was the Morrisons' child? What odds would you give or ask on a $100 bet?

6 Based upon the portions of the opinions you have read (a) what is the *rule of law* that the majority applied in *Morrison v. Jenkins*? (b) What is the *standard of review* the High Court applied? (c) What is the *standard of proof* that an Australian trial judge should apply in a similar paternity/custody case in the future? How do (a), (b), and (c) differ?

7 How does the decision of the High Court differ from the Judgment of Solomon? Which is more rational?

8. An investigation: basic concepts in analysis and evaluation

You are a police cadet in Jonesville on your very first assignment. A report of what sounds like a murder has just been received. A team has been sent out to investigate. You have been instructed to receive and organize all information potentially relevant to the investigation as it comes in from various sources. From time to time you will be asked to make provisional evaluations of the data. You will also be asked to answer some "academic" questions as part of your training.

A

It is reported that:

1 Y was murdered in his home at 4:30 p.m. on January 1st.
2 W_1 says that she saw a person with characteristics, a, b, c, and d enter Y's home at 4:15 p.m. on January 1st.
3 X has characteristics a, b, c, and d.

Assuming that each of these *propositions* is true, answer the following questions:

a Do you suspect that, "It was *X* who murdered *Y*" (*probandum A*, hereinafter "P_a")?
b Are propositions 2 and 3 *relevant* to P_a?
c Do propositions 2 and 3 *prove* P_a to be *true* on the *balance of probabilities*?
d Can you *infer* from W_1's statement that X was in Y's house at 4:30 p.m.?

Give reasons for your answers.

B

Deduction. Using not more than 12 further evidential propositions (such as, W_2 says that he saw X strike Y at 4:20 p.m.) in each instance:

i Construct an argument *proving* that it was necessarily the case that "It was X who murdered Y."

ii Construct an argument *proving* that it was necessarily the case that "It was *not* X who murdered Y."

C

You now have the following additional data:

4 W₂ says that he saw X, who was known to him, running out of Y's home at 4:45 p.m. on January 1st.
5 W₂ says that X was in a state of great agitation.
6 W₃ says that he overheard X on Christmas Day say angrily to Y: "I shall not forget this."
7 A forensic laboratory report states that hairs found on a chair in the room in which Y's body was found are almost certainly X's.

On the basis of propositions 1 to 7, indicate which of the following most closely approximates your current state of belief (select one):

a It is *possible* that X murdered Y.
b It is *more likely than not* that X murdered Y.
c The *odds* are 3 to 1 that X murdered Y.
d It is established *beyond reasonable doubt* that X murdered Y.
e I do not have *any belief* about P_a.

Give reasons for your answer.

D

You now have the following additional data. What difference does each proposition make to the *judgment* you made in (C)? Consider each item first on its own and then in *combination* with each and then all of the other items:

8 W₃, who is X's brother, says that he saw X enter Y's home about 4:05 p.m. on January 1st.
9 W₄ says that he was observing Y's home between 4 p.m. and 5 p.m. on January 1st and that a person who had characteristics a, b, and d was the only person he saw enter and the only person he saw leave during this period.
10 There is no record that X has ever committed a crime of violence.
11 X has two convictions for shoplifting; the most recent occurred five years ago.

Indicate the current state of your belief after considering *each* of these propositions in connection with propositions 1 to 7. State briefly how each of the new items of information and all of them combined affect your belief.

E

Further data. What difference does it make to your state of belief about P_a based on propositions 1 to 11 if *one* of the following items of information is added to your data? Consider each separately and in combination with the others.

12 X claims to have been in a house five miles from the scene of the murder between 2 p.m. and 5 p.m. on January 1st.

13 Z states that she was with X in a house five miles from the murder between 4 p.m. and 4:24 p.m. on January 1st.

14 A new pathologist's report suggests that Y might have died at any time between 2 p.m. and 6 p.m. on January 1st.

15 The same report suggests that the cause of death was probably a blow with a blunt instrument, but could have been from natural causes (such as from striking his head on a table as he fell), but this seems unlikely. No blunt instrument has been found on the premises.

Give reasons for your answers.

F

Ancillary evidence (evidence about evidence). What difference does it make to your state of belief about P_a based on propositions 1 to 15 if *one* of the following items of information is added to your data? Consider each separately and in combination with the others.

16 W_1 is a bank manager?

17 W_2 is very short-sighted?

18 W_2 is Y's brother and stands to benefit financially from Y's death?

19 W_1 seemed to be very nervous and hesitant when questioned by the police?

20 W_3 is a licensed private investigator?

21 Z is a prostitute?

a In what respect or respects is the information about W_1, W_2, W_3, W_4, and Z relevant to an assessment of that witness's *credibility*? Be specific.

b Is any of these witnesses likely to be *biased*?

c How is the new information relevant to your assessment of the likelihood of P_a?

Give reasons for your answers.

G

Revise your *judgment* about P_a in the light of the following *background information*; in each case consider the item separately and then jointly with all the other items in this section.

22 X is female.

23 X is a 65-year-old volunteer social worker.

24 Y was X's son.

25 Y's "home" was an apartment in a building with 20 apartments.

26 Y's home was in an apartment building with three separate entrances.

27 At an identification parade (line-up) held three days after the murder, W_1 failed to identify X.

Give reasons for the effect each proposition and all propositions together have on your judgment.

H

General propositions. In arguments about evidence, several different kinds of *general propositions* play an important role both as discrete steps in an argument and as *background knowledge.* At this stage it is useful to make elementary distinctions between *scientific truths* (such as the law of gravity, that eyewitness identification evidence is often unreliable), *common sense generalizations* (such as that running away is indicative of a sense of guilt), *commonly held beliefs* (such as national or ethnic stereotypes, including prejudices, that suggest that a person of such origins has certain characteristics), and *general background information* bearing on the present case (*case specific generalizations,* such as a *generalization* about X's habits or Y's character).

28 A recent report of empirical research on eyewitness evidence suggests that eyewitness statements reporting identifying characteristics of a suspect made in circumstances approximating those under which W_1 observed a person entering Y's home (proposition 2) are only 100 percent correct in 5 percent of the cases.

29 A recent scientific report suggests that properly conducted laboratory matching of traces of human hair in conditions approximating those upon which the conclusions reflected in proposition 7 were based are correct in over 95 percent of cases.

30 X regularly had afternoon tea with Y on Sundays.

31 Few parents murder their children.

32 Features a, b, c, d were as follows: (a) white hair; (b) approximate height of five feet; (c) a pronounced limp; (d) the wearing of a cheap brown coat.

State all the *generalizations* that you think may be helpful in interpreting the significance of these propositions. Classify each generalization.

I

Construct a list of ten propositions relevant to P_a. Can you think of a more efficient way of *marshaling* the data? If so, describe it.

J

You are the officer who has just been appointed to be in charge of the investigation. Review the information gathered so far:

a Is there any *missing* evidence?
b Is there an *absence of important evidence* about Y and how she met her death?
c Is there any *direct* evidence of the identity of the murderer, if this was murder?
d What *direct* or *circumstantial* evidence is there relating to X's opportunity to kill Y?
e *Imagine* three possible *scenarios* that might explain Y's death. Use these to identify good questions to ask at the next stage in this investigation.
f Construct a *plausible story* incorporating all the data in propositions 1 to 30 that indicates that it was almost certainly X who was the killer. Now construct an alternative, *rival*, story that indicates that it was almost certainly W_3, and not X, who was the killer.
g Can you *eliminate* any of the witnesses as suspects at this stage?

K

Other standpoints.

a You are X's attorney about to interview her for the first time about this event. What information do you hope to obtain from her? Why?
b You are the prosecuting attorney. You have to decide whether to arrest and charge anyone in connection with the murder on the basis of the information contained in propositions 1 to 32. Is it *sufficient* for this purpose? If not, how far short is it of being sufficient?

L

Concepts. (a) Review the glossary at pp. 379–87 below. Elucidate the meaning of each of the following terms as they were used in the context of this exercise: *relevance; probative force; proof; evidence; inference; ancillary evidence; missing evidence; incomplete evidence; credibility; reliability; corroboration; theory of the case; hypothesis; story; elimination; common sense generalization*. In what respects, if any, does their usage in this context differ from ordinary everyday usage and their technical use in legal discourse?

(b) "The law of evidence is a conceptual minefield." Most writers are agreed that it is important to distinguish clearly between "materiality," "relevance," "admissibility," and "weight" (or "probative force"); but there is no agreed terminology and some issues of substance are hidden in some of the debates about words.

One widely-held view might be restated in simplified form as follows: "materiality" concerns what has to be proved for the proponent to succeed (the facts in issue) and is governed by substantive law; "relevance" denotes a direct or indirect probative relation between an evidentiary fact and a *factum probandum* ("tends to support" or "tends to negate") and is a matter of logic; "probative force" denotes the strength of such support or negation; it is based on "experience," but there are few settled criteria for evaluation; questions of "admissibility" concern the exclusion of otherwise relevant evidence and are governed by the law of evidence (including the principles governing judicial discretions to exclude). (Twining (1985) 153.)

This quotation purports to restate "one widely-held view" about the distinctions between materiality, relevance, weight, and admissibility. What are the main points at which this view might be challenged? To what extent do you accept this view?

2

Fact investigation and the nature of evidence

"Have you ever given any attention to the Science of Evidence?" said Mr. Grodman. "How do you mean?" asked the Home Secretary, rather puzzled, but with a melancholy smile. "I should hardly speak of it as a science; I look at it as a question of common sense."

"Pardon me, sir. It is the most subtle and difficult of all the sciences. It is indeed rather the science of the sciences. What is the whole of inductive logic, as laid down (say) by Bacon and Mill, but an attempt to appraise the value of evidence, the said evidence being the trails left by the Creator, so to speak? The Creator has (I say it in all reverence) drawn a myriad red herrings across the track. But the true scientist refuses to be baffled by superficial appearances in detecting the secrets of Nature."[1]

A. Introduction: connecting the dots

Everyone draws inferences from evidence. The dog barks, you infer that someone is approaching the house; a loud horn sounds behind me, I infer that the driver is impatient or angry; there is a peculiar smell in the playroom after last night's teenage party; cigarettes? Hash? Or just leftover pizza? There is a fresh scratch on the front fender of my car with traces of red paint; Aunt Edna has just roared off in her new red Ferrari. There are dark clouds overhead, footprints in the sand, lipstick on the shirt, fingerprints on the steering wheel of a stolen car. All tell tales. Inferential reasoning is a basic human skill.

All disciplines, from archeology to zoology, from history to astronomy, from statistics to decision theory, have largely shared problems of evidence and inference (Twining and Hampsher-Monk, 2003). As Bentham said: "The field of evidence is no other than the field of knowledge" (Bentham 1810:1). Practicing lawyers, policemen, and judges as well as accountants, aeronautical engineers, auditors, intelligence analysts, and anyone involved in diagnosing damaged or faulty motor cars, computers, or human bodies are all involved in analyzing and using evidence as part of their work. Law is different only in that substantive law defines the hypotheses

---

1 Zangwill (1895) (cited by Wigmore as the frontispiece of *The Principles of Judicial Proof*)

to be tested, the propositions to be proved, and formal rules regulate the manner in which cases are prepared and the admissibility and use of evidence.

In recent years, the study of evidence has gained a high profile. In popular fiction, lawyer-novelists have sometimes outsold writers of traditional crime fiction. On television, as well as in bookstores, forensic scientists have joined the ranks of detectives through the works of Patricia Cornwell and programs, such as "Crime Scene Investigation" (CBS television, 2003–). In recent years, international criminal tribunals and truth and reconciliation commissions have proliferated, raising new problems about evidence and story telling. Events in Eastern Europe, Rwanda, South Africa, and Latin America have stimulated an enormous interest in "memory," especially among historians.[2] DNA is in the headlines regularly. In England several police authorities have been won over to FLINTS (Forensic Led Intelligence System), a computer-based tool for investigating multiple crimes, and making links between crimes that were not previously thought to be connected.[3] Evidence was a primary focus of attention in news about Iraq: the weapons inspections, Colin Powell's presentation to the Security Council, the question of links with Al Qaeda, the search for "weapons of mass destruction," and the investigations of the Commission on Terrorism into the tragic events of September 11, 2001 ("9/11").

Perhaps the strongest stimulus came from the terrorist attacks on 9/11. In the postmortem after the attacks on the World Trade Center in New York City and the Pentagon in Washington, D.C., it has been repeatedly alleged that the events could have been predicted because the US intelligence services had received several bits of information but they failed "to connect the dots" (or what Sherlock Holmes referred to as "trifles"). They had enough information to have predicted the event, but lacked the capacity to collate and analyze it. They did not have the capacity to "connect the dots" or methods for identifying as significant a few trifles from the masses of data that flowed into different agencies from a variety of sources. This diagnosis led to a reorganization of the intelligence services, changes in their training, and billions of dollars spent (or misspent) on efforts to develop computer programs aimed at assisting the process of analyzing intelligence data. The problems were encapsulated in the satirical cartoon shown in Figure 2.1.

An article in *The New Yorker* in February 2003[4] reported interviews with leading figures in the CIA and the Pentagon who are concerned with improving intelligence analysis in the aftermath of 9/11. They included Donald Rumsfeld, George Tenet, and Robert Gates. The starting-point was a judgment that American intelligence agencies did not possess the analytic depth or the right methods of analysis accurately to assess possible threats. The diagnosis and the prescriptions were expressed largely in terms that are familiar to students of evidence and inference: the dangers of a commitment to a single hypothesis; the need to distinguish between generating a hypothesis and testing it against the available data; the different problems that arise

---

2 E.g. Nino (1996), Krog (1999), Amadiume and Na'im (2000).
3 Richard Leary (2003).   4 Jeffrey Goldberg (2003) 40–47.

Figure 2.1 *Connecting the dots*

from a surfeit of information and absence of relevant and credible evidence; the difference between ambiguity and incompleteness; the value of alternative interpretations of ambiguous evidence; the dangers of "mirror imaging," that is "projecting of American values and beliefs onto America's adversaries and rivals"; a tendency to confuse the unfamiliar with the improbable; the relationship between a calculus of risk and thresholds of credibility; the likelihood of political bias entering into judgments where the situation is uncertain. These and other problems have been documented by the Commission on Terrorism and others. Though the vocabulary is sometimes different, all of these ideas should be familiar to students of evidence and inference; some of them seem to be derived, directly or indirectly, from Wigmore (1913, 1937) and Schum (1994).

The information that may have been available before 9/11 illustrates some of the difficulties associated with the task of "connecting the dots." Before the terrorists used airplanes as flying bombs to destroy the World Trade Center and damage the Pentagon, the FBI had received information that several foreign nationals from the Mideast, with little or no prior training or experience, had enrolled in different civilian flying schools to learn how to fly large commercial aircraft. It was widely reported that they wanted to learn how to steer and navigate civilian airliners, but not how to make landings or takeoffs in these aircraft, and that they had all paid cash for the lessons.[5] Assuming that these were the facts that had been reported, how might the FBI dots have been connected?

With the wisdom of hindsight, it was clear that the FBI dots, the training requests made by the foreign nationals who sought flying lessons, were significant information that was available before 9/11. Suppose that a well-trained analyst had focused on these dots because of an intuition that they were suspicious. She might have thought about this information by asking and answering the following questions:

1   *Identifying the reasons for suspicion.* This seems suspicious: Why? Answer: because:

   a   A trained pilot of any aircraft needs to know how to take off and land;

   b   Several foreign nationals all doing something unusual in the same time may be acting in a coordinated way and belong to the same organization(s) or group(s);

   c   A person who pays substantial sums of money using cash, rather than a credit card, check, or bank transfer, may be trying to conceal his identity or the source of the funds. Several people doing this simultaneously for the same type of transaction is even more suspicious. The analyst might have identified additional reasons for suspicion, but the reasons identified would have provided a sufficient basis for the next step.

2   *Generating hypotheses.* Why might someone want to be able to fly and navigate a commercial airliner, but not to land or take off?

   a   Innocent hypotheses.

      i   They plan to learn to land and take off later. This is Part I of an unusual training scheme;

      ii   Flying an aircraft is simulated in many video games and these "students" wish to design more realistic games;

      iii   An airline is training non-pilot staff to relieve pilots on long haul flights.

   b   Sinister hypotheses.

      iv   The flights these persons will be on board are for carrying drugs (or other contraband). They do not want to disclose the aircraft's destination to the pilot until the plane is almost there;

      v   The "students" plan to hijack one or more civilian airliners and the hijackers wish to control the flying and navigation prior to landing, but will force the pilot(s) to land at their chosen destination(s);

5   These reports are contested. Staff investigators of the National Commission on Terrorist Attacks Upon the United States reported that, "According to their flight instructors [in San Diego] Hamzi and Mihdhar [two al Qaeda terrorists] said they wanted to learn how to control an aircraft in flight, but took no interest in take-offs or landings." Staff Statement No. 16, "Outine of 9/11 Plot" (2004) at 14. In an earlier statement, they implied that the FBI did not have this information before 9/11. "Contrary to popular belief, Zacarias Moussaoui [the alleged twentieth hijacker] did not say he was not interested in learning how to take off and land. Instead, he stood out because, with little knowledge of flying, he wanted to learn how to take off and land a Boeing 747." Staff Statement No. 10, "Threats and Responses in 2001" (2004). See "Post 9/11 investigations: an exercise" below at pp. 52–53 for a fuller account.

vi It is not intended that the planes should land because they will be blown up in midair;

vii It is not intended that the airliners should land, because they will be used as "flying bombs" directed at specific targets on an analogy with suicide bombers. The list needs to be kept open in case other possible hypotheses are suggested as the inquiry develops, but the hypotheses identified are sufficient to enable the analysts to proceed.

3 *Eliminating some hypotheses.* Hypotheses i and ii are the least plausible, given the number of "students," the secrecy, and the departure from international regulations. Moreover, hypotheses i, ii, and iii could easily be checked. Fairly simple inquiries to determine the identity and background of the students and whether any foreign or domestic airlines had adopted training programs such as those identified in hypotheses i and iii should have enabled the analyst to determine whether they could be eliminated at this stage. The identities of the students and their backgrounds should have enabled the analyst to determine whether hypothesis ii could be eliminated.

4 *Prioritizing the remaining hypotheses.* On the basis of this information alone, the analyst might have provisionally ranked hypotheses iv–vii in terms of seriousness, plausibility, and easiness to check. For example, hypothesis vi is very serious, but it is implausible because it is not necessary for hijackers to take control of a plane in order to blow it up, unless it is planned to blow it up near a target (see hypothesis vii). Hypothesis iv merits investigation, but in terms of the consequences, it is less serious than the remainder.[6] Moreover, that hypothesis ought to have been relatively easy to pursue (and perhaps eliminate) through checks on the identity of the "students" and their associates and through information available to the FBI and to customs and drug enforcement agencies about the use of aircraft in transporting drugs (or other contraband).

The size of the group, the seriousness of the danger, and the relative plausibility of the scenario, given this information, should have suggested to the analyst that hypothesis vii deserves the highest priority, but that hypothesis v also needed to be pursued as a matter of urgency. Of course, the possibility of further hypotheses must be kept open. In focusing on hypothesis vii, there would have been some fairly obvious first lines of inquiry: for example, to what group(s) or organizations(s) do the students belong? Is there any information about the capabilities and intentions of these group(s) or organization(s)? What might be the targets of such attacks? What might be the timing? And so on. The evidence discovered in pursuing the first

6 Prior to 9/11, the FBI probably would have focused its resources on hypothesis iv. Throughout its history, the bureau has focused upon post-event investigations to develop criminal cases. The incentive structure rewarded agents based upon statistics reflecting arrests, indictments, and prosecutions. Control over cases was in the field offices, not FBI headquarters. These and other practices had established a law enforcement culture that constricted the bureau's ability to gather and share information and to use that information for strategic analysis for terrorism prevention. See National Commission on Terrorist Attacks Upon the United States, Staff Statement No. 9, "Law Enforcement, Counterterrorism, and Intelligence Collection in the United States Prior to 9/11." That culture was deeply ingrained and resistant to change. See also Staff Statement No. 12, "Reforming Law Enforcement, Counterterrorism, and Intelligence Collection in the United States."

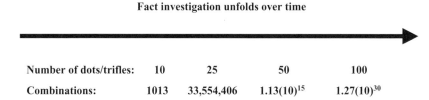

COMBINATIONS OF DOTS OR TRIFLES:

A COMBINATORIAL EXPLOSION

Given N dots/trifles, there are $2^N - \{N+1\}$ possible combinations of two or more of them.

Fact investigation unfolds over time

Number of dots/trifles:	10	25	50	100
Combinations:	1013	33,554,406	$1.13(10)^{15}$	$1.27(10)^{30}$

Figure 2.2 *Possible combinations of two or more dots/trifles*

two lines of inquiry should have enabled the analyst to re-evaluate the plausibility of hypothesis v. Meanwhile, preventive action might have been taken in respect of these "students" before their courses ended.

This example shows that even a single potentially significant piece of information can be used to generate hypotheses, and to eliminate some, through a combination of imaginative reasoning and background knowledge. Each potentially plausible hypothesis can then be used to generate lines of inquiry, specific questions, and to serve as a metaphoric "magnet" for generating other information, which may or may not be already available. However, this report was quite unusual because a piece of isolated information (more accurately a small number of related dots) was sufficient to arouse suspicion, focus attention, and be usable to generate hypotheses. It is much more common that an analyst must sift through large numbers of dots, each of which may seem trivial or insignificant on its own, seeking combinations whose significance is greater than the sum of the individual parts.

There are three basic problems inherent in the task of "connecting the dots." First, we must decide which dots to connect. The number of possible combinations grows exponentially as the number of dots. Figure 2.2 illustrates the difficulties encountered in examining combinations of dots. For example, if there were just fifty dots, there would be more than a million billion $[1.13(10)^{15}]$ possible combinations of two or more dots. In most instances there will be many more than fifty dots to connect; in some cases, there may be thousands or even millions of dots to consider. Clearly, it makes no sense to examine all of these possible combinations, even if we had the fastest conceivable computer. This would be a strategy of examining everything in the hope of finding something. What we need are strategies for better using our imaginations in deciding which dots to combine. The questions posed in the example above provide an example of such a strategy.

Second, combining dots or trifles involves more than just combining single items of information or details. Other dots come in the form of thoughts the analyst has about the meaning or significance of these informational details. Connecting the dots involves combining thoughts as well as potential items of evidence. Third, the analyst must decide what the identifiable combinations of evidential dots and her thoughts about them might mean. Connecting these dots makes it possible to generate hypotheses, but this process is also involved in constructing defensible and persuasive arguments about hypotheses in light of the available evidence.

Post 9/11 investigation: an exercise

According to statements prepared by the National Commission on Terrorist Attacks on the United States and other information published during post 9/11 investigations, agencies of the United States had the following information prior to 9/11.

1   The Federal Aviation Administration had information claiming that, in the 1990s, associates of Usama Bin Ladin were interested in hijacking and using aircraft as a weapon. Moreover, the FAA had considered the potential for terrorist suicide hijackings in the United States not later than March 1998. There was, however, no evidence indicating that the FAA possessed any credible and specific intelligence that Usama Bin Ladin, Al Qaeda, or any other groups were actually plotting to hijack commercial airplanes and use them as weapons of mass destruction. The FAA discounted that threat in presentations that it made to air carriers in 2000 and 2001 because it had "no indication that any group is currently thinking in that direction." Staff Statement No. 3 at 4.

2   On July 10, 2001, the Phoenix office of the FBI sent a report of a field investigation instituted in April 2000 whose purpose was "to advise the Bureau and the New York office [the 'Office of Origin' for the FBI's Al Qaeda program] of the possibility of a coordinated effort by Usama Bin Ladin (UBL) to send students to the United States to attend civil aviation universities and colleges." The memorandum reported that an "inordinate number of individuals of investigative interest" were or had attended civil aviation universities and colleges in Arizona, including Zakaria Soubra, a "hardcore Islamic extremist who views the U.S. as an enemy of Islam." The Phoenix memorandum made many recommendations, including a recommendation that "FBIHQ should discuss this matter with other elements of the U.S. intelligence community and task the community for any information that supports Phoenix's suspicions."[7]

3   On August 15, 2001, the Minneapolis FBI field office initiated an investigation concerning Zacarias Moussaoui. He had entered the country in February and had taken flying lessons at flight school in Oklahoma. On August 13, he began flight

---

7   A redacted copy of the Phoenix memorandum is reproduced in an appendix to the joint report of the U.S. Senate and House Select Committees on Intelligence that conducted a joint inquiry into intelligence activities before and after the terrorist attacks of September 11, 2001 (S. Rept. 107-351 and House Rept. No. 107-792).

training at the Pan American flight training school in Minneapolis. He stood out because, with little knowledge of flying, he wanted to learn how to takeoff and land a Boeing 747. On August 15, he was detained by the Immigration and Naturalization Service on the ground that he was a French national who had overstayed his visa because the FBI agent who handled the case in conjunction with the INS representative on the Minneapolis Joint Terrorism Task Force suspected that Moussaoui wanted to hijack planes. The Minneapolis office sent a summary of the investigation to FBI headquarters on August 18, with a request to the legal attaché in Paris for assistance. The legal attaché responded quickly. According to a letter sent by Special Agent Rowley to FBI director Robert Mueller after the 9/11 attacks, the attaché advised that the French Intelligence had confirmed Moussaoui's affiliation with radical fundamentalist Islamic groups and activities connected to Usama Bin Ladin. ("The 9/11 Commission Report") (2004) (the "9/11 Report") at 273.

4   In September 1999, the Central Intelligence Agency received a report that it had commissioned from the Federal Research Division of the Library of Congress titled, "The Sociology and Psychology of Terrorism: Who Becomes a Terrorist and Why?" (the "CIA Report"). In the executive summary, the authors concluded that "Al-Qaeda's expected retaliation for the U.S. Cruise missile attack against al-Qaeda training facilities in Afghanistan on August 28, 1998, could take several forms of terrorist attack in the nation's capital ... Suicide bomber(s) belonging to an al-Qaeda Martyrdom Battalion could crash land an aircraft packed with high explosives (C-4 and semtex) into the Pentagon, the headquarters of the Central Intelligence Agency (CIA), or the White House ... " CIA Report at 7. None of this information was treated with urgency prior to 9/11.

Questions

1   Put yourself in the position of the hypothetical FBI analyst described above. It is August, 2001. You have the information described in paragraphs 2 and 3 above. Assuming the information excited your suspicions, how would you proceed? Would your hypothesis have differed from those posed above? If so, how and why? What further immediate investigative steps would you have recommended?

2   During the summer of 2001, the FAA, the FBI, and the CIA were aware that there was a heightened risk that terrorists would undertake major attacks in the near future. How would you have designed a system that might have brought all the dots noted above into a single database? If you were an analyst with access to such a database, what questions would you have asked that might have connected these dots?

3   Put yourself in the position of a CIA analyst in the summer of 2001. You recalled and restudied the Library of Congress report and became concerned about the conclusion that al Qaeda might use aircraft as suicide bombs. Using the four-step methodology used by the hypothetical FBI agent, how would you have proceeded? What questions would you have sent to the FBI and FAA and other intelligence agencies to generate information to enable you to eliminate or support your priority hypothesis or hypotheses?

4 Now assume that you had been a supervisory agent in the FBI. You were aware of the generally heightened concern about terrorist threats and you had seen the Phoenix memo and investigative summary sent by the Minneapolis field office. In your capacity as supervising agent you received in late August 2001 the question you submitted in your capacity as a CIA analyst. How would you have responded? What additional actions by the FBI or other agencies would you have recommended? Recognizing that the FBI had limited resources and a culture that tended to "back-burner" investigative requests that were unrelated to the bureau's crime-solving culture, how would you have prioritized these requests? Had your superiors declined to assign these requests the priority you thought they deserved, what if anything do you now think that you would have done?

The examples based on 9/11 developed above illustrate three points that are central to understanding evidence in general, as well as evidence in legal contexts.

i The ingredients of proof in law and in other contexts involve evidence, hypotheses, propositions to be proved, possible explanations, and arguments linking evidence and hypotheses. All of these ingredients must be generated as a result of imaginative reasoning, also called *abductive* reasoning. Generation of these ingredients is a major element of *fact investigation*. But the more familiar logical forms of reasoning, *deductive* and *inductive*, are also required in the testing of hypotheses and in the construction of arguments linking evidence and hypotheses. Computers can be of help in locating and sorting data, but no program has been developed or is likely to be developed to serve as a substitute for the imaginative reasoning possessed by human beings.

ii Such reasoning activities cannot be productive in the absence of knowledge of the major properties or "credentials" of evidence. These credentials – relevance, credibility, and probative (inferential) force – have long been studied in the literature on evidence in the field of law. In fact, there is a rich legacy of knowledge about these credentials that has accumulated in law and that could be taken to greater advantage by persons in many other disciplines as well as by practicing lawyers. This legacy has accumulated over the centuries largely as a result of repeated experiences in the crucible of adversarial encounters in our Anglo-American adversarial system for settling disputes.

iii Evidence varies substantively, or in terms of its content, in a nearly infinite fashion and comes from many different sources. There is a method, however, of classifying forms of evidence that is *substance-blind*. This method allows us to study and analyze evidence without regard to the content of the evidence.

All of these general aspects of the study of evidence are an essential part of understanding evidence in legal and in other contexts. The next part deals with fact investigation, preserving the metaphor of generating dots, trifles, or details and finding potential explanations for those we generate during fact investigation.

Part C identifies and explains the credentials of evidence. The last part explains the importance of using the substance-blind form in examining evidence.[8]

B. Fact investigation: generating dots and explanations for them

One of the most important and difficult tasks in the practice of law is *fact investigation*.[9] Fact investigation involves the generation or discovery of the necessary ingredients of the later process of proof during which the parties present their competing views about "the facts" in some dispute. These ingredients include hypotheses or propositions to be proved, evidence, and arguments linking hypotheses and evidence. Thus, fact investigation involves the analysis, as well as the gathering, of evidence.

Fact investigation may also appropriately be termed *fact inquiry* because a crucial ingredient of fact investigation is the asking of questions. Fact investigation, as an ongoing process, is a *dynamic* activity; it takes place over time, and every episode is unique. The investigator learns different things at different times in response to questions she asks. As fact investigation proceeds, the investigator often has hypotheses in search of evidence and, at the same time, evidence in search of hypotheses. Knowing what questions she should be asking at any given time is rarely obvious, except in hindsight. Often, the most productive questions cannot be asked until she obtains answers to many other questions that may not seem important at the time they are asked.

In contrast, analysis is static. It is necessary at all stages of the process, but it is episodic rather than continuous. The investigator analyzes the then available data and hypotheses to refine the hypotheses (or generate new ones) and to determine whether and how the investigation should be directed or redirected. Given the analysis done, what further questions need to be addressed?

1. Types of logical reasoning and justification

Fact investigation in law shares many attributes that characterize discovery-related activities in other contexts such as science, history, medicine, and intelligence analysis. In any context, investigation and analysis (and proof) require the use of the three standard forms of logic: deductive, inductive, and abductive. Arguments in

---

8 A note on terminology: Lawyers are familiar with terms such as *direct evidence, circumstantial evidence, real evidence, discovery,* and *corroboration,* which have acquired technical legal meanings and have sometimes been the subject of controversy. These terms have different meanings when they are used by logicians, probabilists, newspaper reporters, and others. As this book is about the logic of proof, we have adopted definitions for a few terms (direct, circumstantial, corroboration) that fit this framework and which diverge from technical legal usage. For the sake of precision we have also used a few terms that may be unfamiliar such as *ancillary evidence, probandum,* and *autoptic proference.* All of these terms are defined in the Glossary.

9 The term is taken from the title of a book on fact investigation by Binder and Bergman (1984).

each of these forms can be expressed in the form of a syllogism. In deductive logic, the major premise must be a statement that is universally true:

Deductive: All As are Bs
              X is an A
              X is [necessarily] a B.

In inductive logic, in the sense of practical reasoning, the major premise is not universally true and ordinarily not stated. It is a generalization, a proposition, that may be true "usually," "many times," "more often than not," "sometimes," etc. It can however, be expressed in syllogistic form by articulating the generalization upon which an inference depends.

Inductive: Many As are Bs
              X is an A
              X is probably a B

Abductive reasoning is discussed in detail in the next section. It is the creative process of reasoning. Rather than reasoning from a hypothesis to a conclusion based upon the evidence, it involves reasoning from the evidence to a hypothesis that might explain it.

Abductive: Surprising event A has occurred
              If H were true, A would follow
              There is reason to believe that H might be true.

The applications of these forms of logic are described and illustrated in the materials that follow. For now, it is important to recognize that in legal and most other practical contexts a conclusion based upon the evidence can only be justified as rational through the use of one or more of these forms of logic.

2. Abductive reasoning and the generation of a new idea

In any context, investigation or discovery involves imaginative or creative thought. For many centuries it was assumed that the generation of hypotheses and new ideas involved some species of inductive reasoning. It was not until the late 1800s that questions arose regarding whether new ideas can arise by purely inductive means. It is one thing to justify some hypothesis inductively, based on evidence. But it is quite another thing to say how this hypothesis arose in the first place.

This distinction was considered carefully by Charles Sanders Peirce (1839–1914). Peirce argued that new ideas could not be generated by deductive reasoning, which shows that something is necessarily true. The price paid for necessity in such an argument is the absence of new information, since a deductive conclusion contains nothing that is not already included in its premises. Peirce also argued that new ideas cannot arise strictly on the basis of inductive reasoning. Such reasoning shows that some hypothesis is *probably* true, based on evidence. But this form of reasoning is involved in the justification of a known hypothesis and does not explain how the

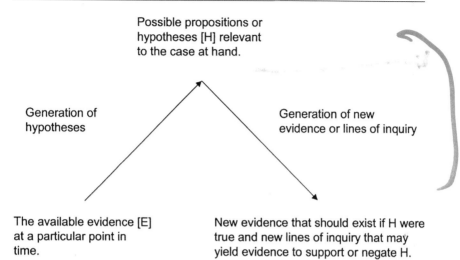

Possible propositions or
hypotheses [H] relevant
to the case at hand.

Generation of
hypotheses

Generation of new
evidence or lines of inquiry

The available evidence [E]
at a particular point in
time.

New evidence that should exist if H were
true and new lines of inquiry that may
yield evidence to support or negate H.

Figure 2.3 *A modified arch of knowledge*

hypothesis was generated or discovered in the first place. Peirce argued that there must be another form of reasoning associated with discovery and the generation of hypotheses or possible explanations. He termed this third form of reasoning *abduction,* by means of which we show that something is possibly or plausibly true.

Peirce associated abductive reasoning with flashes of insight (Peirce (1903) 304):

> The abductive suggestion comes to us like a flash. It is an act of *insight*, although of extremely fallible insight. It is true that the different elements of the hypothesis were in our minds before; but it is the idea of putting together what we had never before dreamed of putting together which flashes the new suggestion before our contemplation.

Peirce went on to put abductive reasoning in the following syllogistic form:

> The surprising fact E_1 is observed;
> *But if hypothesis H were true, E_1 would be a matter of course,*
> Thus, there is reason to suspect that H might be true.

The abductive process is graphically illustrated in the modified arch of knowledge shown in Figure 2.3.[10] Peirce's abductive syllogism defines the upward arm. The downward arm can be similarly expressed in syllogistic form.

> If H were true, then one or more of facts E_2, E_3, and E_4 ought to exist.
> Assume H is true.
> Thus, there is reason to believe that one or more of facts E_2, E_3, and E_4 exist.

10 Philosopher David Oldroyd (1986) developed the original arch of knowledge. As here, he used it as a metaphor to describe the process of investigation and discovery. We have modified it to make clear how the arch can be used to describe the reasoning involved in fact investigation and discovery in legal contexts.

The value of a new hypothesis to an investigator rests not only on its ability to explain evidence she already has; it may also allow her to generate new lines of inquiry that have not been suggested by other hypotheses she had been entertaining. The abductive process is not static. As a result of exploring the lines of inquiry suggested by H_1 or through other inquiries the investigator may discover new facts that require that H_1 be revised or eliminated. For example, the items of evidence, E_2, E_3, and E_4, that ought to have existed if H_1 were true may not exist (or may not be found). In other words, H_1 has failed this test. Instead, her inquiries may lead to the discovery of new items of evidence that makes it necessary to revise H_1. So too, new lines of inquiry suggested by H_1 may result in observations that suggest a new hypothesis, H_2, different from H_1. What we have to imagine are sequences of arches laid side by side as we generate more possible explanations or hypotheses.

A second difficulty with Figure 2.3 involves the nature of the linkage between the initial observation and the hypothesis that the investigator generated to explain this observation. If the analyst is asked to show how some new hypothesis H_1 explains E_1, the phenomenon that allowed her to generate it, she encounters the necessity for constructing an often elaborate argument or chain of reasoning from her observation to this new hypothesis H.[11] For that reason, fact investigation activities always involve *mixtures* of abductive, inductive, and deductive reasoning.

There is a direct connection between the theoretical matters we have just been discussing and the practice of fact investigation in law. It happens that, at the same time Peirce was developing his thoughts about abductive reasoning, across the Atlantic Sir Arthur Conan Doyle was developing the character of Sherlock Holmes. There is no evidence that Peirce and Conan Doyle each knew of the other's work. Though Holmes describes his reasoning feats as "deductions," it is clear that the form of his reasoning was abductive in nature.[12]

3. Generating explanations for dots or trifles

The importance of considering dots or trifles has never been better illustrated than in the exploits of Sherlock Holmes. In the *Boscombe Valley Mystery*, Holmes tells his colleague Dr. Watson (Baring-Gould, 1967, Vol. II, 148), "It was by an examination of the ground that I gained the trifling details which I gave to that imbecile Lestrade, as to the personality of the criminal."

Watson says: "But how did you gain them?"

---

11 The construction of complex arguments based on evidence is discussed and developed in Chapters 3 and 4.
12 A valuable account of the connections between Peirce's abductive reasoning and Holmes's investigative methods is the work of Umberto Eco and Thomas Sebeok (1983). Dr. Bell's observations about a new patient, Holmes's determination that Watson had returned from Afghanistan, and Kemelman's "Nine mile walk" in Chapter 1 provide additional examples of Peirce's abductive reasoning and illustrate the mixture of reasoning forms that are commonly required.

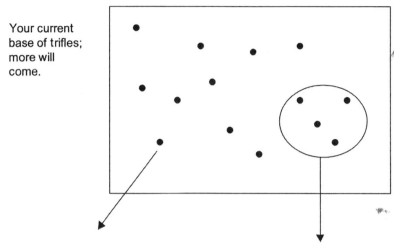

Your current base of trifles; more will come.

Luck: A new hypothesis generated from a single trifle.

A new hypothesis generated from a *combination* of trifles.

Figure 2.4 *Generating hypotheses from dots or trifles*

Holmes replies: "You know my method. It is founded on the observance of trifles."

The "trifles" Holmes mentioned refer to any single dot or detail obtained during fact investigation, whether it comes from a witness or from tangible evidence of some sort.

In fact investigation, the number of trifles mounts up quickly as the process unfolds. In either a criminal or civil case each question posed may lead the investigator to a significant number of trifles. Difficulties arise, as we illustrate in Figure 2.4 above, when she begins the process of trying to make sense out of a rapidly accumulating collection of trifles. In this figure, each dot represents a trifle she has collected.

As Figure 2.4 illustrates, on some occasions you might be fortunate in observing a single trifle that may suggest a new hypothesis – for example, in a criminal investigation fingerprints, DNA samples, shoe prints or other traces that can point to a particular suspect (hypothesis). In most cases, however, the generation of a new hypothesis or possibility is based upon a combination of several or many trifles. This is where the difficulties arise. The number of trifle combinations increases exponentially as the number of trifles gathered increases. The investigator as analyst must determine which trifle combinations to examine. Prescribed methods for analyzing the trifles and for marshaling the investigator's or analyst's thoughts become important at this stage. The principles of logic and the ways they are applied in analyzing evidence in a legal context are presented and illustrated in Chapter 3. Methods of analysis that enable the analyst, be she an investigator or a lawyer preparing for trial, are presented in Chapters 4, 5, and 6.[13]

C. On the credentials of evidence

There are three major characteristics or credentials of an evidential datum that must be established in analyzing its relationship to a hypothesis: *Relevance, credibility*, and *probative [inferential] force or weight*. No trifle comes with these credentials already established; these credentials rest upon arguments constructed by the analysts. For that reason, we must first consider the major ingredients of arguments.

1. Evidential foundations of argument

Arguments consist of evidence, hypotheses, and statements called *generalizations* that justify linkages between evidence and hypotheses. Metaphorically, an argument is a chain of reasoning from evidence to hypotheses. Links in these chains correspond to stages or steps in an argument. Each link exposes a source of possible doubt or uncertainty.

In arguments based on evidence, there is a necessary distinction to be made between evidence of some event and the event itself. In symbols, E* represents evidence (of some kind) about event E. Just because this evidence E* says that event E occurred does not entail that E did occur. In fact, from E* the decision-maker can only infer to some degree that event E did occur. For example, a witness Mary asserts E*, that she saw Harold let the air out of his boss's tires last Monday. Just because Mary makes this assertion does not mean that Harold did let the air out of his boss's tires (event E). Mary's credibility is open to question. The same idea applies to other forms of evidence. For example, Evidence E_2^* in the form of a photograph allegedly shows event E_2, that Frank was in front of the bank shortly before it was robbed on March 4, at 3 p.m. The decision-maker must be concerned about the *authenticity* of this photo. This photo may have been doctored in various ways; it may also have been taken on a different day at a different time. Issues of credibility raise very important sources of doubt, but there are other doubts that arise when we attempt to relate evidence to hypotheses or matters we are trying to prove.

In law a hypothesis is a proposition to be proved (a *probandum*). Probanda occur at several different levels in an argument. A probandum is always a proposition that in principle can be shown to be true or false. Levels of probanda in an argument are illustrated in Figure 2.5.

In a legal case there will be a major or basic probandum at issue which we refer to as the *ultimate probandum*. The rule of law that will be applied to determine whether the plaintiff or the prosecutor is entitled to relief may be viewed as the major premise. The ultimate probandum is the minor premise. If the evidence

---

13 Recent research suggests that how skillful we are at marshaling our *existing* thoughts and evidence influences how skillful we will be in generating *new* hypotheses and *new* lines of inquiry and evidence (Tillers and Schum (1991); Schum (1999)).

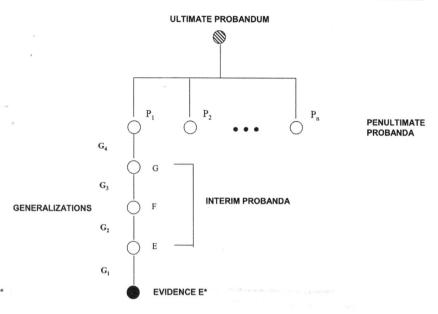

ULTIMATE PROBANDUM

P_1 P_2 ... P_n PENULTIMATE PROBANDA

G_4

G

G_3

GENERALIZATIONS   F   INTERIM PROBANDA

G_2

E

G_1

EVIDENCE E*

Figure 2.5 *Levels of probanda in an argument*

establishes that the ultimate probandum is true to the required degree of certainty, then the verdict must be for the prosecution or the plaintiff. In criminal cases, for example, an ultimate probandum includes all conditions that the prosecution must prove to be true beyond reasonable doubt, in order to justify a conviction. So, in a murder case, the prosecution must prove beyond reasonable doubt: that the victim is dead; that it was an unlawful act that caused the victim's death; that it was the accused who committed that act; and that the accused had the intent required by the law of the jurisdiction in which the murder occurred. In civil cases the ultimate probandum consists of the ultimate facts the plaintiff must plead and prove in order to prevail.

An ultimate probandum is either (rarely) a simple proposition or (usually) a compound proposition that can be broken down into simple propositions, each of which needs to be proved in order to prove the ultimate probandum. These simple propositions are termed *penultimate probanda.* These penultimate probanda are the material facts. The field of law is unique in that the law defines the material facts or the specific propositions or elements that are necessary and sufficient to prove some ultimate probandum.

The evidence E* in Figure 2.5 is linked to penultimate probandum P_1 by a chain of reasoning indicated by propositions E, F, and G. Each of these propositions may be true or false and thus represent a source of doubt interposed between evidence E* and penultimate probandum P_1. These propositions we refer to as *interim probanda.* All probanda, ultimate, penultimate, and interim, are potential sources of doubt or uncertainty. This is what the term *probandum* indicates; they are all matters to be proved.

In Figure 2.5, there are generalizations (labeled G_1 through G_4) that are associated with each link in the chain of reasoning from evidence E^* to penultimate probandum P_1. These generalizations, also called *warrants* (Toulmin, 1964), supply justifications for each reasoning link. Generalizations are commonly "if–then" statements that are *inductive* in nature; that is, they are hedged probabilistically in some way. For example, consider generalization G_2 in Figure 2.5 that licenses the inference of proposition F from proposition E. This generalization might read: "If an event like E occurs, then (usually, frequently, often) an event like F will occur." For example, assume that a police officer testifies in a narcotics case E^* that he observed person X passing a small packet of white powder to person Y at this time and place. From this evidence, the fact finder is asked to infer that X did pass a small packet of white powder to person Y at this time and place. The applicable generalization on which the inference is based might be stated as, "If a police officer testifying under oath says that an event occurred, then this event almost certainly/probably/possibly did occur." Some generalizations may be based on what is referred to as "common sense generalizations" while others are based on specific knowledge of phenomena that the events describe. The kinds of generalizations, as well as various inferential hazards they present, are described in Chapters 3, 4, and 10. These basic argument ingredients make it possible to provide an introductory account of the three basic credentials of evidence.

2. On relevance

When is a trifle evidence? The answer is: when its relevance to some material proposition or matter to be proved in the case at hand is demonstrated. The Federal Rules of Evidence in the United States provide a useful definition:

> *Rule 401. Definition of "Relevant Evidence."* "Relevant evidence" means evidence having any tendency to make the existence of any fact that is of consequence to the determination of the action more probable or less probable than it would be without the evidence.

In order to be relevant, evidence must either make a penultimate probandum more or less probable (or must be relevant to the credibility of a witness or other evidence offered in the case). In short, penultimate probanda supply the touchstones for establishing the relevance of evidence.

There are two important species of relevant evidence – directly relevant evidence and indirectly relevant evidence.[14] These are illustrated in Figure 2.6. Evidence E^* is

---

14 The meaning of directly relevant and indirectly relevant should not be confused with the legal meaning of the direct and indirect evidence. The terms *direct* and *indirect* evidence have different meanings in law. In law, "[d]irect evidence is evidence which, if believed, resolves a matter in issue." McCormick (1999) 278. All other evidence is indirect or circumstantial because "even if the circumstances depicted are accepted as true, additional reasoning is required to reach the desired conclusion." *Id.* (See further below pp. 76–77.)

P$_i$: A penultimate probandum

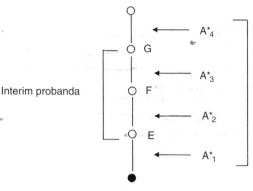

Ancillary [indirectly relevant] evidence on the generalizations at each reasoning stage. Such evidence can either support or undermine a generalization.

Interim probanda

E*: *Directly relevant evidence*

Figure 2.6 *Directly relevant and ancillary evidence*

directly relevant because it is linked directly by a chain of reasoning to a penultimate probandum P$_1$. As a result, E* is said to be *directly relevant evidence* if the chain of reasoning is defensible.

The other four items of evidence A_1^*, A_2^*, A_3^*, and A_4^* are also relevant, but only indirectly so. Although they are themselves not directly linked to a penultimate probandum, they are nevertheless relevant because they each bear upon the strength or weakness of links in the chain of reasoning set up by an item of directly relevant evidence. As a result, these four items are *indirectly relevant or ancillary evidence.*

For example, a witness Willard testifies that defendant Donald was at the scene of the crime when it happened. His evidence is admitted since it bears upon Donald's opportunity to have committed the crime; i.e. it is directly relevant evidence. Then a rebuttal witness Ruth testifies that she was with Willard at a location several miles away from the scene of the crime at the time the crime was committed. If what Ruth says is true, then Willard's assertion cannot be true. Ruth's testimony about Willard's location is relevant because it makes it less probable that Donald had an opportunity to commit the crime. However, Ruth's testimony, when considered in light of Willard's testimony, is also relevant because it diminishes or negates the credibility of Willard's testimony about Donald. In other words, Ruth's testimony is indirectly relevant and is ancillary evidence bearing upon Willard's credibility.

3. The credibility of evidence and its sources

An item of evidence can be either a tangible item or a testimonial assertion. A major question is: To what extent can we *believe* what this evidence says? In other words, and in symbols, if E* represents the evidence we have that event E occurred, the credibility question is: To what extent does E* justify a belief or inference that event

E did actually occur? Unless evidence E* is perfectly credible, it would be a mistake to equate E* and E. Having evidence that E occurred does not entail that E did in fact occur.

There are two forms of evidence that may be relevant in a legal dispute – tangible evidence and testimonial evidence. The attributes that must be considered in assessing the credibility of each form differ.[15] Credibility involves more than one dimension or attribute regardless of what kind of evidence we are considering, but the specific attributes of credibility depend upon what kind of evidence we are considering. Attributes of the credibility of testimonial evidence are quite different from the attributes of the credibility of tangible evidence.

a. Tangible evidence

There are many forms of tangible evidence including objects, documents, sensor images, measurements, and a variety of representations such as charts, maps, and diagrams. All of these kinds of tangible evidence are open to inspection. What they actually reveal in a particular situation is not always obvious.[16] The trouble is that tangible evidence is not always what it seems to be. Documents can be forged, currency counterfeited, images labeled incorrectly, samples of blood mixed up, and drugs planted on persons. There are three important attributes that must be considered in assessing the credibility of tangible evidence.

i. *Authenticity.* Authenticity is the most important element of the credibility of tangible evidence. In law, the party seeking to introduce a document, photograph, or another item of tangible evidence must offer evidence "sufficient to support a finding that it is what it purports to be" (Federal Rule of Evidence 901). To be admissible it must purport to be something that is relevant to a penultimate probandum or to the credibility of other evidence in the case.

There are three major sources of ancillary evidence that may call into question the authenticity of tangible evidence. The first involves evidence that has been deliberately contrived in order to mislead others such as a forged document. Errors in recording, transmitting, or processing evidence is the second source. Tangible evidence may pass through many hands before it is offered at trial. The opportunities for processing or handling errors of various kinds increases with the number of hands a tangible item passes through. Blood samples may be mislabeled or even

---

15 In many contexts including law, the word "reliability" is often used synonymously for the term "credibility." The difficulty is that the term "reliability" has a much more restricted meaning than does the term "credibility." A process of some sort is reliable to the extent that it is consistent, repeatable, or dependable. Thus, you believe your car is reliable to the extent that it will continue to take you where you want to go for some specified time in the future.

16 In many cases, the decision-maker must rely upon the opinions of experts to tell her what event(s) a tangible item reveals. For example, a ballistics expert may express an opinion identifying the weapon from which a bullet was fired and explain how the markings on the bullet enabled him to form that opinion. Experts can be wrong in their interpretation of what event(s) a tangible item reveals. It is the bullet that is tangible evidence; the expert's opinion comes in the form of testimonial assertions whose credibility can only be assessed by reference to the credibility attributes of testimonial evidence. See below at pp. 65–67.

substituted one for another. That is the reason for the requirement that there should be evidence establishing the chain of custody from the time the evidence was discovered (the bloody glove) or generated (an entry into a business record) until the time the evidence is presented at trial. If we do not know all of the links in a chain of custody, we cannot vouch for the authenticity of a tangible item. Finally, the witness whose testimony is offered to establish the authenticity of an item may be mistaken or untruthful.

ii. Accuracy/Sensitivity. Sensing devices of all sorts can supply tangible evidence in the form of images such as photographs and other sensor records. The credibility issue here concerns whether a sensing device provides the degree of resolution necessary for us to discriminate among possible events that may be recorded on the image. In some instances the accuracy of a sensing device can be degraded by inappropriate settings of the device's controls. For example, if a camera is not focused properly, then the image obtained may be blurred. In such cases we may not be able to tell whether the photo does in fact show person X, as the proponent of this evidence claims. Courts admit business records as an exception to the hearsay rule only if the witness who identifies them knows enough about the process for recording the data on which they were based, the process by which they were generated, and how they were stored to enable the other party, through cross-examination, to identify flaws that might undermine the accuracy of the information they contain. This issue of accuracy also applies to demonstrative evidence, such as statistical analyses, results of which can be displayed in graphic or pictorial form. Every student of elementary statistics learns how easy it is to construct inaccurate and misleading graphic accounts of the results of statistical analysis.

iii. Reliability. A reliable process is one that is repeatable, dependable or consistent. For some kinds of tangible evidence, reliability refers to the operating characteristics of the device used to generate it. Such a device is reliable only if it gives the same reading or image on repeated applications of the device. No sensing device can provide reliable readings if the device is not properly maintained. For example, a police radar gun cannot be expected to provide reliable indications of a car's speed if it has not been serviced regularly or if it has been dropped on several occasions. Replicable or repeatable processes form the basis for all statistical analyses. The term "reliability" in statistical analysis refers to the extent of measurement error that is naturally associated with any statistical estimate.

b. The credibility of testimonial evidence

i. *The basis for a testimonial assertion.* An investigator or a lawyer must consider how the witness acquired the data upon which her testimonial assertion is based. The witness may have acquired the data from one or a combination of three sources. For example, person P tells us that event E occurred, and we ask the natural question: How do you *know* that E happened? P can give one of three possible answers. First, she may say, "I observed the occurrence of E for myself." P is claiming *personal knowledge* of the occurrence of event E.

Second, she may say: "I did not observe event E myself, but I learned about its occurrence from person Q." In other words, P obtained information about the occurrence of event E *at second hand* from another person Q. In fact, however, the information obtained by P might have come through sources in addition to person Q. For example, we might ask Q how she obtained information about event E, and she might respond: "I heard about it from person R." If we cannot question R or otherwise discover the *primary source* of information about event E, then P's testimony has no better status than rumor or gossip. P's testimony in this case is *hearsay.* Whether or not such evidence would be admitted at trial depends on the rules regulating the admissibility and use of hearsay evidence. But hearsay evidence is often valuable evidence in advancing fact investigation, even when such evidence might not be admissible later at trial.

Third, P might say: "I did not observe E myself. However, I observed two other events C and D from which I *inferred* that event E also occurred." This is *opinion evidence*, not based on any personal knowledge of event E. The legal requirement that a witness have personal knowledge of events upon which her testimony is based addresses the primary difficulty such opinion evidence poses. The witness ought to tell the decision-maker that she observed C and D so that the decision-maker can decide whether those observations justify an inference that E occurred.[17]

ii. *The credibility attributes of a testimonial assertion.* Assessing the credibility of any testimonial assertion requires consideration of three attributes: *veracity*, *objectivity*, and *observational sensitivity.*

The term "veracity" has caused many difficulties in studies of witness credibility. Suppose witness W tells us that event E occurred and we later discover that it did not occur. This must mean that we now have conclusive evidence that event E did not occur. *Question*: Was W lying to us in his testimony? The correct answer to this question is: "Not necessarily." Witness W might simply have been mistaken in his observation, or was not objective in forming his beliefs. So, a person is being untruthful in testimony only if this person testifies against his/her beliefs. We must be sure that challenges to a witness's credibility are based on the correct forms of ancillary evidence. For example, evidence that a witness has poor eyesight is not a challenge to the witness's veracity.

Now consider the *objectivity* attribute. Suppose we believe that witness W is testifying in accordance with her beliefs. She testifies E*, that event E occurred, and she firmly believes that event E did occur. Now the question is: On what basis did she form this belief? Did she form this belief based on accurate and objective

---

17 In some circumstances, a witness may be permitted to express an opinion, lay or expert, because that is the best or only way the decision-maker can understand the evidence. A lay person might testify, "Harold was sad when the boss fired him," without providing a detailed description of facial expression and behavior that led her to conclude he was sad. A qualified expert might testify, "Based upon a comparison of the DNA in the blood found at the scene and the accused's DNA, it is almost certain that the blood at the scene was the accused's blood," because a non-expert would be unable to understand or interpret the data upon which the expert's opinion was based.

understanding of her sensory evidence, or did she form it on the basis of what she either expected or wanted to occur? An illustration: We are all, on occasion, liable to believe what we either expect or hope will occur regardless of what our senses tell us. By definition, an objective observer is one who forms a belief based on evidence rather than on surmise [expectations] or on desires.

Suppose we now believe that witness W's belief about event E was formed objectively on the basis of sensory evidence. The next question is: How good was this sensory evidence? So, we now come to the credibility attribute we have labeled "observational sensitivity." There is much more to this attribute than just considering the adequacy of a witness's sensory systems: vision, hearing, touch, smell, and taste. Of course it is true that a person may be mistaken in testimony if his visual acuity was poor, and uncorrected, at the time of an observation. But a witness having very acute sensory powers under normal circumstances may still obtain faulty sensory evidence.

Much depends on a witness's general physical condition at the time of an observation. If the person was intoxicated, or under the influence of some narcotic or other chemical substance, we cannot expect this person to make full use of her sensory capabilities. Another general consideration concerns the conditions under which an observation was made. A person having even very acute visual capabilities would not be able to exploit these capabilities under very low levels of illumination. Nor would a person with very acute hearing be able to recognize the content of speech uttered in the presence of strong background noise.

c. Ancillary evidence about testimonial credibility attributes

What is so often overlooked is that the three credibility attributes of ordinary witnesses just discussed are both time and context dependent. For example, witness W might well have been more objective in observations regarding event A than he would have been in observations about event B. Our sensory systems are known to vary in their sensitivity over time. Fortunately, or unfortunately, no one keeps statistical records regarding our veracity, objectivity, and observational sensitivity that might subsequently be used if we show up as witnesses in a legal dispute. To substitute for a lack of any statistical evidence regarding these attributes we substitute a variety of *different* items of evidence we may have about a person that may serve as ancillary evidence regarding attributes of the credibility of ordinary witnesses.

There is no discipline outside of law in which a more extensive effort has been made to record various grounds for impeaching or supporting witness credibility. Figure 2.7 identifies grounds for impeaching and supporting witness credibility that have been compiled over the ages. Each item listed is a form of ancillary evidence bearing upon the credibility of ordinary witnesses, but only some, not all, of these forms of ancillary evidence can be uniquely associated with one of the three credibility attributes we have just discussed.

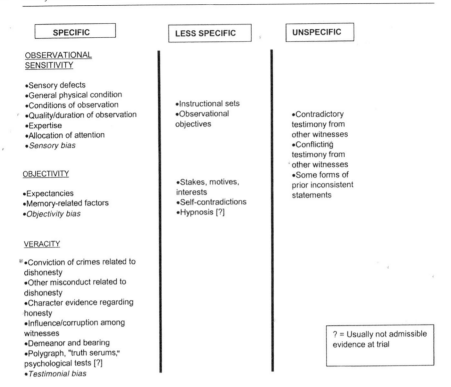

Figure 2.7 *Ancillary evidence concerning attributes of witness credibility*

First consider the column in Figure 2.7 labeled "Specific." Here are forms of ancillary evidence that can be associated specifically with one of the credibility attributes: veracity, objectivity, and observational sensitivity. We have already discussed some of these forms of evidence, but not all of them. In the case of observational sensitivity we must be concerned about the quality and duration of a witness's observation. Did the witness get just a brief look or did he have an opportunity to note details during an observation? Did the witness have any personal characteristics, e.g., poor eyesight, that might have affected her ability to make the observation accurately? Did the witness have any area of expertise that would have allowed her to notice certain important details that would not have been noticed by witnesses lacking that expertise? Was the witness able to allocate full attention to what was being observed, or was she distracted in some way during the observation? Sensory bias refers to various ways in which our vision, hearing, and other senses might have been biased, perhaps by clever forms of deception.

Three specific forms of ancillary evidence are listed under the objectivity attribute. We have already mentioned how one's expectancies may influence beliefs as well as the various memory-related factors we discussed. Memory also affects the objectivity of a witness's testimony. Is there any evidence bearing upon the witness's ability to accurately recall the observations about which she was called to testify? Objectivity bias refers to instances in which a witness may have been biased towards believing an event occurred, or did not occur, regardless of the sensory evidence she obtained.

• Specific veracity-related evidence can involve several matters. Various forms of prior behavior related to dishonesty are admissible under certain circumstances as is any evidence of influence or corruption among two or more witnesses. The demeanor and bearing of a witness while giving testimony may be relevant to her credibility. However, not every composed witness is necessarily being truthful and not every agitated or distraught witness is being untruthful.

Finally, there is a third category of bias we have labeled *testimonial bias*. Regardless of what a witness may believe about the occurrence of event E, this person may have a distinct preference for revealing or not revealing what she believes. Some persons may relish being the bearer of what they believe will be good news to one party or the other. Other persons may have a distinct aversion to being the bearer of what they regard as bad news for one of the parties in contention.

The second column in Figure 2.7, labeled "Less Specific," contains classes of ancillary evidence that may bear upon two of the credibility attributes. For example, instructional sets of the sort mentioned earlier and an observer's objectives may bear upon both observational sensitivity and objectivity. Central processes in the brain exert control over our senses. Indeed, the retinas of our eyes are extensions of our brains. Thus the objectives for which an observation is made can influence visual sensitivity, perhaps by increasing sensitivity. But objectives being entertained at the time of observation may also influence the objectivity with which we form beliefs based on the sensory evidence we obtain. We may be more "primed" to believe one thing rather than another. In addition, any stakes, motives, or interests in observations and testimony can influence both the objectivity with which we form beliefs and our veracity in our testimony about these beliefs.

An important form of credibility-related ancillary evidence concerns self-contradictions, i.e. prior inconsistent statements. A witness may tell a police officer immediately after some incident that event E occurred, but then later tell someone else that event E did not occur. We cannot be sure in such instances whether these self-contradictions involve this witness's objectivity and memory, or whether they indicate untruthfulness. In some instances, events interposed since an observation may cause a person to revise a belief held earlier. The witness may simply be honestly reporting a revised belief. Unfortunately, witnesses are known to "change their stories" for other reasons involving their veracity – e.g., because they were bribed. Finally, the two classes of ancillary evidence with question marks are simply possible forms of credibility-related ancillary evidence that would most likely not be admissible at trial. However, they may be employed during fact investigation.

The column labeled "Unspecific" identifies two of the oldest known forms of evidence challenging credibility: *contradictory* and *conflicting* evidence from other witnesses. Contradictory testimony involves events that cannot happen together;

i.e. they are mutually exclusive. Alibi evidence supplies an example. Joe testifies that defendant Mike was at the scene of the crime in Boston at the time the crime was committed. Later, witness Mary testifies that Mike was with her at this same time in New York City. Mike cannot have been in both places at the same time.

Conflicting or divergent testimony involves testimony about different events that may both have occurred but which favor different possibilities. As an example, we may have evidence that Mike had the intention to commit the crime. But we may also have evidence that Mike did not have the means to commit this crime. Here are some reasons why contradictory and conflicting evidence are unspecific as far as credibility is concerned. Suppose Mary testifies that event E occurred at a certain time. The opposition offers Paul who testifies that event E did not occur at this same time; here is a contradiction since E cannot have occurred and not occurred at the same time. The opposition asserts that Paul has shown that Mary was being untruthful in her testimony. There are two problems, the first of which is the obvious fact that the credibility of both Mary and Paul is at issue. Second, suppose that Paul is indeed correct about the nonoccurrence of event E. This hardly means that Mary was being untruthful; she may have simply made an observational error or was not objective in forming her beliefs based on the observation she made. The same kinds of troubles occur when witnesses provide conflicting testimonies. Finally, some forms of self-inconsistency can be linked to any of the three credibility attributes.

One major purpose of keeping careful track of the assorted grounds for credibility impeachment and support shown in Figure 2.7 is that we may hear arguments about witness credibility that are grounded upon the wrong form of ancillary evidence. Here are just two examples of such difficulties.

1   An opponent offers evidence that impeaches the objectivity of witness Mary by showing that Mary strongly expected to observe event E. But then this opponent says: "We have shown that Mary was not truthful in her testimony." This conclusion does not follow from the evidence given about Mary because she may have truthfully reported what she believed at the time of her observation and what she believed at the time she gave testimony. What is being challenged is Mary's objectivity as an observer and not her veracity in giving testimony.

2   The proponent offers a witness Joe who testifies that event E occurred. The opponent then offers another witness Walter who asserts that Joe was intoxicated at the time of his observation. But then the opponent says: "My evidence from Walter shows that Joe was not truthful in his testimony." There are several troubles here, the most obvious of which is that Joe's alleged intoxication at the time of his observation, if true, influences his observational sensitivity at the time of the event and not his veracity at the time of testimony. Second, the opponent can hardly claim access to truth here since the credibility of Walter is also at issue.

d. Credibility v. competence

The term "competence" has meanings in ordinary discourse that it does not have in law. Synonyms for the word "competence" include: qualified, adequate, appropriate, or suitable. In some contexts other than law no distinction is made between the competence and the credibility of a source of testimonial evidence. There are some situations in which these terms are used synonymously. This invites inferential catastrophe since not all competent persons are credible and not all credible persons are competent. Competence and credibility appear to be independent characteristics. You regard your Uncle Harold as the most honest, objective, and observationally acute person you have ever known. But you would not solicit an opinion from Uncle Harold about a gastrointestinal problem you currently face if he was a truck driver or someone else not having the requisite competence to answer your question. On the other hand, here is Mr. Smith who is regarded as an extremely competent auditor; his opinions are often solicited by well-known industrial organizations. The trouble is that Mr. Smith was privy to an episode of "cooking the books" in an organization, which he later, untruthfully, denies.

In legal terms, an ordinary witness is *competent* if he or she was in a position to make an observation, could understand what was being observed, and could coherently recount the results of this observation. However, the credibility of a witness concerns the extent to which her assertions can be believed. Believability depends upon attributes concerning veracity, objectivity, and observational sensitivity.

4. On the probative force of evidence

The *probative force* of an item or body of evidence answers the question: "How strong is this evidence in favoring or disfavoring some penultimate probandum in the case at hand?" This final major credential of evidence is in many ways the most controversial. Though it is universally recognized that the probative force of evidence is commonly graded in probabilistic terms, there is considerable disagreement among legal scholars and probabilists about how such grading should take place.

Any item of directly relevant evidence must be linked to a penultimate probandum by a chain of inferences. This chain can contain several links. The first link in the chain is always the credibility link. The remaining links are those necessary to demonstrate the relevance of the item to a penultimate probandum. The probative force of an item depends upon the strength of each link in the chain. When there is a mass of evidence to consider, there will be many chains of reasoning to consider. Assessing the probative force of a mass of evidence requires that the probative force of every chain be assessed and that the individual assessments be combined to determine the net probative value of the mass with respect to the ultimate probandum. There are alternative ways in which the probative force of an item of evidence or of a mass of evidence can be assessed. These are discussed in Chapters 8 and 9.

D. A substance-blind approach to evidence

Asked to say how many different kinds of evidence there are, we might be tempted to throw up our hands and say: "The question is foolish; of course there are unlimited varieties of evidence." This would certainly be true if we were considering the substance or content of evidence. By the *substance* or *content* of evidence we refer to the kind of events the evidence supports. For example, an X-ray image, a spent shell casing, a patient's report of pain at a certain location, a passage from a contract, and a reading from an oscilloscope all suggest the occurrence of different kinds of events.

In fact investigation, the investigator may encounter any conceivable kind of evidence. Investigators in the fields of law, history, and intelligence analysis must be prepared to evaluate evidence having any conceivable substance. The problem then is: How can we ever say anything general about evidence if it comes in so many substantive varieties? One answer is provided if we choose to ignore its substance and focus instead on its inferential properties. Two of the three evidence credentials, relevance and credibility, supply us with a very useful scheme for classifying evidence. This classification scheme does allow us to say some general things about evidence that apply regardless of the substance of the evidence.

As a fundamental basis for a substance-blind classification of evidence that rests only on inferential issues, we begin by considering two questions:

1 How does the user or evaluator of an item of evidence stand in relation to the evidence? In answering this question we consider the form or type of evidence we have. Can the user pick it up and look at it or observe it in some other way? Or, does the evidence come from someone else who allegedly made some form of observation? Answers to such questions suggest how we are to establish the credibility or believability of the evidence.

2 How does the event reported in the evidence stand in relation to any probanda the user is considering (including any ultimate or penultimate probanda)? This is a relevance question. It is here that we must distinguish between evidence that has *direct relevance* on some probandum and evidence whose relevance on a probandum is only *indirect*. As we noted, in the latter case we will say that such evidence is *ancillary*. Remember that ancillary evidence is either evidence about evidence or is evidence about the strength or weakness of links in a chain of reasoning.

How any item of evidence is classified on an inferential basis is always relative to a particular context and problem situation. An item of evidence judged to be relevant in one inference task may not be so judged in another. Similarly, the credibility of evidence and its sources are context-dependent. Our belief about a witness's credibility might change across different contexts in which this witness might testify. Relevance and credibility, as credentials of evidence, are not necessarily stationary. During the course of work on some inferential matter, an analyst may have good reasons for changing her mind about either the relevance or the credibility of an item of evidence.

Any useful evidence classification scheme must take account of these two matters. It may happen that a certain item of evidence is used in more than one way in a particular argument. In addition, you may use this item of evidence in different ways

		DIRECTLY RELEVANT	INDIRECTLY RELEVANT [ANCILLARY]
TANGIBLE **(+ or -)**	• Objects •Documents •Images •Measurements •Charts •Maps		
UNEQUIVOCAL TESTIMONIAL (+ or -)	• Direct observation • Secondhand • Opinion		
EQUIVOCAL TESTIMONIAL	• Complete • Probabilistic		
MISSING TANGIBLES OR TESTIMONY			
ACCEPTED FACTS			

Figure 2.8 *Substance-blind forms of evidence*

at different stages of work on a case. Finally, argument construction is a creative act on your part. Thus, there is a natural subjective element in any classification of evidence. How you perceive some item of evidence in a given context might not be so perceived by others, such as your opponent.

A substance-blind classification of evidence, based on credibility and relevance dimensions, is shown in Figure 2.8. Some forms of evidence we have identified might not always be admissible in any trial. But this two-dimensional classification scheme has been useful in thinking about evidence in any context (law or elsewhere) in which it might be used. In addition, you would certainly not disregard certain evidence during fact investigation that you might not be able to get admitted at trial. This evidence, such as objectionable hearsay statements, might have enormous heuristic or abductive value in suggesting new hypotheses and new evidence that is admissible.

The rows in Figure 2.8 arise when we consider how the user or evaluator stands in relation to an item of evidence. In examining this dimension we must attend to the physical properties of evidence, to the manner in which it came into existence, and to the source(s) from which it was received.

First suppose the evidence is *tangible* in the sense that the user can in some way examine it to determine what it reveals. In some cases the user can make such a determination on her own. In other cases, however, the user might need the assistance of an expert in order to determine what some item of tangible evidence reveals. There are, of course, many different kinds of things we can examine for ourselves including objects, documents, sensor images, measuring devices, and a variety of representations such as maps, charts, diagrams, and so on. All of these kinds of tangible evidence are open to our direct examination. What they actually reveal in particular instances is not always immediately obvious.

The plus and minus signs under tangible evidence and under unequivocal testimonial evidence in Figure 2.8 are there to show that both forms of evidence have another property that needs to be recognized. Such evidence can reveal either the occurrence or the nonoccurrence of some event. Evidence revealing the *occurrence* of some event is said to be *positive evidence* (+); that which reveals the *nonoccurrence* of events is said to be *negative evidence* (−). There are some important issues here that bear upon the discovery or generation of evidence as well as upon the inferential use of evidence.

There is no order of precedence between positive and negative evidence as far as either their relevance or their probative force are concerned. Negative evidence, such as tangible or testimonial evidence about the nonoccurrence of an event, can be just as relevant and inferentially forceful as positive evidence about the occurrence of an event. It is common to focus on evidence regarding the occurrence of events and easy to overlook evidence regarding the nonoccurrence of events. In any inferential context, however, it may be as important to inquire about what did not happen as it is to inquire about what did happen. In the mystery *Silver Blaze*, for example, only Sherlock Holmes saw that the fact that the dog guarding the stable did not bark supported an inference that the person who took the horse out of the stable was a person with whom the dog was familiar.

Suppose that the evidence a user receives comes from another person in the form of an assertion that some event of interest occurred or is true. It is customary to call such evidence "testimonial." The credibility of the person making the assertion is always a possible source of doubt and for that reason testimonial evidence is at least two inferential steps from the occurrence or nonoccurrence of events the testimony is offered to support. The same is true with respect to tangible evidence – its credibility attributes (authenticity, accuracy, and reliability) are possible sources of doubt.

There may be even more inferential steps when the evidence is tangible. Suppose that the tangible evidence is a document that the user can examine, such as Agent Dawes's memorandum in *United States v. Able* (pp. 23–27), and that what is of interest in this document is Agent Dawes's assertion that the accountant, Timothy Cooper, had told him that papers in inactive client files had been lost during his move to new offices in 2004. What is tangible is of course the document and not the event to which it refers. In that situation, there are even more inferential steps the user must consider before she reaches a conclusion with respect to events reported.

When a person W testifies about some event we are entitled to inquire about how this person obtained her information about this event. Questions raised in such inquiry are as varied as they are interesting. So, testimonial evidence from a particular person can itself have different grounding. Did the person make a direct observation, get the information at second hand, or is it merely an opinion based on other observations? But testimonial evidence has other characteristics we must recognize. In some situations witness W will give *unequivocal* testimony that a certain event E did occur; W asserts: "Event E did occur." Of course we have uncertainty about whether or not E did occur even though W's testimony is not equivocal or is not hedged in any way. We have already examined some of the specific sources of uncertainty we face as far as W's credibility is concerned (veracity, objectivity, and observational sensitivity).

In other situations a person may give testimony that is *equivocal* in nature. There are at least two ways in which such equivocation may be expressed. In one case we may ask W whether or not event E occurred and W responds by saying such things as: "I couldn't tell," "I don't remember," or "I don't know." Such extreme equivocation may indicate an act of honest self-impeachment on W's part; he actually does not know or remember whether or not E occurred. However, W's extreme or complete equivocation is also consistent with the possibility that W does know or can remember whether or not E happened but, for various reasons, refuses to tell us. In other situations, however, W may hedge or equivocate in less extreme ways. He may state, for example, "I believe it *very probable* that E did occur." In some situations he may attach specific numbers to grade the strength of his belief regarding E; W might assert: "I am 70 per cent sure that E did occur."

Either tangible or testimonial evidence rests, at some stage, upon someone's observations, your own or those of some other person. Again, if no person can be identified who made a relevant observation of an object, event, or situation, our hearing about the occurrence or nonoccurrence of an event may be classed as rumor or gossip. But there are situations in which expected evidence is either not found or is not produced on request and we began to inquire why this is so. Evidence we regard as *missing* may be either tangible or testimonial in nature. An example follows.

You take your car in for routine service and are astonished by the amount you are charged. One expensive item involved replacement of your fuel pump. You ask to see your original pump that was replaced and the mechanic tells you that he discarded it and cannot show it to you. You might easily regard his failure to produce this tangible evidence with some suspicion. Our failure to find evidence where we expect to find it or the failure of persons to produce things or provide testimony can in many cases be regarded as a form of evidence. It is quite important to note that having no evidence about an event is not the same as having evidence that this event did not occur. The distinction between negative evidence and missing evidence is not always made. The distinction is captured by the old saying, "Evidence of absence is not the same as absence of evidence."

Finally, there are other kinds of information we often use as evidence that do not rest upon someone's direct observation. We make frequent use of records we regard as authoritative and we also take certain things for granted without further evidence. In other words, we often make use of what may be regarded as *accepted facts.* One form of authoritative record is an almanac that supplies information about the time of sunrise, lunar phases or times of high and low tide. Other examples include tables of chemical compounds, physical constants, mathematical formulae, and tidal occurrences. If you used such information in an inference task you would ordinarily not be obliged to prove that the information is trustworthy or that someone actually observed it in some way. You would, of course, be obliged to prove that you extracted the correct information from any such authoritative records. Other information often used in an inference is normally accepted without further proof. For example, you would not be obliged to provide further proof about such matters as: Heroin is a narcotic substance; gasoline is a flammable substance; or that the population of New York City exceeds that of Omaha.

Before we consider the column dimension of the taxonomy in Figure 2.8 there is a very important thing to note about the forms of evidence listed in the columns. Evidence that we have may exist in the form of *combinations* of these evidence types. For example, we might have a transcript of a deposition. This is a tangible document that we can examine for ourselves. But this document is a record of testimony given by a witness W. In this recorded testimony W reports that, as a result of a direct observation, he believes that event E occurred at a certain time. Here, of course, we have the authenticity of the document to be concerned about as well as the veracity, objectivity, and observational sensitivity of witness W. Other combinations of the types of evidence shown in the rows of Figure 2.8 are easy to imagine. In every case, we may have some quite difficult credibility matters to consider if we are to believe what these combinations of types of evidence seem to reveal.

The columns in Figure 2.8 arise in response to the question: How does an evidence item stand in relation to the matters at issue in a particular inference? Answers to this question involve the nature of the relevance of the evidence. It will be necessary for us to recall the distinction between directly and indirectly relevant evidence that we illustrated by means of Figure 2.6. The evidence taxonomy in Figure 2.8 differs slightly from the one shown in another work (Schum, 1994, 114–20). This other taxonomy preserves a distinction that has often been made between two forms of directly relevant evidence: *direct evidence* and *circumstantial evidence.* Evidence is often said to be direct if it goes in one reasoning step to a matter revealed in the evidence. If you believe the evidence to be perfectly credible, that settles the matter. Evidence is said to be *circumstantial* if, even though perfectly credible, it provides only some but not complete grounds for belief in some probandum or proposition. In other words, circumstantial evidence, even though perfectly credible, is always just *inconclusive* on some probandum.

The reason why we have not made a distinction between direct and circumstantial evidence is that the term *direct evidence* has several major difficulties.[18] To illustrate these difficulties, we first make use of two "rules" that have been proposed by Binder and Bergman (1984, 77–82). Their two rules are:

Rule 1. All evidence is either direct or circumstantial.
Rule 2. There is no such thing as direct evidence.

The first rule reflects the fact that a probandum or proposition on which an item of evidence may seem direct depends on how we have structured the argument based on this evidence. Second, every argument can be further decomposed to reveal new sources of doubt or uncertainty. Thus, there is arbitrariness associated with any identification of an item of evidence as being direct.

There is just a bit more to be said about ancillary evidence and its inferential use. Recall that evidence is ancillary if it bears upon the strength or weakness of links in a chain of reasoning for evidence being argued as directly relevant. It happens that we must also defend, by argument, the relevance and credibility "credentials" of ancillary evidence. The relevance at issue here concerns whether or not the ancillary evidence we offer actually bears upon the generalizations we assert in defense of the direct relevance of other evidence. The result is that we may often have complex arguments associated with any defense of the relevance and credibility of ancillary evidence.

As Figure 2.8 shows, there are ten possible combinations of the rows and columns. Thus, for example, tangible evidence of some form might be either directly relevant or ancillary in nature relative to some problem and within some particular chain of reasoning. The same is true for the other four basic types of evidence in the remaining rows. The major virtue of the evidence taxonomy we have just presented is that it allows us to characterize any type of evidence without regard to its substance or content.

18 See above p. 62 n.14 and Glossary.

3

Principles of proof

A. Introduction: evidence in legal contexts

Within the common law tradition there has been a tendency to equate the subject of evidence with the law of evidence and to marginalize or neglect other dimensions such as the logic of proof, witness psychology, the evidentiary significance of forensic science, and the role of statistics and of narrative in arguing about and deciding contested issues of fact in legal contexts. In Part B, we first describe the shared assumptions upon which evidence scholars have based their work for two centuries – the Rationalist Tradition – and its importance in contemporary practice and then describe and illustrate the principles that form the basis for the logic of proof.

Part C begins with Wigmore's explanation for his view that mastery of the principles of proof is at least as important as mastery of the rules regulating the admissibility and use of evidence. Part D introduces some terminology basic to understanding those principles. The probative processes and logical principles necessary for analyzing evidence and marshaling arguments in legal contexts are presented and developed in Part E.

B. The Rationalist Tradition[1]

The common law model of adjudication reflects some basic assumptions – assumptions about the nature and proper ends of adjudication, assumptions about the nature of knowledge and the possibility of making accurate present judgments about past events, and assumptions about what is involved in reasoning about disputed questions of fact in forensic contexts. The assumptions underlying contemporary theory and practice, at least as reflected in the writings of those who have specialized in the field of evidence, have persisted with little apparent change since the eighteenth century. Throughout, the accepted assumptions have generally conformed to an ideal type that has been characterized as "the Rationalist Tradition."

An understanding of these assumptions is important to practitioners as well as to scholars. They provide the framework within which rules of procedure and evidence have evolved and within which arguments about the desirability of proposed changes

---

1 For a full account with references, see *Rethinking* 32–91.

will be debated in the future. They represent "first principles" that can usefully be employed by an advocate in urging that a specific rule of procedure or of evidence should be construed in a manner that favors the outcome she seeks – that is, they provide a basis for constructing arguments to persuade a court that the advocate's position is consistent with the assumptions upon which the system is based and that her opponent's is not.

An understanding of these assumptions serves further purposes for law students. The assumptions provide a framework for understanding how the principles of logic and their application in judicial trials fit within the broader contexts of litigation and lawyering processes generally and trial practice specifically. That framework also establishes a basis for understanding how the contemporary rules of evidence and procedure have evolved. It also facilitates understanding the relationships between the formal rules of evidence that regulate admissibility and use and the principles of logic that provide the basis for practical argument and rational justification.

1. The tradition described

The central tenet of the Rationalist Tradition is that the primary objective of adjective (or procedural) law is the achievement of "rectitude of decision" in adjudication, that is to say the correct application of law to facts proved to be true. That tenet has three corollaries that bear upon the present enterprise. First, with respect to disputed questions of fact, the tenet assumes that realization of that objective involves the pursuit of "truth" through rational means.[2] That corollary requires assumptions of two kinds – epistemological assumptions concerning the possibility of making accurate present judgments about past events and reasoning assumptions concerning the principles to be applied to maximize the likelihood that present judgments about past events will be accurate. Second, the Rationalist Tradition reflects a persistent recognition that pursuit of truth has a high, but not overriding, priority as a means to secure justice under law (expletive justice). Third, the model of adjudication is itself instrumentalist in that the pursuit of truth through reason is only a means to achieving the end of expletive justice viewed as the implementation of substantive law.

Given this central tenet, the characteristic assumptions of discourse about evidence within the Rationalist Tradition can be succinctly stated: Epistemology is cognitivist rather than skeptical; a correspondence theory of truth is generally preferred to a coherence theory of truth;[3] the mode of decision-making is seen as

---

2 Critical theorists, postmodernists, and others argue that this is not how judges or juries, in fact, resolve disputed questions of fact. See, e.g., Graham (1987); cf. Twining (1988); see also Nicolson (1994), Siegel (1994). The main "strategies of scepticism" are discussed in *Rethinking*, Ch. 4. Even they, however, would acknowledge that established rules require that decisions resolving such questions must be rationally justifiable.

3 In the view of the authors, philosophical debates about coherence and correspondence theories of truth are not crucially important in this context as the model is flexible enough to accommodate both kinds of theory. Historically most Anglo-American writers on evidence seem to have assumed some correspondence assumptions (Bentham's theory of fictions being a notable exception). Our own position approximates more closely to the "foundeherentism" of Haack (1993).

"rational," as contrasted with "irrational" modes such as battle, compurgation, or ordeal; the characteristic mode of reasoning is induction; and the pursuit of truth, as *a means* to justice under the law, commands a high, but not necessarily an over-riding, priority as a social value.

The basic assumptions that underlie the Rationalist Tradition are summarized in the form of two models in table 3.1.

The first model, Model I, reconstructs a "Rationalist Model of Adjudication"; the second model, Model II, articulates the main epistemological and logical assumptions of standard evidence discourse to be found in specialized secondary writings about evidence in the Anglo-American tradition. Part A of Model I is prescriptive: It states an aspiration and a standard by which actual rules, institutions, procedures, and practices may be evaluated. Acceptance of such standards involves no necessary commitment to the view that a particular system, or some aspect of it, at a particular time satisfies these standards either in its design or in its actual operation. Part B of the model is intended to represent typical claims or judgments of the kind "on the whole the system works well." None of the leading theorists in the Rationalist Tradition were perfectionists who expected one hundred per cent conformity with the ideal. Some were highly critical of existing arrangements and practices.[4]

If the propositions of the second model represent standard elements in rationalist theories of evidence, it should be clear that it is artificial to make a sharp distinction between theories of evidence and theories of adjudication: Generally speaking, the former presuppose or form part of the latter. Although there appears to be less of a consensus in the relevant literature about the ends and the achievements of the Anglo-American system of adjudication than about the logic and epistemology of proof, it is possible to postulate a rationalist model of adjudication as an ideal type that both fits a rationalist theory of evidence and is recognizable as a reasonably sophisticated version of a widely held, if controversial, view. The first model is a modified version of a Benthamite model of adjudication, presented in a way that suggests a number of possible points of departure or disagreement. Although not all leading evidence scholars have been legal positivists and utilitarians, a rationalist theory of evidence necessarily presupposes a theory of adjudication that postulates something like Bentham's "rectitude of decision" as the main objective. There is scope for divergence on a number of points of detail, but not from what might be called the "rational core."

It is reasonable, and sufficient for present purposes, to assert that by and large the leading Anglo-American scholars and theorists of evidence from Gilbert (1754) to Wigmore (and, for the most part, until the present) have either implicitly or explicitly accepted assumptions such as these, although not in this particular for-mulation. Two ideas were shared by all. First, they accepted as given the view that

4 Indeed Bentham, whose *Rationale of Judicial Evidence* (1827) is the main source of the model, made his theory of adjudication the basis for a radical and far-ranging critique of English (and, to a lesser extent, Scottish and continental) procedure, practice, and rules of evidence in his day. See *Rethinking* at 71–92.

the Anglo-American system has adopted a "rational" mode of determining issues of fact in contrast with older "irrational" modes of proof. Second, a particular view of "rationality" was adopted or taken for granted. This view found its classic expression in English empirical philosophy in the writings of Bacon, Locke, and John Stuart Mill.

This account of the Rationalist Tradition has an analytical (as well as an historical) aspect. Analytically, it is an attempt to reconstruct in the form of an "ideal type" an account of a set of basic assumptions about the aims and nature of adjudication and what is involved in reasoning about disputed questions of fact in that context. The test of success of this ideal type is its clarity, coherence, and usefulness as a tool of analysis of evidence discourse and doctrine. But in applying this test, it is important to distinguish between *aspirational* and *complacent rationalism* in respect of adjudication. The claim that the modern system of adjudication is "rational" is a statement of what is considered to be a feasible *aspiration* of the system; it does not necessarily involve commitment to the view that this aspiration is always, generally, or even sometimes, realized in practice. It is commonplace within the Rationalist Tradition to criticize existing practices, procedures, rules, and institutions in terms of their failure to satisfy the standards of this aspirational model.

It is also useful to differentiate a third category, which might be referred to as *optimistic rationalism*. In invoking prescriptive standards, one often makes some judgment about the prospects for attaining or approximating such standards in practice in a given context. In the case of many writers on evidence and judicial process who accepted some variant of Part A of the rationalist model of adjudication, it is reasonable to attribute to them the view that its standards represent a feasible aspiration rather than a remote or unattainable Utopian ideal. Even virulently critical writers such as Bentham and Frank can be shown to have believed that their own favored recommendations would in practice lead to significant increases in the level of rationality in adjudication. They were optimistic rationalists. In brief, almost all the leading writers in the mainstream of Anglo-American evidence scholarship were aspirational rationalists; most were optimistic rationalists most of the time; and many, but by no means all, were fairly complacent about the general operation of the adversary system in their own jurisdiction in their day.[5]

2. Principles of proof, rules of procedure and evidence, and the Rationalist Tradition

Contemporary rules of procedure and evidence make it clear that the assumptions identified in the Rationalist Tradition remain dominant today. Although a detailed analysis is beyond the scope of this book, the importance of those assumptions in understanding contemporary rules can be usefully illustrated here. We offer the illustrations that follow for two reasons – to suggest perspectives that students may wish to consider in studying the formal rules regulating procedure and the

5 For a fuller description, see *Rethinking* 70–82.

Table 3.1 *The Rationalist Tradition: basic assumptions*

Model I A Rationalist model of adjudication	Model II Rationalist theories of evidence and proof: some common assumptions
A *Prescriptive* 1 The direct end 2 of adjective law 3 is rectitude of decision through correct application 4 of valid substantive laws 5 deemed to be consonant with utility (or otherwise good) 6 and through accurate determination 7 of the true past facts 8 material to 9 precisely specified allegations expressed in categories defined in advance by law, i.e. facts in issue, 10 proved to specified standards of probability or likelihood 11 on the basis of the careful 12 and rational	1 Knowledge about particular past events is possible. 2 Establishing the truth about particular past events in issue in a case (the facts in issue) is a necessary condition for achieving justice in adjudication; incorrect results are one form of injustice. 3 The notions of evidence and proof in adjudication are concerned with rational methods of determining questions of fact; in this context operative distinctions have to be maintained between questions of fact and questions of law, questions of fact and questions of value, and questions of fact and questions of opinion. 4 The establishment of the truth of alleged facts in adjudication is typically a matter of probabilities, falling short of absolute certainty. 5 (a) Judgments about the probabilities of allegations about particular past events can and should be reached by reasoning from relevant evidence presented to the decision-maker; (b) The characteristic mode of reasoning appropriate to reasoning about probabilities is induction.

6 Judgments about probabilities have, generally speaking, to be based on the available stock of knowledge about the common course of events; this is largely a matter of common sense supplemented by specialized scientific or expert knowledge when it is available.

7 The pursuit of truth (i.e. seeking to maximize accuracy in fact-determination) is to be given a high, but not necessarily an overriding, priority in relation to other values, such as the security of the state, the protection of family relationships, or the curbing of coercive methods of interrogation.

8 One crucial basis for evaluating "fact-finding" institutions, rules, procedures, and techniques is how far they are estimated to maximize accuracy in fact-determination – but other criteria such as speed, cheapness, procedural fairness, humaneness, public confidence, and the avoidance of vexation for participants are also to be taken into account.

9 The primary role of applied forensic psychology and forensic science is to provide guidance about the reliability of different kinds of evidence and to develop methods and devices for increasing such reliability.

13 weighing of
14 evidence
15 which is both relevant
16 and reliable
17 presented (in a form designed to bring out truth and discover untruth)
18 to supposedly competent
19 and impartial
20 decision-makers
21 with adequate safeguards against corruption
22 and mistake
23 and adequate provision for review and appeal.

B *Descriptive*
24 Generally speaking this objective is largely achieved
25 in a consistent
26 fair
27 and predictable manner.

Note: Prescriptive rationalism: acceptance of A as both desirable and reasonably feasible. No commitment to B.
Complacent rationalism: acceptance of A & B *in re* a particular system.

admissibility and use of evidence in the courts, and to aid students in understanding the role that the principles of proof play in contemporary trial practice.

Contemporary rules clearly reflect the central tenets of the Rationalist Tradition, although recent developments reflect a greater concern for finality and efficiency with concomitant reduced concern for establishing the truth. Consider, for example, the standards specified in the United States Federal Rules of Civil Procedure, Criminal Procedure, and Evidence. The rules governing civil cases are "to be construed to secure the just, speedy, and inexpensive determination of every action."[6] The rules governing criminal proceedings "are intended to provide for the just determination of every criminal proceeding" and are to be "construed to secure simplicity in procedure, fairness in administration, and the elimination of unjustifiable expense and delay."[7] The rules regulating the admission and use of evidence in both kinds of proceedings are to be "construed to secure fairness in administration, elimination of unjustifiable expense and delay, and promotion of growth and development of the law of evidence to the end that truth may be ascertained and proceedings justly determined."[8]

In England, the contemporary rules of civil procedure reflect a similar shift. They have been substantially reformed following the recommendations of Lord Woolf's Final Report on *Access to Justice* (1996). The main concern underlying these reforms was to reduce cost, delay, and complexity; the principal outcome has been to transfer the main responsibility for case management from the parties and their lawyers to the courts. Some consider that the rules will have the tendency to sacrifice concern for rectitude of decision to efficiency. Rule 1 of the Civil Procedure Rules (1999) (CPR) states:

> Rule 1(1) These Rules are a new procedural code with the overriding objective of enabling the court to deal with cases justly.
>
> Rule 1.1(2) Dealing with a case justly includes, so far as is practicable: (a) ensuring that the parties are on an equal footing; (b) saving expenses; (c) dealing with the case in ways which are proportionate (i) to the amount of money involved; (ii) to the importance of the case; (iii) to the complexity of the issues; (iv) to the financial position of each party; (d) ensuring that it is dealt with expeditiously and fairly; and (e) allotting to it an appropriate share of the court's resources, while taking into account the need to allot resources to other cases.[9]

A detailed study of these US Federal Rules would raise interesting questions. Each suggests or states that the ascertainment of truth and the correct application of

---

6 Fed. R. Civ. P. 1.   7 Fed. R. Crim. P. 2.

8 Fed. R. Evid. 102. The position in England is similar. For example, Professor Ian Dennis writes: "Part of the aims of the law of evidence is therefore to articulate the constraints on the principle of free proof which would be logically entailed by the rationalist model of adjudication. Some of the criteria for constraint and their rationale are a matter of considerable and continuing controversy, but certain points seem reasonably plain" (Dennis (2002) 27). Dennis then usefully considers these constraints under four heads: (a) Expense and delay; (b) Procedural fairness; (c) Avoidance of error; (d) Pursuit of other values (*id.* 23–29).

9 For an account and appraisal of the Woolf reforms see Zander (2003) and Jacob (2001).

substantive law is an important objective. Each, however, also states that potentially conflicting values, such as speed and the elimination of unjustifiable delay and expense, are also to be taken into account. None says how the balance is to be struck generally or in specific cases. Nor is it clear why the formulations in the three general codes adopted in the United States through similar processes by the same authorities are different or whether and to what extent the differences in language are intended to have any practical consequences in application.

Partial answers to the questions that might be raised would require consideration of the kinds of aspirations the rules reflect and the reactions generated by current dissatisfaction with the seeming inability of the bench and bar to achieve them. There are few complacent rationalists in modern society. No one seriously claims that the Federal Rules of Civil Procedure have promoted "speedy and inexpensive determinations in every action" that comes before the American federal courts. Quite the contrary, many of those who now vigorously urge a turn to methods of alternative dispute resolution can fairly be characterized as pessimistic rationalists who think the aspirations of Model I can no longer be realized in the traditional model of adjudication. The extent to which plea bargaining is the principal means of resolving criminal proceedings reflects similar dissatisfaction on the criminal side.

Another part of the answer, a more important part for those who expect to practice in the system, may emerge from an understanding that the process through which the Federal Rules were formulated was political and the interests represented in that process reflect divergent views as to how the balance should be struck.[10] As a practical matter, the rules ultimately adopted reflect political compromises, not articulations of principles viewed as theoretically correct. In this context, two points should be noted. First, ambiguity is a form of political compromise – the conflict that cannot be resolved is deferred and left for case-by-case resolution in the courts. Second, and perhaps related, the modern trend has been to expand the discretion of the trial judge and to restrict the scope of review on appeal from decisions on procedural or evidentiary matters. Thus, the political battle is legitimated and proceeds in the courts on a day-to-day, case-by-case basis. How discretion is exercised in construing a rule may largely be a function of the social views of the particular judge, tempered by the persuasiveness of counsel.

These points suggest some perspectives that students may find useful in studying procedural and evidentiary rules. First, modern rules of procedure and formal rules of evidence are relatively recent phenomena. The very lack of complacency

10 The proceedings that led to the adoption of the Federal Rules of Evidence are described in the Senate Judiciary Committee Report that accompanied the bill proposed to enact the rules. S. Rep. No. 1277, 93d Cong., 2d Sess., reprinted in 1974 *U.S. Code, Cong. & Admin. News* 7051–7052, 7054–7055. The political aspect of the history of the Federal Rules of Evidence is emphasized in Wright & Graham (1977) §§5001–5006. Section 5006 deals directly with the drafting history. The legislative history, including the statements of those who appeared at the hearings in the House and Senate, is reproduced in Bailey and Trelles (1980). Amendments to the rules since their adoption are listed in Federal Rules of Evidence (House Judiciary Committee Print 2003) at v–x available at http://www.house.gov/judiciary/committee documents.

is reflected in the frequency with which these rules are amended. Anyone studying such rules at a particular time should pay as much attention to the history of a rule and the political processes by which it reached its present formulation as to the text currently in force. The goal should be to understand the interests and the compromises reflected in the rule. The rules are likely to change during any practitioner's career to reflect changes in the relative political power of those whose interests are affected. In this view, the notes of the advisory committees, the Federal Judicial Center, and the legislative committees concerning rules that were rejected or amended at various stages and the proposals that were rejected may be more revealing than the rule that was actually adopted. In England, both criminal and civil evidence have been a recurrent focus of attention in the past thirty years.[11]

Second, something very similar to the prescriptive norms expressed in Model I remain the norms that define the range within which contemporary debates are conducted. Those who argue for change ordinarily frame their arguments to demonstrate that the changes they seek will enhance the likelihood that truth will be ascertained without imposing further or undue costs or other burdens or, alternatively, that the change will reduce the costs or other burdens or will promote fairness in administration without significantly diminishing the likelihood that truth will be ascertained. Some contemporary theorists argue that the assumptions underlying the model are flawed and are merely political camouflage used to legitimate the *status quo* and that changes are designed to protect or enhance it. Nonetheless, these critics have yet to propose a serious alternative model.[12] For that reason, proposals for change and arguments for construction and application are likely to proceed within the framework of the Rationalist Tradition for the foreseeable future. Thus, as a practical matter, lawyers should develop the ability to use the prescriptive norms effectively in argument.

Contemporary rules of procedure and evidence also make clear the centrality of the principles of inductive reasoning and argument. The Federal Rules of Evidence governing relevance may be fairly viewed as an attempt to codify the assumptions underlying the rationalist theories of evidence and proof. For example, evidence is relevant if and only if it has some "tendency to make the existence of any fact that is of consequence to the litigation more probable or less probable than it would be without the evidence."[13] That rule can only be viewed as mandating a demonstration that requires the application of the principles of inductive logic to persuade a judge that the evidence under consideration, alone or in combination with other evidence, supports an inference or a chain of inferences that increases or decreases the likelihood that a fact of consequence is true. The rule that mandates the admission of relevant evidence unless there exist specified grounds for its exclusion assumes that truth is an objective that can be achieved through rational means and establishes a base for assessing its priority in particular situations.[14]

---

11 For an overview, see Zander (2003) 413–61.   12 See *Rethinking* 77–82.
13 Fed. R. Evid. 401. On the meaning of "fact of consequence," see below, n. 18.
14 Fed. R. Evid. 402.

From that perspective, most of the remaining rules of evidence can be viewed as falling into three categories – rules that justify the exclusion of evidence on the ground that it has improper prejudicial effects that outweigh its probative value,[15] rules that mandate or reflect a cost-benefit analysis to prevent undue delay or consumption of time,[16] and rules that reflect extrinsic policies viewed as overriding the ascertainment of truth as an objective.[17] It should be clear that rules in the first two categories also typically require application of the principles of inductive reasoning to identify the particular improper prejudice that evidence may generate and to frame the arguments that bear upon a comparison of the legitimate probative value and the illegitimate prejudicial effects in the particular case.

We develop the specific uses of the principles in constructing such arguments later. For the moment, it should suffice to note that the principles of practical reasoning and the assumptions upon which they are based will remain central to the common law model of adjudication, notwithstanding any changes that may be made in the formal rules. For that reason, the ability to apply them in analysis and argument is and will remain an essential lawyering skill.

C. Rationale

Wigmore provided the starting-point of our work, and it is important to understand his conception of the subject of evidence in law and how its two main parts (the principles of proof and the trial rules) are related. The following is his opening statement at the start of *The Science*.

§1. **What Is the Science of Judicial Proof?** The study of the principles of Evidence, for a lawyer, falls into two distinct parts. One is Proof in the general sense, – the part concerned with the ratiocinative process of contentious persuasion, – mind to mind, counsel to judge or juror, each partisan seeking to move the mind of the tribunal. The other part is Admissibility, – the procedural rules devised by the law, and based on litigious experience and tradition, to guard the tribunal (particularly the jury) against erroneous persuasion. Hitherto, the latter has loomed largest in our formal studies, – has, in fact, monopolized them; while the former, virtually ignored, has been left to the chances of later acquisition, casual and empiric, in the course of practice. Here we have been wrong; and in two ways.

15 The general principle is stated in Federal Rule of Evidence 403. Rules often have characteristics that reflect justifications from more than one category. Rules 404 and 609, for example, may fairly be viewed as codifications covering recurring situations where the improper prejudicial effects presumptively outweigh the legitimate probative value, but these rules also reflect values unrelated to the pure search for truth, such as the values expressed in the idea of judging "the act not the actor." See *Old Chief v. United States*, 519 U.S. 172 (1997); *R. v. Sang* [1980] A.C. 402 (Eng.).
16 See Rule 403 (the general principle); see also, e.g., Rules 405 (methods of proving character), 701–704 (opinions and expert testimony), 902 (self-authenticating documents).
17 The clearest examples are the rules protecting privileged communications, now reflected in Rule 501, and the constitutional exclusionary rules adopted to regulate improper conduct by law enforcement officers without regard to the often dispositive probative value of the evidence thereby excluded.

For one thing, there is, and there *must* be, a probative science – the principles of proof – independent of the artificial rules of procedure; hence, it can be and should be studied. This science, to be sure, may as yet be imperfectly formulated. But all the more need is there to begin in earnest to investigate and develop it. Furthermore, this process of Proof represents the objective in every judicial investigation. The procedural rules for Admissibility are merely a preliminary aid to the main activity, viz., the persuasion of the tribunal's mind to a correct conclusion by safe materials. This main process is that for which the jury are there, and on which the counsel's duty is focused.

And, for another thing, the judicial rules of Admissibility are destined to lessen in relative importance during the next period of development. Proof will assume the important place; and we must therefore prepare ourselves for this shifting of emphasis. We must seek to acquire a scientific understanding of the principles of what may be called "natural" proof, – the hitherto neglected process . . .

The principles of Proof, then, represent the natural processes of the mind in dealing with the evidential facts after they are admitted to the jury; while the rules of Admissibility represent the artificial legal rules peculiar to our Anglo-American jury-system. Hence the former should be studied first. They bring into play those reasoning processes which are already the possession of intelligent and educated persons. They familiarize the practitioner with the materials most commonly presented in trials at law, and thus prepare him to take up more readily the artificial rules of Admissibility devised by judicial experience for safeguarding legal investigations of fact.

Moreover, this process of Proof is after all the most important in the trial. The trial culminates in either Proof or non-Proof. When the evidence is all in, the counsel sets himself to his ultimate and crucial task, i.e. that of persuading the jury that they should or should not believe the fact alleged in the issue. To do this, he must reason naturally, as all men reason and as juries can be shown how to reason. He must have familiarized himself with the logical processes which men naturally use, and with general experience as to the classes of inferences commonly called for in legal trials. Here he has no use for the artificial rules of Admissibility. Those have been disposed of, at the outset, by the judge. The evidence is in, and the question now is, What is its effect? All the artificial rules of Admissibility might be abolished; yet the principles of Proof would remain, so long as trials remain as a rational attempt to seek the truth in legal controversies . . . (Wigmore, *Science* §1 and 2)

Notes and questions on rules of evidence concerning relevance

1. The definition of *relevance* is the law's codification of the principles of logic. Consider the following provisions of the Federal Rules of Evidence:

Rule 401. Definition of "Relevant Evidence." "Relevant evidence" means evidence having any tendency to make the existence of any fact that is of consequence to the determination of the action more probable or less probable than it would be without the evidence.[18]

18 Strictly speaking, the only facts of consequence in a case are the penultimate probanda (including any probanda asserting an affirmative defense) and probanda undermining or reinforcing the *credibility* of evidence that is relevant to a penultimate probandum.

Rule 402. Relevant Evidence Generally Admissible: Irrelevant Evidence Inadmissible. All relevant evidence is admissible, except as otherwise provided by the Constitution of the United States, by Act of Congress, by these rules, or by other rules prescribed by the Supreme Court pursuant to statutory authority. Evidence which is not relevant is not admissible.

To what extent are the foregoing provisions a codification of principles of "proof"? Are any of the provisions rules of "admissibility"? Would archeologists, historians, and scientists accept the law's definition of relevance for application in their fields? What provisions of the rule deal with problems that are peculiar to courts?

2. Rule 403 of the Federal Rules of Evidence is central. It provides:

Rule 403. Exclusion of Relevant Evidence on Grounds of Prejudice, Confusion, or Waste of Time. Although relevant, evidence may be excluded if its probative value is substantially outweighed by the danger of unfair prejudice, confusion of the issues, or misleading the jury, or by considerations of undue delay, waste of time, or needless presentation of cumulative evidence.

Rule 403 prescribes a "probative equation" the trial court must apply in determining whether an individual evidential proposition should be admitted. The unfair, misleading, or other improper prejudicial effects (PE) of the proffered evidential data must be identified and appraised. The legitimate probative value (PV) must be determined and weighed. Then the court must determine whether the improper prejudicial effects substantially outweigh the legitimate probative value – whether $PE \gg PV$.

a What effects are improperly prejudicial? How should we measure the legitimate probative value?

b Consider propositions 11 and 21 from the exercise at pages 41–43 above. The ultimate proposition to be proved is that "It was X who murdered Y." The prosecutor wishes to offer evidence to show that:

11 X has two convictions for shoplifting; the most recent occurred five years ago.

21 Z [an alibi witness for X] is a prostitute.

Is evidence that supports either proposition relevant? If so, to what "fact that is of consequence" in an action to determine whether "It was X who murdered Y"? Be precise. Would a scientist or an historian consider either proposition relevant? Should either or both propositions be admissible under Rule 403? State the analysis in support of and in opposition to admission precisely.

3. Article IV of the Federal Rules of Evidence is entitled *Relevancy and its Limits.* Consider Rule 404.

Rule 404. Character Evidence Not Admissible to Prove Conduct; Exceptions; Other Crimes

(a) *Character evidence generally.* Evidence of a person's character or a trait of his character is not admissible for the purpose of proving that he acted in conformity therewith on a particular occasion, except;

(i) *Character of accused.* Evidence of a pertinent trait of character offered by an accused, or by the prosecution to rebut the same; . . .

(b) Other crimes, wrongs, or acts. Evidence of other crimes, wrongs, or acts is not admissible to prove the character of a person in order to show that he acted in conformity therewith. It may, however, be admissible for other purposes, such as proof of motive, opportunity, intent, preparation, plan, knowledge, identity, or absence of mistake or accident.[19]

Is Rule 404 a codification of a principle of proof or a rule restricting admissibility and use of logically relevant evidence? If it is a rule of admissibility, what values are served by this departure from the goal of "truth ascertainment"? Consider again propositions 11 and 22 set out above. Would Rule 404 require the exclusion of evidence offered to prove either or both propositions? Does Rule 404 suggest a policy that might enhance an argument that either or both propositions should in any event be excluded under Rule 403?

D. Notes on terminology and inferential relationships

In any inquiry that seeks to determine what happened based upon evidence, the person conducting the inquiry must have or develop a *hypothesis* to be tested (sometimes framed as a question to be answered). Although the hypothesis will often be refined during the investigation and analysis, a meaningful analysis can not be taken without a preliminary hypothesis. In determining whether evidence is relevant, the analyst must answer the question, "Relevant to what?" The "what" is the hypothesis.

In legal contexts, the hypothesis is established by the governing law. In other words, assuming the applicable rule of law is clear, the proposition to be proved is a proposition that includes each of the material facts that must be proved in order to satisfy the conditions specified by the rule. Wigmore adopted and adapted the Latin term "*factum probandum*" (or simply "*probandum*") to designate a proposition to be proved.

If one views the applicable rule of law as the major premise in a deductive argument, then the *ultimate probandum* is the minor premise. For example, a typical statute defining murder might read, "Murder is the unlawful killing of a human being . . . with malice aforethought." That statute might be restated as the major premise of a syllogism as:

If a human being (a victim) is dead, and the victim died as a result of an unlawful act, and it was the accused who committed the act that caused the victim's death, and the person who committed the act acted with malice aforethought, then the accused is guilty of murder.

In a murder case, the *ultimate probandum* would be the proposition that satisfied the requirements of the rule as restated. In "An investigation" presented in Chapter 1

---

19 On character evidence in England, see Dennis (2002) Ch. 18; Zander (2003) 413–33.

at pp. 40–43, the ultimate probandum the prosecution would have to prove might be stated as:

> UP: Y is dead; and Y died as a result of an unlawful act; and it was X who committed the act that caused Y's death; and X acted with malice afore-thought in committing the act.[20]

The illustrations that follow draw upon propositions given in that exercise. To limit the need to refer back, propositions used here have been renumbered.

In almost all instances, an ultimate probandum that is stated in formal terms is a compound statement, a statement containing more than one simple proposition. Under any method of analysis one of the first steps requires that the analyst divide (and sometimes subdivide) the ultimate probandum into simple propositions, what Wigmore called and we will refer to as the *penultimate probanda*. Thus, the penultimate probanda in "An investigation" were that:

1 Y is dead.
2 Y died as the result of an unlawful act.
3 It was X who committed the act that caused Y's death.
4 X acted with malice aforethought in committing the act.

A penultimate probandum is a synonym for familiar terms used in other legal contexts. A penultimate probandum is a *material fact*. (The terms *fact-in-issue* and *ultimate fact* are synonyms in this context.) A penultimate probandum is also a *fact of consequence*, but the term fact of consequence includes more than just the penultimate probanda in a case. For example, when a witness takes the stand her credibility becomes a fact of consequence. So too, inferred propositions, such as the accused had motive or had opportunity, are often called facts of consequence.[21]

All evidential data presented at trial must be presented in a form that the triers of fact can perceive with their senses. This evidence consists of only two types: testimonial assertions made by a witness from the witness stand, that is, oral statements the triers of fact actually hear, and physical objects displayed to the triers of fact or, rarely, other forms of evidential data that can be perceived by one or more of the senses.[22]

To avoid confusion, it is important to have terms that enable us to distinguish evidential data that the jurors (or other decision-makers) will perceive with one of their senses – will hear, see, smell, taste, or touch – from the propositions that the jurors will be asked to infer from those data. Specialized terminology is helpful

---

20 In that problem, the police cadet had an assigned *standpoint*. He was a police cadet assigned, at the outset of the investigation, to analyze information as it was developed. One of the hypotheses the evidence suggested was, "It was X who committed the act that caused Y's death." (*Standpoint* is an important concept that is developed fully in Ch. 4.)

21 See above, n. 18.

22 Stipulated, admitted, or judicially noticed facts might be considered a third class, but these facts are actually inferences that triers of fact are instructed to accept as proven.

because the terms "fact" and "evidence" have many overlapping and imprecise meanings. For example, a lawyer might properly argue that:

a   the *fact* that X had a motive to murder Y is *evidence* that X did murder Y.
b   the *fact* X was in Y's house at 4:30 p.m., the time and place of Y's murder, is *evidence* that X had opportunity to murder Y.
c   W$_3$'s testimony that he saw X running out of Y's house at 4:45 p.m. is *evidence* that W exited Y's house at 4:45 p.m., which in turn is *evidence* that X was in Y's house at 4:30 p.m.

Most listeners would understand each of these assertions notwithstanding the fact that the words "fact" and "evidence" had a different meaning in each.

In a trial, W$_3$'s testimonial assertion about X's departure would be an *evidential datum* – an assertion the trier of fact would hear. The existence of an evidential datum cannot be contested. For example, if a witness testified, "The moon is made of green cheese," the fact that the statement was made could not be disputed. But no one would accept the *inference* that the moon is in fact made of green cheese. Instead, most would *infer* that the witness was lying or was crazy or had a strange sense of humor.

Wigmore adopted the term *autoptic proference* to describe an evidential datum that the decision-makers will perceive with one of their five senses.[23] In the chapters that follow, the terms *autoptic proference* or *evidential datum* are used to identify evidence that the fact-finder will hear or see or otherwise perceive through their senses.

An autoptic proference is only relevant if it makes a fact of consequence more or less probable than it would be in the absence of the autoptic proference. A fact of consequence is always a proposition to be inferred, a *factum probandum*. It is rare, however, that a penultimate probandum can be directly inferred from an autoptic proference. In almost all instances, there are one or more intermediate propositions, probanda, that must be accepted in order to demonstrate the logical relationship between the evidential datum and the penultimate probandum it is offered to support.

Wigmore also used the term "*factum probans*" to describe an inferential proposition that is offered as support for a further inference, a *factum probandum*. It is important to note the terms "*factum probans*" and "*factum probandum*" can refer to the same proposition. Using this terminology, an *autoptic proference* is offered to support a *factum probandum*, which then becomes a "*factum probans*" offered to support a further "*factum probandum*." We have dropped the word "factum," but the terms "*probans*" and "*probandum*" are used throughout the remainder of the book.

The point can be illustrated using propositions presented in "An investigation." For example, from proposition 2, renumbered proposition 5 here, we may assume that at trial:

23 This admittedly awkward term is more precise and broader than the commonly used "real evidence," which is ambiguous.

5 W$_1$ will testify, "I saw a person with characteristics a, b, c, and d enter Y's house at 4:15 p.m. on January 1."

From this autoptic proference, we must first infer the truth of the matter asserted:

6 A person with characteristics a, b, c, and d entered Y's house at 4:15 p.m. on January 1.

Standing alone, neither the testimonial assertion, an autoptic proference, nor the inferred proposition is relevant to the provisional penultimate probandum:

3 It was X who murdered Y.

But there is another autoptic proference, the appearance of X, that the decision-maker would see,

7 X

From which she might infer,

8 X has characteristics a, b, c, and d.

The decision-maker might then *combine* inferred proposition 5 and 6, now each a *probans*, to support a further *probandum:*

9 It was X who entered Y's house at 4:15 p.m. on January 1.

An advocate might urge that proposition 9 supports a further inference:

10 X was in Y's house at 4:30 p.m.

based upon a *generalization:*

11 People who enter a house usually remain for more than fifteen minutes.

That advocate could then argue that the assumed proposition 12 (based on proposition 1 in "An investigation"),

12 Y died in his home at 4:30 p.m. on January 1 as the result of an unlawful act committed by another person,

combines with inferred proposition 10 to support a further inference,

13 X had an opportunity to commit the act that caused Y's death,

which in turn makes the fact of consequence, penultimate *probandum* 3 above,

3 It was X who committed the act that caused Y's death,

somewhat more probable than it would in the absence of the autoptic preferences set out in propositions 5 and 6.

It may be easier to understand the relationships among these propositions if they were depicted in charted form. This can be done using three of the symbols used in the "Chart method of analysis" which is presented in the next chapter. A testimonial assertion that the tribunal will hear from the witness stand is always depicted by a square – □. All other propositions are depicted by a circle – ◯. Autoptic proferences, as opposed to inferred propositions, are identified by placing an infinity symbol – ∞ – beneath the square or circle representing an assertion the fact-finder will hear or a circle depicting an item of evidence that the fact-finder will see or perceive with one of her other senses.

The distinction between "inference" and "proof" also needs to be clarified. An "inference" represents an argument or a claim that there is a logical relationship between two propositions, that one proposition supports the other. In the chart presented below, the relationships depicted show the inferential relationships among the propositions in the keylist. "Proof" (or non-proof) is the result – the conclusion to be reached after the inferences have been evaluated.[24] If we accept the claim that, reasoning from the "bottom up," each of the propositions depicted in the chart makes the proposition above it in some degree more probable than it would be in the absence of the supporting proposition, then we have to concede that the chart accurately depicts the inferential relationships among the charted propositions. That commitment does not entail any commitment to the conclusion that the charted propositions "prove" the penultimate probandum to any specified degree of probability, such as more probable than not or beyond reasonable doubt. Inferential reasoning and argument is the process; proof or non-proof is the result.

A preliminary exercise: State v. Archer (I)

A murder has just been reported and the investigation just begun. You are the prosecuting attorney. The murdered man was named Vern. Detective Paul was the investigating officer. Detective Paul's preliminary report contains the following assertion: "I found a scrap of brown Harris tweed cloth clutched in Vern's right hand." The scrap of cloth has been properly tagged and preserved for use as evidence.

1 Why are Paul's assertion and the scrap of cloth relevant? Formulate as simple propositions the testimonial assertions Detective Paul might make. Formulate the propositions that must be inferred to demonstrate that the autoptic proferences are relevant to a fact of consequence. Using the preliminary charting scheme suggested above, chart the tentative inferences that you would make from this assertion and from the scrap of cloth to guide Detective Paul's investigation.

2 As a matter of logical process, does the analysis of the available evidence from the investigator's standpoint differ from that of the lawyer immediately before trial? If so, how? If not, why not?

---

24 There are standards of proof that are to guide the fact-finder in deciding in whose favor the verdict or judgment in a case should be returned, and there are standards that define the limits of the fact-finder's discretion in making that decision. These subjects are addressed in Ch. 8 below.

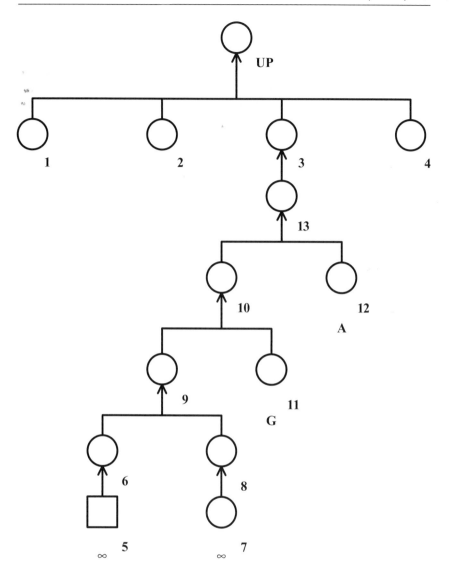

Figure 3.1 *Micro-chart of partial key-list*

E. Probative processes and logical principles

1. Probative processes

Wigmore categorized the main relations between evidentiary propositions in terms of the probative processes for which they might be offered – proponent's assertion (PA), opponent's denial (OD), opponent's rival (OR), opponent's explanation (OE), and proponent's corroborations (PC). These categories establish a vocabulary that is frequently useful in identifying, advancing, and appraising claims that evidence or factual arguments are relevant in particular phases of a case.

When a party offers an autoptic proference at trial, she is a proponent claiming that proffered data support an assertion that is relevant. That is a proponent's assertion (PA). In most instances, the proponent must also claim that that initial assertion supports a further assertion (an interim probandum), which in turn supports a further assertion and so on, until the logical basis for the claim that the proffered datum makes a fact of consequence more or less probable has been demonstrated. In the illustration developed above, the prosecution would offer, as autoptic preferences, propositions 5 and 7 to support proponent's assertions 6, 8, and 9. See key-list and chart 3.1 above.

There are three, and only three, ways that the opposing party, the defendant, could challenge these assertions. He may deny one or more of them, opponent's denial (OD); he may offer evidence supporting a conflicting rival proposition (OR); or he may offer alternative explanations for the proffered datum and inferences, opponent's explanation (OE).

If the investigation begun in "An investigation" proceeded to trial, X might, for example, testify,

14   I did not enter Y's house at any time on January 1,

supporting an inference,

15   X did not enter Y's house at any time on January 1.

Such a testimonial assertion would be classified as an opponent's denial (OD) because it denies the truth of the inference based upon the testimonial assertion that would be made by W_2 based upon proposition 4 in "An investigation,"

16   W_2: I saw X leave Y's house at 4:45 p.m. on January 1,

supporting a proponent's assertion offered by the prosecution,

17   X departed from Y's house at 4:45 p.m. on January 1,

providing additional support for

10   X was in Y's house at 4:30 p.m.

X might also offer autoptic preferences supporting an opponent's rival assertion (OR) based upon proposition 12 in "An investigation":

18   X: I was in a house five miles from the scene of the murder from 2 p.m. until 5 p.m.,

supporting an inference, whose strength would depend upon an assessment of X's credibility,

19 X was in a house five miles from the scene of the murder from 2 p.m. until 5 p.m.,

which would rival the proponent's inferred assertion,

10 X was in Y's house at 4:30 p.m.

Finally, X might offer one or more alternative explanations that weaken the probative value of the proponent's assertion, an opponent's explanation (OE). There are two types of opponent's explanations. The first calls attention to alternative inferences that the proffered datum would also support. For example, in "An investigation," W_3 would testify (P_6),

20 On Christmas Day, I heard X say angrily to Y: "I shall not forget this,"

which the prosecutor might assert supports the inferred assertion,

21 X was angry with Y on Christmas Day,

supporting a further inference,

22 X's anger with Y continued until January 1,

supporting a further inference,

23 X's anger gave him a motive to murder,

supporting the penultimate probandum,

3 It was X who committed the act that caused Y's death.

However, without further evidence, it is clear that there are a number of plausible alternative explanations for X's assertion that are too trivial to support a claim of motive, e.g.,

24 Y may have forgotten to send X a Christmas card, or
25 Y may have embarrassed X at a party or a business meeting,

and so on – and thus tending to explain away and weaken the prosecutor's claim. Opponent's explanations of this kind are implicit in the content or the context from which the proponent's assertion arises and require no other evidential support.

The second kind of opponent's explanation requires further evidence. For example, if the charge that X murdered Y proceeded to trial, counsel for the defense might undermine the probative value of W_1's assertion (P_2) that she saw a person with characteristics a, b, c, and d enter Y's house through cross-examination. If that examination forced W_1 to admit,

22 W_1: I have poor eyesight and was not wearing my glasses on January 1, and
23 W_1: It was dark and it was foggy at 4:15 p.m. on January 1,

counsel could argue that this ancillary evidence supported an opponent's explanation that W's assertion should be discounted because W's observational sensitivity was impaired.

As Wigmore summarized them, the five probative processes applicable to any piece of evidence are:

PA = proponent's assertion of a fact to evidence a probandum;

OE = opponent's explanation of other facts taking away the value of this inference PA;

OD = opponent's denial of the evidentiary fact on which the inference PA is based;

OR = opponent's rival fact, adduced against the probandum, without any reference to the inference PA;

PC = proponent's corroborative facts, negating the explanations OE.

(*Science* (1937) 46)

2. The logical principles

In the adversarial system, all decisions resolving disputed questions of fact must be rationally justifiable. This requirement has two necessary corollaries:

1   The principles of logic – abductive, inductive, and deductive – can be applied to any mass of data that constitutes evidence from which we wish to reconstruct past events in order to resolve disputed questions of fact.

2   The propositions established by these data and those proffered as possible inferred propositions can be articulated and can be organized and marshaled as arguments bearing upon the resolution of such disputed questions of fact.[25]

Some of the principles underlying abductive logic and their application in the investigative phase of any process were presented and illustrated in Chapter 2. They are developed and illustrated here in the context of their application in the legal process.

a. Abductive reasoning. The lawyer must use abductive reasoning in various situations. Early in a case, for example, a lawyer is typically confronted with sparse data or with data supplied by a biased source, the client. The lawyer must ask questions of the data: What hypotheses might account for these data that would be consistent with a result that would advance (or protect) the client's interests? Given the plausible hypotheses, what additional data should be available to confirm or negate them? Frequently, the answers are not apparent. Similarly creative speculation and testing is frequently required when the lawyer is thinking about data that cannot be accounted for by any of the provisional theories under consideration or about data that will support the opposing side's case unless it can be otherwise explained. What the lawyer needs to do in such situations is imagine or construct new hypotheses or possible solutions that may satisfactorily account for the data and then discover

25 For a fuller discussion of the principles and their significance to the adversarial model of adjudication, see Anderson (1991).

sources from which additional evidence to test these hypotheses or solutions might be obtained. This is creative lawyering.

The materials in Chapter 1 included illustrations of abductive reasoning. The "Intelligence analyst" was designed to illustrate abductive reasoning (see pages 3–8). In one interpretation, Solomon employed abductive reasoning in identifying the sword as a useful tool to generate additional evidence that would aid him in deciding the question before him (see pages 2–3). Kemelman and Welt were engaging in abductive reasoning throughout their analysis in "The Nine Mile Walk," especially when they searched for ways to set up and test the hypothesis that the statement concerning a "nine mile walk" reflected events that had actually occurred (see pages 11–18). The exercises in "An investigation" were designed to require the police cadet to engage in abductive reasoning at several stages (see pages 40–45). Although not the focus, each of the other exercises in Chapter 1 contains illustrations of abductive logic or requires its use to "solve" the problem presented or both.

After discovery is over[26] and all planned investigations have been completed, the lawyer is confronted with the task of analyzing the available evidence to identify, construct, and appraise arguments that can be used to persuade the tribunal that the necessary ultimate probandum has or has not been proved with the degree of certainty required by the applicable standard of proof.[27] In theory, the evidence is as complete as it can be, and the lawyer is only required to analyze a fixed and defined mass of data. The primary method of reasoning required at this stage is inductive reasoning. Can the data be marshaled to provide compelling support for the inferred propositions necessary to the client's success in the case at hand?

There is, however, a continuing need for abductive reasoning in preparing for and presenting a case at trial. In preparing for trial, a lawyer uses abductive reasoning to identify an opponent's explanations that she may use to explain away assertions based upon evidential data the opposing party is likely to offer and to identify explanations that she must anticipate opposing counsel may suggest to weaken or undermine assertions based upon evidential data she will offer. At the trial stage, the lawyer can invoke the process of opponent's explanation (OE) to suggest to the tribunal alternative hypotheses that might explain away damaging evidence offered by her opposing counsel. After the trial has begun, however, it is ordinarily too late to seek new evidence that might support one or more of those explanations and make it a true rival that might more effectively undermine the proponent's case. Abduction is critical in the early stages, when there remains time for investigating the possibilities before committing to a specific theory on which the case will be tried. Induction becomes central when the possibilities have been identified and explored and the data are as complete as is feasible. The unexamined possibility first seen and raised at trial is ordinarily a sign of desperation or inadequate preparation.

---

26 In England "discovery" is now referred to as "disclosure."
27 On standards of proof, see Ch. 8.

b. Deductive reasoning. Deductive logic is the process by which we apply a universal major premise to a particular factual proposition, a minor premise. The classic illustration is: All men are mortal; Socrates is a man; therefore, Socrates is a mortal. If the major and minor premises are true, it necessarily follows that the conclusion is true. In a legal case, the applicable rule of law is the major premise and the ultimate probandum is the minor premise. In the last section, we presented a rule of law defining murder, a major premise, and the ultimate probandum that must be proved to satisfy that rule, a minor premise (at pages 90–91). If the ultimate probandum was true, then it would necessarily be the case that the accused is guilty of murder.

c. Inductive reasoning.[28] In analyzing the available evidential data and identifying and marshaling the inferences that those data support in preparing for trial, the lawyer relies primarily on inductive reasoning. The examples drawn from "An investigation" developed in the preceding section (at pages 96–98) illustrated the process of inductive reasoning. The nature of that form of reasoning is developed further in the discussion of generalizations that follow.

d. Generalizations. There is a necessary relationship between deductive and inductive reasoning that every lawyer should understand.[29] The primary mode of reasoning in analyzing the relationships between a specified mass of evidential data and a proposition to be proved may be inductive, but effective analysis of those relationships requires the application of a form of quasi-deductive reasoning.

Wigmore noted the essential point:

[E]very inductive inference is at least capable of being transmuted into and stated in the deductive form, by forcing into prominence the implied law or generalization on which it rests more or less obscurely. (*Science* (1937) 21)

The point requires further development.

i. The importance of generalizations.[30] "Generalizations . . . represent the glue that hold our arguments together" (Schum (1994) 82). Every inference is dependent upon a generalization. The inductive form of an inference can be converted to a quasi-deductive form by identifying and articulating the generalization upon which it depends. Thus, classically, Descartes's "I think; therefore I am" depends on the generalization that might be formally stated as "All persons who think are persons who exist" and converted to a syllogistic form:

All persons who think are persons who exist.
I am a person who thinks.
Therefore, I am a person who exists.[31]

---

28 We follow Wigmore and John Stuart Mill in using "induction" to refer to inferential reasoning that, in this context, is mainly concerned with reasoning towards and justifying conclusions about particular past events. See generally Walton (1989) and (2002).
29 This is also true of abductive logic. See above at pages 56–58.
30 The roles generalizations play in analysis and argument are explored in greater depth in Ch. 10.
31 Or, to parallel Descartes's elegant simplicity: All who think are; I think; therefore, I am.

In practice, it is rare that the generalization upon which the justification for an inference depends is a universally true proposition. Usually they have fuzzy quantifiers such as, "people who enter a house *usually* remain for more than fifteen minutes."

In most contexts, inductive reasoning operates intuitively. The reasoner does not consciously identify the generalizations upon which her inferences depend, unless she is required to justify her conclusions. Even then, she will often find it hard, probably impossible, to articulate the precise generalization upon which an inference relied, as opposed to articulating an after-the-fact generalization that she believes justifies her conclusion. For example, a student might report to her teacher that her friend John did not attend class today because his car would not start, urging the teacher to conclude that John's absence should be excused because it was caused by circumstances beyond his control. The teacher might inquire, "How do you know his car would not start?" The student might reply, "Because John told me so." The teacher might continue the inquiry: "Why does the fact that he told you his car would not start justify the conclusion that his car, in fact, would not start?" Forced to justify her inference, she might claim, "Based upon my past experience with John, I believe John's assertions are almost always true and accurate."

In a legal context, it is frequently important to identify the generalization upon which an inference depends to determine the strength or the plausibility of the inference and to identify potential fallacies. Both the importance and the potential dangers can be simply illustrated.

Many people would accept the generalization, "In most instances, a person who has committed a violent crime will flee from the scene of that crime." In "An investigation," the cadet learns (P_4): "W_2 says that he saw X, who was known to him, running out of Y's home at 4:45 p.m. on January 1." Y was murdered in the house at 4:30 p.m. and proposition 4 supports an inference that X was fleeing from the scene of that crime shortly after it was committed. If the generalization identified above were applicable, the cadet might argue that this shows it is likely that X murdered Y. But that argument would be fallacious. The generalization so framed cannot logically be applied to justify that inference. The only basis upon which an inference from X's "flight" to X's guilt can be justified is by the far weaker generalization: "In some instances, a person fleeing from the scene of a serious crime is the person who has committed that crime."[32] Given the number of plausible explanations, other than guilt, why someone might flee from the scene of a violent crime, the evidence provides, at best, only weak support for the inference that X murdered Y.

32 The more detailed "flight" chain of inferences is: "Analytically, flight is an admission by conduct, and its probative value as circumstantial evidence of guilt depends on the degree of confidence with which four inferences can be drawn: (1) from defendant's behavior to flight; (2) from flight to consciousness of guilt; (3) from consciousness of guilt to consciousness of guilt concerning the crime charged; and (4) from consciousness of guilt concerning the crime charged to actual guilt of the crime charged." *U.S. v. Myers*, 550 F.2d 1036. 1039 (5th 1977) (noted as leading case in *McCormick on Evidence*, §263 (1999)).

ii. *A note on the nature of generalizations*. Generalizations can be classified using three axes — a generality axis, a reliability axis, and a source axis. The end points of the generality axis are marked by generalizations in the most abstract form and generalizations that have been made specific to the precise case or context in which they are to be applied. For example, the abstract, "In some instances a person seen fleeing from the scene of violent crime may be guilty of that crime," as opposed to the context specific, "It is possible that a person dressed in a suit and tie who was seen emerging from a ten-unit apartment building and walking rapidly toward a bus stop 100 yards from the building shortly after a victim had been brutally beaten with a hammer in that building may be guilty of the crime."

At one end of the reliability axis are scientific laws (such as the law of gravity); well-founded scientific opinions (such as the conclusions of a qualified forensic expert based upon comparison of specimens of handwriting alleged to have been written by the same individual); and widely shared conclusions based upon common experience (for instance, everyone knows that a driver must stop for a red light). In the middle are commonly held, but unproven or unprovable, beliefs (for instance, fleeing the scene of a crime is evidence of a guilty conscience). At the other end are biases or prejudices that may be strongly held irrespective of available data (for instance, women do not make good trial lawyers; men are generally poor single parents; whites cannot fairly sit as jurors when a black is on trial, etc.) and less strongly held but still operative beliefs (for instance, a person's actions usually conform to her motives).

Finally, the source axis may range from generalizations based upon repeated personal experience to those based on acquired knowledge to "synthetic/intuitive" generalizations[33] whose source the person formulating the generalizations cannot identify. Based upon personal experience, the authors believe that, "In Miami, Florida, the sun shines for some period of time on most days of the year." Based upon their studies the authors believe, "Gravitational force is proportional to the masses, and inversely proportional to the square of the distance between them." Although none of the authors could identify its source, each accepts the generalization, "In some instances a person seen fleeing from the scene of a violent crime is the person who committed that crime."

Wigmorean analysis provides a technique for identifying and making explicit the generalizations involved at each step of an argument. At the same time, that analysis may cumulatively seem like an invitation to extreme skepticism. It regularly provides strong ammunition for attacking an opponent's argument and for questioning one's own. So many generalizations seem so vulnerable in so many respects that one may be led to the conclusion that all arguments about evidence are built on shifting sands. Whether such skepticism is philosophically tenable, however, is not an immediate concern for the practicing lawyer. In our experience, students of Wigmorean analysis often go through a skeptical phase, in which they doubt whether any argument can

---

33 The term and its origin are developed further in Ch. 10.

ever be strong. However, after doing some exercises they usually conclude that it is possible to construct cogent arguments that can even satisfy the standard of "beyond reasonable doubt."

A good lawyer must be able to assess the relative strengths and weaknesses of his or her own case as well as those of an opponent's case. For present purposes it is sufficient to note that, in legal contexts, reliance upon generalizations that fall far short of certainty is an inevitable aspect of even the strongest case. The common law model of adjudication assumes as much, and rarely will an argument be of any value if it is limited to demonstrating that one's opponent's case falls short of perfection. The skepticism of the disappointed perfectionist has little value in a system that is explicitly based upon standards that require only less than perfect proof. In litigation, the question is not "Is it certain?", but rather, "Does it conform to the best available judgment that can be reached based upon the evidence provided in light of the stock of knowledge and beliefs commonly held in the particular society at the time the case is tried?" In that context, Wigmorean analysis simply provides analytic tools for identifying and analyzing background generalizations. The capacity to use those tools effectively is an essential part of sound lawyering.

3. Application of the principles in legal disputes

An offer of evidence always involves one (or more) of the probative processes Wigmore described – assertion, explanation, rival, denial, or corroboration. But the logical structure of the argument from evidential data to proposed conclusion will differ in ways unrelated to the probative process being invoked. These structures are important in two respects. First, they are central to questions on how specific arguments, or the arguments in a case-as-a-whole, should be evaluated in reaching a judgment. These are questions that Wigmore did not address in any detail. They have become prominent in the current debate over the nature and role of probabilistic reasoning in forensic contexts. Second, the structures have considerable practical importance for the lawyer who must analyze evidence to identify and appraise the arguments that can be made in any case. We have largely deferred the problems associated with evaluation and probabilistic reasoning to chapters 8 and 9 and the appendix on probability.[34] But it is important to identify and explain five central concepts and their significance in analysis before proceeding – *conjunction, compound* (and *complex*) propositions, *convergence, corroboration,* and *catenate* inferences.

   a. Conjunction. In order to succeed in a civil or a criminal case, a party may have to establish each of several facts in issue or merely to establish one of a number of facts in issue in the alternative. Thus, in a standard murder case, the prosecution typically has to prove (A) that the victim is dead, (B) that the death was caused

---

34 Appendix I, "Probability and Proof: Some Basis Concepts" by Philip Dawid, Professor of Statistics, University of London, appears at www.cambridge.org/9780521673167.

by an *actus reus,* (C) that the accused committed the *actus reus,* and (D) that the accused acted with criminal intent. Each of these is a necessary element in the prosecution's case. On the other hand, it is sufficient for the defense to establish reasonable doubt by undermining the probability of any of these penultimates or by offering credible evidence in support of any one of a series of defenses, such as (E) self-defense, (F) insanity, or (G) provocation. To put the matter formally, to succeed in a typical murder case, the prosecution has to establish beyond reasonable doubt that *A and B and C and D* are true, each of which is a *necessary* condition, and it is *sufficient* for the defense to show either that one of these conditions has not been established beyond reasonable doubt or that defense *E or F or G* has not been negated beyond reasonable doubt by the prosecution. In a civil case, the ultimate *probandum* may include alternative conditions, disjunctive penultimate probanda, such that the proponent need only establish one of the alternatives in order to recover – for example, that the equipment that caused the plaintiff's injury was *either* negligently designed *or* negligently manufactured.

In every case, a lawyer must first determine, at least provisionally, the ultimate *probandum* that must be established (or avoided). Thus, counsel for the plaintiff in *Sargent v Southern Accident Company* (pages 28–31) would have identified that she must find evidence sufficient to establish that it was more probable than not that: (A) Upham Sargent is dead, and (B) he suffered an accidental injury, and (C) the accidental injury was the sole cause of his death, and (D) he died within 90 days of the accidental injury, and (E) Upham Sargent was the insured under a $500,000 insurance policy issued by the Southern Accident Company, and (F) Porter Sargent is the sole beneficiary under that policy. Each of the component propositions is, to some degree, analytically, but not statistically, independent of the others and must be supported, at a minimum, by evidence sufficient to withstand a motion for a directed verdict. Parsing the ultimate *probandum* into its individual elements is a necessary first step in the analysis that a lawyer must perform in any case.

b. Compound (or complex) propositions. Sometimes an intermediate *probandum* may also contain a number of elements, each of which is supported by separate evidence. In such instances, the question arises, how should one assess the strength of the proposition as a whole? Although similar to conjunction, in legal contexts different considerations apply to assessing the strength of compound propositions that are intermediate *probanda* as opposed to assessing the strength of the ultimate *probandum* for a case-as-a-whole.

Initially, the analytic task for the lawyer is to identify and to parse such intermediate propositions into their component parts and to reduce each component to a simple proposition. This task has two aspects. In the abstract, the task must be performed in order to analyze with precision which evidence bears upon which component, so that the support for each may be properly appraised. There is also a strategic aspect. How the compound proposition and each of its components should be framed typically is a function of strategy as well as logic. Logic specifies necessary, but rarely sufficient, conditions that must be satisfied. For present purposes, however, it is enough to note that the division of any compound or complex proposition into its simplest constituent parts is necessary to sound analysis.[35]

The kind of analysis required in dealing with compound intermediate propositions ordinarily differs from that required to identify and separate the elements in an ultimate *probandum* in ways that are significant. Once the lawyer has identified a potential ultimate *probandum* in a case, the task of subdividing it into its separate elements and reducing them to simple propositions is primarily a task similar to the task of parsing the holding in an appellate decision. Identifying compound intermediate propositions that may be necessary or possible steps in an argument requires more.

The distinction and its importance can be illustrated with the example developed above (pages 94–98). In that example, the prosecution alleged,

3   It was X who committed the act that caused Y's death,

and has offered evidence supporting two intermediate propositions:

10   X was in Y's house at 4:30 p.m.
12   Y died in his home at 4:30 p.m. on January 1 as the result of an unlawful act committed by another person.

Neither proposition 10 nor 12, standing alone, supports (or is even relevant to) proposition 3. If they are combined to form the proposition "X was in Y's house at 4:30 p.m., and Y died in his home at 4:30 p.m. on January 1 as the result of an unlawful act committed by another person," the resulting compound proposition supports proposition,

13   X had an opportunity to commit the act that caused Y's death,

which in turn supports proposition 3.

It is important that lawyers recognize the parts of an argument where such combinations are necessary because doubts about proposition 10 and about proposition 12 must, in some manner, combine to increase the doubt about proposition 13. Putting aside questions concerning how such doubts should be combined in reaching a judgment about that proposition, it is clear that the presence of independent sources of doubt creates possibilities for effective argument that no lawyer should overlook. This requires careful analysis.[36]

---

35   The distinction between compound and complex propositions raises questions that can be deferred until we turn explicitly to problems of evaluation in Chs. 8 and 9. As used here, complex propositions are compound propositions in which the truth or falsity of each component element is independent of the truth or falsity of the others.

36   The difficulty of the analytic task is enhanced by the fact that the presence of a compound proposition in argument is often concealed (intentionally or unintentionally) by the language commonly used in argumentation. The prosecutor, for example, might argue, "The evidence shows that X was in Y's house at 4:30 p.m., when the murder occurred." Counsel for the defense must have foreseen the likely argument and have identified that it involves the combination of two simple propositions in order to plan a response that effectively illustrates the need to consider and combine any doubts that exist as to each of the component propositions. See also note 38 below (for an illustration of how the seemingly simple proposition, "Y was murdered in his house at 4:30 p.m.," might usefully be divided into three further simple propositions).

Propositions developed through investigations are often complex propositions. For example, based upon proposition 4 in "An investigation," the prosecutor can anticipate that W_2 would testify,

28   W_2: I saw X, whom I know, running out of Y's home at 4:45 p.m. on January 1.

This testimonial assertion needs to be broken down into three component propositions because each is relevant for a different reason.

29   W_2: I know X (relevant to credibility of identification).
16   W_2: I saw X leave Y's home at 4:45 p.m. on January 1 (relevant to presence in home at 4:45 p.m. and thus to opportunity).
30   W_2: X was running when he left Y's home at 4:45 p.m. on January 1 (relevant to flight).

The importance of this kind of analysis should be clear.

   c. *Convergence.* A logician provided a useful definition of convergence: "Two items of circumstantial evidence converge when both facts, independently of the other, [support the] probability [of] the same conclusion."[37] For example, consider two propositions:

9   It was X who entered Y's house at 4:15 p.m. on January 1, and
17   X departed from Y's house at 4:45 p.m. on January 1.

Either proposition, if accepted as true, would support the inference,

10   X was in Y's house at 4:30 p.m.

The two *converge* to strengthen this inference.

   Again putting aside questions concerning the degree of additional strength provided when two propositions converge, it should be clear that convergence raises analytical issues, in addition to credibility, that are different from those raised by testimonial corroboration. In the illustration, the lawyer may and should examine possible explanations unrelated to the credibility of the witnesses – for instance,

32   X may have left Y's house before 4:30 p.m. to run an errand and returned sometime after 4:30 p.m. and before 4:45 p.m.

It is also important to note that an argument that is strengthened because two propositions *converge* to support a third is an argument that can never be strengthened and must ordinarily be *weakened* because two propositions *combine* to form a compound proposition that is a necessary step in the arguments in a case. For example, if accepted as true, propositions 6 and 16, and the assertions made by W_1 and W_2, support inferences that *converge* to strengthen proposition 10, "X was in Y's house at 4:30 p.m. on January 1." That proposition *combines* with the proposition 12, "Y died in his home at 4:30 p.m. on January 1 as the result of an unlawful act

37 Cohen (1977) 94.

committed by another person," to support proposition 13, "X had an opportunity to commit the act that caused Y's death," which provides a necessary step in the prosecution's argument that the evidence establishes X's guilt. The resulting compound proposition, can, however, be no stronger than its constituent parts and must, in some sense, be weaker where the evidence leaves ground for doubt about each of the parts.[38]

d. Corroboration. The same logician considering the concept in the context of judicial disputes gave it a narrower meaning that, for present purposes, is useful: "At its simplest testimonial corroboration occurs when two witnesses both testify, independently of one another, to the truth of the same proposition."[39] For example, if a new witness, W_6, testified,

31 W_6: I also saw a person with characteristics a, b, c, and d enter Y's house at 4:15 p.m. on January 1,

that would corroborate W_1's testimony,

5 "I saw a person with characteristics a, b, c, and d enter Y's house at 4:15 p.m. on January 1,"

and, in some degree, strengthens the inference,

6 A person with characteristics a, b, c, and d entered Y's house at 4:15 p.m. on January 1.

It is important to recognize the distinction between convergence in general and corroboration in particular. Corroboration in this narrow sense focuses the analysis on credibility. The lawyer who wishes to challenge a proponent's assertion supported by the independent testimony of two witnesses must begin by examining possible sources of error that may diminish the credibility of either or both witnesses – such as that the conditions under which the observation took place were not suitable for accurate perception (lighting, distance, eyesight, etc.); the witness's memory is not reliable (lapse of time, reliability of the witness with respect to other events, etc.); or the witness has a motive to lie (animosity toward X, fear of prosecution, etc.). By limiting corroboration to this narrower meaning, the starting-point for analysis is clarified. That limitation also makes it possible to maintain an analytically useful distinction between corroboration and convergence.

e. Catenate inferences. Catenate inferences are "chains" of inferences, a condition that exists when there is more than one step in the reasoning necessary to show

---

38 In theory, the strength of a compound proposition can never be greater than the strength of the weakest of its constituent parts. If I am absolutely certain that Y was murdered in his house at 4:30 p.m., but I think it only slightly more probable than not that X was in Y's house at 4:30 p.m., I can at most conclude that the compound proposition is slightly more probable than not. If I also have doubt about (i) whether Y was, in fact, murdered, or (ii) whether his death occurred in the house, or (iii) whether the time of death was 4:30 p.m., my doubts must in some manner combine to diminish the degree of certainty with which I could accept the compound proposition as proven. We address problems of this kind in Chs. 8 and 9 and the appendix on probability.
39 Cohen (1977) 94.

the relationship by which a probans supports a probandum. An argument from an autoptic proference to a fact of consequence almost invariably involves (and can always be restated to involve) catenate rather than simple inferences. For example, the first step in any inferential chain from a testimonial assertion must always be the truth of the matter asserted – e.g., from the fact that W_2 testified,

16   W_2: I saw X leave Y's house at 4:45 p.m. on January 1,

we infer that,

17   X departed from Y's house at 4:45 p.m. on January 1,

and then infer that,

10   X was in Y's house at 4:30 p.m on January 1.

Two points follow from this that should be noted. First, sound analysis requires that the lawyer identify and articulate each step in the chain of inferences necessary to reason from an autoptic proference to a fact of consequence. The step omitted is the possible source of doubt not identified, the "weak link" unseen, the possible point of attack unnoted. Second, creativity and judgment are required in analyzing and articulating the steps in an inferential chain. The best practical guide in this context is that the lawyer should seek to identify every condition that may give reason for doubt about the claim that probans A supports probandum B. Each ground that raises a plausible basis for doubt indicates that there is a necessary step in the inferential chain that should be examined.

f. *Combining Evidentiary Propositions: Integration.* Most factual arguments involve the use of different logical structures – inferences that are corroborative, convergent, or catenate, or the product of a combination of two (or more) simple propositions – in demonstrating the proposed relationships between discrete evidential data and the *probandum* urged. As a practical matter it is important to be able to recognize the distinctions and their significance.

The simple inference from each testimonial assertion to the truth of the fact asserted focuses attention on credibility as the most significant source of possible doubt. The presence of two or more testimonial assertions that are *corroborative* may diminish the likelihood that credibility can be plausibly attacked (perhaps to a point where further explorations are not justified), but it cannot eliminate it. Where two circumstantial propositions *converge* to strengthen a third, the lawyer must consider possible explanations unrelated to credibility and possible sources of evidence that might support one of these explanations or support a rival inference.

Where two propositions *combine* to support a further inference, the lawyer must recognize that the support cannot be stronger than the weaker of the two and must look for further possibilities that may explain or rival the proposed probandum – for instance, that X was present in the house at the time of the murder, but a third party intruder, acting independently, was the person who committed the act that caused Y's death. She should focus her investigations accordingly. The fact that multiple steps are required in an argument from evidential data to proposed conclusion signals the need for further investigation before the case is tried and makes it possible to identify and eliminate or cumulate sources of doubt that can be used in argument at trial.

Those distinctions make it possible to frame more clearly some issues of considerable importance – namely, questions about how doubt at each stage of an argument should be considered in reaching a judgment whether a probandum has been proven to the required degree of certainty. If there is any ground to doubt credibility of W_1 (proposition 5) or W_6 (proposition 31) or their ability to identify accurately the characteristics of the person they say they saw enter Y's house at 4:15 p.m. in the circumstances present, there must be some ground to doubt the inferences they support, that a person who had the same characteristics as X entered at 4:15 p.m. Assuming there is some doubt, how should these doubts and the additional doubt created by limiting qualifications on the generalization, proposition 11, "People who enter a house *usually* remain for more than fifteen minutes," affect the assessment of the likelihood that proposition 10, "X was in Y's house at 4:30 p.m.," is true? How then should those doubts be combined with any doubts about the time, place, or cause of Y's death in evaluating the strength of the inference that Y had an opportunity to commit the act that caused Y's death and how can they be accumulated in reaching a judgment about the penultimate probandum, "It was X who murdered Y"?

These are important questions. They have been the subject of extensive (and sometimes heated) debate among scholars holding different theories of probability. They are obviously significant to a lawyer in a criminal case who must argue to a jury that ultimate probandum in that case has or has not been proved "beyond a reasonable doubt." Those questions are addressed in Chapters 8 and 9.

The chart and other methods of analysis presented in this book do not address these questions. The principles of proof developed in this chapter and the chart method of analysis presented in the next chapter can be used and applied to any case because they are independent of any of the contending theories of probability. With a few adjustments, probability theorists from any of the schools may use the principles and the method to analyze and organize the evidence in a case in a manner that facilitates the development of their ideas on how the particular parts and the whole should be evaluated. As a practical matter, the principles and the methods Wigmore presented, as refined and developed here, can readily be adapted to facilitate the analysis, construction, and appraisal of arguments about disputed questions of fact that are the concern of the analyst.

The exercise continues: State v. Archer (II)

The Prosecutor's Standpoint

The investigation of Vern's murder continues (see page 94 above). You remain the prosecuting attorney. The investigative reports submitted by Detective Paul to date include the following extracts:

In response to the housekeeper's call, I was dispatched to Vern's home at 8:15, Monday morning. The housekeeper said she had arrived at 8:00 a.m. and discovered Vern's body lying on the living room floor. The living room was a shambles. Upon examining the body, I found a scrap of brown Harris tweed cloth clutched in Vern's right hand. (I extracted the scrap of cloth, placed it in an evidence bag, marked and sealed the bag, and subsequently delivered it to the police evidence custodian.)

. . . After learning that Vern had been wealthy and that his sole surviving heir was a nephew named Archer, I proceeded to Archer's house to interview him. I arrived at 5:30 p.m., Wednesday. Archer stated he had been at home and had gone to bed early on Sunday and had gone directly to work Monday morning.

. . . As I was departing, I observed a brown Harris tweed jacket in Archer's front closet. It had a hole in the upper right hand sleeve.

. . . At 7:30 a.m., Thursday, I returned with a warrant to search Archer's home. I seized the jacket, placed it in an evidence bag, and sealed and marked the bag. A visual comparison of the scrap of cloth found in Vern's hand and the jacket shows that the scrap and the jacket are the same color, texture, and weave. The scrap fits in the hole in the upper right sleeve of the jacket . . .

On the strength of this and other evidence, Archer has been arrested and indicted for the murder of Vern. You are now preparing for trial and planning what further investigations should be done. Your current provisional ultimate probandum is: "It was Archer who murdered Vern." For today, you are *only* concerned with the relationship between the propositions supported by the scrap of cloth, the jacket, and Paul's anticipated testimony with respect to these two items.

1   Create and number a keylist of simple propositions which you could elicit as testimonial assertions from Detective Paul and the circumstantial propositions you would argue that the trier of fact should infer directly from these testimonial assertions and the scrap of cloth and the jacket and label. Each proposition should be phrased as a simple declarative statement to which the trier of fact might assign a truth value (for instance, true or false, probable or not probable). Each proposition representing a testimonial assertion or a physical object must be an autoptic proference the jury will hear or see.

2   Given the ultimate probandum, "It was Archer who murdered Vern," identify each intermediate proposition the trier of fact must infer in order to conclude that the evidential propositions you have listed support the conclusion that the ultimate probandum is true.

3   *Abduction:* We are concerned here only with the scrap of cloth, the jacket, and the circumstances in which each was discovered. In light of these facts and the analysis you have developed, what additional evidential data might be available to strengthen or weaken the inference that P is true? State precisely the plausible hypotheses that should be investigated and specific evidence you would direct Paul to seek to support (or eliminate) each.

4   *Defense Counsel's Preliminary Standpoint.* You have been appointed to represent Archer. You have not met him. The prosecution has given you Paul's reports. You

have, of course, performed the same analysis as the prosecutor in order to evaluate the case and to determine what information you will seek from Archer and what other investigations you will make. Formulate a list of propositions that might explain away the prosecutor's proposed inferences. Do the facts as reported by Paul suggest any possible propositions for which there might be evidential support and which would involve the rival or denial processes? List the potential propositions. Classify each proposition on your list as opponent's explanation (OE), denial (OD), or rival (OR).

4

Methods of analysis

A. Introduction

The principles of inductive logic are the common tools of practical reasoning and are important to anyone who must make decisions based upon incomplete and fallible data. These tools are specially important in many professions. Society holds professionals to a higher standard of reasoning because, ordinarily, their decisions can significantly affect the interests of individuals or society as a whole, and they are supposed to be competent to make such decisions. In one view, the highest standards may reasonably be required of doctors and lawyers. They undertake to solve problems of great importance for individuals, and their work in the aggregate is critical to society.

Every profession that engages in fact analysis and reasoning must develop ways of recording and organizing the data in forms suitable for analysis and use. This is surely true for lawyers. At every stage, the lawyer must engage in analysis. Has my client provided me with sufficient facts to state a claim for relief or a basis for a defense? What additional evidence should I seek to test and strengthen my client's case? Given the evidence available to both sides, can the data be marshaled to persuade the relevant decision-maker that my client is entitled to satisfactory relief?

Analysis must ordinarily precede use, and a system designed to record and organize data in a manner that facilitates analysis will ordinarily differ significantly from a system designed to facilitate the effective, post-analysis use of that data. The lawyer then needs a system under which the data can be organized and marshaled for presentation in the appropriate context, be it counseling, negotiation, or trial. Here, the nature of the forum in which the evidence and arguments will be presented dictates the requirements for a system to order and organize the available data for its intended use.

Lawyers have developed a variety of systems for recording and organizing data. The filing system in a lawyer's office is designed to ensure information received on each matter and the products of any analysis or research are organized to facilitate retrieval for use. Chronologies have long been recognized as a useful device for organizing factual information for analysis. Over the past two decades, lawyers (and other professionals) have developed sophisticated record management and indexing systems to facilitate analysis, often augmented by computerized support systems.[1] So too, they have developed devices such as the trial book to organize the data for effective presentation to a tribunal in light of the analysis done. There has, however, been far less attention devoted to articulating the principles and protocols that should be applied in analyzing factual data in legal (and other) contexts in order to enhance the quality and the completeness of the analysis.

In this chapter, we present a generalized set of procedures, a protocol, that we think may usefully be applied in any method of analysis. In Chapter 5, we present a simplified version of Wigmore's chart method of analysis and show how the protocol can be adapted and applied to use that method. In Chapter 6, we describe the outline method of analysis and the uses of narrative and chronologies as analytic devices. In that chapter, we also describe how and when the different methods and devices can be used in the context of a case to be litigated and tried.

B. The methods and a protocol for their use

1. Methods of analysis and analytic devices

In this book we present two methods of analysis – the "chart method" and the "outline method." A "method of analysis" in this context is a method for recording and organizing data and for specifying the logical relationships among the propositions and how they can be marshaled to support or negate a fact of consequence. Each method of analysis results in a distinct product. The distinctive feature of the chart method is that the principal products are a key-list and a chart. The "key-list" contains all of the evidential and inferential propositions that can be marshaled to support or undermine the ultimate proposition to be proved, the ultimate probandum. The "chart" uses symbols to depict the claimed logical relationships between these propositions. (See page 139 below for an illustration.) The product of the outline method of analysis is an outline that simplifies the complex proposition that is the ultimate probandum into simple propositions, the penultimate probanda, and uses them as the major headings in the outline. The major headings are then divided and subdivided into necessary intermediate propositions until the analyst reaches the evidential propositions – the propositions that express what the decision-maker will hear or see, if and when the case is tried.

We also describe two analytic devices – chronologies and narratives.[2] An "analytic device" is a tool that aids in developing lines of inquiry for or in testing the quality and

---

1 On June 14, 2004, a search for "litigation support" using GOOGLE generated more than 290 sites where programs or information could be found.
2 Wigmore thought that narratives constituted a separate "method of analysis" (*Science*, 821). For reasons described below, we maintain that narrative complements analysis but is not an alternative to analysis. Although narrative serves many purposes, we characterize it here as an analytic device to emphasize its role in the analytic process and reduce the temptation for the analyst to "skip" the more rigorous and demanding methods of analysis in favor of just constructing stories.

completeness of an analysis. Converting all of the available data into propositions ordered in a strict chronology, at any stage, simplifies the task of discovering story possibilities that can be constructed from the available evidence. It simplifies the task of discovering gaps that need to be filled. Narratives serve similar functions. For example, when an analysis of the available evidence has been completed shortly before trial, the question becomes: Can the analysis be converted into a coherent narrative that is consistent with the theory of the case and that accounts for the available evidence, but that does not depend upon facts for which there is no evidence? In contrast, when the analysis has been done at the investigative stage, the question may be: Does a narrative derived from that analysis reveal gaps that need to be filled or suggest additional lines of inquiry that need to be pursued? Constructing chronologies and plausible narratives that might be true at that stage can facilitate imaginative reasoning of the kind described in Chapter 2.

The methods of analysis are complementary rather than rival. Each has special advantages for specific purposes at various stages of a case. For each, the quality of the product can be enhanced by the careful application of a specified set of procedures in its construction and use. We believe that every lawyer should be familiar with both methods, with the purposes for which each is best suited, and with the procedures, the protocol, by which each may be used to maximize its advantages, as well as with the ways in which the analytic devices can be used to facilitate and enhance the resulting product.

2. A seven-step protocol for analysis: a generalized account

In the context of a legal dispute, three questions must always be addressed:

1 What is the ultimate proposition that must be proved?
2 What are the data that are available?
3 What are the plausible and defensible relationships between these data and the ultimate proposition?

A method of analyzing evidence is basically a heuristic device for responding to these questions. As such, the device should have two components – (i) a practicable method for organizing and conducting the analysis and (ii) a system for recording or expressing the results of the analysis in a usable form.

Experience suggests that the quality of an analysis and the resulting product are enhanced if those engaged in the task observe a known and systematic protocol. We believe the quality of the analysis of evidence in a legal dispute and the product that results from that analysis are likely to be enhanced if a systematic set of procedures is regularly employed. The protocol we have developed has seven steps:

1 Clarification of standpoint;
2 Formulation of the potential ultimate *probandum* or *probanda;*
3 Formulation of the potential penultimate *probanda;*
4 Formulation of the theories of the case;

5 Recording the available data;
6 Preparing the product(s); and
7 Refining and completing the analysis.

Step 1. *Clarify the standpoint* of the analyst by giving clear and precise answers to four questions: Who am I? At what stage in what process am I? What materials are available for analysis? What am I trying to do?

Standpoint is always a function of four dependent variables – time, objective (or purpose), materials available for analysis, and role. In academic law instruction, the point in time is typically post-trial and post-appeal. For the practitioner and, with appropriate exercises, for the student, the exercise may focus upon any stage: reviewing a trial record for appeal, developing a closing argument based upon evidence given, preparing a matter for trial based upon a completed investigation, investigating a matter in preparation for litigation or trial, evaluating a client's claims in order to aid the decision whether to litigate, or even advising a client on proposed conduct or on how to structure proposed conduct with respect to the prospect of future litigation.

The standpoint is also a function of the objectives of the analysis. These can usefully be divided into three main classes: organizational, evaluative, and advocacy objectives. One of the main values of a rigorous method of analysis is as a tool for organizing or ordering or structuring the evidence and the inferences derived from it, as a preliminary to pursuing some other objective, such as evaluating the "net persuasive effect" of the evidence or converting the analysis into a form suitable for the presentation of an argument in a forum, e.g., in a negotiation or at a trial.

For Wigmore, and for most academic analyses, the objective is ordinarily to evaluate the evidence offered or reported to determine whether a case was rightly or justifiably decided with reference to some articulated standard – for instance, given the substantive law and the burden of proof the court found applicable, did the evidence support the factual conclusion necessary to sustain the result reached? This evaluative analysis may be done for different purposes – to determine whether the lawyer could have done better on closing argument or on appeal, whether the rules of admissibility operated to further or frustrate an inquiry to determine truth, etc. But all such exercises start from the assumption that the evidence presented to the trier of fact or the facts reported by the appellate court are fixed.

For example, the *O. J. Simpson* case is history. If we were to take the standpoint of a historian examining the trial record, we would need to differentiate the question, "Was the verdict justified?" from the question, "What actually happened?" It is one thing to ask, "Was the jury justified in acquitting Simpson on the basis of the evidence and arguments presented at trial?" It is another to ask, "Could the prosecution have presented a stronger case at the trial than they in fact did?" And still another to ask, "On the basis of all the evidence available today, can it now be established that it is beyond reasonable doubt that O. J. Simpson was guilty of the murder of Nicole Brown Simpson?"

An advocacy objective is typically dominant when the student or the lawyer seeks to perform the analysis to assist in determining an appropriate course of conduct. What additional investigation or discovery should I seek to strengthen (or weaken) inferences necessary to the development of my client's (or my adversary's) case? What evidence must I highlight, and what evidence must I seek to exclude or minimize to develop my theory of the case?[3]

The objectives that can be achieved are limited by the materials available for analysis. If the available material is a report of a decision by a court of appeal, the analyst can only determine whether the decision was supported by the facts that the court chose to report. She cannot determine whether the evidence presented at trial was sufficient to support a determination that the accused was guilty. She cannot determine whether the court fairly summarized the evidence. If the material is the trial record from a decided case, the analyst might examine the competency of counsel in structuring and marshaling the evidence and arguments. She might be able to make a judgment about whether the evidence was sufficient to enable the fact-finder (judge or jury) to determine that the ultimate probandum was or was not proven to the required degree of certainty. She could not, however, determine whether the accused was guilty or innocent because she does not have access to the evidence that was not discovered or presented. The failure to identify an objective that can be achieved based upon the materials available is a common error that can have serious consequences. Midway in a project, the analyst may discover that the objective specified cannot be achieved with the data available. Either the objective must be amended (often not possible) or the job must be redone.

A fourth variable is role. Role is always implicit once the objective is chosen. But it may be useful to consider the variable separately both to clarify objectives and to reveal possible personal biases of the person doing the analysis. For example, the lawyer preparing for trial must examine the evidence from three standpoints and three roles in order to do the job completely: first, the role of advocate for her client; second, the standpoint and role of her opponent; and, finally, the role and standpoint of the trier of fact. What is her opponent likely to adopt as his theory of the case? To what extent will the triers of fact share the generalizations (or biases) upon which the probative force of her analysis and marshaling of the evidence depend?

It is always important to define standpoint carefully from the outset and at each stage of the case. For present purposes, let us assume the role is that of a lawyer engaged to represent a client with respect to a contested matter, the outcome of which appears likely to depend upon the resolution of disputed questions of fact

3 The concept of a "theory of the case" and related concepts are further developed below at page 118.

(as opposed to a dispute over the controlling legal principles). Throughout, the lawyer's purpose will be to aid the client in determining and achieving the best possible outcome. Under this assumption, standpoint will vary according to the stage at which an analysis of the state of the evidence is undertaken.

The objective of the analysis, and the tools available and useful, will also differ at different stages of a case. For example, at a first interview the lawyer will be listening and probing for facts that will make it possible to frame provisional ultimate *probanda* as hypotheses. At that stage, these hypotheses will be tested by questions framed to determine whether there appears to be evidence available that would support each of the necessary elements of the hypotheses.

Step 2. *Formulate* carefully and precisely *the potential ultimate probandum or probanda.* This does not come as naturally to students as an experienced lawyer might expect. It is surprising how often students fail to see that this is a crucial preliminary step that provides the focal point for the whole analysis. Without an ultimate probandum there is no touchstone of relevance; if it is incorrectly or loosely formulated, the ensuing analysis is correspondingly vulnerable.

The first step then must be to formulate (or identify) the controlling propositions of law. The substantive propositions constitute the major premises; the ultimate *probandum* or *probanda* are the minor premises – those propositions of fact which, if found proven to the required degree, compel or support the conclusion that the party with the burden must prevail. Two caveats are important. First, the ultimate probandum should ordinarily be phrased in a way that respects the burden of proof. The lawyers for O. J. Simpson did not have to prove that he was not guilty; it was the prosecution's burden to prove that he was. Second, the ultimate probandum should not include the standard of proof. The probative force of the evidence cannot be charted. The propositions defining the burden of proof come into play after the analysis has been completed and the task shifts to an evaluation of the probative force of the evidence.[4]

In the O. J. Simpson case,[5] the ultimate probandum had to be derived from the rule of law defining first degree murder. Under Section 187(a) of the California Penal Code, "Murder is the unlawful killing of a human being . . . with malice aforethought." That section might be rephrased as the major premise of a syllogism:

---

4 It should be clear that analysis and evaluation cannot be completely compartmentalized in practice. As the analyst constructs an argument, she automatically appraises its strength. It is, however, useful to maintain the distinction in applying the protocols for analysis. See Chs. 8 and 9 below.

5 *People v. Simpson*, No. BA0987211, California Superior Court (L.A. 1995). Schmalleger (1996) contains a useful and detailed (albeit slightly biased) account of the trial, including significant portions of the trial transcript. Transcripts from the trial are available on-line at Westlaw Database OJ-TRANS. The trial record also appears, and in an organized and more user-friendly way, at www.simpson.walraven.org/. Several of the Famous American Trials series, including a useful version of the evidence in the O. J. Simpson Trial, are available at http://www.law.umkc.edu/faculty/projects/ftrials/ftrials.htm.

If a human being, a victim, is dead, and the victim died as a result of an unlawful act, and it was the accused who committed the act that caused the victim's death, and the person who committed the act that caused the victim's death acted with malice aforethought, then the accused is guilty of murder.

For the murder of Nicole Brown Simpson ("NBS"), the ultimate probandum had to be a proposition that satisfied the conditions of that major premise. That proposition might be framed in the abstract as:

NBS is dead; and NBS died as the result of an unlawful act; and it was Orenthal James Simpson ("OJS") who committed the act that caused NBS's death; and the person who committed the acts that caused NBS's death acted with malice aforethought.

Step 3. *Formulate the potential penultimate probanda.* Ordinarily the ultimate probandum or probanda are complex propositions with more than one condition that must be satisfied. Determining the penultimate probanda, initially and at a minimum, requires that the analysts convert the complex ultimate probandum into a compound proposition and partition (and often sub-partition) that proposition into its component simple propositions. Once these penultimate probanda have been tentatively formulated, the lawyer should be in a position to visualize the overall structure of the case.

In the *O. J. Simpson* case, framing the penultimate probanda requires partitioning the ultimate probandum until it has been reduced to its elements expressed as simple declarative sentences, e.g.:

1 NBS is dead.
2 NBS died as the result of an unlawful act.
3 It was OJS who committed the act that caused NBS's death.
4 The person who committed the acts that caused NBS's death acted with malice aforethought.

Step 4. *Formulate the provisional theories of the case.* The theory of the case is the logical statement formulated as an argument supporting one or more conclusions about the case as a whole. In *Simpson*, the only penultimate probandum in dispute was proposition three (identity): It was OJS who committed the act that caused NBS's death.[6] In that case, a central problem for the prosecution was to develop a credible theory that would explain why OJS would have committed the

---

6 *Simpson* provides a good illustration of the importance of developing a coherent and consistent theory. Theoretically, defense counsel could have disputed proposition 4 (intent) by claiming the person who murdered NBS acted in the heat of passion. As a practical matter, the theory that the defense adopted forced them to take the position that proposition 4 was irrelevant to the defense. The defense denied that it was OJS who did the stabbing and offered evidence suggesting that there were others who might have done it. Having committed themselves to a reasonable-doubt-about-proposition 3 theory, they could not credibly argue that it was not OJS, but if it was OJS he was acting in the heat of passion. A trial lawyer may develop alternative theories, but she may not present conflicting theories, at least not in a jury trial.

murders – to identify a credible motive.[7] The prosecution elected to proceed on a theory of control, a theory that might be summarized as follows:

> OJS had expressed jealous rage resulting in violence in his attempts to control NBS and prevent her from finally severing their relationship. His continuing jealous rage gave him a motive to murder her as the ultimate act of control, and the brutal manner in which she was murdered by multiple stab wounds shows that she was murdered by someone acting in a rage. OJS was the only person who had acted against NBS in a jealous rage. He had a motive to try to maintain his control and to prevent NBS from acting independently, and he went to her house to kill her as the ultimate act of control. Therefore, it was OJS who murdered NBS in a jealous rage.[8]

Partitioning the ultimate probandum into simple declarative sentences that constitute the penultimate probanda identifies the principal "facts of consequence" in the case.[9] The specification of a provisional theory of the case makes it possible to use a penultimate probandum as a "magnet" to attract the relevant evidential propositions.

For example, in order to prove that "it was OJS who committed the acts that caused NBS's death," the prosecution had to prove that OJS had an opportunity to commit the acts. Thus, the analyst might look for evidential propositions bearing upon the time of NBS's death and the time OJS was subsequently observed because they would be relevant to the proposition, "OJS had an opportunity to commit the violent acts that caused NBS's death."

A post-trial analyst might use the "opportunity magnet" to examine the database – the evidence admitted during the trial. Using that magnet, her key-list would include relevant evidential propositions derived directly from the data. For example, Pablo Fuentes, who lived near NBS's house, testified that he had heard the plaintive wail of a dog at 10:15 p.m. on the evening the murder was committed. Other witnesses testified that they later had found NBS's dog wailing and with blood on its paws. From these propositions, the jury might have inferred the propositions necessary to demonstrate the logical relationship of those evidential propositions

---

7 The prosecution does not have to prove motive in a criminal case; it is not a penultimate probandum. Motive, if it exists, is relevant to show it was the accused who committed the act that caused the victim's death. It may also be relevant to intent. In *Simpson* and in many cases, however, it is difficult, sometimes impossible, to persuade a jury to convict without providing a persuasive reason explaining why the accused did it.

8 See Schmalleger (1996) 57–59 (excerpt from "The Prosecution's Opening Statement"). There were alternate theories that the prosecution might have chosen. For example, the prosecution team reportedly considered, but rejected, an "exploding bomb" theory: OJS went to NBS's house that evening intending to vent his anger by committing an act of vandalism, such as slashing the tires on her car. His anger "exploded" when he found NBS with another man, Ronald Goldman (RLG), in the yard in front of her house.

9 Once a witness has taken the stand, her credibility also becomes a fact of consequence. It should be clear that all of the evidential data offered at trial must be relevant to either one or more penultimate probanda or to the credibility of a witness. See Chapter 2 on relevance (pages 62–63) and testimonial credibility (pages 65–70).

to a penultimate probandum – e.g., the plaintive wail of the dog that belonged to NBS and had blood on its paws supported an inference that the wailing was caused by the dog's discovery that its mistress was dead, supporting the further inference that the murder occurred at or shortly after 10:15 p.m. Detective Vanetter testified that it took five minutes to drive from NBS's house to OJS's house. Alan Park, a chauffeur who was waiting for OJS, testified that a recently showered and calm and collected OJS emerged from his house at 11:00 p.m. to be driven to the airport. This testimony and the evidence supporting an inference that NBS died at 10:15 p.m. provided the basis upon which the prosecution had to persuade the jury that OJS had an opportunity to commit the murders – i.e. that he could have been present at NBS's house at 10:15 p.m. and still have returned home, showered, disposed of his bloody garments, collected himself, and emerged from his house at 11:00 p.m.

In other instances, it may be easier to start with an evidential proposition and reason "upward" to develop the inferred propositions that clarify its relevance. In the previous example, an analyst might initially ask why the testimony about a dog's wailing at 10:15 p.m. was relevant, and work upward until she saw that it was relevant to establishing the time of NBS's death and that establishing the time of NBS's death was necessary to determine whether OJS could have had an opportunity to kill NBS. Often, the need to reason upward occurs when pieces of the puzzle are "left over" – i.e. evidential data that seem relevant remain unused after the penultimate "magnets" have been applied to the entire mass of available evidential data. The process of fitting these leftover pieces into the puzzle often forces revisions of the theory and penultimate probanda.

Until the final analysis is complete, the theories must remain provisional, subject to revision as the analysis proceeds. If the problem is a complex one involving a mass of evidence, it is highly likely that there will be a range of possible theories each of which could lead the analysis in significantly different directions. In order to make the task manageable, it may be necessary to eliminate some possibilities and concentrate on one or more specific theories. Even historians and scientists do not have infinite time and resources to pursue endless lines of inquiry. Typically advocates have to develop a provisional theory that will guide their analysis at an early stage. Until the analysis is complete, they must remember that the theory is provisional and remains open to being revised or even changed as the analysis proceeds.

The task of the lawyer is simpler than that of other analysts, such as the historian or the intelligence analyst. The lawyer has an opponent who will try to organize and marshal the evidence to prevent her adversary from prevailing. The lawyer can often limit the number of potential theories that should be examined by formulating the strongest potential theory or theories of the case for her opponent. The theories that need to be examined are those that, given the available evidence, hold the most promise in light of the plausible theories that her opponent may use.[10]

---

10 In Chs. 6 and 10 we shall explore in some detail the nature of such theories, their relationship to "story," "situation," and "theme" in the context of advocacy, and their functions at different stages of litigation.

Step 5. *Recording the available data.* The evidential data must be recorded in propositional form. The dynamic nature of the development of a case over time makes it necessary that the lawyer have some adaptable generic devices that can be employed to record the data in an organized form and that can be expanded as the case develops. One common device of this kind is the chronology. Chronologies can be developed in two forms. One form is a chronology based upon the individual witnesses, documents, or other items of evidence. For each potential witness and exhibit place the events that can be asserted or shown in chronological order. The other form is a master chronology, which places each of the propositions supported by the data in a temporal sequence, indexed to the witnesses or documents by which they are to be established. So ordered, these propositions describe the events that are known or believed to have occurred in the precise sequence in which they occurred. Such a chronology sets the events and documents in the order in which they occurred, the order in which most people think.

As an analytic device, the chronology serves two functions. It helps the lawyer see where there are temporal gaps that need to be filled or explained. Moreover, it helps the lawyer see narratives, "story possibilities," that might explain the events taken as a whole. Both devices enable the lawyer to identify areas where further investigation is necessary and should be productive. Because the chronology is ordered temporally, it can be revised and expanded as new evidential data are obtained.[11] In most cases, a lawyer should begin to develop a master chronology rather early. Later in the case, a fully developed chronology may provide the framework for presenting the theory of the case as a story in the opening statement.

Throughout all stages of the process, steps 1 through 5 are reflexive. The analyst needs to have a provisional ultimate *probandum* to identify possible theories and to establish some basis for selecting lines of investigation that are likely to produce relevant evidential data. At the outset, however, the lawyer needs some factual assertions (ordinarily the client's statements) in order to identify potentially applicable principles of law that will enable her to frame ultimate and penultimate *probanda* as provisional hypotheses. The hypotheses so framed and the provisional theory adopted will guide further investigation, and that investigation, in turn, is likely to generate data that will require that the *probanda* and the theory be revised or that new or additional ones be provisionally adopted.

Two points merit emphasis. First, in processes such as interviewing and investigation, these four steps are likely to be useful in differing sequences. Second, at any stage where the lawyer undertakes a comprehensive analysis to determine the state of the case at that time, each step will be required even though the probanda are provisional and the data incomplete.

---

11 Some cases require alternative or additional generic devices. For example, if the location at which the events occurred is critical, physical diagrams or models may be important analytic devices. So too, in a products liability case, engineering models and blueprints may be necessary. In other complex cases, devices from other fields may be useful – for example, economic analysis in an antitrust case or statistical analysis in an employment discrimination case.

Step 6. *Preparing the product(s).* The product produced is a function of the method chosen – a key-list and chart in the chart method or an outline for the outline method. These methods and analytic devices overlap in ways that make it possible to convert material generated by an analytical device into the product of one of the methods of analysis and to transfer material recorded for one method into the product of the other. For example, the propositions in a master chronology are propositions that will appear in an outline and propositions from the chronology and the outline will appear in a key-list and chart.

Step 7. *Refining and completing the analysis.* Whatever the product, the objective is to develop a logically sound analysis that, in light of the analyst's specific objectives, organizes a mass of evidence and identifies the inferences necessary to relate all significant relevant data to the ultimate proposition in issue. Typically, the process of revision and refinement is continuous, with judgments previously made being revised in each succeeding step of the analysis to deal with any gaps discovered or flaws in the reasoning that are revealed as the process proceeds. It is, however, the chart and key-list, or the outline completed through step 6, that makes it possible to analyze and evaluate the case-as-a-whole and to test the judgments initially made. This is where the true value of the analysis as both intellectual exercise and practical work emerges most clearly. For that reason, the final analysis of the whole should be done as a separate step.

Exercise

Read and review the O. J. Simpson problem in Chapter 1. Prepare a list of the propositions concerning opportunity in chronological order. Develop an opportunity theory that would support the prosecution's claim that the evidence showed beyond reasonable doubt that OJS could have murdered NBS and RLG. Develop a defense theory that would support the defense's claim that it cannot be established beyond reasonable doubt that OJS could have murdered NBS and RLG. Both the prosecution and the defense theories must account for the three thumps that Kato Kaelin testified he had heard around 10:45 p.m. and the black man in dark clothes that Alan Parks testified he had seen approaching the house at 10:55 p.m.

5

The chart method

A. The chart method: an overview

The chart method of analysis is the most rigorous of the three methods of analysis identified above. It is a technique that enables the analyst to construct, test, and reconstruct arguments about questions of fact. It requires that the analyst articulate every step in an argument, breaking down the argument into simple propositions, and then mapping or "charting" all the relations between those propositions and the penultimate probanda (or the components of a hypothesis). The logic is simple; the complexity lies in the materials to be analyzed and in identifying the relationships between the propositions in an extensive argument based on a mass of conflicting evidence. The logic is binary: Every relevant proposition either tends to support or tends to negate a single hypothesis or conclusion (the ultimate probandum). The technique is dialectical: The aim of the chart-maker should be to construct the most cogent possible argument for and against the ultimate conclusion and to relate the opposing arguments within a single coherent structure.

The chart method structures the analysis at two levels – the macroscopic level and the microscopic level. The macroscopic level involves structuring the "top" of the chart. The ultimate and penultimate probanda must be determined based upon the law and, usually, restated after the analyst has formulated a provisional theory of the case. The penultimate probanda help the analyst identify which of the main propositions must be established to support each of the penultimate probanda. Ordinarily, there are subordinate probanda that can be immediately identified. For example, in a murder case the central question often is, "Was it the accused who committed the act that caused the victim's death?" In such a case, the analyst must recognize that any evidence that supports an inference that the accused had opportunity or motive may be important. The subordinate propositions become metaphorical magnets the analyst can use in sorting the evidence and organizing different phases of the argument into discrete, manageable sectors. The key lies in anchoring the arguments about the case as a whole in a defined standpoint, clear questions, and precisely formulated hypotheses or conclusions.

The microscopic level requires precise and detailed analysis of the evidential data for each important phase of the argument. This "microscopic analysis" is arduous and time-consuming work. However, with practice, the analyst learns some basic principles of economy, by identifying crucial or important phases within an argument and focusing mainly on these. If a person's jugular vein is severed, death is almost inevitable. In advocacy "going for the jugular" means concentrating one's attack on the weakest point in an opponent's argument or, more positively, building up support for a proposition which, if established, will ensure success. The chart method of analysis is particularly useful for identifying potentially key propositions that can be used to build or destroy a case.

The two main products that distinguish the chart method from other methods of analysis are a "key-list" of all the propositions used in the argument and a detailed map showing how propositions inferred from the evidential data can be logically marshaled to provide the strongest arguments in support of and against the ultimate probandum. The method is disciplined and systematic, but a chart is a picture of the chart-maker's beliefs about what constitutes the strongest argument. Judgment, selection, skill, and analytical capacity are required at every stage. The chart method is an aid to disciplined analysis, construction, and criticism of arguments; it should not be viewed as a substitute for thinking.

B. The seven-step protocol for the chart method: a detailed account

Mastering Wigmore's chart method of analysis is similar to mastering any complex analytical skill. In learning it, you should try to cultivate the habit of going through a regular sequence of operations step-by-step. Steps 1 through 4 and 7 are common to all methods; steps 5 and 6 must be adapted to the chart method. To provide a solid foundation, we present a more detailed account of each of the steps, adapted to the chart method, using the *United States v. Able* case from Chapter 1 (page 23).

Step 1. *Clarifying standpoint.* The analyst must answer the four basic questions at the outset of any analysis project: Who am I? At what stage in what process am I? What materials are available for analysis? What am I trying to do? The consequences of failing to respond carefully to each of these questions can be dramatic and traumatic in applying the chart method. At some point in trying to develop the charted analysis, usually after the investment of substantial time and effort, the deficiency is more likely to become apparent because the precision required for the chart method makes it far more difficult to overlook any deficiencies.

For purposes of learning how to apply the chart method, it is often helpful to adopt the standpoint of a historian making an *ex post facto* judgment about what happened (the event) on the basis of a finite body of evidence. In this context, a historian might define and pursue a single objective – the construction and evaluation of the arguments for and against a specific conclusion. For example, she might seek to answer the question: Could a rational fact-finder have concluded that the evidence in the *Sacco and Vanzetti* (page 21) case, after the revelation that bullet III could not have been fired from the gun that fired bullets I, II, and IV, established beyond a reasonable doubt that it was Sacco who fired the shot that killed Berardelli?[1]

Adopting the standpoint of a historian can serve to isolate the tasks of analysis and evaluation from other tasks. Historians do not have to concern themselves with procedural technicalities, admissibility, questions of role, tactics, ethical constraints, or other "noise" factors to the same extent as participants in actual trials. On the other hand, historians do not have a formal concept of materiality that defines the ultimate probandum.[2]

In analyzing trial records, law students often find it difficult to keep separate the concept of the original event (Did X happen?) and the proceedings at trial, which may have involved lack of due process, poor or unethical advocacy, or bias or prejudice on the part of the judge or jury (Did the evidence presented justify the result?). None of the latter factors should influence a historian's judgment about the original event. Trial records are useful sources of evidence for a historian, but they may involve "noise" factors that are irrelevant to a historical judgment about the original event rather than the trial.

In *Able*, our standpoint might be stated as follows. Who are we? We are the lawyers representing Richard Able in *United States v. Able*. The case is ready for trial and discovery has closed. The evidence in the case file is the only material available. We are preparing the case for trial and seek to marshal the available evidence and inferences to maximize the likelihood that Able will be found not guilty.

Step 2. *Formulating the ultimate probandum.* For every case, the lawyer must identify the rule or rules of law that will (or that she believes will) control the case and formulate a proposition or propositions of fact, the ultimate probandum, that must be proved in order to satisfy the conditions required by the rule or rules. For *United States v. Able*, we could have looked at the Internal Revenue Code for the proposition of law that the government's ultimate probandum must satisfy, but for present purposes we need only look at the indictment. Because the court has denied Able's motion to dismiss, it was established for this case, at the trial level, that the facts alleged in the indictment, if proved, are sufficient to support a guilty verdict.[3]

---

1 See Schum and Kadane (1996) for a full analysis.
2 Of course, historians are not of one kind. They too have to be concerned with objectives, biases, and context. Even for the historian standpoint, role and objectives need to be defined with precision. See Twining and Hampsher-Monk (2003), esp. Geller, "The Last Wedge" (at 122) and Anderson, "Wigmore Meets 'The Last Wedge'" (at 140) for an illustration of the application of the chart method to a historical problem. Other published applications of the chart method include Anderson (1999) (Huddleston); Dingley (1999) (The Ballpoint case – cf. the approach of Feteris (1999) to the same case); Wigmore, *Science* (Umilian and Hatchett).
3 Our motion to dismiss the indictment would have asserted that the indictment failed to allege facts sufficient to state a violation of Section 7201 of the Internal Revenue Code, i.e. that it failed to allege an ultimate probandum that satisfied the conditions mandated using Section 7201 as a major premise. Given our standpoint, the issues raised by that motion are matters to be considered by appellate counsel in the event Able is convicted.

Thus, from the indictment the ultimate probandum can be formulated:

1 Richard Able ("RA") knowingly filed a false federal tax return for the year 2003 ("the 2003 return") with intent to defraud the government of income tax due and owing on not less than $45,000.

Step 3. *Formulate the potential penultimate probanda.* The ultimate probandum for *United States v. Able* can be divided into seven penultimate probanda:

2 RA knowingly filed a false income tax return for the year 2003.
3 RA filed a tax return for the year 2003.
4 The tax return that RA filed for 2003 was false.
5 RA knew his 2003 tax return was false when he filed it.
6 At the time RA filed his 2003 tax return, he intended to defraud the government of income tax due and owing on not less than $45,000.
7 RA owed the government taxes on an additional $45,000 at the time he filed his 2003 tax return.
8 RA intended to defraud the government of the taxes due and owing at the time he filed his 2003 tax return.

In *United States v. Able* the law was reasonably clear. However, situations often arise in which it is not certain how a court will interpret the applicable law. For instance, in *Sargent* (page 28) it is not clear how a court will interpret the insurance policy: Would being killed by a bear or dying from starvation count as an "accidental injury"? Such questions need to be researched, but if research does not provide a clear answer, how is the analyst to proceed? There is no easy way out. As a rule of thumb one needs to prepare alternative arguments based on "pessimistic" and "optimistic" interpretations of the applicable law, bearing in mind that the most pessimistic interpretation is likely to be the foundation for the strongest case that one's opponent is likely to present.

Step 4. *Formulate the provisional theories of the case* (and choose the strategic ultimate, penultimate, and intermediate probanda that best fit the theory or theories). For any case, the analyst must formulate what she sees as the strongest provisional theories of the case for both sides. This is necessary for two reasons. First, the advocate needs to know the theory she is most likely to confront in order to assess how the evidence will be marshaled against her client. Second, if the opposing theory is not developed, the advocate may wind up developing a theory that misses the point, a theory that attacks a "straw man."[4]

4 If the problem is a complex one involving a mixed mass of evidence, it is likely that there will be a range of possible theories each of which would lead the analysis in significantly different directions. In order to make the task manageable, it may be necessary to eliminate some possibilities and concentrate on one or more specific theories. Even historians and scientists do not have infinite resources to pursue endless lines of inquiry. Typically advocates have to settle for one theory (or at least a limited number) at a fairly early stage. The precise timing of such choices naturally varies according to circumstance. On the relationship between stories, theories, and themes see Ch. 10 below.

Thus, for *United States v. Able*, in order to effectively develop a theory for the defense, we need to identify the theory that the prosecutors are likely to adopt. For the government in Able, the theory is likely to be:

Prior to leaving practice in 2002, RA was earning more than $450,000 per year. When he became a professor, his income dropped precipitously. The amount he needed to support the lifestyle he wanted to maintain and meet his other obligations exceeded the amount that the law school paid him. His income for 2003 was $170,000 – $125,000 from the law school and $45,000 in fees. In order to avoid paying the additional amount that was due as a result of the $45,000 in fees he had received, RA filed a false tax return that only reported the $125,000 he had earned as salary and from which an amount sufficient to satisfy the taxes due on that amount had been withheld. Thus, RA knowingly filed a false tax return for 2003 with intent to defraud the federal government of the taxes that were due and owing on the additional $45,000 he had received as fees.

Given the probable theory the government will adopt, the strongest provisional theory for Able might be:

RA fully disclosed all his income to Timothy Cooper, his accountant, and relied upon Cooper to prepare and file his pre-signed return. RA informed Cooper he had received $125,000 in salary from the law school at their first meeting. On April 12, his girlfriend, Jane Evans, delivered a letter to Cooper's office advising him that RA had also earned $45,000 in fees. With that letter RA enclosed a blank tax return that he had signed and a signed check payable to the Internal Revenue Service with the amount left blank. In that letter, RA advised Cooper that he was going to be out of town until after April 15, 2004, and instructed Cooper to complete the return and to insert in the check the amount that was due to the government. Thus, RA did not know that the tax return Cooper prepared and filed was false and RA fully intended to pay any additional taxes that were due and owing on the $45,000 he had received as fees.

Having identified these provisional theories, it is possible to strategically reformulate the penultimate probanda to simplify the analysis by rephrasing propositions 3, 4, 5, 7, and 8 to focus the analysis more precisely on the material facts that are in dispute:

3 An income tax return for the year 2003 ("the 2003 return") signed by RA was filed.
4 The 2003 return was false.
5 At the time the 2003 return was filed, RA knew that the 2003 return was false.
7 At the time the 2003 return was filed, RA owed the government taxes on the $45,000 RA received as fees during the year 2003.
8 At the time the 2003 return was filed, RA intended to defraud the government of the taxes due and owing on $45,000.

As restated, only penultimate probanda 5 and 8 are in dispute. These propositions should be the analyst's "targets" in analyzing and marshaling the evidence . This macroscopic analysis of the case is depicted in charted form in Figure 5.1.

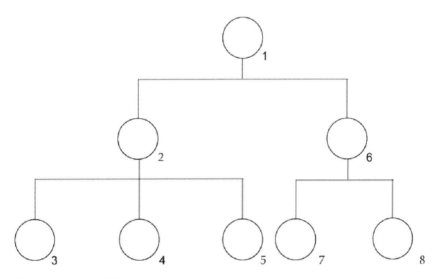

Figure 5.1 *Chart (Able)*

Step 5. *Formulate the key-list.*

   a. *What is a key-list?* A key-list is a numbered list of propositions of three kinds. First, there are the propositions developed and refined at the macroscopic level – the ultimate and penultimate probanda and propositions identified as necessary in light of the provisional theory adopted, e.g., that OJS had a motive to murder NBS. Second, there are propositions that can be directly inferred from the evidential data, e.g., from an autoptic proference of the 2003 tax return, we can infer that the tax return reported that RA only earned $125,000 in 2003. Third, the list includes all the intermediate proponent's assertions, opponent's explanatory, rival, and denial propositions, and any propositions the proponent may use to undermine the opponent's propositions or to strengthen her assertion in light of the opponent's attacks. Collectively, the key-list must include every proposition that the analyst concludes is important to the arguments in support of and against the ultimate probandum. The list is a key-list because every symbol in the chart has a number that identifies the proposition on the key-list which it depicts.

   b. *Formulating the propositions.* The first step is to identify those items of evidential data that are available to be offered and convert them into simple propositions – i.e. propositions involving only one condition and susceptible to the response "true/false," "proven/not proven," "probable/not probable," etc. The next step is to identify each inferred proposition that is necessary to show how an evidential proposition supports or undermines a fact of consequence – a penultimate probandum or the credibility of a witness's assertion. The process is not as mechanical as it might seem. The analyst must confront two types of difficulty.

First, formulating the propositions on a key-list involves more than merely making explicit what was perhaps formerly implicit or only partially expressed. It also involves refinement of expression, analogous to what is involved in drafting a statute or formal document on the basis of a rough set of instructions. Indeed, the formulation of the ultimate probandum may well require the same level of drafting skill and precision. The formulation of evidential data into key-list propositions does not require, for most practical purposes, the same degree of precision and rigor as the drafting of legal instruments. The point at which precision becomes pedantry typically depends on context. But the analogy with drafting is nevertheless useful.

Second, identifying and formulating the intermediate inferential propositions necessary to establish the relevance of an evidential proposition to a fact of consequence (a penultimate probandum or a proposition bearing upon the credibility of a testimonial assertion or an item of tangible evidence) is ordinarily the hardest and most important task. For example, the endorsement by the Las Vegas branch of Able's bank on the $25,000 check that Richard Able received from the New York law firm supports a chain of inferences leading to an inference that RA had motive to file a false tax return to avoid paying taxes on that amount. But the weaknesses in that argument become apparent only if the intermediate inferential steps necessary to support motive are identified with precision – i.e. RA gambled with all or substantially all of the $25,000 supporting a further inference that RA lost all or substantially all of the $25,000. The explanations that undermine the strength of these inferences – i.e. RA may not have gambled or may have gambled with only a modest amount, and RA may have won or may have quit after he had lost an amount he could comfortably afford – and the generalizations that make them plausible are not apparent absent precision.

There are no fixed rules for drafting propositions, but it is possible to give some guidance by way of advice. For example: Be precise. Be clear (avoid ambiguities). Normally, each proposition on the key-list should make one point only, and this should be signaled (for example, "It was OJS who killed NBS" rather than "OJS killed NBS"). So too, where possible, propositions should be stated in the affirmative rather than the negative. Trying to chart a negative creates difficulties that should be unnecessary. Choose an appropriate level of generality for each proposition. So far as possible, use language that signals clearly the connections with immediately adjacent propositions. Be succinct and strive for economy – a cogent argument needs to be well structured, economical, and clear. Again, skill in drafting a key-list involves art as well as science.

c. *Selecting propositions to be included.* From the universe of data available, the key-list may (and probably must) be limited to what is relevant to the ultimate probandum. But visualizing what is relevant requires an intuitive application of the inductive process we are trying to make explicit. Beware of cutting out potentially relevant material too early; err on the side of over-inclusion in the first cut. It is simple to strike unnecessary evidentiary propositions from the key-list after the chart is complete; it may well be impossible to see significant relations if necessary data have been omitted.

The process of developing and organizing the key-list is also reflexive. The ultimate and penultimate probanda suggest intermediate probanda we want to reach. But the evidential proposition may also suggest direct and intermediate inferences and combinations whose relevance will be apparent only when formulated. The propositions on the list should be ordered "logically," but there is a danger that too early an effort at structure and coherence will cause us to overlook important hypotheses.

Several points deserve further comment. First, identifying standpoint and recognizing the limits it imposes are crucial. For example, if the project calls for the analysis of a decided case such as *Morrison v. Jenkins* (page 31), the data available for analysis are fixed. Nothing can be added. The role of the analyst is analogous to the role of a historian. In this context, all the evidence has been collected. The exercise then is to analyze a given mixed mass of evidence that constitutes the data upon which the decision was based in light of a declared ultimate probandum. If this standpoint is adopted, the natural next step is to compile a key-list. This involves identifying, formulating, and ordering the reported propositions that are relevant to the ultimate probandum or probanda as given, as well as any unstated inferential propositions necessary to demonstrate the relevance of each reported proposition.

If the standpoint is that of an advocate, however, the problem of selection must be addressed. Selection implies a given collection of pre-existing propositions from which one chooses those that are relevant. But even where there is a finite body of material for analysis, such as a pre-trial collection of depositions and documents, the propositions are not already there, lined up like candidates on parade. A complex process of extracting, individuating, and making explicit statements in propositional form is involved, allowing considerable scope for both choice and creativity. To be sure, there may be statements in the record that may be lifted verbatim into a key-list, but these are likely to be exceptional.

Selection also requires more than sorting out the relevant from the irrelevant. A proposition is relevant if it has some probative connection with an ultimate probandum, that is, it tends to support, tends to negate, or tends to explain that probandum either directly or indirectly. Relevance is a necessary condition for inclusion of an evidential proposition on a key-list, but it is not a sufficient condition. There is an almost infinite possibility of regress and of more and more minute analysis of any body of evidentiary materials. Inclusion in a key-list inevitably involves making judgments of importance (non-triviality) that go beyond mere theoretical relevance. Wigmore's *Science* does not, and probably could not, provide a clear set of criteria of importance. The importance criterion is simple to state, but difficult to apply. The final product must include all, but only, those propositions that are important in light of the theory of the case the advocate has adopted and the theory that she anticipates opposing counsel will adopt. Again, in the preliminary stages, caution must be exercised: Weeding is easier than inserting.

It is often difficult to judge whether to include generalizations on the key-list. For example, it would clutter the key-list and obscure the argument if every generalization that serves as a warrant for an inference is included in the key-list. For example, the proposition that X testified to Y tends to support Y because of the generalization, "Testimonial evidence is usually true." These and other common generalizations are usually left unstated.

On the other hand, an argument or its strength may depend upon a generalization that is not obvious and that may be disputed. For example, in "The Nine Mile Walk" (pages 11–17), Welt asserts, "An inference can be logical and still not be true . . . Give me any sentence of ten or twelve words, and I'll build you a logical chain of inferences that you never dreamed of when you framed the sentence." Kemelman challenges Welt with the sentence, "A nine mile walk is no joke, especially in the rain." Later in the story when it appears Welt's inferences may be true as well as logical, he asks Kemelman, "Where did you get that sentence?" Kemelman responds, "It was just a sentence. It simply popped into my head." Welt immediately argues, "It couldn't have! It's not the sort of sentence that pops into one's head." Welt's argument depends upon an experience-based generalization that was not apparent until he explained it: "If you had taught composition as long as I have, you'd know that when you ask someone for a sentence of ten words or so, you get an ordinary statement such as 'I like milk' – with the other words made up by a modifying clause like, 'because it is good for my health.' The sentence you offered related to a *particular situation.*"

One value of the chart method is that it enables the analyst to make explicit what is normally left implicit. Because of the dangers and uncertainties surrounding generalizations in the context of argumentation, it is good discipline to articulate at least those generalizations that may play a significant role in the argument and that are not obvious or are vulnerable to attack.[5]

d. *Ordering the propositions on the key-list.* The propositions on the final key-list should be ordered, to the extent feasible, so that the structure of the argument is apparent on its face. The easiest type of key-list for the reader to use is one that presents the propositions in a form that conforms to the outline method of analysis (discussed in Chapter 6, below). The penultimate probanda are the main headings, and the supporting propositions are organized in a way that outlines the argument under that heading.

This is not always feasible and, in some cases, it may facilitate the analyst's work to adopt other organizing principles. For example, some analysts prefer to first extract and individuate all of the evidential propositions onto the key-list before beginning to identify the inferential propositions necessary to demonstrate their relationships to the penultimate probanda (or to credibility). Clearly, if the chart is the end product, there is no logical necessity for order within the key-list: The chart defines the order. But practically, reading the key-list and working through a chart

---

5 *Huddleston* provides another illuminating example. See Chapter 1 at page 19 above.

are both enhanced if the propositions on the list are ordered logically. Common sense, taking into account the purpose of the effort and the needs of the audience, is likely to be a safe guide.

Step 6. *Preparing the chart(s).* The end products are the chart and the key-list. The actual mechanics required to draw a chart are always laborious. They are especially laborious in one's first attempts. The struggle is not only with the logic, but also with recalling the correct symbols and laying it all out on paper. Based upon our experiences and those of our students, we offer some suggestions that may aid those embarking on a project for the first time.

a   After clarifying your standpoint, always start by charting the ultimate and penultimate probanda and work "down" as far as your provisional theory allows. This will serve several purposes: It will help you to visualize the structure of the case; it will let you plan the space allocations for the chart or charts; and it may show you ways of reorganizing parts of your key-list. (The macroscopic chart of Able above at page 128 provides a simple example.)

b   Break the chart into sectors, and complete one sector at a time. If the evidential propositions related to a particular penultimate probandum seem manageable in number, chart them first. Do the charting in "sector charts" on separate sheets of $8^1/_2'' \times 11''$ paper[6] and then identify these sector charts on a chart of your ultimate and penultimate probanda. For example, in the *Simpson* case, the lawyers might have charted the propositions bearing on opportunity as one sector. In the macroscopic charting of the ultimate and penultimate probanda, under proposition 3, "It was OJS who committed the act that caused NBS's death," the analyst would have had, as one of the principal supports, the proposition, "OJS had an opportunity to commit the act that caused NBS's death." Under the symbol for that proposition, the analyst might have put "See chart B." It is annoying to see a new relationship or possibility after you have charted fifteen propositions in a sector; it is devastating to encounter the same problem after you have charted 150 propositions on a single sheet of paper. Moreover, the final product is easier to work with (and store) if it fits in a binder or standard file.

c   Do not assume that an autoptic proference or a proposition will appear only once in the chart. A logic chart is not a jigsaw puzzle in which each piece fits in only one place. Do not assume that a piece of evidence supports only one inference. For example, the prior tax returns in *United States v. Able* not only support inferences about how much money he made as a partner in a law firm, but also support an important defense inference – Able regularly relied upon accountants to prepare his income tax returns.[7]

d   At every stage, check that each inferential relationship charted involves a genuine inference. The best test is to ask whether the claimed inference is necessary to address

---

6 Most students draw their draft chart by hand, and those who are not comfortable with computer drawing must draw their final charts in the same way. There are standard logic templates that have the necessary symbols. Using protractors with $8^1/_2'' \times 11''$ graph paper facilitates the manual drawing process.

7 The use of the same proposition to support different parts of an argument creates a significant risk of "circularity," as illustrated by the analysis of *Huddleston*. See Anderson (1999) 468.

a real doubt. This step is critical. The function of the chart is to enable the preparer and the audience to spot flaws not previously apparent in the analysis and to enable the advocate to correct or emphasize the flaw.

e Detect and avoid common charting errors. It is important to remember that an argument is different from a chronological table or a story. The relations between propositions on a key-list in logical analysis are based upon relevance: propositions tend to support or tend to negate other propositions. A common error in microscopic analysis is using propositions to tell a story in terms of temporal relations ("and then," "and then" ...) or causal relations ("x happened because y happened"). Such errors can easily be detected when the propositions are charted. They are often depicted as a "string of pearls" all supporting a single proposition. On a chart, there is a single node with five or ten nodes depicted as each providing independent support for that node. If ten witnesses assert they saw X enter Y's house at 4:15 p.m., the relationships are correctly depicted. Otherwise the string indicates a problem. Alternatively, they are depicted as a vertical string of pearls – e.g., a single testimonial assertion supporting a catenate chain of five or more inferential steps supporting a single conclusion. Again, it is possible to have that many nodes in a chain, but it is so rare as to excite immediate suspicion.[8]

Step 7. *Refining and completing the analysis.* The chart and key-list are means not ends. As a guide to work, the first five steps have proven useful in practice. But at each step the judgments made and the analysis were necessarily tentative. The end is to develop a logically sound analysis that, in light of the analyzer's specific objectives, organizes a mass of evidence and charts the inferences necessary to relate all significant relevant data to the ultimate proposition in issue. Typically, the process of revision and refinement is continuous, with judgments previously made being revised in each succeeding step of the analysis. But the chart and key-list completed through step 6 provide the first real opportunity for analyzing and evaluating the case-as-a-whole and testing the judgments initially made. This is where the true value of the analysis as both intellectual exercise and practical work emerges most clearly. For that reason, the analysis of the whole should be done as a separate step.

Time permitting, this step should not be undertaken immediately and, in practice, should ordinarily be a collegial activity. Lay the record, the key-list, and the chart aside for a few days. Ask a fellow student or a partner to read the record, the key-list, and the chart to see if he or she can follow it, attack it, offer fresh insights. Then, using the first six steps as a guide, work through the materials and refine or adjust the key-list and chart as necessary.

For the trial lawyer, this is obviously and necessarily a continuous process. The early phases of an investigation have suggested a tentative theory: The available evidence, in light of established legal principles, suggests a plausible theory by which a desirable ultimate proposition might be proven. But new supporting and

---

8 Other common errors are described and illustrated at the *Analysis* website.

conflicting data will be added, and the analysis and theory must be continuously revised. Indeed, the key-list and chart that the lawyer used in preparing for trial must be finally reviewed and revised in light of the evidence actually admitted and excluded during the course of the trial in order to prepare for closing argument. The utility of the key-list and chart, in that context, is that it makes it possible for the lawyer to see immediately the effect of the evidence unexpectedly admitted or excluded on the theory of the case as previously developed and charted.

The final step should produce a product that accounts for all the significant relevant data that are available and that precisely and clearly identifies the logical organization and inferences necessary to relate those data to the ultimate probandum. In the aggregate, it establishes and makes available for critical review the lawyer's theory of the case and in practice it provides the foundation for preparing and executing the next task in the case at hand.

C. The symbols and their use

Wigmore's chart method employs a system of symbols specifically designed to make it feasible to depict the evidence and arguments that bear upon the material facts in a legal dispute in graphic form. In this section, we first present the symbols and discuss their use. We then address the question: Do the benefits justify the effort?

1. The basic Wigmorean palette[9]

The modified Wigmorean charting system or palette presented in this book requires only eight symbols. Five are likely to be required for any chart:

- □ the square for depicting testimonial assertions;
- ○ the circle for depicting circumstantial evidence or inferred propositions;
- > the open angle to identify an argument that provides an alternative explanation for an inference proposed by the other side;
- ◁ a vertical triangle to identify an argument that corroborates a proposed inference;

    a line to indicate the "direction" of a proposed inferential relationship
- ↑ between or among propositions – a vertical line indicates "tends to
- ← support"; horizontal lines indicate "tends to negate or weaken." The direction from evidential data to asserted inferences is always up, from bottom to top. Directional arrows are only occasionally necessary where the line standing alone might be misunderstood.[10]

---

9 We use the term "palette" as it has been adopted in computer jargon. Programs now exist for constructing charts by using a specified palette of symbols, such as the basic Wigmorean palette described in this section. See note 14 below and references cited there.

10 Each of these is a standard logic symbol that can be drawn using commercially available plastic templates.

The nature of a judicial trial makes it necessary to have symbols to identify the kinds of evidential data or the source of the propositions the tribunal will be asked to take as the basis for the arguments advanced. Wigmore specified two, and we have found a third useful:

∞ (6) an infinity symbol to identify testimonial assertions that the fact finders will hear or other autoptic preferences they will perceive with their other senses;

¶ (7) a paragraph symbol to identify facts the tribunal will judicially notice or otherwise accept without evidential support; and

G (8) the letter "G" to denote a generalization that is likely to play a significant role in an argument in a case, but that is not a proposition that will be supported by evidence or that the tribunal will be formally asked to notice judicially.

These symbols satisfy the three conditions necessary for a chart method. First, the system makes it possible to distinguish between the principal types of evidential data that will be presented to the tribunal – testimonial assertions, tangible evidence, and judicially noticed facts – and to identify generalizations upon which particular arguments depend.

Second, the system makes it possible to chart the five different *probative processes* (above pages 94–98) involved in adjudicated cases. Proponent's assertion can be depicted by the use of lines to depict the relationships between a probans and the probandum that the proponent claims it supports. The opponent's explanation can be depicted by the use of the open angle, to chart the data or generalizations offered to support a proposition that provides an alternative explanation for a proponent's assertion. The opponent's denial and the opponent's rival can be depicted by the use of squares and circles to depict the opponent's argument and the use of a line and directional arrow to depict the claim that they combine to support a proposition that detracts from the related proponent's assertion – that is, the use of a directional arrow, pointing away from the proponent's assertion and toward the rival or negative proposition the opponent has advanced.

Although rare, the distinction between "proponent's corroboration," as a probative process, and "corroboration," as a logical structure, can sometimes be important to an advocate preparing for trial or an analyst concerned with showing at what stages evidence was introduced at trial. In that context, an additional symbol to identify the proponent's corroboration as a separate probative process is useful. This may be done by the use of a vertical triangle connected by a line (with or without a directional arrow) to the proponent's assertion that it reinforces to show the context in which the evidential data reinforcing the proponent's claim were or will be presented. This additional symbol makes it possible to distinguish between the principal support for a proponent's assertion and the corroborating support available if, and perhaps admissible only if, the opponent challenges that assertion.

Finally, the use of lines and directional arrows makes it possible to identify the steps and inferential relationships in an argument in which it is claimed that propositions are logically related – that is, to depict what Wigmore called the probative relations among evidential data and circumstantial propositions in a case and to present a chart (or series of charts) showing these relationships for a case-as-a-whole. If the analyst stipulated that the direction of the inferential relationships depicted is upward unless otherwise indicated then directional arrows are only necessary for identifying rival or denial propositions. See chart 5.2 below.

2. The chart method illustrated

These eight symbols are sufficient to construct a chart that depicts the possible arguments in a case. That point is illustrated by the key-list and chart that follow. The key-list takes the propositions from "An investigation" (above, page 40) that were used to illustrate different logical structures typically involved in making inferences and adds some additional propositions for the defense. The ultimate probandum in the case remains, "It was X who murdered Y." The key-list and chart were prepared from the standpoint of a lawyer early in the investigation trying to identify and analyze the arguments that might be made from the available evidential data to support the intermediate probandum, "X was in Y's house at 4:30 p.m. on January 1" – the time and place of the alleged murder of Y. The chart illustrates how these basic symbols might be employed to depict arguments that could be made, based upon the available data and how the different probative processes might be depicted within a single chart. The key-list and chart will also lay the foundation for some additional points developed below.

Two points merit immediate note. First, the arguments developed in the key-list and depicted in the chart represent only one approach that the prosecutor might have taken. For example, she might have decided (and might still decide) that W_2 should be called before W_1, so that the convergent testimony might be juxtaposed as support for P_2 without holding W_2 in reserve until W_1 had been impeached. Similarly, she might have identified other generalizations she thought more significant.

Second, the example in Figure 5.2 presents a simple key-list and a chart that fits comfortably on a single page. In a more complex case, it would ordinarily be necessary to divide the argument into sectors and then to chart the sectors on different sheets of paper. For example, it is often useful to chart credibility separately. If that is done, the chart of the propositions bearing upon a witness's credibility would culminate in one proposition (or in some cases, two) expressing the analyst's judgment as to the impact on the witness's credibility. In the credibility chart, the analyst would insert an open angle (if the analysis undermines the witness's credibility). If there is evidence reinforcing the witness's credibility or undermining the attack, the analyst would insert a vertical triangle (if there is evidence that reinforces credibility) or a further open angle (if there are generalizations or evidential data that can be marshaled to undermine the attack on the witness's credibility). In such a case, only the open angle(s) and the vertical triangle would be appended to the credibility node for each assertion the witness makes with a reference to the sector chart, e.g., "see chart 15," where the micro credibility analysis is depicted.

Partial key-list for "Preliminary opportunity chart"

1 Y is dead; and Y died as a result of an unlawful act; and it was X who committed the act that caused Y's death; and X acted with malice aforethought in committing the act.
2 Y is dead.
3 Y died as a result of an unlawful act.
4 It was X who committed the act that caused Y's death.
5 X acted with malice aforethought in committing the act.
6 X had an opportunity to commit the act that caused Y's death.
7 X had a motive to murder Y.
8 There is other evidence support proposition 4.
9 Y was murdered in his home at 4:30 p.m. on January 1.
10 W_1 will testify, "I saw a person with characteristics a, b, c, and d enter Y's house at 4:15 p.m. on January 1."
11 W_1 saw a person with characteristics a, b, c, and d enter Y's house at 4:15 p.m. on January 1.
12 A person with characteristics a, b, c, and d entered Y's house at 4:15 p.m. on January 1.
13 X has characteristics a, b, c, and d.
14 Characteristics a, b, c, and d were as follows: a. white hair; b. approximate height of five feet; c. a pronounced limp; d. the wearing of a cheap brown coat.
15 G: Few people walk with a pronounced limp.
16 It was X who entered Y's house at 4:15 p.m. on January 1.
17 People who enter or leave a house usually remain or have been in that house for at least fifteen minutes.
18 It may have been someone other than X, who had characteristics similar to X's, who entered Y's house at 4:15 p.m.
19 W_2 will testify, "I know X."
20 W_2 knows X.
21 W_2 will testify, "I saw X leave Y's home at 4:45 p.m. on January 1."
22 W_2 saw X leave Y's home at 4:45 p.m.
23 X left Y's house at 4:45 p.m.
24 X was in Y's home at 4:30 p.m. on January 1.
25 X will testify, "I was in a house five miles from the scene of the murder between 2 p.m. and 5 p.m. on January 1."
26 X was in a house five miles from Y's house between 2 p.m. and 5 p.m. on January 1.
27 Z will testify, "I was with X in a house five miles from Y's house between 4 p.m. and 4:24 p.m. on January 1."
28 Z was with X in a house five miles from Y's house between 4 p.m. and 4:24 p.m. on January 1.
29 X was not in Y's house at 4:30 p.m. on January 1.

30 ¶: It gets dark after 4:00 p.m. on January 1.

31 W_1's observational sensitivity may have been impaired.

32 At an identification parade (line-up) held three days after the murder, W_1 failed to identify X.

33 A recent report of empirical research on eyewitness evidence suggests that eyewitness statements reporting identifying characteristics of a suspect made in circumstances approximating those under which W_1 observed a person entering Y's home (proposition 2) are 100 percent correct in only 5 percent of the cases.

34 W_1's memory and objectivity are open to question.

35 W_1 seemed to be very nervous and hesitant when questioned by the police.

36 G: People who are very nervous when they are being questioned by the police may not be sure that their statements are true.

37 G: It is normal to be very nervous when being questioned by the police about a serious crime.

38 W_1's veracity may be questioned.

39 The credibility of W_1's identification of the person who entered Y's house is open to serious question.

40 W_1 is telling the truth as he recalls it.

41 W_1 is a bank manager.

42 G: Bank managers are almost always truthful.

43 G: Most people would notice and recall that a person they had seen walked with a pronounced limp.

44 It is highly probable that W_1 did see a person with characteristics a, b, c, and d enter Y's house at 4:15 p.m. on January 1.

45 W_2 is very short-sighted.

46 W_2's observational sensitivity may have been impaired.

47 W_2 knew that X regularly visited Y's house.

48 Y was X's son.

49 W_2 is Y's brother.

50 X is also W_2's mother.

51 G: It is probable that a brother would know about regular visits between his mother and his brother.

52 G: When someone sees a person, who has the characteristics of a person known to be a regular visitor, leave a house, he or she is likely to conclude that the person leaving is the person known to be a regular visitor.

53 W_2's expectations (objectivity bias) may have caused him to misidentify the person he saw leave Y's house at 4:45 p.m.

54 W_2 stands to benefit financially from Y's death.

55 G: A mother is usually a beneficiary of her son's estate.

56 X is probably a beneficiary of Y's estate.

57 G: Persons who are convicted of murder cannot receive any part of the victim's estate.

58 The benefit to W_2 would probably increase if X were convicted of Y's murder.

59 W_2 has a motive to lie.

60 W_2's veracity is open to doubt.

61 W_2's identification of Y is open to serious challenge.

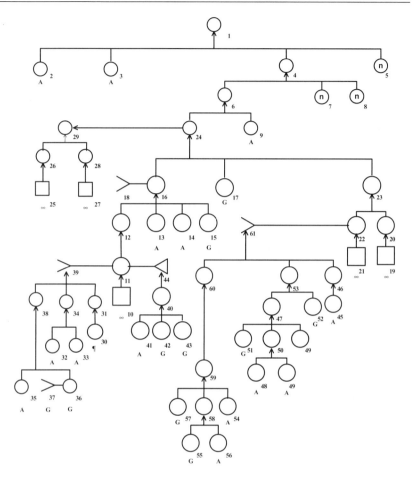

"A" = a proposition reported to the police cadet and assumed to be true.
"n" = not charted

Figure 5.2 *Key-list and chart ("An investigation")*

The specified procedures are designed to enhance the rigor and enable the "charter" to see possibilities and problems that otherwise might have passed unnoticed. The resulting product makes it possible for others, as well as the "charter," to provide rigorous critique and appraisal of the arguments advanced. But the procedures and the charting systems can only complement, never substitute for, the intellectual skill and judgment of the lawyer.

Exercise

1 You are the young prosecutor charged with presenting the government's case in *Able*. Review the case file (at pages 24–27). Analyze Able's credibility, using the attributes of credibility presented in Figure 2.7 (above at page 68) and prepare an organized list of

the questions you ask Able on cross-examination to focus the jury's attention on the identified bases for doubting all of the important testimonial assertions you anticipate that Able will make during his direct examination, if he takes the stand.

2   Switch: You are the defense attorney who will represent Able at trial. You have done the same analysis and have identified questions you think a competent prosecutor would ask. How would you suggest Able respond to each question? Are there any opponent's explanations you could offer to undermine any of the points developed by the prosecutor's attack? Is there evidence you might present that would reinforce Able's credibility? If so, prepare a key-list and chart the propositions identified. On that basis, prepare an organized list of the questions you would ask on redirect and specify the witnesses you might call to reinforce the credibility of his assertions.

3. Additional symbols, conventions and their utility

The key-list and chart presented above provide a foundation for appraising the utility of other symbols and conventions that might be used in charting a particular problem. The utility of additional symbols and conventions is largely a function of the objectives of the person applying the method and of the characteristics of the particular problem. We have identified further symbols and refinements that have proven useful when the standpoint is that of a lawyer preparing for trial. We discuss specific symbols and other conventions and appraise their utility in the paragraphs that follow.

There are three symbols that are frequently useful to the lawyer conducting an analysis in preparation for trial. As a practical matter, facts are often stipulated to be true by the parties ("S"); admitted by the pleadings ("A"); or not subject to genuine dispute ("U"). They should, however, be employed with caution and precision. Stipulated and admitted facts ordinarily can and must be formally introduced and published at trial, albeit without testimony or other autoptic proference. Facts that are not subject to dispute must nevertheless be supported by admissible evidence unless they have been established by formal admission or stipulation. Precision is necessary to ensure that those who might rely on the chart in preparing for trial are not misled.

Every case will differ. The standard conventions may often need to be supplemented or adapted by case-specific conventions in a complex case. For example, in cases in which questionable hearsay or propensity evidence has been or may be admitted, two additional conventions may be useful. First, hearsay can be depicted by placing a square inside the circle depicting an out-of-court assertion the declarant allegedly made. So too, if there is or was a dispute over the admissibility of certain evidential data it is often useful to shade or color code the evidential data and the inferences to be derived from those data so that the actual or potential effect of that evidence may readily be identified.[11] Indeed, in some cases there may be more than

---

11 See, e.g., *Chambers v. Mississippi*, 410 U.S. 284 (1973) and *Crawford v. Washington*, 124 S. Ct. 1354 (2004) (cases in which the admissibility of hearsay evidence was the central issue).

one kind of evidential data whose admissibility or use could be challenged, such as a case involving both hearsay and propensity evidence that was or may be offered,[12] or cases in which the same kind of evidence may be challenged on different grounds, such as a case involving more than one witness testifying to an out-of-court assertion in which different exceptions to the hearsay rule may apply.[13] In such cases, multiple colors or shadings may be useful.

Students embarking on the construction of a chart should realize that the standard conventions for the charting system may have to be modified or supplemented for the particular chart. But they should also recognize that it is important to articulate precisely any modified or special conventions adopted, so that others familiar with the standard conventions may understand and appraise the product. As in bridge, special conventions are likely to cause trouble unless they are understood by your partner.

To achieve the latter objective, we advise students to begin with the simplified Wigmorean eight-symbol system or palette described above and to explain carefully any additional symbols or conventions they adopt in constructing a particular chart. The particular advantages of that system are three. The system was specifically designed for charting the evidence in a legal dispute. The system employs symbols that can be constructed with standard logic templates that are readily available. Moreover and more important, computer software for the construction of charts using this system has already been developed and will be further refined in the future.[14]

4. Three advantages of symbols and charting

Like other symbol systems, the chart method imposes a barrier to those who would use it. They must first master the symbols and their definitions and the protocols specified for their use. Mastering such a system is hard work. This poses a question that has thus far only been partly addressed: Are there significant advantages that can be realized by the use of symbols to chart the evidence and arguments in a legal dispute that cannot be as easily achieved by other means? The answer is, in our view, a firm "Yes." We develop the basis for this view below.

The chart method, described above, has three essential advantages. First, it requires the person doing the analysis to identify and articulate precisely each proposition that she claims is a necessary step in the arguments in a case. The value to be achieved is precision. Second, the method requires that the person employing

---

12 See *United States v. Abel*, 469 U.S. 45 (1984) (a case involving hearsay and extrinsic evidence with an improperly prejudicial propensity effect offered to question the credibility of a witness).

13 See *Tome v. United States*, 513 U.S. 150 (1995) (a case involving hearsay statements from the same declarant offered through different witnesses, where the potential exception depended upon the status of the witness).

14 New technology has begun to make an impact. Construction of Wigmore evidence charts is facilitated through the use of graphic devices such as Microsoft PowerPoint[TM] and the Presentation application in Appleworks[TM] 5 and 6. See further Appendix III on the website.

it specify with precision each step in each argument being advanced. This makes it possible to appraise each argument rigorously. Third, it provides a method of marshaling all the relevant and potentially relevant data in a complex case into a single, coherent, and clear structure in the form of an argument.

The use of symbols and charting is, in our view, necessary to realize all three advantages simultaneously and to realize the second and third fully. The chart is a graphic depiction of the arguments in a case-as-a-whole (or of a complex set of arguments bearing on a particular aspect of a case). The specific arguments advanced and their support are shown in a form that makes it simple to see and appraise the structure and content of the arguments being advanced. The chart also makes it possible to specify the evidence and arguments likely to be advanced in opposition or available for corroboration in a form that facilitates analysis and appraisal of the parts and the whole of the specific argument under study and its relationship to other arguments in the case-as-a-whole. In short, the chart and key-list are devices that make it possible to present all the evidence and arguments in a form that facilitates analysis, understanding, and appraisal.

Wigmore's chart method of analysis, as we have modified it, serves the same functions and has the same advantages as the symbols and related methods of analysis established in other fields.[15] It facilitates understanding, analysis, and appraisal precisely because it employs a format that focuses upon the precise steps in the arguments advanced and makes it possible to depict the results of the analysis of a complex problem in a concise form. In our view, a method that employs symbols and charting is the only method that makes it possible to present all the arguments in a case in a form and format that enhances clarity and understanding and that best facilitates rigorous appraisal and critique.

Any system that satisfies the necessary conditions for analyzing and charting the available evidence in a case will, in its nature, involve complexity and require considerable effort for mastery and application. Computer drawing systems and other systems under development may well reduce the now formidable mechanical effort required to draw and revise the charts for a complex case in much the same way that word processing software has reduced the mechanical effort necessary to construct and revise complex documents. Those efforts will not, however, significantly reduce the amount of intellectual skill and energy necessary to conduct the analysis and marshal the resulting arguments.

---

15 The product of the chart method has advantages similar to those Whitehead identified in explaining the advantages of using symbols in mathematics: "It is not only of practical use, but is of great interest. For it represents an analysis of the ideas of the subject and an almost pictorial representation of their relations to each other." With a well constructed key-list and chart, "by the aid of symbols, we can make transitions in reasoning, almost mechanically by the eye, which would otherwise call into play the higher faculties of the brain." This is so because the system of symbols employed in the chart method has the property that Whitehead identified as crucial to a good system: "It should be concise, so as to be visible at one glance of the eye [and] the juxtaposition of important symbols should have an important meaning." Whitehead (1939), 58, 60–62.

The exercise continues: State v. Archer (III)

1. Defense counsel's standpoint

Preparation of Archer's defense to the charge he murdered Vern continues. [Review the facts already developed and analyzed in the exercise on *State v. Archer* (II) (page 109) above.] The statement made by Archer at his initial interview included the following extracts:

> On the Sunday on which Vern was murdered, I spent the day at home. It rained all day so I worked around the house and read the Times. I went to dinner at a neighborhood restaurant around 6:00 p.m. I returned shortly after 7:00 p.m. and watched television. I went to bed after the 10 o'clock news. I slept till 7:30 Monday morning. Because it was still raining, I did not arrive at work till 10:30 a.m....
>
> ... I have never owned a brown Harris tweed jacket, and I don't know how the jacket Detective Paul found came to be in my closet...
>
> ... I invited two couples from my office and my girlfriend to my house for dinner on Saturday evening. The party lasted till about 11:00 p.m. No one visited me at home on Sunday or Monday. Tuesday afternoon, Mr. Boswell, Uncle Vern's former partner, called. He said Detective Paul had interviewed him and had also interviewed Mr. Carl. Carl and Vern had been friends until Carl's sister committed suicide when Uncle Vern refused to marry her. Boswell suggested the three of us should get together. I invited them to stop by that evening after dinner for drinks. They came around 9:00 p.m. and stayed till 11:00 p.m. I guess they just wanted to reassure me that, even though each of them hated the old skinflint, neither had murdered him. We all felt vulnerable because each of us had stayed home alone that Sunday...
>
> ... I don't recall exactly what Boswell or Carl was wearing, but I do recall that it was a crisp, chilly evening and that they were wearing coats and jackets when they arrived. I think I would have noticed if either had left without his coat...

You have since received a copy of the coroner's report, which fixes the time of Vern's death between 11:00 p.m. and midnight Sunday.

For the moment, your analysis continues to focus upon the scrap of cloth and the jacket and the circumstances in which each was found. The ultimate probandum remains: "It was Archer who murdered Vern." You obviously want to obtain and present evidence that will preclude the jury's finding that proposition to have been proven beyond a reasonable doubt.

a   Using the prosecution's propositions developed for *State v. Archer* (II) (with any amendments you now think appropriate), identify and frame the penultimate and strategic propositions you think the prosecutor will attempt to support with the evidential propositions relevant to the scrap of cloth, the jacket, and the circumstances in which each was found. Again, with such revisions as now appear necessary, do a preliminary chart showing the relationship between these propositions. (Polishing the chart comes later.)

b   As defense counsel, the rival probandum for the defense is: "It was someone other than Archer who murdered Vern."[16] Archer's statement read with Paul's can be analyzed from two standpoints: It suggests several hypotheses that should be investigated, but it also provides certain facts to which Archer can testify directly. Obviously, you must be concerned with both standpoints, but before planning the further investigations, we must analyze the evidential data in hand.

  i   Formulate your standpoint as counsel for the defense. State and number the ultimate probandum and penultimate probanda the prosecution must prove. Formulate the strongest theory for the prosecution and for the defense. Add any defense propositions that would directly undermine one or more of the penultimate probanda that the prosecution must prove.

  ii Identify and formulate a defense key-list of evidential propositions available from Archer's and Paul's statements that appear relevant to explain away, deny, or rival the inferences the prosecution may seek to establish. Identify and formulate as simple propositions the circumstantial inferences your evidential propositions suggest. Order these propositions as best you can and number each. (It may simplify the charting task if you use different numbers from those used to label the prosecution propositions you have identified and formulated – for instance, if you have 25 prosecution propositions, start your defense list with number 50 and proceed.) Label each proposition opponent's explanation (OE), opponent's rivalry (OR), or opponent's denial (OD).

  iii Chart the propositions on the key-list, first to depict the strongest argument for the prosecution; then depict the strongest arguments for the defense to undermine the prosecution's argument and to develop a rival theory adopted for the defense. Depict the additions to the prosecution chart made by adding symbols for your propositions to the chart.

2. Defense investigation

Now formulate as hypotheses the additional intermediate probanda that will guide your investigation. What, if any, additional questions do you have for Archer? Or for Paul (assuming he would respond)? What information do you need from or about Boswell? Carl? Assuming time and resources are limited, how would you organize the investigation?

---

16 Evidence supporting this rival proposition need only make it a plausible hypothesis to demonstrate that the evidence cannot be marshaled to establish beyond a reasonable doubt that it was Archer who murdered Vern.

6

Outlines, chronologies, and narrative

The outline method of analysis and its variants are more familiar to practicing lawyers. They have the advantage that they are easier to use than the chart method, although it is harder to maintain the rigor that the chart method requires. In addition to these two methods of analysis, there are two analytic devices in common use, narratives and chronologies, that complement and facilitate the use of both methods of analysis. In Part A of this chapter, we describe and illustrate the outline method of analysis. In Part B, we describe the analytic devices and discuss their utility. In Part C, we discuss how and with what effect the methods and devices can be used at various stages of a litigated case. In Part D, we describe the essential tools by which the products of an analysis may be converted into forms useful to a lawyer at any stage of a case.

A. The outline method of analysis

One of the strengths of the outline method is its utility in organizing the evidence and arguments. In the outline, each of the penultimate probanda is a main heading in the outline. For example in the *Simpson* case, the outline would begin:

I NBS is dead.
II NBS died as the result of an unlawful act.
III It was OJS who committed the act that caused NBS's death.
IV The person who committed the acts that caused NBS's death acted with malice aforethought.

Given the prosecution's provisional theory of the case, the central fact in dispute was the third penultimate probandum. The outline under that heading might continue:

III It was OJS who committed the act that caused NBS's death.
  A The Physical Evidence: OJS was present at the scene when the act was committed.
  B Motive: OJS had motive to kill NBS.
  C Opportunity: OJS could have committed the murder.
    1 NBS was murdered at 10:15 p.m. or shortly thereafter.

a The plaintive wail of NBS's Akita dog establishes that NBS and RLG were murdered at approximately 10:15 p.m. on June 12.
   i PF testimony, I heard the plaintive wail of a dog at 10:15 p.m. on June 12.
   ii It was NBS's dog that wailed.
     (a) Other residents testified that they found a white Akita dog with blood on its paws.
     (b) Other witnesses testified that the Akita belonged to NBS.
   iii Generalization: It is highly likely that a dog that discovers its owner's bloody body will begin wailing plaintively.

2 OJS had 35 to 40 minutes between the time NBS and RLG were murdered and the time he emerged from his house for a limousine ride to the airport.
a The murder was committed at 10:15 p.m. (See III.C.1)
b OJS came out of his house to go to the airport at 11:00 p.m., dressed in stone-washed jeans and a white-collared shirt with a black coat, with no visible evidence of blood or other signs that he had been in a struggle.
c It takes about five minutes to drive at the speed limit from NBS's townhouse to OJS's house (Vannatter).

3 Generalization: 40 to 45 minutes is almost certainly enough time for a murderer who stabbed two victims to death to drive to his home five minutes from the scene of the crime and to remove and pack the blood-stained clothing he had worn at the scene, without leaving significant trace evidence, and to shower, dress, and compose himself for a trip.
a OJS could have driven from NBS's condominium to his house, removed and packed the blood-stained clothing he had worn at the scene, without leaving significant trace evidence, showered and dressed and composed himself for a trip in less than 45 minutes.

The provisional outline of Point III is incomplete. The outline could be expanded to account for all of the relevant evidential data and organized to show how it supports the penultimate probanda in the case, and conventions could be adopted that would make it possible to enter propositions that tend to explain away or rival the inferences supporting proposition III. If the outline is started at the outset of a case, it can readily be updated as new information is obtained by the insertion of additional propositions. As a working tool it is far easier to maintain and update an outline than it is to do and re-do a chart.

Exercise

In the *Simpson* case, Kato Kaelin testified he heard three loud thumps on the wall outside his bedroom in back of the house at approximately 10:45 p.m. Alan Park testified that he saw a six-foot African-American male weighing about 200 pounds dressed in dark clothing enter the house 5 or 6 minutes before OJS emerged to go to the airport. On cross-examination, Mr. Park acknowledged that the person he saw might have been dressed in a black robe.[1] How would you include these statements and the inferences they support in the outline supporting proposition III.C?

B. Analytic devices: chronologies and narratives

Chronologies can be used to test completeness of an analysis at any stage of an investigation. In most cases, it is useful to construct three kinds of chronologies – witness-by-witness chronologies, document and other tangible evidence chronologies, and a master chronology. A witness chronology puts every event to which a witness could testify in chronological order. This serves three purposes. It provides a basis for assessing the completeness and consistency of the witness's likely testimony. Are there additional facts that this witness should know? Are there ambiguities or inconsistencies that need to be clarified and resolved? Second, it provides a basis from which the lawyer can identify ways in which the witness's testimony can be presented in the most dramatically and strategically effective way. Where does this witness's testimony fit in the story to be established (or refuted) at trial? Can it be organized to present a coherent and dramatically effective chapter in that story? Third, the witness (and tangible evidence) chronologies provide the basis for constructing the master chronology.

In most cases the documents or other items of tangible evidence will be used to establish or confirm that an event occurred. The check Richard Able cashed on December 20, 2001, establishes that Able received $25,000 income prior to the end of the 2001 tax year. It also could be used to establish that Able was in Las Vegas on that date. In some cases, the date on which a document or other item of tangible evidence was prepared or discovered may be important. For example, the date on which a deposition was taken or a letter written may be crucial, apart from their contents, if either is offered as a prior consistent statement to rebut a charge of recent fabrication or improper motive. The statements in such a document may be used to establish the truth of the matter asserted only if the statement were made prior to the date on which the motive to fabricate arose.[2] The fact that Detective Paul found the brown Harris tweed jacket in Archer's closet only two days after Vern had been murdered limits the period during which Archer could claim that the jacket was left there by someone else. A tangible evidence chronology provides the other basis for constructing the master chronology. It also may provide confirmation for an event to which a witness may testify, and it may identify gaps or inconsistencies in a witness's testimony that need to be filled or resolved.

The master chronology places all events that are or may be relevant to the case in the order in which they occurred. At the early stages of a case, it enables the analyst to identify gaps that require further investigation and hypotheses that should be

---

1 Schmalleger (1996).
2 See Rule 801(d)(1)(B) of the United States Federal Rules of Evidence and *Old Chief v. United States*, 519 U.S. 172 (1997).

explored. At the later stages of a case, it becomes a device for testing the completeness of the chart or outline the analyst has prepared. Throughout, it is a device for recording evidential propositions that should be considered in constructing a key-list or an outline. At any stage, it provides the basis for identifying story possibilities in the evidence.

The narrative, as an analytical device, can be used to construct logical stories that could be supported by the evidence. A narrative is a device that complements, but cannot substitute for, a detailed analysis. Once the analyst has identified and refined her ultimate and penultimate probanda and has developed her provisional theory of the case and constructed a master chronology and a key-list and chart or a detailed outline, the logical story possibilities for each side are ordinarily easy to identify. In using the narrative as an analytical tool, the analyst is interested in constructing stories that order the evidence so that it logically supports her theory of the case.

In early stages of an investigation, the narrative further assists the analyst in identifying gaps that must be filled in order to present evidence that supports the narrative. It also further enables her to use the narrative to identify hypotheses to be explored. In the later stages, the analyst will seek to construct a story that is supported by and accounts for all of the evidence she intends to present to the decision-maker and one that cannot be effectively undermined by the evidence she anticipates her opponent will present. Ultimately, the objective is to create a story that the fact-finder will accept as the most plausible (or, for the prosecution in a criminal case, the only plausible) story of what happened that is supported by the evidence.

The analyst must, however, be able to identify the logical weaknesses of the narrative that she proposes to adopt and of the narrative that she anticipates her opponent is likely to craft. The objective is to develop a persuasive narrative that is not only consistent with and supported by the evidence, but that also minimizes the possible points on which it is vulnerable to attack. She must also identify the weaknesses of her opponent's anticipated narrative account in order to plan how she can persuade the fact-finder that it is flawed or in any event less plausible than the narrative she advocates. It is the atomistic analysis developed through the chart or outline methods that makes this possible.

Exercise

1   In *Simpson*, the prosecutor's narrative argued that the African American male in dark clothing who entered the house five or six minutes before OJS emerged at 11:00 p.m. was OJS returning from NBS's condominium, the scene of the crime.[3] Based upon the analysis you developed for the preceding exercise, account for these facts in a narrative

3 Schmalleger (1996).

that provides greater support for proposition III.C and that is less vulnerable to attack.

2   From the evidence available in *United States v. Able*, it would be a simple matter for the prosecution to develop a narrative that would support a headline statement of the theory: "High Liver Comes on Hard Times; Lawyer Turned Law Professor Cheats on Taxes to Maintain Exciting Lifestyle." It would be equally simple for the defense to develop a narrative that would support the headline: "Government Prosecutes Innocent Taxpayer for Accountant's Error." Each has significant weaknesses that opposing counsel could use to attack it. Develop the narratives and then identify the significant weaknesses in each. Could the prosecution develop a revised theory of the case and a different narrative that were equally strong, but that are less vulnerable to attack? Could the defense? How?

C. The litigation context

The chart and outline methods of analysis are complementary. The initial analysis is likely to employ the outline method. The penultimate probanda are the main headings in the outline. If the question is, "Do we have enough information to justify filing a complaint?" an outline is frequently the most effective way to organize the available and the anticipated data. As a device, the master chronology is a key-list of evidential propositions ordered chronologically. The ordering makes it possible to see conflicts and gaps without preparing a chart. It also makes it possible to transform the evidence and possible inferences into a narrative account. Outlines, chronologies, and narratives are fluid; each can readily be updated and revised to account for new evidence as it becomes available. The chart method, however, is static: It is the most rigorous method for determining and assessing, at a particular point in time, the extent to which the evidence can be marshaled to support or undermine an ultimate probandum, but its products will remain the most time-consuming to develop and revise. Against that background, we discuss the uses and limits of the methods and the devices at various stages of litigation.

1. The stages of a case and the methods of analysis

Defining the protocols for the methods of analysis does not answer three practical questions of considerable importance. Which methods and devices are most useful for recording the products of analysis over time as the case develops? At what stages is a complete analysis worthwhile? Which method of analysis is likely to be most useful at each of those stages?

Logical analysis is required at all stages from initial interview through settlement, trial, or appeal. Most office procedures used by lawyers have as one of their purposes recording particular aspects of the analysis in a retrievable and usable form. A memorandum documenting the results of an interview reports facts that the lawyer thinks may be relevant. An outline for a deposition sets forth areas in which the lawyer has concluded that the deponent may be able to testify or provide other information that will lead to evidence that is relevant to facts that must be established to support or confound the possible ultimate probandum that has been identified. The memorandum of law is a device by which lawyers typically document the research necessary to enable them to frame or revise the potential ultimate probandum in a case. The case file itself is a device for compiling and maintaining such products in an organized manner. Good lawyers have systems for maintaining case files that are designed to organize the information in a form that facilitates ongoing analysis. From this perspective, all these are subordinate devices for analysis.

An outline that organizes the available evidence by penultimate probanda is a device that enables the lawyer to determine the state and sufficiency of the available evidence at any stage. The form may differ, but the basic requirement for such a device is that it serves as a precise index. It must identify each element that must be proved under the theory provisionally adopted and each witness and exhibit that is thought relevant to establishing or confounding that element. It should also include a summary description of the evidence that the witness or exhibit is expected to provide that is relevant to that element. It should identify each of the intermediate probanda, each item of evidential data that is, alone or in combination, necessary to show the logical relation of the item to the penultimate probandum it supports. Such an outline is an adaptable tool. Information provided by new witnesses or documents can be inserted as discovered, and the lawyer can use the device to identify particular necessary elements for which the evidence seems inadequate or altogether lacking and to determine where investigative efforts should be concentrated.

At various stages, systematic analysis of the evidence for the case-as-a-whole is also necessary. Most lawyers would probably agree that there are at least three stages in a litigated case at which such systematic analysis is appropriate – before the first factual pleading is filed, before the decision to forego further discovery or investigation is made, and before the case is tried. In the first stage, the outline method is ordinarily sufficient. The importance of the decisions that must be made at the latter two stages may make it necessary that the chart method be employed. We examine the first two stages in some detail and describe methods of analysis that seem appropriate for each. We comment upon final trial preparation only briefly here, reserving a more detailed description for Chapter 12.

a. The pleading stage

Before the complaint or indictment is filed, the lawyer for the plaintiff or the government should be satisfied that facts can be alleged that, if proved, would justify a favorable judgment as a matter of law. The lawyer should also have a reasoned basis for believing that she has, or is likely to be able to obtain, evidential data that support each of the necessary allegations. These data should be at least sufficient to withstand a motion to dismiss the complaint or for judgment on the pleadings. In order to frame the complaint, the lawyer must have a provisional theory or theories of the case. That is, the lawyer must have identified one or more propositions of substantive law; in light of the information available, she must have framed one or more ultimate probanda that would bring the case within the scope of the legal rule or rules identified; and she must have a reasoned basis for concluding that the available facts, if accepted, would logically entitle the plaintiff or the government to the relief sought. Even under notice-pleading rules, the plaintiff or prosecuting authority must, at a minimum, allege the ultimate facts necessary to justify the outcome sought. These allegations are, in effect, the penultimate probanda necessary to support the theory or theories of the case provisionally adopted. Cost-benefit analysis reinforces the professional standards that require the lawyer to have a good faith basis for believing that there is evidential data available sufficient to support each of the necessary allegations before suit is filed or specific defenses are asserted.

On the other hand, time constraints and inaccessibility usually combine with cost considerations to make it impracticable to develop and analyze the evidential data fully before filing the first pleading. Much of the potential evidence may be obtainable only through discovery, and one function of the pleadings is to define the disputed issues of fact, in order that the parties and the court do not devote needless time to considering facts that are not in dispute. Nonetheless, at this stage, the lawyer should have rather carefully articulated statements of the provisionally adopted ultimate probandum or probanda and should have identified and articulated the provisional penultimate strategic probanda for each. The questions then become: What evidential data do I have that support the inferences necessary to argue that each of the penultimate probanda has been proved? From what sources do I reasonably think I can obtain the additional evidence necessary to establish or strengthen the required inferences?[4]

Many lawyers use an outline format for this stage. The ultimate probandum, the penultimate probanda, and the supporting intermediate and evidential propositions are organized in outline form, albeit in a somewhat summary fashion. The concern here is the sufficiency of the allegations and the existence of a good faith basis for believing they are provable.

b. Before the close of discovery and investigation

In the early stages of a dispute and throughout the investigative stages, abductive reasoning is at least as important as inductive and deductive reasoning. Like Kemelman in "The Nine Mile Walk" (above, page 11) or the police cadet in "An investigation" (above, page 40), the lawyer is a detective looking for possibilities suggested by the evidence or the nature of the case. In the early stages, the real danger is that the lawyer will settle too quickly upon a single theory of the case and, often for that reason, will fail to identify or consider additional sources of evidence that might be

---

4 The lawyer should also have memoranda documenting the legal research and analyses that support what have been identified as the controlling propositions of law from which the ultimate probanda have been derived.

explored. No analytic devices can be a substitute for the creative thought needed during this (or other) phases of a case, but they can aid the lawyer in seeing gaps and weaknesses that may warrant further investigative effort.

These dangers indicate the need for a comprehensive and structured analysis before the investigative phase ends or is abandoned. Is there sufficient evidence with respect to each necessary element of the ultimate probandum to withstand a motion for a directed verdict at the close of the plaintiff's, prosecutor's, or defendant's case? Can the evidential data be organized to support a compelling argument that each of the elements has been proven to the required standard? Have any possible sources of important data been overlooked? The lawyer must have a means of answering each of these questions in a rigorous fashion before the opportunity for further investigation ends.

It is at this point that a comprehensive and detailed method is necessary. The outline – expanded to include every significant proposition that would appear on a key-list – is a necessary device for responding to the first question and may provide significant aid in responding to the second and third. The chart method is for some, including the authors, a device for depicting the logical relationships among the propositions in a manner that permits more rigorous analysis and appraisal. In many cases, micro-charts of crucial points coupled with a detailed outline might suffice. For example, the evidential data bearing on OJS's opportunity would have been and still is a good candidate for a detailed charted analysis.

Application of one or both of these methods also provides the foundation for a more rigorous use of narrative. A narrative, in this context, provides a method for reorganizing the data in a form that enables the lawyers involved to make a reasoned judgment concerning the second inquiry: Can the available evidential data be organized and presented in a form that makes a compelling logical argument for the result sought? A narrative forces the lawyer to organize and present the analysis in a familiar form. Placing aside rhetorical devices and dramatic organization, the narrative method is designed to organize the evidence into a coherent story that is logically supported by the evidence, which will enable the lawyer to assess whether a jury would be likely to understand and, more important, be persuaded by the theory it is intended to illustrate.[5]

c. Final trial preparation

If the analysis justifies a decision to end the investigative phase, the lawyer has presumably prepared the analysis upon which she will rely at trial. All the data have been analyzed, and the inferences have been organized in relationship to the ultimate probandum. The data are as complete as possible or feasible. What remains is presentation. Key-lists and charts, outlines, chronologies, and narratives serve

---

5 It is this virtue that, in the authors' view, makes it appropriate that the narrative method be employed to complement and supplement other methods. Using the narrative method alone is dangerous. The danger is that the "story" will take over, and the lawyer will pay inadequate attention to the detail necessary to support each step in the argument.

additional strategic and practical functions when the task is organizing the data for trial or other use. These functions and the other devices typically employed in trial preparation are sufficiently important that they are developed more fully in Chapter 12.

A further point should be emphasized. The utility of the chronologies and narratives is not limited to final trial preparation. They may be employed at any stage for appraisal and to facilitate translating the current state of the analysis into a statement that facilitates use in other aspects of a case – in counseling a client about the strengths and weaknesses of the case; in stimulating imaginative reasoning at the investigative stages of a case; in persuading opposing counsel that a favorable settlement is in the best interests of the opposing party; in identifying additional witnesses or other evidence that might strengthen a case; or in persuading a judge that the case requires a trial on the merits. Moreover, the notion of "narrative" and the related notions of "theory of a case," "story," and "theme" are featured today in many contemporary discussions of litigation theory and practice. Consideration of the methods and devices and their utility requires preliminary consideration of these related ideas also.

D. Theories, themes, stories, and situation-types

In order to prepare or to present a case, counsel for each of the parties must develop a strong logical *theory* of the case. In most cases, especially those to be tried by a jury, counsel must develop recurring *themes* that will serve as points of emphasis and reinforcement with respect to crucial parts of the case. In each case, counsel must use the theory adopted and the themes identified to construct a compelling *story* of what the evidence in the case shows. In most cases, counsel will be better able to develop and test their theories, themes, and stories by identifying and describing a general *situation* into which the case fits as illustrated by the story that reinforces the need to find the facts in a way that supports the result counsel seeks. We discuss these concepts in greater detail in chapters that follow. For present purposes, we need to draw fairly precise distinctions between four notions and identify the ways in which methods of analysis contribute to their development.

The *theory of a case*, in advocacy, is the *logical* statement of the case-as-a-whole selected by counsel from the available alternatives, in light of opposing counsel's anticipated theory and in light of counsel's choice as to theme and story. The theory should be capable of statement in the form of a series of syllogisms that demonstrate that the desired conclusion is necessarily true, given the controlling legal principle and the available evidence and assuming the truth of the proposed inferences.

The theory of the case is a product of analysis. For the Wigmorean lawyer, the key-list and chart enable her to test her provisional theories and revise those theories until she has settled on the theory that provides strongest support for her client's position and is least vulnerable to attack by opposing counsel, the theory that will enable her to marshal the evidence that provides the strongest support for the conclusion that the ultimate probandum has (or has not) been proved. The theory adopted must be capable of statement in logical form. The lawyer should be able to organize the data and marshal the arguments in syllogistic form to demonstrate that, if all of the generalizations upon which the required inferences depend are valid, the ultimate probandum must be accepted as proven to a certainty (or as incapable of being proven to the required degree of certainty). In that sense the theory of the case is a matter to be tested by logic.[6]

Theme: An English barrister described the theme of a case better than we could:

Having decided on a theory, you must pick a theme to fit that theory. You must have two goals in mind: First, why the other side is responsible for what happened and second, why your client is not. For example, big business at its intolerant and unimaginative worst; on the other hand, no one is perfect; there is a limit to the care and foresight which the ordinary man like your client cannot be expected to possess, etc.[7]

Frequently, the theme is announced as the headline at the beginning of the opening statement. For example, counsel might begin her opening statement in *Sargent v. Southern Accident Co.* (above, page 28) with the assertion: "This is a story about a heartless insurance company that chose to prolong the agony of grieving parents by refusing to pay the amount due under the policy for which they had paid until they proved the obvious – that their son is dead."

Sometimes a theme may be expressed in a sentence or phrase that is used repeatedly for emphasis. For example, in *Simpson* one of the prosecutors challenged OJS to put on the bloody glove that had allegedly been worn by the murderer and found behind his house. It did not fit. Throughout his closing, defense counsel sounded the theme, "If it doesn't fit, you must acquit," every time he identified items of the prosecution's evidence that could plausibly be interpreted as not supporting OJS's guilt.

The same barrister described the relationship between analysis and the development of theory and theme and emphasized their importance as follows:

A primary task in any litigation is to develop a cohesive theory and theme of the case. The theory should be that explanation of the facts which shows logic requires your side to win and the theme should be that explanation of the facts which shows the moral force is on your side. This strategy should provide a framework for assimilating the facts in a manner which is most advantageous to your client. Since there are generally some harmful facts in any litigation, you should choose a strategy which does not rely on these facts and which makes such facts irrelevant . . .

Selecting a theory is simply one aspect of careful preparation and is the *sine qua non* of effective litigation. Without a coherent framework provided by a carefully considered strategy, the most exhaustive preparation, the most cogent argument, and the most sympathetic case will be unavailing. While a cohesive theory cannot take the place of

6 The term "theory of the case" or "case theory" is used in several different ways. For a good discussion, see Palmer (2003) Ch. 5.
7 Bennett (1986).

thorough preparation and a favorable set of facts, it is the glue which holds together the other elements required for successful litigation.[8]

The selection of the best theory of the case and its conversion into a compelling narrative account, however, require more than logical analysis from the standpoints of the proponent and opponent. It requires an understanding of the human and physical material available as witnesses and other autoptic proferences and of the significant generalizations likely to influence a jury in a case of this kind. These are the materials by which the *story* of the case as a whole must be presented and from which the necessary themes can be established.

A *story* is a narrative account of a succession of events, ordinarily presented in the chronological order in which they occurred, presented as a meaningful whole.[9] Three elements are essential to the usage adopted here – a story is a narration of events arranged in a time sequence; the narrated events are abstracted from their disposition in the evidence presented at trial; and they are presented as a meaningful totality.

In this usage, the "story of a case" would be the advocate's narration of events abstracted from the evidence and arranged in a sequence to persuade the fact-finder that the story told is the most plausible account of what "really happened" that can be constructed from the evidence that has been or will be presented. In advocacy, the story must not include elements that are logically inconsistent with the theory of the case and must be a plausible account, the main elements of which find support in the evidence.

It should be clear that construction of stories from the available evidential data may be useful at any stage of the analysis. The master chronology and the narrative are independently useful analytic devices. Both can reveal gaps in the evidence at a time when further investigation or discovery might enable the advocate to fill them before trial. More, however, is required of a story in the context of a trial. It must be a story the fact-finder, judge, or jury will find compelling. Typically the story is first told as part of the opening statement, and is retold and urged as the only or most probable account in closing argument.

Situation. We shall use the term "situation" where what is being described or depicted is a state of affairs at a given moment of time as contrasted with a sequence of events. A description of a situation is like a still photograph; a story is like a moving picture. Both may be included in a narrative account. In this connection, we have deliberately avoided using "scene," because it tends to be used ambiguously in lawyers' talk. A "scene" may refer to a place (as in "the scene of the crime") or to an

8 Id. at 1–2.
9 Two definitions offered by literary theorists are useful in the present context. In one view, a story is a narrative of particular events arranged in a time sequence and forming a meaningful totality. Adapted from P. Ricoeur (1981) 278–79. In another, the notion of story is limited to "the narrated events, abstracted from their disposition in the text and reconstructed in their chronological order, together with the participants in the event[s]." S. Rimmon-Kenan (1983) 3. See *Rethinking*, Ch. 7, "Lawyers' Stories" (for a fuller discussion of the role of story in advocacy and adjudication).

episode or part of a story (as in a scene in a play) or to a static situation (as in "he set the scene before outlining the plot"). Although when used with precision "scene" is often a useful term, loose usage glosses over distinctions that are important for purposes of analysis.

In using situation sense, the advocate or judge categorizes the facts of the present case as a *type* of situation and describes it at a level of generality and using language that makes it fit some recognizable general rule or principle that will justify the desired outcome in *this* case.[10] Consider, for example, the persuasive force of this famous passage from a judgment of Lord Denning:

> Did the accountants owe a duty of care to the plaintiff? ... They were professional accountants who prepared and put before him these accounts, knowing that he was going to be guided by them in making an investment in the company. On the faith of these accounts he did make the investment whereas if the accounts had been carefully prepared, he would not have made the investment at all. The result is that he has lost his money.[11]

Similarly, an advocate, in presenting her client's story in a case involving disputed issues of fact, might seek to characterize it as creating a situation in which the theory and themes come together in a pattern that compels the result sought. For example, an advocate might characterize the situation as one involving a *professional* advising a *non-professional* and that professional *expecting* the advice to be *relied* upon.

The relationship between constructing theories, telling stories, and describing situations, on the one hand, and constructing and analyzing arguments about evidence, on the other, raises an important issue concerning the relationship between story telling and atomistic analysis. Many trial lawyers and decision theorists believe that juries (and other fact-finders) make "holistic" judgments – that they are persuaded by stories. In this view, juries choose between the two stories presented by the contending lawyers (or adopt a variant of their own) and decide the case accordingly. We largely agree with this view.[12]

In our view atomistic analysis is fundamental to story construction in the adversarial system because:

> *In principle,* the adversarial system is designed to assure *generally sound* processing of information and resolution of questions of fact *because* it assigns primary responsibility for atomistic analysis and evaluation to the contending lawyers and *appropriately* restricts the amount of information and the manner of its presentation to the ultimate decision maker, be it judge or jury.[13]

---

10 Situation in this usage is often similar to Karl Llewellyn's notion of "situation sense," which he developed in the context of appellate arguments about disputed questions of law. K. Llewellyn (1960) 121–32, 268–74 . Note that "situation" in this context is not necessarily confined to static states of affairs.
11 *Candler v. Crane Christmas* [1951] 2 K.B. 164 at 176.
12 See *Theories of Evidence* 183–85, 226; *Rethinking,* at 219–61.
13 Anderson (1991) 785.

The point to be recognized is that the common law adversarial model of adjudication allocates roles and functions in an appropriate fashion. The primary responsibility for analysis is among the responsibilities assigned to the lawyers. It is they who analyze the data; construct and critique hypotheses and arguments; and develop what they see as the strongest theory of the case on each side. They marshal the evidence and arguments that best support (or confound) the contending theories. On the basis of that analysis, they construct the stories that they will urge the ultimate decision-maker to adopt and identify points on which the opposing side's best story is likely to be most vulnerable.

In this model, using stories as the basis for decision is efficient. In the common law model the trial is a separate and isolated event. The lawyers for the contending adversaries present the evidence that they have culled from the universe of available and potentially relevant data and present the contending theories, arguments, and stories that they have selected and developed. The contending stories and the lawyers' arguments attacking and defending each story provide, in principle, a sound method of processing information to aid the judge or jury in resolving, efficiently, finally, and accurately, the factual issues necessary to a fair judgment. So long as the analysts have done their jobs well, it is hard to see why we would want a system that would require the ultimate decision maker to replicate, rather than assess, their work as a basis for resolving disputed questions of fact necessary to reach a judgment on the case as a whole.[14]

The process by which juries or other fact-finders choose between stories is logical. The evidence is rarely conclusive. If there are genuine factual disputes, the fact-finder must form a belief by testing the available stories against a recollection of the evidence and an assessment of the likelihood that a particular story is the most plausible version of what really took place in light of their commonly held beliefs or other generalizations. The nature of closing argument is to reassure the fact-finder that the evidence "logically" makes one story the most plausible and to focus its attention on the inconsistencies and logical fallacies in the opponent's story in relation to the central legal principles laid down by the judge. Of necessity (because of such factors as time and audience attention span), the lawyers must strike for the jugular: Normally, only the weakest links in the opposition's chain of inferences and only those that cut against belief in its story-as-a-whole can be attacked; there is neither time nor purpose for attack on secondary detail. The making of such a focused argument, however, must be preceded by logical, atomistic analysis and be combined with judgment.

Atomistic analysis remains a central tool for identifying the plausible story possibilities, for checking them for consistency and coherence, and for choosing among them. It remains necessary, even though all must concede it is not sufficient. In that light, the contribution of the story-theorists is to focus attention upon the

14 See Anderson (1999) 47 (for a comparison of the adversarial and inquisitorial systems as models of decision-making).

relationships between the logical theory of a case, the dramatic themes by which the theory may be developed most plausibly in trial, and the story-as-a-whole.

State v. Archer (IV): *the exercise concludes*

The facts remain as developed through *State v. Archer* (III) (above, page 143). The prosecutor has learned that Archer hosted the party on Saturday, the day preceding the murder, and that Boswell and Carl had drinks at Archer's house on the Tuesday after the murder. Through Detective Paul's interviews and investigations, she has also learned that the termination of the partnership between Boswell and Vern was initiated by Vern and left Boswell embittered and that Carl believed that Vern's refusal to marry his sister had caused her to commit suicide.

1. The prosecution standpoint

a   *Theory of the case.* Based upon the available data, state the theory of the case that you now think a competent prosecutor should seek to develop. The statement should compel the conclusion that Archer is guilty, if the facts assumed are accepted as true. It should rely, however, only on those facts that are most likely to be accepted in light of the evidence available to the prosecution and the defense. The statement should take no more than a paragraph or two.

b   *Story of the case.* On the basis of the theory developed, construct the story that you could argue is the only plausible story of what happened. Assuming that further investigation did not undermine your provisional theory, this would be the story of the evidence that you could recommend that the prosecution develop in her opening statement. Again, compress the essential account into a couple of paragraphs.

c   *Themes for the case.* Identify and state the one or, at most, two best themes the prosecutor might rely upon in presenting the case, if the provisional theory and story withstand further investigation.

2. The defense standpoint

Assume the standpoint of counsel for the defendant. Through further interviews, counsel for the defense has also learned that Boswell was bitter over what he perceived as Vern's wrongful termination of their partnership and that Carl blamed Vern for his only sister's death. In appraising the case for the defense, you would have made an assessment of the prosecution's case similar to that developed in response to item one of this exercise. Now repeat the exercise for the defense (a) stating the provisional theory of the case for the defense in narrative form, (b) constructing the most plausible story for the defense at this stage, and (c) identifying the one or two most promising themes defense counsel might choose to develop.

7

Analyzing the decided case: anatomy of a *cause célèbre*

A. Introduction

Rex v. Bywaters and Thompson is one of England's most famous *causes célèbres.* On January 9, 1923, Frederick Bywaters and Edith Thompson were hanged for the murder of Edith's husband Percy, just three months and six days after his death. The case is an example of rough as well as speedy "justice." Public opinion at the time and subsequent commentators have been divided on the question whether Edith was guilty as charged and on a number of subsidiary issues.

In our experience, *Bywaters and Thompson* is a particularly good vehicle for classroom consideration of modified Wigmorean analysis for several reasons:

a It is interesting in itself;
b It is a good test of macroscopic analysis not only because it involves a complex mixed mass of evidence, but also because uncertainties about the law relating to aiding and abetting, conspiring and incitement, raise challenging questions about precisely what it was that the prosecution had to prove in order to establish a case that was sufficient to support a conviction in respect of Edith;
c There were several possible theories of the case available to each side;
d Several key phases of the evidence, including some passages in Edith's letters, invite careful microscopic analysis; and
e Some of the key evidentiary issues relate to what Jerome Frank called "wild facts," that is to say issues relating to such elusive matters as motive, intent, the characters and relationships of the main actors, and the language of lovers. Edith's letters in particular provide an excellent test of the uses and limitations of careful analysis. As one student put it: "If you can analyze Edith's prose, you can analyze anything."

The materials presented here are a selection from the trial record of the proceedings as published in the Notable British Trials Series (F. Young, 2nd edn., 1951). This is only some of the evidence in the case, but it is sufficient for present purposes. We recommend that students read through the materials as a whole to orient themselves and to form a general impression and then work systematically through the record using the questions at pages 220–23 as a guide. The main disputed issue at the trial was and has remained: Was Edith guilty as charged in the first indictment? The prosecution did not proceed with the second indictment, but it raises some interesting issues and provides some clues to the prosecution's strategy at trial.

There is an extensive secondary literature on the case.[1] We recommend, however, that you work through the material before considering secondary literature, which might serve as a diversion from the enterprise of applying modified Wigmorean analysis to a particularly complex and elusive body of evidence and of appraising the method in the context of analyzing a decided case.

Our experience has been that *Rex v. Bywaters and Thompson* is a particularly good vehicle for learning how to analyze a complex mixed mass of evidence. The questions at the end of this chapter are designed to follow the seven step protocol for the chart method (Chapter 5, above). The case also provides useful illustrations of several points about standpoint, theory and theme, "jugulars," stories and generalizations (see below, Chapter 10), and much else besides. However, many other trial records, some rather less complex, are suitable for the purpose. So too are hypothetical trial problems such as *Wainwright* and *Weller* (below, pages 326–9, 343–78). In our experience, the following cases also work well either for discussion in class or for written exercises. They are backed up by relevant literature, including the full trial record: *Sacco and Vanzetti*; *Leo Frank*; *Roger Tichborne*; *New Jersey v. Hauptman* (the Lindbergh Baby case); *Louise Woodward* (the Boston nanny case), the *Lockerbie* bombing or *O. J. Simpson*.[2]

B. The trial of Bywaters and Thompson

(F. Young, ed. 2nd edn, 1951) (excerpts)

1. Preliminary matter

a. The indictments

[*Copy Indictment No. 1*]

The King
Against
Frederick Edw[D]. Francis Bywaters
and Edith Jessie Thompson.
Central Criminal Court.
Presentment of the Grand Jury.

---

1 See, for example, Weis (1988); *Rethinking* (1994) Chs. 8 and 9; the powerful novel by F. Tennyson Jesse, *A Pin to See the Peepshow* (1934, 1979); and Weis and Twining in Twining and Hampsher-Monk (2003) Ch. 2.

2 For bibliographical references see the References section at pages 388–95. The range of usable materials is vast. Based on our experience of teaching we recommend the following guidelines for selection: (1) Primary materials (e.g. trial records) are preferable to secondary sources; (2) The case should be sufficiently complex to illustrate the value of macroscopic analysis as a tool of fact management; (3) There should be a historical doubt about the outcome. This is important to maintain student interest and to illustrate the dialectics of argument. (4) It is not necessary to analyze the whole of a complex case. It is enough to identify the ultimate and penultimate probanda and competing theories of the case ("the top of the chart") and then select a few phases of the argument for microscopic analysis.

F. E. F. BYWATERS and E. J. THOMPSON are charged with
the following offence: –
STATEMENT OF OFFENCE.
MURDER.
Particulars of Offence.
F. E. F. BYWATERS and E. J. THOMPSON on the 4th day of October, 1922,
in the County of Essex, and within the jurisdiction of the Central Criminal Court
murdered Percy Thompson.

[Copy Indictment No. 2] [3]

The King
Against
FREDERICK EDW^D. FRANCIS BYWATERS
and EDITH JESSIE THOMPSON.
Central Criminal Court.
Presentment of the Grand Jury.
F. E. F. BYWATERS and E. J. THOMPSON are charged with
the following offences: –

FIRST COUNT:
STATEMENT OF OFFENCE.
Conspiracy to Murder contrary to sec. 4 of the Offences against the Person Act,
1861.
Particulars of Offence.
F. E. F. BYWATERS and E. J. THOMPSON on the 20th day of August, 1921, and
on divers days between that date and the 2nd day of October, 1922, in the County of
Essex, and within the jurisdiction of the Central Criminal Court, conspired together
to murder Percy Thompson.

SECOND COUNT:
STATEMENT OF OFFENCE.
Soliciting to Murder contrary to sec. 4 of the Offences against the Person
Act 1861.
Particulars of Offence.
E. J. THOMPSON on the 10th day of February, 1922, and on divers days
between that day and the 1st day of October, 1922, in the County of Essex, and
within the jurisdiction of the Central Criminal Court, did solicit and endeav-
our to persuade and did propose to F. E. F. BYWATERS to murder Percy
Thompson.

---

3 Indictment No. 2 was not proceeded with.

THIRD COUNT:
STATEMENT OF OFFENCE.
Inciting to commit a misdemeanour.
Particulars of Offence.

E. J. THOMPSON on the 10th day of February, 1922, and on divers days between that day and the 1st day of October, 1922, in the County of Essex, and within the jurisdiction of the Central Criminal Court, did unlawfully solicit and incite F. E. F. BYWATERS unlawfully to conspire with her, the said E. J. Thompson, to murder Percy Thompson.

FOURTH COUNT:
STATEMENT OF OFFENCE.
Administering poison with intent to murder contrary to sec. 11 of the Offences against the Person Act, 1861.
Particulars of Offence.

E. J. THOMPSON on the 26th day of March, 1922, in the County of Essex, and within the jurisdiction of the Central Criminal Court, did administer to and cause to be taken by Percy Thompson certain poison or other destructive thing unknown with intent to murder the said Percy Thompson.

FIFTH COUNT:
STATEMENT OF OFFENCE.
Administering a destructive thing with intent to murder contrary to sec. 11 of the Offences against the Person Act, 1861.
Particulars of Offence.

E. J. THOMPSON on the 24th day of April, 1922, in the County of Essex, and within the jurisdiction of the Central Criminal Court, did administer to and cause to be taken by Percy Thompson a certain destructive thing, namely, broken glass, with intent to murder the said Percy Thompson.

b. Dramatis personae

The Trial
Within The
Central Criminal Court,
Old Bailey, London,
Wednesday 6th December, 1922.

Judge –
Mr. Justice SHEARMAN.
Counsel for the Crown –
The Solicitor-General,

Mr. Travers Humphreys.

Mr. Roland Oliver.

(Instructed by the Director of Public Prosecutions.)

Counsel for the Prisoner Frederick Bywaters –

Mr. Cecil Whiteley, K. C.

Mr. Huntly Jenkins.

Mr. Myles Elliott.

(Instructed by Mr. Barrington Matthews.)

Counsel for the Prisoner Edith Thompson –

Sir Henry Curtis Bennett, K. C.

Mr. Walter Frampton.

Mr. Ivor Snell.

(Instructed by Mr. F. A. S. Stern.)

c. Leading dates in the case

1914	– Edith Graydon employed at Carlton & White's, London.
1915 Jan. 15	– Percy Thompson married to Edith Graydon.
1918 Feb.	– Frederick Bywaters joins Merchant Service.
1920 July	– The Thompsons move to 41 Kensington Gardens, Ilford.
1921 June	– Bywaters goes with them to Shanklin, I.O.W.
1921 June 18	– He returns to live with them as a lodger.
1921 Aug. 5	– He quarrels with Thompson and leaves.
1921 Sept. 9	– He leaves in S.S. Morea for the East (Correspondence between Bywaters and Mrs. Thompson).
1921 Oct. 29	– Bywaters returns to England.
1921 Nov. 3	– He visits the Thompsons.
1921 Dec. 1 I	– He sails again in the Morea (Correspondence continued).
1922 Jan. 6	– He returns home.
1922 Jan. 20	– He sails again.
1922 Feb.	– Correspondence continued.
1922 March	– Correspondence continued.
1922 March 16	– Bywaters returns home.
1922 March 31	– Bywaters sails again in the Morea.
1922 April	– Correspondence continued.
1922 March	– Correspondence continued.
1922 May 25	– Bywaters returns in the Morea.
1922 June 9	– Bywaters sails again for the East.
1922 July	– Correspondence continued.
1922 August	– Correspondence continued.
1922 Sept. 23	– Bywaters arrives at Tilbury, works on ship, and sleeps at home.
1922 Sept. 25	– He meets Mrs. Thompson.

1922 Sept. 29	– He leaves ship and goes to his mother's home.
1922 Oct. 2	– He meets Mrs. Thompson by appointment.
1922 Oct. 3	– They have tea at Fuller's, and leave together at 5.15 p.m. The Thompsons go to the theatre. Bywaters spends the evening at the Graydons, and leaves about 11 p.m. Percy Thompson murdered at Ilford about midnight.
1922 Oct. 4	– Mrs. Thompson visited by police 3 a.m. Bywaters arrives at his mother's house early a.m. He goes to town. He spends the evening at the Graydons, where he is arrested. Statement to police. Mrs. Thompson arrested.
1922 Oct. 5	– She makes a statement. Post-mortem on the body of Thompson. Bywaters is charged, and makes a second statement.
1922 Oct. 9	– Knife found in Seymour Gardens.
1922 Oct. 12	– Letters found in Bywaters' chest on board S.S. Morea.
1922 Nov. 3	– Thompson's body exhumed. Post-mortem.
1922 Nov.	– Bywaters and Mrs. Thompson before Magistrate. Committed for trial.
1922 Dec. 6–11	– Trial at the Old Bailey.
1922 Dec. 21	– Appeals of Bywaters and Mrs. Thompson heard and dismissed.
1923 Jan. 9	– Frederick Bywaters hanged at Pentonville. Edith Thompson hanged at Holloway.

2. The judgment on Thompson's appeal: *Rex v. Thompson* (1922)

Royal Courts of Justice, Thursday, 21st December, 1922.

Court of Criminal Appeal.
Rex
v.
Edith Jessie Thompson.
Before – The Lord Chief Justice of England,
Mr. Justice DARLING, and
Mr. Justice SALTER.

Judgment

The Lord Chief Justice – This appellant, Edith Jessie Thompson, was convicted at the Central Criminal Court, together with the last appellant, Frederick Edward Francis Bywaters, of the wilful murder of Percy Thompson, and she was sentenced to death. She now appeals against conviction. The charge against her was in point of law that she was what is called a principal in the second degree; that is to say, that she was a person present at the commission of the offence who aided and abetted the commission of the offence, and, to put it in a slightly different way, the point of the charge against this woman was that she incited and aided and abetted the commission of this crime upon the night of the 3rd day of October. Now, before I come to deal with the argument that has been presented on behalf of the appellant by Sir Henry Curtis Bennett, it is necessary, as shortly as possible, to review some of the facts of this essentially commonplace and unedifying case. The appellant, Edith Jessie Thompson, is twenty-nine years of age. She is the daughter of a Mr. Graydon, and seven years ago she married Mr. Percy Thompson, the man now dead, the only person who in this case excites any sympathy.

At the time of his death he was thirty-two years of age. They lived in a part of a house at Ilford, called No. 41 Kensington Gardens; and the evidence was that the appellant and her husband were not on good terms with each other. She was employed as manageress of a firm of milliners in Aldersgate Street, where she received a salary of £6 a week in addition to a bonus. Some time ago, a considerable time ago, the appellant made the acquaintance of Bywaters, a young steward on a liner, whose case was dealt with this morning. He had stayed with them elsewhere and in their own house, and it is quite obvious from many portions of the evidence that the terms upon which she and Bywaters had come to be, long before the 3rd October of this year, were terms of the most culpable intimacy. Bywaters was from time to time absent on his ship. It is not necessary even for the sake of clearness to examine closely the chronology in the case; but there were periods when he was at home and there were periods when he was away, and the periods when he was away are to a great extent covered by a remarkable and deplorable correspondence, full of the most mischievous and perilous stuff. In August of last year Bywaters, according to the evidence, made a statement to his mother about the unhappy life of Mrs. Thompson, and the evidence showed, if the jury accepted it, as they apparently did, that on more than one occasion Bywaters had called at the warehouse where Mrs. Thompson was employed, that he had kept up this protracted correspondence with her. The letters which are actually made exhibits began with the 11th of August, 1921, and they continue right down to the 2nd October, 1922 – that is to say, the day before the commission of the crime – and the evidence further was that after an absence of some weeks, Bywaters began a new period of leave on the 29th September last. There was evidence that he was with the appellant at a neighbouring teashop upon that day; and again upon Tuesday, the 3rd day of October. That was the day upon which the crime was committed. On that Tuesday, the 3rd October, the appellant and her husband went to a theatre with the husband's uncle, Mr. Laxton. Upon that same evening Bywaters went to the house of the appellant's father; and it appears to have been mentioned at that house that the Thompsons had gone to the theatre. Bywaters left about ten o'clock or a little after ten. Somewhat later the appellant and her husband, with Mr. Laxton, went to the Piccadilly Tube station, about a quarter to eleven. There, it was said, they were apparently on good terms, and it is clear from what followed that they made their way home by train to Ilford. Shortly before midnight a Miss Pittard was walking with Mr. and Mrs. Clevely from Ilford station, and their way took them through a road called Belgrave Road, and when they were between De Vere Gardens and Endsleigh Gardens, both places not far from Kensington Gardens, where the Thompsons' own house was, Mrs. Thompson came running to him. She was agitated and incoherent. She said – "Oh, my God, will you help me, my husband is ill; he is bleeding." And she said he was on the pavement and asked those persons to go or take her and get a doctor. They took her to the house of a doctor, Dr. Maudsley, and then Mrs. Thompson ran back. A witness was called named Webber, who lived about 30 or 40 yards away from that place, and he said that as he was going to bed he heard a woman's voice, a voice which he now recognised as Mrs. Thompson's voice, calling in piteous tones, "Oh, don't, don't." He went outside, and three or four minutes later he saw three persons coming from Dr. Maudsley's house. Mrs. Thompson was in front running and sobbing. He followed, and found Mrs. Thompson and Mr. Thompson. He asked her if he could help, and she said, "Don't touch him, don't touch him; a lady and a gentleman have gone off for a doctor." Miss Pittard and Mr. Clevely then came up, and they found the appellant kneeling down by Mr. Thompson, who was lying upon the footpath in Belgrave Road with his back propped against the wall. The place was dark. Mr. Clevely struck a match, and Miss Pittard asked Mrs. Thompson what had happened; and the appellant answered, "Oh, do not ask me; I do not know. Somebody flew past, and when I turned to speak to him blood was pouring out of his mouth." A few minutes later Dr. Maudsley arrived, and he found that Mr. Thompson was dead. He thought he had been dead then about ten minutes. Mrs. Thompson was standing by his side, and he described her as being confused, hysterical, and agitated. He asked her if Mr. Thompson had been ill coming home, and she said "No." He told her that Mr. Thompson was dead, and she said, "Why did not you come sooner and save him?" The doctor made no examination then. He saw the blood. He did not see any wound, but he sent for the police. A police sergeant took the appellant to her house, and on the way she said, "Will he come back? They will blame me for this." Now, the place where the body was found was about 50 yards from the Thompsons' house and 1250 yards from Ilford station. It was an indirect way from the station to the house. The police came, took the body to the mortuary and undressed it, and it was examined; and a great number of wounds were found upon it. The most serious wounds were three stabs, apparently inflicted from behind, one of which penetrated down to and opened the gullet. Mr. Thompson's brother was sent for, and shortly before two o'clock in the morning he arrived at Mrs. Thompson's house. She told her brother-in-law that Mr. Thompson was walking along and suddenly came over queer and said "Oh!" and that on the way from the station he had complained of pains in his legs, and that she had met a lady and gentleman and had gone for a doctor, and when they got back he was dead.

At three o'clock in the morning two police sergeants went to Mrs. Thompson's house and saw her. She was asked if she could explain what had happened on the road, and she said, "I do not know, I cannot say; I only know that my husband suddenly dropped down and screamed out 'Oh!' I then rushed across the road and saw a lady and gentleman, and asked them if they would help me, and they went with me for the doctor." She was asked whether she could account for the cuts on her husband's neck, and she said, "No. We were walking along, and my husband said 'Oh,' and I said 'Bear up,' thinking he had one of his attacks." He then fell on her, and walked a little further. He then fell up against the wall and then on the ground. She was asked if her husband carried a knife, and she said "No." She was asked if she was carrying a knife in her handbag, and she said "No." She was also asked if she or her husband saw or spoke to any person in Belgrave Road, and she said, "No; I did not notice any one." About eleven o'clock in the morning of the 4th October Inspector Hall saw Mrs. Thompson at her house, and she told him: "We were coming along Belgrave Road and just passed the corner of Endsleigh Gardens when I heard him call out, 'Oh, er,' and he fell up against me. I put out my arms to save him, and found blood which I thought was coming from his mouth. I tried to hold him up. He staggered for several yards towards Kensington Gardens and then fell against the wall and slid down. He did not speak to me; I cannot say if I spoke to him. I felt him, and found his clothing wet with blood. He never moved after he fell. We had no quarrel on the way; we were quite happy together. Immediately I saw blood I ran across the road to a doctor's. I appealed to a lady and gentleman who were passing, and the gentleman also went to the doctor's. The doctor came and told me my husband was dead. Just before he fell down I was walking on his right hand side on the inside of the pavement nearest the wall. We were side by side. I did not see anybody about at the time. My husband and I were talking about going to a dance." That evening Mrs. Thompson was taken to the police station, and on the 5th October she made a statement which became exhibit No. 3 at the trial. I shall not read it all; but it is to be observed that in that statement made when she went to the police station she says this: "I have always been on affectionate terms with my husband. I remember Tuesday, the 3rd October, we both went to our respective businesses that day; I met my husband by appointment at a quarter to six in Aldersgate Street." She then describes how they went to the theatre and how they came home; and then she describes or purports to describe what took place, and she says, amongst other things, this – "I cannot remember whether I saw any one else there or not. I know there was no one there when he staggered up against me." She went on to speak of Bywaters and her knowledge of Bywaters. She said, "I am not in possession of any letters he wrote to me. I have destroyed them all, as is customary with me with all my correspondence. When he was at home in England we were in the habit of going out occasionally together without my husband's knowledge." According to that statement she had not seen Bywaters that night; she did not associate Bywaters with what had taken place, and she was on good terms with Mr. Thompson, her husband. Now it happened that at the police station she saw Bywaters, who had been taken to the police station, and was in the library as she passed, and she then said, "Oh God, oh God, what can I do? Why did he do it? I did not want him to do it. I must tell the truth." And then she made a further statement, which is exhibit No. 4. In that short statement she said this – "When we got near Endsleigh Gardens a man rushed out from the Gardens and knocked me and pushed me away from my husband. I was dazed for a moment. When I recovered I saw my husband scuffling with a man. The man who I know as Freddie Bywaters was running away. He was wearing a blue overcoat and a grey hat. I knew it was him although I did not see his face." The two were afterwards charged together. The knife with which these wounds had been inflicted was found in a neighbouring drain, and I do not think I need dwell upon the rest of the evidence. Dr. Spilsbury said that all the wounds except the one on the arm of Mr. Thompson were stabs.

The appellant Bywaters gave evidence first, and Mrs. Thompson gave evidence, and I shall have to refer in a moment to the denials she made. She said, among other things, that she first fell in love with Bywaters in September, 1921, and that she had told her husband that she had given him cause for divorce. The jury, having heard the whole of the evidence, both that which I have summarised and much else, came to the conclusion that the appellant was guilty of wilful murder.

Now, what are the pleas that are put forward on behalf of the appellant in this appeal? Sir Henry Curtis Bennett at the outset stated, and very frankly stated, that before he came into Court this morning he had decided to abandon that ground of appeal which rested upon the allegation that this appellant and Bywaters ought to have been tried separately, but were in fact tried together. That ground of appeal is not persisted in. But Sir Henry says – he puts it in more than one way, but it is really the same contention illustrated and sought to be enforced from different points of view – that in order that this appellant might properly be convicted of this crime there ought to be evidence showing not merely that as between her and Bywaters there was a community of purpose in this matter, but that that community of purpose continued right up to the crucial moment when the crime was committed; and in regard to that complaint Sir Henry relies especially upon two matters. He relies first upon the letters and the use to which they were put or not put; and secondly, he relies upon certain portions in the summing up, where he says the learned judge not only misdirected the jury in the sense of inviting them to find what they could not find, but also omitted to direct the jury in the sense that he did not adequately put before the jury what the defence of the appellant was. With regard to the letters, in the opinion of this Court there was more than one ground upon which the use of these letters could be justified. It is enough for the present purpose to say that they could be justified upon this ground – that by means of them the prosecution were seeking to show that continuously over a long period, beginning before and culminating in the time immediately antecedent to the commission of the crime, Mrs. Thompson was, with every sort of ingenuity, by precept and by example, actual or simulated, endeavouring to incite Bywaters to the commission of this crime. I am not going to read those letters. There is a great mass of them. Many of them were read at the trial. They begin in the summer of 1921, and they continue until the 2nd October, 1922; that is to say, they continue until the day before the day upon which this crime was committed. Now, what is it that those letters may reasonably be regarded as showing? First of all, they show a passionate and, in the circumstances, a wicked affection between Mrs. Thompson and Bywaters. Secondly, they contain what purport to be accounts of efforts which have been made, sometimes without the assistance of Bywaters, sometimes with the assistance of Bywaters, to get Mr. Thompson out of the way. Thirdly – and this is a thread that runs through the whole skein of these letters – there is the continual entreaty and hope that that which they both desire will somehow be accomplished. Now, in the opinion of the Court, the theory that these letters, so far as they purport to describe attempts made upon the life of Mr. Thompson, are mere nonsense – "Vapour," as Bywaters calls them – "Melodramatic nonsense," as learned counsel has thought fit to call them – is a theory which cannot be accepted. But however that may be, if the question is, as I think it was, whether these letters were evidence of a protracted, continuous incitement to Bywaters to commit the crime which he did in the end commit, it really is of comparatively little importance whether the appellant was truly reporting something which she had done, or falsely reporting something which she merely pretended to do. I am not going to read them; it is not necessary; but reference may, perhaps, be made to one of them, which is the last. By this time Bywaters was back in this country. The appellant and Bywaters were meeting. They had ample opportunity of conversation and arrangement of any plan in which they might be interested; and upon the 2nd of October the appellant wrote to him – "I tried so hard to find a way out of to-night, darlingest, but he was suspicious and still is. ... We ought to be able to use great big things for great big love like ours." And again – "Darlint, it is funds that are our stumbling block – until we have those, we can do nothing." That is not the only passage in the later correspondence in which the appellant refers to the importance of money. Then she goes on – "Darlint do something to-morrow night will you? something to make you forget. I'll be hurt I know, but I want you to hurt me – I do really – the bargain now seems so one-sided – so unfair – but how can I alter it." And finally, the last passage – "Don't forget what we talked in the tearoom. I'll still risk and try if you will – we only have $3^3/_4$ years left darlingest." Now, it cannot be said that those letters were not evidence against the appellant in support of the charge which the prosecution were making up against her.

Taking that long summing up as a whole, and reading one part with the rest of what the learned judge says, in the opinion of this Court it is not possible to found upon it any unfavourable criticism. The case was clearly put before the jury. There was simple evidence, partly direct evidence, partly evidence from which inference might properly be drawn; and upon that evidence, in a case which exhibits from beginning to end no redeeming feature, the members of the jury have convicted the appellant. In the opinion of this Court there is no reason to interfere with that conviction, and this appeal must be dismissed.

3. Evidence from the trial: the Prosecution

a. Extracts from testimony (including statements made by the accused)

Examination of John Hancock

JOHN HANCOCK, examined by Mr. TRAVERS HUMPHREYS – I am a detective constable. I received a number of letters from Inspector Hall, which I examined and had copied. There were also a number of newspaper cuttings in some of the letters. On 9th October I found a knife (exhibit No. 1) in a drain on the north side of Seymour Gardens, Ilford, about 250 yards from Kensington Gardens, Ilford. I handed it to Inspector Hall. I did not find any sheath. It is an English knife. I received three letters from the witness Miss Jacobs (exhibits 14, 30, and 51). These letters are signed by Bywaters. I searched the house at 41 Kensington Gardens, and I found a bottle (exhibit 61) in a small drawer in Mr. and Mrs. Thompson's bedroom. It has a label, "Aromatic tincture of opium." I handed the bottle to Mr. Webster, the analyst.

Cross-examined by Sir H. CURTIS BENNETT – Altogether I found 62 letters, including telegrams, and of these 32 have been put in as exhibits in this case. In the different letters there were some 50 enclosures, cuttings from newspapers, referring to a variety of subjects. Of those cuttings about ten referred to cases which were more or less in the public eye at the time. I have with me a list of the names of the cuttings. It includes the following: –

The Poisoned Curate.	Women who Hate all Men.
Curate's Household of Three.	Do Men like Red Haired Women?
Helping the Doctor.	Does Courtship Cost too Much?
The Poisoned Curate.	Do Women Fail as Friends?
Drugs for Brother in Hospital.	Advent of Loveless Women.
Event of the Season.	University Mystery.
Two Women.	False Friendship.
Battle of Calves and Ankles.	An Ideal Love Letter.
Patient killed by Over-dose.	Women on the Rack.
Girl's Drug Injection.	Women who Always Act.
Fuel Control and Love-making.	Girl's Death Riddle.
Holiday Death Pact.	Men and Marriage.
My Sweet Offer.	Masterful men.
Flat Mystery.	Winner Her; Winning Him
Their Married Life.	Asking her twice.
Rather the Devil for a Father.	July Marriages.
Defence in Disputed Baby Case.	The Wedding Season.
Crimes against Love.	Keeping Her.
Chicken Broth Death.	What does She Do with Him?

Poisoned Chocolates.
Do Women Dislike the Truth?
Do not Marry a Genius.
Dangerous Women.
Woman the Consoler.
The Ideal Dance Partner.
The Best Wines that I have drunk.

The little bottle which has been produced, containing aromatic tincture of opium, was found by me in the small drawer in the chest of drawers in the bedroom which was occupied by both Mr. and Mrs. Thompson. I did not see any of Mr. Thompson's collars and ties in that drawer. It contained envelopes, notepaper, photographs, and gloves. I could not say whether it was his drawer or her drawer.

Examination of Richard Sellars

RICHARD SELLARS, examined by Mr. TRAVERS HUMPHREYS – I am a divisional detective inspector of police, K. Division. At 11 a.m. on 4th October I saw Mrs. Thompson at her house, 41 Kensington Gardens, Ilford. I said to her, "I am an inspector of police. I understand you were with your husband early this morning in Belgrave Road. I am satisfied he was assaulted and stabbed several times." She said, "We were coming along Belgrave Road, and just past the corner of Endsleigh Gardens, when I heard him call out, 'Oh-er,' and he fell up against me. I put out my arms to save him, and found blood, which I thought was coming from his mouth. I tried to help him up. He staggered for several yards towards Kensington Gardens, and then fell against the wall and slid down; he did not speak to me. I cannot say if I spoke to him. I felt him, and found his clothing wet with blood. He never moved after he fell. We had no quarrel on the way; we were quite happy together. Immediately I saw blood I ran across the road to a doctor's. I appealed to a lady and gentleman who were passing, and the gentleman also went to the doctor's. The doctor came, and told me my husband was dead. Just before he fell down I was walking on his right hand side, on the inside of the pavement, nearest the wall. We were side by side. I did not see anybody about at the time. My husband and I were talking about going to a dance." At that time Mrs. Thompson was in an agitated condition. About 7 p.m. on the same day I saw the prisoner Bywaters at the Ilford police station, and took possession of the overcoat he was wearing, which is the one now produced. I saw Mrs. Thompson again a little later in the same evening, after she had made her first statement to me, and I afterwards took her to the Ilford police station. I spoke to her again on the next day, 5th October, and asked her if she would give me any further information regarding her husband's assailant. She said, "I will tell you if I possibly can," and she made a voluntary statement which was typewritten, read, and signed (exhibit No. 3). That statement is as follows: –

Statement of Edith Jessie Thompson

EDITH JESSIE THOMPSON, 41 Kensington Gardens, Ilford, age 28, married, states –

My husband's name is Percy Thompson. He is a shipping clerk employed by Messrs. O. J. Parker & Co., Peel House, Eastcheap, E. C.

I am employed by Carlton & Prior, millinery manufacturers, 168 Aldersgate Street, E.C., as a book-keeper. We have been married six years and have no family. We were married in the beginning of the year 1916. In that year my husband joined the London Scottish Regiment, he was discharged as medically unfit a few months later and did no foreign service. I have always been on affectionate terms with my husband. I remember Tuesday, 3rd October 1922. We both went to our respective businesses that day. I met my husband by appointment at a quarter to six, in Aldersgate Street, that day, we went to the Criterion Theatre, we there met my uncle and aunt, Mr. and Mrs. J. Laxton, we left the Theatre about 11 p.m., we all four went to the Piccadilly Circus Tube, we there separated, my husband and I went to Liverpool Street, and we caught the 11.30 train to Ilford, we arrived at Ilford about 12 o'clock, we then proceeded along York Road, Belgrave Road and when we got between De Vere and Endsleigh Gardens, (we were walking on the right hand side) my husband suddenly went into the roadway, I went after him, and he fell up against me, and called out "oo-er." He was staggering, he was bleeding, and I thought that the blood was coming from his mouth. I cannot remember whether I saw anyone else there or not. I know there was none there when he staggered up against me. I got hold of my husband with both hands and assisted him to get up against the wall. He stood there for about a minute or two and then slid down on to the footway, he never spoke, I fell on the ground with him. I cannot remember if I shouted out or not. I got up off the ground and ran along to Courtland Avenue, with the intention of calling Dr. Maudsley, but on the way I met a lady and a gentleman and I said to them something to this effect, "Can I get a doctor or help me, my husband is ill." The gentleman said, "I will go for the doctor." Dr. Maudsley arrived shortly after, although it seemed a long time. The doctor examined my husband and said that he was dead. An ambulance was sent for and the body was removed. I was accompanied to my home by two Police Officers.

I know Freddie Bywaters, I have known him for several years; we were at school together, at least I wasn't but my two brothers were. He is residing with his widowed mother at 11 Westow St., Norwood. He is a ship's writer and periodically goes away to sea. He has been for a very long time on visiting terms with my family. In June, 1921, Bywaters came to reside with my husband and myself at No. 41 Kensington Gardens. He came as a paying guest. I think he paid 25s. or 27s. 6d. per week. He was with us up to the beginning of August, 1921. I remember August Bank Holiday, 1921. My husband and I quarrelled about something, he struck me. I knocked a chair over. Freddie came in and interfered on my behalf. I left the room and I do not know what transpired between them. As far as my recollection goes, Freddie left on the following Friday, but before he left my husband and he were friends again. We have been in the habit of corresponding with one another. His letters to me and mine to him were couched in affectionate terms. I am not in possession of any letters he writes to me. I have destroyed all as is customary with me with all my correspondence. The letters shown to me by Inspector Hall and addressed to Mr. F. Bywaters are some of the letters that I wrote to Freddie, and were written to him without my husband's consent. When he was at home in England, we were in the habit of going out occasionally together without my husband's knowledge. This statement has been read over to me. It is voluntary and it is true.

(Sgd.) EDITH THOMPSON

Examination of Richard Sellars, Continued

After making that statement, Mrs. Thompson and I left the room; I took her to the matron's room. In doing so we passed the library, where Bywaters was detained. She saw him as she passed, and she said, "Oh, God; oh, God, what can I do? Why did he do it? I did not want him to do it." She further said almost immediately after, "I must tell the truth." She was hysterical, and I said, "You realise what you are saying; what you might say may be used in evidence." She then proceeded to make a statement, which again was written down and signed (exhibit No. 4). It is as follows: –

Statement of Edith Thompson

When we got near Endsleigh Gardens a man rushed out from the Gardens and knocked me away and pushed me away from my husband. I was dazed for a moment. When I recovered I saw my husband scuffling with a man. The man whom I know as Freddie Bywaters was running away. He was wearing a blue overcoat and a grey hat. I knew it was him although I did not see his face.

Examination of Richard Sellars, Continued

After taking Bywaters' coat from him, it was examined by Dr. Drought, and after he had examined it I said to Bywaters, "We shall detain you and retain possession of your overcoat." He said, "Why, I know nothing about it." He commenced to speak further, and I said, "If you wish to make a statement, it will be better to put it in writing." I cautioned him, and he made a statement which he signed in my presence (exhibit No. 5).

Statement of Frederick Edward Francis Bywaters

4th October, 1922.

FREDERICK EDWARD FRANCIS BYWATERS, 11 Westow Street, Upper Norwood, aged 20, Laundry Steward, states –

I have known Mr. Percy Thompson for about four years and his wife, Edith, for about 7 years. Mr. Thompson is a shipping clerk; his wife is in a millinery business, and they reside at 41 Kensington Gardens, Ilford. I stayed with them from June 18th, 1921, to the 1st August, 1921. The first week that I was there, I was there as their guest and the remaining weeks I paid 25s. per week. The cause of my leaving was that Mr. Thompson quarrelled with Mrs. Thompson and threw her across the room. I thought it was a very unmanly thing to do and I interfered. We had a quarrel and he asked me to leave, and I left. I had always been exceedingly good friends with Mrs. Thompson. I was also on visiting terms with the mother of Mrs. Thompson, a Mrs. Graydon, who resides with her husband and family at 231 Shakespeare Crescent, Manor Park. After I left Mrs. Thompson I went back to reside with my mother at my present address. On the 7th September, 1921, I got a position as writer on board the s.s. "Morea." I sailed on the 9th September and returned to England the end of the following month. Shortly after I came back from the voyage I called on Mr. and Mrs. Thompson at their address. Mrs. Thompson received me quite friendly, Mr. Thompson a little coldly, but we parted as friends. The same evening I called on Mrs. Graydon and I there again saw Mr. and Mrs. Thompson, who were visiting her. I have never called upon Mr. and Mrs. Thompson since that time. I have met them once or twice at Mrs. Graydon's since, the last time being in June last. Since that date I have never seen Mr. Thompson. I have met Mrs. Thompson on several occasions since and always by appointment. They were verbal appointments. On Monday last I met her by appointment at 12.30 at Aldersgate Street. We went to lunch at the Queen Anne's Restaurant, Cheapside. After lunch she returned to business and I have not seen her since. Mr. Thompson was not aware of all our meetings, but some of them he was. I have known for a very long time past that she had led a very unhappy life with him. This is also known to members of Mrs. Thompson's family. I have written to her on two occasions. I signed the letters Freddie and I addressed her as "Dear Edie." On the evening of Monday, 2nd October, I called on Mrs. Graydon and stayed there till about 10 o'clock. I never mentioned the fact that I had lunched with Mrs. Thompson that day, and as far as I know Mr. Thompson was not aware of it. I left my home yesterday morning about a quarter to twelve. I was dressed in the same clothes that I am now wearing. I went up West and remained there until the evening. I was alone and never met anyone that I knew. I then went to Mrs. Graydon's, arriving there about 7. I left about 11 o'clock, my impression is that it had gone 11. Before leaving I remember Mrs. Graydon's daughter Avis saying that Percy (Mr. Thompson) had 'phoned her up, and I gathered from the observations she made that he was taking his wife to a theatre that night and that there was other members of the family going. When I left the house I went through Browning Road, into Sibley Grove, to East Ham Railway Station. I booked to Victoria which is my usual custom. I caught a train at 11.30 p.m. and I arrived at Victoria about 12.30 a.m. I then discovered that the last train to Gypsy Hill had gone; it leaves at 12.10 a.m. I had a few pounds in money with me but I decided to walk. I went by way of Vauxhall Road, and Vauxhall Bridge, Kensington, Brixton, turning to the left into Dulwich, and then on to the Crystal Palace, and from there to my address at Upper Norwood, arriving there about 3 a.m. I never noticed either 'bus or tram going in my direction. On arriving home I let myself in with a latchkey and went straight to my bedroom. My mother called out to me. She said. "Is that you, Mick?"

I replied, "Yes," and then went to bed. I got up about 9 a.m. and about 12 I left home with my mother. I left my mother in Paternoster Row about half past two. I stayed in the City till about 5. I then went by train from Mark Lane to East Ham, and from there went on to Mrs. Graydon's, arriving there about six. The first time that I learned that Mr. Thompson had been killed was when I bought a newspaper in Mark Lane before I got into the train to go to East Ham. I am never in the habit of carrying a knife. In fact I have never had one. I never met a single person that I knew from the time that I left Mrs. Graydon's house until I arrived home. Mrs. Thompson has written to me two or three times. I might have received one letter from her at home. The others I have received on board ship. I have destroyed these letters. She used to address me as "Dear Freddie," and signed herself "Peidi." I occupy the back bedroom on the top floor at my address, and that is where I keep all my clothing. When I said that I was dressed in precisely the same clothing yesterday as I am to-day, I meant it to include my undergarments, with the exception of my collar and handkerchief, which are at home.

This statement has been read over to me, is voluntary and is true.

(Sgd.) FREDERICK E. F. BYWATERS

Examination of Richard Sellars, Continued

Having made some further inquiries, I again saw Bywaters on the evening of 5th October, and said to him, "I am going to charge you and Mrs. Thompson with the wilful murder of Percy Thompson." He said, "Why her? Mrs. Thompson was not aware of my movements." I said, "If you wish to say anything, I will take it down in writing." I again cautioned him. He made a statement, which I read to him, and which he signed. It is exhibit No. 6, and it is dated 5th October –

Statement of Frederick Bywaters

FREDERICK BYWATERS states –

I wish to make a voluntary statement. Mrs. Edith Thompson was not aware of my movements on Tuesday night, 3rd October. I left Manor Park at 11 p.m. and proceeded to Ilford. I waited for Mrs. Thompson and her husband. When near Endsleigh Gardens I pushed her to one side, also pushing him further up the street. I said to him, "You have got to separate from your wife." He said, "No." I said, "You will have to." We struggled. I took my knife from my pocket and we fought and he got the worst of it. Mrs. Thompson must have been spellbound for I saw nothing of her during the fight. I ran away through Endsleigh Gardens, through Wanstead, Leytonstone, Stratford; got a taxi at Stratford to Aldgate, walked from there to Fenchurch Street, got another taxi to Thornton Heath. Then walked to Upper Norwood, arriving home about 3 a.m. The reason I fought with Thompson was because he never acted like a man to his wife. He always seemed several degrees lower than a snake. I loved her and I could not go on seeing her leading that life. I did not intend to kill him. I only meant to injure him. I gave him an opportunity of standing up to me as a man but he wouldn't. I have had the knife some time; it was a sheath knife. I threw it down a drain when I was running through Endsleigh Gardens.

Examination of Richard Sellars, Continued

Later the two prisoners were charged with the murder of Percy Thompson. When the charge was made Thompson made no reply, while Bywaters said, "It is wrong, it is wrong." On 12th October I received a ditty box (exhibit No. 8), from Sergeant James. The prisoner Bywaters gave me the key which opened the box. I received from Inspector Page, of New Scotland Yard, and also from Sergeant Hancock a number of letters. Inspector Hall also handed to me three letters written by Bywaters. I have seen Bywaters write, and to the best of my belief exhibits Nos. 14, 30, and 31 are in his handwriting.

Cross-examined by Mr. CECIL WHITELEY – Bywaters was taken to the Ilford police station on the evening of 4th October.

Were you in sole charge of this case, or was there any other officer concerned? – Superintendent Wensley came down, but I was practically in sole charge of it. He was not present with me at every interview I had with Bywaters. He was present with me when Bywaters gave the long statement (exhibit No. 5). He was not present when I took the statement No. 6. When Bywaters was brought to the station in the evening of the 4th Superintendent Wensley and I were there, and we both saw him. We were in the company of Bywaters that evening for about an hour and a half. Practically the whole of that period was occupied by the taking of the statement. There was a typist present in the room.

You do not suggest that this was a statement dictated by Bywaters? – Practically. He wished to make a statement, and I said we would take it down in writing.

No questions asked? – Yes.

Is it not clear from the statement itself that questions were put to him and his answers are incorporated in that statement? – Not wholly, practically. Both Superintendent Wensley and I asked the questions. We left Bywaters about nine o'clock. I do not think either of us saw him again that evening; I do not remember seeing him. I believe he slept in the library that evening. On the next day, 5th October, about 3 p.m., I took a statement from Mrs. Thompson (exhibit No. 3). The second statement of Mrs. Thompson (exhibit No. 4) was taken about half-past four or quarter to five.

Was it before those two statements that Mrs. Thompson saw Bywaters and said, "Why did he do it; I did not want him to do it"? – Yes, after she was returning from the room where she was taken. Superintendent Wensley was not present when she said that. No steps were taken by the police to prevent Mrs. Thompson and Bywaters seeing each other.

It was after Mrs. Thompson had seen Bywaters, and after she had made the statement (exhibit No. 4) that you went back into Bywaters' room and the statement (exhibit No. 6) was taken? – Yes. I wrote it down myself. Before that statement was taken I told him that I was going to charge him and Mrs. Thompson with this crime.

By Mr. JUSTICE SHEARMAN – Did you know by that time that he had seen that she was there too? – Yes.

You told us that she caught sight of him, but nobody has told us that he caught sight of her. Do you know if he did? – I could not say, because my attention was centred on her.

Cross-examination continued – I certainly think that Bywaters did see Mrs. Thompson, but I cannot say positively.

No doubt they had seen one another, and the very first thing he said, directly you said that both of them were going to be charged, was, "Why her? Mrs. Thompson was not aware of my movements"? – Yes.

And when you charged them both together that evening Bywaters said, "It is wrong; it is wrong"? – Yes.

Cross-examined by Sir H. CURTIS BENNETT – I first of all saw Mrs. Thompson at 11 a.m. on 4th October, the morning that Mr. Thompson died, and at that time she made a statement which I noted in my notebook. At that time she had no knowledge, as far as I know, that any inquiries were being made as regards Bywaters. She did not say anything about anybody having knocked her or pushed her aside. After making that statement I asked her to come to the police office, and she was kept there from twelve o'clock on the 4th until the afternoon of the 5th, when I took from her the long statement (exhibit No. 3).

At that time, as far as you know, she had no knowledge that Bywaters was at the station? – I could not say, but I should not think so.

Nobody had told her as far as you know? – No, but I gleaned that she did on account of the letters.

What? – I gleaned that she did on account of the letters. The letters were on the table where we took the statement, and she must have known on account of Bywaters's letters.

By Mr. JUSTICE SHEARMAN – She identified her own letters to Bywaters.

Cross-examination continued – She identified them in the statement (exhibit No. 3). That statement took about an hour and a half. After the statement was taken she had to pass the room where Bywaters was being detained in order to get to the matron's room.

Directly she saw Bywaters there she said this, "Oh, God, oh, God, what can I do? Why did he do it? I did not want him to do it"; and then almost immediately afterwards, "I must tell the truth"? – Yes.

And then it was that, having said "I must tell the truth," you cautioned her, and then she said, "When we got near Endsleigh Gardens a man rushed out from the gardens and knocked me away, pushed me away, from my husband. When I recovered I saw my husband scuffling with a man. The man, who I knew as Freddie Bywaters, was running away. He was wearing a blue overcoat and a grey hat. I knew it was him, although I did not see his face." That is right? – Correct.

So that directly she had in fact seen Bywaters was at the station she made this second statement? – Yes.

Examination of Leonard Williams

LEONARD WILLIAMS, examined by Mr. ROLAND OLIVER – I am a detective of K Division. On 6th October I took the prisoner Bywaters and certain property from Ilford to Stratford Police Court. When at the Court he said, pointing to the property, "Have you a knife there?" I said, "No." He said, "Have they found it?" I said, "I do not think so." He said, "I told them I ran up Endsleigh Gardens, but coming to think of it after I did it I ran forward along Belgrave Road towards Wanstead Park, turning up a road to the right. I am not sure whether it was Kensington Gardens where they lived or the next road. I then crossed over to the left side of the road, and just before I got to the top of Cranbrook Road end I put the knife down a drain; it should be easily found."

Concluding Remarks

The Solicitor General – That will be the case for the Crown.

[The letters, exhibits Nos. 49, 12, 62, 27, 13, 15, 16, 20, 50, 17, 18, 19, 21, 22, 51, 23, 66, 67, 68, 24, 53, 25, 69, 26, 52, 63, 54, 28, 55, 47, 48, 58, 59, 9, 60, 10, 64, 14, 30, 31, were read.]

Sir H. CURTIS BENNETT – The jury, of course, will understand that in addition to those letters there are 33 other ones on which the prosecution do not rely and which are not put in.

[At the conclusion of the case for the Crown, a selection of Edith Thompson's letters to Bywaters and three letters from him to Thompson were read out in open court by Travers Humphreys, one of the junior counsel for the Crown. It is said that his reading of the letters was "not unsympathetic."]

b. Index to selected exhibits

(Letters from Edith Thompson and Frederick Bywaters
put in Evidence at the Trial.)

Exhibit	Date	Page
9	30th September, 1922	200
10	No date	202
12	20th August, 1921	–
13	3rd January, 1922	181
14	1st December, 1921	–
15	10th February, 1922	183
15a	9th February, 1922	184
15b	8th February, 1922	–
15c	5th February, 1922	–
15d	6th February, 1922	–
16	22nd February, 1922	–
17	1st April, 1922	188
18	24th April, 1922	184

Exhibit	Date	Page
19	1st May, 1922	185
20	14th March, 1922	–
20a	10th March, 1922	–
21	15th May, 1922	–
21a	13th May, 1922	–
22	18th May, 1922	–
22a	10th May, 1922	–
22b	6th May, 1922	–
23	23rd May, 1922	–
24	13th June, 1922	189
25	20th June, 1922	192
26	4th July, 1922	195
27	No date	180
28	19th September, 1922	–
30	No date	–
31	No date	–
47 & 48	22nd September, 1922	199
49	11th August, 1922	179
50	No date	–
51	No date	–
52	14th July, 1922	196
53	14th June, 1922	191
54	12th September, 1922	198
55	No date	199
55a	20th September, 1922	199
58 & 59	25th September, 1922	199
60	No date	200
62	No date	–
63	28th August, 1922	198
64	No date	202
66	6th June, 1922	189
67	7th June, 1922	–
68	9th June, 1922	–
69	26th June, 1922	194

c. A selection of Thompson's earlier letters

Exhibit 49:

August 11th, 1921.

Darlingest, – Will you please take these letters back now? I have nowhere to keep them, except a small cash box, I have just bought and I want that for *my own letters only* and I feel scared to death in case anybody else should read them. All the wishes I can possibly send for the very best of luck to-day,

From Peidi.

Exhibit 27:

[Copy]

Envelope – Unaddressed.

Have told you before I put 10/- eh way on 'Welsh Woman' for the M'chester Cup, just because you liked it. I expect you know the result. The favourite won and it (the favourite) was the only horse I really fancied, but as it was only 5 to 2 starting price, I didn't think it was worth the risk and then the dashed thing won.

Darlint, its a good job you are winning some money at cards, for I can't win any at horses.

I have won 14/9 on one race since you have been gone, I've forgotten which one it was.

I've enclosed you several cuttings, please read them darlint, and tell me what you think of them. The one I've marked with a cross I think very true indeed, but I'd like to know what you think about it.

The part about 'a man to lean on' is especially true. Darlint, it was that about you that first made me think of you, in the way I do now. I feel always that were I in any difficulty, I could rely and lean on you. I like to feel that I have you to lean on, of course I dont want to really but its nice to know I can, if I want to. Do you understand? Note the part, 'always think of her first, always be patient and kind, always help her in every way he can, he will have gone a long way to making her love him.'

Such things as wiping up, getting pins for me etc, all counted, darlint. Do you remember the pin incident, on Aug. 1, darlint and the subsequent remark from him 'You like to have someone always tacked on to you to run all your little errands and obey all your little requests.' That was it, darlint, that counted, obeying little requests – such as getting a pin, it was a novelty – he'd never done that . . .

'It is the man who has no right, who generally comforts the woman who has wrongs.' This is also right darlint isn't it? as things are, but darlint, its not always going to be is it? You will have the right soon wont you? Say Yes. . .

The last 2 Fridays I have been to the Waldorf and on the first occasion it was very foggy – all the trains were late, so had a taxi right to the avenue and got to Mother's at 10.20. He wasnt coming for me so I didnt matter much – but I expect they wonder what I do. I have promised to go to the 'Cafe Marguerite' to dinner tonight. Can you guess with whom? God knows why I said Id go, I dont want to a bit especially with him, but it will help to pass some time away, it goes slowly enough in all conscience – I dont seem to care who spends the money, as long as it helps me to dance through the hours. I had the wrong Porridge today, but I dont suppose it will matter, I dont seem to care much either way. You'll probably say I'm careless and I admit I am, but I dont care – do you? I gave way this week (to him I mean,) its the first time since you have been gone. Why do I tell you this? I dont really know myself, I didnt when you were away before, but it seems different this time, then

I was looking forward – but now well I can only go from day to day and week to week until Jan. 7th – then thoughts and all things stop. How have you got on with 'The Guarded Flame.' I expect by now you have it interesting –. I have persevered with 'Felix' and have nearly finished it. Its weird – horrible and filthy – yet I am very interested. You'll have to read it after I have finished. I believe if I read this letter through before I sealed it you'd not receive it darlint, I feel that Id tear it up, it doesn't seem to me that Ive been talking to you at all – just writing to you, but I feel like that today, and I know its rotten because you get this letter for Xmas and it wont be a very nice present will it darlint, but its the best I can do. Perhaps I'll leave this letter open and see how I feel by Wednesday, the last day for posting it.

Darlint, Monday – I recd greetings from you and a note 'I cant write to you' and Ive been expecting to talk to you for a long time I wanted to I wanted you to cheer me up – I feel awful – but I know darlint if you cant well you cant – that's all to be said about it, but I always feel I cant talk to you when I start, but I just say to myself he's here with me, looking at me and listening to what I am saying and it seems to help darlint, couldnt you try and do this, I feel awfully sad and lonely and think how much you would be cheering me up but perhaps you'll think I'm selfish about it all and I suppose I am, but remember when you are thinking badly or hardly of me your letters are the only thing I have in the world and darlint, I havnt even all those.

We had – was it a row – anyway a very heated argument again last night (Sunday). It started through the usual source, I resisted – and he wanted to know why since you went in August I was different – 'had I transferred my affections from him to you.' Darlint it's a great temptation to say 'Yes' but I did not. He said we were cunning, the pair of us and lots of other things that I forget, also that I told lies about not knowing you were coming on that Sat. He said 'Has he written to you since he has been away,' and when I said 'No' he said 'That's another lie.' Of course he cant know for certain, but he surmises you do and Im afraid he'll ring up and ask them to stop anything that comes for me so I must get Jim on my side. You know darlint I am beginning to think I have gone wrong in the way I manage this affair. I think perhaps it would have been better had I acquiesced in everything he said and did or wanted to do. At least it would have disarmed any suspicion he might have and that would have been better if we have to use drastic measures darlint – understand? Anyway so much for him. I'll talk about someone else . . .

Goodbye for now darlint, I'll try and be more cheerful when I write to Marseilles. You say 'Dont worry'– just dance – If I only could.

PEIDI.

Exhibit 13:

Envelope – Mr. F. Bywaters, P.O. R.M.S. "Morea," Plymouth.
[Postmark – London, 3 Jan. 22.]

Darlint, I've felt the beastliest most selfish little wretch that is alive. Here have I been slating you all this trip for not talking to me and I get all those letters from Marseilles darlint, I love them and don't take any notice of me, I know I am selfish – and you ought to know by now, I told you haven't I ? heaps of times. Now what have I got to talk to you about, heaps of things I believe – but the most important thing is, that I love you and am feeling so happy that you are coming back to England, even tho perhaps I am not going to see you – you know best about that darlint, and I am going to leave everything to you – only I would like to help you, can't I. Of course he knows you are due in on the 7th and will be very suspicious of me from then, so I suppose I won't be able to see you – will I? You know darlint, don't have the slightest worrying thoughts about letters as "to be careful I've been cruel" to myself I mean.

Immediately I have received a second letter, I have destroyed the first and when I got the third I destroyed the second and so on, now the only one I have is the "Dear Edie" one written to 41, which I am going to keep. It may be useful, who knows? By the way I had a New Year's card, addressed to me only from "Osborne House, Shanklin."

About the 15th darlint, which will be the 14th as that is the Sat: I am going – *as far as I know,* I have to book the seats this week.

Darlint, I've surrendered to him unconditionally now – do you understand me? I think it the best way to disarm any suspicion, in fact he has several times asked me if I am happy now and I've said "Yes quite" but you know that's not the truth, dont you.

About the photos darlint, I have not seen them, so I don't understand about "waiting for you" please destroy all you don't want and when you come to England, show me what I look like, will you yes, I was glad you promised for me, darlint, as I most certainly should have refused myself and I should have hated myself for refusing all the time. Darlint, I never want to refuse you anything, its lovely for me to feel like that about you, I think by this you can understand how much I love you.

The French phrase darlint, if I can remember rightly was "I cant wait so long, I want time to go faster."

You used iron and I used my heel and its such a long time ago, or seems so, since I asked a question, to which your "I did that" is the answer, that, I have forgotten what my question was. Yes, darlint I did wonder about you and the "Cale" and was nursing all to myself quite an aggrieved feeling against you for not telling me, but your letter explained. I feel glad you didn't transfer, darlint Ive got no special reason for feeling glad – but I am. About the fortune teller – you have never mentioned "March" before darlint, you've said "Early in the New Year," are you gradually sliding up the year to keep my spirits up? darlint, I hope not I'd sooner be sad for ever and know the truth, than have that expectant feeling of buoyancy for a myth.

Darlint I'll do and say *all* and everything you tell me to, about friend, only remember not to do anything that will leave me behind by myself.

About the Stewardess, Im glad you went to the cabin with her, what is it I feel and think about you? I have *someone* to lean on – if I need anyone, and she had too darlint, hadn't she? someone to lean on and help her, even against her own inclinations.

I know I am right? Darlint, I didnt think it fair about the fight altho most people are disgusted with boxing (women I mean) I always tried to look upon it as something strong and big and when you told me about that I thought. If amateurs even do that sort of thing, then professionals must and I felt disappointed.

Thanking you for those greetings darlint, but you wont always be "The man with no right" will you – tell me you wont – shout at me – make me hear and believe darlint, about that "Do you" I believe I felt about the worst I have ever felt when that happened I think when I noticed what I had done I had a conscience prick and felt "I dont care what happens and I dont suppose he does really" but you would care wouldnt you darlint? tell me yes, if I really thought you wouldnt darlint I shouldnt want to die, I just want to go mad.

Why have you never told me what you thought of your own photos darlint, you are a bad bad correspondent really darlint I absolutely refuse to talk to you at all next trip, if you dont mend your ways. Darlint, are you frightened at this – just laugh at me. . .

PEIDI.

Exhibit 15:

Envelope – Mr. F. Bywaters, P. & O. R.M.S. "Morea," Aden.
[Postmark – London, 10th Feb. 22, 2.30 p.m.]

Darlint – You must do something this time – I'm not really impatient – but opportunities come and go by – they have to – because I'm helpless and I think and think and think – perhaps – it will never come again.

I want to tell you about this. On Wednesday we had words – in bed – Oh you know darlint – over that same old subject and he said – it was all through you I'd altered.

I told him if he ever again blamed you to me for any difference there might be in me, I'd leave the house that minute and this is not an idle threat.

He said lots of other things and I bit my lip – so that I shouldn't answer – eventually went to sleep. About 2 A.M. he woke me up and asked for water as he felt ill. I got it for him and asked him what the matter was and this is what he told me – whether its the truth I dont know or whether he did it to frighten me, anyway it didnt. He said – someone he knows in town (not the man I previously told you about) had given him a prescription for a draught for insomnia and he'd had it made up and taken it and it made him ill. He certainly looked ill and his eyes were glassy. I've hunted for the said prescription everywhere and cant find it and asked him what he had done with it and he said the chemist kept it.

I told Avis about the incident only I told her as if it frightened and worried me as I thought perhaps it might be useful at some future time that I had told somebody.

What do you think, darlint. His sister Maggie came in last night and *he told her,* so now there are two witnesses, altho' I wish *he* hadn't told her – but left me to do it.

It would be so easy darlint – if I had things – I do hope I shall.

How about cigarettes?

Have enclosed cuttings of Dr. Wallis's case. It might prove interesting darlint, I want to have you only I love you so much try and help me PEIDI.

Exhibit 15a:

Extract from *Daily Sketch,* 9th February, 1922, page 2, column 1.

With headnote: –
"Curate's Household of Three.
"Mystery of his Death still unsolved.
"Wife and Doctor.
"Woman asked to leave the Court during man's evidence."

"Death from hyoscine poisoning, but how it was administered there is not sufficient evidence to show."

This was the verdict last night at an inquest at Lingfield after remarkable evidence and searching cross-examination.

The three principal figures in the case are –

The Rev. Horace George Bolding (39), curate of Lingfield (Surrey) Parish Church, found dead on his bed in his dressing-gown on January 4. Described by parishioners as "Happy, jovial, one of the best of good fellows, and a regular sport."

Mrs. Bolding, about 35, the widow, who was in London with the only child, a boy, at the time of her husband's death.

Dr. Preston Wallis, a ship's surgeon, who, separated from his wife, had stayed some time with the Boldings, and who was called to the bedroom and found the curate dead.

On page 15, column 3, the report is concluded with the following headnote: –
"Helping the Doctor.
"Why Curate's wife often went about in his Chair.
"Practice that dwindled."

Exhibit 18:

Envelope – Mr. F. Bywaters, P. & O. R.M.S. "Morea," Aden
[Postmarks – London, E.C., Apr. 24, 1922, 5.30 p.m.; Aden, 7 May, 1922.]

I think I'll tell you about the holidays darlint – just what I did – do you want to know? or will you say its all ordinary common place talk – I suppose it is – but after I have discussed the ordinary things, I may be able to really talk to you. On Thursday we left at 1 and I went to the Waldorf to lunch and stayed on until the dance tea – I only danced once – a fox trot – I don't feel a bit like dancing darlint – I think I must be waiting for you. We left the Waldorf at 6.20 and met Avis at 6.30 and went with her to buy a costume – getting home about 9.

On Friday I worked hard all day starting that "Good Old fashioned English housewife's occupation of spring cleaning," not because I liked doing it – or believe in it, but because I had nothing else to do and it helped to pass the time away. I started about 9.30 and went to wash and dress about 20 to 6 – .

Dad took us to the E.H. Palace to the Sunday League Concert in the evening and we stopped the night at 231.

In return for this I booked for us all at Ilford Hippodrome on Saturday. The show was good and a girl – in nurses uniform appearing with Tom Edwards sang "He makes me all fussed up."

Of course Avis remarked about you and the song also Molly was sitting behind us with another girl and a boy – is she affected in her conversation? She was very much on Saturday and I wondered if it was put on for my special benefit.

Avis came back to stay the rest of the holiday with us. Bye the way, we, (she and I) had a cup of tea in bed on Sunday – we always do when she is stopping with us.

Mother and Dad came over to me to dinner – I had plenty to do. On Monday Mr. and Mrs. Birnage came to tea and we all went to the Hippodrome in the evening. Bye the way – what is "Aromatic Tincture of Opium" – Avis drew my attention to a bottle of this sealed in the medicine chest in your room.[4]

I took possession of it and when he missed it and asked me for it – I refused to give it him – he refuses to tell me where he got it and for what reason he wants it – so I shall keep it till I hear from you.

I used the "light bulb" three times but the third time – he found a piece – so I've given it up – until you come home.

Do you remember asking me to get a duplicate of something – . I have done so now.

On Sunday we were arguing about the price of "Cuticura." Avis is quite certain when she bought it, not for herself, (her owns words) it was 10 $\frac{1}{2}$. Mother said when she bought it for you it was 1/- and I said the same.

The remark was passed – "you all in turn seemed to have bought it for him.". . .

Exhibit 19:

Envelope – Mr. F. Bywaters, P. & O. R.M.S. "Morea," Port Said.
[Postmark – London, E.C., May 1, 1922, 6.15 p.m.]

Darlingest Boy I know,

If you were to hear me talk now you would laugh, I'm quite positive and I should be angry – I've got practically no voice at all – just a little very high up, squeak.

It started with a very sore throat and then my voice went – it doesn't hurt now – the throat is better but it sounds so funny. I feel like laughing myself but altho you'd laugh darlint you'd be very kind wouldn't you? and just take care of me. I know you would without asking or you answering – but you can answer because I like to hear you say it.

About those fainting fits darlint, I don't really know what to say to you.

---

4 The room Bywaters had occupied when he lodged with the Thompsons. – Ed.

I'm beginning to think it's the same as before – they always happen 1st thing in the morning – when I'm getting up and I wasn't ill as I should have been last time, altho' I was a little – but not as usual.

What shall I do about it darlint, if it is the same this month – please write and tell me I want to do just what you would like.

I still have the herbs.

"I like her she doesn't swear."

This is what you write – do you like her because she doesn't swear or was that bit an afterthought. I'm wondering what you really think of a girl – any girl – even me who says – damn and a few stronger words sometimes – or don't these words constitute swearing as you hear it.

Of course I was glad you did as you did with her. I should never be glad at any other way darlint, whatever the object or the end in view.

Talking about "Felix" darlint can't say I was disappointed in the end because I didn't expect very much of him. You say you expected him to do a lot for Valevia – I didn't – he was too ordinary – too prosaic to do anything sensational – he'd do anything in the world for her if it hadn't caused comment but when it did – he finished. Do you remember the railway station scene when her husband appeared, and took command of the proceedings. Felix was nowhere and he allowed himself not only to go home, but to be ordered to go home by Mr. Ismay. What were your feelings for Mr. Ismay – did you like him? About the word you starred – I can't say I actually know the meaning of the word only of course I guess but you can tell me darlint I certainly shan't ask anyone else.

Darlint isn't this a mistake "Je suis gache, ma pauvre petite amie." This is how you wrote it.

I was glad you think and feel the same way as I do about the "New Forest." I don't think we're failures in other things and we musn't be in this. We musn't give up as we said. No, we shall have to wait if we fail again. Darlint, Fate can't always turn against us and if it is we must fight it – You and I are strong now We must be stronger. We must learn to be patient. We must have each other darlint. Its meant to be I know I feel it is because I love you such a lot – such a love was not meant to be in vain. It will come right I know one day, if not by our efforts some other way. We'll wait eh darlint, and you'll try and get some money and then we can go away and not worry about anybody or anything. You said it was enough for an elephant. Perhaps it was. But you don't allow for the taste making only a small quantity to be taken. It sounded like a reproach was it meant to be?

Darlint I tried hard – you won't know how hard – because you weren't there to see and I can't tell you all – but I did – I do want you to believe I did for both of us.

You will see by my last letter to you I havn't forgotten the key and I didn't want reminding – I didn't forget that – altho' I did forget something last time didn't I altho it was only small.

We have changed our plans about Llandudno – it is too expensive we are going to Bournemouth July 8th, and while Avis was over last night he asked her to come with us. The suggestion was nothing to do with me – it was his entirely and altho' I wouldn't have suggested such a thing for the world – I'm glad – because if things are still the same and we do go – a third party helps to make you forget that you always lead the existence we do.

Au revoir for the week end darlint.

The mail was in this morning and I read your letter darlint, I cried – I couldn't help it – such a lot it sounded so sad I cried for you I could exactly feel how you were feeling – I've felt like that so often and I know.

I was buoyed up with the hope of the "light bulb" and I used a lot – big pieces too – not powdered – and it has no effect – I quite expected to be able to send that cable – but no – nothing has happened from it and now your letter tells me about the bitter taste again. Oh darlint, I do feel so down and unhappy.

Wouldn't the stuff make small pills coated together with soap and dipped in liquorice powder – like Beechams – try while you're away. Our Boy had to have his thumb operated on because he had a piece of glass in it that's what made me try that method again – but I suppose as you say he is not normal, I know I feel I shall never get him to take a sufficient quantity of anything bitter. No I haven't forgotten the key I told you before.

Darlint two heads are better than one is such a true saying. You tell me not to leave finger marks on the box – do you know I did not think of the box but I did think of the glass or cup whatever was used. I wish I wish oh I wish I could do something.

Darlint, think for me, *do*. I do want to help. If you only knew how helpless and selfish I feel letting you do such a lot for me and I doing nothing for you. If ever we are lucky enough to be happy darling I'll love you such a lot. I always show you how much I love you for all you do for me. Its a terrible feeling darlint to want – really want to give all and everything, and not be able to give a tiny little thing – just thro' circumstances.

You asked me if Deborah described her feelings rightly when she was talking about Kullett making love to her.

Darlingest, boy, I don't think all the feelings can be put on paper because there are not words to describe them. The feeling is one of repugnance, loathing not only of the person but of yourself – and darlint when you think of a man and a woman jointly wrote that book it's not feasible that the words used would be bad enough to express the feelings. The man Author wouldn't allow the woman Author to talk too badly of Kullett – do you think? I still think that nobody can express the feelings – I'm sure I couldn't – but they are there, deeply rooted and can never be plucked out as circumstances now are unless they (the circumstances) change. Did you notice any similarity in 2 girls names in two books that you recently read and the utter dissimilarity in their natures (I don't think I spelt that word rightly) I didn't know that you would be in London a month this time – altho I had a little idea.

That month – I can't bear to think of it a whole four weeks and things the same as they are now. All those days to live thro for just one hour in each.

All that lying and scheming and subterfuge to obtain one little hour in each day – when by right of nature and our love we should be together for all the 24 in every day.

Darlint don't let it be – I can't bear it all this time – the pain gets too heavy to bear – heavier each day – but if things were different what a grand life we should start together. Perhaps we could have that one week I could be ill from shock – More lies – but the last. Eh darlint.

Do experiment with the pills while you are away – please darlint.

No we two – two halves – have not yet come to the end of our tether.

Don't let us.

I'm sorry I've had to use this piece of paper but the pad was empty – I sent the boy for a fresh one and they will have none in until tomorrow.

We have started on the 5th week of your absence now – each week seems longer than the last and each day the length of two.

Do you know darlint that the Saturday I usually have off when you are home is Whit Saturday and I shan't be able to see you nor on the Monday following.

Three whole days – and you so near and yet so far – it musn't be darlint – we musn't let it somehow.

Good bye now darlint I can't write any more. You said you have a lump – so have I in fact its more than a lump now.

Good bye until Marseilles next week. I do always love you and think of you.

PEIDI.

Exhibit 17:

Enclosure in letter, dated 1 April 1922.

Dont keep this piece.

About the Marconigram – do you mean one saying Yes or No, because I shant send it darlint I'm not going to try any more until you come back.

I made up my mind about this last Thursday.

He was telling his Mother etc. the circumstances of my "Sunday morning escapade" and he puts great stress on the fact of the tea tasting bitter "as if something had been put in it" he says. Now I think whatever else I try it in again will still taste bitter – he will recognise it and be more suspicious still and if the quantity is still not successful – it will injure any chance I may have of trying when you come home.

Do you understand?

I thought a lot about what you said of Dan.

Darlint, don't trust him – I don't mean don't *tell* him anything because I know you never would – What I mean is don't let him be suspicious of you regarding that – because if we were successful in the action – darlint circumstances may afterwards make us want many friends – or helpers and we must have no enemies – or even people that know a little too much. Remember the saying, "A little knowledge is a dangerous thing."

Darlint we'll have no one to help us in the world *now* and we musnt make enemies unnecessarily.

He says – to his people – he fought and fought with himself to keep conscious – "I'll never die, except naturally – I'm like a cat with nine lives" he said and detailed to them an occasion when he was young and nearly suffocated by gas fumes.

I wish we had not got electric light – it would be easy.

I'm going to try the glass again occasionally – when it is safe Ive got an electric light globe this time.

d. Thompson's later letters
Exhibit 66:
[COPY TELEGRAM.]
Office of Origin – Barbican, London City. Office Stamp – Tilbury, 6 June, 1922, Essex.
Handed in at 10.36. Received here at 10.52.
To – Bywaters, Steamer Morea, Tilbury Dock.
Failed again perhaps 5 o'clock to-night.

Exhibit 24:
Envelope – Mr. F. Bywaters, P. & O. R.M.S. "Morea," Marseilles, France
[Postmark – London, E.C., 13th June, '22, 4.30 p.m.]
Darlingest Boy,

I'm trying very hard – very very hard to B.B. I know my pal wants me to.

On Thursday – he was on the ottoman at the foot of the bed and said he was dying and wanted to – he had another heart attack – thro me.

Darlint I had to laugh at this because *I knew* it couldn't be a heart attack.

When he saw this had no effect on me – he got up and stormed – I said exactly what you told me to and he replied that he knew thats what I wanted and he wasnt going to give it to me – it would make things far too easy for both of you (meaning you and me) especially for you he said.

He said hed been to 231 and been told you had said you were taking a pal out and it was all a planned affair so was the last Thursday you were home and also Tuesday of last week at Fenchurch Street – he told them at 231 a pal of his saw us and by the description he gave of the man I was with it was you.

That's an awful lie darlint because I told him I went to F St. for Mr. Carlton and saw Booth and spoke to him and I asked him the next day if Booth mentioned me and he said no – nothing at all.

We're both liars he says and you are making me worse and he's going to put a stop to all or any correspondence coming for me at 168. He said "It's useless for you to deny he writes to you – because I know he does" – hence my wire to you regarding G.P.O.

He also says I told him I wrote to you asking you not to see me this time – he knows very well I said last time – but I think he has really persuaded himself I said this time.

I rang Avis yesterday and she said he came down there in a rage and told Dad everything – about all the rows we have had over you – but she did not mention he said anything about the first real one on August 1st – so I suppose he kept that back to suit his own ends Dad said it was a disgraceful thing that you should come between husband and wife and I ought to be ashamed. Darlint I told you this is how they would look at it – they don't understand and they never will any of them.

Dad was going to talk to me Avis said – but I went down and nothing whatever was said by any of them. I told Avis I shd tell them off if they said anything to me I didn't go whining to my people when he did things I didn't approve of and I didnt expect him to – but however nothing was said at all.

Dad said to them "What a scandal if it should get in the papers" so evidently *he* suggested drastic measures to them.

On Friday night I said I was going to sleep in the little room – we had a scuffle – he succeeded in getting into the little room and on to the bed – so I went into the bathroom and stopped there for $^1/_2$ an hr – he went downstairs then and I went into the little room quickly – locked the door and stopped there all night – I shd have continued to do so – but even a little thing like that Fate was against us – because Dad was over on Sat. and asked me if he could stay the night – suggested he should sleep with *him* in the big bed – but Dad would not hear of it – so sooner than make another fuss – I gave in.

On Saturday he told me he was going to break me in somehow – I have always had too much of my own way and he was a model husband – and in future on *Thursdays* the bedroom was to be cleaned out.

He also told me he was going to be master and I was to be his mistress and not half a dozen mens (his words) I dont exactly know how to take this – Darlint, do you know Avis said to me – Miss M'Donald saw you with Freddy last week – of course I denied it – but she described my frock – anyhow it turned out to be on Wed. – so of course it was all right – but you see – we are seen and by people who know us and cant hold their tongues Avis said she was upset because you had gone for good – she said she could hardly realise it. She also said that *he* said at 231 "I thought he was keen on you (Avis) – but now I can see it was a blind to cover his infatuation for Edie."

Darlint its not an infatuation is it? Tell me it isn't.

I don't think theres anything else heaps of little things were said that I cant remember but you can judge what they were – because you know me and *him*.

Im writing a letter to Marseilles darlint – this is only a summary of events.

Exhibit 53:

Envelope – Mr. F. Bywaters, P. & O. R.M.S. "Morea," Marseilles, France.
[Postmark – London, E.C., 14 June, 1922.]

Darlint Pal,

[First paragraphs omitted.]

I wonder how my own pal is feeling – I'm feeling very blue myself – an inactive sort of drifting feeling, that can't be described – I suppose its really reaction – I longing to hear from you next Monday – I hope its a lot.

On our birthday you will be left Aden on your way to Bombay – you'll be thinking of a girl whose best pal you are in England wont you – I'll think of you – all day every little minute – and keep on wishing you success as I cant be – Perhaps you can and as you say you are still hoping darlint – so shall I. Time hangs so dreadfully and just because I want to work it away we are not busy this week and are leaving at five. I suppose we shall thro the Summer now. Darlint, how can you get ptomaine poisoning from a tin of salmon? One of our boys Mother has died with it after being ill only three days.

One year ago today we went for that memorable ride round the island in the char-a-banc do you remember? Last night when I went to bed I kissed you goodnight in my mind because that was the first time you kissed me.

Darlint this month and next are full of remembrances – arnt they?

I went to 49 last night and sat and listened to ailments for about 2 hours – its awfully exhilarating especially when you feel blue. I also had a small row with them. He asked why Graham never came to see us and I said "Why do you ask for him to come round when you know he's not allowed to."

This led to words of course and I was told that neither his mother nor his Father would tell him not to speak to me – my retort was that I knew his Father would not but It would take more than any of them to convince me his mother would not, and I wish to God I didnt have to go there – I feel really bad tempered when I come away.

I was taken faint in the train this morning – I didnt quite go off though – On Saturday I'm going to see a Doctor, I think it is best that I should – I dont like doing these silly things in public places – I've got my costume home – it looks very nice – Im ever so pleased with it – but I dont want to wear it – I wish you would see me in it – what would you like me to do? Next week I'll be writing to the other end of the world to you darlint – I wish you didnt ever have to leave England, even if I didnt see you I should feel happier and safe because you would be near – but the sea and Australia sounds years and years apart, I do so much want my pal to talk to and confide in and my own man to lean upon sometimes . . .

always,
PEIDI.

Exhibit 25:

Envelope – Mr. F. Bywaters, P. & O. R.M.S. "Morea," Sydney, Australia.
[Postmark – London, E.C., June 20, 1922, 1.30 p.m.]

Darlingest *Boy I know*,

This time last year I had won the sweep stake for the Gold Cup, this year I have lost £1: 10/- eh way Kings Idler and the result is Golden Myth at 7 to 1, Flamboyant 20 to 1, and Ballyheron 8 to 1. I'm not going to bet any more – even in horse racing the fates are against me.

You get into Marseilles tonight I wonder how you're feeling darlint, very blue – or not feeling anything at all – just drifting – its hard either way isn't it?

I wish you had taken me with you darlint – I don't think I will be able to stay on here all alone – there seems so much to contend with – so long to "dance" when you'd rather die and all for no definite purpose. Oh I'll pack up now, I can't talk cheerfully – so I shan't talk at all goodnight darlint.

It's Friday now, darlint nearly time to go, I am wondering if you remember what your answer was to me in reply to my "What's the matter" tonight of last year.

I remember quite well – "You know what's the matter, I love you" . . . but you didn't then darlint, because you do now and its different now, isn't it? From then onwards everything has gone wrong with our lives – I don't mean to say it was right before – at least mine wasn't right – but I was quite indifferent to it being either right or wrong and you darlint – you hadn't any of the troubles – or the worries you have now – you were quite free in mind and body – and now through me you are not – darlint I am sorry I shouldn't mind if I could feel that some day I should be able to make up to you for all the unhappiness I have caused in your life – but I can't feel that darlint – I keep on saying to myself that "it will – it shall come right" – but there is no conviction behind it – why can't we see into the future?

When you are not near darlint I wish we had taken the easiest way – I suppose it is because I can't see you – can't have you to hold me and talk to me – because when you are in England I always want to go on trying and trying and not to give up – to see and feel you holding me – is to hope on, and when I can't have that I feel a coward. The days pass – no they don't pass, they just drag on and on and the end of all this misery and unhappiness is no nearer in sight – is anything worth living for?

There are 2 halves in this world who want nothing on earth but to be joined together and circumstances persistently keep them apart – nothing is fair – nothing is just – we can't even live for ourselves – can we?

I suppose the week end will pass somehow – the only thought that helps is that you will talk to me on Monday.

Goodbye darlingest boy – I do wish you were here.

Its Monday now darlint, that day you came up and took me to lunch at the Kings Hall do you remember?

Things are very quiet here and Mr. Carlton has taken 2 or 3 days off this week. He told me he would come up about Thursday – to fix up the outing on Saturday – that was the day last year that you and Avis came to an understanding – I wonder if that's the right way to put it.

Nothing happened over the week end darlint except that Dad came up on Saturday and did not go home in the evening. It's becoming a regular thing now – I wonder why?

When you are in Australia – darlint you will tell me all you do and where you go – everything – I want to know.

I shall be in Bournemouth when you're in Australia think about me darlingest boy – it won't be the holiday I anticipated will it? I certainly shant learn to swim neither shall I be playing tennis it won't be nice at all – because I shan't even be able to escape things and beings by going up to town each day – but it's one of those things that have to be gone thro in this life I lead and all the railings against it won't alter a tiny bit of it – so I must dance thro somehow. Are you going to see Harold? if you do, try and knock a bit of sense into him please darlint pour moi and write and tell me what he is doing, – how is he getting on – everything – he writes such nonsense that you can't tell from a letter what he really is doing. He's written to Doris Grafton and tells her, he is sending over her passage money and she is to come out and marry him – and a lot more of rot like that – darlint I'm sure he's not normal sometimes.

See what my pal can do for me, please.

Won't you have a long time to wait for a letter from me this time, Darlint? I have been looking at the mail card and see you do not arrive in Australia until July 22nd – I'm so sorry – I wish I could afford to cable you a long long letter to somewhere before Sydney, or better still, to be able to phone to you and hear you say "Is that Peidi?"

I went to see a doctor on Saturday he asked me lots of questions – could he examine me etc – I said no – then he said are you enciente? to which I replied "No, I think not," but explained to him how I felt. Eventually he came to the conclusion that I have "chronic anaemia" – which will probably turn to pernicious anaemia if I am not careful.

I asked him exactly what this was and he said, "all your blood every drop turns to water."

I also asked him if it was a usual thing for any one to have and he said "No" only much older people suffer with it; as a rule – only younger people, when they have had an accident and lost a lot of blood, have you had one? he said.

I said "No" – because it wasn't really an accident and I didn't want to tell him everything – he might have wanted to see my husband.

But I expect thats what has really caused this anaemia – because I lost an awful lot of blood.

The doctor says I must drink Burgundy with every meal – 4 glasses a day – I don't know how I am going to do that – I hate the stuff.

He has given me some medicine as well and a box of pills to be taken until I am ill. Darlint are you disappointed it is only that? tell me please.

I've just come back from getting the Marseilles Mail at the G.P.O.

What an utterly absurd thing to say to me "Don't be too disappointed."

You can't possibly know what it feels like to want and wait each day – every little hour – for something – something that means "life" to you and then not to get it.

You told me from Dover that you were going to talk to me for a long time at Marseilles and now you put it off to Port Said.

You force me to conclude that the life you lead away from England – is all absorbing that you havn't time nor inclination to remember England or anything England holds.

There were at least 5 days you could have talked to me about – if you only spared me 5 minutes out of each day. But what is the use of me saying all this – it's the same always – I'm never meant to have anything I expect or want. If I am unjust – I am sorry – but I can't feel anything at present – only just as if I have had a blow on the head and I am stunned – the disappointment – no, more than that – the utter despair is too much to bear – I would sooner go under today than anything.

All I can hope is, that you will never never feel like I do today – *it's so easy to write* "try to be brave" its so much harder to be so, nobody knows – but those who try to be – against such heavy odds.

It's more to me than anything on this earth – to read what you say to me – you know this darlint, why do you fail me? What encouragement is it to go on living and waiting and waiting.

Perhaps I ought not to have written this – perhaps I ought to have ignored having a scrap only, altogether – but how I feel and what I think I must tell you always.

Darlint I hope you will never never never feel as miserable as

PEIDI.

Exhibit 69:

[COPY MARCONIGRAM.]

Deld. Date: 26 June, 1922.

No. 2   MOREA.   26 Jun. 1922.

      P   7

Handed in at: London. 13.35.

V.W.B. 10/2 A.G.S.

Via Eastern Radio – 26th.

To – BYWATERS, Steamer Morea, Bombay radio.

M H R 27621 PEIDI.

Exhibit 26:

Envelope – Mr. F. Bywaters, P. & O. R.M.S. "Morea," Freemantle, Australia.
[Postmark – London, E.C., 4 July, 1922.]

Darlingest Boy

First of all last Sunday week a lady I don't know her name – we all call her "2 jam pots high" asked after – "that nice curly headed boy." We met her in Ilford in the evening – I said when I last saw you – you were quite well. I wasn't by myself Darlint – *he* was with me.

I felt quite jealous that she should remember you all this time. Then last Wednesday I met your mother and she cut me. I wasn't prepared for it either – I saw her coming towards me and thought "as she spoke to me last time we met that there is no reason why she shouldn't this time." And as she came up I just smiled, bowed, said "How do you do" – she just took no notice whatever and walked on. I can't explain how I felt – I think I wanted to hit her more than anything – things get worse and worse – instead of just a tiny bit better each day.

On Thursday afternoon I went to the G.P.O. for the Port Said Mail and encountered the first man that I saw before – he handed me a registered envelope from you (which contained the garters – thank you very much darlint) and told me if I had an address in London I couldn't have letters addressed to the G.P.O. – I told him I hadn't – but I don't think he believed me anyway he didnt give me your Port Said letter and I hadnt the patience to overcome (or try to) his bad temper.

I went again on Monday and got it a different man was on duty – when I read it – I didnt feel very satisfied darlint it didnt seem worth waiting all that time for – 24 days – however I wont talk about it – you ought to know by now how I feel about those things.

In one part of it you say you are going to still write to me because it will help, in another part you say – "Perhaps I shant write to you from some ports – because I want to help you." I dont understand – I try to – but I cant – really I cant darling – my head aches – aches with thinking sometimes.

Last Friday last year – we went to see "Romance" – *then* we were pals and this year we seem no further advanced.

Why arnt you sending me something – I wanted you to – you never do what I ask you darlint – you still have your own way always – If I don't mind the risk why should you? whatever happens cant be any more than this existence – looking forward to nothing and gaining only ashes and dust and bitterness.

I'm not going to ask dad about you at all – I not going to say anything to anybody – they can all think the worst of me that is possible – I am quite indifferent.

Miss Prior is on holiday and the only person in this world that is nice to me is Mr. Carlton – I have had 2 half days off and am having another to-morrow afternoon – all this time off makes me think of last year – when you were with me – rushing home to see you.

I've had a brandy and soda some mornings – about 11-30 and a half bottle of champagne between us – other mornings and I learn such a lot of things that are interesting too.

This morning on the station I saw Molly – talking and laughing with Mr. Derry – in case you dont remember the name – it's the little man in the "White Horse."

I've never seen her talk to him before altho she has passed me on the platform talking to him several times (me talking to him I mean) I bowed – said good morning to him as I passed and have since been wondering if they have told each other what they know about me.

Never mind, a little more bad feeling cant hurt – there is such a lot of it to contend with will you tell me if youd rather I didnt write?

PEIDI.

Have you studied "Bichloride of Mercury"?

Exhibit 52:

Envelope – Mr. F. Bywaters, P. & O. R.M.S. "Morea," Colombo.
[Postmark – London, W.1., July 14, 1922, 7.15 p.m.]

Darlingest boy – you worry me so much – what do you mean you say "I want to be in England to look after you." I can understand that and I want you to be here also – but you then say "I want you to look after me too"... Whats the matter darlint, are you ill? is anything the matter that I could help you in at all. I do believe youve been ill – oh darlint why are you such miles away – why arent we together – so that I could help you. Would you like a pillow? the pillow that only Peidie can give you – Id love to have you here now so that I could give it you. Do tell me whats the matter darlingest boy – I shall worry and worry all the time until you write and tell me. Its Thursday and Ive just come from the G.P.O. with the Aden mail. Isnt it late this time darlint it's usually in on a Monday or at latest Tuesday. However Ive got it and thats all that really matters Darlingest boy didnt I say a long time ago "Dont trust Dan." Of course I didnt mean that in the sense you have told me he couldnt be trusted in but my instinct was right wasnt it? You will be careful wont you darlint pour moi? I dont want to ever know or think that my own boy is in any predicament of that sort – because Ill be too far away to help wont I? The thought of anything like that makes my blood cold – Ill be always worrying. Im writing this letter rather early to Colombo – because Im going away tomorrow and I shant have an opportunity of writing to you again for a fortnight. Perhaps I could manage a letter card tho anyway you'll understand wont you darlint pal? I dont mind a bit pencil as long as its words on paper – it doesn't matter – because they're what you say and think and do – a letter darlint is like food only you have food everyday to keep you alive and I have a letter every how many days? 14 sometimes and I have to keep alive on that all that time. About Bella Donna – no I dont agree with you about her darlint – I hate her – hate to think of her – I dont think other people made her what she was – that sensual pleasure loving greedy Bella Donna was always there. If she had originally been different – a good man like Nigel would have altered her darlint – she never knew what it was to be denied anything – she never knew "goodness" as you and I know it – she was never interested in a good man – or any man unless he could appease her sensual nature. I don't think she could have been happy with nothing – except Baroudi on a desert island she liked – no loved and lived for his money or what it could give her – the luxury of his yacht the secrecy with which he acted all bought with his money – that's what she liked.

Yes she was clever – I admire the cleverness – but she was cunning there is a difference darlint, I don't admire that – I certainly don't think she would ever have killed Nigel with her hands – she would have been found out – she didn't like that did she? being found out – it was that secret cunning in Baroudi that she admired so much – the cunning that matched her own.

If she had loved Baroudi enough she could have gone to him – but she liked the security of being Nigel's wife – for the monetary assets it held.

She doesn't seem a woman to me – she seems abnormal – a monster utterly selfish and self living.

Darlint this is where we differ about women.

I usually stand up for them *against* you and in this case its the reverse but honestly darlint I dont call her a woman – she is absolutely unnatural in every sense.

You do say silly things to me – 'try a little bit every day not to think about me – doesn't that 'trying' ever make it worse – it does for me always.

About the 'age' passages in 'The Fruitful Vine' – I marked them because as I read they struck me as concerning you and I.

Darlint I didn't do it with malice every passage in any book I read that strikes me as concerning 2 pals I mark – it doesn't matter what they are about.

I hadn't mentioned the subject any more had I?

My veriest own lover I always think about the 'difference' when I'm with you and when I'm away sometimes when I'm happy for a little while I forget – but I always remember very soon – perhaps some little thing that you might say or do when we're together reminds me. Sometimes I think and think until my brain goes round and round. 'Shall I always be able to keep you.' 8 years is such a long time – it's not now – it's later – when I'm 'Joan' and you're not grown old enough to be 'Darby.' When you've got something that you've never had before and something that you're so happy to have found – you're always afraid of it flying away – that's how I feel about your love.

Don't ever take your love away from me darlint – I never want to lose it and live.

If it gets less and gradually fades away – don't let me live to feel without it. It feels a bigger fuller greater love that I have for my own and only lover now.

PEIDI.

Exhibit 63:

Envelope – Mr. F. Bywaters, P.O., R.M.S. "Morea," Port Said.

[1^1/$_2$d. stamp – London, E.C., Aug. 28, 6.15 p.m., 1922.]

Darlingest boy, today is the 27th and its on a Sunday, so I am writing this in the bathroom, I always like to send you greetings on the day – not the day before or the day after.

Fourteen whole months have gone by now, darlint, its so terribly long. Neither you nor I thought we should have to wait all that long time did we? although I said I would wait 5 years – and I will darlint – its only 3 years and ten months now.

Many happy returns and good luck darlingest boy – I cant wish you any more can I? every day I say 'Good luck to my Pal' to myself.

PEIDI.

Exhibit 54:

Envelope – Mr. F. Bywaters, P. & O. R.M.S. "Morea," Marseilles, France.

[Postmark – London, E.C., Sept. 12, 1922, 5.30 p.m.]

Darlint Pal,

I've got nothing to talk to you about – I can't think about anything at all – I can't even look forward to seeing you. Now you are nearing England – I keep contrasting this home coming with the previous ones. I have been buoyed up with hope, bubbling with excitement Just existing with an intense strung up feeling of seeing you and feeling you holding me in your two arms so tightly that it hurts but this time everything seems different. I don't hear from you much you don't talk to me by letter and help me and I don't even know if I am going to see you.

Darlint, I'm an awful little beast I know – I don't want to be either – but I feel so hopeless – just drifting – but if you say 'No I won't see you' then it shall be so, I'm quite reconciled to whatever verdict you send forth and shall say to myself 'It is for the best it must be so.'

Darlint you do love me still tho' don't you? and you will go on loving me even if we don't meet. Things here are going smoothly with me – I am giving all – and accepting everything and I think am looked upon as 'The Dutiful Wife' whose spirit is at last bent to the will of her husband.'

This isn't sarcasm or cynicism its exactly how I feel. I had a little letter from you – by what you said it was written on the 28th of July Ive had nothing – further there are heaps and heaps of questions in my letters to you.

I wonder if you will answer them, or are they already *dismissed*? On Saturday I was so ill. I had to stop away – its not very often I give in so much as stopping away from business but on Saturday I really had to I'm quite alright now tho' darlint.

I don't think I told you I bought a fur coat – at least part of it. It was 27 gns. and I had £13 saved up – so I borrowed £15 from the account and am paying it back at £1 per week – the debt is only £10 now.

Also I've had to fall back on wearing lace shoes – no don't make a face darlint, they are rather nice ones – I wanted grey and could get nothing at all in my usual style – only with one or two straps across – and I don't like these – even if they hid my foot I shouldn't – they look loud, so I bought lace ones, only to wear with cloth clothes tho' darlint – not with silk.

Yesterday you were at Suez – I suppose you got my Port Said letters there and on Friday or Saturday, you will get these – I think the mail facilities favour you more than me darlint.

Darlingest pal – do let me hear an awful lot from you next week – I'm just existing now – I shall live then.

Darlingest, only lover of mine – try to cheer me up.

PEIDI.

Exhibit 55:

Darlint Pal, please try and use-pour moi, and dont buy a pouch, je vais, pour vous – one of these days.

(ad) PEIDI–

Exhibit 55a:

Extract from *Daily Sketch*, 20th September, 1922, page 2, column 4.
With headnote –

"Chicken Broth Death."
"Rat Poison Consumed by Fowl Kills Woman."

The report states –

"That death was due to consuming broth made from a chicken which had eaten poison, containing a rat virus, was the medical explanation at the resumed inquest at Shoreditch yesterday on Mrs. Sarah Feldman (34) of Reliance Square, Horton."

Exhibits 47 and 48:

[TELEGRAM.]
Office of Origin – London City, S. Office Stamp – Tilbury,
Essex, 25 Sep. 22.
Handed in at 9.28. Received here at 9.48

To – Reply Paid Bywaters Steamer Morea, Tilbury Dock.

Can you meet Peidi Broadway 4 p.m.
Envelope addressed – Bywaters, s.s. "Morea." Reply Pd.

Exhibits 58 and 59:

[TELEGRAM.]
Office of Origin – London City, S. Office Stamp – Tilbury,
Essex, 25 Sep. 22.
Handed in at 10.3 a.m. Received here at 10.16 a.m.

To – Bywaters, Steamer Morea, Tilbury Docks.

Must catch 5.49 Fenchurch Reply if can manage.

Exhibit 9:

[ORDER.]

From Carlton and Prior,
168 Aldergate Street,
London, E.C.1.

September 30, 1922.

Come in for me in $\frac{1}{2}$ an hour.

PEIDI.

Exhibit 60:

Plain envelope.

Darlingest lover of mine, thank you, thank you, oh thank you a thousand times for Friday – it was lovely – its always lovely to go out with you.

And then Saturday – yes I did feel happy – I didn't think a teeny bit about anything in this world, except being with you – and all Saturday evening I was thinking about you – I was just with you in a big arm chair in front of a great big fire feeling all the time how much I had won – cos I have darlint, won such a lot – it feels such a great big thing to me sometimes-that I can't breathe.

When you are away and I see girls with men walking along together – perhaps they are acknowledged sweethearts – they look so ordinary then I feel proud – so proud to think and feel that you are my lover and even tho' not acknowledged I can still hold you – just with a tiny 'hope.'

Darlint, we've said we'll always be Pals haven't we, shall we say we'll always be lovers – even tho' secret ones, or is it (this great big love) a thing we can't control – dare we say that – I think I will dare. Yes I will 'I'll always love you' – if you are dead – if you have left me even if you don't still love me, I always shall you.

Your love to me is new, it is something different, it is my life and if things should go badly with us, I shall always have this past year to look back upon and feel that 'Then I lived' I never did before and I never shall again.

Darlingest lover, what happened last night? I don't know myself I only know how I felt – no not really how I felt but how I could feel – if time and circumstances were different.

It seems like a great welling up of love – of feeling – of inertia, just as if I am wax in your hands – to do with as you will and I feel that if you do as you wish I shall be happy, its physical purely and I can't really describe it – but you will understand darlint wont you? You said you knew it would be like this one day – if it hadn't would you have been disappointed. Darlingest when you are rough, I go dead – try not to be please.

The book is lovely – it's going to be sad darlint tho', why can't life go on happy always?

I like Clarie – she is so natural so unworldly.

Why ar'nt you an artist and I as she is – I feel when I am reading frightfully jealous of her – its a picture darlint, just how I did once picture that little flat in Chelsea – why can't he go on loving her always – why are men different – I am right when I say that love to a man is a thing apart from his life – but to a woman it is her whole existence.

———————————

I tried so hard to find a way out of tonight darlingest but he was suspicious and still is – I suppose we must make a study of this deceit for some time longer. I hate it. I hate every lie I have to tell to see you – because lies seem such small mean things to attain such an object as ours. We ought to be able to use great big things for great big love like ours. I'd love to be able to say 'I'm going to see my lover tonight.' If I did he would prevent me – there would be scenes and he would come to 168 and interfere and I couldn't bear that – I could be beaten all over at home and still be defiant – but at 168 it's different. It's my living – you wouldn't let me live on him would you and I shouldn't want to – darlint its funds that are our stumbling block – until we have those we can do nothing. Darlingest find me a job abroad. I'll go tomorrow and not say I was going to a soul and not have one little regret. I said I wouldn't think – that I'd try to forget – circumstances – Pal, help me to forget again – I have succeeded up to now – but its thinking of tonight and tomorrow when I can't see you and feel you holding me.

Darlint – do something tomorrow night will you? something to make you forget. I'll be hurt I know, but I want you to hurt me – I do really – the bargain now, seems so one sided – so unfair – but how can I alter it?

———————————

About the watch – I didn't think you thought more of that – how can I explain what I did feel? I felt that we had parted – you weren't going to see me – I had given you something to remind you of me and I had purposely retained it. If I said "come for it" you would – but only the once and it would be as a pal, because you would want me so badly at times – that the watch would help you not to feel so badly and if you hadn't got it – the feeling would be so great – it would conquer you against your will.

Darlint do I flatter myself when I think you think more of the watch than of anything else. That wasn't a present – that was something you asked me to give you – when we decided to be *pals* a sort of sealing of the compact. I couldn't afford it then, but immediately I could I did. Do you remember when and where we were when you asked me for it? If you do tell me, if you don't, forget I asked.

How I thought you would feel about the watch, I would feel about something I have.

It isn't mine, but it belongs to us and unless we were differently situated than we are now, I would follow you everywhere – until you gave it to me back.

He's still well – he's going to gaze all day long at you in your temporary home – after Wednesday.

———————————

Don't forget what we talked in the Tea Room, I'll still risk and try if you will – we only have $3^3/_4$ years left darlingest.

Try & help

PEIDI.

Exhibit 10:

[ORDER.]

From Carlton and Prior,
168 Aldersgate Street,
London, E.C.1.

————19.

Wait till one he's come.

PEIDI.

Exhibit 64:

Plain envelope.

Darlingest boy, thank you –

I know what you say is really true, but darlint it does feel sometimes that we are drifting. Don't you ever feel like that – and it hurts so – of ever so much.

Yes, we are both going to fight until we win – darlint, fight hard, in real earnest – you are going to help me first and then I am going to help you and when you have done your share and I have done mine we shall have given to each other what we both "desire most in this world" ourselves, isn't this right, but darlint don't fail in your share of the bargain, because I am helpless without your help – you understand.

Darlint, this is the one instance in which I cannot stand alone I cannot help myself (at first) – the one instance when I want a man to lean on and that one man is and can only – always – be you.

Please, please darlint take me seriously – I want you to – I wanted you to before and you didn't. Tell me when you see me next time that you will darlint, *for certain,* remember Peidi is relying on *you* and *you* understand me and know I mean what I say and tell me you know I *wont fail* or *shirk* when the time or opportunity comes.

———————————

Darlint you say you are looking forward to Thursday night, is this really true? somehow I feel it isnt, I have done ever since the 9th and when I think about it I feel more so about it. You have not asked me all the time you've been home to go with you – except to a dance – which I refused – because I want to wait for that time – that *first dance* until it will be a real pleasure, *without* any pain and it can't be just now darlint can it? and when you said you'd take me to lunch and then didn't come and I'm wondering – I can't help it darlint if I've done right in asking you to take me out. And apart from this feeling that I have, there is that ever present question of money – darlint you've never told me this time once about money – what you had and what you spent and I felt hurt – horribly darlint, especially about the suit – last time you told me about the coat – but not this time – why the difference darlint?

And as I haven't any money to give you, at least not much and perhaps you havn't any I wish you weren't going to take me out darlint and even now its not too late – if you'd only tell me, be quite frank about it darlint, I'll understand – surely you know I will. I didn't intend to mention this darlint, but neither you nor I must harbour thoughts that each other doesn't know, must we, we must be one in thoughts and wishes and actions always darlint, so I have. Please understand how I feel and know I love you.

PEIDI.

[Bywaters' letters omitted]

4. Evidence from the trial: the Defence

a. **Extracts from cross-examination of Bywaters**

Did you then tell him that you were in love with his wife? – No.

Did you suggest any grounds upon which either she or he was to obtain a divorce? – No.

Was divorce mentioned? – Divorce or separation was mentioned.

Were you not at this time attempting to keep back from him all suspicion as to your relations with Mrs. Thompson? – No, I was not attempting to keep it back.

Did you ever tell him up to that time? – No.

Had you and Mrs. Thompson at that time spoken about suicide? – Yes.

Do you remember when that proposal was abandoned? – Abandoned? Yes. Was it abandoned? – Yes, the pact of suicide was abandoned.

It is referred to in exhibit No. 62, the letter of 18th November, 1921 –

All I could think about last night was that compact we made. Shall we have to carry it thro'?

Was that pact of suicide abandoned after that letter? – I never really considered it seriously.

May we take it from that time forward there was no more thought of the suicide pact? – Oh yes, there was; it was mentioned.

But not really entertained by you? – No.

Do you say from that time forward the only idea in your mind or hers was divorce or separation? – Or suicide on her part.

But the suicide, I put to you, after that letter was not seriously entertained? – Not by me, but by her it was.

Except for the suicide on her part you say that you or she only contemplated separation or divorce? – That is true, or me to take her away.

Was the removal of her husband ever mentioned by her to you? – No.

Never? – Never.

Did it ever occur to you that that was a way in which you and she might come together? – No.

Did her letters suggest it to you? – No.

Did you tell your learned counsel that you read her letters as melodrama? – Some.

What was it you understand as melodrama? – She had a vivid way of declaring herself; she would read a book and imagine herself as the character in the book.

Do you mean that you read her references to poison as melodrama? – Some as melodrama; some as general knowledge.

General knowledge? – Yes.

I don't understand that. What did you understand when she mentioned a particular poison? – To what are you referring?

Are you aware, or do you remember, that she mentioned several times a poison in her letters? – Yes.

Did that suggest to you a dose of poison might kill her husband? – No.

It did not occur to you? – No.

Did you not read those letters as meaning that the idea was in her mind? – No.

Did she ever make an actual proposal to you that you and she might go off together? – Yes.

When did she first make it? – I suppose it was about the November when I came home.

Did you agree to the proposal or did you reject it? – I said, "Wait and see what happens."

What were you going to wait for? – To see if she could get a separation or divorce.

And how long were you going to wait? – A period of five years.

Did you ever mean to do anything to make a divorce possible? – No.

You had no intention of taking any action? – No.

Will you turn to the letter of 1st April, exhibit No. 17. "I thought a lot about what you said of Dan"? – I had told Mrs. Thompson about a friend of mine named Dan.

That is all you had told her? – I told her of some of his business that he had told me. I had not told him anything about myself and Mrs. Thompson.

Then will you follow while I read –

> Darlint, don't trust him – I don't mean don't tell him anything because I know you never would – what I mean is don't let him be suspicious of you regarding that – because if we were successful in the action – darlint circumstances may afterwards make us want many friends – or helpers and we must have no enemies – or even people that know a little too much. Remember the saying "A little knowledge is a dangerous thing."

What was "the action" that she there refers to? – Suicide, as far as I remember.

But, Bywaters, read it again. What does "the action" mean? – Mrs. Thompson had proposed to me that she did not want to make my life as unhappy as hers. She said she would sooner kill herself.

Do you really suggest that "the action" means suicide? – As far as I remember, yes, it means suicide.

Are you quite clear it does not mean crime? – I am positive of that.

I am coming back to that letter. Look now at exhibit No. 50. This is written before 31st March and you had been home for about a fortnight at the end of January and again for a few days at the end of March? – Yes

Read what Mrs. Thompson says in that letter –

> This time really will be the last time you will go away – like things are, won't it? We said it before darlint I know and we failed – but there will be no failure this next time darlint, there mustn't be.

Had there been a failure? – Yes.

What had you tried that had failed? – Separation or divorce.

Does it occur to you what was the best way to get a divorce if that was all you wanted? – Yes, I know the best way of getting a divorce.

What was the best way of getting a divorce for Mrs. Thompson from her husband? – To provide Mr. Thompson with the information he needed.

Why did you not try? – Because he would not accept.

Did you provide him with the information? – She had.

Had she provided him with the information to enable him to get a divorce? – She said she would provide him with the information to get a divorce.

Had she tried to give him the information to get a divorce? – She said she would do it.

My question was had she tried to get a divorce from her husband? – She had suggested to him she wanted a divorce, and she would provide him with the information he required if he would come to terms.

I suggest to you that "failure" there refers to the same thing as "action" in the other letter – that Mrs. Thompson had tried to poison her husband and had failed? – And I say that that is not true.

What you say is that it refers to information or a statement she had thought of making to her husband to make him divorce her? – Yes, or separation.

Were you and she really anxious that he should know that you and Mrs. Thompson were lovers? – He did know.

From what time did he know? – I do not know he exactly knew we were lovers. He knew we were fond of each other.

Did you not do your best to keep it from him from start to finish? – Oh no.

Will you turn to the letter of 3rd January, 1922, exhibit No. 13 –

> Immediately I have received a second letter, I have destroyed the first and when I got the third I destroyed the second and so on, now the only one I have is the "Dear Edie" one written to 41, which I'm going to keep. It may be useful, who knows?

Was that the letter of 1st December, exhibit 14, beginning "Dear Edie" and signed "Yours very sincerely, Freddy"? – Yes.

Was that the customary way in which you wrote to Mrs. Thompson at that time? – No.

Was that letter written in that form in order to disarm suspicion? – No.

Did you understand from the passage I have just read from the letter of 3rd January that she was going to use that letter to disarm suspicion? – No.

Did you understand what was meant when she said "It may be useful – who knows"? – I do not know.

Would the letter be any use to get a divorce or separation? – I think that she is referring to the latter.

I take it you would agree with me the letter would not be useful for that purpose? – I do not agree with you. I never said that.

You do not follow me. You agree with me that that letter which says "Dear Edie," and finishes "Yours very sincerely" would be of no use to enable either her or you to get a divorce? – That letter was not meant to be a means of getting a divorce. It was a letter conveying Christmas greetings.

Did you understand what she meant when she said "This letter may be useful; I will keep it?" – She may have kept this to show to her sister Avis; that was one of the reasons that I wrote it.

Then you did write it to blind somebody? – Oh yes.

Did the subject of poisons ever occur in your conversations with her when you were at home? – Sometimes.

In what connection? – General conversation; knowledge.

Who mentioned poisons? – If she had been reading anything and poison was mentioned, and any matter that she would not understand, she would ask me what it meant.

Did you know anything about poison? – I did not know very much.

Did she appear to be interested in poison? – No, not particularly.

Did it ever strike you it occupied a prominent place in her mind? – No more than other things.

Did you take an interest in poison? – I was fond of chemistry when I was at school.

But chemistry and poison are two different things? – Poisons deal with chemistry. Poisons come in chemistry.

Did you take any interest in poisons as poisons? – No.

Did you keep up your interest which you say you had in chemistry? – No, I did not. She knew of that interest, though; her brother used to join me.

Do you suggest then that the mention of poison in your conversation and in your letters was due to the fact that she knew you were interested in chemistry? Is that your explanation? – No, my explanation is this: if she had been reading something and it occurred to her, if I had been in her presence she would have asked me what it was. If I was not there, she put it in writing.

Do you remember a document which you wrote out containing the troy weights, exhibit 57? "60 milligrams= 1 grain, 18 grains= 1 gramme, 30 grammes= 1 oz." Is that your handwriting? – Yes.

When did you write it? – I could not say.

Why did you keep it? – Because it is useful in general knowledge.

Had that any connection with the request she made to you to experiment with pills? – Oh no.

Turn back to the letter of 1st April, exhibit No. 17, and listen to this paragraph –

He was telling his Mother etc. the circumstances of my 'Sunday morning escapade' and he puts great stress on the fact of the tea tasting bitter 'as if something had been put in it' he says. Now I think whatever else I try it in again will still taste bitter – he will recognise it and be more suspicious still and if the quantity is still not successful it will injure any chance I may have of trying when you come home. Do you understand?

What did you understand about that passage? – That she had taken the quinine and it tasted bitter.

Look at it again –

He puts great stress on the fact of the tea tasting bitter 'as if something had been put in it' he says.

To whom did it taste bitter? – Mrs. Thompson.

Do you suggest that, Bywaters? – I do.

Do you suggest that is how you understood the letter when you received it? – I do.

Now I think whatever else I try it in again will still taste bitter – he will recognise it and be more suspicious still.

Do you still adhere to what you say, that she is speaking of her taste? – Yes.

What did you understand him to be suspicious of? – That she was attempting to commit suicide.

Did you understand her to mean that she would tell him that her tea tasted bitter and she was about to commit suicide? – Possibly she would.

Is that your understanding of that passage? – That is.

Look at the letter of 1st May (exhibit 19) –

I don't think we're failures in other things and we mustn't be in this.

Did you understand what that referred to? – Yes.

What? – Well, if you read further, "We mustn't give up as we said."

What was that? – Give up trying for a separation or divorce.

We must learn to be patient. We must have each other darlint. It's meant to be I know I feel it is because I love you such a lot – such a love was not meant to be in vain. It will come right I know one day, if not by our efforts some other way. We'll wait eh darlint, and you'll try and get some money and then we can go away and not worry about anybody or anything. You said it was enough for an elephant.

Do you remember saying that? – Yes.

Did you say that in writing or in speech? – In speech.

Are you clear about that? Did you say it in a letter or in a conversation when you were at home? – I really do not remember whether it was in conversation or in a letter.

And what was it you said was enough for an elephant? – The quinine I had given Mrs. Thompson.

For what had you given her quinine? – She had been wanting me to get her something with which to commit suicide, as she did not want to make my life as unhappy as hers. To satisfy her craving I said I would get her something, and I gave her quinine.

It is your suggestion that in May, 1922, you were lending your assistance to her desire to commit suicide? – Her suggestion.

You say you gave her this quinine because she wanted something with which to commit suicide. Is that right? – Yes, that is so.

Did you give her quinine with that object? – I did.

Were you therefore willing to help her to commit suicide? – No, I knew she could not hurt herself with quinine.

You were playing with her ideas? – I was pulling her leg.

> You said it was enough for an elephant. Perhaps it was. But you don't allow for the taste making only a small quantity to be taken. It sounded like a reproach was it meant to be?

That is your explanation, that you were playing a joke upon her? – That is so.

She goes on –

> Darlint I tried hard – you won't know how hard – because you weren't there to see and I can't tell you all – but I did – I do want you to believe I did for both of us . . . I was buoyed up with the hope of the 'light bulb' and I used a lot.

Did you understand that as referring to a dose she herself took of broken glass? – Possibly, yes. She was trying to persuade me to give her something with which to commit suicide, and I refrained. I gave her this quinine so that she would not take anything herself.

But in the next passage that I have called your attention to she refers to another specific –

> I was buoyed up, with the hope of the 'light bulb' and I used a lot – big pieces too.

Did you understand that to mean that she had taken glass? – I understood that to be a lie from her to me.

You understood, even if it was a lie, that what it was a lie about was what she had taken herself? – Oh, yes.

By Mr. JUSTICE SHEARMAN – Look at it. Was she lying about what her husband had taken or what she had taken herself? – I say she was lying about what she had taken herself.

b. Further extracts from the cross-examination of Bywaters

Look at the letter written on 1st October (exhibit No. 60) at the end –

> Don't forget what we talked in the Tea Room, I'll still risk and try if you will – we only have $3\frac{3}{4}$ years left darlingest.

What did you understand the risk was that she was prepared to run? – The risk of being knocked about when she was asking for separation or divorce.

What was the risk that you were to run, "I will still risk and try if you will"? – "If you will let me."

How was she going to run the risk of being knocked about by telling her husband she was going with you? – No, by asking for a divorce or separation.

Then you did in fact meet her and never went near her husband? – I kept away; I did not want further trouble.

You met her at Fullers in the afternoon of 3rd October? – Yes.

Did you have any conversation about her husband? – No.

Did you not refer to him? – Only that she was going to the theatre.

She did tell you that she was going to the theatre? – Yes.

And she told you which theatre? – Yes.

After you left her I understand you went straight to the Graydons? – Yes.

Were you carrying your knife when you went there? – I was.

Did you carry that knife everywhere while in England? – Yes.

Did you ever use it for anything? – Cutting string or cutting things handy.

Is that the purpose for which you carried it? – I bought that – it may be handy at any time.

A knife of that size and character? – Yes, handy at sea.

Handy at sea, but was it handy at home? – Yes.

c. Extracts from the examination of Thompson

The next letter I want you to look at is the one dated 20th August, 1921 (exhibit 12) –

> Come and see me Monday lunch time, please darlint. He suspects.

What did you mean by "he suspects"? – I meant that my husband suspected I had seen Bywaters; I think it was on the Friday previous to that date. I usually saw him on Fridays, and I continued to see him until he sailed on 9th September. He came back in the end of October, and remained in this country until 11th November. After he sailed I corresponded with him, and among other letters I wrote exhibit 62, which is undated.

> All I could think about last night was that compact we made. Shall we have to carry it thro'? Don't let us darlint. I'd like to live and be happy – not for a little while, but for all the while you still love me. Death seemed horrible last night – when you think about

it darlint, it does seem a horrible thing to die, when you have never been happy really happy for one little minute.

What compact were you referring to in that letter to Bywaters? – The compact of suicide. We had discussed the question of suicide some time previous to the writing of this letter; I cannot state when.

What was said about it? – That nothing was worth living for, and that it would be far easier to be dead.

Had you discussed any particular means of committing suicide? – I believe we had.

After Bywaters had sailed on that voyage did you send him from time to time cuttings out of the papers? – I did. They were generally cuttings of sensational matters appearing at the time. Amongst the cuttings that I sent there was an account of an inquest upon a girl, Freda Kempton, who had died through taking an overdose of cocaine.

In your letter of 14th March, 1922 (exhibit 20), you say –

Enclosed are some cuttings that may be interesting. I think the 'red hair' one is true in parts – you tell me which parts darlint. The Kempton cutting may be interesting if it's to be the same method.

What were you referring to there? – Our compact of suicide.

Look at the letter (exhibit 27) where you say –

I had the wrong Porridge to-day, but I don't suppose it will matter, I don't seem to care much either way. You'll probably say I'm careless and I admit I am, but I don't care – do you?

What were you referring to? – I really cannot explain.

The suggestion here is that you had from time to time put things into your husband's porridge, glass, for instance? – I had not done so.

Can you give us any explanation of what you had in your mind when you said you had the wrong porridge? – Except we had suggested or talked about that sort of thing and I had previously said, "Oh yes, I will give him something one of these days."

By Mr. JUSTICE SHEARMAN – Do you mean that you had talked about poison? – I did not mean anything in particular.

Examination continued – We had talked about making my husband ill.

How had you come to talk about making your husband ill? – We were discussing my unhappiness.

Did that include your husband's treatment of you? – Yes.

Now you say you probably said that you would give him something? – I did.

Did you ever give him anything? – Nothing whatever. My husband took porridge in the mornings. It was always prepared by Mrs. Lester, and never by me.

Further on in that same letter (exhibit 27), you say –

> You know darlint I am beginning to think I have gone wrong in the way I manage this affair. I think perhaps it would have been better had I acquiesced in everything he said and did or wanted to do. At least it would have disarmed any suspicion he might have and that would have been better if we have to use drastic measures.

What were you meaning by the "drastic measures" you might have to use? – Leaving England with Bywaters.

Look now at the letter of 3rd January, 1922 (exhibit 13), where you say –

> Immediately I have received a second letter, I have destroyed the first and when I got the third I destroyed the second and so on, now the only one I have is the "Dear Edie" one written to 41, which I am going to keep. It may be useful, who knows?

Why were you keeping that letter? – I wanted to show it to my people if I were asked if I had heard from Mr. Bywaters for Christmas. It was a letter wishing me all good wishes for Christmas and my people were certain to ask if I had heard from him. Otherwise I did not keep Bywaters' letters, it being a habit of mine to destroy letters that I had received.

d. Further extracts from the examination of Thompson

Turn now to your letter of 28th August (exhibit 63) –

> Darlingest boy, to-day is the 27th and it's on a Sunday, so I am writing this in the bathroom, I always like to send you greetings on the day – not the day before or the day after. Fourteen whole months have gone by now, darlint, it's so terribly long. Neither you nor I thought we should have to wait all that long time did we? altho' I said I would wait 5 years – and I will darlint – it's only 3 years and ten months now.

What did you mean by that – it is only three years and ten months to what? – To wait.

For what? – To live with Mr. Bywaters or go away with him, or be with him only.

Had you made arrangement with Bywaters to wait for five years? – Yes.

What was to happen at the end of five years? – If he was not in a successful position to take me away or had not in the meantime found me something to go to – well, we should part.

Mr. JUSTICE SHEARMAN – The other witness's story was that they wanted to commit suicide, and he said, "Put it off five years," which seems to be the one sensible thing I have heard.

(To Witness) – Was that discussed when you wanted to commit suicide together, that you should put it off and wait five years to see how he was getting on? – We might have discussed that, but I do not remember about it.

Examination continued – I was quite prepared to wait five years.

Will you turn to exhibit 28, where you say –

> Yes, darlint, you are jealous of him – but I want you to be – he has the right by law to all that you have the right to by nature and love – yes darlint be jealous, so much that you will do something desperate.

What do you mean by doing something desperate? – To take me away at any cost, to do anything to get me away from England.

Look at exhibit 60. Do you remember the day on which you wrote that letter? – I think it was probably on the Monday, 2nd October. I saw Bywaters on the Monday, but I could not be certain whether it was before or after the writing of the letter. On the Saturday I had told him of my engagement to go to the theatre on the Tuesday. It is quite probable that that engagement was made a fortnight before.

In that letter you say –

> Darlint – do something tomorrow night will you?something to make you forget. I'll be hurt I know, but I want you to hurt me – I do really – the bargain now seems so one-sided – so unfair – but how can I alter it.

"To-morrow night" was the night you were going to the theatre. What had Bywaters to forget? – That I was going somewhere with my husband.

What was he to do to make him forget that? – I wanted him to take my sister Avis out.

You say, "I will be hurt, I know." What did that mean? – I should have been hurt by Bywaters being with a lady other than myself.

In that letter you also say –

> Darlingest find me a job abroad. I'll go tomorrow and not say I was going to a soul and not have one little regret.

Did that really represent your feelings at that time, that you were prepared to go abroad with him at once? – Yes. We had discussed it on the Saturday.

Look at the end of that letter –

> Don't forget what we talked in the Tea Room, I'll still risk and try if you will.

What had you discussed in the tearoom? – My freedom.

Had you at any time from the month of June, 1921, to the month of October of this year any desire for Bywaters to commit any injury on your husband? – None whatever. Bywaters returned from his last voyage on 23rd September, but I did not see him until Monday, the 25th. I saw him again during that week and at nine o'clock on Saturday, the 30th. I left him to do some shopping, and then I rejoined him, and was with him until mid-day. We spent the morning in Wanstead Park. I did not see him again on the Saturday or the Sunday. I saw him on Monday, 2nd October, I think at 2.15, outside 168 Aldersgate Street, and we lunched together. After lunch I returned to business. I saw him again in Fullers about five o'clock that afternoon, and I believe I had a coffee with him. I stayed with him until about quarter to seven, when I returned home. I did not see him again that night.

During the time you were with Bywaters on the Saturday and the Monday, apart from discussing a separation, did you discuss your husband at all? – No, I did not.

Was there any mention or any indication of a possible assault being committed on him? – None whatever. On Tuesday, 3rd October, I went to business as usual, and I saw Bywaters about 12.30, when we lunched together. I saw him again about quarter-past five, and was with him for about quarter of an hour. After leaving him I met my husband in Aldersgate Street, and we went straight west – about quarter to six I think it was. We had a slight meal together before going to the theatre.

Did you anticipate, or had you any reason to think, that you would see Bywaters again that day or not? – None whatever. I had made arrangements to see him on the following day at lunch time at 168 Aldersgate Street.

e. Extracts from cross-examination of Thompson

Had you any doubt when you were asked by the police about it that it was Bywaters who was there and was the man? – No, I had not.

May I take it that when you made the long statement (exhibit 3) you left out Bywaters' name in order to shield him? – I did so.

Did you also say this in the statement: "I have always been on affectionate terms with my husband"? – I cannot say that I actually said that. The statement was made as question and answer.

I think it was read over to you and you signed it? – It might have been, yes.

At any rate, is the statement true or untrue? – It is untrue.

If you left Bywaters out of that statement in order to shield him, were you afraid that if you brought his name into it he would be suspected? – I was not afraid of anything. I left it out entirely.

Why? What were you afraid of if you did not know your husband had been stabbed? – I was not afraid of anything.

What were you going to shield him from? – To have his name brought into it.

Were you not going to shield him from a charge of having murdered your husband? – I did not know my husband was murdered.

Did you not know that your husband had been assaulted and murdered? – The inspector told me, but I did not realise even at that time that he was dead.

Inspector Hall had told you then that your husband was dead? – He had.

When you told those untruths and left out Bywaters, were you not attempting to shield him from a charge of having murdered your husband? – I did not even know my husband had been murdered. When I say that I did not know, I mean that I did not realise it.

I will ask you again, what were you attempting to shield Bywaters from? – From being connected with me – his name being brought into anything.

Now, Mrs. Thompson, is it not the fact that you knew that Bywaters was going to do something on this evening and that these two false statements were an attempt to prevent the police getting wind of it? – That is not so.

Now I will go back to the early stages of your relationship with Bywaters. Do you agree with me that it was in June of 1921 that you first fell in love with Bywaters? – No, I did not.

Do you put it in November? – September, I said.

Look at your letter of 28th August, 1922 (exhibit 63), where you say –

> Fourteen whole months have gone by now, darlint, it's so terribly long. Neither you nor I thought we should have to wait all that long time.

Does that not satisfy you that you and Bywaters declared love to each other in June, 1921? – Not at all.

You deny that? – Yes.

When did you first begin to address him as your lover? – It is just what you mean by "your lover."

The terms in which a woman does not write to any man except her husband? – I cannot remember.

Did you from the first time you realised you were in love with Bywaters take an aversion to your husband? – For the first time, did you say?

Did you ever take an aversion to your husband? – I did.

Can you tell me the date? – I think it was in 1918.

Then both before and after you and Bywaters fell in love with each other you hated – is that too strong a word – your husband? – It is too strong.

Did your aversion to him become greater when you fell in love with Bywaters? – I think not.

Were you happy with him after you fell in love with Bywaters? – I never was happy with him.

Did you behave to him as if you were happy? – On occasions, yes.

Did your husband repeatedly ask you if you were happy? – He did.

And did you tell him you were happy? – I did.

Was that to deceive him? – It was to satisfy him more than to deceive him.

Did you seriously at that time intend to leave your husband or to give him cause for divorce? – I did.

Did you ever tell him you had given him cause for divorce? – I did.

When, for the first time? – I cannot remember.

Were you afraid your husband would find out anything between you and Bywaters? – What do you mean by "anything"?

Were you frightened that your husband would find out anything between you and Bywaters? – Except that we were meeting and he might come and prevent us meeting.

But if you had told your husband that you had given him ground for divorce, what were you afraid of beyond that? – I was afraid of my husband coming to my place of business and making scenes as he had threatened.

You had told your husband that you had been unfaithful to him, or would be unfaithful to him, and given him grounds for divorce? – I did.

Had he made scenes at your business when you told him that? – No, he did not, but he had threatened to do so.

What was the risk you were running, the risk you so often mentioned to Bywaters? Look at your letter of 4th July (exhibit 26) –

> Why arnt you sending me something – I wanted you to – you never do what I ask you darlint – you still have your own way always – If I don't mind the risk why should you?

What risk? – That was the risk of Mr. Bywaters sending me something instead of bringing something.

Why was that a risk? – Well, it would be a risk for me to receive anything.

Not a risk to receive a letter? – I did not say a letter.

What was it? – Whatever Mr. Bywaters suggested.

Why should you think there was a risk in his sending you something? – I did not know that I should personally receive it.

Why should there be a risk in a friend or even a lover sending you a letter or a present? – I did not say it was a letter.

What was it? – Something Mr. Bywaters suggested.

Did he suggest it was a dangerous thing? – No.

Why did you think it was a dangerous thing? – I did not think it was a dangerous thing.

Why did you think there was a risk? – There was a risk to anything he sent me that did not come into my hands first.

Did you think it was because somebody would think there was a *liaison* going on between you and him? – No, only you would not like anything private being opened by somebody previous to yourself.

You were afraid somebody might have thought there were improper relations between you and him. Is that what you are referring to? – No.

I understand you did not mind your husband knowing you and Mr. Bywaters were lovers? – We wanted him to realise it.

The more it came to the knowledge of your husband the more likely you were to achieve your design of divorce or separation; is that the fact? – No, that is not so. The more it came to his knowledge the more he would refuse to give it me; he had told me that.

In the passage I have read you were asking Bywaters to send something which he had said, according to you, he was going to bring? – That is so.

What was it? – I have no idea.

Have you no idea? – Except what he told me.

What did he tell you? – He would bring me something.

Did he not say what the something was? – No, he did not mention anything.

What did he lead you to think it was? – That it was something for me to give my husband.

With a view to poisoning your husband? – That was not the idea, that was not what I expected.

Something to give your husband that would hurt him? – To make him ill.

And it was a risk for your lover to send, and for you to receive, something of that sort? – It was a risk for him to send me anything he did not know came to my hands first.

And a special risk to send you something to make your husband ill. You appreciate that? – Yes, I suppose it was.

You were urging Bywaters to send it instead of bringing it? – That is so.

Was that in order that it might be used more quickly? – I wrote that in order to make him think I was willing to do anything he might suggest, to enable me to retain his affections.

Mrs. Thompson, is that quite a frank explanation of this urging him to send instead of bring? – It is, absolutely. I wanted him to think I was eager to help him.

By Mr. Justice Shearman – Eager to do what? – Eager to help him in doing anything he suggested.

That does not answer the question, you know.

Cross-examination continued – He suggested giving your husband something to hurt him? – He had given me something.

Given you something to give your husband? – That is so.

Did the suggestion then come from Bywaters? – It did.

Did the suggestion come in a letter or in a conversation? – I cannot remember.

Did you welcome it when it came? – I read it. What? – I read it and I studied it.

Did you welcome the suggestion that something should be given to your husband to make him ill? – I did not.

Did you object to it? – I was astonished about it.

Did you object to it? – I did, at the time.

And although you objected to it you urged Bywaters to send it more quickly than he intended? – I objected at the time. Afterwards I acquiesced.

From the time you acquiesced did you do all you could to assist Bywaters to find something which would make your husband ill? – I did not.

Did you try to prevent him from finding something to make your husband ill? – I could not prevent him; he was not in England.

Did you try? – I do not see how I could have tried. Did you discourage him? – I did, at first.

And afterwards did you encourage him? – No.

Look at your letter of 1st April (exhibit 17). What is the meaning of the injunction in that letter, "Don't keep this piece"? – I cannot remember now.

Shall I help you to remember, if you read the next passage? – It may not have referred to that piece.

Look at the original letter. You see that that injunction is written on the top of a new page? – Yes.

Did you intend Bywaters not to keep that piece of paper? – No.

"Don't keep this piece"? – I think you will see there has been something attached to that piece of paper. There are distinctly two pin marks there.

You dispute my suggestion to you that "Don't keep this paper" refers to the piece on which the following is written? – I do.

Look at the next paragraph. It is about giving your husband something bitter. I think you told your learned counsel that was an imaginary incident? – Yes.

Do you mean that you imagined it, or that your husband did? – I imagined it.

Do you mean you invented the incident altogether for Bywaters' information? – I did.

Can you tell me what the object of that was? – Still to make him think I had done what he suggested.

By Mr. JUSTICE SHEARMAN – Had done what? Given your husband something? – Yes.

Cross-examination continued – Was it with the same object that you wrote the paragraph lower down, "Don't tell Dan." You say –

> What I mean is don't let him be suspicious of you regarding that – because if we were successful in the action –

Does that refer to the proposal that Bywaters had made, that you should make your husband ill? – I think not.

What do you think it refers to? – The action of my going away to live with him unmarried.

> I'm going to try the glass again occasionally – when it is safe. I've got an electric light globe this time.

When was it likely to be safe? – There was no question of it being safe; I was not going to try it.

Why did you tell Bywaters you were going to try it when it was safe? – Still to let him think I was willing to do what he wanted.

You are representing that this young man was seriously suggesting to you that you should poison and kill your husband? – I did not suggest it.

I thought that was the suggestion? – I did not suggest that.

What was your suggestion? – He said he would give him something.

By Mr. JUSTICE SHEARMAN – Give him something in his food; you answered my question a little while ago that it was to give him something to make him ill? – That is what I surmised, that I should give him something so that when he had a heart attack he would not be able to resist it.

You are suggesting now that it was Bywaters who was suggesting that to you? – Yes.

And you did not do it? – No, never.

Cross-examination continued – Why were you urging Bywaters to do something if the suggestion really came from him? In your letter of 10th February (exhibit 15) your first sentence is, "You must do something this time"? – I was not referring to that at all. I was referring to him getting me something to do, a position of some sort abroad.

Let us see what the rest of the letter was. The fourth paragraph is the one that relates to the incident of your husband waking up and asking you for water as he was feeling ill. Was that a true incident? – Absolutely true.

Why did you hunt for the prescription? Was that to prevent a similar incident? – Probably. I did not think it was wise for him to do those things.

Was your anxiety so that you should get hold of the prescription and avert the catastrophe of taking an overdose? – Yes.

Do you mean you were really frightened about your husband's overdose? – I was.

Then can you explain to me the meaning of the next sentence –

I told Avis about the incident only I told her as if it frightened and worried me as I thought perhaps it might be useful at some future time that I had told somebody.

Was it true that you were frightened and worried, or was it acting? – No, that was true.

You were frightened and worried? – I was.

Why did you take special pains to tell Avis as if you were frightened and worried? – I was worried and frightened and told my sister.

Why was it likely to be useful to pretend that you were frightened and worried? – If anything had happened to my husband it would have been much better for somebody else to know besides myself.

And you thought it would have been much better for you, if you poisoned your husband, if you professed anxiety to Avis previously? – I had no intention of ever poisoning my husband.

Look at the next paragraph –

What do you think, darlint. His sister Maggie came in last night and he told her [I suppose "he" is your husband] so now there are two witnesses, although I wish he hadn't told her – but left me to do it.

Now, that is to say you wanted again to create the impression that you were frightened by your husband's attacks? – I did not want to create the impression. I was frightened.

It would be so easy darlint – if I had things – I do hope I shall.

What would be easy? – I was asking or saying it would be better if I had things as Mr. Bywaters suggested I should have.

What would be easy? – To administer them as he suggested.

"I do hope I shall." Was that acting or was that real? – That was acting for him.

You were acting to Bywaters that you wished to destroy your husband's life? – I was.

By Mr. JUSTICE SHEARMAN – One moment, I do not want to be mistaken. Did I take you down rightly as saying, "I wanted him to think I was willing to take my husband's life"? – I wanted him to think I was willing to do what he suggested.

That is to take your husband's life? – Not necessarily.

Cross-examination continued – To injure your husband at any rate? – To make him ill.

What was the object of making him ill? – I had not discussed the special object.

What was in your heart the object of making him ill? So that he should not recover from his heart attacks? – Yes, that was certainly the impression, yes.

The Court adjourned.

C. Comments

Arguments about the degree of Edith Thompson's guilt or innocence can never now be finally settled. One thing is incontrovertible, i.e. the aura of sexual prejudice (as palpable as anti-Semitism, apartheid, or any other form of paranoia), which pervaded the court when she was tried. Even her co-defendant Bywaters may have been an indirect victim of it. He was presented as the helpless prey of an evil woman and in that role attracted some sympathy; but if murder had been done his was undoubtedly the hand that committed it. Thus the people who were determined that Edith should swing for it could not have got her without getting him too. (Elaine Morgan (1979))

Age is eternally jealous of youth; impotence is jealous of passion; law is jealous of liberty; those who have found happiness within the pale are apt to look with suspicion and misgiving on those who dare to seek and find happiness without the pale. Intellect affects to despise emotion; yet a real and deep emotion, however wayward, is a more vital thing than are the sterile and negative barriers within which, necessarily, but in vain, the social state tries to confine it. That is why we have Courts of law, for a world ruled only by emotion would be a dreadful place. The lesson of it all surely is never to let emotion escape from its own sphere, to wander into the dreadful wilderness that ends in the Court and the prison house. Mr. Justice Shearman frequently referred to Bywaters as "the adulterer," apparently quite unconscious of the fact that to people of Bywaters's generation, educated in the ethics of dear labour and cheap pleasure, of commercial sport and the dancing hall, adultery is merely a quaint ecclesiastical term for what seems to them the great romantic adventure of their lives. Adultery to such people may or may not be "sporting," but its wrongness is not a matter that would trouble them for a moment. Sinai, for them, is wrapped in impenetrable cloud. And if we are not prepared to adapt the laws of Sinai to the principles of the night club and the *thé dansant*, I see no other alternative but to educate again our young in the eternal verities on which the law is based. (Filson Young (1951))

No one can say
That the trial was not fair. The trial was fair, Painfully fair by every rule of law,
And that it was made not the slightest difference. The law's our yardstick, and it measures well.

Or well enough when there are yards to measure. Measure a wave with it, measure a fire, Cut sorrow up in inches, weigh content. You can weigh John Brown's body well enough, But how and in what balance weigh John Brown? (*John Brown's Body*, by Stephen Vincent Benet (1961))

D. Notes and questions on Rex v. Bywaters and Thompson

A. Some threshold questions

1 "Love letters cannot appropriately and should not be used as evidence in a court of law." Do you agree?

2 What, in your view, are the main problems in using love letters as evidence in a case of this kind?

3 (a) What issues of admissibility of evidence could have been raised by the defence in respect of the letters?

(b) Was it open to the judge to admit some letters but exclude all or parts of others?

B. Clarification of standpoint

(Who am I? At what stage(s) in what process am I? What am I trying to do?)

4 (a) Identify six significantly different standpoints for a Wigmorean analysis of *Bywaters and Thompson.*

(b) Before starting on the exercise, state what you would expect to be the main differences in the analysis of the case from each of the six different standpoints.

(c) Which, if any, of the standpoints insures a whole-hearted commitment to truth?

C. Ultimate probanda

5 (a) What were the ultimate *probanda* for each of the counts in Indictment No. 2?

(b) What were the ultimate *probanda* for the charge in Indictment No. 1?

(c) Which of the offences charged in Indictment No. 2 are included in the offence charged in Indictment No. 1?

6 (a) From the standpoint of counsel for the Crown, what issues of substantive law had to be decided in order to frame the two indictments? In order to make the decision to proceed on Indictment No. 1?

(b) From the standpoint of the defense, were there any additional questions of substantive law that needed to be resolved in order to prepare the defense?

(c) From the standpoint of the historian, are there issues of substantive law on which you would need advice in order to do a thorough analysis of the evidence in relation to the question: Was Edith responsible for the death of Percy?

7 In order to convict Edith Thompson of murder, was it necessary for the prosecution to prove (a) that Frederick Bywaters murdered Percy Thompson? (b) that the specific attack was premeditated? Both?

D. Penultimate probanda, theories, and themes

8 (a) Formulate, in not more than 150 words each, two alternative "theories of the case" from the standpoint of (a) the prosecution; (b) the defense.

(b) Identify two or three themes that would be suitable in presenting and supporting each theory at the trial.

9 Outline the main hypotheses favoring the prosecution and those favoring the defense that an historian might want to analyze in light of the evidence available in terms of the concepts presented here. How might these differ from the theories of the case of each side?

E. The chart method: application and appraisal

10 (a) Was it (i) necessary (ii) sufficient with respect to the charge of murder for the prosecution to prove attempted murder by poison or broken glass (Counts 4 and 5 of Indictment No. 2) on prior occasions? To what issue(s) in respect of the charge of murder are such allegations relevant?

(b) Construct a key-list and chart of the prosecution's main theories of the case.

(c) Construct a key-list and chart of the defense's argument in relation to the proposition: "Freddy's attack on Percy was premeditated." Is this an example of a "jugular" argument?

11 What "aids" or techniques of textual interpretation are helpful in analyzing the letters in *Bywaters and Thompson*?

12 Compile a key-list and chart of propositions in respect of the following passages:

(a) Exhibit 60: "Don't forget what we talked in the Tea Room … Try and help."

(b) Exhibit 15: "It would be so easy Darlint – if I had things – I do hope I shall. How about cigarettes?"

(c) Exhibit 19: "I was buoyed up with the hope of the 'light bulb' and I used a lot. … I wish oh I wish I could do something."

(d) Exhibit 17. All the potentially significant statements.

13 (a) In relation to Exhibit 17 (above, page 188) René Weis wrote:

> That this piece of fantasy could ever be construed as part of a premeditated murder plot defies belief. Bywaters knew it was a fiction and that she had herself tasted the quinine in the tea to be able to give an accurate account of Percy's complaint. In the court the jurors were told that "the passage is full of crime". Yes, as long as it is understood that "crime" means "imaginary crime". It is never easy to separate fact and fiction in Edith's extensive and intense correspondence, and though outside evidence is available to help distinguish one from the other, the more intimately acquainted the reader becomes with the correspondence, the more complex its rash interweaving of fact and fiction is bound to appear. In most of our lives blurring is not uncommon. It is not always harmless. But it is seldom the matter of life and death into which it developed here. (Weis (2001: 105). Compare *Rethinking* at 316–18.)

Construct an argument to show that this letter is relevant evidence to support at least one important *probandum*.

(b) A pin-hole has been noticed at the top of Exhibit 17, but no attachment has been found. Has this any evidentiary potential?

14 (a) What bearing, if any, does the character of each of the main protagonists have on the case as a whole?

   (b) Strictly on the basis of the available evidence give a description of Edith's character (i) which favors the prosecution's case; (ii) which favors the defense's case.

   (c) Is it possible to give an account of Edith Thompson's character which is (i) neutral; (ii) impartial; (iii) falsifiable; (iv) false; (v) completely true; (vi) simply factual?

   (d) Can the letters be interpreted to suggest that the relationship between Edith and Freddy underwent significant changes over time? If so, does this help the defense or the prosecution case?

15 Can you imagine any theories, techniques or developments in (a) logic; (b) psychology; (c) textual analysis; (d) forensic science; (e) computer applications: (f) medical knowledge; (g) other fields of inquiry which could settle once and for all any of the outstanding central questions concerning *Bywaters and Thompson*?

F. Uses and limitations of the chart method

16 In your view, can the chart method deal adequately with:

   (a) cryptic, vague, or ambiguous statements in letters;

   (b) the character of important protagonists;

   (c) probability judgments;

   (d) factors, such as public opinion, that influenced the atmosphere of the trial;

   (e) the language of love;

   (f) photographs of Edith;

   (g) the demeanor of witnesses;

   (h) absence of relevant information;

   (i) common sense generalizations?

17 In what respects, if any, is Wigmore's method useful in analyzing *Bywaters and Thompson*?

G. Concepts:

18 Using examples from *Bywaters and Thompson*, elucidate and illustrate the following concepts and distinctions:

   (a) Propositions of fact; normative propositions; speculative statements; opinions; background generalizations.

   (b) Facts in issue; disputed facts; *factum probandum; factum probans.*

   (c) Hard facts; wild facts; undisputed facts; hypotheses; stipulated facts.

   (d) Relevance; materiality; admissibility.

   (e) Evidence; inference; proof.

   (f) Quantum; cogency.

   (g) Probability judgments; plausible statements; a credible witness.

   (h) Conjunction; convergence; corroboration; catenate inference.

   (i) Observational capacity; veracity; witness bias.

   (j) Legal guilt; moral guilt; moral responsibility.

   (k) Wigmore's five probative processes: PA; OD; OR; OE; PC.

H. Other dimensions

19 In the story of *Bywaters and Thompson*, viewed as a total process involving a flow of decisions and events, what in your view were crucial decisions, especially mistaken decisions, made by each of the main protagonists?

20 A group of supporters of Edith Thompson is planning to petition the English Criminal Cases Review Commission to reconsider her conviction. Leaving aside the issue whether this case happened too long ago, an important element in such a review would be whether there is significant new evidence to render the conviction unsafe. Use your imagination to identify what kinds of new evidence might be helpful in this context, if it were available.

21 The Lord Chief Justice stated in regard to the route followed by the Thompsons on the evening of October 3: "It was an indirect way from the station to the house." (above, page 166). There is nothing in the record of the trial to support this statement, which is contradicted by contemporary maps and by the fact that the Thompsons were not alone in taking this route. So this appears to be an invented "fact." What is the significance, if any, of this point? Could this count as "new evidence"?

22 To what extent did prevailing attitudes toward women play an important part in the story?

23 After observing her and talking with her over several weeks after her conviction, the prison governor of Holloway was convinced of Edith Thompson's innocence. Assess the value of such evidence from the point of view (a) of an historian (b) of the Home Secretary, considering clemency.

8

Evaluating evidence

A. Introduction

The preceding chapters focused upon the logic of proof and methods for analyzing evidence in a variety of contexts – for example, analyzing the evidence in an ongoing investigation or in a decided case or in preparing for trial. It should be clear, however, that developing the strongest theory of a case and determining how the evidence can best be marshaled to support a probandum necessarily requires that the analyst make evaluative judgments. So far, we have not directly addressed the problems of or techniques for evaluating the probative value of evidence or the strength or cogency of arguments about particular aspects of the evidence or about the evidence in a case-as-a-whole. This chapter and the next focus upon those problems and techniques.

A lawyer must confront the problems at every stage of a case. For instance, in a civil case, from the initial interview onward, the lawyer must assess the weight and force of the evidence that is available and that is likely to become available. Should the case be taken? Filed? Pursued? Is the case ready for trial or is further investigation or discovery justified or required? Given the available evidence and the operative law, should the case be settled and, if so, on what basis? At trial, the questions concern both the lawyers and the decision-makers. Does the particular evidence proffered have such probative value that it should be admitted notwithstanding any improper prejudicial effects that it may have? Is the evidence as a whole sufficient to warrant submission of the case to a jury? Does the evidence prove the claim to the required standard? The lawyer must argue and the appropriate decision maker must decide these questions based upon an assessment of the probative value or force of the parts or the weight of the whole of the evidence.[1] Similar questions arise in criminal processes from the start of an investigation through trial, appeal, and beyond.

---

1 The terms "probative value," probative force," and "weight" do not have generally accepted meanings. In this book, "probative value" and "probative force" are used where the discussion focuses on the value or force of particular items of evidence. "Weight" is used where the discussion focuses on a mass of evidence.

Questions such as these pose fundamental issues that are of concern to lawyers, judges, and others interested in the processes by which disputed questions of fact are adjudicated. A central issue may be stated thus: Do the standards of decision provide meaningful guidance for those who must apply them in the process or for those who would appraise the outcome of the process? For lawyers, the question is central because the standards establish the framework within which they must advise clients, make decisions, and frame arguments to courts and juries. For judges and juries, the question is central because the standards define the range of their discretion and purport to provide meaningful guidance for the exercise of that discretion. For those concerned with adjudication as an aspect of the judicial system, the question is central because the operation of the standards in some measure determines the extent to which the system is or could be viewed as rational and fair.

Standpoint is central for lawyers addressing questions such as these. Lawyers are the primary decision-makers with respect to questions of procedure and strategy. The lawyer's objective must be to decide how to construct arguments that will persuade other decision-makers that, from their respective standpoints, the decision sought is the decision that they should make. Other decisions must be made or approved by clients, by opposing counsel and their clients, by arbitrators, by judges, or by juries. The lawyer's role varies; it may be to advise or to persuade or negotiate.

For that reason, the kinds of questions that a lawyer must consider in constructing arguments to persuade others are extensive. To identify a few: Is the client risk-adverse, risk-neutral, or risk-preferring? The decision to settle or accept a plea or try a case is ultimately the client's not the lawyer's. In the United States, the lawyer must consider questions such as: Does the judge have to run for re-election? If so, can she reasonably be expected to rule against the prosecution and police on important issues or on a regular basis? Is the judge a federal judge appointed for life who can make unpopular decisions without worrying about her position or livelihood. If so, does she have ambitions to be promoted to the court of appeal or to be appointed to high office in the executive branch? What generalizations are the jurors selected likely to hold and which generalizations can the jury as a whole be persuaded to accept in evaluating the evidence and the competing stories constructed by the lawyers? In England the questions are less obvious, but the lawyer must still consider the background of the decision-makers.

In this chapter, we establish a framework that lawyers (or others) might use in addressing questions such as these at all stages of a case. In Part B, we describe techniques for evaluating and constructing arguments about the weight or the probative value of evidence. That part describes the traditional vocabularies that lawyers and judges use in expressing their views on the probative value of particular segments of the evidence or on the weight of the evidence as a whole. In Part C, we examine standards for decision, standards for pretrial decisions that lawyers and clients must make, and standards for decisions in adjudication. Those standards provide the framework within which arguments about the probative value or weight of the available evidence must be constructed and resolved. Those standards guide lawyers in evaluating evidence and framing arguments to persuade others that the available evidence measured by the applicable standard compels the decision the lawyer seeks.

B. Evaluating the weight and probative force of evidence

1. No rules of weight

Until recently most legal scholars have accepted the view that evaluation of evidence can rarely be governed by rules. That view can be traced to the earliest views expressed by theorists of evidence through the present day. For example, if Jeremy Bentham had had his way, there would have been no binding rules of evidence at all:

> To find infallible rules for evidence, rules which insure a just decision, is, from the nature of things, absolutely impossible; but the human mind is too apt to establish rules which only increase the probabilities of a bad decision. All the service that an impartial investigator of the truth can perform in this respect is to put legislators and judges on their guard against such hasty rules.[2] (J. Bentham (1825) 180)

Bentham's views have not prevailed. But his "anti-nomian" thesis has been much more successful than is generally acknowledged. With only a few exceptions, there is an almost total absence of formal regulation in respect of evaluating evidence or, to put it differently, the Anglo-American law of evidence has almost no rules of weight. Thayer's statement of the predominant view would be accepted by most courts and scholars today:

> The judicial office is really one of administration . . . While these are some of the chief characteristics of legal reasoning, it will be noticed that they are only, in the nature of them, so many reasonable accommodations of the general process to particular subject-matters and particular aims. Amidst them all the great characteristics of the art of reasoning and the laws of thought still remain constant. As regards the main methods in hand, they are still those untechnical ways of all sound reasoning, of the logical process in its normal and ordinary manifestations; and the rules that govern it here are the general rules that govern it everywhere, the ordinary rules of human thought and human experience, to be sought in the ordinary sources, and not in law books. (Thayer (1898) 274–75)

Wigmore was even more explicit on this issue:

> The rules of Admissibility have nothing to say concerning the weight of evidence when once admitted. The relative weight of circumstantial and testimonial evidence, therefore, does not present itself in this place. Indeed, it can be said that there are no rules,

---

2 The nearest he ever came to qualifying this view is in the following passage: "To take the business out of the hands of instinct, to subject it to rules, is a task which, if it lies within the reach of human faculties, must at any rate be reserved, I think, for the improved powers of some maturer age." (Bentham (1827) vol. 1, 44)

in our system of Evidence, prescribing for the jury the precise effect of any general or special class of evidence. So far as logic and psychology assist us, their conclusions show that it is out of the question to make a general assertion ascribing greater weight to one class or the other. The probative effect of one or more pieces of either sort of evidence depends upon considerations too complex. Science can only point out that each class has its special dangers and its special advantages. (1 Wigmore on Evidence §26 (Tillers Rev. 1983))

To say that there are no rules of weight means that the law does not prescribe general rules concerning the weight or cogency of particular types of evidence such as confessions, eyewitness identification evidence, or fingerprints. There are, however, ways in which some limited control is exercised over evaluation of evidence. For example, in many common law jurisdictions a judge has a duty to warn the trier of fact about the potential unreliability of eyewitness identification evidence.[3] In England directions to a jury may include advice on evaluation of certain phases of the evidence and such guidance is sometimes included in specimen directions prepared by the Judicial Studies Board. Judges may withdraw a case from a jury on the grounds of insufficient evidence (see below). Bentham drew a sharp distinction between rules addressed to the will (binding) and instructions addressed to the understanding (guidance). Almost without exception this distinction is maintained by the law of evidence throughout the common law world.

2. Traditional modes of expressing weight and probative force

There is a useful analogy between grading examinations and evaluating evidence. One obvious point of similarity has to do with the extent to which both modes of decision-making are susceptible to rational guidance, justification, and criticism. We all hope that grading is not a completely arbitrary, irrational, hit-or-miss process; but few would deny that there is an inescapable personal element at the point of decision. So with the weighing of evidence. Less obvious is the point that, in discussing what is involved in the conscientious marking of examinations and the weighing of evidence, it is important to distinguish among a number of questions. In examining, we distinguish between conventional modes of *expressing* marks or grades (percentage; alphabetical grading; pass/fail); *standards* required for attaining a particular result (e.g., the standards for the pass mark, for awarding a distinction or credit); the *criteria* used in awarding marks or the *reasons* for making particular evaluations (e.g., marks given for accuracy, originality, or good analysis or subtracted for errors, omissions, or even illegibility); how to *combine judgments* about grades, especially when they are based on multiple criteria; and the extent to which such criteria can be embodied in *rules*.

In evaluating evidence, we need to make some similar distinctions. In particular we need to distinguish among the following questions, even though they are intimately related in both theory and practice:

---

3 *E.g., R. v. Turnbull* [1977] Q.B. 224 (CA).

1   How can we express assessments of weight (the *vocabulary* of evaluation, analogous to a marking scheme)?
2   What are the *standards for decision* of factual issues (cf. the pass mark)?
3   How can judgments of weight and probative force be *combined*?
4   What are the *criteria for evaluating* the probative force of individual items of evidence or the weight of a "mass" of evidence in a given case (cf. *reasons* for awarding or debiting marks or awarding a particular overall grade)?
5   To what extent *could* the law of evidence prescribe *rules of weight or evaluation* (cf. marking rules)?

Whatever the possibility of developing principles of evaluation, there is an established vocabulary by which degrees of persuasion and probative force are expressed in forensic and other contexts. It is perhaps noteworthy how little the vocabulary has changed over the past two centuries.

> In the first place, it has been observed by a very learned Man, that there are several Degrees from perfect Certainty and Demonstration, quite down to Improbability and Unlikeliness, even to the confines of Impossibility; and there are several Acts of the Mind proportioned to these degrees of Evidence, which may be called the Degrees of Assent, from full Assurance and Confidence, quite down to Conjecture, Doubt, Distrust and Disbelief. (J. Gilbert (1754) 1)

> Certainty, absolute certainty, is a satisfaction which on every ground of inquiry we are continually grasping at, but which the inexorable nature of things has placed forever out of reach. Practical certainty, a degree of assurance sufficient for practice, is a blessing, the attainment of which, as often as it lies in our way to attain it, may be sufficient to console us under the want of any such superfluous and unattainable acquisitions. (Bentham (1827) vol. 5: 351)

> In talking about inferences, it is common to resort to metaphor: We talk of the *weight* of the evidence, of prejudicial effect *outweighing* probative value, of the persuasive *force* or the probative *force* of an argument, of the *strength* of support, or of a *weak* case. Yet we do not normally seek to express differences or to measure such matters in terms of grams or ohms or watts or volts or pounds per square inch or other physical measures.

There is a variety of contexts in which judgments concerning evidence are commonly expressed as probability judgments, although not always identified as such. For example, it is common to express probability judgments on a conventional scale of 0 to 1. Similarly, the strength of a judgment may be expressed in terms of percentages (e.g., it is 60 percent probable that X is the murderer); or of wagering odds (e.g., I would bet three to one that X is the murderer). There are also standard formulations by which beliefs are expressed in subjective (I am *confident* that X is the murderer) or objective (the evidence *strongly* supports the conclusion that X is the murderer) terms that connote a probabilistic judgment.

The conventions for marking examinations illustrate, in an analogous context, some of the concerns that the use of the term "probability" raises. The adoption of a convention that expresses marks or grades in terms of numbers or Roman or Greek letters or some other mode of expression (e.g., Excellent – Worthless) tells us little or nothing of the criteria used for making such judgments. In expressing judgments about evidence or exam papers, however, using numbers makes it easier, and more tempting, to add, subtract, multiply, or perform other mathematical calculations to create an appearance of precision and objectivity; but whether a particular mode of calculation or whether calculating at all is appropriate are separate questions. Some of the central debates in the theory of evidence address such questions in respect to weighing or assessing the probative force of evidence. These controversies are introduced in Chapter 9. In this chapter, we are concerned with only three questions: First, what are the *conventions* for expressing decisions or judgments about probative force or weight, independently of any particular *criteria* for arriving at such decisions or judgments? Second, what are the *criteria* or *standards* the decision-maker is to use in making the required decisions and judgments? Third, what, if any, is the legal significance of the various criteria and standards?

In legal discourse, terms that connote an assessment of *probability* are commonly invoked. Lawyers, judges, and commentators also talk of the *credibility* of evidence and of witnesses, of the *plausibility* of an argument, and of the *likelihood* that an event occurred or will occur. In some contexts, such terms are used synonymously with probability.[4] For purposes of the present chapter, we shall use the term "probability" in its conventional sense as a general term for expressing judgments about the probative force and effect of evidence without any necessary commitment to any particular *criteria* for assessing the correctness of particular judgments of probability; in short we shall use the term broadly to embrace both "objective" and "subjective," mathematical ("Pascalian") and nonmathematical ("Baconian"), theories of probability.

Against that background, one might construct a "probability table," which grades both mathematical and nonmathematical probability judgments on a ten-point scale.

For different purposes the number of gradations are sometimes increased or reduced. For example, most English university law faculties express marks in percentages, but according to convention the normal range is on a 50-point scale, for almost no one gets more than 80 percent and only disastrous performances rate less than 30 percent. A standard alphabetical system of marking along the sequence A++, A+, A . . . C++, . . . F has approximately 20 gradations, sometimes extended by the craven insertion of queries (e.g., B-??, B+?+). Some examinations have two grades: Pass/Fail. In the present context the moral is clear: The mode of expressing

---

4 For some people, however, the term "probability" is indissolubly associated with certain forms of mathematical reasoning and calculation so that to them it seems paradoxical, even heretical, to talk of "nonmathematical probabilities." In this view, it may be perfectly acceptable to claim that it is inappropriate to quantify the plausibility of an argument, the criminal standard of proof, the credibility of a witness, or the likelihood of some claim being true (though this is, perhaps, more controversial), but any judgment of probability must by definition be expressed or at least capable of being expressed numerically. These views are discussed in Ch. 9.

Table 8.1 *A probability table*

Chance	Frequency	Wager	Belief (subjective)	Strength of Support (objective)	Marks
1.0	100%	No Contest	I know	Beyond peradventure	A+
.9	90%	9-1	I am positive	Overwhelming	A
.8	80%	8-2/4-1	I am sure	Cogent	A−
.7	70%	7-3	I am confident	Strong	B+
.6	60%	6-4/3-2	I think	More likely than not	B
.5	50%	Evens/1-1	I wonder whether	Evenly balanced	B−
.4	40%	4-6/2-3	I suspect	Not very likely	C+
.3	30%	3-7	I surmise	Unlikely	C
.2	20%	2-8/1-4	I doubt that	Weak	C−
.1	10%	1-9	I very much doubt that	Minimal	D+
.0	0	0	I disbelieve	Nil	D/F

judgments concerning degrees of probative force is usually a matter of convention, in which there is no magic in the numbers.

The moral for lawyers and law students should be clear. Judges and juries must in some way "grade" the evidence each time they are required to make an evaluative decision concerning evidence, whether the decision takes the form of a judge's deciding whether the improper prejudicial effect substantially outweighs the probative value of proffered evidence or the jury's deciding whether the evidence establishes the defendant's guilt beyond a reasonable doubt or whether it shows that the plaintiff's ultimate probandum is more probable than not. In practice, these judgments are ordinarily *expressed* on a binary scale – evidence is admitted or not admitted, objections are sustained or overruled, the jury's verdict is guilty or not guilty, for the plaintiff in a specific amount or for the defendant. Nonetheless, both judges and juries are expected to weigh the evidence in terms of probabilistic assessments of the probative force of the parts and of the whole. For that reason, lawyers must know and be able to frame their arguments using the conventional vocabularies by which such arguments and judgments are expressed.

C Standards for decision

Traditional works on the law of evidence tend to focus on the contested jury trial and the standards of proof that are applicable to adjudicative decisions at first instance, notably the civil standard (balance of probabilities, preponderance of evidence) and the criminal standard (proof beyond reasonable doubt). These are, of course, very important. However, if one adopts a total process model of litigation that involves a variety of specific decisions by different participants pre-trial and post-trial, as well as at trial, other standards for decision also need to be considered.

Adjudicative decisions are indeed a focal point of litigation, both because they are important in themselves and because they "cast a long shadow" on other decisions that precede or come after them. For example, a decision to prosecute or to plead not guilty must take into account the likelihood of a decision to acquit or convict by the trier of fact. This in turn requires an assessment of the net persuasive effect that the evidence would be likely to have on the trier of fact. Similarly, many post-conviction decisions have to treat the decision of the trier of fact as given or, exceptionally, to consider whether it should be overturned. Nevertheless, it is important to bear in mind that both analysis and evaluation are typically involved in all these decisions and that evaluation is typically governed by different standards with respect to the different kinds of decisions that must be made.

In this context, there are three propositions that should be axiomatic. First, there are accepted standards that are intended to provide guidance for almost every decision that requires consideration of evidence in a legal context. Second, almost all those decisions require not only that the evidence be analyzed so that potential logical relationships may be identified, but also that it be evaluated to determine the relative strength of the inferences for which it may logically be claimed to provide some support. Third, however articulated, the standards for decision are usually framed in terms intended to provide guidance in evaluation as well as analysis.

From the standpoint of the practitioner there is a further distinction that should be equally axiomatic. The standards for decision can be usefully separated into two categories. In one category are those standards that are prescribed to impose limits on the decision-maker's exercise of discretion; for instance, standards of review such as whether the evidence was logically sufficient to support the decision below. In the other category are those standards intended to guide a decision-maker in the exercise of assigned discretion, such as a standard that the jury must be satisfied beyond a reasonable doubt in a criminal case. The axioms and the importance of the distinctions are illustrated in the sections that follow.

1. Lawyering standards

The resolution of any legal dispute may require decisions by at least five kinds of decision-makers: the parties (or clients), their lawyers (including prosecutors), the trial judge, jurors, and appellate judges. There are standards established by conventional wisdom, ethical norm, or legal rule for virtually every decision that must be taken at any stage of the process. The purpose of this section is to illustrate this point briefly with reference to examples of lawyer-client decisions and of pretrial decisions that are ordinarily made by lawyers.

a. Standards for lawyer-client decisions

In the common law system of adjudication, clients and lawyers, as well as adjudicators, are decision-makers. Ethical considerations, rules of professional conduct, and practical realities dictate that there is a variety of decisions in which the lawyer and the client must participate; these rules identify decisions on which the lawyer must ordinarily defer to the client. Many of these decisions depend significantly upon an assessment of the state of the known evidence and its probable effect upon the decision-maker, such as a defendant's decision to accept a proposed plea bargain or to waive or to seek or demand a trial by jury.

In civil cases, lawyers ordinarily apply some rather straightforward utilitarian standards in making decisions about whether a claim should be pursued, settled, or abandoned. Many of these decisions require that the available and potentially available evidence be evaluated in order to assess the likelihood that one party will prevail on liability questions and the probable value to that party of the damages or other relief that would be awarded if liability is established. These determinations must then be balanced against the potential risks and probable costs involved in pursuing the claim.

Standards for deciding whether to undertake a case and whether and on what basis to settle it may illustrate the point. Decision theorists and economists have tried to develop utilitarian standards that they argue should serve to guide lawyers and clients in evaluating and settling a legal dispute. A simplified approach might be stated as follows:

> Most cases should be settled, and the decision to take, prosecute, or settle a case can be reduced to a simple set of formulae that should be commonplace among lawyers. In almost every instance, there are only four variables that need be considered – the state of the law, the state of the evidence, the amount or value of the possible recovery, and the legal fees and costs likely to be incurred in achieving the result. At any time during a case, the lawyer's assessment of the probability that the court will apply a specific rule of law and of the probability that the then available evidence will persuade the fact-finder to impose liability upon the defendant under that rule provide a basis for calculating the probability that liability, "PL," will be imposed. The elements or heads of damages as a matter of law and the evidence available to prove the amount of damages recoverable in the particular case should suffice to enable a competent lawyer similarly to assess the probable amount of the anticipated damage award, "PD," at any stage. What is left is for the lawyer for each side to estimate the legal costs and fees, "CF," likely to be required, from that point forward, to litigate the matter to conclusion. This information should suffice to enable the lawyers for each side to make a reasoned assessment of the probable value of the case, "PV," at any stage.

In their simplest form, these decisions can be expressed for American litigation as follows:

For plaintiff: $PV = (PL \times PD) - CF$ (as assessed by plaintiff and his or her counsel)

For defendant: PV = (PL × PD) + CF   (as assessed by defendant and his or her counsel)

Although mathematics provides tools of sufficient sophistication to deal with more variables and may provide greater sophistication in reaching decisions, basic principles for evaluating the typical case can be simply devised and might be expressed as follows:

1. In ordinary circumstances, no lawyer should undertake a case for a potential plaintiff unless PV > 0 by an amount sufficient to compensate for the fact that the client will lose the estimated amount of the costs and fees and for the costs and burdens (economic and psychological) incidental to pursuing the claim.
2. In ordinary circumstances, cases should be settled whenever the sum of the future costs and fees to both sides exceeds the difference between the probable values as assessed by the clients and their respective lawyers, or whenever:

[PL × PD (plaintiff)] – [PL × PD (defendant)] ≤ CF (pff) + CF (def)

If lawyers understood simple decision analysis, there might be fewer trials, wealthier clients, and the economy would have eliminated substantial transaction costs.

Questions

1 The standards above are offered to guide lawyers (and clients) in the exercise of discretion. What, if any, standards define the limits of that discretion?
2 Review *Sargent v. Southern Accident Company* (page 28).
   a What factors should a lawyer have considered in deciding whether she should undertake to represent the Sargent family? Should it have made a difference, from her standpoint, whether she ordinarily charged an hourly rate or a contingent (percentage of recovery) fee for her services? Assuming either arrangement was permissible and was agreeable to the Sargent family, how should the lawyer have decided which method of charging was preferable? Which of the factors that she should have considered require an assessment of the evidence as it bore upon the probable outcome of the case?
   b From the standpoint of the Sargent family, what advice should they have required from the lawyer before deciding whether to pursue the claim or to retain this specific lawyer for the matter? Suppose the lawyer advised that her firm would undertake the matter for actual costs (deposition transcripts, filing fees, etc.) plus either a standard hourly billing rate of $200 an hour or a contingent fee of thirty percent (30%) of the amount recovered? If the Sargents liked the lawyer, how should they have proceeded to decide upon the fee? What legal or ethical duties would the lawyer have in advising the Sargents with respect to this decision?
   c Assume (1) that the lawyers representing the Sargents had agreed to represent them for a fee of $200 an hour plus any amounts expended for costs and the firm representing the insurance company had agreed to represent it for a fee of $150 an hour plus any amounts expended for costs; (2) that the Sargents have paid their lawyers $20,000 in fees and $10,000 for costs to date and that the insurance

company paid their lawyers $15,000 in fees and $10,000 for costs to date; (3) (i) that the lawyers for the Sargents have estimated that they will need to spend 60 more hours to prepare and try the case and that the costs from this point through the end of the trial will be about $8,000 and (ii) that the lawyers for the insurance company have given similar estimates of the fees and costs to be incurred if the case is tried.

  i How should the claims supervisor have proceeded to decide upon the maximum amount the company should offer to settle the case before trial? What strategy would you have employed as counsel for the company to achieve a successful settlement?

  ii How should the Sargents have decided on the minimum amount they would accept to settle the case? What strategy would you have employed as counsel for the Sargents to achieve a successful settlement?

 d How would the formulae for deciding to take or settle a case differ under a system that requires the losing party to pay the winning party's legal costs and fees ("the costs follow the event")? In view of this analysis, what policies are furthered by each of the systems?

b. Standards for lawyers' decisions

The significance of lawyer decisions and the extent to which these decisions are subject to standards are matters that are not frequently analyzed in books on evidence or trial practice. Ordinarily it is the lawyers who effectively direct the course of pre-trial pleading and discovery. By their discovery decisions, lawyers have the power to impose burdens on or to frustrate the legitimate objectives of the adverse party to the litigation. Similarly, lawyers have the power to impose significant burdens on the court as well as on the adverse party through their decisions concerning which motions should be filed and how vigorously each should be documented and pursued. In the United States, there is substantial literature and other evidence suggesting that lawyers involved in large cases use these powers for reasons that may be largely unrelated to achieving a prompt and fair adjudication of a disputed claim.[5] Some examples should illustrate the point.

(i) The decision to file a complaint

The range of a lawyer's discretion in filing a complaint (or other pleading) in a civil case has been the subject of extensive litigation in the United States. Lawyers are the officers of the court who make the final decision to file a civil complaint. American law prescribes standards (either directly or through the rules of the profession) that they are required to apply in deciding whether to initiate a case and, if so, what allegations may properly be made in an initial or subsequent pleading. For example, Rule 11 of the Federal Rules of Procedure in the United States provides:

---

5 See, e.g., John D. Shugrue, "Identifying and Combating Discovery Abuse," 23 Litigation No. 2 (Fall 1997) 10 (for an illustration and description); see also Symposium Conference on Discovery, 39 Boston Coll. L. Rev. (1998) 517–840 (for a more comprehensive overview).

Rule 11 – Signing of Pleadings, Motions, and Other Papers; Representations to Court; Sanctions

(a) Signature. Every pleading, written motion, and other paper shall be signed by at least one attorney of record in the attorney's individual name, or, if the party is not represented by an attorney, shall be signed by the party. Each paper shall state the signer's address and telephone number, if any. Except when otherwise specifically provided by rule or statute, pleadings need not be verified or accompanied by affidavit. An unsigned paper shall be stricken unless omission of the signature is corrected promptly after being called to the attention of the attorney or party.

(b) Representations to Court. By presenting to the court (whether by signing, filing, submitting, or later advocating) a pleading, written motion, or other paper, an attorney or unrepresented party is certifying that to the best of the person's knowledge, information, and belief, formed after an inquiry reasonable under the circumstances, –

(1) it is not being presented for any improper purpose, such as to harass or to cause unnecessary delay or needless increase in the cost;

(2) the claims, defenses, and other legal contentions therein are warranted by existing law or by a nonfrivolous argument for the extension, modification, or reversal of existing law or the establishment of new law;

(3) the allegations and other factual contentions have evidentiary support or, if specifically so identified, are likely to have evidentiary support after a reasonable opportunity for further investigation or discovery; and

(4) the denials of factual contentions are warranted on the evidence or, if specifically so identified, are reasonably based on a lack of information or belief.

(c) Sanctions. If, after notice and a reasonable opportunity to respond, the court determines that subdivision (b) has been violated, the court may, subject to the conditions stated below, impose an appropriate sanction upon the attorneys, law firms, or parties that have violated subdivision (b) or are responsible for the violation.

ii. The decision to prosecute

Section 9-27.220.A of the United States Justice Department's *United States Attorneys' Manual* specifies the standard that should be observed in deciding whether to prosecute:

The attorney for the government should commence or recommend Federal prosecution if he/she believes that the person's conduct constitutes a Federal offense and that the admissible evidence will probably be sufficient to obtain and sustain a conviction, unless, in his/her judgment, prosecution should be declined because:

1. No substantial Federal interest would be served by prosecution;
2. The person is subject to effective prosecution in another jurisdiction; or
3. There exists an adequate non-criminal alternative to prosecution.

The standard in England and Wales is similar. Under *The Code for Crown Prosecutors*,[6] there are two tests which must be satisfied before a prosecution is

6 The Code can be found at http://www.cps.gov.uk/publications/docs/codeeng.pdf.

initiated – the evidential test and the public interest test. The two are summarized in sections 5.1 and 6.2 of the Code.

> 5.1 Crown Prosecutors must be satisfied that there is enough evidence to provide a 'realistic prospect of conviction' against each defendant on each charge. They must consider what the defence case may be, and how that is likely to affect the prosecution case.
>
> ...
>
> 6.2 The public interest must be considered in each case where there is enough evidence to provide a realistic prospect of conviction. A prosecution will usually take place unless there are public interest factors tending against prosecution which clearly outweigh those tending in favour. Although there may be public interest factors against prosecution in a particular case, often the prosecution should go ahead and those factors should be put to the court for consideration when sentence is being passed.

Both sets of standards are clearly written as guides to the exercise of discretion. The legal limits of that discretion are unclear.

iii. Other pre-trial decisions

A further aspect of lawyers' decisions should be considered. There is frequently a tension between the lawyer's duties to the client (e.g., to pursue the client's objective zealously within the bounds of the law) and the lawyer's duties to the court and to opposing counsel and their clients (e.g., not to assert claims or take actions for purposes of delay). The duty to the client is likely to push the lawyer to ignore standards intended to guide discretion, such as the "good faith basis in fact" standard, and to exercise discretion in favor of the client unless satisfied that the exercise violates the standard establishing legal limits in a manner that is likely to be detected and result in sanctions or other adverse consequences.

For example, in 1969, the United States and, later, several private parties filed separate civil actions alleging that International Business Machines Company ("IBM") had violated various provisions of the antitrust laws. A few years later, IBM's chairman is reported to have quipped that IBM's Vice President for Legal Affairs had the only office with an unlimited budget, and that he had already over-spent it. IBM and its law firm are reported to have assigned more than 20 lawyers to the case and to have instructed them that every debatable issue was to be litigated to the maximum extent permitted by law. Pre-trial motions and discovery took six years. The trial on liability alone lasted more than six additional years. After 12 years and a change in the administration, the Justice Department dropped its suit, stipulating it was "without merit." Most of the private plaintiffs were unable to pursue their claims successfully. In one view, decisions by IBM and its lawyers to pursue every point to the maximum and the resulting delays ultimately controlled the outcome.[7] What standards other than costs can or should be applied to limit lawyers' discretion in

---

7 See Watson and Petre (1990) 376–89 (for a description from the client's standpoint).

making decisions in litigation? This ethical tension is apparent in many decisions lawyers must make.

Questions

1 Does Rule 11 of the Federal Rules of Civil Procedure establish standards intended to guide the lawyer in her exercise of discretion or standards designed to confine the limits of that discretion? Does the rule provide a clear standard governing a judge's decision to impose sanctions or merely standards designed to aid the judge in the exercise of discretion?

2 The standards established to guide prosecutors in deciding whether a prosecution should be initiated are, by their terms, intended as guides to the exercise of discretion. What standards should define the limits of that discretion and who should have authority to enforce them?

2. Standards for decisions in adjudication

Prior to or during trial, a party may ask the judge to dispose of all or part of the case as a matter of law – for instance, through a motion to dismiss or for summary judgment or for a directed verdict. During a trial, counsel for the parties will regularly call upon the judge to resolve disputes concerning the admissibility of evidence. At the close of the evidence, counsel will attempt to persuade the fact-finder that the evidence does or does not satisfy the prescribed standard and requires a verdict favorable to his or her client. Generally, the loser may appeal to a higher court claiming that errors by the trial judge or jury in applying the standards for assessing the parts or the whole of the evidence require outright reversal or at least a new trial. In this section, we discuss the significance of the standards governing adjudicative decisions such as these.

a. Standards for decisions disposing of a case as a matter of law

Prior to trial the parties to a case may ask the court to dispose of the case as a matter of law on the ground that there are no disputed facts the resolution of which could affect the outcome. A defendant may move to dismiss the complaint on the ground that the facts alleged, if true, do not state a claim for which the law provides a remedy. In a civil case, either party may move for judgment on the pleadings on the ground that the facts alleged or admitted in the pleadings, when viewed most favorably to the opposing party, establish as a matter of law that the relief must be or cannot properly be granted. At any time prior to a civil trial, with the additional evidence obtained through discovery or presented by affidavit, either party may ask the court to grant summary judgment on the ground that the then existing state of the record establishes that no fact material to a determination of the outcome as a matter of law is subject to any genuine dispute.

Each of these motions asserts a claim that there is no factual dispute to be resolved and that all facts necessary to a final application of the proper legal principle are admitted or have been placed beyond reasonable challenge. The standard for decision on such motions is whether the claimant is right: If there are no material facts in dispute, the court should finally dispose of the case by applying the correct principle of law.[8]

At various stages in a trial, the judge may be asked to terminate the proceedings and rule in favor of one of the parties. When the prosecution or the plaintiff has finished presenting evidence and has rested, the defendant may ask the trial court to rule that the evidence is insufficient to support a conviction or a judgment for the plaintiff. When the defendant has rested, either the defendant or, in a civil case, the plaintiff may ask the court to rule either that the evidence is insufficient or that it points so overwhelmingly in one party's favor that there is no reason to proceed further.

The standard that the trial judge is to apply again requires a determination whether any fact material to the outcome is subject to genuine dispute. A motion attacking the sufficiency of the evidence asks the court to determine that the evidence is so slight that no rational trier of fact could reach a favorable conclusion to the degree of certainty required by the applicable standard of proof. A motion asking for a directed verdict or an early judgment on other grounds asks the court to determine that the evidence is so weak or, in a civil case, so overwhelming that under the applicable standard of proof rational fact-finders could not disagree on the correct result.

In theory, an appellate court applies the same standard and need not accord any deference or special weight to the trial judge's decision on such claims. The appellate court, so the theory goes, is as capable as the trial court in identifying and applying the correct legal principle, and as capable as the trial court in determining whether the evidence left room for rational debate as to any fact necessary to the judgment reached.[9] The important points, for present purposes, are two. Logical analysis is a necessary condition to effective argument. It is not, however, a sufficient basis either for argument or for predicting or explaining decisions.

b. Standards for decisions on admissibility

We address the relationship between the principles of proof and the law of evidence in Chapter 11. It should be apparent, however, that many rules of evidence are standards intended to guide the trial judge in exercising her discretion in deciding whether evidence should be admitted or its use limited.

One of the basic principles underlying the rules and defining the extent of the judge's discretion under those rules is that a judge should exclude evidence whose

---

8 In theory, this involves no discretion, and an appellate court applies the same standard in assessing the trial court's decision, but cases such as *Robinson v. Diamond Housing Corp.*, 267 A.2d 833 (D.C. Ct. App. 1970), and *Robinson v. Diamond Housing Corp.*, 463 F.2d 853 (D.C. Cir. 1972) (reversing the decision of the District of Columbia Court of Appeals) make it clear that there is an element of discretion involved even here.

9 As the *Diamond* decisions in the trial court and on appeal illustrate, the extent to which appellate practice conforms to established theory is at least open to debate.

improper prejudicial effects substantially outweigh its legitimate probative value. Precise analysis of the inferences that a particular item of evidence might support is necessary to identify both its improper prejudicial effects and its legitimate probative value.

How should a Wigmorean lawyer approach the task of identifying and arguing the probative value and prejudicial effects that the court should consider in deciding whether particular evidence should be admitted or excluded? The first step in the equation requires identification of the inferences that are claimed to give the evidence legitimate probative value. The second requires identification of the improper prejudicial effects that the evidence may have. The results of this analysis establish the framework for arguments about whether the improper prejudicial effects substantially outweigh the legitimate probative value of the evidence in the context of this case.

Establishing probative value begins with analysis. To what fact of consequence in the litigation is the proffered evidential data relevant? The kind of analysis and its importance in this context may be illustrated by an example drawn from *United States v. Richard Able*.[10] Given the parties' respective theories, the only penultimate probanda open to dispute were:

5   At the time the 2003 return was filed, RA knew that the 2003 return was false.
8   At the time the 2003 return was filed, RA intended to defraud the government of the taxes due and owing on $45,000.

The prosecution would seek to introduce as part of its evidence the cancelled check for $25,000 issued by the law firm to Able with endorsements showing it was cashed at a Citibank branch in Las Vegas. Its relevance is clear. The cancelled check shows that Able received $25,000 on December 20, 2002, and that this amount was income. That check combined with evidence showing the salary Able received from the law school and the two other checks combine to support an inference that Able received $170,000 income during 2002 ($125,000 salary, $25,000 from the Law Firm, and $20,000 from other consulting work) – one of the penultimate probanda the government must prove. This analysis, at least provisionally, also establishes that the probative value of the evidence is high: Absent evidence of forgery or the like, the cancelled check would appear to establish, and to be necessary to establish, a central fact of consequence to something approaching a certainty.

The government would also claim that the endorsement made the check relevant to motive. On its face, the claim is plausible. The number of the steps in the chain of inferences necessary to demonstrate that relevance makes it clear that its probative value with respect to motive is slight (page 129).

In the face of that analysis, what bases would be open to counsel for Able to object to permitting the jury to see the endorsement on the check? The analysis necessary to

10 The case is at page 23; review also pages 125–28 (macroscopic analysis), pages 126–27 (theory of the case), and page 129 (preliminary analysis of the endorsement on the check for $25,000).

respond requires an understanding of the kinds of improper prejudicial effects that provide proper bases for arguments opposing the admission of particular evidence. The key is identifying effects that the law identifies as improper.[11]

A standard articulation requires the court to consider effects of the evidence that might cause "unfair prejudice, confusion of the issues, or misleading the jury, or ... undue delay, waste of time, or needless presentation of cumulative evidence."[12] That standard requires first an analysis of inferences supported by the evidence other than those that demonstrate its relevance, and then an identification of policies or reasons that renders the alternative inferences improperly prejudicial.

The nature of the task and some of the policies and reasons can be illustrated by an analysis of the endorsement on the cancelled check from the standpoint of counsel for Able. The endorsement showing that Able cashed the check on December 20 in Las Vegas supports a number of inferences:

> Able cashed a large check in Las Vegas, therefore Able was a gambler, therefore Able is a risk taker.
>
> The amount of the check supports an inference that Able stayed at a fancy hotel and gambling casino, therefore Able is a high liver.
>
> Only five days before Christmas, Able cashed a check in a city built for gamblers and in a state which has legalized prostitution, therefore Able is not the kind of person who respects the traditional ways of celebrating an important family and Christian holiday.

Depending upon the views represented in the jury, any or all of these inferences could be damaging to Able. At the same time, an inference that Able was a gambler and a high liver, in light of his income for the year, supports a chain of inferences pointing toward motive and hence to knowledge and intent. Are these inferences in any way improper?

The argument that they are unfairly prejudicial stems from the policies that underlie the rules governing character evidence. Although casino gambling may be legal in Las Vegas, it is likely to be viewed as a character defect in states where it is illegal (including the hypothetical New State), supporting an inference that Able is a bad person. So too, gambling may be regarded as establishing a propensity to take risks, and the jury might infer that Able's propensity to take risks made it likely that he took the risk of filing a false tax return to defraud the government. These inferences have some logical force, but they conflict with the policies of individuated justice that underlie the character evidence rule. Able is not on trial for gambling or high living, and the jury's deliberations may be unfairly prejudiced or the issues confused if this evidence is admitted.

This analysis has identified some prejudicial effects that are improper. The standard formulation of the rule, however, would require that Able's counsel persuade

---

11 It should be clear that any evidence that supports one side of a dispute should ordinarily have an adverse effect on the other. Sometimes in ordinary usage such adverse effects are called "prejudicial." This is misleading because, absent other factors, there is nothing improper about these effects.

12 Federal Rule of Evidence 403.

the trial judge that the danger created by improper prejudicial effects substantially outweighs the legitimate probative value of the law firm's check, which directly supports, and is probably the strongest evidence with respect to, an element of the offense – the amount of income Able received in 2002.

Assume that Linda Davis had died before the trial and that Able's counsel agreed to stipulate to the fact that Able received $25,000 from the law firm in 2002 and, if desired, to stipulate to the admission of a copy of the front of the check with a further stipulation that Able cashed it in December 2002. In that case, Able's lawyer could persuasively argue that the identified improper prejudicial effects substantially outweigh any legitimate probative value of the endorsement with respect to motive, and the argument would have considerable force.[13]

The example has isolated a piece of evidence and analyzed it apart from the case as a whole. Assume that Linda Davis had not died and was available at trial. In that situation, it should be apparent that an assessment of the arguments about the endorsement would depend upon Linda Davis's testimony. If Davis, for example, testified that Able took her to Las Vegas for a gambling spree and that the two did gamble heavily and lost and spent most of the balance of the $25,000 enjoying Las Vegas's other attractions, the prosecution's argument for admission would be far stronger. If, on the other hand, Davis proffers testimony consistent with Able's report of the events to his counsel, Able's lawyer may have a strong argument to exclude much of Davis's testimony as well as the endorsement.[14]

Three points deserve emphasis. First, an assessment of the probative value of an item of evidence requires a precise identification and analysis of each of the inferential steps necessary to relate it to a fact of consequence. Second, an identification and appraisal of the possible improper prejudicial effects ordinarily requires a similar analysis. Third, the analysis must examine the particular evidence in the context of the case as a whole. A Wigmorean chart demonstrates at a minimum that the bits of evidence in a case are so interconnected that decisions with respect to a particular item of evidence may have a significant effect on the whole. A blown fuse is going to affect more than the socket that caused it to blow.

So far the analysis has focused upon arguments designed to persuade the trial judge to sustain an objection claiming that the prejudicial effects of the endorsement substantially outweighed their probative value. Even with this rather detailed analysis, would a decision by the trial judge overruling either or both objections be likely to cause an appellate court to overrule the judgment were Able convicted? If the

---

13 Perhaps such force that a refusal by the trial court to accept to exclude the evidence would exceed the limits of the broad discretion conferred upon her by Rule 403. See *Old Chief v. United States*, 519 U.S. 172 (1997).

14 If Able's counsel succeeds in persuading the court to exclude the endorsement from evidence during the prosecution's case, the question could arise again if Able took the stand. If Able were to testify to facts supporting an argument that he was a fiscally and socially conservative individual, the prosecutor would likely re-offer the endorsement on rebuttal, arguing that Able's testimony had opened the door and placed his character in issue and had made the credibility of his assertions facts of consequence in the litigation and that the re-offered evidence had thus obtained a probative value that could no longer be successfully disputed.

trial judge were to sustain both objections, and if Able were found not guilty by the jury, the prosecution could not appeal and thus could not even challenge the decisions. The message is, if the lawyer does not win it at trial, it is highly unlikely that she will ever win it.

The analysis also illustrates the distinction between standards for decisions that serve as guides for the exercise of discretion and those, such as the standards of review, that define the limits within which that discretion must be exercised. From the standpoint of the lawyer, the former are useful primarily as articulations for framing cogent arguments to persuade the trial judge how discretion should be exercised; the latter are useful only where the lawyer can satisfy an appellate court that the trial judge exceeded the limits of the discretion permitted – a rare occurrence.

c. The case as a whole: burdens of proof and the civil and criminal standards

The distinction brought out by Gilbert between objective degrees of cogency and subjective degrees of persuasion or belief[15] is reflected in orthodox discourse about standards of proof. Thus the ordinary civil standard of proof is typically articulated in seemingly "objective" terms ("balance of probabilities," "preponderance of evidence") while the criminal standard is almost universally expressed in terms of the state of mind of the trier of fact ("proof beyond reasonable doubt" or "you must feel sure of the prisoner's guilt," as Goddard L.C.J. put it in *Regina v. Hepworth and Fearnley* [1955] Q.B. 600, 603).[16] The purpose of this section is to raise some questions about the meaning and role of these standards, how far they can be taken at face value as clear guides to decisions, and whether the distinction between objective and subjective criteria is of any practical importance. Chapter 9 addresses the question whether any or all of these standards can and should be treated as embodying probabilistic notions that are susceptible, at least in theory, to mathematical calculation.

There are common standards prescribed to guide the fact-finder in assessing the evidence as a whole. Under the standard commonly prescribed for civil cases, the fact-finder must determine whether the plaintiff has proved all the elements of the ultimate probandum by a preponderance or on the greater weight of the evidence or whether, on a balance of probabilities, the elements of the ultimate probandum are more probably true than not. On the criminal side, the fact-finder must determine whether the evidence establishes the elements of the offense and the defendant's guilt beyond a reasonable doubt. These are the basic standards by which fact-finders must evaluate the overall weight of the evidence.

There is an important preliminary question: Are standards of proof rules of law? If not, what are they? Both English and American discussions, by judges and commentators, abound with statements to the effect that it is impossible to give any precise meaning to the civil and criminal standards of proof, that to attempt to do so

---

15 Above page 228.
16 See the model direction by the Judicial Studies Board in England: www.jsboard.co.uk/specdir/. Discussed by Roberts and Zuckerman (2004) 363–64.

is otiose and may be dangerous and, as Sir Rupert Cross put it: "It is to be hoped that such questions . . . will never be allowed to become the basis of prescribed rules" (Cross (1979) 116). Yet, as we shall see, there is not only a very extensive theoretical debate about the meaning and rationale of the various standards, but also, as Chief Justice Burger acknowledged in *Addington v. Texas*, "even if the particular standard-of-proof catch-words do not always make a great difference in a particular case, adopting a 'standard of proof' is more than an empty semantic exercise" (441 U.S. 418, 423–25 (1979)).

Closely related to the above is the question: How many standards of proof are there in ordinary litigation? Here there seems to be a divergence of views among the authorities. In the United States it is now widely accepted that there are at least three distinguishable standards: proof beyond reasonable doubt, proof on the preponderance of evidence, and an intermediate standard variously expressed as proof by "clear and convincing," "clear, cogent, and convincing," or "clear, unequivocal, and convincing" evidence.

In England, on the other hand, the predominant view is that there are only two standards, but that there are different degrees of proof within each standard. Denning, L.J., as he then was, stated the matter as follows:

> The difference of opinion which has been evoked about the standard of proof in recent cases may well turn out to be more a matter of words than anything else. It is of course true that by our law a higher standard of proof is required in criminal cases than in civil cases. But this is subject to the qualification that there is no absolute standard in either case. In criminal cases the charge must be proved beyond reasonable doubt, but there may be degrees of proof within that standard. As Best, C.J., and many other great judges have said, "in proportion as the crime is enormous, so ought the proof to be clear." So also in civil cases, the case may be proved by a preponderance of probability, but there may be degrees of probability within that standard. The degree depends on the subject-matter. A civil court, when considering a charge of fraud, will naturally require for itself a higher degree of probability than that which it would require when asking if negligence is established. It does not adopt so high a degree as a criminal court, even when it is considering a charge of a criminal nature; but still it does require a degree of probability which is commensurate with the occasion.[17]

Is there any practical difference between the United States and English positions? It is commonly said that it would be unreasonable to expect the trier of fact to demand the same level of proof for a minor traffic violation as for a conviction for murder and that in civil cases involving allegations of dishonesty or adultery or illegitimacy, for example, a higher degree of probability is required than mere preponderance of evidence. That some such deviations are and should be applied is generally acknowledged, but there is a remarkable lack of clarity about the rationale(s) for such deviations and about the degree of deviation that is indicated in

---

17 *Bater v. Bater* [1951] P. 35, 36–37; cf. *Re H (Minors)* [1996] A.C. 563 (HL) criticized by Dennis (2004) 396–98.

each kind of case. Many judicial dicta suggest that the degree of probability may depend on the seriousness of the consequences to the subject of the allegation (for instance the stigma or likely harmful consequences of a judicial finding of adultery or fraud or paternity). Are these views reconcilable?[18]

d. Appellate review: standards for limiting discretion

The limits of the fact-finder's discretion here are of two types. First, the trial or the appellate court may intervene if it is satisfied either that the evidence is insufficient to support a finding for a claimant or that the evidence eliminates all material factual questions, either because it so overwhelmingly points to one conclusion that reasonable persons could not differ as to the correct conclusion or because it does not establish any genuine dispute with respect to a material issue of fact and the question concerns only the identification and application of the proper rule of law.[19] The prescribed standards for decisions of this type emphasize analysis, but require evaluation as well. For example, sufficiency is typically couched in terms of logical sufficiency, but it is clear that in most cases, the court is being asked to evaluate the opposing evidence and to discount strength of the claimed inferences to something approaching zero value. Second, if the evidence was logically sufficient and leaves questions of fact open for decision, the appellate court (or the trial judge after a jury trial) may set aside the factual determination only if it can declare from the evidence that the decision was clearly erroneous, against the manifest weight of the evidence, or unsafe. However framed, the standards for legal intervention in such circumstances are clearly designed to protect the fact-finder's discretion and to limit the occasions for intrusion.

The standards of review make it clear that the standards of proof are, from the trial lawyer's standpoint, merely guides to aid the fact-finder in exercising discretion. An appellate court may not reverse a jury's verdict unless it is satisfied that no rational jury could have reached the verdict it did on the evidence before it under the standard of proof applicable. Stated differently, so long as the evidence was logically sufficient to satisfy the standard and support the verdict, and not so overwhelmingly one-sided as to eliminate all genuine issues of material fact, the jury's discretion, in theory, has no effective limits.[20]

Policies favoring finality and judicial efficiency have led the courts to mandate similarly broad discretions for trial judges as fact-finders. In the United States federal

---

18 See the discussion in Roberts and Zuckerman (2004) 360–73.
19 Neither standard may be applied against the defendant in a criminal case, and it is generally agreed that the jury has a discretion to acquit that cannot be effectively overruled. However, in England, the Criminal Justice Act 2003, Part 10 authorizes the Court of Appeal to quash an acquittal for an offence (which appears on a list of serious offences) if "new and compelling evidence" has later come to light.
20 In England the standard for review in criminal appeals is now governed by section 2 of the Criminal Appeal Act 1995, which states: "Subject to the provisions of this Act, the Court of Appeal (a) shall allow an appeal against conviction if they think that the conviction is unsafe; and (b) shall dismiss such an appeal in any other case." On the debate leading up to this provision see Zander (2003) 658–75.

courts, for example, a court of appeals may not reverse a decision even when all three judges agree that they would have resolved the factual issues differently. Reversal of a factual finding is permissible only when the reviewing court determines that it is "clearly erroneous."[21] And a finding is only "'clearly erroneous' when … the reviewing court on the entire record is left with the definite and firm conviction that a mistake has been committed"(*Icicle Seafoods Inc. v. Worthington*, 475 U.S. 709 (1986)). Even then, the reviewing court may ordinarily not substitute its own factual findings for those of the trial court.

The standards of review concerning admissibility decisions also leave broad discretion in the trial court. The standard of review for decisions involving balancing tests is "abuse of discretion." Even if the reviewing court is satisfied that the trial judge exceeded the limits of the discretion allowed or otherwise erred in admitting or excluding evidence, the counsel must still satisfy the court that the error affected a substantial right of the appellant and had or may have had an effect on the outcome, such that the error cannot be properly classified as harmless.

In one view, standards of review such as these are the only operative rules of law regulating actual determinations. In that view, so long as the trial judge's and jury's decisions fall within the broad range of discretion allowed by these rules of law, these decisions are final. That view, however, is subject to at least two further qualifications. First, most appellate judges are fully able to interpret rules and marshal facts sufficiently to justify a reversal in any case in which they deem that appropriate. This qualification emphasizes the range of discretion and the power conferred upon the appellate courts. Second, the view fails to acknowledge adequately the extent to which judges and jurors take the standards seriously in attempting to exercise discretion responsibly. Stated differently, defining the range within which discretion may be exercised under various standards does not define the range within which discretion typically is exercised under those standards.

The view and its qualifications are important for those who would be trial lawyers. The view emphasizes the range of discretion available and defines the framework within which arguments may be constructed and made. It also emphasizes the importance of analysis and argument in the trial court. The qualifications serve as necessary cautions. The discretion at all levels is exercised by the men and women who act as decision-makers. The advocate must frame her arguments in a manner that takes account of the standpoint of the particular decision-makers to whom they will be addressed and recognizes the psychological and other non-legal factors that may be operative.

21 Fed. R. Civ. P. 52(a) (standard stated); *Anderson v. City of Bessemer City*, 470 U.S. 564 (1970) (standard applied).

Probabilities, weight, and probative force

A. Introduction

There are no conclusions reached in legal disputes that can be stated with absolute certainty. Consequently, the use of probabilistic concepts is as common in inferences in law as it is in inferences in other contexts. Probabilistic judgments concerning various matters in law are usually made verbally. For example, forensic standards of proof involve verbal probabilistic hedges such as "beyond reasonable doubt," "clear and convincing evidence," and "probable cause." In some contexts it is supposed that probabilistic judgments will always be stated numerically either using numbers on the conventional zero–one probability scale or in terms of odds. But in other contexts, law for example, such numerical judgments are quite difficult to make and justify because the events of concern either happened or did not happen on exactly one occasion. We cannot play the world over again a thousand times to determine the frequency with which these events have happened in the past. On only rare occasions in law can probabilities be determined by counting the frequency with which some event has occurred in the past.

There are basically five reasons why, in any context including law, conclusions based on evidence are necessarily probabilistic in nature. The first is that our evidence is *always incomplete*, we never have all of it. The second is that evidence is commonly *inconclusive*. This means that the evidence may to some degree favor more than one proposition at issue to some extent, or be consistent with the truth of more than one proposition at issue. Evidence we have is often *ambiguous*; we cannot decide what the evidence is telling us or what information it conveys. No better examples of ambiguous evidence exist than are found in the letters Edith Thompson wrote to Freddy Bywaters (see Chapter 7). Bodies of evidence are commonly *dissonant*; some of the evidence may favor one proposition while other evidence favors another proposition. Finally, evidence comes to us from *sources who/that have every gradation of credibility shy of perfection*. These five matters influence how the force of evidence is assessed, and they also influence how forensic standards of proof are stated.

There have been many attempts to relate verbal assessments of probability to ranges of numerical probabilities. For example, what range of numerical probabilities corresponds with someone's saying "very likely"? One of the best known efforts of this kind was undertaken by Sherman Kent who, for many years, was termed the "Dean" of American intelligence analysts. Based on extensive empirical studies involving many intelligence analysts, Kent generated intervals of probability numbers that corresponded with a variety of verbal hedges intelligence analysts employ such as "very probable," "probable," "improbable," and "very improbable." But efforts to equate verbal probabilistic hedges and intervals of numerical probabilities are rarely taken seriously. The reason is that probability intervals advertised as being equivalent to a verbal hedge may fail to be persuasive or useful to any given person. In addition, such scales have been formed using just the conventional views of probability. As we note in this section, there are other views of probability that should be taken seriously.

Certain probabilistic judgments in law involve the use of metaphors, some of which lead us to the essential topic in this section: the probative "weight," "force" or "strength" of evidence. As noted in Chapter 2, a major credential of evidence is its probative weight, force or strength. We now consider the task of assessing this important credential of evidence. Unfortunately, there is no settled way in which this credential should be assessed and graded; there is considerable controversy associated with these tasks. There appear to be only two uncontroversial characteristics of the force, weight or strength of evidence. The first is that gradations of the probative force of evidence have *vector-like* properties; that is, evidence may point in a certain *direction* (toward a certain proposition or probandum) with a certain force or strength. The second is that gradations of the force or weight of evidence are always expressed probabilistically in some way. Here is where the major controversy lies since there are quite different views about how evidential weight or force ought to be assessed in probabilistic terms. So, considering the force or weight credential of evidence is where probability enters our discussions. We now briefly consider some basic issues concerning probability and the force or weight of evidence. A more extensive discussion of probability appears in the Appendix by Professor Philip Dawid on the website.

B. Flirtations involving law and probability

Probability is an example of a discipline that, somewhat paradoxically, has a very long past but a very short history. There is evidence that cave dwellers in Paleolithic times used various devices (such as rudimentary dice) either for games of chance or to foretell the future. Subsequent legal and religious works, such as the Talmud and the Bible, make reference to probability and its determination in very simple situations. But it was not until the early 1600s that we have the first records of serious attempts to calculate probabilities. Blaise Pascal (1623–1662) is usually credited with being the first person to attempt to calculate probabilities associated with games of chance. This marks the beginning of mathematics being used with reference to probability. However, at this same time, persons in other fields began to take an interest in whether probability calculations could be made regarding events other than those involving games of chance. For example, merchants became interested in determining the probability that their cargoes would arrive safely at their destinations. Historians became interested in determining the probability that past events having historical significance had actually occurred as recorded in ancient documents. Theologians became interested in determining probabilities associated with past events having religious significance, particularly those involving miracles. What is of interest to us, however, is that some legal scholars in the 1600s began to take an interest in probabilities, particularly those associated with what they termed the *credibility-testimony* problem.

One problem of interest to early jurists concerned how strongly our belief that a certain event occurred ought to increase as we obtain testimony about this event's occurrence from additional witnesses. Testimony about the same event from two or more witnesses was then said to be *concurrent* testimony; in Chapter 2 we used the term *corroborative*[1] with reference to such testimony. It was recognized at the time that how strongly our belief increases with successive testimony depends upon the credibility of each one of the witnesses. Another problem of interest concerned what was then called *successive* testimony. Person A tells Person B that an event occurred; B tells C, C tells D, and so on. The issue was: how certain can we be that the event, as reported by the last person in this chain, actually occurred? You recognize this last person's testimony (what we presently have) as being *secondhand* or *hearsay* evidence. Theologians were especially interested in successive testimony. Among the matters of interest to them was the extent to which belief in some past religious event might naturally decay over time as testimony about this event was passed from one generation to the next, either orally or in written form. In the case of successive testimony, the extent of the decay in belief depends upon the credibility of each person or source in a chain of sources.

Thus began a long drawn out flirtation between law and probability.[2] This initial flirtation did not immediately ripen into a torrid romance. Some early scholars were not at all convinced that the complexity of matters such as the credibility-testimony problem could ever be captured in probabilistic terms. In addition, for many years probabilists have linked probability only to those situations involving replicable events for which we can obtain estimates of probabilities by *counting* or *enumeration*. Unfortunately, this does not apply to most of the events that are of interest to legal scholars and practitioners which tend to be unique, singular or one-of-a-kind. As noted above, we cannot play the world over a thousand times to determine the number of occasions a defendant actually committed the crime for which he/she is now charged. Nor can we play the world over again to determine the number of occasions on which a defendant may have committed repeated instances of the same crime. Within evidence scholarship in law, during the past

---

1 On the ambiguity of the term "corroboration," see the Glossary.
2 Good assessments of the historical beginnings of the flirtation of law and probability are to be found in the works of Lorraine Daston (1988) and Barbara Shapiro (1982, 1991).

30 years or so, there has been considerable debate about applications of probability in the field of law. This debate has been particularly intense because there are now alternative views about what a probability means in the first place. Here is a very brief review of some of the issues that are currently being addressed in this continuing debate.

If there is now a romance between law and probability, it is often a stormy one. One reason is that probabilists (and others) cannot agree about what constitutes a "rational" approach to drawing conclusions from evidence having the five characteristics noted above. Their disputes have only intensified debates among legal scholars about the extent to which probability theories have anything of value to offer scholars and practitioners in law. The so-called "probability debates" in law have been underway now for over *thirty* years. What made contemporary legal scholars begin to debate among themselves about probabilities? Identifying the exact stimulus for any human activity is no easy task. Here is a brief summary of works emerging during the law–probability flirtation in recent times.

Developments were taking place in probability theory during the 1970s that have forever changed the face of probability. Some very old ideas were challenged within probability theory itself. Debates among probabilists about the merits of these new ideas added considerable vigor to discussions about probability that took place among legal scholars. The probabilistic reasoning tasks required in legal and in many other contexts are far too rich for us to expect that all of this richness can be captured within the confines of any single theory of probability. Papers by Ekelof (1964), Williams (1979), Eggleston (1979), Twining (1980), and a book by Cohen (1977) raised issues that gave rise to a conference on probabilistic issues in law that took place in Durham, England in 1982 (Twining, 1983). In 1984 and 1988, Adrian Zuckerman, of the Oxford University Law Faculty, organized two conferences on probability and evidence in the field of law. Probabilists as well as legal scholars attended both conferences. In 1986 and in 1990, Peter Tillers (Cardozo Law School) held conferences on probability and evidence in law at Boston University Law School and at Cardozo Law School. Papers given during these two conferences were published in special issues of the *Boston University Law Review* (Tillers and Green (1986), also (1988)) and in the *Cardozo Law Review* (Tillers (1990)).

One focal point of much discussion about probabilities in law was the *Collins* Case.[3] The major issue in this case was one of identification. According to witnesses, a white female assaulted and attempted to rob an older woman. The female assailant escaped from the scene in a car driven by an African-American male. Witnesses described various details of the two participants and of the car in which they fled the scene. A white female and an African-American male, meeting these descriptions, were subsequently arrested and brought to trial. The prosecution hired a probabilist named Edward O. Thorp to calculate a *statistical* estimate of the probability that

---

3 *People v. Collins* (1968 Cal. 2d 319).

any two persons would have the same characteristics as those described by the witnesses (and possessed by the defendants). The probability estimate that Thorp calculated was *very* small. On this basis, the prosecution argued that the two persons in custody must have been the ones who committed the crime. To shorten a long story, some probabilists immediately argued that Thorp's calculations were quite inappropriate and legal scholars argued about the justice of what was later called "a trial by numbers."

In 1970, in the wake of the *Collins* Case, appeared an article in the *Harvard Law Review* by Finklestein and Fairley entitled: "A Bayesian Approach to Identification Evidence." The authors attempted to provide what they believed would be a more satisfactory approach to calculating identification probabilities. Several probabilists had also written papers that were justly critical of Thorp's calculations in the *Collins* Case. A year later, in 1971, came a resounding rebuttal to Finkelstein and Fairley written by Professor Lawrence Tribe, also in the *Harvard Law Review*. Tribe's piece was entitled: "Trial by Mathematics: Precision and Ritual in the Legal Process." Tribe essentially argued against any use of numerical probabilities, as a matter of policy, in settling matters at trial. Tribe advanced three main reasons for this: (1) As a matter of communication, so long as judges and jurors can be assumed to be innumerate, they should not be addressed in a language they cannot understand; (2) Mathematical arguments are likely to be overly seductive or prejudicial because seemingly "hard" quantified variables will tend to push out "soft" non-quantitative variables; and (3) It is politically improper to quantify certain matters, such as an acceptable level of risk of conviction of the innocent. In this debate about probabilities between jurists, Tribe seems to have won the day.

But Tribe's victory served only to stimulate other legal scholars to write about probabilistic issues. If Tribe believed he had put probability to rest in the field of law, he was mistaken. An influential paper by Richard Lempert on relevance (1977) considers how the weight of evidence should be graded in probabilistic terms. In this work Lempert advised other legal scholars and practitioners not to ignore research on probabilistic reasoning regardless of what Professor Tribe said about the evils of mathematics. Lempert's essential argument was that probabilistic analyses of evidential issues could be very informative to jurists in a variety of ways. Lempert's work was very influential in arousing interest in probabilistic issues on the part of other evidence scholars in law.

Each view of probability we will describe allows us to capture unique and important elements of this intellectual richness. Each view has something valuable to say; but no single view says it all. Within the field of law, and in other fields as well, debate about probability and the force of evidence continues.

C. Probability and the force or weight of evidence

In this section are four different probabilistic conceptions about ways of assessing the probative force or weight of evidence.

1. Conventional probability and Bayes's Rule

There are three basic axioms upon which this conventional view of probability rests:

- Probabilities are either positive numbers or are zero (there are no negative probabilities).
- The probability of a sure event (one certain to happen) is 1.0.
- If two events cannot happen jointly, the probability that one or the other occurs is equal to the sum of their separate probabilities.

Taken together, these three properties simply say that probabilities are numbers between zero and one (inclusive) and that they are additive across mutually exclusive events (those that cannot occur together or jointly). But all probabilities rest upon what we know or assume at the time they are either calculated or judged; and they may change in light of new information we obtain. Thus, all probabilities must have some means by which they can be revised or updated in light of, or conditional upon, new information. In the conventional view of probability there exists the concept of a *conditional probability* that shows one way of revising a probability in light of new information. One very important consequence of these three axioms and how a conditional probability is defined is called *Bayes's Rule* or *Bayes's Theorem* (named after the eighteenth-century English clergyman Thomas Bayes, who first described its properties).[4]

Suppose that we want to reassess the probability of a probandum in light of a new item of evidence. This probability is called a *posterior probability* because it concerns the probability of this proposition *after* we have obtained this new evidence. In order to determine this posterior probability, we need to have two ingredients. The first, called a *prior probability*, expresses how sure we were that this proposition is true *before* we received this new evidence. The second, called a *likelihood*, allows us to express how strong or forceful is this new evidence in changing our prior probability into a posterior probability. As we now illustrate, the force or weight of evidence in conventional probabilities is graded by considering *ratios of likelihoods*.

For example, suppose the probandum of interest is: It was Nicola Sacco who shot the payroll guard Alessandro Berardelli. We must of course consider the alternative proposition that it was not Nicola Sacco who shot Alessandro Berardelli. Here is an item of evidence we must now take into consideration: The bullet that killed Berardelli was fired through a 32-caliber automatic pistol that Sacco was carrying when he was arrested. Here is a picture of how the probative weight or force of this evidence is graded in probabilistic terms using a ratio of likelihoods.

Shown in Figure 9.1 are two likelihoods. The first expresses how likely it is that the bullet that killed Berardelli was fired through Sacco's automatic, given that Sacco *did* shoot Berardelli. The second expresses how likely it is that the bullet

---

4 Equations for Bayes's Rule and some exercises involving its use appear in the Appendix on Probabilities and Proof.

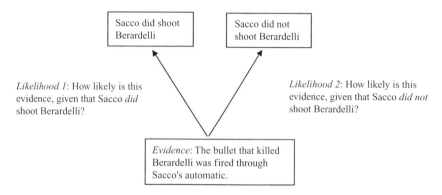

Figure 9.1 *Illustrating a likelihood ratio method for grading the probative force of evidence*

that killed Berardelli was fired through Sacco's automatic, given that Sacco *did not* shoot Berardelli. We first notice that this bullet evidence is *inconclusive.* The bullet may have been fired through Sacco's automatic, but it may have been another person who fired Sacco's automatic. We are concerned of course about the credibility of the bullet evidence. Perhaps this bullet was not fired through Sacco's automatic (as the prosecution claimed).

The probative force of this bullet evidence depends on the relative sizes of the two likelihoods shown in Figure 9.1. If we believe Likelihood 1 is greater than Likelihood 2, then we are saying that this bullet evidence favors the proposition that it was Sacco who shot Berardelli. How strongly the evidence favors Sacco shooting Berardelli depends on how many times larger is Likelihood 1 than Likelihood 2; this is why we consider their ratios. If we believe that Likelihood 2 is greater than Likelihood 1, then we are saying that this bullet evidence favors the proposition that Sacco did not shoot Berardelli. How strongly this evidence favors Sacco not shooting Berardelli depends on how many times larger is Likelihood 2 than Likelihood 1. If the two likelihoods are equal, this says that the bullet evidence has no probative force at all, since it is equally likely under both propositions at issue.

The example shown in Figure 9.1 concerns a likelihood ratio approach to grading the probative force of just a single item of evidence. But this approach can also be used to grade the probative force of bodies of evidence of various sizes. For example, in the *Sacco and Vanzetti* case we might form a likelihood ratio for the entire mass of evidence generated in this case. Here we would ask the question: Is this aggregate evidence more likely if Sacco and Vanzetti were guilty as charged than it would be if they were not guilty as charged?

Lempert (1977) argued that this way of expressing evidential force or weight is entirely consistent with how FRE-401 defines relevance. Evidence is relevant if it allows us to revise, upward or downward, our probability of some proposition. This is exactly what a likelihood ratio expresses. It shows the extent to which an item or body of evidence allows us to revise a prior belief (before new evidence) to form a posterior belief (after taking the new evidence into account).

A likelihood ratio approach to grading the probative force of evidence has many virtues. In a Wigmore chart, an argument linking evidence to some proposition or probandum involves, among other things, revealing all the sources of doubt or uncertainty we believe to lurk between the evidence and the proposition whose proof is being sought. Each source of doubt represents a link in the chain of reasoning we have constructed to link evidence with what we are trying to prove from it. Expanded forms of likelihood ratios allow us to combine all recognized sources of doubt in assessing the probative force or weight of evidence. Some of these sources of doubt concern the credibility of the source of the evidence. Other sources of doubt concern links in chains of reasoning we construct to defend the relevance of the evidence on the proposition at issue. So, likelihood ratios allow us to combine both the credibility and relevance ingredients of the probative force of evidence.

Another major virtue of grading probative force or weight in terms of likelihood ratios is that such methods allow us to capture for study and analysis a very wide array of evidential and inferential subtleties that reside just below the surface of even the simplest of evidence-based reasoning tasks. In Chapter 2 we provided an account of the recurrent substance-blind forms and combinations of evidence. Likelihood ratio analyses of the probative force of these forms and combinations of evidence provide valuable insights about the consequences of having various beliefs concerning the probabilistic ingredients required in assessing the probative force of these forms and combinations of evidence (see further Schum, 1994, Chs. 6, 7, and 8).

2. Evidential support and evidential weight: non-additive probabilistic beliefs

The likelihood ratio approach just described rests on the three axioms mentioned in introducing this approach. These three axioms were first proposed by the Russian mathematician A. N. Kolmogorov (1933). Axioms forming the basis for any formal system are statements that the proponent believes are self-evident and that should be accepted as such by everyone else. From a set of axioms various consequences are deduced. Modern probability theory now provides a vast array of very useful consequences that have been deduced from Kolmogorov's three basic axioms, including Bayes's Rule. However, not everyone will necessarily accept as self-evident what another person proposes as axioms. Shafer (1976) rejected Kolmogorov's third axiom involving additivity in relation to probability judgments that are necessary for the unique events so commonly encountered in the field of law. In Shafer's system there is a quite different interpretation of what the weight of evidence means. Following is an example of his concerns about Kolmogorov's additivity axiom and what it says about probabilistic beliefs and the probative weight or force of evidence.

Suppose you have read the entire transcript of the Bywaters and Thompson trial, as discussed in Chapter 7, and are asked to judge the probability, on all this evidence, that Edith Thompson was guilty of the charge against her. She either conspired with Freddy Bywaters to kill her husband Percy on the particular occasion on which Percy was killed, or, over time, she incited Freddy to kill Percy on some unspecified occasion. Suppose you judge this probability to be 0.6. Now, consider the proposition that Edith is not guilty of this charge. Edith cannot be guilty and not guilty at the same time; these two events are mutually exclusive. Further, they are exhaustive; as far as legal deliberations are concerned, one of these events must be true. So, if asked what the probability is that Edith was not guilty, Kolmogorov's rules state that you must say that this probability is 0.4, since the conventional probabilities for mutually exclusive and exhaustive events must sum to 1.0. If you had been a member of the jury in this case, you would almost certainly not have voted to convict Edith, since your assessed probability of her guilt seems quite far below a proof "beyond reasonable doubt."

Reflecting on your task of assessing these probabilities, Professor Shafer argues that this additivity requirement puts a burden on you that you might not be willing to accept. The conventional system of probability requires that you must always commit all of your probabilistic belief to mutually exclusive and exhaustive events; you cannot hold back any of your belief or leave it uncommitted. Another way of saying this is to say that you must be completely decisive in expressing your beliefs; your probabilistic assessments must not reflect any indecision on your part. However, suppose that you cannot decide what some of the evidence against Edith really means. Take Edith's letters to Freddy for example. Do they mean that she herself had contemplated or even tried, without success, to kill Percy? Or, are they simply manifestations of her fantasies about being rid of an abusive husband for whom she no longer had any affection? A third possibility is that there is no connection between Edith's letters to Freddy and the events surrounding Freddy's killing of Percy. A major feature of Shafer's approach to probabilistic reasoning is that it provides for instances in which you can deliberately withhold some of your probabilistic belief. In other words, you are entitled to be indecisive in situations in which, among other factors, you cannot decide what some of the evidence really means.

To illustrate further some of the consequences of being able to withhold some of your probabilistic beliefs, we first need to examine Shafer's views about what the probative weight or force of evidence really means. His interpretation of this credential of evidence is quite different from the likelihood ratio interpretation we examined above. On Shafer's view, the weight of evidence means the *support* this evidence provides to propositions at issue. The more support evidence provides to some proposition the greater the weight of this evidence. Shafer employs numbers between zero and 1.0 (inclusive) to indicate the degree of support or weight, but he does so in a way that is not consistent with the Kolmogorov axiom for additivity. Suppose we let U = the ultimate probandum that Edith Thompson is guilty of the charge against her; then **not** $- U$ = the negation of U or the possibility that Edith is not guilty of the charge against her. Following is an example of what you are permitted to do using Shafer's system.

Consider just the letters that Edith wrote to Freddy; let L be the evidence of these letters. To what extent do these letters, as evidence, support U or $not - U$? Let S_L be the support you will assign to these possibilities based on letter evidence L: Here is an example of how you can assign S_L.

$$\{U\} \quad \{not - U\} \quad \{U, not - U\}$$
$$S_L: \quad 0.6 \quad\quad 0.1 \quad\quad\quad 0.3$$

These support assignments say that you believe Edith's letters support her guilt to degree 0.6 and *her being not* guilty to degree 0.1. But, what does the support of 0.3 you have assigned to $\{U, not - U\}$ mean? First, read the expression $\{U, not - U\}$ as: Edith is guilty or Edith is not guilty. The value of $S_L = 0.3$ you have assigned to $\{U, not - U\}$ indicates the degree of *indecision* on your part about whether her letters support Edith's guilt or support Edith's being not guilty. In other words, this is the degree of your evidential support, indicated by S_L, that you have held back or have not yet committed to either U or to $not - U$ specifically. You can regard $S_L = 0.3$ for $\{U, not - U\}$ as indicating the degree of your support that could favor either U or $not - U$ but which one you cannot presently decide.

Observe in the example above that your present beliefs about U and $not - U$, based on letter evidence L, do not sum to 1.0, as would be required in conventional probability. If you had been using Bayes' Rule, your posterior probabilities for U and $not - U$, based on letter evidence L, would be required to sum to 1.0. You can in fact assign support S to propositions or probanda in ways that capture a wide assortment of belief states that we all experience. This is one of the major virtues of Shafer's system. Here is an example of an extreme belief that you can capture using Shafer's system; it involves the concept of *ignorance* as *lack of belief*. Using Edith's letters to Freddy again, suppose that after reading these letters you believe that they are sufficiently ambiguous that you simply cannot decide whether they specifically favor U or $not - U$ to any degree at all. In other words you cannot commit any of your belief specifically to either of these possibilities. In this case, your S_L assignment would look like this:

$$\{U\} \quad \{not - U\} \quad \{U, not - U\}$$
$$S_L: \quad 0 \quad\quad 0 \quad\quad\quad 1.0$$

What this support assignment says is that you are presently completely indecisive about the extent to which the letter evidence supports either U or $not - U$ specifically and so you have completely withheld all of your support from either one of these possibilities. You presently have no grounds for saying that this letter evidence specifically supports U or supports $not - U$.

It is entirely fair to ask what the consequence is, in the above example, of having assigned $S_L = 0$ to both U and to $not - U$ specifically. The answer to this question requires us to compare Shafer's support scale with the scale in the conventional probability system. First, here is a listing of interpretations that can be placed on the end points of the conventional probability scale:

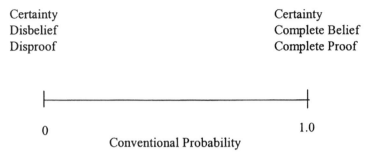

Figure 9.2 *Conventional probability scale*

Figure 9.3 *Evidential support scale*

On this conventional probability scale the value 1.0 means that an event is certain to occur or you have a complete belief that this event will occur. The probability value zero means that an event is certain not to occur or that you disbelieve that this event occurred. We discuss the proof-disproof dimension on this probability scale momentarily when we consider the third view of what is meant by the weight or force of evidence. But on an evidential support scale for S there is an entirely different meaning attached to the zero point; this scale is shown in Figure 9.3.

The major distinction between conventional probabilities and Shafer's support assignments is that zero no longer represents disbelief but lack of belief. In the conventional system of probability, a probability of zero assigned to some proposition means that this proposition is completely dead; it cannot be resuscitated by any further evidence, regardless of how strong this evidence might seem. In other words, we cannot say that we disbelieve some proposition and then later say we believe it. But we can say that a lack of belief means something entirely different than disbelief. We can go from a lack of belief to some degree of belief if our evidence supports this change. So, propositions assigned S = 0 are not forever dead as they would be if they were assigned conventional probabilities.

Finally, since an axiom of conventional probability is violated in Shafer's system, we should not expect to see Bayes's Rule being the means for revising our beliefs about propositions in light of further evidence. In Shafer's system there is a rule called Dempster's Rule that allows us to combine support assignments assigned to different items or bodies of evidence. Dempster's Rule allows us to go from a lack of belief to some degree of belief in a proposition in light of further evidence (see further Shafer (1976), Schum (1994) 225–43).

3. Baconian probability and completeness of evidential coverage

Centuries ago, Sir Francis Bacon proposed the idea that we would be wasting our time trying to prove some general hypothesis or proposition just by accumulating evidential instances favorable to this hypothesis. Regardless of how many results favorable to this hypothesis we have accumulated, all it takes is one demonstrably unfavorable result to disprove this hypothesis. What Bacon argued was that we would be far better off performing evidential tests designed to eliminate any hypothesis we are considering. The hypothesis that best resists our most concerted efforts to eliminate it, as well as any other hypotheses, is the one in which we should have increasing confidence. This strategy has become known as *induction by elimination*. The best known development of Bacon's method was by John Stuart Mill (1843).

It will not do of course in eliminative testing to perform the same test over and over again. This may increase our belief about the reliability of this single test, but it will not increase our belief regarding the extent to which any hypothesis holds up in many circumstances. In the testing of drugs for their possible toxicity to human beings we need to determine whether a drug continues to be non-toxic under such conditions as various levels and spacing of dosages, the age and sex of the recipients of the drug, and possible interactions with other drugs a person might be taking. In short, eliminative testing also needs to be *variative* in nature. The more different conditions under which a hypothesis holds up, the more confidence we can have in it.

John Stuart Mill was not successful in showing how conventional probability is applicable in eliminative and variative testing. Nor was the philosopher Karl Popper later on, who also advocated eliminative testing, successful in relating conventional probability to such testing. Popper did, however, claim that science should strive for improbable hypotheses that provide us with the most surprising deductions of new phenomena (Popper, 1968). Development of a system of probability expressly congenial to eliminative and variative induction awaited the work of L. Jonathan Cohen. In Cohen's major work (1977), he advocated a system of probabilities that we now call Baconian to acknowledge their linkage to Bacon's original ideas about eliminative and variative testing. In Cohen's Baconian probability system, evidence is *relevant* only if it serves to eliminate one or more hypotheses or propositions being considered. Such elimination, however, is usually only tentative since later evidence may act to explain away the eliminative properties of an earlier item of evidence on a certain hypothesis.

Cohen's Baconian probabilities differ considerably from ordinary probabilities as illustrated on the scale in Figure 9.2. First, as in Shafer's support S scale, a Baconian probability of zero has a different meaning as shown in Figure 9.4. On this Baconian

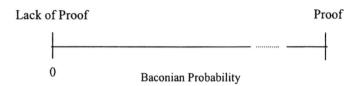

Figure 9.4 *A Baconian probability scale*

scale zero means *lack of proof* rather than disproof. A Baconian probability of zero for some hypothesis can be revised upward since we can go from lack of proof to some proof if justified by evidence. Notice that we have not put any number to be associated with the upper end of the Baconian scale. The reason involves several additional properties of Baconian probabilities.

Cohen's Baconian probabilities have only *ordinal* properties. What this means is that we can compare them to see which is larger but we cannot perform any algebraic operations on them (those involving addition, subtraction, multiplication, or division). A Baconian probability for some hypothesis or proposition increases as this hypothesis passes more eliminative and variative evidential tests. But the tests may not all be comparable since they involve different matters. Thus, for example, we cannot say that the Baconian probability of hypothesis H_1, which has passed four tests, is twice as large as the Baconian probability of hypothesis H_2, which has only passed two tests. The reason is that the tests passed by these hypotheses may not be comparable in terms of their importance or eliminative potential. In short, there is no natural unit of Baconian probability as assumed in conventional probabilities or on Shafer's support scale.

We now come to the most important property of Baconian probability as far as concerns the probative weight or force of evidence. In the eliminative and variative testing of hypotheses, it is altogether important to consider *how many* different tests have been performed and how completely our testing has involved all relevant matters that anyone could think of. In testing the toxicity of a drug, for example, regardless of how many other tests drug X has passed, we will not have confidence in its being non-toxic if we have failed to check to see whether it remains non-toxic when taken with other drugs or if we ignore its possible long-run effects. In a Baconian view of probabilistic reasoning the weight of evidence depends in large part on how many questions there are that remain *unanswered* by the evidence we have. In short, the Baconian weight of evidence is related to *how complete has been the coverage* of evidence on matters recognized to be relevant in the inference at hand. Here is a picture of the Baconian interpretation of the probative weight or force of evidence; it involves the "inferential limb" on which we find ourselves when we attempt to draw a conclusion from evidence.

Suppose on the basis of a collection of evidence we decide to conclude that hypothesis H is true. Figure 9.5 illustrates the inferential limb we find ourselves on when we draw this conclusion. The length and strength of this limb depends upon

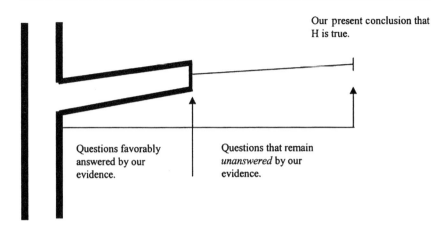

Figure 9.5 *Illustrating the Baconian weight of evidence*

two things. First, the strong part of our inferential limb depends on how much credible evidence we have that is favorable to hypothesis H. Second, the weak part of our inferential limb depends on how many questions regarding the likeliness of any of our hypotheses remain *unanswered* by the evidence we have. Baconian probabilities take both of these matters into account. Answers to some of these unanswered questions may in fact be favorable to our chosen hypothesis H; but other answers may not be at all favorable to H. We cannot know which ones and how many will also be favorable until we ask the questions. The basic reason why we do not put a specific number on the right-hand end of the Baconian probability scale in Figure 9.4 is that we ordinarily do not know how many tests of hypothesis H are possible. We can only list those unanswered questions that we have recognized.

Cohen's system of Baconian probability is the only system that takes specific account of how completely the evidence we have covers matters recognized to be relevant in the testing of hypotheses we entertain. Such information is not conveyed, for example, by Bayesian posterior probabilities, even if they are very large and near 1.0. Cohen argues that in judging the probative force of evidence we cannot ignore how much evidence we have and how completely it covers questions relevant to matters at issue. It happens that Cohen's major work (1977) is especially directed at inferences in the field of law. In this work, he has assembled a large collection of anomalies and paradoxes he says are associated with attempts to apply conventional probabilities to inferences in law. A discussion of the anomalies and paradoxes Cohen identified appears elsewhere (Schum, 1979). His work generated widespread discussion and much controversy among legal scholars as well as probabilists. Not all of the troubles he mentioned were viewed as anomalous or paradoxical. But we should not ignore what he has told us about the importance of evidential completeness in grading the probative weight of evidence.

4. Wigmore and the fuzzy weight of evidence

Wigmore was no probabilist, but he did understand that the linkages between probanda in chains of reasoning are probabilistic in nature. This is why we have said that a chain of reasoning involves sources of doubt or uncertainty. He described the strength of these probabilistic linkages in words rather than numbers. This is something that we all do on many occasions when we wish to convey to others our beliefs about the likeliness of events when we have no basis for assigning precise numerical probabilities to these events. But Wigmore also used the term "force" in describing the strength of these probabilistic linkages. He used different symbols attached to his arrows linking probanda. One symbol meant "weak probative force"; another symbol meant "strong probative force"; another meant "provisional probative force"; and there were others. One criticism frequently directed at Wigmore's methods concerns his never providing any method for combining all of these verbal probabilistic force gradations in reaching a conclusion about the aggregate force of some mass of evidence.

Wigmore died in 1943, only 22 years before the development of "fuzzy logic" by Professor Lotfi Zadeh. In a celebrated paper in 1965, Zadeh asked us all to recognize how much imprecision is rampant in our inferences, decisions and other activities. In probabilistic reasoning, for example, we so often attach words rather than numbers to indicate the strength of our conclusions, since we have no basis for providing precise single probabilities or even intervals of probabilities. Such probabilities Zadeh has called "fuzzy probabilities" recognizing their imprecision. Wigmore's methods for grading probative force are examples of fuzzy probabilities or hedges. What is especially interesting about Zadeh's work is that he provides methods for combining fuzzy gradations of various things. Following is just one example of Zadeh's concerns about the fuzziness rampant in our everyday reasoning.

Suppose you hear the following argument: "If a person is *overworked* and *underpaid*, then this person is *probably not very satisfied* with his/her job." We hear arguments like this all the time; Zadeh calls such reasoning "inexact" or "approximate." All the words italicized in the sentence above are fuzzy ingredients; there is no precision here regarding any of these ingredients. Fuzzy probabilistic qualifiers abound in the field of law, for example: beyond reasonable doubt, balance of probabilities, clear and convincing evidence, and probable cause. All these forensic standards of decision are necessarily fuzzy since we are unable to provide precise and uncontroversial numerical probabilities, of any kind, to associate with them. In many situations we may not be able to improve upon Wigmore's fuzzy gradations of the probative force of evidence. All of the views we have examined have been criticized in various ways. Zadeh's work on fuzzy logic has not escaped criticism. Susan Haack (1996) questions the philosophical bona fides of fuzzy logic and also points out that applications of fuzzy logic designed to cope with imprecision involve mechanisms that do induce precision.

In summary, we have provided four quite different interpretations of what is meant by the probative force, weight or strength of evidence. Each view tells us something valuable about this important credential of evidence, but no single view says all there is to be said. Likelihood ratios from Bayes's Rule allow us to capture many interesting and important evidential and inferential subtleties and are consistent with what FRE-401 says regarding relevance. Shafer's direct assessments of evidential weight as evidential support allow us to be indecisive in hedging conclusions and to withhold portions of our beliefs, and they allow us to capture important judgmental characteristics that are very common. Baconian interpretations of the probative force of evidence alert us to the importance of considering how much evidence we have and how completely it covers matters we recognize as relevant in inferences we make. Questions we have not yet answered are just as important in inferences as those for which we have obtained evidential answers. Finally, Wigmore's fuzzy gradations of the force of evidence are certainly in keeping with the many other fuzzy interpretations of uncertainties encountered in the field of law.

10

Necessary but dangerous: generalizations and stories in argumentation about facts[1]

> Since, then, our inferences from fact to fact depend upon our belief in general rules of connection between fact and fact, generalizations about the way things happen in nature, the work of criticizing inferences resolves itself into that of criticizing general-izations. (Sidgwick (1884) 9)

We have seen that generalizations are almost always necessary as warrants for every step in inferential reasoning, but that they can often be shown to be the weakest points in an argument (Chapter 3). Similarly, we have seen that stories are not just an alternative to analytical approaches such as the chart method, but rather complement them in important ways (Chapter 6). According to some psychologists and practitioners stories are psychologically necessary to decision-making about issues of fact. Yet another strand in the literature suggests that stories are wonderful vehicles for "cheating" in the process of persuasion in legal contexts. In this chapter we look in more detail at the nature of generalizations and stories, their role in fact-determination, some reasons why they can be labeled dangerous, some links between these dangers, and practical techniques for navigating them in litigation.

A. Generalizations

1. Reprise and introduction

Generalizations are warrants that serve as the "glue" that links an item of evidence to a particular interim or ultimate *probandum* by showing that it is relevant (*Foun-dations* 81–83, 109). We have previously examined the role of generalizations in arguments about evidence. In Chapter 3 we identified the role that generalizations perform in the application of the principles of logic in constructing and analyzing arguments. The materials from *R. v. Bywaters and Thompson* illustrated the kinds of covert roles that generalizations based upon prejudice may play, roles that make them dangerous. Chapters 8 and 9 presented current views on how evidence may be evaluated in various contexts. All of those views depend upon the evaluator's

---

1 This chapter is based in large part on two articles (Twining, 1999, and Anderson, 1999). Some of the themes are further developed in *Bazaar*, Chs. 12–16.

assessment of the strength (the degree of certainty) with which the generalizations upon which the arguments being evaluated depend can be expressed.

In this chapter we integrate these materials and present a more comprehensive analysis of the roles generalizations play. In the next section, we focus on how the degree of certainty affects the use of generalizations in determining how evidence should be evaluated. In Section 3, we examine the ways in which generalizations can be classified and the differences that stem from those classifications. The legitimacy of the common law adversary system of dispute resolution depends in some part on an assumption that there is a cognitive consensus, an assumption that members of society share a core of basic information and view the world in similar ways. We describe and assess this view in Section 4. Section 5 identifies the dangers that stem from the use of generalizations. We conclude with an examination of generalizations from the practitioner's standpoint.

2. Degrees of certainty

Perhaps all and certainly most inferences from particular to particular depend upon an unstated generalization.[2] When the usually covert generalization is made explicit, the inductive reasoning upon which the proposed inference depends can be translated into a quasi-deductive form, and that forces into prominence the generalization being assumed as a major premise. However, generalizations are usually hedged in some way:

> In reasoning from E* to E at the first step, I might assert the following: If we have evidence that an event occurred, this event *usually* (*often, sometimes, frequently,* etc.) did occur. Thus I believe we have some degree of license to reason from evidence E* to E, the event(s) reported in the evidence. But notice that I have hedged this generalization or warrant; I did not say: When we have this evidence that an event occurred, this event necessarily occurred. If it is inconclusive, evidence about some event does not allow me to say that the occurrence of the event is certain. Which hedge I choose depends upon the strength of my own belief based upon experiences I have had in evaluating this kind of evidence. At this stage I might say: If something like E happens then something like F *usually* (*often, sometimes, frequently,* etc.) happens ... (Schum, *Foundations*, 81–2)

If one were able to quantify the frequency of an event with reasonable confidence, one could formally convert a generalization that is hedged into the major premise of a syllogism:

> In all cases of X there is a 0.7 probability (70% likelihood) of Y
> This is a case of X
> Therefore Y is 0.7 probable.

2 Anderson and Schum are in the "all" camp (see pp. 100–101 above); Twining draws the line at "certainly most."

However, such estimates need to be treated with great caution: What is the basis for the estimate? Who is making the estimate? Might it be biased, purely speculative or otherwise unreliable? Is it an example of false precision? And so on.

> However, an inference openly based on a fuzzy generalization is conspicuously weak:
>
> X and Y sometimes occur simultaneously
> This is a case of X
> Therefore Y may have occurred simultaneously.

It is important to distinguish between the strength of support for a generalization and its probative force if it is accepted as true. Here we find an interesting feature of the operation of generalizations in the kind of argument with which we are concerned: the more cautious a generalization, the more plausible it is likely to be, but the weaker the support that it gives to the probandum.[3] For example, using the example of the disparity of age between Edith and Freddie, the generalization, "All older women dominate all younger men in all circumstances," would give strong support to the *probandum*, "Edith dominated Freddie in all circumstances," if it were true. But it clearly is not true. On the other hand, a proposition such as: "In intimate relationships the older partner tends to be the dominant partner" is more plausible, but it is very vague and at best gives weak support to the *probandum* that Edith incited Freddie to murder her husband.

Moreover, there are many other possible generalizations that might be imagined, some pointing in the opposite direction. Consider again the differences in age between Edith and Freddie. We could move by a number of different routes from this fact to the intermediate *probandum* that Edith influenced Freddie. There are several possible generalizations about the relations between an older woman and a younger man. A lawyer might argue that in such relationships, for example: (a) older women tend to *dominate*, (b) older women are *insecure*, (c) older women are *demanding*, (d) older women are more inclined to *take initiatives*, (e) older women play the role of a mother substitute, and so on. Each of these could provide a significantly different route to support or negate an argument concerning the existence, extent, and effect of Edith's influence over Freddie. Furthermore, each of these generalizations could also lead to other intermediate *probanda* about motive or intent or something else.

It appears from the argument that counsel for the prosecution in *Bywaters and Thompson* selected (a). Why? Perhaps, because it provides stronger support for the intermediate *probandum* "Edith dominated Freddie or Edith influenced Freddie." But upon reflection, perhaps backed by research, we might conclude that there is stronger support for one of the other generalizations (b) through (e). To repeat: it

---

3 It is not quite correct to say that the probative force of a generalization varies inversely with the strength of support for it, because some universal or near-universal generalizations are well founded.

is important to distinguish between the strength of support for the generalization and the probative force of the generalization, if it is accepted as true.

There are further complexities. Edith and Freddie can be characterized in gender-neutral terms: as partners, lovers, persons, for example. The context can be characterized in a way that hedges the generalization: in intimate relationships, in love affairs, or more vaguely in relationships of this kind. Each of the elements could be expressed in heavily loaded emotive terms. To give a crude example: An ageing adulteress will manipulate a naive adolescent.

The important point here is that, for the lawyer, the choice of formulation is crucial. The precise, specific formulation may set up an irrefutable syllogism compelling the conclusion sought, if the decision-maker accepts the generalization in that form as true. But in most cases, the generalization will not be that well established nor that widely shared nor very precise. Probably no one believes that "All older women dominate all younger men all of the time," and some potential jurors would probably reject such a generalization even in a much weaker form.

3. Types of generalizations

Generalizations can be categorized in different ways for different purposes. In Chapter 3, we identified three axes that could be used in classifying generalizations – a generality (or level of abstraction) axis, a reliability (or degree of certainty) axis, and a source (or basis) axis. There is a fourth axis that should also be viewed as a part of that classification scheme – what might be called a commonality axis. The commonality axis refers to how widely the generalization would be accepted or shared within the particular community in which a disputed question had to be resolved.

At one end of the commonality spectrum are generalizations that are shared only by a small number of people. Examples might be drawn for generalizations falling along any of the other three axes – e.g., generalizations expressing the prejudice that underlay the hatred that separated the Capulets and the Montagues; generalizations acquired by experience or study necessary to fully understand and accurately evaluate the performances of world-class athletes; or the generalizations understood only by astrophysicists trying to evaluate data being generated by the Hubble telescope.

At the other end of the spectrum are generalizations that are universally or widely shared within the relevant community. Examples clustering at this end of the spectrum are similarly diverse – e.g., generalizations based upon prejudices of the kind that have resulted in "ethnic cleansing" in Rwanda or the former Yugoslavia; generalizations originally based upon scientific or mathematical principles that are now shared generally in most communities – e.g., any object dropped will fall until it reaches the ground or some other surface; generalizations derived from common experience – e.g., all lighted stove burners are very hot.

In most discussions of generalizations in legal and other contexts, generalizations have been described and classified without taking into account the variable revealed by placing them along the axes identified above. As a result, the categories commonly used to describe generalizations are overlapping, imprecise, and ambiguous, and the descriptions employed often conceal, rather than disclose, differences that are important. Nonetheless, lawyers and others who must work with generalizations in constructing and critiquing arguments about disputed questions of fact must be aware of the descriptions commonly used and of the roles that generalizations so described have played and will play in such arguments and critiques.

Generalizations can be categorized in different ways for different purposes. In the context of arguments about questions of fact, it is useful to categorize them in terms of source and reliability. From the standpoint of a lawyer, it is useful to distinguish between two main types: (a) case-specific generalizations contrasted with (b) background generalizations, which in turn can be classified roughly in terms of their reliability – scientific/expert, general knowledge, experience-based, and synthetic-intuitive (or belief) generalizations. In the context of argumentation in legal processes different considerations apply to each category. Generalizations can be placed on a spectrum of reliability ranging from well-tested and generally accepted propositions, such as those associated with the law of gravity, to largely untested and sometimes untestable intuitions, such as the generalizations upon which the view that running from the scene of a crime is evidence of guilt, to unfounded biases based upon false stereotypes – such as prejudices based on gender, race, class, or age.[4]

a. Case-specific generalizations

These may be used explicitly or implicitly in argument in a particular case. They may include descriptions about personal habits or character, or local practices (how newly born babies are labeled in this hospital), or allegations of a general nature, such as "The employer-defendant in this case regularly discriminated against women in its employment practices."

Case-specific background knowledge may be a mixture of particular and general information, such as Welt's use of "local knowledge" in relation to bus time tables and the Old Sumter Inn in "The Nine Mile Walk" (above, page 11). A composite picture of Edith's character as a successful businesswoman and a forceful person might be used to bolster a generalization to the effect that she was the dominant partner in her relationship with her lover.

Such generalizations may become operative in a specific case, although frequently they remain in the background. They may be supported by explicit evidence adduced, for example, in an employment discrimination case. But often they may also be inferred from the background beliefs of the decision-makers, as, for example,

4 A classic example is *Bradwell v. Illinois*, 83 U.S. 130 (1872) (affirming decision by Illinois Supreme Court that women could not be admitted to the bar): "The paramount destiny and mission of women are to fulfil the noble and benign offices of wife and mother. That is the law of the Creator. And the rules of civil society must be adapted to the general constitution of things, and cannot be based on exceptional cases" (Bradley, J., concurring at 141–42).

may have been true about sexual prejudices among jurors at the trial of Bywaters and Thompson.[5] They may be and frequently are a product of both.

Especially if they are supported by evidence, case-specific generalizations tend to push out or trump background generalizations. For example, in *Bywaters and Thompson* it was important for the prosecution to prove that Freddie's attack on Percy was premeditated, for that would support the proposition that he acted in pursuance of a conspiracy or because of Edith's incitement. The main evidence in support of this was the highly ambiguous tea-room letter (Exhibit 60) and the fact that he was carrying a knife. The probative value of this last fact would be considerably weaker if it could be shown that Freddie was in the habit of carrying the knife wherever he went. Freddie claimed this, but his credibility was weak. If Edith's counsel had called one of Freddie's shipmates as a witness to support this case-specific generalization, that would have weakened the prosecution's case very significantly. In the event, both sides had to rely on contradictory or divergent background generalizations. The prosecution argued that "Possession of a knife of this kind was in itself suspicious," and that "No reasonable man living in London carries a knife like this in his pocket." The defense argued: "It is not strange for a seafaring man visiting foreign countries, to purchase a knife," and "There are few sailors who do not possess a knife." (See Figure 10.1.) A witness-backed case-specific generalization about Freddy's habits in this respect would have been much more persuasive than any of these background generalizations.[6]

The evidence necessary to establish many case-specific generalizations will ordinarily be admitted automatically. Edith *was* 28, Freddie *was* 20, and both sat before the jury. It is difficult to see how counsel for the defense could have prevented the jury from learning that "Edith is older than Freddie." In such a circumstance, counsel must determine what generalizations this fact may evoke in the jurors' minds (e.g., "older women dominate younger men") and how to enhance or diminish their effect. Often important case-specific generalizations may have to be established by evidence.

It is also possible that evidence might be adduced to enhance or diminish the strength of generalizations that might otherwise be held or accepted by the triers of fact. For example, psychologists might today be employed to examine Edith and Freddie and, on that basis, might be able to express an opinion about whether Edith did or could influence Freddie's conduct in important matters. Similarly, social science survey techniques might conceivably today enable lawyers to produce evidence as to what proportion of seafaring men habitually carried knives in their coat pockets. The attempt to prove such case-specific generalizations raises an array

5 "Mrs Thompson was hanged for immorality" is a remark attributed to her counsel by several commentators.
6 Anderson (1999) also uses the term "context-specific" generalizations to refer to background generalizations that have been made more concrete in the context of a particular case. This is different from case-specific generalizations about habits, practices, character etc., which are, or at least should be, based on particular evidence.

Prosecution	Defense
1. The attack was premeditated.	14. When B arrived at Belgrave Road, he had no intention of killing P.T. (110, 142).
2. The murder weapon was a knife owned by B (not disputed).	
3. B put the knife in his pocket in order to kill P.T. (137).	15. B's carrying of the knife was innocent (142).
	16. *B always carried the knife with him.*
17. a. B contradicted himself. (38–53) b. B's bias.	17. B's testimony (53).
4. *Possession of a knife of this kind is in itself suspicious* (104).	
5. The knife was a deadly weapon (35), a dagger (151), a stabbing instrument (151), a dreadful weapon (132).	18. The knife was an ordinary sheath knife used for many purposes (53).
6. a. The knife (exhibit 1.34).	6. b. The knife (exhibit 1.34).
7. The evidence of the wounds (22–23).	19. B's testimony (implicit, 53).
	20. Foster's (tool merchant's) testimony (32).
8. The knife was not a convenient thing to carry about (132, 137).	21. The knife fitted conveniently in the inside pocket of B's overcoat (137).
	22. B's testimony (implicit, 53).
23. [Nothing is known re size of coat.]	23. The coat (exhibit 29).
9. B purchased the knife in order to kill P.T.	24. B purchased the knife for an innocent purpose.
	25. B purchased the knife over a year before the attack. 20. Consistent with Foster's testimony above.
10. No evidence that B showed it to anyone (132, 139).	10. a. No reason why B should have shown it to anyone (137).
11. *If he had possessed it for long, there would have been evidence of jocular remarks* (132).	
26. a. B's bias b. No corroborating evidence (132).	26. B's testimony (39, 53, 110).
12. B. was a ship's clerk, not a sailor (editorial intervention!) (110).	27. *It is not strange for a seafaring man, visiting foreign countries, to purchase a knife* (110, 140). 28. B took the knife abroad with him. 29. B's testimony (53).
13. *No reasonable man living in London carries a knife like this in his pocket* (140).	30. *There are few sailors who do not possess a knife* (110, 140).

Figure 10.1 *Reconstruction of arguments about the knife (B and T)*

of problems concerning availability, admissibility, and utility that are frequently treated in standard texts on evidence and trial practice. However, it is quite unrealistic to expect to use experts for the great majority of propositions used in arguments about judicial evidence, even when there is potentially applicable scientific material.

b. Background generalizations

Karl Llewellyn wrote:

> [W]hen Michael and Adler divided knowledge into two essential categories: "common sense" and "scientific knowledge," they overlooked... that the matter does not thus cleave neatly into *two* significant areas, but that it stretches out or sprawls instead between two poles. At the one pole is ignorance and *pure* guess. At the other pole is solid and thoroughly systematized scientific knowledge. "Common sense" is, so to speak, in the South Temperate Zone. Uncommon sense, ordered, pondered on with care, and tested out once and again in inconclusive but still illuminating corrective careful tests – that is so to speak, in the North Temperate Zone. Knowledge does not have to be scientific, in order to be on the way toward Science. Neither does it have to be scientific in order to be extremely useful. (Llewellyn (1936) 22)

In the absence of experts or other direct evidence, we fall back on background generalizations. In the Rationalist Tradition it is assumed that the triers of fact, including jurors, come already equipped with a largely shared "stock of knowledge," which is the main source of warrants for making inferences in arguments about questions of fact. This equipment is commonly described as "general experience," "background knowledge," "common sense," or "society's stock of knowledge." Again we need to ask, whose experience, sense, or knowledge? As we shall see, each of these expressions is somewhat misleading if it is used to refer to the totality of the individual and communal beliefs that are used as warrants for inferential reasoning.

What is advanced as knowledge, common sense, or shared beliefs is too varied to be susceptible to precise classification. The bases for such generalizations are as varied as the sources for the beliefs themselves – education, direct experience, the media, gossip, fiction, fantasy, speculation, prejudice, and so on. In legal contexts it is useful to draw broad distinctions between different kinds of generalizations according to their perceived reliability in a given society at a given time, bearing in mind that there is a continuum that ranges from uncontested scientific truths, through "knowledge" based on more or less established forms of expertise, to largely uncontested general knowledge, to less established "common sense" generalizations, to beliefs that are based on limited experience, faith, speculation, myth, or prejudice. Although these are quite rough categories, it is important to realize that they can operate quite differently in arguments about questions of fact in legal contexts.

c. Scientific knowledge and expertise

Scientific generalizations are based upon scientific knowledge and research. They vary in terms of their reliability. There are those based upon the "laws of science" (e.g., the applications of the law of gravity to prove how long it took the victim's body to strike the sidewalk after he was pushed out of the sixteenth-story window). There are those based upon well-established principles (e.g., the body of scientific knowledge upon which fingerprint identification is based). There are those extrapolated from research findings that are less well-established or are recognized as less reliable (e.g., voice print identification or the nature of the relationship between prenatal smoking and birth defects). Typically, these are generalizations that are established by expert witnesses who testify both as to one or more case-specific generalization, that are relevant (e.g., to establish that the deceased died at 4:30 p.m.) and, if required, to the scientific generalizations that support that conclusion.

The courts have come to rely increasingly on scientific and other expert evidence. This in turn has generated problems about the qualifications of experts, the probative helpfulness of expert evidence, how to deal with novel and contested "scientific" findings, the role of experts in testifying directly to ultimate and penultimate probanda ("the ultimate issue" problem), and the tensions between the fallibilism of science and the need for finality in adjudication.[7] It was estimated that by 1990 over 70 percent of civil jury trials in the United States involved expert evidence and the proportion has been growing. DNA and other advances in forensic science and technology have already made a profound impact on the investigation and prosecution of crimes and alleged miscarriages of justice. This trend is bound to continue. The leading comparative law scholar, Mirjan Damaska, has predicted:

> Let there be no mistake. As science continues to change the social world, great transformations of factual inquiry lie ahead for all justice systems. These transformations could turn out to be as momentous as those that occurred in the twilight of the Middle Ages, when magical forms of proof retreated before the prototypes of our present evidentiary technology.[8]

d. General knowledge

General knowledge generalizations are generalizations that would be generally accepted as well established in a given community: Palm trees, rain, and high humidity are common in Miami, Florida; transactions in securities traded on the New York Stock Exchange are accurately summarized in the *Wall Street Journal*; most pubs in England are affiliated in some manner with a brewery, and so on. Many such generalizations are so widely known or believed in the particular community that they

---

7 Haack (2004).
8 Damaska (1997) 151. It is beyond the scope of this book to explore the complex issues relating to scientific and expert evidence in detail. However, questions of competence and admissibility are touched on in Ch. 11 and some problems relating to statistical evidence are included in Appendix I (Probabilities and Proof).

will simply appear in argument without any formal request that they be noticed. Many will fall under the doctrine of judicial notice (see below). Others may require some proof, but all share the characteristic that they will be accepted as largely indisputable at the time and place of the trial.[9]

e. Experience-based generalizations

Sometimes people confidently claim to "know" something on the basis of firsthand experience. Some such experience-based generalizations may be widely shared in a community. Some may be based on extensive firsthand experience (Llewellyn's idea of "horse sense").[10] Most Miami residents have learned from experience that torrential rain showers may fall with little advance indication. Others are individual generalizations, based on isolated events, sometimes involving unwarranted extrapolations from individual experiences. For example, someone who has been unfairly treated by the police may, rightly or wrongly, conclude that all or most police officers are not to be trusted. If the individual is a juror, the generalization may affect the outcome, irrespective of its validity. Someone who has had an unpleasant experience with someone from another race or class may develop negative views about all members of that race or class. Such beliefs are best treated as unwarranted beliefs or prejudices rather than as being genuinely based on experience.

f. Synthetic-intuitive generalizations (belief generalizations)

Many "common sense" generalizations can be usefully categorized as beliefs that a person synthesizes or intuits from her stock of knowledge and beliefs. Sometimes an individual can explain the sources from which she synthesized the generalization. Frequently, however, the intuitive predominates – the individual cannot identify the source of the generalization or explain why she believes that it is sound.

The generalizations necessary to support the inferences that flight from the scene of a crime is evidence of guilt are examples of "synthetic-intuitive" generalizations. We are not aware of any tests that claim to have verified these generalizations. Nonetheless, the generalization "persons who have committed a crime often flee from the scene of that crime" seems intuitively right – at least to some middle class people.[11] In its weakest form, we might accept the transposed generalization upon

9 Of course, what passes for knowledge in a given society at a particular time may later be shown to be untrue. For example, in an earlier era, it was "generally known" that the earth was flat. In an appropriate case, evidence that a person was on a ship that was last seen sailing over the horizon might have been sufficient to establish that the person was dead. To talk of beliefs "passing for" knowledge at different times involves no commitment to a strong relativist position in epistemology. On "the passes for fallacy" (the fallacy that because what passes for the truth is often no such thing, it follows that there is no objective truth), see Haack (1998) 93.

10 "Horse-sense is the kind of highly informed, distinctly *un*common, better-than-common, expert but not scientifically demonstrable know-what and know-how which a David Harum had about horses and other horse-traders" (Llewellyn, unpublished manuscript (1950) cited in Twining (1973) 503).

11 Note that if someone sees another person running in the vicinity of an event, such as a fight or motor accident, to call it "flight" involves an inference: the person could be running *to* somewhere

which flight inferences depend, "persons who flee from the scene of a crime are *sometimes* persons who are guilty of that crime." The generalization thus framed could provide only weak support for an inference that the person seen fleeing from the scene of a specific crime was the person who committed that crime: "That person *may be* the person who committed the crime." There often seems to be no clear basis for our acceptance of these generalizations, apart from a synthesis or an intuition based upon our personal "stock of knowledge" or "common sense." This is clearly fallible, but it may be all that we have to rely on.[12]

One of the claims for Wigmorean analysis is that by making explicit what is usually left implicit it readily exposes weak points in argument. In marking students' exercises in this kind of analysis, we regularly look for non sequiturs in their arguments. Very often the non sequitur is based on a faulty generalization, like the one in Figure 10.2.

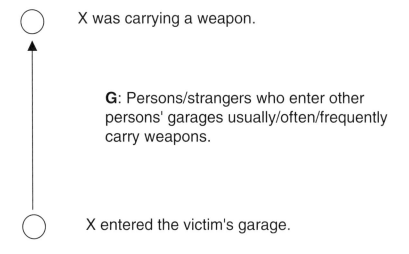

Figure 10.2 *Foolish generalizations*

This generalization, once articulated, would seem absurd on its face to most people. Constructing generalizations to show disconnects in chains of reasoning is a very useful device when evaluating an argument.

(e.g. to summon help), running *from* the scene or running *past* it, for example, a jogger who happened to be passing near the scene of the event when it happened. Some people might interpret running from the police as good sense rather than an indication of guilt.

12 A fairly representative statement of the orthodox view is as follows: "More often assumed than articulated is the premise that jurors must rely on common sense, or the knowledge and experience which they share with the community generally. But 'common sense' is frequently wrong ... Our everyday experience of the world comes in crude, unrepresentative chunks, with causal relations hopelessly obscured, and with prejudice, superstition, and self-interest inextricably intertwined in perception" (Bitterman (1956) A-16). "This is no argument for not using common sense. We operate in judicial institutions with the best we have and the inescapable necessity of making concessions to the shortness of life" (Levin and Levy (1956) 141–42).

4. Judicial notice and cognitive consensus

a. Judicial notice

In most jurisdictions there are rules concerning "judicial notice," that is to say "facts which need not to be proved." For example, the Federal Rule 201(b) provides: "A judicially noticed fact must be one not subject to reasonable dispute in that it is either (1) generally well known within the territorial jurisdiction of the trial court or (2) capable of accurate and ready determination by resort to sources whose accuracy cannot reasonably be questioned." Similarly a leading treatise on the law of evidence in England and Wales states:

> A judge may take judicial notice of facts which are matters of common knowledge and which could not be the subject of serious dispute. Hence it would be pointless and wasteful to require evidence of them. Hypothetical possibilities of notorious facts are limitless: textbook writers frequently cite as illustrations the date of Christmas and the death of Queen Victoria as facts which would be judicially noticed. Reported cases contain many examples. The courts have taken judicial notice of the fact that by the laws of nature, a fortnight is too short a period for human gestation; that cats are kept for domestic purposes; that London streets carry a large volume of traffic, so that a boy employed to ride a bicycle through them runs a risk of injury; that the reception of television is a common feature of domestic life enjoyed primarily for the purposes of recreation; and that one of the popular forms of entertainment on television is a series of reconstructed trials which have a striking degree of realism. (Dennis (2002) 424–45. Citations omitted)

The idea of judicial notice should not be confused with background knowledge or "common sense generalizations." It is both wider and narrower. It is wider in that it includes knowledge of specific facts (that Lima is the capital of Peru; that the old Sumter Inn is nine miles from Hadley) (above, page 13). It is narrower because a great deal of "common sense" or "society's stock of knowledge" is not well founded and its accuracy can reasonably be questioned.

Once articulated, many "common sense generalizations" appear dubious on their face or are open to challenge on a variety of grounds. If so, they technically fall outside the scope of the doctrine of judicial notice. But in practice prosecutors, plaintiffs, defense counsel, and courts regularly rely on such beliefs, not because they are well founded, but because there is no practicable alternative.

b. Cognitive consensus

Writers on evidence talk of "a stock of knowledge" and tend to postulate a high degree of "cognitive consensus." The following passage deserves to be treated as the *locus classicus* for this view:

> The inductivist analysis, [...] presupposes only that when a juryman takes up his office his mind is already adult and stocked with a vast number of commonplace generalizations about human acts, attitudes, intentions, etc., about the more familiar

features of the human environment, and about the interactions between these two kinds of factors, together with an awareness of many of the kinds of circumstances that are favourable or unfavourable to the application of each such generalization. Without this stock of information in everyday life he could understand very little about his neighbours, his colleagues, his business competitors, or his wife. He would be greatly handicapped in explaining their past actions or predicting their future ones. But with this information he has the only kind of background data he needs in practice for the assessment of inductive probabilities in the jury-room. He does not need to have tacitly ingested a mass of quantitative or numerical statistics for this purpose. Nor does he need implicitly to remember some sophisticated mathematical algorithm in order to compute the probabilities from the data. The inductive probability of the proposed conclusion on the facts before the court depends just on the extent to which the facts are favourable to some commonplace generalizations that connect them to the conclusion.

Not that jurymen are incapable of disagreeing with one another in their assessment of the probability with which a proposed conclusion has been proved from undisputed facts. But on any rational reconstruction of their disagreement (when prejudice, personal sympathy, sectional spite, and other irrational factors may be disregarded) the disagreement must normally be due to differences of opinion about the kinds of circumstances that are favourable or unfavourable to the application of some particular common sense generalization. The main commonplace generalizations themselves are for the most part too essential a part of our culture for there to be any serious disagreement about them. They are learned from shared experiences, or taught by proverb, myth, legend, history, literature, drama, parental advice, and the mass media. When people ceased to believe that those who had insensitive areas of skin were in commerce with the Devil, it was symptomatic of a major cultural change. Similarly, so long as the jurymen at a criminal trial are the accused's peers his case has a reasonable chance of being judged correctly by them, while if they belong to a different culture they are more likely to misjudge it even when trying to be fair. But there is still room for occasional disagreement, even within the same culture, about the kinds of circumstances that are favourable or unfavourable to the application of some particular common sense generalization. (L. Jonathan Cohen (1977) 274–76)

This passage has been criticized as presenting a rather complacent view about common sense generalizations. It should be apparent that Cohen is making an argument based on a collection of general knowledge and synthetic-intuitive generalizations that he assumes are so widely shared among the audience of scholars, lawyers, and judges to whom the argument is addressed that they do not merit further documentation or development. The main criticisms that have been advanced can be summarized as follows:[13]

First, Cohen assumes that all jurors (and defendants) are male or sexless. But even within a given culture and class a cross-gender cognitive consensus cannot always be assumed on such matters as domestic violence, rape, equal pay, or more generally. Moreover, in a dynamic multi-class, multi-cultural society one cannot

---

13 For a recent sympathetic critique see Stein (2005).

assume an extensive cognitive consensus across classes or cultures or even within cultures. The idea of a cognitive consensus involving a common stock of knowledge or beliefs is highly problematic.[14]

Second, and perhaps most important, standard versions of inferential reasoning are species of propositional logic. One infers conclusions from premises that are expressed as propositions. When we talk of "background generalizations" as the warrants or the glue in this kind of argument, there is a tendency to assume that we draw these from our stock of knowledge as ready-made propositions. But this is psychologically implausible. Instead an individual's or a community's stock of beliefs is unlikely to be stored in the form of a neatly categorized code or data base:

> A "stock of knowledge" does not consist of individual, empirically tested, and readily articulated propositions: rather, both individually and collectively, we have ill defined agglomerations of beliefs that typically consist of a complex soup of more or less well-grounded information, sophisticated models, anecdotal memories, impressions, stories, myths, proverbs, wishes, stereotypes, speculations, and prejudices. Fact and value are not sharply differentiated. Nor are fact, fantasy and fiction. Nor can one take for granted either consistency or coherence within an individual's or a society's "stock of knowledge." (Twining (1999) 362; *Bazaar*, 456)

Third, insofar as an individual's or a group's stock of beliefs is like a bouillabaisse, it does not seem like an environment conducive to maintaining clear distinctions between is and ought, fact and value. Stereotypes, proverbs, and stories typically have an evaluative element – that is often their main point.[15] Cohen's formulation does not make sufficient allowance for the relationship between values and facts in this kind of context – the influence of bias, prejudice, values, and so on, on perceptions of social facts. Cohen assumes that empirical generalizations can readily be distinguished from judgments of value.

Fourth, the statement is over-simple in other respects; for example, it does not distinguish among different examples of generalizations in relation to their scientific status or empirical base, their level of generality, or the extent to which they are "purely" factual or contain other components – speculative or evaluative. So too, it does not adequately distinguish among firmly held beliefs, matters on which people have vague ideas, matters on which they are open to suggestion, and matters on which they are agnostic or would register as "don't knows."

So we need to recognize that the idea of a cognitive consensus involving a common stock of knowledge or beliefs is highly problematic. However, Cohen's position can be defended up to a point. He allows that there is not a social consensus about everything; that the stock of knowledge is relative to a given society, and by implication to

---

14 In the context of "globalization" the idea can be extended beyond a plural or a multi-cultural society to the point that for many purposes we can no longer treat societies, countries, or nations as self-contained units with clear and stable boundaries. However, John Rawls's useful idea of an overlapping consensus can be used to curb tendencies to exaggerate the extent to which stocks of belief in fact vary across "cultures" (Rawls (1987); discussed GLT 69–75).

15 *Bazaar* Ch. 16.

particular subgroups within a society; and that the stock of knowledge can change over time. He points to the notion that with collegial decision-making, especially by a jury, the stock of knowledge is a pool drawn from all the members' "experience."[16] Moreover, in certain kinds of decision-making, the triers of facts are selected because of their special knowledge and/or values, for example, in jury selection, at least in the American system. So too, in arbitration it is typical to choose people for their expertise – that is, some special subcategory of general experience, or to choose people because of their biases or absence of bias or because they represent certain kinds of interests, with a view to having a balanced panel that may find a middle way – for instance, one trade unionist, one representative of management, and one "neutral" (who may or may not be an expert).

From the standpoint of the lawyer, both the view and the criticisms are important. Lawyers must identify from the evidence what generalizations may affect the decision-makers and how commonly and strongly held these generalizations are likely to be among them. They must rely in part upon their own stock of knowledge as members of the community, such knowledge about the specific decision-makers as they can legitimately acquire through *voir dire* or otherwise, and such additional knowledge as they may be able to acquire by study.

5. Dangers of generalizations

As Sidgwick observed, linking generalizations are often the main source of doubt in an argument. One of the claims for the chart method is that by forcing articulation of what is being (or might be) argued, one can more readily spot weak points in the argument.[17] In the course of discussion we have seen some examples of weak generalizations. Here is a summary list of some of the main weaknesses one can expect, especially in relation to experience based and synthetic-intuitive generalizations.

Generalizations are dangerous[18]

Generalizations are dangerous in argumentation about doubtful or disputed questions of fact because they tend to provide invalid, illegitimate, or false reasons for accepting conclusions based on inference. They are especially dangerous when they are implicit or unexpressed. For example:

i The warranting generalization may be *indeterminate* in respect of:
   a frequency or universality (all/most/some);
   b level of abstraction;
   c defeasibility (exceptions, qualifications);
   d precision or "fuzziness";

16 Some support for the consensus idea is to be found in writings about the jury in which research suggests that the tendency is toward consensus formation in that kind of decision-making (Abbott and Ball (eds.) (1999) Ch. 20).
17 A useful technique for showing the weakness of an argument is to show that it relies on a generalization that, once articulated, is obviously foolish (see above, page 272).
18 This section is adapted from Twining (1999) 356–58.

e empirical base/confidence (accepted by scientific community; part of everyday firsthand/vicarious experience, speculative, etc.);

ii It may be unclear as to identity (which generalization? There may be rival generalizations available to each side in a dialogue), or source (whose generalization? e.g. male/female experience in domestic violence cases).

iii When articulated, a generalization may be expressed in value-laden language or in loaded categories.

iv There are several reasons for treating such ideas as "common-sense generalizations" and "society's stock of knowledge" with great caution.

Some of the more obvious ones are as follows:

a By no means all the beliefs in a social stock of knowledge will satisfy even quite relaxed tests of warranted beliefs. What passes as common sense is often easily shown to be untrue.

b A high degree of consensus about the contents of the social stock of knowledge or beliefs cannot be taken for granted, especially in a plural or a stratified society. The extent of cognitive consensus varies according to time and place.

c What is commonly referred to as a society's "stock of knowledge" typically consists of a complex mixture of "scientific facts," impressionistic beliefs, stereotypes, myths, proverbs, and so on. Value judgments (including prejudices, racist or gender stereotypes) may be masquerading as empirical propositions.[19]

d The content of a "stock of knowledge" does not consist solely or mainly of ready-made generalizations, still less of empirical generalizations. Beliefs may be embedded in stories, examples, experience, etc., which are particular and which may not have been articulated in general terms. There is often considerable indeterminacy about what moral or general lesson or other generalization(s) may or will be extrapolated from such material.

e What officials, including courts, are prepared to recognize as "common sense" may not correspond with what most people in a given society in fact believe. Even in an open society some beliefs may be repressed as not being socially acceptable, politically correct, or otherwise proper. A regime may be "in advance" of public opinion in respect of such matters as gender, race, or class or vice versa. In repressive societies official versions of the truth may diverge very substantially from what people in fact believe.

6. Generalizations: the practitioner's standpoint

Evaluating the strength of an argument or assessing the net persuasive effect of the evidence as a whole ordinarily depends upon the significant generalizations that the decision-maker will or can be persuaded to apply. In all cases the decision-maker(s) will bring an array of generalizations (i.e. a stock of beliefs) that will affect and may control decisions of disputed questions of fact. It is accordingly important that lawyers identify generalizations that will or may play a role in a case and how

19 See page 275 above.

that role can be most effectively enhanced or minimized. This requires that they identify how significant generalizations will enter the case; for instance, through the evidence or as part of the knowledge and beliefs that the fact-finder brings to the case. It is the latter that presents the more difficult practical and theoretical questions.

In preparing an argument for a decision-maker, the lawyer must first identify and appraise the most significant generalizations that are available to either side to enhance or diminish the strength or force of the potential arguments. Ordinarily, this poses no special difficulty with respect to what we have classified as scientific and as general knowledge generalizations. The questions whether a claimed scientific generalization is well accepted or whether the evidence and an opinion necessary to establish it as a basis for argument are admissible poses questions of a kind that are familiar to lawyers and judges.[20] Similarly, generalizations that are truly accepted on the basis of general knowledge in the relevant community must be viewed as established or simply shown and thus as operative in the case. The challenge here is for the advocate to use or to counter such generalizations effectively. The remaining kinds of generalizations present different and more subtle problems.

a. Case-specific generalizations

The advocate typically must confront several problems with case-specific generalizations. They must first be identified and then decisions must be made to appraise the likelihood that the evidence that will invoke them will be admitted. Facts of the sort that Edith was 28 and Freddie was 20 will either be admitted or be apparent to the trier of fact. The facts that Freddie had long been employed as a clerk on ocean-going ships and that he was in fact carrying a knife on the evening of the murder are almost certainly going to be admitted in evidence at some stage of the proceedings. It is the lawyer's job to identify the possible background generalizations these facts may evoke and to decide how they may be shaped and used in argument. In contrast, it is not clear whether evidence of Richard Able's cocaine use or the extent to which evidence concerning the events at the disco and those surrounding his cashing the $25,000 check at a gambling casino will be admitted. Able's lawyer must not only identify the possible generalizations that would be evoked, but must also plan arguments that confront the various contingencies.

b. Experience-based and synthetic-intuitive generalizations

Experience-based and synthetic-intuitive generalizations raise the same problems, but they also pose an additional difficulty. A lawyer may be able to gather in advance of trial significant information about the individual judge's experience and about significant beliefs and biases that may influence that judge's perception of the evidence. In a case tried by a jury, however, the problem is more complex. The lawyer's primary opportunity to learn about and shape the experience-based and belief

---

20 On admissibility of expert evidence see p. 300 below.

generalizations likely to influence the trial outcome will occur during jury *voir dire* and selection.

c. Formulation and appraisal

In addition to problems of identification and appraisal, however, there is the problem of formulation. This is a problem common to generalizations of all types, and it is peculiarly a problem that lawyers can shape through argument. The formulation of the generalization can vary in a number of respects: It can be framed as a universal or as a propensity statement or as something less than that (see above); it can be stated with varying degrees of precision; it can be stated at different levels of generality; it may contain an explicit or implicit judgment of value; the choice of words may be relatively neutral or mildly or strongly emotive; there may be expressed or implied exceptions or qualifications.

For the lawyer, the choice of formulation is crucial. The precise, specific formulation may set up an irrebuttable syllogism compelling the conclusion sought, if the decision-maker accepts the generalization in that form as true. But in most cases, the generalization will not be either that well established or that widely shared and will probably be defeasible. No one believes that "All older women dominate all younger men all of the time," and some potential jurors would probably reject such a generalization in its weakest form.

In analyzing a generalization that plays a potentially important role in an argument one can adopt a procedure similar to doing a detailed microscopic analysis of a selected phase of an argument for a Wigmorean chart: clarify standpoint; specify the proposition to be justified; specify the proposition or propositions offered as the basis for its justification; identify and articulate the generalization(s) on which the justification depends; submit the generalization(s) to the various tests that have been discussed above.[21] Perhaps the main points can usefully be synthesized into a rough working protocol as follows:

Protocol for assessing the plausibility and validity of a generalization in the context of an argument

Standpoint: counsel for defense (pre-trial) in respect of an opponent's potential generalization

1 Will the generalization be stated expressly or merely implied?

    A. Express
2 If expressly, is it precise?
3 Is it ambiguous?
4 Is it stated as a universal or is it qualified by a hedge as to frequency (usually/often/sometimes)?

21 For a detailed discussion, illustrated with reference to *Huddleston v. United States*, see Anderson (1999) 461–77.

5 Is it an empirical generalization (capable of being shown to be true or false)?

6 Is it expressed in value laden or emotive terms?

7 What is the empirical basis for the generalization: scientific evidence/general experience/common sense/speculation/prejudice?

8 Can the truth of the generalization be reasonably disputed?

9 Can you articulate a rival generalization that points in the opposite direction/supports a different conclusion?

10 Does the least vulnerable/most plausible version of the generalization offer strong/moderate/weak/negligible support to the inference?

B Implied

11 Articulate the most persuasive version of the implicit generalization.

12 Submit it to the tests of precision, ambiguity, hedges, empirical, value laden, empirical basis, disputability, rival, strength of support.

B. Stories necessary, but dangerous

We have seen in Chapter 6 that stories and story telling are central to fact determination. A well-grounded story is crucial to organizing and presenting a persuasive argument. But like generalizations, story telling is vulnerable to abuse. It may be true that stories and story telling are psychologically necessary to decision-making in legal contexts, but they are dangerous in that they often can be used to violate logical standards, appeal to emotion rather than reason, and subvert legal principles and conventions.

Empirical research by Bennett and Feldman (1981), Pennington and Hastie (1993), and others suggests that American juries determine "the truth" about alleged past events mainly by constructing and comparing stories rather than critically evaluating arguments from evidence. These findings have been confirmed in other disciplines (e.g., medical diagnosis and history) and extended to fact determination by legal professionals and the police (e.g., Wagenaar et al. (1993)). Simply put, the widely accepted thesis is that human beings need stories in order to make certain kinds of decisions and, more generally, to make sense of the world.

The literature is less clear about the exact functions of story construction and comparison. Bennett and Feldman say they are used to fill in gaps; others suggest in order to be satisfied, triers of fact need to explain human motivation and action, even when motive is not a material fact, or when the facts to be determined relate to a static situation or a single "simple" fact such as identity. There is scope for disagreement as to whether stories are psychologically necessary in all situations involving fact determination in legal contexts (e.g., identity in a motiveless murder), but there seems to be a consensus that they are in practice felt to be very important a great deal of the time.

Story telling can also be shown to be dangerous in legal contexts in that it can be, and is often, used to violate or evade conventional legal norms about relevance, reliability, completeness, prejudicial effect, etc.[22] It is widely regarded as appealing to intuition and emotion and as a vehicle for "irrational means of persuasion." Examples of such dangers include:[23]

   i sneaking in irrelevant facts;
   ii sneaking in invented or ungrounded facts;
  iii suggesting facts by innuendo;[24]
  iv focusing attention on the actor rather than the act;[25]
   v appealing to hidden prejudices or stereotypes;
  vi telling the story in emotionally toned language;
 vii telling a story that may win sympathy for the speaker or the victim but is irrelevant to the argument;
viii making use of dubious analogies;
  ix subverting lawyers' distinctions between fact, law, and disposition and, more generally, fact and value; and
   x good stories pushing out true stories.[26]

Most of these points are illustrated in the materials in Chapter 1 and in the questions and exercises at the end of this chapter. As with generalizations, one can develop a rough working protocol for testing the plausibility, coherence, and evidentiary support for a story, based upon the following questions:

Protocol for assessing the plausibility, coherence, and evidentiary support for a story

Standpoint: counsel (on either side) preparing for trial

Is the story fully articulated? Or is it largely implied? If so, what exactly is the story? If articulated:
Is the story internally consistent?
Is there any evidence in this case that seems to conflict with the story?
To what extent does the evidence in the case support this story?
Are there any elements in the story not supported by evidence? To what extent are they based on speculation?
Does the story sneak in expressly or by innuendo:

   Any irrelevant facts
   Any invented facts
   Any inadmissible facts?

---

22 Such norms include: judge the act not the actor; consider only relevant evidence; argue from evidence, not speculation; and keep separate questions of fact, law, and disposition.

23 For a detailed account see *Rethinking* Ch. 7, *Bazaar* Chs. 12–16.

24 See Ch. 1, B 4 Sam's Party.

25 To give a simple example: at common law, evidence of disposition or bad character (such as prior convictions) is not normally admissible to support a criminal charge, but character is often an important but implicit part of a story (FRE 404–6). On the changes introduced in England by the Criminal Justice Act, 2003 see Roberts and Zuckerman (2004) 511–15; on the controversy behind these changes, see Zander (2003) 413–22.

26 *Bazaar* Ch. 14.

Can the story be told in a neutral way or does it expressly or impliedly involve value judgments?

Does it appeal to hidden prejudices or stereotypes?

Does the story fit some familiar story, such as Cinderella or the parable of the Prodigal Son or Lady Macbeth? If so, what is the relevance of this?

Does the story cast any of the actors in a bad light in a way that subverts the principle: judge the act, not the actor?

Does the telling of the story distort the facts so that a good story (entertaining, funny, exciting etc.) squeezes out a less interesting true story?

Does the story purport to "make sense" of the original episode or the motivation of one or more principal actors?

Is the story calculated to win sympathy for the victim/complainant/accused beyond what is supported by particular evidence?

Insofar as the story goes beyond the data, is it supported by plausible background generalizations?[27]

C. The relationship between stories and generalizations

If generalizations and stories are both necessary, but dangerous, how are they connected? It might be objected that the two theses apply to different spheres of discourse. Generalizations are logically necessary in the context of rational argument; stories are psychologically necessary in the context of human decision making. The logical "dangers" are different from the dangers of poor "judgment."

The relationship between logic and psychology in relation to decision-making is a very large subject. Here, we confine ourselves to two points. First, some of the functions of story telling are to do with human interaction and communication, and are not performing a function in an argument. For example, in oral presentation by an advocate, stories may legitimately be used to attract and retain interest, set a comprehensible context, and provide concrete illustrations to assist understanding. They may, of course, be used to distract attention or win sympathy for the speaker or the victim independently of what is at issue and so on. So, some of the functions and dangers are to do with communication rather than argumentation.

However, stories also seem to have a place within arguments and questions can be asked about the legitimacy, validity, or cogency of their place in this context. Some of the allegations about the dangers of stories seem to be appealing to standards of rationality. For example, a story-winning sympathy for the speaker independently of the issue can be criticized as irrelevant to the argument; where a good story

---

27 In *Anchored Narratives* (1993) three Dutch psychologists, Wagenaar, Crombag, and Van Koppen, usefully link stories and generalizations. However, they greatly exaggerate the importance of generalizations as direct "anchors" for stories, for generalizations should only be used to play this role in the absence of particular evidence to support the story. Particular evidence will nearly always give stronger support than a background generalization. A story is as vulnerable to attack as the generalizations that support it. See further *Bazaar* Ch. 13.

pushes out a true story, it can be criticized on the ground its attraction is to do with something other than truth (e.g., excitement, reassurance, titillation), and undue weight is being given to it. (See *Bazaar* Ch. 14.) Where a story is used to fill in gaps in the evidence, its justificatory force may be little or none, and it seems odd to claim that an argument about a question of fact is bolstered by claiming the situation is analogous to a work of fiction or a parable (*Bazaar* Ch. 16).

One version of this position may be restated as follows: In ordinary life and in making important decisions we need stories in order to "make sense" of the world and of particular past events; in factual inquiries, including adjudication, for a story to be accepted as true it needs to be warranted by (or anchored in) evidence. A well-formed story needs to be coherent, but to be true, it must be both plausible and backed by particular evidence. Plausibility is tested by background generalizations; the truth of specific factual conclusions is tested by reasoning from particular evidence.

There are also important examples, mainly in the Anglo-American literature on advocacy and adjudication, of claims that stories play a crucial role not merely in respect of presentation and rhetoric, but analytically as part of an argument. For instance, in a much cited paper, John W. Davis maintained, "in an appellate court the statement of the facts is not merely a part of the argument, it is more often than not the argument itself" (Davis (1953) 181). Similar statements have been made by Karl Llewellyn, James Boyd White, and other American jurists.[28] The precise meanings of such statements are not always clear, but it is reasonable to interpret them as maintaining that such notions as stories need to be accommodated within a conception of rational argument in legal contexts. Such claims are controversial, but if, for the sake of argument, we accept them as plausible, the question remains: What is the relationship between stories and generalizations in this context?

Perhaps the main link lies in the idea of "a stock of knowledge." As we have seen, a "stock of knowledge" does not consist of individual, empirically tested, and readily articulated propositions, still less of empirical laws.[29] Beliefs may be embedded in stories, examples, and experiences that are particular and may not have been articulated in general terms. There is often considerable indeterminacy about what moral or general lesson or other generalization(s) may or will be extrapolated from such material.

Generalizations may be indeterminate as to their application; stories may be indeterminate as to their significance. There is an intimate interaction between the general and the particular in all arguments about questions of fact. One aspect of the relationship between generalizations and stories can be usefully analyzed with greater precision. Generalizations are, by definition, general; stories are particular.[30] There is, as every lawyer knows, an intimate relationship between general rules and particular cases. Similarly, as every theologian and moralist should know, there is

28 *Rethinking* Ch. 7.   29 Above, pages 274–76.
30 On the definition of a "story" see above, page 155.

an intimate relationship between parables (and other morality tales) and their significance. That significance can be expressed in such terms as the point or the moral or some other general lesson or idea that it illustrates. Stories appeal strongly to the imagination. Part of that appeal lies in their concreteness and their particularity. That power can be undermined if the moral or point is spelled out or otherwise made explicit. Why this should be so is crucial in the present context.

The idea of precedent as a source of law is an especially clear illustration of the interaction between the general and the particular.[31] Because precedents are especially important in the common law, there has been much theorizing and controversy about "the problem of the *ratio decidendi*." We need not venture into that old controversy here because on several relevant points there is widespread agreement. "The facts" of a case are particular. The facts, at least in a hard case, give rise to a question of law. Such questions of law should be expressed in general terms, not "Is the defendant guilty or liable?" but "In circumstances of this type, is the defendant guilty or liable?" In deciding the particular case, the court gives an authoritative answer to the question(s) of law. That answer may be explicit or implicit.

The relationship between the facts, the issue(s), and the answer can be formally restated as follows: the facts = X happened; the issue = if X happens, then what? (legal consequence); the answer = whenever X happens, then Y.

In this formulation X is a constant despite the transition from particular to general. This transition from a particular situation to general questions and a general answer involves a shift from "this was the situation" to "in situations of this type, the law prescribes … " The crucial point in this context is that X is a constant. In short, X=X=X.

One of the main problems in interpreting cases is that the level of generality of X is indeterminate. The same applies to "the moral" of parables and morality tales. But if the facts are known, and if X=X=X, how can X be clear at the particular level, but unclear at the general level? The answer is, of course, that how exactly the facts are to be categorized is also indeterminate. X represents a particular situation seen as a type. How precisely that situation should be interpreted, what elements are material, and what is the best or an appropriate description of the situation is a matter of interpretation. And, since X=X=X, the problem of interpreting X is almost constant.[32]

Descriptions of situations are typically expressed in language. The choice of language is not significant solely because of the more or less obvious rhetorical potential of emotive or value laden terms. For example, a categorization may be judged appropriate because it reflects the way a significant reference group thinks or talks (for instance, using the concepts of a particular trade to describe the situation in a commercial case), or because it corresponds with or fits, explicitly or implicitly,

31 For a longer account, see *Bazaar* Ch. 16.   32 Twining and Miers (1999) 307–8.

some general principle or policy (for example describing a situation in a way that brings out that a non-expert was relying on the judgment of an expert in a reasonably proximate relationship).[33] This idea of choosing appropriate categories to describe particular fact situations is at the core of Karl Llewellyn's important, but elusive, idea of "situation sense."[34]

Some of the alleged "dangers" of stories shared with generalizations include, for example, presenting unsupported facts as if they were anchored or appealing explicitly or implicitly to biases or prejudices. Perhaps the most obvious common element is indeterminacy: Indeterminacy as to what exactly is being argued or is the general significance of the particular example. For example, what precisely is the moral of the parable of the prodigal son? Indeterminacy is generally presented as a weakness in an argument. But, as John Wisdom points out, one of the attractions of case by case argument is that one is not forced to define the boundaries of X in advance.[35] It can be valid and sensible to say, "This is a clear case of X" without *defining* X. That is part of the key to understanding the attraction of precedent at common law. It is a form of argument by analogy which does not commit the arguer to a position beyond what is needed for the case at hand.

D. Generalizations, stories, and themes: questions and exercises

The materials in Chapter 1 contain a great deal that is directly relevant to points made about stories and generalizations in Chapter 3 and this chapter. At this stage it may help to draw a lot of threads together by revisiting some of these examples.

Generalizations

Review the material on the testimony of Officer Connolly in the *Sacco and Vanzetti* case (Ch. 1, C4a) to the effect that during his arrest Sacco attempted on several occasions to put his hand under his overcoat in spite of being warned not to. Figure 10.3 is a reconstruction of the prosecution's argument that Connolly's testimony supported the conclusion that Sacco took part in the robbery and murder at South Braintree on April 15, 1920. Each step in the chain of inferences involves an implicit generalization as a warrant.[36]

---

33 This example is based on Lord Denning's famous "persuasive" categorization of the facts in *Candler v. Crane Christmas & Co.* [1951] 1 All E. R. 428, which was concerned with whether there is ever a duty of care in respect of negligent misstatements causing financial loss:

They were professional accountants who prepared and put before him these accounts, knowing that he was going to be guided by them in making an investment in the company. On the faith of those accounts he did make the investment, whereas, if the accounts had been carefully prepared, he would not have made the investment at all. The result is that he has lost his money. *Id.* at 431.

34 Llewellyn (1960) 230–34, discussed in *Rethinking* 230–32.

35 Wisdom (1956), (1974) at 38–40.   36 *Foundations* 88–90.

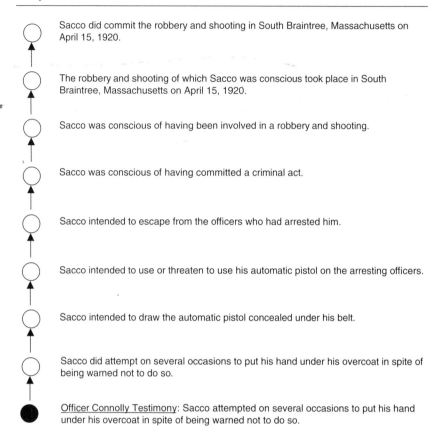

Sacco did commit the robbery and shooting in South Braintree, Massachusetts on April 15, 1920.

The robbery and shooting of which Sacco was conscious took place in South Braintree, Massachusetts on April 15, 1920.

Sacco was conscious of having been involved in a robbery and shooting.

Sacco was conscious of having committed a criminal act.

Sacco intended to escape from the officers who had arrested him.

Sacco intended to use or threaten to use his automatic pistol on the arresting officers.

Sacco intended to draw the automatic pistol concealed under his belt.

Sacco did attempt on several occasions to put his hand under his overcoat in spite of being warned not to do so.

Officer Connolly Testimony: Sacco attempted on several occasions to put his hand under his overcoat in spite of being warned not to do so.

Figure 10.3 *Vanzetti: Connolly's testimony*

1 Adopting the standpoint of counsel for Sacco:
  a Articulate the least vulnerable formulation of the generalization that is needed as a warrant for each step in the chain of inferences;
  b Classify each generalization according to the scheme suggested in Chapter 10 (e.g., case-specific, scientific/expert, etc.);
  c Assess the plausibility, reliability, and probative force of each generalization in this context;
  d How might counsel for Sacco deal with this item of evidence (i) in cross-examination of Connolly; (ii) in closing?
2 Review the materials and questions in Chapter 1 Section B, especially B1 (Solomon), B3 (Joseph Bell and Sherlock Holmes), B4 (Sam's Party), and C3a (The Brides in the Bath). In respect of each, identify, formulate, and categorize the explicit or implicit generalizations involved in the reasoning and assess their plausibility in their respective contexts.
3 Review *Sargent v. General Accident Co.* (Ch. 1, C6). From the information provided and drawing on different kinds of generalizations, can you construct a plausible argument that:

a   Upham Sargent was suicidal;

b   Given the length of the Nottaway River, an experienced outdoors man like Upham Sargent would have the skills to find his way back to safety without getting lost, unless he has sustained a serious injury.

4   Review the case of *Huddleston v. United States* (C3b). Consider carefully Question 2 (a–d).

5   Joseph Bell and Sherlock Holmes (B3).

a   To what extent does the reasoning of Joseph Bell rely on specific local knowledge, background generalizations, case-specific generalizations? Can these categories be clearly distinguished in this context?

b   What generalizations are implicit in Holmes's reasoning towards the conclusion that Watson had been in Afghanistan? What is the weakest point in this chain of reasoning?

Stories

1   "The Nine Mile Walk" (Ch.1, C2). Kemelman has produced a splendid example of imaginative reasoning that has led to identifying two suspects, but it is a long way from proving the case against either of them. Assuming for the sake of argument that one of the suspects is in fact the murderer, construct an account of his movements during the past 24 hours that explains why he was in Hadley and why he made the remark about the nine mile walk. Bear in mind that any alibi claims can probably be checked fairly easily and that if he is caught lying this will weaken his position. Does the strategy of your story rely mainly on denial (OD), rival (OR), or explanation (OE)?

2   Review the quotation from Lord Denning in *Miller v. Jackson* (Ch. 1, C3c).

a   How many examples of using a story to "cheat" can you find in this text, read by itself?

b   Would your answer be different if the following "facts" were added: At the time Lintz was a depressed former mining village in County Durham; the Millers had a small child; the Millers were not the only people who had complained about the cricket; no evidence was adduced at trial about the attitude of the cows.

Stories and argument

In an appellate court, the statement of the facts is not merely a part of the argument, it is more often than not the argument itself. (John W. Davis (1940))

It is trite that it is in the statement of facts that the advocate has his first, best, and most precious access to the court's attention. The court does not know the facts, and it wants to. It is trite among good advocates, that the statement of the facts can, and should in the very process of statement, frame the legal issue, and can and should, simultaneously produce the conviction that there is only one sound result. It is as yet less generally perceived as a conscious matter that the pattern of the facts as stated must be a simple pattern, with its lines of simplicity never lost under detail; else attention wanders, or (which is as bad) the effect is submerged in the court's effort to follow the presentation or to organize the material for itself. (Karl Llewellyn (1962) 341–42)

[W]e can say that both the history and the tapestry are in this respect like a law case: the lawyer knows that to prove his (or her) case he must not only demonstrate the truth or probability of certain propositions of fact; he must present to the judge or juror a way of looking at the cases as a whole that will make sense; and it must "make sense" not merely as a matter of factual likelihood, but as a predicate to judgment, as a basis for action. While a case can in a technical sense be refuted by disproving one element or another, in practice the lawyer knows that he must do more than that: he must offer the judge or juror an alternative place to stand, another way of making sense of the case as a whole. To do his job, that is, the lawyer must both engage in an accurate retelling of the facts and make his own claim for what they mean. (James Boyd White (1985) 160)

Questions

1   Are these passages concerned with questions of fact or questions of law or both?
2   How can a statement of facts be an argument?
3   Give an example of a persuasive statement of facts.
4   a   Consider the case of *In re the Estate of James Earl Warren* in Chapter 12: Construct a persuasive story on behalf of James Warren Jr.
    b   Many students preparing to try this case immediately see an analogy with the Parable of the Prodigal Son (St Luke, Ch. 15). They suggest that it could provide a powerful theme for one side, especially in closing argument.
        i   What is the moral or point of the parable?
        ii Which side might use it to support their case in *Warren*?
        iii What fact of consequence in the *Warren* case might the analogy with the parable be used to support?
        iv How can the behavior of a father in Palestine in the time of Christ be *relevant* to making a judgment about the behavior of a father in the United States in the late twentieth century?
        v   How can a fictitious story that is nearly 2000 years old be used as evidence in a modern case?
        vi Can you think of a modern story that might be used to support the other side?[37]
5   *Edith Thompson.* Construct a story about Edith's relationship with Freddie and Percy that casts persuasive doubts on the prosecution case and is backed in all important respects by evidence reproduced in Chapter 7.
6   It is said that good stories often ease out true stories. Give three examples.

37   These issues are discussed in *Bazaar* Ch. 12.

11

The principles of proof and the law of evidence

A. Introduction

The purpose of this book is to provide a theoretical and practical foundation for mastering some specific analytical skills relating to the construction and criticism of arguments about disputed questions of fact. It is not a book about the law of evidence, but a central theme has been that the principles of proof and the law of evidence are intimately related. Like Wigmore, we believe that understanding the principles of proof is a valuable, perhaps a necessary, foundation both for understanding the rules and learning how to use them in practice.

At several points this interdependence has been made explicit. Chapters 1 and 2 illustrate the extent to which the two subjects share the same basic concepts; for example, relevance, materiality, weight/probative force, admissibility, inference, credibility, corroboration, prejudicial effect, and so on. In Chapter 3, we saw how nearly all secondary writers on evidence, including all the leading treatise writers, have worked within a framework of shared assumptions, which we called "The Rationalist Tradition." Those assumptions are common to the principles of proof and the basic principles of the law of evidence in common law countries. We also saw how relevance and weight are governed by "logic and general experience" rather than formal rules and that relevance is the main test of admissibility of evidence. As questions of admissibility are increasingly determined by exercise of judicial discretion and application of balancing tests in the circumstances of a particular case (for example the weighing of prejudicial effect against probative value), so too the logic of proof and the practical operation of rulings on admissibility have increasingly converged. In Chapter 8, we looked further at the idea that there are no rules of weight, and we considered different standards of proof, review, and appeal in the context of weighing evidence. In Chapter 10, we considered briefly scientific generalizations and judicial notice. All of these topics are central to understanding the law of evidence.

In this chapter we will seek to synthesize these ideas by presenting a coherent overview of the law of evidence as developed by Wigmore's teacher, James Bradley Thayer, and use this as a framework for integrating the principles of proof and the technical rules of evidence. We then present an overview of the approach to analyzing for admissibility under the Federal Rules of Evidence. The chapter ends by proposing a general protocol for analyzing any problem of admissibility.

B. What is the law of evidence? A Thayerite overview[1]

In the Anglo-American tradition there have been four principal attempts to develop an explicit general theory of the law of evidence. Gilbert tried to subsume all the rules of evidence under a single principle, the "best evidence rule";[2] Bentham saw the existing technical rules as an illogical and indefensible morass, and he argued that there should be no binding rules at all within the framework of the Natural System of Procedure; Stephen tried to find a coherent rationale for the whole of the law of evidence in the principle of relevancy. Thayer admired Stephen's enterprise but agreed with Sir Frederick Pollock's judgment that it represented "a splendid mistake."[3] Relevance was a matter of logic, not law and "The law has no mandamus on the logical faculty."[4] Thayer treated the rules of evidence as a mixed group of exceptions to a principle of freedom of proof.

Nearly all modern writers on evidence in the common law world have accepted some version of Thayer's thesis, and it has more or less explicitly provided the basis for most subsequent attempts to codify this branch of the law, including the Federal Rules of Evidence.[5] Accordingly, Thayer is the natural starting-point for interpreting the current position.

The Thayerite conception of the law of evidence has a strikingly narrow focus. It concerns processes *in court*; it is restricted to what facts may be presented to the court by whom and the manner of their presentation. It is not directly concerned with pre-trial and post-trial events. Over time, many topics previously included in books on evidence were exiled to procedure, pleading, or substantive law and, in the United States, to constitutional law. Underlying this conception are sharp distinctions between materiality, relevance, admissibility, and cogency, each of which is governed by a different set of criteria. In constructing an argument on an issue of fact, a four-stage intellectual procedure has to be followed, with each stage belonging to a different sphere of discourse and allocated to a specific functionary. Thus in a contested jury trial the standard pattern is as follows:

1   What are the facts to be proved? (Facts in issue, ultimate *probanda*, material facts are all synonymous in this context.) This is the issue of *materiality*. It is governed by *substantive law* and is to be determined by the judge.
2   Of any fact offered as evidence or potential evidence: Does this fact tend to support or tend to negate one or more of the facts in issue? This is the question of relevance; it is governed by logic and general experience, and is a matter for the judge.

---

1 This section is adapted from *Rethinking* 188–96.
2 Gilbert (1754).   3 Pollock (1899).   4 Thayer (1898) 314.
5 For an interesting gloss on Thayer's account of the shift from "irrational" to "rational" modes of proof see Murphy (1999) 334–38.

3 Of any fact offered as evidence or potential evidence: Is there a rule or principle that
   requires that this item of relevant evidence should be excluded or its use limited
   because *either*
   (a) it belongs to a *class* of inadmissible evidence; *or*
   (b) it would be contrary to the policy of the law to admit this in the circumstances of
        the case?
   This issue of *admissibility* is governed by the law of evidence, and is a question for the
   judge.
4 What *weight* should be given to this item of evidence (or the evidence as a whole) in
   the circumstances of the case? This is the issue of *evaluation of weight* (or cogency or
   probative force); it is governed by "logic and general experience," and is a matter for
   the jury or other trier of fact. An alternative interpretation is that the criteria for
   weight of evidence are provided by probability theory, of which there are many
   versions (see above, Chapter 9).

Thayer's surgical narrowing down of the scope of the law of evidence was inspired
ground-clearing. He then molded what remained into a simple and coherent system,
based on two principles:

(1) That nothing is to be received which is not logically probative of some matter
requiring to be proved; and
(2) that everything which is thus probative should come in, unless a clear ground of
policy of law excludes it.[6]

The first principle (the test of relevance) is *exclusionary*, but it is not strictly speaking
part of the law of evidence: "It is not so much a rule of evidence as a presupposition
involved in the very conception of a rational system of evidence."[7] The second principle is *inclusionary* and is the basic principle of the law of evidence. It mandates
the reception of evidence supposed to be logically relevant to the facts in issue,
subject to exceptions prescribed by law. The main role of technical rules of evidence
is to prescribe the scope of the exceptions to the general inclusionary principle.
Thayer's explanation for the perceived complexity of the subject was essentially historical. While the exclusionary rules were logically exceptions to a general principle
of inclusion, the historical process was different:

What has taken place, in fact, is the shutting out of the judges of one and another thing
from time to time; and so, gradually, the recognition of this exclusion under a rule.
These rules of exclusion have had their exceptions; and so the law has come into the
shape of a set of primary rules of exclusion; and then a set of exceptions to these rules.[8]

These exceptions, and exceptions to exceptions, were justified on disparate grounds:

Some things are rejected as being of too slight a significance, or as having too conjectural
and remote a connection; others, as being dangerous in their effect on the jury, and
likely to be misused or overestimated by that body; others as being impolitic, or unsafe

6 Thayer (1898) 530; cf. id. 266.   7 Id. 264–65.   8 Id. 265.

on public grounds; others on the bare ground of precedent. It is this sort of thing, as I said before – the rejection on one or other practical ground, of what is really probative – which is the characteristic thing in the law of evidence; stamping it as a child of the jury system.[9]

Three points about Thayer's conception of the scope of the law of evidence deserve emphasis. First, the core of Thayer's view of the law of evidence is concerned with the regulation of *reasoning* about disputed questions of fact at trial.[10] The law of evidence consists mainly of artificial limitations on free enquiry and ordinary reason in the process of arguing about and justifying decisions on such questions. Since the law, by and large, leaves judgments about relevancy and weight to logic and general experience, the "excluding function" is the main role of the law of evidence.

Secondly, the converse of this last proposition is not the case. The law of evidence is only one of several grounds for excluding evidence. In litigation the issues are artificially and sharply defined in advance by substantive law and pleading; historians, physical scientists, and others have no strong concept of materiality to limit their enquiries in such ways. More evidence is excluded on grounds of irrelevance than for any other reason; but relevance is a matter of logic, not law, even if lawyers tend to interpret relevance more strictly than most. It should also be remembered that Bentham, who wished to abolish all formal rules of evidence, was in favor of exclusion of evidence if it was irrelevant or superfluous or its adduction would have involved preponderant vexation, expense or delay judged by the standard of utility in the circumstances of the case.

Thirdly, Thayer indicates that questions of weight are not and should not be governed by rules of law, but they are subject only to "the ordinary rules of human thought and experience, to be sought in the ordinary sources, and not in the law books."[11] In short, the law prescribes almost no rules for the evaluation of evidence.[12]

By and large, subsequent treatise writers and codifiers have followed Thayer in accepting a fairly restrictive view of the law of evidence, but have followed Wigmore in including all or most of the "borderline" topics, such as presentation of evidence, burdens and presumptions, and appellate review.[13]

The Thayerite theory can be interpreted as stating that the law of evidence consists of a series of disparate exceptions to a principle of free proof. If a body of law is conceived as constituting a series of exceptions to a single principle, it would

---

9 Id. 266.
10 Chapter VI is entitled "The Law of Evidence, and Legal Reasoning as applied to the Ascertainment of Facts."
11 Thayer (1898).   12 See above, Ch. 8.
13 *Rethinking* Ch. 6 quotes a useful formulation by an Australian lawyer, Philip McNamara (1986), which presents a summary overview of the canons of Australian law of evidence in the spirit of Thayer under nine basic heads. This is helpful in concretizing Thayer's theory, but is not included here as it does not represent modern US law in respect of a few specific details.

seem natural to start by elucidating the nature and scope of that principle, before considering the exceptions. What, then, is "free proof"? In the present context, one can give a relatively straightforward answer that fits the Thayerite view of the law of evidence. "Free proof" means an absence of formal rules that interfere with free enquiry and natural or common sense reasoning. In the adversary system, where the parties have primary control over what evidence is presented in what form and what questions are or are not put to witnesses, the freedom of enquiry by judge, jury, or other triers of fact is strictly limited. It is for the parties to determine whom and what they see or hear, but not how they evaluate and reason from evidence. This "freedom" is largely the freedom of the parties and to a lesser extent that of the judge, jury, or trier of fact.[14] This conception of "free proof" is entirely compatible with the Thayerite picture of the law of evidence.

We saw in Chapter 3 that Thayer's disciple, Wigmore, treated the principle of proof and the law of evidence as two complementary parts of a single subject, what he called judicial evidence. The principles of proof, said Wigmore, were anterior to and more important than what he called the "Trial Rules." It is worth revisiting both elements in this claim. Wigmore argued that it was better to study the principles of proof *before* studying the rules. This was not merely because it seems sensible to study a basic principle before considering exceptions to it. More important, the principles of proof are logically anterior to the law of evidence, as well as providing many of their underlying rationales (insofar as they had a rational basis). Thayer had made essentially the same point when he claimed that these two basic principles of evidence (the exclusionary and inclusionary principles) were not so much part of the law of evidence as necessary presuppositions of a rational system of evidence.[15] The exclusion of irrelevant evidence was a matter of logic not law, and there was a general presumption in favor of admitting all relevant evidence. In order to have a clear view of the law of evidence, one needs first to understand these two basic principles of proof.

In our experience, Thayer and Wigmore have both been proved right, but like many other teachers of evidence, we have extended the focus of attention beyond the courtroom and the contested trial to cover all phases of litigation, from investigation to post-trial decisions. This is not only because the law of evidence "casts a long shadow," but also because inferential reasoning is an important part of many pre- and post-trial decisions. It is for this reason that we have adopted a "total process"

14 This is, of course, rather different from Bentham's model of the Natural System of Procedure, which was more inquisitorial in nature. Nevertheless, Bentham's attack on all binding rules of evidence, his "anti-nomian thesis," provides the classic picture of a system of free proof in adjudication: no rules excluding classes of witnesses or of evidence; no rules of priority or weight or quantum; no binding rules as to form or manner of presentation; no artificial restriction on questioning or reasoning; no right of silence or testimonial privileges; no restrictions on reasoning other than the general principles of practical reason; no exclusion of evidence unless it is irrelevant or superfluous or its adduction would involve preponderant vexation, expense, or delay in the circumstances of the particular case. For a detailed discussion see Twining (1985) Ch. 2.

15 Thayer (1898) 264–65.

model of litigation (both civil and criminal) and have emphasized the importance of differentiating the standpoints of different participants at different stages of legal processes as well as of different kinds of outside observers.

C. One law of evidence?

Our approach in this book combines the ideal type of the Rationalist Tradition, a total process model of litigation, principles of proof, methods of marshaling arguments, and a substance-blind approach to the credentials of evidence, especially relevance, credibility, and probative force. It also deals with the relationship between generalizations, narrative, and argument. All of these transcend differences between evidentiary problems in civil, criminal, and other contexts. They represent the general part of the study of evidence in law within the tradition of Thayer and Wigmore. However, detailed study of the technical rules of evidence needs to be sensitive to the differences between procedural and institutional contexts and to the different rationales and policies underlying criminal and civil proceedings and other kinds of litigation. Indeed, in most civil law systems the rules of evidence are treated as part of procedure, and civil, criminal, and administrative procedural systems belong to different specialisms. In England, especially since the decline of the civil jury, most courses on evidence focus almost exclusively on evidence in criminal proceedings. One of the leading textbooks is now called *Criminal Evidence*.[16] This trend has probably gone further in England than in most common law countries.

In the United States, the situation is more complex for there have been conflicting trends. Evidence is still treated as a single subject in most books and courses, partly because the jury is still important in civil cases and because the Federal Rules cover both civil and criminal evidence. However, in dealing with questions of admissibility and proof, constant attention must still be paid to the different underlying principles, policies, and rationales of civil and criminal litigation. Furthermore, the impact of constitutional law on criminal procedure has promoted the separation of civil and criminal evidence. However, some important constitutional issues are treated more in courses on criminal procedure or constitutional law than in courses on evidence, whereas in England the impact of the European Convention on Human Rights and the Human Rights Act 1998 can hardly be ignored in a course on evidence.

---

16 Roberts and Zuckerman (2004). Evidentiary issues arise in all types of proceeding, in all types of legal processes and at every stage. However, Roberts argues that the subject becomes more manageable and coherent if one focuses on one type of proceeding – viz. criminal process (Roberts (2002)). We agree that it is desirable to integrate the law of civil and criminal evidence with their different procedural contexts, but would reiterate that the logic of proof is highly transferable across legal traditions, procedural contexts, and even disciplines. We included exercises involving different stages of criminal process, intelligence scenarios, and other non-legal examples to emphasize this transferability.

D. Linking the principles of proof and the law of evidence: relevance as the main bridge

As we have seen, the logic of proof is an important element in studying, for example, judicial notice, similar facts, prejudicial effect/probative value, burdens and standards of proof (and for other decisions),[17] and presumptions. The increasingly important subject of scientific and expert evidence is a good peg on which to hang some of the central epistemological questions concerning evidence.[18] However, the main bridge between fact analysis/the principles of proof and legal doctrine is supplied by the topic of relevance because:

a Relevance is the most important mechanism of exclusion.
b The principles of proof are anterior to the other exclusionary rules because they deal with the exclusion of relevant evidence. In other words, the question of relevance needs to be determined as a preliminary to considering whether a particular exclusionary rule applies to a particular item of potential evidence.
c To understand relevance involves understanding the principles and characteristics of inferential reasoning.
d The law of evidence can be treated as a coherent whole by Thayer's inclusionary and exclusionary principles, which are expressed in terms of relevance within a basic framework of argumentation.

Many modern course books treat relevance as the first topic to be studied on the law of evidence. They often devote substantial space to it. While staying with the idea that relevance is the core of both the logic of proof and the rules of evidence, we have tried in this book to present a broader and more coherent foundation to the study of the rules. It is important that this should be more than just a preliminary topic to be studied at the beginning of a course and then forgotten; rather the approach needs to be an integral part of the detailed study of most standard topics in an evidence course.[19]

E. Analyzing for admissibility[20]

The connection between the principles of proof and exclusionary rules is clear if we think in terms of argumentation. If an item of evidence is inadmissible, this means that it may not be part of an argument and so it has no place on the chart. The

17 On the broader concept of "standards for decision" see above, Ch. 8.
18 Roberts 324–28. The links between epistemology and scientific evidence have been brilliantly explored by the philosopher Susan Haack. See especially Haack (2003) Ch. 9 and Haack (2004).
19 A similar point is made by Paul Roberts. In arguing for more attention to be paid to relevance, he suggests that after a preliminary consideration at the start of a course, the lessons can be reinforced by explicit consideration of it in relation to other topics such as previous misconduct evidence, hearsay, and silence. (Roberts (2002) 306–7). See further Roberts and Zuckerman (2004), *passim*. For an illustration see pages 341–43 below.
20 This heading echoes the title of the excellent Ch. 8 of Palmer (2004), which deals with this subject in more detail but at a general level.

exclusionary rules tell us what may or may not be part of an argument. Since these formal rules work to exclude relevant evidence, relevance is always a preliminary issue. But relevance can only be determined in relation to a material fact or another fact of consequence. In other words the ultimate and penultimate probanda need to be established before either questions of exclusion because of irrelevance or other grounds of inadmissibility can be determined.

Thus where an issue of admissibility arises, questions of relevance arise twice: relevance to a fact of consequence and relevance to credibility. Often the initial question of relevance may be unproblematic. For example, in a murder case a confession, "I killed Charlie," is obviously directly relevant to opportunity and identity, though it may not tell us anything about criminal intent or a possible defense. But the prosecution must first lay a foundation, by introducing evidence that the confession was voluntary.

Sometimes the argument can become quite complicated and it may be helpful to use a Wigmorean approach to clarify an issue of admissibility. For instance, in the case of *R. v. George Joseph Smith* (the brides in the bath murders) the prosecution had plenty of evidence of motive and opportunity, but there was not much evidence to support the propositions that Smith caused the death of Bessy Munday and that he did so with criminal intent. The prosecution successfully argued that evidence of the deaths of two other brides by drowning in similar circumstances was admissible. The passage from the peroration in the closing speech by Thomas Bodkin QC for the Crown is powerful as rhetoric, but it masks a quite complex argument.[21] One can reconstruct the argument in Wigmorean terms as follows: *Standpoint*: counsel for the prosecution arguing that details of the deaths of two other brides are admissible.

Ultimate probandum: GJS murdered Bessie Munday.

1   GJS caused BM to die by drowning[22]
2   GJS acted with criminal intent
3   There was a large aggregation of resemblances between the deaths of BM and two other recent brides
4   The aggregation of resemblances could not have occurred without design.
5   The combination of factors a–l is too uncommon to be a coincidence. (G)[23]
6   In all three cases factors a–l were present

21   See above, Ch. 1, C3a.
22   This could be disaggregated into two propositions relating to cause and identity: A person caused BM's death by drowning; it was GJS who caused BM's death. Identity was not really in question in the case.
23   The factors emphasized by Bodkin were (a) going through a form of marriage; (b) the ready money of the woman was withdrawn or realized; (c) a will was drawn in favor of GJS absolutely; (d) the will was drawn by a stranger to the testatrix; (e) the victim either insured her life or had property that made this unnecessary; (f) there was a visit to a doctor, which was unnecessary given the physical condition of the patient; (g) the woman wrote letters to relatives on the night before she died or on the same night; (h) the prisoner was the first to discover the drowning; (i) the door was unfastened and the water was not drawn off until after the doctor had been; (j) the prisoner put forward demonstrably that he had been shopping and absent from the house in which his wife was lying dead; (k) the prisoner disappeared after the event; (l) the prisoner achieved or attempted to achieve monetary advantage as a result of the death.

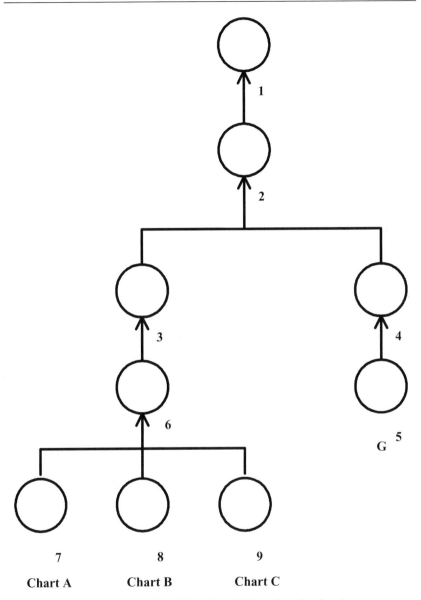

Chart A   Chart B   Chart C

Figure 11.1 *R. v. George Joseph Smith* (admissibility of similar facts)

7 In case I factors a–l were present (foundational facts)
8 In case II factors a–l were present (foundational facts)
9 In case III factors a–l were present (foundational facts)
10 Chart A: the evidence supporting 7
11 Chart B: the evidence supporting 8
12 Chart C: the evidence supporting 9.

Several points are worth noting about this example. First, the argument about design supports three material facts (causation, identity, and criminal intent). Second, a crucial step in the argument involves a generalization about coincidence. In this case, it seems very plausible, but arguments from coincidence are frequency arguments that can easily be abused.[24] Third, this case should be distinguished from similar fact arguments that involve "propensity" as a step in the reasoning. Such cases, which have caused a great deal of difficulty in all common law countries, can also be usefully analyzed by the chart method.[25] Here the argument was about coincidence to support design and did not involve any reference to the character of the accused. Today, such cases all need to be analyzed in terms of prejudicial effect versus probative value.[26] Fourth, part of the strength of the argument in this case arises from a synergy between individual pieces of evidence: several of the common factors support the proposition that Smith had so arranged things that he stood to gain financially, i.e. he had a motive, which further supports design, identity, and intent.

At a general level one can analyze most issues of admissibility by asking four questions, as follows:

1 Does this evidence raise a potential issue of admissibility? (e.g., evidence of circumstances of two other murders.)
2 If so, what is the purpose for which it is being tendered? (To what fact(s) in issue is this evidence relevant? In *Smith* both cause of death and criminal intent.)
3 What are the facts relevant to the question of admissibility of this evidence? (Sometimes referred to as "foundational facts"; e.g., the facts that in each case factors a–l were present.)
4 What evidence tends to prove the existence of the foundational facts? (e.g., the evidence that factors a–l were present in Case I and Case II.)[27]

---

24 E.g., *R. v. Clark* [2003] E.W.C.A. Crim. 1020 (Sally Clark, multiple cot deaths, discussed in Appendix I on the website).
25 See Acorn (1991).
26 See, however, the Criminal Justice Act 2003, sections 101 and 103: bad character is admissible where "it is relevant to an important matter in issue between the defendant and the prosecution," subject to a general condition of "fairness." For a good discussion see Roberts and Zuckerman (2004), suggesting that for most purposes this legislative intervention "reads like a convoluted restatement of existing legal principles" (517).
27 For an extended protocol under the US Federal Rules, see below, Figure 11.2.

F. Analysis under the United States Federal Rules of Evidence

The Federal Rules of Evidence, enacted as law in the United States (the "Federal Rules"), provide a good vehicle to illustrate the relationship between analysis of evidence and rules of evidence because all of the basic rules are prescribed in statutory form in a unified code.[28] Unlike most common law jurisdictions, the rules do not have to be taken from separate codes regulating civil and criminal procedure or distilled from piecemeal legislation or appellate decisions or treatises by recognized authorities.[29] Having authoritative statements of the rules collected and organized as a coherent code simplifies the task.

The rules of evidence fall into three overlapping categories. In the first are rules adapting the principles of proof to the judicial context. In the second are rules designed to regulate the probative process by identifying improper prejudicial effects that may result from the admission and use of particular kinds of evidence and requiring that the trial court weigh those effects against the legitimate probative value of the evidence in the case before it. In the third category are rules that require the exclusion of evidence without regard to its probative value based upon policies that override the importance of establishing truth. Some rules do not fit neatly into just one category; an analysis of their application requires consideration of factors from two or sometimes all three categories. Nonetheless, the categories provide a useful starting-point for considering the relationship between analysis of evidence and the application of the rules of evidence prescribed by law.

1. Rules codifying the principles of proof and regulating their application in judicial trials

Rules 401 and 402 codify the principles of proof. Under Rule 401, evidence is relevant if it has any tendency to make a fact of consequence more probable or less probable than it would be in the absence of that evidence. There are only two kinds of facts of consequence in any case – the facts that are defined as material by the applicable rules of substantive law, and the credibility of evidence once it has been admitted. Whether an item of evidential data is relevant can only be demonstrated by applying the principles of logic developed above in Chapter 3. Under Rule 402, all relevant evidence is admissible, unless it is excluded or its use is limited by the Constitution of the United States, by statute, or by another of the Federal Rules.

Trials in the United States and other common law systems, especially jury trials, are designed to be single, continuous events whose beginning point (opening statements) and end points (closing statements, jury instruction, deliberation, and verdict or decision) are defined in advance. They are not open-ended inquiries of the kind undertaken in science and other disciplines. They are closed inquiries in

---

28 Fed. Rules Evid., 28 U.S.C.A; also available at http://judiciary.house.gov.
29 For the confusing fragmentation of sources of the law of evidence in England, see any standard text, e.g., Roberts and Zuckerman (2004).

which decision-makers may not have any training or expertise in analyzing evidence to resolve disputed questions of fact. For that reason, additional rules are necessary to regulate the admission and use of evidence in that context.

A moderate modern Benthamite or a trained investigator in another discipline would accept some of these rules as sensible adaptations. They would probably accept as reasonable the requirement that a witness have personal knowledge of the matter about which she testifies (Rule 602), that she testify under oath subject to the penalties for perjury (Rule 603), that a witness expressing an opinion must demonstrate that she is qualified by training or experience to express the opinion and, in the case of experts, that the opinion be based upon reliable principles reliably applied to reach the proffered conclusion (Rules 701–705).[30]

Most scientists and historians would also recognize the principle that their investigations must be limited to some degree by efficiency concerns. Resources are finite, and a conclusion, however provisional, must be reached at some point. The need for efficiency is greater in the jury trial context and, for that reason, they would probably recognize that rules adopted to promote efficiency must be more stringent than might be appropriate in other contexts. Rule 102 articulates efficiency as one of potentially conflicting goals that should be considered in applying the rules of evidence. Efficiency is one of the grounds used to justify the limits on the kinds of evidence that may be used to prove relevant character traits imposed by Rules 405 (methods of proving character), 608 (character and conduct of witness), and the rule authorizing a court to take judicial notice (Rule 201).

The application of these rules usually requires considerable analysis of the particular evidence to determine whether any of the efficiency based rules should be applied to admit or to exclude or limit the use of that evidence.

Questions

1   Which of the other Federal Rules can be justified, at least in part, based upon having as one of their objectives the promotion of efficiency?
2   Which of these rules would a scientist or historian recognize as a sensible limitation on the evidence that may be received in a trial?
3   Rule 403 is based in part on efficiency concerns: "Although relevant, evidence may be excluded if its probative value is substantially outweighed . . . by considerations of undue delay, waste of time, or needless presentation of cumulative evidence." What limits on the judge's discretion to exclude relevant evidence based upon these considerations would a scientist or historian suggest that appellate courts adopt and impose?

---

30 Three decisions, *Daubert v. Merrel Dow Pharmaceuticals, Inc.*, 509 U.S. 578 (1993); *General Electric Co. v. Joiner*, 552 U.S. 166 (1997); and *Kumho Tire Company, Ltd. v. Carmichael*, 526 U.S. 137 (1998), have made questions about the admissibility of scientific or expert evidence a major area of litigation and scholarship in the United States.

4   Scientists and historians often decline to seek some kinds of evidence based upon the considerations expressed in the quoted portion of Rule 403. What limits should be imposed upon the scientist's or the historian's exercise of discretion not to seek additional evidence based upon these grounds, and how should those limits be enforced?

5   Who has the broadest discretion to exclude evidence based upon the quoted consideration, with impunity: the trial judge, the scientist, or the historian?

2. Analysis and the rules designed to regulate the probative processes

The prejudicial effects that the Federal Rules were designed to regulate can be analyzed using a spectrum that has two ends. At one end are limitations based upon efficiency concerns such as those described above. At the other end are kinds of evidence that can be characterized as having improper prejudicial effects only because the admission and use of such evidence would conflict with policies deemed more important than the probative value such evidence might have in establishing truth. The fact that a city repaired a crack in the sidewalk after a citizen had broken her leg when it caused her to stumble would be relevant as evidence having a tendency to show the city recognized that the condition was dangerous and that it was a condition that could have been easily fixed. If the city thought that repairing the crack might increase the likelihood that it would be held liable for the citizen's injuries, it might leave it unrepaired until the issue had been resolved. We want the city to fix the dangerous condition as soon as possible. Rule 407 excluding evidence of subsequent remedial measures offered to prove negligence, culpable conduct, a defect in a product or its design, or the need for a warning or construction was adopted to implement this policy. Rules 408 (excluding evidence of settlement discussions to prove liability or the amount of damages), 409 (limiting the use of evidence of payment of medical or similar expenses), 410 (limiting the use of evidence of pleas and plea discussions), and 411 (limiting the use of evidence of liability insurance) were all enacted to further similar policy objectives, notwithstanding the probative value such evidence might have with respect to facts of consequence that are disputed in a particular case.

It is important to note that none of these rules excludes the evidence in all circumstances. For example, a trial judge has discretion to admit evidence of subsequent remedial measures if the evidence is offered for other purposes such as proving ownership or control. For that reason, arguments about the admissibility or use of evidence covered by these rules require that counsel seeking to have such evidence admitted must be able to analyze and articulate the inferences that demonstrate that the evidence has probative value for purposes other than the purpose prohibited by the rule. Similarly, opposing counsel must be able to identify the impermissible prejudicial effects the rule was enacted to avoid and to construct and articulate arguments that will persuade the trial judge that the identified improper prejudicial effects outweigh the legitimate probative value of the evidence. This requires careful analysis of the particular evidence and of the different inferences it might support.

Rules such as these, or the reasons given for their enactment, identify as a matter of law the effects that are improperly prejudicial. But when the question is whether the improper prejudicial effect outweighs the legitimate probative value of the proffered evidence, skill in microanalysis and the use of the logical principles provide the tools necessary to construct persuasive arguments bearing upon that issue.

Exercise

Rule 407 specifies that the evidence of a subsequent remedial measure is not admissible to prove negligence or culpability (an improper prejudicial effect), but it is admissible to prove ownership or control (a legitimate probative value). Assume Mr. Smith was injured when his car crashed as a result of a large hole in a graveled road that connected Farmer Jones's house to the highway. The next day, Farmer Jones filled the hole and put new gravel on the road. Smith sued Jones, and Jones alleged the road was owned by her neighbor, and thus the neighbor was responsible for its maintenance and repair. At trial, Smith calls a witness who will testify that she saw Jones fill the hole and regravel the road on the day after Smith's accident. Jones argues that the evidence is inadmissible to prove that he was negligent or culpable. Smith argues it should be admitted to prove Jones's ownership and control of the road.

1 What test should the court apply in deciding whether the improper prejudicial effects the evidence will have as evidence of Farmer Jones's negligence and culpability require that it be excluded notwithstanding its legitimate probative value as evidence that Jones owned and controlled the road and was responsible for repair? Should the court require that Jones satisfy it that the improper prejudicial effect outweighs the legitimate probative value? Substantially outweighs? Is at least equal to the probative value? Given the congressional policy that led to the enactment of the rule, should the court require that Smith satisfy it that the probative value outweighs the improper prejudicial effects? Substantially outweighs? Is at least equal to or greater than the prejudicial effects?

2 In addressing this issue, is the court deciding a question of law or a question of fact? Is it applying the rule or using the rule as a guide to the exercise of discretion? If the court admits the evidence, can that decision be reversed on appeal? What if it excludes the evidence?

3 As counsel for either of the parties, what other evidence would you ask the trial judge to consider in deciding whether to admit the witness's testimony? What additional evidence might strengthen the argument that the evidence should be excluded? What additional evidence might strengthen the argument that the evidence should be admitted? If counsel for one of the parties had looked for, but been unable to find, additional evidence that might affect the balance and had reported her efforts to the

court, should the court consider the unavailability of the evidence? If opposing counsel admitted he had not even looked for additional evidence relevant to the issue, what, if any, weight should the court give to this failure?

Rule 403 articulates the general test under which relevant evidence may be excluded. Evidence may be excluded if the improper prejudicial effects of that evidence substantially outweigh its legitimate probative value. Most of the remaining rules authorizing the exclusion of relevant evidence, or the imposition of limitations on evidence for the purpose for which such evidence may be used, can be explained as recurring situations in which judicial experience has shown the inherent improper prejudicial effects of specific kinds of evidence by a margin sufficient to justify the exclusion of that kind of evidence or the imposition of limitations on its use. The problems presented by *United States v. Able* illustrate these points.

Rule 404(b) reflects a social judgment that evidence that an accused has committed a crime other than the crime charged will create a substantial risk that the jury will convict the accused based upon a judgment that she is a bad person deserving of punishment, notwithstanding any weaknesses in the other evidence offered to establish guilt of the charged crime. "We try the act, not the actor." Rule 404(b) also recognizes, however, that evidence of another crime may also have a legitimate probative value with respect to relevant facts, such as motive or identity. In such circumstances, the judge has discretion to admit evidence of the other crime, notwithstanding its improper prejudicial effects.

Evidence that Able used cocaine was relevant to motive, which in turn is relevant to intent to defraud. Cocaine is an expensive drug, and the decline in Able's income substantially exceeded the decline in his expenses. On the other hand, there is a substantial possibility that at least some jurors would vote to convict Abel (a) for his cocaine use, or (b) in a belief that it was beyond reasonable doubt that he *either* used cocaine *or* he intended to defraud the government by filing a false tax return and, thus, deserved to be punished, or (c) because a person who violates the law by using cocaine is a person who has a propensity to violate the law, and for that reason Able's illegal cocaine use increases the likelihood that he illegally filed a false tax return to an extent that justifies overlooking weaknesses in the other evidence of guilt offered by the government.

Able also illustrates the role that microanalysis plays in constructing arguments about the admissibility and use of evidence. In the absence of reliable evidence concerning the quantity and price of the cocaine Able used, the legitimate probative value of cocaine use with respect to financial motive was diminished, but the improper prejudicial effects remained great. So too, (a) the number of steps in the inferential chain necessary to demonstrate the relevance of the fact that the $25,000 check from the law firm was cashed in Las Vegas in December to the existence of a motive to falsify Able's tax return the following April and (b) the plausible explanations for each of those inferential steps made it possible to construct a strong argument that the improper propensity effects of the endorsement evidence, standing alone, and the likelihood the jury would misvalue that evidence, substantially outweighed any legitimate probative value it had with respect to motive. See page 129 above.

Questions

1   George Joseph Smith was charged with the murder of Bessie Mundy. The relevance and legitimate probative value of evidence that two of his other "brides" drowned in similar circumstances is discussed and charted above. The improper prejudicial effects are not. Were there any improper prejudicial effects other than the obvious propensity effects? Assuming Rules 403 and 404(b) had been in effect, construct an argument demonstrating that the improper prejudicial effects of that evidence outweighed its legitimate probative value.

2   Smith was not indicted for the other murders. Why not? Consider the following proposal to amend Rule 404(b) by adding the following as the second sentence of that rule:

> Evidence of another crime shall not be admissible unless the accused has either (i) pled guilty to or been convicted of that crime or (ii) had been indicted and is being tried for that crime as part of the case in which such evidence is offered.

> Should the proposed amendment be adopted? Why or why not? Justify your position.

3   When the prosecution seeks to introduce evidence of another crime or bad act, how much evidence should it have to produce to establish that the other crime or act occurred and that the accused was responsible for it? Proof beyond reasonable doubt? Clear and convincing evidence? A preponderance of the evidence? Some evidence? See *United States v. Huddleston*, 485 U.S. 681 (1988) for the answer under the Federal Rules. See Anderson (1999a) for a Wigmorean critique of the answer and the reasoning used to justify it.

3. Analysis and mandatory exclusionary rules

Evidence obtained in violation of rights guaranteed by the Constitution and evidence discovered as a result of such a violation may not be admitted against the accused in a criminal trial no matter how strong its probative value may be. This rule excludes evidence obtained in violation of the fourth amendment's prohibition of unreasonable searches and seizures or of the fifth amendment's privilege against self incrimination.[31] Often such evidence is not only highly probative of the accused's guilt, but also evidence without which the case cannot be prosecuted – e.g., without the 20 kilograms of cocaine found in the accused's apartment through a search that was subsequently declared unreasonable, the government could not prosecute the

---

31 U.S. Const., amends. IV and V.

accused for possession with intent to distribute. The current rationale for the rule is that exclusion is required to deter police misconduct.[32]

The application of the constitutional exclusionary rule has always required analysis of the evidence bearing upon the circumstances in which the challenged evidence was obtained. The party opposing admission of evidence on the ground that it was unlawfully seized must produce evidence of the circumstances surrounding the search and marshal the available inferences to demonstrate that it was an "unreasonable search." The Supreme Court has enhanced the need for careful analysis of the facts (and has diluted the rule) by decisions such as those creating special rules authorizing the search of an automobile,[33] and those establishing an impeachment exception to the exclusionary rule authorizing the use of unlawfully obtained evidence to impeach the credibility of an accused who takes the stand.[34]

The other principal source of rules excluding probative evidence are the rules establishing privileged communications. Information provided by an accused to her lawyer about what happened is likely to be highly probative or likely to identify sources from which dispositive evidence of guilt might be obtained. So too, statements an accused might make to his physician in order to enable her to treat her gunshot wounds would almost certainly have probative value in determining whether she was a participant or an innocent bystander in a bank robbery in which a number of bank employees and customers had been shot. Society has decided rules prohibiting the discovery or use of communications between lawyer and client, doctor and patient, priest and penitent are necessary to achieve other important ends, notwithstanding the limits they impose upon the gathering and use of probative evidence. The application of these rules also requires analysis of the underlying facts. Did the communication occur during the existence of the privileged relationship? Did it fall within the scope of that relationship? And so on.

4. A Wigmorean protocol for analyzing problems in the use and admissibility of evidence under the Federal Rules and its application

Figure 11.2 describes a seven-step protocol for analyzing problems in the use and admissibility of evidence. That protocol can be used to illustrate the relationship between analysis of evidence and the rules prescribed by law to regulate the admissibility and use of evidence. The admissibility and use problems presented by hearsay evidence are among the most interesting and complex problems addressed by the Federal Rules. We begin with a description of the problems from an analytic perspective. We conclude with an application of the protocol to a concrete hearsay problem.

---

32 The rationale originally had a second prong. Exclusion was necessary to protect the integrity of the courts, that is the courts should not be dealing in stolen evidence. The original rationale and its evolution through the Court's decision are described in LaFave (2004) §3.1(b).
33 The origin and development of the automobile rules are described in LaFave (2004) §3.7.
34 Id. at § 9.6. For an analysis of the impeachment exception, see Kainen (1992).

1   What is the ultimate probandum for the case in which the proffered evidence is being offered? What are the penultimate probanda?

2   To what fact of consequence is the proffered evidence relevant? Specify the necessary inferential steps.

3   Is there a rule of evidence that the opponent could invoke to challenge the admissibility or use of the proffered evidence? If so, specify the rule, and make the argument, initially in syllogistic form.

4   What, if any, are the arguments that the proponent of the evidence may make to avoid the application or minimize the effect of the rule or rules? Begin by challenging the opponent's rule-based argument.

5   Unless it is clear (and it rarely is) that the evidence must be excluded under the rule or rules invoked, what is the legitimate probative value of the proffered evidence? What are its improper prejudicial effects?

6   What is the strongest argument that can be made to persuade the court that the improper prejudicial effects ("PE") substantially outweigh (or outweigh) the legitimate probative value ("PV")? That is that PE ≫ PV? What is the strongest argument the proponent could make to diminish the PE and enhance the PV in order to persuade the court that the PE do not substantially outweigh the PV?

7   Should the proffered evidence be admitted? If admitted should its use be limited? Why?

Figure 11.2 *A Wigmorean protocol for analyzing problems in the use and admissibility of evidence*

a. The hearsay problem[35]

A rule preferring live testimony rather than hearsay finds strong support in the logical principles of proof. In any case in which a statement made by a declarant, otherwise than while testifying, is offered to prove the truth of the matter asserted, the number of steps in the inferential chain increases and the sources of possible error multiply. Consider, for example, the testimony of William in a case in which Sam is accused of murdering John: "I heard Donald say, 'I saw Sam shoot John.'" In determining whether Donald said, "I saw Sam shoot John," the decision-maker must consider William's credibility and the factors that might affect his veracity, his objectivity, and his observational sensitivity. In doing so, they must answer four questions creating at least four possible sources of error. Did William believe he had heard Sam's statement at the time at which William testified? Did William have any expectations that might have caused him to misinterpret Donald's statement? (For example, Donald may have already suspected that it was Sam who murdered John and, for that reason, he may have thought he heard "Sam" when in fact Donald actually said, "I saw Pam shoot John.") Given the lapse of time, did William accurately remember what he heard John say? Was William's hearing good and was he close enough to hear what John said? Figure 11.3 depicts an investigative key-list

---

35   This section is based upon the more comprehensive account and analysis of the hearsay problem developed in Schum (1992).

Key-list for investigative chart

1 William will testify, "I heard Donald say, 'I saw Sam shoot John.'"
2 William heard Donald say, "I saw Sam shoot John."
3 Donald said, "I saw Sam shoot John."
4 The credibility of William's testimonial assertion may be open to substantial doubt.
5 Veracity: Are there any reasons to doubt William's veracity?
6 Does William have a motive to lie?
7 Are there other factors, such as a prior conviction or William's reputation for honesty, that would support an inference that he was a dishonest person?
8 Objectivity: Are there objective factors that create doubts about the accuracy of William's report?
9 Did William have any expectancies that might have caused him to misinterpret Donald's statement? (For example, William might have had a strong suspicion that it was Sam who shot John and for that reason, he may have thought he heard "Sam" when in fact Donald said, "I saw Pam shoot John.")
10 Are there any factors upon which to question William's recollection?
11 Observational sensitivity: Are there any factors that may create doubts about William's ability to hear what Donald said?
12 Are there reasons to question William's ability to hear, e.g., impaired hearing, wax in his ears, etc.?
13 Do the external conditions under which William claims to have heard Donald speak provide reasons to doubt William's ability to hear what Donald said, e.g.: Was the statement during happy hour in a crowded bar? Was the statement directed to William or did he just overhear what Donald heard said to another person?

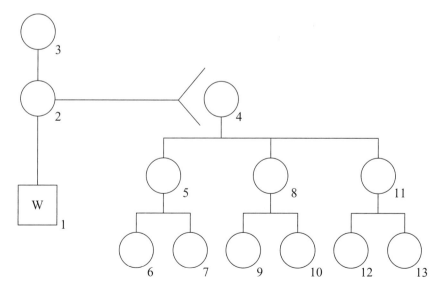

Figure 11.3 *An investigative key-list and chart*

and chart that an attorney might use to guide her search for evidence upon which to base her cross-examination of William.

The central distinction between live testimony and hearsay is the availability of the right to cross-examine the live witness.[36] The attorney for Sam can cross-examine William to ensure that the jury is aware of any factors that might call into question William's veracity, objectivity, or observational sensitivity. She could cross-examine William to eliminate any ambiguities that might be created by his other testimonial assertions. There is no ambiguity in William's testimony reporting what John said and, assuming counsel's cross-examination did not develop reasons to question William's credibility, a jury might infer, but could only infer, that Donald said, "I saw Sam shoot John."

Donald's statement, if admissible, would clearly be offered to prove the truth of the matter asserted. From the statement the jury would be asked to infer that (a) Donald saw Sam shoot John and from that inference that (b) Sam shot John and from that inference, combined with inferences from evidence concerning the cause of John's death, that (c) it was Sam who committed the act that caused John's death.

The logical foundation for a rule excluding hearsay or limiting its use stems from the fact that the jury will not hear Donald say, "I saw Sam shoot John," and Sam's attorney cannot cross-examine John to ensure that the jury is aware of any factors that may call into question his credibility attributes that might raise doubts about his veracity, the objective accuracy of his statement, or his observational sensitivity.[37] Any or all of these factors might have diminished Donald's credibility, but the jury must assess his credibility without knowing whether or which of these factors existed. The sources of doubt about the truth and accuracy of William's testimony must be multiplied by the sources of doubt about the truth and accuracy of Donald's assertion, sources about which the jury lacks information necessary to appraise their significance. That is the logical problem created by the admission of hearsay. Analysis of the evidence is necessary to demonstrate that the number of steps in the inferential chain necessary to establish relevance diminished the probative value of the statement and how the inability to present factors that might affect the jury's appraisal of the declarant's credibility creates, at a minimum, a substantial prejudicial effect that is improper by dramatically increasing the likelihood that the jury will overvalue or be misled by the assertion.[38]

Most defined exceptions to the hearsay rule are also grounded in logic. These exceptions are based upon the view that it is possible to identify circumstances in which some statements are made that provide intrinsic indicia of reliability

---

36 Another distinction that is important is that the decision-maker is able to observe the demeanor and reactions of the witness while she is being examined.

37 Rule 806 was adopted to diminish these sources of doubt by permitting the opponent of the evidence to introduce some extrinsic evidence to attack the credibility of a declarant whose assertion has been admitted under an exception to the hearsay rule.

38 The United States Supreme Court has decided that the Confrontation Clause, U.S. Const., amend. VI, prohibits the admission of hearsay testimonial assertions such as William's report of what John said, *Crawford v. Washington*, 541 U.S. 36 (2004).

sufficient to justify their admission, notwithstanding the absence of the declarant. These exceptions also reflect a policy that not only the indicia of reliability, but also the necessity that the statement be admitted, are to be considered. As the need increases, the indicia of reliability required are often reduced. For example, the need for the admission of a dead declarant's dying declaration concerning the cause of her death is usually high. Unless someone else was present, there may be no other evidence. The declarant is unavailable, and the statement, if true, has substantial probative value. The indicia of reliability, however, are weak. The only apparent indicia are based upon one or both of two generalizations:

1 People who fear God are unlikely to lie when they believe death is imminent.
2 The imminence of death concentrates the mind and diminishes the capacity to fabricate.

Neither of these generalizations has been empirically justified, and both can be rebutted by a counter-generalization:

3 A person who believes that death is imminent also believes that this is her last chance to get even or bring down a person she hates.[39]

A similar analysis could be made of each of the other exceptions under Federal Rules 803 (Availability of Declarant immaterial) and 804 (Declarant unavailable) other than the exception for former testimony codified in Rule 804(b)(1) (where admissibility is justified based upon indicia of accuracy and considerations of fairness in light of necessity).

Exercise

Figure 11.4 is a graph on which the need for the admission of hearsay statements and the intrinsic indicia of reliability can be plotted. The authors have depicted their view of the need and indicia of reliability for two of the exceptions – Rules 806 (business records) and 804(b)(2) (dying declarations). Review the other exceptions created by Rules 803 and 804, and use the graph to depict your view of need and indicia of reliability that might be used to justify the exception.

b. The protocol applied
In *United States v. Able* (pages 23–28), the government gave Able's counsel a three-page memorandum prepared by FBI Agent Dawes stating that he had interviewed Timothy Cooper in August 2004 and that, among other things, Cooper had told him that Cooper had merged his accounting practice in July 2004 and that his secretary had lost or thrown out some materials, such as notes and work papers, contained in inactive client-files. According to the memorandum, Cooper told Dawes that Able

39 Even if Mrs. Shepard had believed that death was imminent, she may have stated that Dr. Shepard had poisoned her in order to bring down her faithless husband so that he would not be able to marry the mistress with whom he had tormented her. See *Shepard v. United States*, 290 U.S. 96 (1933), for a full account of her statements and the context in which they were made.

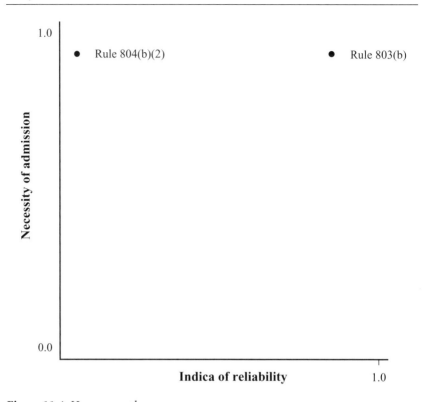

Figure 11.4 *Hearsay graph*

was listed as an inactive client at the time. Dawes's memorandum reported that Cooper could not tell from examining the file whether any materials from Able's file had been discarded.

Dawes's memorandum also reported that Cooper had no recollection of how the signing of Able's return was handled, but Cooper said that he usually mailed two copies of a return to his clients with an envelope addressed to the Internal Revenue Service and a note instructing them to review, sign, and mail the completed returns by April 15. The memorandum reports that Cooper could not find a copy of such a note with the copy of Able's 2003 return in his files. Cooper reported that the file contains no information about any income other than Able's salary, and that Cooper did not recall Able informing him that he had received any other income.

The problem included the following additional facts:

> On cross-examination, Cooper testified that he did not recall seeing Able's April 11 letter; that had his office received it, it would have been in the client-file he maintained for Able, and it is not; that his files were perfectly maintained; that he does not recall discussing any papers being lost in his 2004 move; and that he has never seen Agent Dawes's memorandum and it does not refresh his recollection.

Are Agent Dawes's memorandum and the statement it reports that Cooper made admissible?

How the protocol set out in Figure 11.2 could be used to develop an answer to this question is illustrated below.

1   **What is the ultimate probandum for the case in which the proffered evidence is being offered? What are the penultimate probanda?**
    The ultimate and penultimate probanda in *Able* were formulated in Chapter 5 (at page 126). The ultimate probandum was:
    1   Richard Able ("RA") knowingly filed a false federal tax return for the year 2003 ("the 2003 return") with intent to defraud the government of income tax due and owing on not less than $45,000.
This was partitioned and repartitioned into seven penultimate probanda.
    2   RA knowingly filed a false income tax return for the year 2003.
    3   RA filed a tax return for the year 2003.
    4   The tax return that RA filed for 2003 was false.
    5   RA knew his 2003 tax return was false when he filed it.
    6   At the time RA filed his 2003 tax return, he intended to defraud the government of income tax due and owing on not less than $45,000.
    7   RA owed the government taxes on an additional $45,000 at the time he filed his 2003 tax return.
    8   RA intended to defraud the government of the taxes due and owing at the time he filed his 2003 tax return.

2   **To what fact of consequence is the proffered evidence relevant? Specify the necessary inferential steps.**
    a   Cooper's statements that papers were lost from his inactive client files when he moved his office and that Able was an inactive client at that time are relevant to two facts of consequence. First, these statements support an inference that the April 11 letter might have been lost during the move. That inference supports an opponent's explanation that accounts for the fact the letter was not in Cooper's file at the time the FBI approached him. That explanatory proposition is relevant because it makes the inference that Able's letter was not delivered to Cooper's office, an inference that was supported by evidence that the letter was not in the file and by Cooper's assertion that his files had been perfectly maintained. For that reason, the explanatory proposition increases the probability that Able's letter was delivered to Cooper's office, which in turn makes it more probable that Able intended to disclose and intended that Cooper include the additional $45,000 in his tax return and thus makes it less probable that: "2. RA knowingly filed a false income tax return for the year 2003," or that: "8. RA intended to defraud the government of the taxes due and owing at the time he filed his 2003 tax return," two of the penultimate probanda the government must prove.
        Second, the statements are also relevant to Cooper's credibility because they are prior statements that are inconsistent with the testimony he gave on the witness stand. Since both statements cannot be true, the probability that his testimonial

assertions are true is diminished. Since the credibility of a witness who has testified is also a fact of consequence, both statements are relevant.

b The Dawes memorandum. The assertions made in Dawes's memorandum are relevant to show that Cooper in fact made the statements which the memorandum reported he had made. Because Cooper's statements are relevant to three facts of consequence, evidence that he made those statements is also relevant to those facts of consequence.

3 **Is there a rule of evidence that the opponent could invoke to challenge the admissibility or use of the proffered evidence? If so, specify the rule, and make the argument, initially in syllogistic form.**

Both statements fit squarely into the definition of hearsay.

a Cooper. Under Rule 801(a) a statement that is an oral assertion made by a declarant other than while testifying that is offered to prove the truth of the matter asserted is hearsay. Here Cooper is a declarant who made two assertions to Agent Dawes during an interview, each of which is being offered to prove the truth of the matter asserted, i.e., that papers from Cooper's inactive client files were lost during a move in 2003 and that Able was an inactive client at that time. Both statements are hearsay and hearsay is not admissible under Rule 802.

b The Dawes memorandum. The two relevant written assertions made in the Dawes memorandum (identified above) are only relevant if they are offered to prove the truth of the matter asserted, namely that Cooper made the statements during the interview that the memorandum reports that he did. Dawes is the declarant and each of the written assertions that Dawes made prior to trial is being offered to prove the truth of the matter asserted. Each is hearsay and Rule 802 prohibits their admission.

4 **What, if any, are the arguments that the proponent of the evidence may make to avoid the application or minimize the effect of the rule or rules? Begin by challenging the opponent's rule-based argument.**

Rule 802 does not prohibit the admission of any of the statements.

a Cooper: Rule 613(b) authorizes the admission of extrinsic evidence of a prior inconsistent statement of a witness if the witness has been afforded an opportunity to explain or deny the existence of the same. The Dawes memorandum is extrinsic evidence that Cooper made the two prior inconsistent statements. Cooper was confronted with and afforded an opportunity to deny or explain those statements when he was cross-examined. The statements are offered to undermine Cooper's credibility, not to prove the truth of the matter asserted, and for that purpose, they are not hearsay. They are relevant, and Rule 402 requires that they be admitted. If the assertions made by Dawes in the memorandum are admissible then the assertions attributed to Cooper are also admissible.

b The Dawes memorandum: The assertions made by Dawes in his memorandum are not hearsay. Under Rule 801(d)(2)(D)(2), a statement offered against a party is not hearsay if the statement was made by the party's agent concerning a matter within the scope of the agency made during the existence of the relationship. The statement is being offered by the defendant against his party-opponent, the United States.

At the time he interviewed Cooper, Dawes was an FBI agent employed by the United States. Conducting and documenting interviews in a criminal investigation is within the scope of an FBI agent's employment. Dawes has testified that he wrote the memorandum. Any statements made in that memorandum are excluded from the definition of hearsay by Rule 801(d)(2)(D)(2).

Moreover, the statements made in the memorandum would in any event be admissible under Rule 803(5) (recollection recorded). Assuming he followed FBI procedures, Dawes will testify that he dictated the memorandum immediately after the interview with Cooper and that he reviewed and corrected the draft no later than the following day. The substance of the memorandum was made when it was fresh in his memory and, given his training and the procedures he followed, there is ample evidence to show that the memorandum reflects his knowledge correctly. Thus the memorandum could in any event be read to the jury, and the jury could consider the statements Dawes made as evidence of the truth of the matters he asserted.

5   **Unless it is clear (and it rarely is) that the evidence must be excluded under the rule or rules invoked, what is the legitimate probative value of the proffered evidence? What are its improper prejudicial effects?**

The only legitimate probative value of the statements is the probative value of Cooper's inconsistent statements with respect to the credibility of the assertions he made while testifying. The primary improper prejudicial effect stems from the fact that the jury is likely to use these statements as evidence of the truth of the matter asserted, notwithstanding any instructions the court may give telling them that they are not to consider them for that purpose.

6   **What is the strongest argument that can be made to persuade the court that the improper prejudicial effects ("PE") substantially outweigh the legitimate probative value ("PV")? That is that PE ≫ PV? What is the strongest argument the proponent could make to diminish the PE and enhance the PV in order to persuade the court that the PE do not substantially outweigh the PV?**

a   The government. The jury is likely to consider the statements for the truth of the matter asserted and infer that Able's letter may have been one of the papers lost. Apart from the fact that the rules prohibit consideration of Cooper's assertions for the truth of the matter they assert, the jury has no foundation upon which to accurately appraise the value of these statements for three reasons. First, it is likely that Cooper learned of the alleged loss from his secretary, in which event the jury is basing its assessment of hearsay within hearsay within hearsay – and so extending the inferential chain to its breaking point. Second, the support that these statements provide for an inference that Able's letter was one of the papers lost is both weak and ambiguous. The jury will have no evidence indicating the extent of the problem. If five pieces of paper were lost during a move of 5,000 files, the likelihood that Able's letter was among them is remote. If the boxes containing the inactive client files fell off the truck and the papers in those files scattered with the wind, the likelihood that Able's letter was among the papers lost would be high. But without any evidence to place the problem in context, it is almost certain the jury will misvalue this evidence.

b   Able. Cooper's credibility is central. If the jurors accept his testimony about the perfection with which he maintained his files, the likelihood that they will find Able guilty will increase dramatically. If they have evidence before them showing that he either lied or has a seriously defective memory, they are likely to discredit all his testimony and the likelihood they would find Able guilty will decrease accordingly. The probative value of this evidence is high. The government's cynicism about the ability and willingness of the jurors to follow the instructions the court gives them is hardly ground for penalizing the defendant. There are no irremediable improper prejudicial effects and certainly none that could substantially outweigh the probative value of this evidence.

7   **Should the proffered evidence be admitted? If admitted should its use be limited? Why?**

This could well be the first question in the protocol. Most lay persons can make a sound judgment about whether certain evidence should be admitted. Those trained in analysis have a more developed "common sense" and basis for their "gut feelings." But most of the time, most of us would get it right even if we did not know the intricacies of the rules of evidence and their application. In that context, the answer here is easy: Yes, the evidence should be admitted.

That conclusion can easily be justified under the policy upon which the hearsay rule and its exceptions were based. Given that the source of the information about Cooper's statement is an FBI agent, it is almost certain that Cooper made the assertions attributed to him and that those statements were true. FBI agents do not reach out to gather evidence that will make the prosecutor's task more difficult. If they report evidence that favors the defense, it is almost certain their report is accurate or understates the evidence. Cooper should not be permitted to lie with impunity and, if his memory is that bad, the jury should have that information in deciding how much reliance they may fairly place on any testimony he gives that implicates Able in the alleged crime. Having made that assessment, defense counsel's task is to figure out how to get in under the rules and the prosecution's task is to decide whether and how strongly she wishes to oppose the admission of the evidence.

Exercise

Apply the protocol to determine whether proposition 6 in "An investigation" – "W3 says that he overheard X on Christmas Day say angrily to Y, 'I shall not forget this'" – could or should be admissible if X is tried for the murder of Y. Would the trial judge have to consider the limitations imposed by *Crawford v. Washington* in resolving that issue? Why or why not?

12

The trial lawyer's standpoint

A. A Wigmorean lawyer prepares for trial

The purpose of this part of the chapter is twofold. First, we want to set Wigmorean analysis in general and the chart method in particular in the context of trial preparation and practice in the United States.[1] All competent lawyers use and apply the principles of proof in preparing a case and all use one or more devices to consolidate the results of their analysis. The chart method is simply an additional and a more methodical and rigorous device, one that requires making explicit what might otherwise be left implicit. Second, we want to describe the processes and devices lawyers commonly use to translate and reorganize the products of their analysis of the law and facts into a form suitable for use at trial. We start by describing some such devices and conclude with a brief discussion of ways in which the products of analysis are translated into the tools of advocacy.

1. Of charts and other analytic devices

All phases of the trial lawyer's work involve two fundamental and related processes: analysis of law and analysis of fact. At all points from the initial interview onward, the lawyer uses her existing legal knowledge to probe for facts that may be relevant to the case at hand. These facts in turn suggest further inquiries: the potentially applicable legal principles may be expanded, narrowed, or refined by research and analysis. The facts known and the products of the legal research and analysis may suggest additional lines of factual inquiry. The process is reflexive and continuous. The analytic component of this process continues through closing argument (and beyond). The evidence is in and closed. Given this finite body of evidential data and given the law the trier of fact will apply, how can the evidence be most effectively organized and marshaled to support the inferences the lawyer advocates that the trier should accept? In theory, however, the investigative process ends as the trial begins. The lawyers for each of the parties have a common set of legal principles to work with – in the jury trial context, the jury instructions. Each of the lawyers

---

1 We chose the United States for two reasons. First, jury trials are more common in the United States than in England, especially in civil cases. Second, preparing for a jury trial calls upon all of the analytic and other skills that this book seeks to develop.

316 Analysis of Evidence

has a defined and relatively settled body of evidential data. There may be variables to be resolved: Which of the contending legal principles will be adopted or applied? Which of the evidential data will be admitted? Which excluded? But in theory, the available chips are all on the table. And the theory comes close enough to reality to make the model useful.[2]

Under this model, a lawyer trained in the chart method of analysis would have identified the available evidential propositions; charted the possible inferential relationships; and prepared a set of strategic charts, each reflecting her judgments on how to maximize the probability that her theory of the case will be accepted and to minimize the risk that opposing counsel will achieve their objectives.[3] Collectively, the final product would be designed to account for all the foreseeable variables. If these legal principles are accepted, take this road; if that evidence is excluded, fall back to this position and follow this alternative path. The extent to which reality falls short of the theory merely increases the number of possible variables that counsel must anticipate and for which she must plan. Although few lawyers fully chart their cases, all use other devices to facilitate their analysis and organization of the data. For example, most lawyers analyze and cross-reference the evidential data each witness can supply. What precise testimonial assertions can this witness make? To what allegations in the pleadings or to what fact required to be proved under the jury instructions is each relevant? What other assertions or evidential data exist to corroborate or discredit such allegations or facts? Are they or can they be made admissible?

From this witness-by-witness and exhibit-by-exhibit analysis, every lawyer must develop a composite which she can use to analyze the case as a whole. Where the dispute involves past events, one of the most useful analytical tools is the master chronology. Set every event described in the testimonial assertions and documents in the sequence in which they are alleged to have occurred. Such a chronology makes two objectives possible. It presents the events in the order in which they supposedly occurred, the order in which most people think, and thus makes it possible to construct stories that the evidence supports. It also makes it easier to identify gaps and conflicts in the evidence. Similarly, in a criminal or personal injury suit, the physical setting where the central events occurred is often critical, and most lawyers will reconstruct the events through diagrams or models. Both kinds of composites are nothing more than devices to fix the alleged events in time and space and to

---

2 In theory, through meticulous investigation and use of discovery mechanisms, both lawyers should have a firm idea of the data available for presentation. In fact, the theory can never be fully realized and sometimes not even approached. Not all facts are ever discovered in civil cases, and legal as well as practical limitations leave much to be learned during trial on the criminal side. (See discussion below.)

3 Lawyers rarely use the chart method fully in practice because it requires too much time. Less rarely, lawyers use the method to chart particular phases of an argument. Lawyers who have been trained in the chart method, the most rigorous method of analysis, develop skills that are useful in any method of analysis. Two of the authors have taught law students the chart method of analysis for more than 20 years, the other for more than five years. Almost all students have enthusiastically acknowledged the benefits of the course.

make them concrete. Both are necessary tools for organization and analysis. Both are common tools. Both are compatible with Wigmore's general approach.[4]

The chart, as a method of analysis, does not replace other devices; it simply provides an additional and rigorous method for analyzing facts and constructing and testing arguments at any point in the process. The Wigmorean lawyer will have his or her witness-by-witness proposition lists cross-referenced to each other and to the pleadings and law; an exhibit-by-exhibit proposition list similarly cross-referenced; and, where appropriate, a series of diagrams and other composites. One point merits emphasis: All such devices require application of the principles of proof.

As final preparation for trial begins, every lawyer uses one or more of the compilation devices: A master chronology, a model, a map; an index of the evidential facts by legal principle and allegation in the pleadings; and so on. Such systems have long been commonplace among competent trial lawyers. For example, Elihu Root is reported to have developed a seven-document system in the late nineteenth century that, with some adaptation, is similar to those in use today. Under the Root-Stimson system, lawyers assisting in trial preparation were required to prepare seven documents: (1) a *pleadings chart* to identify, allegation by allegation, which facts alleged in the pleadings had been admitted, denied, stipulated, etc., in order to identify the material facts-in-issue for trial; (2) a *master chronology* organizing the facts in chronological order and identifying the witnesses or documents by which each will be proved; (3) an *abstract of the documents* to be used, arranged chronologically or, where appropriate, by subject matter; (4) a *preliminary analysis* in outline form that identified every proposition to be proved at trial and identified the witnesses and documents by which each was to be proved; (5) the *trial book* developed from these documents; (6) a *memorandum of law* for the court outlining counsel's view of the central facts in issue and controlling law to be applied; and (7) the *proposed jury instructions* counsel will ask the court to give. Although developments, such as the move to notice pleading, the expanded scope of discovery, and the introduction of new technologies, require some modification, the description of that system makes it clear that the basic approaches are timeless. Then to apply the chart method simply provides the Wigmorean lawyer with an additional device and skills for rigorously ordering the available data and precisely analyzing their relationships to the ultimate propositions to be proved.

2. The trial book: an organizational device

None of these devices, however, organizes the available data in a form suitable for presentation at trial. The final pre-trial step must be to reorganize the data

---

4 Complex cases may require additional or different devices. For example, many cases require expert analysis and testimony. The data must be collected and organized to facilitate this analysis and presentation for the specific case at hand. The point, however, should be clear: All competent lawyers use appropriate devices to organize the facts at various stages in the preparation of a case for trial.

in a manner that will facilitate its use at trial. The most common device used for this is the lawyer's "trial book." The "trial book" is simply a lawyer's device for organizing what he or she needs to try a particular lawsuit. Typically, it will include pleadings, checklists, copies of documents to be introduced and statements or depositions to be used, outlines for opening and closing, outlines or anticipated "scripts" for direct and cross-examination of witnesses, jury instructions, and memoranda of law addressing significant problems likely to arise during the particular trial.

The trial book serves three kinds of functions. First, preparation of the book is a systematic way to prepare for trial. The lawyer is forced to analyze what she needs for each segment of the trial from *voir dire* through closing and verdict. The lawyer is also forced to organize the materials into a whole. Like the production book for a play, the trial book enables the participants to see the parts and the whole and to visualize concretely whether the whole makes sense. Second, during the trial, the trial book is a ready reference. The trial book has everything the lawyer needs in one place, organized to facilitate easy use. Finally, also during trial, the trial book serves as a checklist and an organized vehicle for keeping track of what has been and what needs to be done. Counsel (counsel's partner) can check off that essential questions have been asked, that items of documentary evidence have been not only identified but also admitted into evidence. The lawyers can keep notes on particular witnesses and for reference in closing argument. This section describes the components typically included in a trial book and the relationships between each component, the other analytic devices, and the actual phases of the trial.[5]

1. The preliminary memorandum: an overview of theory, theme, and strategy. The lawyer must go into trial with *a theory of the case*. In this context, the theory of the case must combine the legal theory, the factual theory, and a strategic theory on how the evidence and arguments should be presented at trial. In preparing the final chart, the Wigmorean lawyer either knows the legal principles the trier of fact will apply or has made judgments about those the trier can be persuaded to apply.[6] He or she has identified the central facts-in-issue, the penultimate probanda that are in dispute, that must be proved (or challenged). The charts have made it possible

---

5 The trial book may take many forms: An indexed notebook, a series of folders, or in a complex case, an entire file cabinet or several boxes, today, the portable computer into which documents, deposition transcripts, and other material have been loaded with programs that make it possible to search and find particular items almost instantaneously. Many trial advocacy manuals have sections that describe the author's view of how a trial notebook should be organized. See for example Mauet (2005) 34–37 or Haydock and Sonsteng (1999).

6 This presentation focuses on preparing a case in which the outcome hinges on disputed questions of fact. Many cases, especially in public law areas, hinge upon how disputed questions of law will be resolved. Some cases, of course, depend upon the resolution of questions of fact and of law, which occasionally remain unanswered as the trial begins. The structure of the trial book and its components vary with the function to be served, but the lines of attack and organization are always similar to those described here.

to identify the plausible logical theories that appear to offer sound opportunities to persuade the trier of fact that the ultimate *probanda* have (or have not) been proven. The rules of admissibility have been analyzed to determine the evidential data that is likely to be admitted and how it may be used at trial. This analysis provides the material from which the lawyer must choose the theory of the case (and perhaps alternative and fall-back theories) that will be used at trial. The objective must be to choose the theory most likely to maximize the probability of a successful (and to minimize the risk of an adverse) outcome for the client.

The lawyer must also know by that time the characters and materials she must use to present the facts at trial and must have made judgments on the relative plausibility of the *stories* that could be developed to make the theories dramatically coherent and effective. With this background, the lawyer must also decide what *themes* can be established and used to develop the available theories and reinforce the stories. In this context, themes make explicit the concept of persuasive presentation. Who are the good guys? The bad guys? What ideas need emphasis to create an impression that will enhance the jury's willingness to accept the story chosen?

In preparation for trial, the lawyer must consider and make strategic judgments in choosing among the available theories, the possible themes, and the plausibility of the resulting stories as a whole. The lawyer at this stage must choose a theory and themes that are consistent with each other and that reinforce the desired story and then must organize the evidence so that it can be presented at trial in a manner that will make themes and theory come together as a dramatically effective and plausible story-as-a-whole. The preliminary memorandum is a device to document and test the choices made and to provide an overview of the parts that follow.

Components of a preliminary memorandum typically include:

a   *The introduction. A short summary and outline:* Who is suing whom for what on what basis? What does the "whom" want and on what basis? What are the one or two central facts, the jugular facts, or legal questions upon which the case hinges? How will these be addressed? How is the memorandum organized?

b   *The facts.* The facts distilled to those essential to the theory and presented to tell the story and illustrate the chosen themes.[7] (The uses of stories and themes are addressed in Chapters 6 and 10.) The task here requires skills similar to those necessary for the art of preparing the statement of facts in an appellate brief.[8] Typically, these are the intermediate *probanda* that counsel believes will be

---

7 Many courts require a pre-trial memorandum designed both to identify and narrow the facts and legal questions in dispute and to establish the parameters of the evidence to be offered. Because it is "published" to the court and opposing counsel, the strategic considerations differ; otherwise, its functions are similar.

8 See, e.g., Llewellyn, "Argument: The Art of Making Prophecy Come True," in Llewellyn (1960) 236–55. On the role of theory, story, theme, and situation-sense in the broader litigation context, see above at pages 153–58.

established by testimonial assertions and real evidence admitted at trial, presented in a narrative form that hopefully compels the conclusion that the ultimate *probandum* has been proved or not proved. Each assertion is typically indexed to the witness(es) or exhibits from which the evidential data will be drawn. The function of the statement is to provide a touchstone of relevance in planning and conducting the trial; not a comprehensive regurgitation of the evidence, but also not so abstract a compilation that neither theory nor theme is clear.

c *The law.* The summary articulation of the law the lawyer expects the court to apply or instruct the trier-of-fact to apply to the facts. Here again, the focus is upon the lawyer's theory of this case, not simply a persuasive regurgitation of the law for all possible theories or a summary of the jury instructions. Typically, both parties in their pleadings have articulated a variety of theories of liability and defense. If pre-trial preparation has not eliminated or ordered the significance of most of those theories, the lawyer's job has not been done. Here the lawyer is setting out his or her considered judgment as to what will constitute the law of this case – the legal assumptions against which the trial is to be organized and presented.

d *Strategy, problems, and solutions.* The theory, story, theme, facts, and law have been organized, not only in light of what the lawyer has to work with, but also in anticipation of what opposing counsel has and how she can and will use it. Here counsel presents the major strategic judgments made, the critical challenges anticipated, the possible solutions identified, and the fall-back positions selected. For example, in the prosecution of Archer for the murder of Vern, if the prosecution has determined that Archer stood to inherit considerable wealth as a result of Vern's death, that fact plus the scrap of cloth and the jacket may be the central facts in the prosecution's theory and theme. (Review the facts in *State v. Archer [III]*, pages 142–44.) If the defense counsel has determined that evidence is available to suggest that Baker believed he had been cheated when Vern broke their partnership or that Carl thought Vern caused his sister to commit suicide by breaking off the engagement, those facts plus the Tuesday visit may be central to the defense theory and theme. The admissibility of the evidence supporting these inferences on either side may be open to challenge, in which event the entire strategy of each side might hinge upon how the court will rule on these admissibility questions. Here, counsel would identify the problems, how each is to be resolved, and, where necessary, what the best fall-back position would be.

In sum, the preliminary memorandum presents the lawyer's best judgment on how the case can and should be presented. Prior to trial, it constitutes his or her touchstone in organizing the other components of the trial: Is this testimony consistent with the theory, story, and theme? Consistent with the strategy? Is it necessary? What function does it serve? During the trial, it is the ready reference that enables the lawyer to revisualize the forest after a day of cutting trees and wandering down unexpected paths. How do I get back on the main path tomorrow?

2. *The trial components.* The trial lawyer will have outlines and checklists for every component of the trial, typically organized in the sequence they will be used.

The following notes describe the kinds of materials that might be included in each segment of a trial book and how the pre-trial devices might be used in developing them.

a *Jury selection.* If the case is tried to a jury in the United States, each lawyer will need a checklist, charts, and questions to guide him or her in jury selection. The development of the materials will depend upon the particular jurisdiction's and judge's (i) rules and attitudes about the function and scope of *voir dire* questioning and about the lawyer's role in the process and (ii) procedure for exercising challenges. Given these, the lawyer must make judgments about the characteristics and backgrounds of the "best" and "worst" kinds of jurors for the particular case. The lawyer wants jurors who will understand the theory, respond to the themes, and be governed by the generalizations upon which both depend. The lawyer's judgments on prospective jurors may be guided by scientific inquiry, past experience, or biases and "lore" (lawyers' generalizations). Of course, while the manifest function of *voir dire* is to *select* a jury, it is often used in practice to serve other functions, such as to educate or establish rapport with the potential jurors.

b *Preliminary matters.* In almost all complex cases and in some jurisdictions, all pre-trial motions and other matters are resolved before the trial begins. In some jurisdictions, counsel may make pre-trial motions and address "housekeeping" matters – e.g., to invoke the rule excluding witnesses from the courtroom until they have testified or to ask how freely may counsel move about the courtroom – before opening statements. Indeed, where permitted counsel may wish not to disclose her position on some issues until the last possible moment for strategic reasons. Often, such motions seek to resolve an evidentiary issue where counsel does not want her opponent to mention the evidence in opening statement – e.g., motions to exclude evidence of a prior crime or bad act under Rule 404(b) of the Federal Rules of Evidence. This section of the trial book would identify the matters to be addressed or that may be raised by opposing counsel before opening statements and would include summaries of the arguments to be made and the supporting authorities and, to the extent possible, opposing authorities counsel may have to address.

c *The opening statement.* There are many views about the significance of an opening statement and what it should include. But its content is ordinarily a function of two variables: the central facts (as identified in the preliminary memorandum) and the lawyer's strategy. Rarely would a lawyer include facts not identified as central to her theory of the case; often strategy will dictate holding back some of these. The object is to present the facts necessary to understand the theory of the case and to establish the central themes to be developed, but it may be necessary to avoid areas where counsel is uncertain how the trial will develop.[9] But ordinarily the opening is where the foundation for theory and theme are established. Within the limits imposed by

9 At the extreme are those occasional criminal defenses where the nature of the defense depends largely upon how the prosecution develops its case or where counsel is seeking to keep the defense cards concealed. There the defense opening may be little more than a peroration calling upon the jurors to keep open minds and reminding them that the burden is on the government to prove its case beyond any reasonable doubt and that the defendant need not even take the stand.

strategic and ethical considerations, the opening statement is also when the lawyer tells the *story* and establishes the *themes* she expects to develop through presentation of evidential data and to emphasize in closing argument. Its structure and delivery are functions of these objectives, plus rhetorical and communication considerations. In addition, the opening statement ordinarily lays out the program and storyline for the "play" to follow; for example, who will be witnesses and what they will contribute. The trial book will, at a minimum, include a checklist of points to be covered and an outline for counsel's speech.

d   *The Evidence.* The evidence sections of the trial book ordinarily follow the order in which witnesses and exhibits will (or in which counsel anticipates they will) be called or used.

i   The opening party (plaintiff or prosecution) will typically have for each witness:

a   A statement of objectives to be achieved through this witness and a checklist. (What components of the theory must be established through this witness? Which evidential assertions on the key-list *must* be adduced here? How can this witness contribute to establishing the planned themes?)

b   A "script" of proposed questions and anticipated responses or, more likely, an outline of the testimony to be elicited from each witness, organized to bring out the central points in a dramatically effective way and structured to place emphasis on the propositions essential to the theory in a manner that develops the themes,[10] including questions sufficient to establish the necessary foundation for each exhibit to be introduced through that witness.

c   Copies (or abstracts) of any documents or other real evidence to be introduced, identified, or used through the witness.

d   A set of notes addressing various objections or other points of law likely to arise with references to cases or other authorities that counsel will use or anticipate her opponent will use with reference to the folder containing copies of those cases.

e   Copies (or abstracts) of any prior statements or transcripts of depositions that the witness gave at an earlier time.

ii   Opposing counsel's trial book will contain for each of those witnesses:

a   A statement of counter-objectives. (Is the witness to be discredited? Can this witness be compelled to make assertions that are on the defense key-list or that will place the testimony on direct in a different context? And so on.)

b   A "script" of questions for anticipated cross-examinations or, more likely, a point outline indicating the lines of questioning that may be developed.

---

10   Few experienced lawyers "script" the anticipated dialogue. For that reason and because "scripting" may raise serious ethical concerns, many trial practice teachers do not require it and some do not permit it. In the context of teaching the art of questioning, however, scripting can be a valuable exercise for students because the art of direct examination is far more difficult than most young lawyers perceive. To present a dramatically effective and coherent conversation without using leading questions while assuring that the proper foundations are laid to establish the competence of the witness does not come naturally. Anderson and others teaching practice skills have found that the development of the necessary skills is accelerated if a proposed "script" is actually written out in advance of the examination and is available for pre- or post-performance critique.

c Documents or exhibits that the witness may be called upon to identify or that may, if permitted, be introduced during cross-examination.

d Law notes for objections, with references to authorities.

e Prior statements or deposition transcripts that may be used to refresh the witness's recollection or impeach his or her credibility.

iii For the defense case, the sections of the trial book are the same, but the roles are reversed. Counsel for the defense are concerned with direct examination of witnesses and introducing exhibits; counsel for the plaintiff or the government are concerned with cross examination of witnesses and blocking.

iv The roles again shift for any rebuttal. The notes and copies for planned motions, stipulations, and other problems are interspersed appropriately.

Interspersed in the witness-by-witness sections, the trial book will ordinarily contain copies of documents to be admitted and published and facts to be introduced by stipulation or by judicial notice with appropriate notes on the objectives to be achieved and the legal problems to be confronted in each instance. Finally, both sides will have outlines for motions to be made (or anticipated) at the close of the plaintiff's or prosecution's case (or at earlier stages) with supporting authorities.

e *The closing statement.* For the trial book, an abstract and a speaking outline: But here the *theory, theme,* and *law* must be interwoven; the *plausible story* told. Based upon the evidential propositions established and the lawyer's assessment of the best theory and theme now available, the closing argument is developed. The analysis developed in the Wigmorean chart and developed as the outline for the plausible story must, at the close of trial, be adjusted (mentally) for surprises that occurred during the trial. The task is translating the analysis into a persuasive story and argument.

f *Miscellaneous.* Every trial book will also contain other materials that may be necessary, but will not be presented at trial – e.g., (i) a checklist of exhibits with space to record whether each was identified, admitted (with or without objection), or rejected (and on what basis); (ii) a master checklist to keep track of all the evidence to be introduced or opposed to assure that the essential data have been included; (iii) copies of any pre-trial papers that may be necessary at trial; (iv) the pleadings or pre-trial order, as a touchstone for relevance; the admissions, as the basis for introducing facts without testimony; (v) the objections or other law problems the court ruled upon before trial; and (vi) the jury instructions tendered (or to be tendered), approved, and rejected.

3. The trial book: an art form

Master chronologies, diagrams, key-lists, and charts are all devices for organizing and analyzing the available data. The skills required to prepare each go beyond the mechanical, beyond the logical analysis; art and judgment are required for each. So too, the trial book. The trial book should be a central organizational and analytical device. It is the final pre-trial vehicle through which the lawyer puts the case together.

During the trial, it constitutes the lawyer's "bible." But a trial is more than a mere presentation of facts and legal principles; judges and juries are neither computers nor logicians. The trial is an art form.

The dramatic play and the theater provide useful artistic metaphors for the trial and courtroom. In this metaphor, the trial book is the producer-director's master production book. The lawyer's roles are awesome. She is the editor-producer-director. The facts available to each player must be edited and organized for dramatic effect as well as logical relevance. The actors must be rehearsed or prepared. The sequence in which each will appear and in which the story is to unfold must be planned and determined. The conventions of the "theater" must be analyzed to determine how to protect and enhance the one play and restrict and limit the options available to the other. All this must be planned before trial. During the trial, the lawyers take on additional roles as stage managers and major actors. And only rarely is there an opportunity to test the production on the road – the first performance is typically the last. Two plays are competing on the same stage for one audience. One play (deserved or not) will get rave reviews; the other will be consigned to oblivion.[11]

The metaphor can be carried too far. The conventions are ethical as well as legal. The system depends on the players observing established norms of conduct whose violation might not be noticed by the judge-critic, but on whose existence the entire system relies. But even so limited, the metaphor illustrates the art required in preparing the trial book and presenting the evidence and argument at trial.

The trial book is central. It identifies the theory, story, and themes to be developed at trial and the plan for their development. It creates and defines the sequence in which witnesses and other evidence will be presented to maximize their dramatic effect in relation to the theory, story, and themes chosen. But it also establishes the detail: planning, sometimes scripting, the dialogue (witness examination); outlining, sometimes scripting, counsel's soliloquies (opening and closing); identifying the physical exhibits (a scrap of cloth, a coat, a wheelchair, a map, a model, etc.); and specifying the manner in which each will be presented and used. The more complete the book, the less the stage manager has to carry in her head during the trial.

And it should be clear that during the trial, the lawyer as actor, producer, and stage manager will have enough to do and is likely to lose the theory and theme and fail to present the story unless the production book is at hand and is a competent work of art as well as a complete reflection of the mechanics. Logical analysis and organization are always necessary conditions; never sufficient.

---

11 The metaphor should not for a moment obscure ethical responsibility of the lawyer. Not only is the trial a play with real consequences in terms of just and unjust outcomes, but also at every stage the lawyer must remember that the law and the profession impose obligations intended to advance the ascertainment of truth. Nonetheless, with that admonition, the dramatic metaphor is useful.

B. Two simple cases

1. Suggested format

Two mini-trial problems that are the basis of this exercise were developed for use in the Inns of Court School of Law in London for training would-be barristers. They take the form of a modified solicitor's brief to a barrister. They also represent compact exercises by which the course-to-date can be put together.

The problems are designed so that, where appropriate, a class can be divided into two-person law firms, for example, Law Firms A, B, C, and D. In an eight-person exercise, the Law Firms would be paired in the following manner. Law Firms B and D would represent the prosecution (or supply the prosecution witness); Law Firms A and C would represent the defendant (or supply the defense witness). The trial pairings would thus be:

Police v. Weller	*Police*	*v.*	*Weller*
Counsel Firm:	B		C
Witness Firm:	A		D
Police v. Twist	*Police*	*v.*	*Twist*
Counsel Firm:	D		A
Witness Firm:	C		B

The full exercise would have three parts:

1 Each firm would prepare a complete key-list and chart for the case it is to present.
2 Each firm would prepare a trial book.[12] An entire trial book should be less than ten typewritten pages doublespaced.
3 Each case would be tried using the following rules:
   a *Time allowances:* (i) opening statements – two minutes each; (ii) direct and redirect – five minutes per witness; (iii) cross – three minutes per witness; (iv) closings – five minutes each. (The total time consumed by each trial should not exceed 30 minutes.)
   b *Division of responsibility:* One member of each firm would *open* and conduct the *cross-examination* of the opposing side's witness; the other would conduct the *direct* and will *close*.
   c *The law:* The statutes defining the alleged offenses are set out at the end of the two problems. Students should assume the law governing traffic offenses and negligence is otherwise the same as that in their jurisdiction. Students outside the United Kingdom should remember that the law in England requires drivers to drive in the left lane and that the "near side" is the passenger side on the left, and the offside is the driver's side on the right.

The trial can be conducted as *a jury trial* in the United States or before a bench of magistrates in England and Wales. The non-participating members of

---

12 The trial book should contain all those actions necessary to try the assigned case.

the class can constitute the jury or magistrates for each trial. Names and pronouns should be changed to conform to the gender of the parties and witnesses in each trial.

2. Materials for *Police v. Weller*

Brief to Counsel for the Prosecution

IN THE HAVERING MAGISTRATES COURT

Police

v.

Samuel Weller

Counsel has herewith:

1. Statement of P.C. 21X Heep.
2. Police Plan

The Defendant is charged with (a) driving without due care and attention contrary to section 3 of the Road Traffic Act of 1972 and (b) failing to comply with a traffic signal (give way sign) contrary to section 22 of the Road Traffic Act 1972. The Defendant has the following previous convictions:

19.3.last	Camberwell Green Magistrates Court: Pedestrian Crossing
	Fine £10 Licence endorsed.
11.12.last	Marlborough Street Magistrates Court: Traffic Signal
	(Automatic Traffic Signal)
	Fine £25 Licence endorsed.

Counsel is instructed accordingly.

P.C. 21X Heep will say:[13]

At 12.05 hours on December 28 last I was standing on the corner of Acacia Drive South and Sussex Road in North Woodford. Sussex Road is the major road, and there are "give way" signs 15 yards from the junction of Acacia Drive South and North and Sussex Road. There are markings on the road surface at the junction. I saw a Singer Gazelle motor car being driven along Acacia Road North towards the junction. I estimated its speed to be 30 m.p.h. The driver made no attempt to slow down until he was about 8 feet from the junction when he appeared to brake heavily. The vehicle stopped with the front about 8 feet onto the north carriageway of Sussex Road. A Jaguar motor car travelling east on Sussex Road was forced to swerve violently to its offside in order to avoid the Singer. I went over to the driver of the Singer who identified himself to be Samuel Weller aged 19, of 24 Marine

---

13 Counsel and the witness should assume that this is a quotation of a statement made and signed by the Officer in his police report.

Drive, Sandwich. I cautioned him, and he said, "I'm sorry officer; I don't know this neighbourhood." I told him he would be reported with a view to his prosecution for careless driving and failing to obey a traffic sign. At the time of the incident the sun was shining, but the road surface was wet from recent rain. Counsel should assume that this is a statement made by Officer Heep.

Brief to Counsel for Defendant

IN THE HAVERING MAGISTRATES COURT

Police

v.

Samuel Weller

The Defendant is charged with:

1. Careless Driving contrary to section 3 of the Road Traffic Act 1972.
2. Failing to comply with a traffic signal contrary to section 22 of the Road Traffic Act 1972.

The Defendant wishes to plead Not Guilty to both charges. Counsel is asked to appear for the Defendant and endeavour to secure his acquittal, but if he be convicted, to enter a plea in mitigation. Samuel Weller of 24 Marine Drive, Sandwich, Kent will say:

On Sunday, December 28, last,[14] I was driving in my Singer Gazelle motor car on my way home from Epping where I had stayed the previous night with friends. At Woodford I lost my way and found myself driving through side roads. This was about midday. It had been raining but had stopped and the sun had come out. The roads were wet. At one time I was driving due south – the sun was low in the sky and was being reflected off the road surface so that it was difficult to see ahead. When I reached the junction of Sussex Road and Acacia Drive, I did not notice the cross roads ahead – it seemed to me that the road went straight ahead. I was travelling about 25 m.p.h. When I was about 20 yards from Sussex Road, I noticed the road and braked heavily. I stopped at the line, although my bumper may have been over the line. A car went by from my right at that stage, and swerved. That was an unnecessary action because my car presented no obstacle or danger. I did not notice the give way sign or the markings on the road, but I was half blinded by driving into the sun. A police officer who apparently had been standing at the corner, came over and told me I would be reported for reckless driving. I told him I had been blinded by the dazzle from the road.

I have two endorsements within the last year:

---

14 Assume that December 28 last was a Sunday.

Police plan – *Weller*

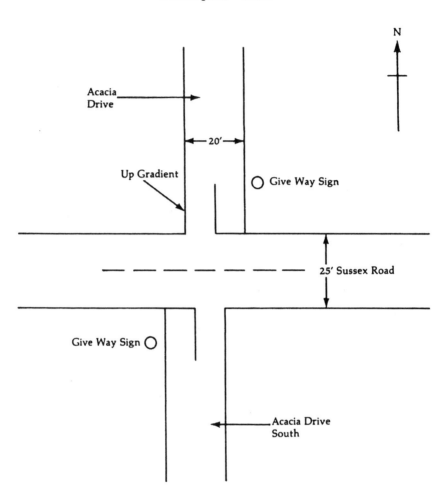

| 19.3.last | Camberwell Green Magistrates Court: Pedestrian Crossing Fine £10 Licence endorsed. |
| 11.12.last | Marlborough Street Magistrates Court: Traffic Signal Fine £25 Licence endorsed. |

I am nineteen years old and passed my test last February. I am at the moment a fitter but I hope to start working for my uncle on his minicab business next month. I also need my licence to take my girl friend out and I consider that my social life will be gravely restricted if I do not have a motor. I hope to bring a letter from my uncle to the court.

3. Materials for *Police v. Twist*

Brief to Counsel for the Prosecution

IN THE WESTON MAGISTRATES COURT

Police

v.

Oliver Twist

Counsel will find herewith:

1. Statement of W.P.C. 213 D. Abbott
2. Sketch Plan of the area

The Defendant is charged that he:

1. On the 8th day of December last in the Petty Sessional Division of Hayes, Middlesex, on a public road named Yeading Lane at the junction with Boundary Road did drive a motor vehicle to wit: an Austin 1100 motor car YMP 100A without due care and attention, contrary to section 3 of the Road Traffic Act 1972.

2. On the 8th day of December last in the Petty Sessional Division of Hayes, Middlesex, while driving a motor vehicle, to wit, an Austin 1100 motor car YMP 100A, at the junction of Yeading Lane and Boundary Road did fail to comply with the indication given by a prescribed traffic sign lawfully placed on or near the said Yeading Lane, contrary to section 22(1)(b) of the Road Traffic Act 1972.

3. On the 8th day of December last in the Petty Sessional Division of Hayes, Middlesex, drove a motor vehicle, to wit, an Austin 1100 motor car YMP 100A, the cylinder capacity of which did not exceed 50 cubic centimetres and the rear offside tyre of the which did not have a tread showing throughout three-quarters of the breadth of the said tread and round the entire circumference of the tyre, contrary to regulation 98(1)(b) of the Construction and Use Regulations 1972 and sections 34, 65 and 40 of the Road Traffic Act 1972.

W. P. C. 213 D. Abbott "C" Division will say:

At approximately 4.32 p.m. on the 8th December last, I was driving a police car west along Boundary Road Hayes Middlesex approaching the junction with

Yeading Lane. At the same time the defendant Oliver Twist was driving his Austin 1100 YMP 100A north along Yeading Lane towards the junction. There is a stop sign and a double line on Yeading Lane. He failed to stop at the double white line and a collision took place between the front offside of the Austin and the front nearside of the police car. There are no other witnesses. Visibility from the centre of the mouth of Yeading Lane east in the direction of Ealing is 60 yards.

On 8th December, I was driving police car PVR 207E west along Boundary Road, Hayes in Middlesex on an emergency call. As I approached the junction of Yeading Lane (which was to my left) an Austin 1100 motor car YMP 100A suddenly drove into my path. I applied my brakes, skidded and stopped 60 yards from the junction on the wrong side of the road. Damage to my vehicle was to the front nearside, with scrape mark along the whole nearside. I returned to the scene of the accident where I saw Oliver Twist (aged 21). He agreed he was the driver of the vehicle which collided with my car. I cautioned him and he said "I'm sorry. I never saw you." Damage to his car was to the front offside. I noticed the rear offside tyre was bald. Notice of intended prosecution was sent to the Defendant by recorded post on 20th December. I have since returned to the scene to check the relevant distances.

Twist has 2 previous convictions:

21st December (two years before the event)	Ealing Magistrates Court, Excess Speed £10 L.E. (Licence endorsed)
15th July (the year before the event)	Harrow Magistrates Court. Excess Speed £25 L.E.

Brief to Counsel for Defendant

IN THE WESTON MAGISTRATES COURT
26th January 1981

Police
v.
Oliver Twist

Counsel will find herewith:

1. Summonses against the Defendant (to be imagined)
2. Statement by the Defendant
3. Sketch Plan

Instructing solicitors request counsel to act for the Defendant Oliver Twist who has been charged that he:

1. On the 8th day of December last in the Petty Sessional Division of Hayes Middlesex on a public road named Yeading Lane at the junction with Boundary Road did drive a motor vehicle to wit: an Austin 1100 motor car YMP 100A without due care and attention, contrary to section 3 of the Road Traffic Act 1972.

Sketch plan – *Twist*

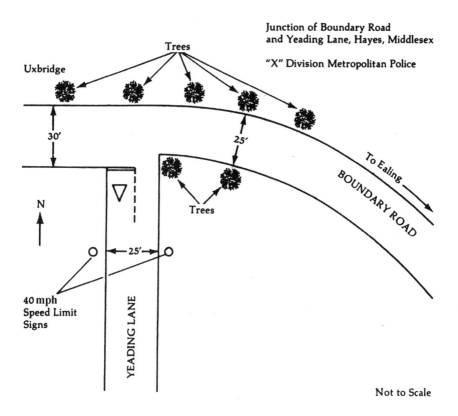

Junction of Boundary Road
and Yeading Lane, Hayes, Middlesex

"X" Division Metropolitan Police

Uxbridge

Trees

30'

25'

To Ealing

BOUNDARY ROAD

N

Trees

25'

40 mph
Speed Limit
Signs

YEADING LANE

Not to Scale

2. On the 8th day of December last in the Petty Sessional Division of Hayes Middlesex while driving a motor vehicle to wit an Austin 1100 motor car YMP 100A, at the junction of Yeading Lane and Boundary Road did fail to comply with the indication given by a prescribed traffic sign lawfully placed on or near the said Yeading Lane, contrary to section 22(1)(b) of the Road Traffic Act 1972.

3. On the 8th day of December last in the Petty Sessional Division of Hayes Middlesex drove a motor vehicle, to wit an Austin 1100 motor car YMP 100A the cylinder capacity of which did not exceed 50 cubic centimetres and the rear offside tyre of which did not have a tread showing throughout three-quarters of the breadth of the said tread and round the entire circumference of the tyre, contrary to regulation 98(1)(b) of the Construction and Use regulations 1973 and sections 34, 65 and 40 of the Road Traffic Act 1972.

The Defendant admits driving with a defective tyre but intends to contest the remaining charges.

Counsel is referred to the Defendant's statement herewith for full details of what occurred. Instructing solicitors understand that the visibility from the centre of the mouth of Yeading Lane east in the direction of Ealing is 60 yards. Counsel is asked to appear for the Defendant.

Oliver Twist of 203 Uxbridge Road, Ealing, W5 will say:

I am aged 21 and work at the Ace Motors Garage in Ealing as a salesman. It is essential for my job that I keep my licence. On 8th December I drove along Yeading Lane to the junction with Boundary Road. I was going home from a party at the garage. The weather was bad – pouring rain. The sun had set and it was dark. I stopped at the junction but could not see clearly to my right. The view was obscured by (a) a large tree and (b) a bend in the road. I began to edge carefully out looking both ways. Suddenly a police car came tearing from my right and hit me. I saw the police car before it hit me and I had stopped. I was half out in the nearside lane of Boundary Road when the collision occurred. I don't remember what the policewoman said, but she was very annoyed and discourteous. She told me she was going to throw the book at me when I tried to explain what happened. She scrutinised my car and found that the offside rear tyre was bald.

I admit the tyre is bald. I do not admit I was guilty of any other summonses and I wish to plead NOT GUILTY to all the others. I did not receive the notice of intended prosecution until the day after Boxing Day. I do not remember the police officer giving me verbal notice of intended prosecution.

I have two previous convictions for driving offences:

21 December (two years prior to event)	Ealing Magistrates Court. Excess Speed £10 L.E. (Licence endorsed)
15th July (one year prior to event)	Harrow Magistrates Court. Excess Speed £25 L.E.

Road Traffic Act 1972

S3. Careless, and Inconsiderate, Driving

If a person drives a motor vehicle on a road without due care and attention, or without reasonable consideration for other persons using the road, he shall be guilty of an offence.

S22. Drivers to Comply with Traffic Directions

(1) Where a constable is for the time being engaged in the regulation of traffic in a road, or where a traffic sign, being a sign of the prescribed size, colour and type, or of another character authorized by the Secretary of State under the provisions in that behalf of the Road Traffic Regulation Act of 1967, has been lawfully placed on or near a road, a person driving or propelling a vehicle who –

(a) neglects or refuses to stop the vehicle or to make it proceed in, or keep to, a particular line of traffic when directed so to do by the constable in the execution of his duty, or
(b) fails to comply with the indication given by the sign,

shall be guilty of an offence.

(2) A traffic sign shall not be treated for the purposes of this section as having been lawfully placed unless either –

(a) the indication given by the sign is an indication of a statutory prohibition, restriction or requirement, or
(b) it is expressly provided by or under any provision of this Act or of the Road Traffic Regulation Act of 1967 that this section shall apply to the sign or to signs of a type of which the sign is one;

and where the indication mentioned in paragraph (a) of this subsection is of the general nature only of the prohibition, restriction or requirement to which the sign relates, a person shall not be convicted of failure to comply with the indication unless he has failed to comply with the said prohibition, restriction or requirement.

(3) For the purposes of this section a traffic sign placed on or near a road shall be deemed to be of the prescribed size, colour and type, or of another character authorized as mentioned in subsection (1) above, and (subject to subsection (2) above) to have been lawfully so placed, unless the contrary is proved . . .

C. The art of plausible proof: theory, story, and theme revisited

1. Introduction

1. *Some questions.* What are the central facts in dispute in *Weller*? Is it possible to develop a *theory* which, if accepted, would compel both the conclusion (a) that Weller was *not* driving without due care and attention, and the conclusion (b)

that Weller did *not* fail to comply with the give way sign? From the standpoint of counsel for the prosecution, if the court had directed you to proceed on only one of the charges which would you have chosen? Would counsel for defense have been pleased by your decision? Are the same disputed facts central to both charges? What difference would it have made if either the events had occurred on July 28 or they had occurred in Nairobi, Kenya? These are questions that can be answered only by analysis. In the context of *Weller*, the analysis necessary to respond requires creative analysis, abductive as well as inductive reasoning.

Analysis of the evidence in *Twist* should have yielded similar questions with one exception. Presumably, the analysis would not be as dramatically affected had the events occurred in July or in Nairobi. An analysis of *Twist* is likely to lead counsel to focus more attention on evidence that bears upon the credibility of the two witnesses than was appropriate in *Weller*. Why? Again these are questions that fall primarily within the domain of analysis. A comparison between the kinds of analysis needed in *Twist* with that needed in *Weller* should make it clear that technical skill and defined protocols provide necessary tools but do not eliminate the need for creativity and judgment.

Analysis that identified and yielded answers to questions such as those posed above should have enabled counsel to define the plausible *theories* available for each side in either case. Those theories in turn may have suggested, but did not dictate, the way in which the evidential data and arguments could be presented to develop an effective *story* consistent with the *theory* chosen. Does the *story* that either counsel in *Weller* might properly have chosen have as strong or dramatic a *plot* as the stories that might appropriately have been developed in *Twist*? Did you anticipate that the story presented by counsel for the police was likely to be significantly different from that developed by counsel for Weller? How similar did you expect the competing stories to be in the trial of *Police v. Twist*?

The choice of a *theory* and a *story* in the two cases also illustrates the importance of *theme*. Does counsel for Weller have to attack the conduct and motives of Officer Heep in any significant way? Did the record provide material suggesting that such an attack could have been successfully mounted? Would the attack have been consistent with a sound defense *theory* or *story*? What were the appropriate *themes* in *Weller*? Contrast your responses to these questions with the responses you would give concerning the themes that counsel for Twist should try to establish in the cross-examination of Officer Abbott and should emphasize in opening and closing arguments. If you participated in the full exercise, review your own performance and those of your colleagues in light of your responses. How would you do the job differently next time?

2. *Some notes.* The materials that follow illustrate theories and stories that might have played an important role in famous (or in one instance fictional) trials. For the most part, these materials are more interesting as literature than prose in presenting principles of proof and methods of analysis. As you read each, however, ask yourself

how extensive and detailed an analysis of the evidence would have been necessary to enable a lawyer to select and develop themes and stories for cases in which real interests of real parties were at stake.

2. More food for thought

a. K. Llewellyn: Who are these men?[15]

Who are the two men whose names recur, whose lives and honor are the immediate stake in all this story?

Nicola Sacco, an Italian, resident in Massachusetts from his eighteenth year. A solid workman, who learned his trade outside of hours, a shoeworker, a "good cobbler" and "edger." A simple-hearted devoted husband and father. A lover of nature – who in prison found difficulty writing to his friends unless blue sky heartened and cheered him through the bars. An idealist, bent on improving the lot of working-men, so strong, so unafraid in his convictions that on trial for his life, before a jury whom he knew to be prejudiced against such views, he preached his beliefs, prepared to be a martyr to his faith.

Nicola Sacco (the same Nicola Sacco?), a foreigner discontented with our institutions, yet content to abide among them. One who forsook all decent views for Socialism, even for Anarchism. Living and earning here, yet fleeing to Mexico in fear of being drafted to defend the country. The user of a false name. A man who would lie lightly to his employer to cover up a morning on leave that he had spent in talk and not on business. A gun-toter. An agitator. A man too indifferent to American ways to seek during 12 years of freedom to learn English decently, too stupid to learn English decently during seven years in jail. An associate of that Vanzetti whom we know to have been convicted of an attempted holdup in Bridgewater.

Bartolomeo Vanzetti, a man who had forsaken his home in Italy and a good living with a farmer-family whom he loved, because his conscience would not let him be a party to exploiting men. A man who, though without wife and children, astonished his neighbors by his steadiness and effort at his work. A man who, ready to throw himself into the place of danger in defense of his fellows, was chosen to go up to New York to discuss the further defense of Salsedo, a radical held incommunicado by the Federal authorities in their wild deportation drive of 1920; that Salsedo whose "questioning" is suspected of having driven him to seek relief in suicide. Vanzetti, a man whom person after person, of judgment, insight, and sensibility, learned to know after the time of his imprisonment; and whom each of those who learned to know him came to honor, respect, admire, even love. A man framed up before the

---

[15] Llewellyn (1962) Ch. 20. This was originally prepared as part of an unpublished study of the Sacco-Vanzetti case. The present portion has been published in Michael and Wechsler (1940) 1085, and in Joughin and Morgan (1948). The Michael and Wechsler notes [hereinafter designated "Michael & Wechsler"] have been retained. See *Commonwealth v. Sacco*, 255 Mass. 369, 151 N.E. 839 (1926), 259 Mass. 128, 156 N.E. 57 (1927), 261 Mass. 12, 158 N.E. 167 (1927). The full record of all the proceedings has been published as *The Sacco-Vanzetti Case* (1929). For discussions of the case, see Frankfurter (1927); Kadane and Schum (1996).

present trial (on a charge made against Sacco, too, until for Sacco an unshakable alibi was proved) in order to make easy the conviction in the case in hand.

Bartolomeo Vanzetti (the same Bartolomeo Vanzetti?), a radical leader, a speech-maker, an anarchistic agitator; closely concerned with that Salsedo who was dangerous enough to induce the Federal authorities to hold him incommunicado till, seemingly, he confessed his guilt by suicide. A guntoter, Vanzetti, as well. A man convicted previously of another desperate crime of violence. A man the more dangerous because of his brains and gift of leadership. A draft-dodger. A liar, who lied copiously and confessedly on his arrest. A believer in violence. An associate, a sympathizer, a "comrade" of those radicals who threatened and even exercised outrageous violence in efforts to terrify the authorities into giving him up without punishment.

Opinions differ, you may observe, about these two. Two things are certain: they were Italians and radicals; they were accused of murder.

From one angle, it makes no difference which of these two views of these two Italians you accept. Angel or devil, a man has a claim to a fair trial of his guilt. Angel or devil, he has a claim to a fair trial, not of his general social desirability, but of his guilt of *the specific offense* charged against him. Such is the letter of our law.

b. Bywaters and Thompson: Who is this woman?

What kind of person is Edith Thompson? She pictures herself as a great romantic lover, as someone who is prepared to risk anything "for a great big love like ours." But she is deceiving herself as she deceived others: just as again and again she lied to her husband, to her family, to the police, even to her lover, so more often than not she deluded herself. Consider her first as a wife and as a lover: She did not marry for love; when did she show affection or sympathy or mercy or remorse for her husband? She refused him companionship, she refused him sex, she refused him children. She made no effort to make her marriage work or to save it. She valued her job above her home, above her husband's life, even above her love for Freddy – why else did they not elope? And what kind of lover is she? She complains, she nags, she coaxes, she flatters, she wheedles; she dominates and manipulates this younger man who is more straightforward and less clever than she is. When she is feeling insecure she is, on her own admission, prepared to lie to him, to make up stories, to keep back presents, even to claim that she has tried to kill her husband. She values money and respectability above her love for Freddy and, when the crunch comes, she ditches him and puts the blame on him in order to save her skin: she denies her love. Who's the loyal pal, the real lover in the end?

No, this idea of a great romantic love is a great delusion. What is the truth? Edith Thompson is a calculating, manipulative woman who used others – including Freddy – for her own ends. She's a competent business woman, a manager. She regularly looks to the future, she calculates. Her world is full of plans and pacts and plots and schemes. Plans for secret assignations, for getting a job abroad, for persuading Percy to divorce her, for suicide, and even for murder. There are telegrams and notes and prearranged signals, and, again and again, a desperate, persistent searching for ways to get rid of Percy without being found out – "when the time comes we shall need friends," "we shall need witnesses," she says; of course she wants fun, adventure, risk, even love of a sort: so long as it does not involve sacrifice of security, money, or respectability. What kind of great romantic is this who is not prepared to sacrifice anything except her husband and her lover?

Questions

1   For what kind of audience is this intended? What clues are to be found in this passage? Is it consistently addressed to the same audience?
2   (a) What is the main purpose of the argument? (b) To what specific *probanda* is the passage relevant?
3   In what ways does this strongly support the relevant *probanda*? Suggest ways in which the strength of the support might be increased within this particular framework.
4   Identify elements in the passage that are clearly and unequivocally supported by the evidence (a) of Edith's own words (b) by other evidence.
5   Identify elements in the passage that (a) are not supported by any evidence; (b) involve exaggeration; (c) can be contradicted or explained away or rivaled.
6   Redraft the passage within the framework of the same theory of its function in order to improve it.
7   Compose an alternative picture of Edith's character, based on a significantly different theory. Make clear what you have in mind in respect to audience, relevance, and function; how it strengthens the case as a whole; and how strongly it is supported by evidence.
8   Analyze this passage and your own in terms of how far there is a tension between logic and appeals to emotion and how far they mutually sustain each other.
9   In what respects does this passage violate ethical norms or principles of fairness in argument?

c. Is Ford Motor Company guilty of killing girls with a Pinto?[16]

The flat northern Indiana farmland is lifeless now. Only the naked oaks and maples break the emptiness, their branches standing like skeletons against the foreboding winter sky. A stubble of dead, farrowed cornstalks sticks through the snow, and there is no sound except for the wind. But the trees were full and green on that August afternoon in 1978, and the cornstalks stood high and ready to bear. The land was alive that day, as alive as the three Ulrich girls.

Donna Ulrich, 18, from Roanoke, Ill., was visiting her cousins Judy and Lynn Ulrich in Osceola, a little town just outside Elkhart in northern Indiana. The girls were close – bound by blood, age, and interests. Donna was only a day older than Judy. Lynn was two years younger. All three were deeply religious, their social

---

[16] B. Dart, Atlanta Constitution, Jan. 28, 1980, §A.

lives revolving around church and school. That afternoon they were driving over to Goshen, about 20 miles southeast, to a volleyball practice at the First Baptist Church.

Judy was driving them in her new yellow Pinto – new to her, that is, for the Ulrichs were the seventh owners of the 1973 model Ford. Earl Ulrich, a carpenter, was helping his daughter pay for the used car as a sort of a high school graduation present. The little car was good on gas, he figured when deciding to buy it, and it was made by American workers, by gosh.

The girls left Osceola about 5:45 p.m., chattering about summer jobs and future plans. Judy was working as a waitress at Farrell's Ice Cream Parlor over in South Bend. She aimed to enter a commercial college that fall to study interior design. Donna was going to do volunteer church work. Lynn, a high school junior, was working part time as a cashier at the Park and Shop Supermarket in Osceola. All three were excited about going to South Dakota the next week for a Missionary Church youth camp.

On the way, they stopped at the Checker Self-Serve gas station in Dunlap, an unincorporated township, to fill up. Then they headed on, laughing and talking.

Likely no one knows for sure why the Ulrich girls turned around and headed back towards home on Highway 33 – the stretch of five-lane blacktop between Elkhart and Goshen. There was probably car trouble, for Judy had the Pinto's red emergency blinkers flashing and the car was only going between 10 and 17 mph in the right-hand lane. They might've wanted to get off the highway – which was crowded with vacationers in motor homes – but they couldn't. Eight-inch curbs prevented any exit.

Suddenly, bearing down on them was a customized 1972 Chevy van – with a 350 cubic-inch engine, a "Peace Train" logo and mural of a train on the panels, and a two-by-six wood plank for a bumper.

The Ulrich girls never saw the Chevy van.

Levi Hochstetler was out in the barn, settling in some new brooder chicks, when he heard the noise. A tool-and-die maker by trade, Hochstetler is a bit of a farmer at heart and works a lot in the outbuildings behind his rambling white house, which sits alongside the railroad that runs parallel to Highway 3.

A crash startled him that August afternoon. Then came an explosion. He ran to the roadside, but the thick black smoke kept him from seeing exactly what had happened: He ran back to the barn and got a fire extinguisher.

He could see the burning car when he got back. Inside a ring of groundfire, a blackened body lay beside it.

"Help me! Oh, please help me!" pleaded the body that was Judy Ulrich.

Hochstetler saw that her foot was caught between the car door and rocker panel. He tried to open the burning door but couldn't. Then there was another man there, pushing open the door with a stick. Hochstetler pulled the girl out of the fire.

"Thank you! Thank you!" Judy told him.

Only then did Hochstetler feel the throbbing in his hands. He looked and saw them covered with second-degree burns. He had heard screams, horrible screams, earlier, he remembered now. Perhaps they had come from onlookers.

James Fry, a Goshen fireman, arrived with the rescue squad. He looked into the blackened Pinto and saw a girl, Donna Ulrich, dead in the front seat. Only later would he find out that Lynn Ulrich was also dead in the crushed rear of the burned car.

With his partner, he went to aid Judy. In 14 years on the job, the graying potbellied fireman had seen a lot of accidents, even people cut in two by a train. But never had he seen anyone burned as badly as this girl.

An Elkhart ambulance arrived then, and sped off with the injured girl to the bigger hospital there. But Judy Ulrich had burns over her entire body. She remained lucid and alert, but her condition worsened. Doctors decided to take her to the burn center at St. Joseph's Hospital in Fort Wayne, 75 miles away.

Judy was awake and talking for most of the trip. The medical attendants with her said she didn't complain much about pain.

But she asked questions, ones they found hard to answer. "How're Lynn and Donna doing? Are they all right?" "Will this keep me from having children?" Then, finally, "Am I going to die?"

Tears rolled down a male nurse's cheeks as he listened to Wanda Lumpkin, the other nurse, comfort the dying girl by quoting a scripture from the faith they shared.

"When thou passest through the waters, I will be with thee; and through the rivers, they shall not overflow thee."

"When thou walkest through the fire, thou shalt not be burned; neither shall the flame kindle upon thee."

"For I am the Lord thy God, the Holy one of Israel, thy Savior."

Questions

The excerpt comes from a newspaper story about the criminal prosecution of the Ford Motor Company for reckless homicide based upon their allegedly having sold Pintos with knowledge that their gas tanks were likely to explode if the car was struck in the rear. Consider the excerpt as part of an opening (or a closing) statement in a wrongful death action by the Ulrichs against the owner and driver of the Chevy van and the Ford Motor Company.

1 From the standpoint of plaintiff's counsel: Who are the witnesses and what other evidence will be necessary to support this statement of the "facts"? Are there any assertions that appear to be incapable of proof; that is, assertions for which no evidential data could be offered that would support the assertion as a reasonable inference? Identify them. Are there any facts of which the court might take or permit the jury to take judicial notice? Identify them.

2 From the standpoint of defense counsel: Assuming plaintiff's counsel begins with the assertion, "Ladies and gentlemen of the jury, here is what I think the evidence will show (has shown)," are there any valid bases for objecting to this statement or any parts of it? What parts are objectionable and on what bases?

3 The statement does not include facts suggesting why Ford Motor Company should be held responsible. Assume that you have experts who will testify, and documents showing Ford's engineers knew, that at an additional cost of $25 per unit Ford could have installed a buffer between the rear bumper and the gas tank that would have reduced the probability from one in ten to one in 50 that the gas tank would have exploded from a comparable impact. Assume also that such buffers were known to federal regulatory authorities, but were not required by applicable standards and were not generally installed by United States auto manufacturers. Invent additional facts that seem plausible inferences. In a two-paragraph statement of the facts, using Mr. Dart's style, supplement his statement to show the jury why Ford should be held liable.

4 Assume that Dart's story (with your two-paragraph addition) was told to the jury by counsel for the plaintiff as the opening statement. Assume that each of the following propositions is a statement of law the court will include in the instruction to the jury:

   i In order for the manufacturer of an automobile to be liable for the death of another, the jury must find:
      a That the automobile or its components were defectively designed, manufactured, or assembled; and
      b That, but for the specific defect in the design, manufacture, or assembly of the particular automobile or component the death would not have occurred.

   ii In order to find that an automobile or a component thereof was defectively designed, the jury must find that the manufacturer knew or should have known at the time the automobile was assembled:
      a That the automobile or component was capable of causing significant injury if improperly designed; and
      b That a design for the automobile or component was available and could be employed at a non-prohibitive cost that would have materially reduced the probability that an injury would occur or that the consequences from such an injury would be so severe.

   iii In determining whether a design was defective, the jury may consider industry practices and any federal safety standards applicable in the automobile manufacturing industry at the time as evidence of the state of the art in such designs.
      a Prepare a key-list and a chart showing the strategic ultimate and penultimate *probanda* (i.e., through step 3) that you believe counsel for plaintiff should attempt to prove.
      b Translate your analysis into a brief (preferably one paragraph) statement of the logical theory plaintiff's counsel would be applying if he or she adopted your key-list and chart.

5 Story and theme: Dart's story is both dramatic and coherent. Identify five background generalizations he used or on which his story depends. Identify the characteristics that

two of the principal witnesses would have to demonstrate on the stand (if they were to be consistent with the characterizations the story has suggested).

6   The defense. Using the same assumptions and assuming in addition that the defense witnesses will be credible and capable characters: (a) Prepare a key-list and chart of the strategic ultimate and penultimate *probanda* you would use for the defense theory. (b) Translate your analysis into a brief (preferably one paragraph) statement of the logical theory defense counsel would be using if your analysis were adopted.

7   Story and theme: Prepare a brief opening statement consistent with your theory that develops the most favorable story and themes that Ford might reasonably attempt to establish.

8   Assume the trial was to take place primarily in Elkhart, Indiana, mid-size city.

D. Two more complex trial problems

1. Introduction

The two trial problems that follow are based upon problems developed for the National Trial Competition in the United States in 1981 (*Wainwright*) and 1982 (*Warren*). They provide material suitable for a culminating exercise in a course that focuses upon analysis of evidence for potential trial lawyers. (In the appended materials, dates should be advanced to make the problems current.)

The suggested exercise has four parts – the preparation of a complete key-list and chart for one of the problems, the development of a complete trial book based on that analysis, the trial of the case so prepared, and the preparation of a post-trial critique. The following guidelines illustrate how the full exercise could be implemented.

1   Students undertaking the exercise would form two-person law firms, and each firm would choose (or be assigned) to represent one of the parties in one of the problems and to serve assigned roles as witnesses for one side in the other problem.

2   Each firm would analyze the evidence in light of the law given in the jury instructions and develop a complete key-list and chart for the case from the standpoint of lawyers preparing for trial.

3   Each firm would prepare a trial book containing all components specified above at pages 318–23. The preliminary memorandum should refer to propositions on the key-list as well as the appropriate portions of the record and should explain the theory and themes adopted in light of the possibilities identified by the chart. The "script" for anticipated direct and cross of each witness should identify the proposition(s) on the key-list that each testimonial assertion is intended to support (or confound), and each document or other item of real evidence should be similarly indexed to the key-list.

4   Each firm would then try its case to a jury composed of other members of the class under the following rules:

   a   *Witness preparation.* Witnesses should know their statements thoroughly and be familiar with the entire record. Of necessity, each witness will have to make inferences with respect to relevant facts not adequately specified in the statements. Witnesses should attempt, within the bounds of fairness and integrity, to draw inferences favorable to the theory that counsel for their side of the case are attempting to develop. In pre-trial preparation, counsel may *suggest* plausible inferences by the use of *leading questions,* but they are *bound* by the witness's responses. On cross-examination, the witness must reveal any instructions received from counsel in preparation. Opposing counsel may not, however, object to any testimony on the ground that it is not in the statement or the record.

b *Other evidence and law.* No real or demonstrative evidence other than that contained in the problem (or provided by the instructor as a supplement) may be used. Pre-trial stipulations and rulings and the jury instructions set forth in the record may not be challenged, although legal arguments may be advanced during trial to support particular constructions where appropriate.

c *Motions.* No written motions will be received, and preliminary oral motions will be looked upon with disfavor. No rights or objections are waived by failure to present them before the trial commences.

d *Division of responsibility.* Each side shall call its two designated witnesses during its case-in-chief. (Only if adequate time remains and the presiding judge is satisfied that the interests of justice will be served thereby, may the other side's witnesses thereafter be called as additional and adverse witnesses.) Each member of the firm will conduct the direct examination of one of its designated witnesses and the cross-examination of one of the other side's designated witnesses. The one member who conducts the direct or cross-examination is responsible for responding to and making objections to exhibits and testimony offered through that witness as appropriate. One member of the firm shall open; the other shall close. Each planned motion made during trial, for a directed verdict or the like, shall be argued only by the member of the firm who makes it.

e *The trial: order and time allotments for proceedings*[17]
   i Opening statements. Each side shall give an opening statement that may not exceed five minutes.
   ii *Case-in-chief.* Each side shall have an aggregate of not more than 30 minutes, including time devoted to arguments on motions or objections and to the introduction and publication of documents and other evidence, to present its case-in-chief.
   iii *Cross-examination.* Cross-examination of each witness may not exceed ten minutes, including time devoted to arguments on motions or objections.
   iv *Rebuttal evidence.* Ordinarily, rebuttal evidence will not be permitted. If the plaintiff or prosecution has time remaining from its case-in-chief and if the presiding judge concludes that fairness so requires, rebuttal may be permitted. This should be done only in the exceptional case where the plaintiff's or the prosecution's counsel have been unfairly surprised because evidence has been offered by the defense that could not reasonably have been anticipated.

17 Based upon one of the authors' extensive experience in coaching teams for the competition, these time limits are more than adequate for well-prepared teams. The time allotments specified in the National Trial Competition Rules are more generous: ten minutes for opening statements; forty-five minutes for each side's case-in-chief; fifteen minutes for cross-examination of each witness; plaintiff's rebuttal, time remaining; and closings, ten minutes for each side.

v *Closing.* Each side shall give a closing argument that may not exceed ten minutes. Counsel for the plaintiff or prosecution may reserve up to five minutes of that allotment for rebuttal argument.

vi *Verdict.* The jury should attempt to reach a verdict, and thereafter counsel and the jury should discuss the case. The nature of this discussion should reflect the fact that the jurors are Wigmoreans.

5 Each firm should prepare a post-trial memorandum critiquing the analysis and the theory, story, themes that they developed before trial in view of their effectiveness at trial and should specify what changes they would make in preparing a similar case in the future.

2. The criminal case: *United States v. Wainwright*

IN THE UNITED STATES DISTRICT COURT
FOR THE TERRITORY OF COLUMBIA

UNITED STATES OF AMERICA VS. HORACE WAINWRIGHT	CRIM. NO. C-XX-001

Indictment

THE GRAND JURY CHARGES:

Count One

On or about October 19, last year, within the Territory of Columbia, on land under the exclusive jurisdiction of the United States, the Defendant, Horace Wainwright, did, with malice aforethought, unlawfully shoot and kill Terry Dobbs with a gun. (Violation, Title 18, United States Code, Section 1111.)

Count Two

On or about October 19, last year, within the Territory of Columbia, on land under the exclusive jurisdiction of the United States, the Defendant, Horace Wainwright, while engaged in the commission of an unlawful act not amounting to a felony, to wit, the assault of Harold Clark by striking Clark's head with a gun, did unlawfully shoot and kill Terry Dobbs with such gun. (Violation, Title 18, United States Code, Section 1112.)

Count Three

On or about October 19, last year, within the Territory of Columbia, the Defendant Horace Wainwright, while engaged in the commission of a lawful act which might produce death, to wit, confronting Harold Clark, Terry Dobbs and Carlos Blanca with a gun, without due caution and circumspection, and through gross negligence, and having actual knowledge that his conduct was a threat to the lives of others, or having knowledge of such circumstances as could reasonably be said to have made foreseeable to him the peril to which his acts might subject others, did unlawfully shoot and kill Terry Dobbs with such gun. (Violation, Title 18, United States Code, Section 1112.)

A TRUE BILL
/s/ Lucius Coleman
FOREMAN, GRAND JURY

Stipulations

The Government and the Defendant agree and stipulate as follows:

1 The Court has full and complete jurisdiction of the subject matter and of the parties. For purposes of this Competition, the Territory of Columbia is a location within the exclusive, special maritime and territorial jurisdiction of the United States. No issue will be raised concerning the applicability of federal law to this case. The subject incident occurred within the Territory of Columbia.

2 No issue will be raised concerning the sufficiency of the indictment.

3 No Speedy Trial Act questions are involved in this case, and none will be considered or raised.

4 Each witness statement was given under circumstances where the penalty of perjury would apply.

5 Prior to making any statement, the Defendant was given all appropriate warnings and was fully advised of his rights.

6 Dr. Joseph Jiminez is the chief medical examiner, duly licensed and qualified to determine the cause of death. The doctor, if present, would testify under oath that he performed an autopsy on the deceased who died as a result of a .44 caliber gunshot wound to the chest. The bullet entered in the area of the heart, went slightly downward, straight into the body from front to back, and struck the heart killing the deceased immediately. Because there was no powder residue on deceased or his clothes, the gun had to be at least 20″ from the deceased when it was fired. The deceased had a blood alcohol content of 0.15 or 1.5 times the 0.10 level at which all experts and the medical profession agree is the standard recognized level of intoxication. In other words, anyone who reaches 0.10 will be intoxicated regardless of their individual tolerance. The deceased was in excellent health. There were no other wounds. The bullet was recovered from the heart and turned over to Special Agent Kelso.

Statement of Harold Clark

My name is Harold Clark. I attend the University of Columbia where I am majoring in management. I am 21 years old and in my third year of college. Last night I picked up my friend, Carlos Blanca, a foreign student who plans to return to Spain, where his home is. Also, I picked up Terry "Bull" Dobbs and took him to the Octoberfest. We all called him "Bull" because he was short and well built. I picked up Terry at his home. We were good friends. We went to the Beer Garden and had a few beers.

I think I had four or five. Actually it could have been seven or eight. I took my own mug. We saw three girls whom we knew and bought them a few beers and were taking them home to their sorority house. On the way, I told them that I knew of this eccentric old man that lived at the end of the street. I grew up just a few blocks away in a much poorer area. The word was this old fellow was about half crazy and scared to death and kept building fences and stuff to keep people out of his yard. I thought it would be fun just to drive by and show them where he lived. We went down Trails End Road and drove around the cul-de-sac. Bull said, "let's don't bother him." This was after I may have yelled something like "Hey old man, how is everything in your stockade tonight?" Then we left and took the girls home.

After we took the girls home, I said, "let's go back there just for fun." It was about 2:30 a.m. and we really weren't going to do anything bad. My Spanish friend was sitting in the right front seat and Bull was seated directly behind me. I was driving. We drove around the cul-de-sac one or two times. I don't remember anybody yelling anything. The old man came out so we stopped in front of the house next door to see what he would do. He opened the gate and came toward us. He had a flashlight in his hand and I couldn't see what else he was holding. It never occurred to me that he had a gun. However, as he got close to the car he said, "What are you punks doing here? I may show you young whippersnappers a thing or two." Bull said, "He's got a gun." I quickly reached over to put the car in first gear. The car has a four-on-the-floor gearshift. About that time I was hit real hard up side my head. I heard a loud sound. Somebody yelled "let's get out of here." The next thing I knew I was driving down the street, and Carlos said, "Bull's been shot and I think he's dead." I guess he was dead. He never moved or said anything. I went straight to the hospital, which was not too far away, and from there we called the police and told them what had happened.

I don't know if the old man meant to shoot and kill Terry or not. I do know that he hit me plenty hard and I was dazed pretty good while I was driving away. In fact, there is still a big scar on my head. He must have wanted to hurt me pretty bad by hitting me so hard. I don't know why he would do this. None of us really knew him and we hadn't done anything but drive down to the end of the street like lots of other people I know. In fact, we were in my car in the street. We weren't even on his property.

I feel real bad about what happened. Bull's father was a police officer and was shot and killed last year by a robber. Bull worked part time to help support his mother. He was a straight "A" student and was getting ready to graduate with a music degree. He never hurt a fly and was the nicest guy I knew. After he drank a few beers that night, he was as friendly as I have ever seen him. In fact, he didn't want to go down to the end of the street either time. Once he said, "let's just leave the old man alone." This is really all I know.

/s/ Harold Clark
Harold Clark

Subscribed and sworn before me, a notary public, on October, 20.

/s/ Carol Smith,
Notary Public.

Offense Report of Special Agent Kelso

I was working homicide in the district that includes Trails End Road during the night shift on October 19, last year. I have been a homicide special agent for ten years and have worked this area during all that time. I know the neighborhood very well, and I am familiar with many of the people that live there. At 3:20 a.m., while cruising the area, I received a call to go to 10 Trails End Road to question a Mr. Wainwright, whom I knew, about a shooting. As I got to the door, Mr. Wainwright was getting ready to leave his house. I immediately asked him what had occurred and he told me he accidentally shot his gun when a boy, who was in a car and who had driven to his house several times that night, went for a weapon. In fact I said, "A young man is dead, he was shot, do you know anything about this?" He said, "Yes, I must have done it, my gun went off when I was protecting myself from the driver who was going for a weapon. I didn't mean to hurt anybody."

I later talked to the driver, Harold Clark. I examined his car and his tires matched perfectly the fresh skid marks in the cul-de-sac as well as the tire tracks in the ditch. My diagram shows where the car was parked in relation to Mr. Wainwright's gate.

I took a statement from Mr. Wainwright and what he said about the past shootings at his house is true. I saw his window and the speaker at his gate after they were shot out. Also, I know he called the police a lot about cars coming up to his property.

I found no weapon on any of the boys or in the Pontiac. The Pontiac has a four speed floor shift. The boy, Clark, was coherent, but walked a little unsteadily, smelled of beer and probably was intoxicated. He had been drinking. Mr. Wainwright turned over the gun. It was a .44 caliber pistol. The bullet from the autopsy was the same as the remaining bullets in the gun. There was one empty hull.

Mr. Wainwright's gun is a "single action" revolver. Ordinarily, to fire it you must first cock the hammer and then pull the trigger. Of course, if you pulled the trigger back and held it and the hammer was moved back and then fell closed, the gun would fire. The gun can be fired with the hammer closed, but it takes a terrific blow to the hammer. I tested it. I am also very familiar with all types of pistols and their operation. In my opinion, the hammer must have been cocked when the gun fired and Mr. Wainwright's finger must have been inside the trigger guard.

Mr. Wainwright is old. He has never been in any trouble before from his criminal history. Neither the deceased nor the driver had any criminal record or previous arrests. The Spanish boy spoke little English and was to return to Spain the next week. He was finishing up a thesis for a masters degree in French at the University.

Interviews with neighbors in Houses 1, 2, and 3 were unproductive. House 1 is vacant and for sale. House 2 occupants were out of town. Mr. and Mrs. Jones in

House 3 were home and in bed. They heard nothing. Their bedroom is in the back of their home.

Dated October 28.

/s/ L. I. Kelso
Special Agent L. I. Kelso

Statement of Sally Williams

My name is Sally Williams. I live at 34 Trails End Road. I am a retired school teacher. I live alone. I am 58 years old.

Last night I was sleeping in my upstairs front bedroom. It was a cool night, but I had the window open. Some time after midnight I saw a small foreign car come up to the cul-de-sac and go around the circle very fast. The car returned about thirty minutes later and did this again. I must have gone back to sleep. Around 2:00 a.m. I saw a white car come up that looked like a two-door sports model. I think it was a Pontiac. The car went around the cul-de-sac one time squealing its tires. I heard one of the male occupants yell, "Hey you old goat, what if we ran through that silly looking fence?", or something like that. Something else may have been said. I just don't remember. I heard a noise like metal hitting metal.

Then sometime about 3:00 a.m. (I looked at my clock) I saw the same kind of car come to a stop in the little ditch in my front yard. I just stayed by my front window and looked out. Then I saw my neighbor, Mr. Wainwright, open the gate and come toward the car. It looked like he had something in his right hand. I know he was carrying a flashlight in his left hand because it was turned on. He walked up to the car and said something to the effect of, "What are you doing here." One of the boys said something. I can't remember what, but he was very belligerent. I am sure of that. The car was facing outward toward the street, and I couldn't see what happened next, but I heard a gun discharge. Then someone said, "Let's go quick," and the car spun a lot of mud and came flying out onto the street. Then Mr. Wainwright looked around the neighborhood and walked back to his gate. I don't know what happened next. I guess I should have called the police, but I did not know that anybody had been shot. Besides, I have heard shots fired around the end of the street on several previous occasions.

Mr. Wainwright's wife used to be a friend of mine, but since she died he sort of stays to himself. It seems like he is always building a big fence or putting lights out there or some kind of gadget on his gate. He seems like a nice old man, but he really doesn't have much to say. I have never known him to do anything violent or wrong before and he has got a good reputation for being a peaceable citizen. He doesn't like kids or anyone driving around his home at night. He is always complaining about that.

I also wish people would quit racing around that cul-de-sac late at night. Sometimes, it keeps me awake. I don't know of any of the other neighbors that have been shot at or had their houses shot at, but Mr. Wainwright did show me where

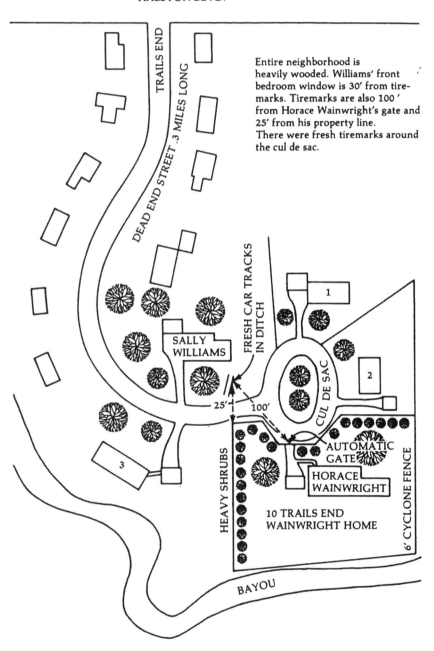

HALSTON BLVD.

TRAILS END

DEAD END STREET .3 MILES LONG

Entire neighborhood is
heavily wooded. Williams' front
bedroom window is 30' from tiremarks. Tiremarks are also 100 '
from Horace Wainwright's gate and
25' from his property line.
There were fresh tiremarks around
the cul de sac.

FRESH CAR TRACKS
IN DITCH

SALLY
WILLIAMS

1

2

CUL DE SAC

25'   100'

AUTOMATIC
GATE

HORACE
WAINWRIGHT

HEAVY SHRUBS

3

10 TRAILS END
WAINWRIGHT HOME

6' CYCLONE FENCE

BAYOU

Prepared by Special Agent L. I. Kelso

Blowup of Cul de Sac

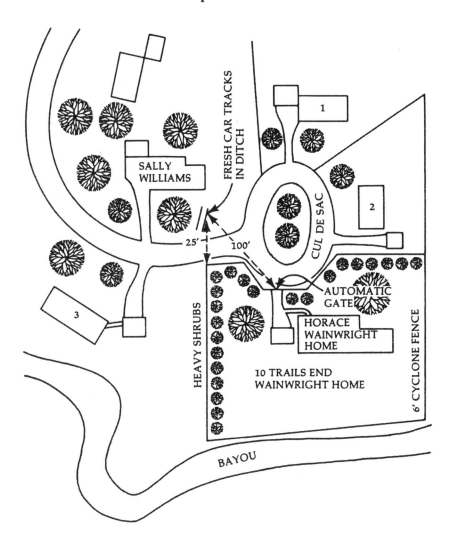

Prepared by Special Agent L. I. Kelso

his home had been fired into once and also where his fence was broken by a car running over it.

I don't know any of the boys in the car. I did hear one boy say, "Come on, let's go, let's leave the old geezer alone." This was when the car was in the ditch maybe one minute before Mr. Wainwright walked out. This is really all I know, heard, or saw that night.

/s/ Sally Williams
Sally Williams

Subscribed and sworn before me, a notary public, on October, 22.

/s/ Carol Smith,
Notary Public.

Statement of Horace Wainwright

My name is Horace Wainwright. I am a white male, age 73. I live alone at 10 Trails End Road. My wife died last year, and I am a widower. We bought this house two years ago because we wanted privacy and by living at the end of this dead end street in this wooded neighborhood, we thought we could enjoy my final years of retirement in the same general area where we were both raised. Although the overall neighborhood has deteriorated, our street is nice and well kept.

Soon after we purchased our home, we found that kids and adults liked to drive their cars at night to the cul-de-sac at our property entrance. They would drive up and couples would park, kids would relieve themselves, and sometimes the kids drove all over my yard. They would honk and yell bad things. They made me mad and I installed a 6' cyclone fence. After this they would still drive up and honk and yell obscenities. About a year and a half ago, one guy drove through my fence. Then, about one year ago, someone fired a rifle through the downstairs kitchen window while we were asleep. I then installed lights in my trees, an automatic gate with a lock, and a speaker phone at the entrance.

Maybe around Christmas, some kids fired some more shots. My wife had a heart attack the day after and died in the hospital two months later. Just last August, someone shot out my speaker phone with a shotgun, and one of my lights was shot out one month ago.

I have lived in fear and the police have been called many times. In fact, Special Agent Kelso, who I am giving this statement to, works this area and investigated most of these shootings.

Tonight, like many weekend nights, it started back again. At 1:00 a.m. a car drove up and ran into my fence. It was the same car the dead boy was later in. I ran out and saw that it was a white Pontiac two-door sports car. It bent my fence, but didn't break it. The car came back two or three more times and spun its tires and went around and around the cul-de-sac. The guys yelled obscenities. I heard them call me a "dirty old s.o.b." and one said, "We'll just come over this pissant fence you old lush." They left the next to last time around 2:30 a.m. At 3:00 a.m. they came back and spun the wheels and honked so I got my old long tom .44 pistol called a thumb buster. It's a single action revolver and the only gun I have. "Single action" means that ordinarily the hammer must be cocked before you pull the trigger to fire. I went out to ask them to leave and scare them. I noticed their car parked in the ditch of my neighbor's yard, I guess 50′ from my front gate. I walked up to the car to get the license number. Someone in the car said, "Hey fink face, you want to have some fun?" I said, "Get out of here." My hand was trembling.

The driver had his hands on the wheel and then he suddenly reached for something between the seats with his right hand. I thought he grabbed a weapon. I had a flashlight in my left hand turned on him. The gun was in my right hand. I don't think the hammer was cocked. I didn't want to shoot him so I hit him in the head with the barrel of the pistol. I guess the gun went off right then. There were three boys in the car. The passenger in front yelled, "Get out of here, he shot Bull."

The car dug out of the ditch and left real fast. I went back to the house. I didn't know what to do. Finally about 3:30 a.m., I put on my pants and coat and was going to drive to the police sub-station and tell them what happened. As I walked to my car Special Agent Kelso was coming up the walk, so here I am. I don't think I knew any of the three men in the car. I do know they came to my house many times that night.

I have read the above statement and it is true and correct.

/s/ Horace Wainwright
Horace Wainwright

Subscribed and sworn before me, a notary public, on October, 20.

/s/ Carol Smith,
Notary Public.

Court's Instructions to the Jury

Members of the Jury:

You have now heard all of the evidence in the case as well as the final arguments of the lawyers for the parties. You, as jurors, are the judges of the facts. But in determining what actually happened in this case, that is, in reaching your decision as to the facts, it is your sworn duty to follow the law I am now in the process of defining for you.

The indictment or formal charge against a Defendant is not evidence of guilt. Indeed, the Defendant is presumed by the law to be innocent. The law does not require a Defendant to prove his innocence or produce any evidence at all. The Government has the burden of proving him guilty beyond a reasonable doubt, and if it fails to do so you must acquit him. But, while the Government's burden of proof is a strict or heavy burden, it is not necessary that the Defendant's guilt be proved beyond all possible doubt. It is only required that the Government's proof exclude any "reasonable doubt" concerning the Defendant's guilt.

A "reasonable doubt" is a real doubt, based upon reason and common sense, after careful and impartial consideration of all the evidence in the case. Proof beyond a reasonable doubt, therefore, is proof of such a convincing character that you would be willing to rely and act upon it without hesitation in the most important of your own affairs. If you are convinced that the accused has been proved guilty beyond reasonable doubt, say so. If you are not convinced, say so.

While you should consider only the evidence in the case, you are permitted to draw such reasonable inferences from the testimony and exhibits as you feel are justified in the light of common experience. In other words, you may make deductions and reach conclusions which reason and common sense lead you to draw from the facts which have been established by the testimony and evidence in the case. You may also consider either direct or circumstantial evidence. "Direct evidence" is the testimony of one who asserts actual knowledge of a fact, such as an eyewitness. "Circumstantial evidence" is proof of a chain of facts and circumstances indicating either the guilt or innocence of the Defendant. The law makes no distinction between the weight to be given to either direct or circumstantial evidence. It requires only that you weigh all of the evidence and be convinced of the Defendant's guilt beyond a reasonable doubt before he can be convicted.

It is charged in Count One of the indictment that on or about October 19, last year, in the Territory of Columbia, the Defendant, Horace Wainwright, with malice aforethought, and by means of shooting, unlawfully killed Terry Dobbs, in violation of Title 18, Section 1111 of the United States Code. Section 1111 of Title 18 of the United States Code declares, in part, that:

> "Murder is the unlawful killing of a human being with malice aforethought."

If the act of killing is done with a premeditated intent willfully to take a human life, the offense is murder in the first degree. If the act is done without such premeditated intent, the offense is murder in the second degree. You will note that the indictment contains no allegation that the Defendant acted with premeditation. Consequently, the offense charged is that of murder in the second degree. Two essential elements are required to be proved in order to establish the offense of second-degree murder:

> First, the act or acts of killing a human being unlawfully;
> Second, doing such act or acts with malice aforethought.

"Unlawfully" means contrary to law. So, to do an act "unlawfully" means to do willfully something which is contrary to law and without legal justification. An act is done "willfully," if it is done voluntarily and intentionally, and with the specific intent to do something the law forbids; that is to say, with bad purpose either to disobey or to disregard the law.

"Malice aforethought" means an intent, at the time of a killing, willfully to take the life of a human being, or an intent willfully to act in callous and wanton disregard of the consequences to human life; but "malice aforethought" does not necessarily imply any ill will, spite, or hatred towards the individual killed. "Malice," as the term is used here, is but another name for a certain state or condition of a person's mind or heart. Since no one can look into the heart of another, the only means of determining whether or not malice existed at the time of a killing is by inference drawn from the surrounding facts and circumstances, as shown by the evidence in the case. If it is shown that the Defendant used a deadly weapon in the commission of a homicide, then you may find, from the use of such weapon, in the absence of mitigating circumstances, the existence of the malice which is an essential element of the offense. You are not obliged so to find, however.

The law permits the jury to find the accused guilty of any lesser offense which is necessarily included in the crime charged in the indictment, whenever such a course is consistent with the facts found by the jury from the evidence in the case, and with the law as given in the instructions of the Court. So, if the jury should unanimously find the accused "not guilty" of the crime charged in Count One of the indictment, then the jury must proceed to determine the guilt or innocence of the accused as to any lesser offense which is necessarily included in the crime charged.

The crime of murder in the second degree, which is charged in Count One of the indictment in this case, necessarily includes the lesser offense of voluntary manslaughter. Section 1112(a), Title 18 of the United States Code defines manslaughter as follows: "Manslaughter is the unlawful killing of a human being without malice...: Voluntary – Upon a sudden quarrel or heat of passion." Two essential elements are required to be proved in order to establish the offense of voluntary manslaughter:

First: The act or acts of killing a human being;
Second: The doing of such act or acts voluntarily and without legal justification or excuse.

If the jury should unanimously find the accused "not guilty" of both the crime of murder in the second degree and the lesser included offense of voluntary manslaughter, then the jury must proceed to determine the guilt or innocence of the accused as to Count Two of the indictment, which charges that he is guilty of involuntary manslaughter in that on or about October 19, [last year], in the Territory of Columbia, the Defendant, Horace Wainwright, while engaged in the commission of an unlawful act not amounting to a felony, to wit, the assault of Harold Clark by striking Clark's head with a gun, did, unlawfully shoot and kill Terry Dobbs with such gun, in violation of Title 18, Section 1112(a) of the United States Code. Section 1112(a) provides in part: "Manslaughter is the unlawful killing of a human being without malice...: Involuntary – In the commission of an unlawful act not amounting to a felony..."

Two essential elements are required to be proved in order to establish the offense of involuntary manslaughter charged in Count Two of the indictment.

First: The act or acts of killing a human being unlawfully;
Second: Doing such act or acts while engaged in the commission of an unlawful act not amounting to a felony.

You are instructed that Title 18, Section 113(a)(4) of the United States Code prescribes punishment for the commission of (1) assault by striking, beating, or wounding. The punishment prescribed is less than the minimum punishment prescribed for the commission of a felony. Consequently, assault by striking, beating, or wounding and simple assault are unlawful acts not amounting to a felony within the meaning of Title 18, Section 1112(a) of the United States Code. If a person actually strikes a blow while committing an assault, the offense is that of assault by striking. This offense requires neither a particular degree of severity in the injury inflicted nor the specific intent to cause serious injury. However, the prosecution must establish the absence of just cause or excuse for the Defendant's conduct if evidence of just cause or excuse is presented.

If the jury should unanimously find the accused "not guilty" under Count Two of the indictment, then the jury must proceed to determine the guilt or innocence of the accused as to Count Three of the indictment. It is charged in Count Three of the indictment that on or about October 19, last year, within the Territory of Columbia, the Defendant, Horace Wainwright, while engaged in the commission of a lawful act which might produce death, that is confronting Harold Clark, Terry Dobbs and Carlos Blanca with a gun, without due caution and circumspection, and through gross negligence, unlawfully shot and killed Terry Dobbs, in violation of Title 18, Section 1112 of the United States Code. Section 1112(a) also provides: "Manslaughter is the unlawful killing of a human being without malice . . . : Involuntary . . . in the commission in an unlawful manner, or without due caution and circumspection, of a lawful act which might produce death."

Three essential elements are required to be proved in order to establish the offense charged in Count Three of the indictment.

First: The act or acts of killing a human being unlawfully;
Second: Doing such act or acts while engaged in the commission of a lawful act which might produce death, without due caution and circumspection;
Third: Actual knowledge of the Defendant that his conduct was a threat to the lives of others, or knowledge of such circumstances as could reasonably be said to have made foreseeable to him the peril to which his acts might subject others.

The term "without due caution and circumspection" is equivalent to the term "gross negligence." Gross negligence means more than ordinary simple negligence.

Gross negligence requires proof beyond a reasonable doubt of a wanton or reckless disregard for human life.

With regard to all counts of the indictment, you are instructed as follows:

In this case, the Defendant has relied in part upon the defense of self-defense. If the Defendant was not the aggressor, and had reasonable grounds to believe and actually did believe that he was in imminent danger of death or serious bodily harm from which he could save himself only by using deadly force against his assailant, he had the right to employ force, including deadly force in order to defend himself. By "deadly force" is meant force that is likely to cause death or serious bodily harm. In order for the Defendant to have been justified in the use of force or deadly force in self-defense, he must not have provoked the assault on him or have been the aggressor. Mere words, without more, do not constitute provocation or aggression. The circumstances under which he acted must have been such as to produce in the mind of a reasonably prudent person, similarly situated, the reasonable belief that the other person was then about to kill him or to do him serious bodily harm. In addition, the Defendant must have actually believed that he was in imminent danger of death or serious bodily harm and that deadly force must be used to repel it.

If evidence of self-defense is present, the Government must prove beyond a reasonable doubt that the Defendant did not act in self-defense. If you find that the Government has failed to prove beyond a reasonable doubt that the Defendant did not act in self-defense, you must find the Defendant not guilty. In other words, if you have a reasonable doubt whether or not the Defendant acted in self-defense, your verdict must be not guilty.

If the Defendant had reasonable grounds to believe and actually did believe that he was in imminent danger of death or serious bodily harm and that deadly force was necessary to repel such danger, he would be justified in using deadly force in self-defense, even though it may afterwards have turned out that the appearances were false. If these requirements are met he could use deadly force even though there was in fact neither purpose on the part of the other person to kill him or do him serious bodily harm, nor imminent danger that it would be done, nor actual necessity that deadly force be used in self-defense.

If the Defendant had reasonable grounds to believe and actually did believe that he was in imminent danger of death or serious bodily harm and that deadly force was necessary to repel such danger, he was not required to retreat or to consider whether he could safely retreat. He was entitled to stand his ground and use such force as was reasonably necessary under the circumstances to save his life or protect himself from serious bodily harm. However, if the Defendant could have safely retreated but did not do so, his failure to retreat is a circumstance which you may consider, together with all other circumstances, in determining whether he went farther in repelling the danger, real or apparent, than he was justified in doing under the circumstances.

Even if the other person was the aggressor and the Defendant was justified in using force in self-defense, he would not be entitled to use any greater force than he had reasonable grounds to believe and actually did believe to be necessary under the circumstances to save his life or avert serious bodily harm. In determining whether the Defendant used excessive force in defending himself, you may consider all the circumstances under which he acted. The claim of self-defense is not necessarily defeated if greater force than would have seemed necessary in cold blood was used by the Defendant in the heat of passion generated by an assault upon him. A belief which may be unreasonable in cold blood may be actually and reasonably entertained in the heat of passion.

In this case, the Defendant has also relied in part upon the defense of accident. If evidence of accident is present, the Government must prove beyond a reasonable doubt that the discharge of the Defendant's gun was not accidental. If you believe that the Defendant, while engaged in the commission of a lawful act and while using due caution and circumspection, accidentally discharged the gun which caused the death of Terry Dobbs, or if you have a reasonable doubt thereof, then you should find the Defendant "not guilty" on all counts of the indictment.

Any verdict must represent the considered judgment of each juror. In order to return a verdict, it is necessary that each juror agree thereto. In other words, your verdict must be unanimous. It is your duty as jurors to consult with one another, and to deliberate in an effort to reach agreement if you can do so without violence to individual judgment. Each of you must decide the case for yourself, but only after an impartial consideration of the evidence in the case with your fellow jurors. In the course of your deliberations, do not hesitate to re-examine your own view and change your opinion if convinced it is erroneous. But do not surrender your honest conviction as to the weight or effect of the evidence solely because of the opinion of your fellow jurors, or for the mere purpose of returning a verdict.

3. The civil case: *The Estate of James Dale Warren*

NO. 10-05-XX[18](A)

IN THE MATTER OF THE ESTATE	IN THE DISTRICT COURT OF
OF	LAMA COUNTY, NOCONA 81st
JAMES DALE WARREN, Deceased	JUDICIAL DISTRICT

Original Petition for Contest of Will

NOW COMES Susan Warren Gearhart, acting as Plaintiff and Contestant herein, and brings forth this her Original Petition for Contest of Will, to contest the validity of a purported Will filed for probate by Defendant and Proponent herein, James

---

18 The original problem was dated 1980. We have increased the sums involved to reflect inflation up to 2003. We recommend adjusting the figures and the dates on the exhibits to reflect the year before the case is tried.

Dale Warren, Jr., and in support of such Contest would respectfully show to this Honorable Court and jury the following:

1   This Contest is brought as an ancillary proceeding to the Application for Probate of a purported holographic Will of James Dale Warren, Deceased, dated October 31, last year, filed by the Decedent's son, James Dale Warren, Jr., in Cause No. 10-05-XX, pending, on November 4, last year.

2   By order of the Court, it has been adjudged and decreed that the purported Will dated October 31, last year, bears the signature of James Dale Warren, Deceased, and satisfies the formalities of the laws of the State of Nocona for the making of a legally binding holographic will. By further Order of the Court, it has been adjudged and decreed that the parties to this proceeding, Susan Warren Gearhart, Contestant, and James Dale Warren, Jr., Proponent, are the sole legal heirs of James Dale Warren, Deceased, and as such, the parties have proper standing and interest for this proceeding.

3   As grounds for her Contest of Will, Contestant would show to this Honorable Court and jury that the purported October 31, last year Will of her father, James Dale Warren, Deceased, was executed at a time and under such circumstances when he was not of sound mind and did not possess sufficient capacity to make a will. Because the decedent lacked testamentary capacity, as that term is defined by law, at the time of his execution of the purported October 31, last year Will, said document is not the valid Will of James Dale Warren, Deceased, and is therefore null and void.

4   As additional and/or alternative grounds for her Contest of Will, your Contestant would show this Honorable Court and Jury that the purported October 31, last year Will of her father, James Dale Warren, Deceased, was executed at a time and under such circumstances that James Dale Warren, Jr. exercised over the decedent and over the mind and will of the decedent such influence or dominion as prevented the alleged Will from being the decedent's own free will and constituted it instead the will of the Proponent. Because the decedent executed the purported October 31, last year Will under the proponent's undue influence, as that term is defined by law, said document is not the valid Will of James Dale Warren, Deceased, and is therefore null and void.

WHEREFORE, PREMISES CONSIDERED, by reason of the above and foregoing, your Contestant must generally deny the allegations in support of probate offered by Proponent's Application for Probate, and Contestant prays that the purported October 31, last year Will of James Dale Warren, Deceased, be denied admission to probate and be declared null and void on the grounds of lack of testamentary capacity and/or undue influence with respect to the execution thereof, and Contestant prays further that she be given such other relief, at law or in equity, to which she may be entitled and for which she will ever pray.

Respectfully submitted,

Portia Lawson,
Attorney for Contestant, Susan Warren Gearhart

Answer to Petition for Contest of Will

NOW COMES James Dale Warren, Jr., acting as Defendant and Proponent herein, and files this Answer to the Petition for Contest of Will and would respectfully show the Court and jury the following:

1 Paragraph 1 is admitted.
2 Paragraph 2 is admitted.
3 Paragraphs 3 and 4 are denied, and your Proponent would show that there is no legal or factual basis upon which the Last Will and Testament of James Dale Warren, Deceased, dated October 31, last year, should be declared null and void or denied admission to probate.

WHEREFORE, PREMISES CONSIDERED, Proponent/Defendant prays that the Original Petition for Contest of Will be denied and that this Court enter judgment for Proponent in accordance with the facts and law and for such other and further relief to which he may be entitled.

Respectfully submitted,

Renaldo Palmer,
Attorney for James Dale Warren, Jr.

Stipulations

1 It is stipulated by and between the parties hereto that at the time of the trial hereof, Contestant will herself take the stand and will call, as her only other witness, Pat Duffey.
2 It is stipulated by and between the parties hereto that at the time of trial hereof, Proponent will himself take the stand and will call, as his only other witness, Ernest Potter.
3 It is stipulated by and between the parties hereto that the text of the May 26, last year Will and Testament executed by James Dale Warren on May 26, last year is as follows:

May 26

Last Will and Testament

I, James Dale Warren, do hereby make this my Last Will and Testament. I revoke all prior wills, as it is my intent at this time to write my Last Will and Testament before I go on to my reward. Being of sound mind and sound body, I hereby leave to my devoted and faithful daughter, who has cared for me for many years, the interest and principal of my $100,000 savings account, and our family home at 4250 Riverside Lane. I also leave to Susan all of my other property of any kind, except that I leave to my grandchildren my old beagle, Cassandra, because I know they will continue to care for her.

/s/ James Dale Warren
Happy Valley, Nocona

4. It is stipulated by and between the parties hereto that the text of the October 31, last year Will is as follows:

October 31

This is my last will and I revoke all others. I am of sound mind but I am going to die. I leave all of my estate and property of any to my dear son, Jim, because he needs $50,000 to start a new life except for Mary's jewelry and family china which I leave to Susan who is traveling with her husband.

/s/ James Warren

5. It is further stipulated that the letter written by James Warren, Sr., to James Warren, Jr., on October 13, last year, reads as follows:

October 13

Dear Son,

Thanks for your phone call last night. It meant a lot to me to hear from you and to learn that you are not bitter about the fact that I could not be a father to you when you were growing up. Your half sister, Susan, has remarried recently, to a guy named Bill Gearhart. He is a stockbroker, not very successful, but enough to take care of Susan and the kids. I have been here in this Home since April, and I don't mind it too much, except I really miss watching Kim and James grow up. I love them like they were my own.

I have thought about your problem of needing a grub-stake to produce your new play. I have decided to find a way to help you. It would really make me feel wonderful if I could help you do something great in your life.

I really look forward to your next phone call and especially to your promised visit in the near future.

Dad

Please write me at: James Warren
Room 13
1500 Lama Lane
Happy Valley Nursing Home
Happy Valley, Nocona

6. It is further stipulated that, at the time of his death, the value of the Estate of James Dale Warren was $525,000 and consisted of

Cash and Certificates of Deposit	$ 100,000
Pension Fund Annuity Death Benefit	$ 150,000
Property at 4250 Riverside Lane	$ 250,000
Personal Property	$ 50,000
Liabilities for final hospital costs	
and for funeral expenses, etc.	$ (25,000)
Net assets	$ 525,000

7. It is further stipulated that Pat Duffey is a qualified witness under Rule 702 of the Federal Rules of Evidence for the purposes of this trial.

Statement of Susan Gearhart

My name is Susan Warren Gearhart. I live at 4250 Riverside Lane, Happy Valley, Nocona. I am thirty-nine years old. My father was James Dale Warren, and my mother was Mary Warren, who is now deceased. I have a half-brother named Jim from my father's first marriage to Elizabeth Warren, who, as far as I know, is dead. My father and Elizabeth Warren were divorced when my half-brother was about two years old.

Ten years ago on July 4, last year, I married Bill Gearhart. Bill is my second husband, and my first husband's name was Tom Smith. By Tom Smith, I had a son, James Warren Smith, who is now twelve years old, and a daughter, Mary Kimberly Smith, who is now ten years old. When Tom and I married, we continued living in my father's home with him, since my mother had recently passed away, and I didn't want to leave my father all alone. Tom was a salesman, and he was on the road a lot, so it worked out well for me to live at home and have Dad there to help raise the kids when they came along. About a year after Kim was born, Tom Smith divorced me, and I continued to live there with my father in our family home on Riverside Lane. Actually, I have never lived anywhere other than on Riverside Lane, except for the times when I was away at school.

My dad's health began to fail long ago, and I never felt comfortable leaving him alone in the house for the last four or five years. I had discussed moving out of the house with him, but he was very opposed to it, especially since he enjoyed having Jamie, his namesake grandson, and Kim there with him. He was a very devoted grandparent, and my children were extremely devoted to him. I know he would never have failed to include me and my children in his will, if he were in his right mind.

When I was growing up here in Happy Valley, I had an almost perfect relationship with my parents, and they had a wonderful relationship with each other. My father told me that he and Elizabeth had gotten a divorce because he couldn't stand her constant bad temper, complaints and nagging. He never spoke kindly of her. As for my half-brother, Jim, my dad told me he had been sending child support for the first twenty years of Jim's life and had never gotten a thank you for anything from Jim or Elizabeth. It seemed to hurt him that Jim never wrote to thank him for the presents my father used to send him. He was a very ungrateful boy. I can remember that he used to telephone our house back when he was in high school, and he would always be rude to me and my mother. He would say something like, "Let me speak to the old man." Sometimes my dad would be in when Jim would call, and my dad would always get really upset after their conversations. My dad always said that each telephone call was for the purpose of asking for money to buy something extravagant, like a car or a travel ticket. When I was just about right out of high school, Jim decided to come to Happy Valley, probably to try to borrow money again. By then, my mother was very ill and suffering from a nervous condition caused by her medication, and I prayed

Jim would not show up to upset our household. I warned Mother in advance that he might possibly show up, because I thought it might be harmful to her to be surprised by his visit. Sure enough when he showed up, he was something of a surprise.

When Jim arrived at the front door, he was wearing filthy rags and had a long beard and long hair. I reluctantly let him in after he told me who he was, and I took him into my father's study and introduced my dad to Jim. I think they had met a few times over the years, but I doubt that he could have recognized Jim as his own son on that day. I then left the room, and the only thing I heard about their conversation was when I walked by and heard Jim saying things about how tough it was to be a poor student and that he would appreciate any help my father might give him. My father then announced a principle that I had often heard him say, and that was, "A man ought to make it on his own, or not at all." The rest of what I heard were just a few mumblings which sounded kind of like an argument to me. I don't recall how long Jim was there. When Jim left my father's study, he walked out into the hall and asked me if I would give him a ride. As I headed for my coat, he asked me also to see if I could pick up some money for him to use or else he just might have to stay around a few days. I then went upstairs and got some money I had been given as a present. When we got in the car, Jim asked me again for some money, and I gave it to him and told him that he should use it to leave town and that he should not come back to upset my family any more. I should have listened to him at the time, because he laughed at me and told me that he would be back and that he would get whatever he wanted out of the old man.

Over the next several years, Jim never called one time that I know of to speak with my dad, and he never wrote any letters that I saw, either. I don't think he ever came to visit, because I certainly didn't see him. I have heard from other people that Jim turned out to be a drug addict, and I think he was on drugs the day he came to see my dad way back there, or at least he looked like it. My dad never talked about him or Elizabeth to me after that visit, and we continued to have a good life together, until my dear mother died when I was about twenty-three years old. Two years later, I married Tom Smith, and he moved into my house, so I could continue to take care of my dad.

Several years after my divorce, I met Bill Gearhart, and we were engaged for over a year before we finally married. My dad was aware that I was going to marry Bill, but he never really said very much about it to me. I don't think he liked Bill, but then he never thought anyone was good enough for his daughter – just a typical father. The only comment he ever made to me was after Bill and I got married, he seemed a little surprised that Bill would be willing to live in another man's home, in the same house where I had been married and living with Tom Smith, and he repeated his old philosophy that a man should succeed on his own or not at all.

On many occasions, my father used to tell me that it was his intention to leave the home on River Lane to me so that I could raise Jamie and Kim properly. The home is worth probably $250,000 in today's market in Happy Valley. He also told me he wanted me to have everything else of his in return for the years I had spent taking care of him. We had a wonderful relationship, and it certainly came as no surprise to me that I would be his sole beneficiary in his will. On May 26, last year, I was with him when he sat down and wrote out a will leaving the house and everything to me.

My dad's health had gotten to be really poor, and it seemed to me that he would be much better off where nursing care would be available in the event anything serious happened. The doctors told me he had all sorts of problems which could at any moment result in an emergency, which is, of course, what finally did happen to him when he had the stroke. After Bill and I married, sometimes he would go with me to the nursing home to visit my dad, but of course Dad paid the most attention to Jamie and Kim when we visited. I was there practically every day, and I felt he was really happy there, or I would have taken him back home with me. My dad had a roommate named Ernie Potter, whom he seemed to like quite a bit, although Mr. Potter always seemed to be flaky and sour-acting when I saw him. Certainly my father never objected to me about staying at the nursing home instead of living in his home with me and the kids.

Sometime in the middle of the summer, my half-brother called to tell me he wanted to speak with my dad. I can't really recall when it was, it could have been anytime during the summer months. I told him where Dad was and gave him the address where he could write to him. I know he later called my husband one day while I was visiting with my dad and asked for the information again, telling Bill that he had lost it. Bill gave him the phone number and address where my dad could be reached. So far as I know, he never bothered to call or write, at least my dad never mentioned it if he did.

On October 28, last year, I received a phone call from the Happy Valley Nursing Home just as I finished feeding old Cassie. At that time, I learned that my dad had suffered a stroke, which they believed to be a mild stroke, and that they were going to put him in the hospital wing for treatment and observation. I rushed on down to the hospital and stayed with him all of the time that they permitted me to during that day. He really wasn't quite right on that day, and he didn't act like himself at all. He was having a terrible time talking and he was weepy and depressed. I was very worried about him, but the nurses kept telling me he was doing very well. I was never able to talk with the doctors before I left to go home that night.

On the next morning, I was on my way to the hospital to see my dad and spend the day with him, when I was involved in a terrible car accident. The guy ran a stop sign and hit me broadside. I hit my nose on something and broke it, which gave me two black eyes later on. It also caused me to cut my lip and my forehead, and I really looked horrible. Also, I broke several ribs and could barely breathe. I was taken to Valley Hospital in an ambulance, where I was admitted for treatment of my injuries. I called Bill at work and told him about it and told him to call the hospital to advise them that I would not be there because of my injuries. I also told Bill that he should instruct the nurses and doctors not to mention my injuries to my dad, because it would upset him under the circumstances. When Bill got to the hospital to see me, he had already called the Happy Valley Hospital and had told them of my situation. Bill also told me that the nurses said not to worry about Mr. Warren, because he was in very good condition. At some point in time, Bill went over to the Happy Valley Hospital to check up on my dad, and he told me my dad had been sleeping peacefully when he saw him.

On October 30, 1 called my dad's room twice, hoping to speak with him. I had decided that maybe I would tell him I had caught a cold or something and that I would not be able to visit with him because it might be contagious. A man answered the phone and told me that Mr. Warren was doing very well, but that he could not talk on the telephone because of doctor's orders and that Mr. Warren couldn't really speak very well anyway. I asked the man to tell my dad that I had called and that I would call him back. I also asked the man to give my dad best wishes from his grandchildren. The man did not tell me his name, I am certain, and I did not find out until later that it was probably my half-brother, Jim. By October 31, my face was really black and blue, and I looked absolutely frightening. I again concluded I simply could not possibly go to visit my dad in that condition. I was discharged from the hospital during the afternoon of October 31, and stayed at home. Again, I called my dad's room and was told by the same male voice just about the same story, and now I believe that it was my half-brother, Jim, to whom I spoke. I also called the nurses' station and spoke with a nurse by the name of Pat Duffey, with whom I had been casually acquainted back in high school. She had heard about my accident and asked me how I was doing. I explained to her that I had been discharged from the hospital, but that I looked too awful to come to visit my dad. She reassured me that my dad appeared to be in pretty stable condition. She suggested that 1 should put on some makeup and come in to visit my dad whenever I felt like I could, because she explained that it had been her experience that stroke patients could not be considered really stable for a few weeks after an initial problem. I believe that telephone call was between 4:00 and 5:00 p.m. in the afternoon of October 31, [last year].

Around 11:30 that evening, Pat Duffey called me to tell me that my dad had taken a terrible turn for the worse and that his condition had resulted in his receiving a great deal of emergency care and attention, but to no avail. She told me my dad had passed away. She also told me that my brother was there and would be able to take care of all of the arrangements and details and for me not to worry about coming to the hospital that night if I didn't feel able. I was shocked to learn of my brother's presence, and told her that I did not have any idea that he had been there at all. Pat Duffey told me she was surprised that I did not know of it and had assumed that I had known that he had been there constantly for three days hovering over my father. Bill and I immediately went to the hospital to take care of everything, and by the time we arrived at the hospital, Jim was no longer there.

/s/ Susan Warren Gearhart
SUSAN WARREN GEARHART

SUBSCRIBED AND SWORN TO Before me by the said Susan Warren Gearhart on this 28th day of January, current year.

/s/ Patricia A. McNulty
NOTARY PUBLIC
My Commission Expires at Death.

Statement of Pat Duffey, R.N.

My name is Pat Duffey. I live alone at 3737 South Street, Happy Valley, Nocona. I am thirty-seven years old, and I have been employed as a primary care nurse in the Happy Valley Nursing Home Hospital since I obtained my M.S.N. at Nocona University. I am occasionally assigned to be the nurse on duty in the nursing home wing of Happy Valley Nursing Home, but usually my duties involve only the hospital wing. I have known James Warren since April 15, when he moved to the Home.

On the 27th through the 31st of October of last year, I covered the morning shifts for a nurse who was ill who was assigned to the Home wing. My regular shift at the hospital was the 3-11 shift, which I also worked that week.

On the morning of the 28th of October, James Warren had a mild stroke in his room at Happy Valley Nursing Home, and he was immediately moved to the hospital wing for special care for his condition. That evening, I checked on him and found his daughter, Susan, with him. He was in stable condition, physically, but he was mentally slightly disoriented, which is typical of the stroke patients which I have attended. He was being medicated to keep him calm to avoid his being excessively frustrated by his confusion. I observed him become somewhat depressed about his inability to speak properly at times. He was sort of childlike in his dependency on his daughter. For example, he began to cry when she tried to go home, and she had to stay until he went to sleep.

Next morning I received a call on duty at the Home, and it was Bill Gearhart telling me about Susan's accident. Shortly thereafter, I met Jim Warren and told him about the accident. I told him to please not mention it to James Warren, and he assured me that he had no intention of bringing up Susan or her accident to Mr. Warren.

On October 30 and 31, I saw Jim Warren in his father's room throughout my entire 3–11 shifts. I noticed on the 30th of October that he had shaved off the beard and mustache which he had on the first day, and I also noticed that he was wearing new clothes. He had brought in several flower arrangements and other gifts for his father. I assumed he was very devoted to his father, because each time I would go into the room, on the 30th of October, Jim would be sitting on the side of the bed, or standing at the side of the bed, telling his father details about his being a playwright and some of the stories he had written. On the 30th, Mr. Warren seemed to improve quite a bit in his speaking ability, and once during my shift, he asked me quite plainly to find out why Susan had not come to see him since his stroke. I realized that he was still a little disoriented and confused when he made that comment, but at least his speech was getting better.

On the 31st of October, I checked on Mr. Warren immediately after beginning my 3–11 shift. Jim Warren was still in his father's room talking to him constantly. When I walked into the room around 3:30, I saw that Mr. Warren was holding a pen in his hand and a blank sheet of paper was in front of him. I assumed he couldn't speak well and that he was going to try to write things he wanted to say. I took Mr. Warren's blood pressure and had to remove the pen from his hand. At that time, Mr. Warren was able to say a few words which were reasonably well articulated, and I don't recall him saying anything that didn't make sense or anything like that. I remember only that he stated that he was very tired when I asked him how he was feeling.

As I left the room, I saw Mr. Warren motion to his son, and Jim Warren got up and put the pen back into his father's hand and started talking to him again.

At the nurses' station, while one of the nurses was complaining about all of the drugs missing lately, I answered a call from Susan Gearhart inquiring as to her father's condition. I tried to be reassuring to her in order not to worry her too much, just in case her injuries were still severe. However, I felt uneasy about her father's condition and encouraged her to attempt to come to the hospital to visit him if she felt she could. I feel terrible about not having mentioned to her at that time that Jim Warren was there, but I really didn't know the relationship between the two. I'm sure if I had mentioned that he was there, this whole thing wouldn't have happened to her.

Each time I went back to see Mr. Warren for the remainder of my shift until about 7:00, he was asleep, or at least appeared to be, except for once when I looked in and saw him writing on a piece of paper with Jim standing beside him helping him to write. I couldn't say whether Jim could have read the words on the paper from his position or not, and I think I observed that occurrence shortly before we served dinner, although I really can't say for sure when it was.

Around 7:30 p.m., Jim Warren came running out to the nurses' station and said his father appeared to be getting very weak and was having difficulty breathing. He was really panic-stricken. From that point on, James Warren's condition went steadily downhill, and nothing we did seemed to do any good. Jim Warren stayed in the room until we ordered him to leave, because he was extremely emotionally upset and kept saying, "Please, Dad, not now, Dad," and things to that effect. The doctor walked out to tell Jim Warren of his father's death, and I went to the telephone to advise Susan Gearhart. It was at the time of that first telephone conversation that I first mentioned Jim Warren's presence to her and learned she had known nothing of his being in town.

I stood there and observed the doctor as he filled out the attached clinical summary. It is a report the doctors always prepare promptly upon the discharge of our patients in the routine or regular course at the hospital. After it was prepared, it was placed in the permanent file we keep on every patient that is treated in the hospital.

/s/ Pat Duffey PAT DUFFEY

SUBSCRIBED AND SWORN TO Before me by the said Pat Duffey on this 19th day of January, current year.

/s/ Patricia A. McNulty
NOTARY PUBLIC
My Commission Expires at Death.

Statement of Ernest Potter

My name is Ernest Potter, I am seventy-five years old, and I reside at the Happy Valley Nursing Home – all of which is against my will. About the only good thing that's happened to me since my daughter stuck me here in the so-called Happy Valley is that I met up with James Warren, rest his soul. We spent a lot of time together, and we got to be really good friends before he died. I never had much use for his daughter, Susan, and I think it was mutual judging from the way she used to stare at my crippled hand and my wheel chair like I was something from outer space. It was always a wonder to me that my friend James continued to look forward to her visits, which were pretty frequent, just as though she hadn't run him out of his own house and home and dumped him in a nursing home. I expect he might have looked forward to her visits mainly because he was crazy about his grandchildren, Kim and James. You could look around his side of our room and tell that from all the pictures he kept hanging on the wall of those kids. The only time we ever talked about James's son, Jim, was when he would talk about how disappointed he was that Jim had turned out to be a starving artist trying to make it as an actor. He told me he had the guilties about divorcing Jim's mother, Elizabeth Warren, right after young Jim was born, since he never spent any time being Jim's father after that. I used to try to talk him out of worrying so much about his kids, since I didn't think they were apparently very worried about him at the time, especially after old Susan married "the Golddigger," as James used to call him. Once or twice the Golddigger, Bill Gearhart, would come along with little Susan to visit James, and I could see James immediately change into a bad mood. He would either get depressed or red-faced angry, and pretty soon they'd be arguing like they always did about how much high-living Bill Gearhart was doing. I remember one day they had a really big argument about the fact that the Golddigger had put the kids into a private school, which James thought was too expensive and would turn the kids into pampered weaklings.

A couple of months before James passed away, rest his soul, he got a phone call from his son, Jim, from New York. It really did him a lot of good, kicked his spirits up pretty high. From what I heard, a part of the conversation concerned Jim's asking for some help, because I heard James say, "It's about time I did something for my own son, so don't be ashamed of asking." They talked for about half an hour, and James hung up and said to me, "Well, Ernest, I've still got a chance to be a father to my son, and I'm going to do it this time." We talked a lot longer, about how glad he was to have heard from Jim.

Right then, he sat down and wrote a letter, to Jim I think, although I don't know whether he mailed it.

I'll never forget the day James had his stroke, right there in our room, and I called the people in charge at the Home and told them he was bad sick, and that was on October 28, last year, right after breakfast. As soon as they came and got James and took him around to the hospital wing of the Home, I went through James's telephone number book until I found his son's number in New York. I called him and told him that his dad had had a stroke. Early the next morning, Jim arrived from New York and came directly to my room to thank me for having called him and to visit with me about his dad. Then he went on up to the hospital wing to visit with his dad, and I didn't see him again until the morning of the 31st of October.

I never did see that Susan, and I don't know if she even bothered to come by to see James in the hospital, but I do know the nurses said they had called her to tell her that he had apparently suffered a stroke. I never heard from anybody where she was, but I think it would have done James some good to get to see his grandchildren if she had bothered to bring them up there.

On the morning of October 31, last year, Jim came by my room and told me that James wanted me to come in for a visit, and Jim told me that he had been with his father constantly since he had arrived. Jim then rolled me around to the hospital wing and we went in to see James together. James looked tired and not well at all. He told me he was glad to see me, and we just talked a little bit generally. He seemed to be at peace with himself. He told me he had really enjoyed spending some time with his son, Jim, at last, and that he had something really important to do that I could help him with. He told me he wanted me to come back after supper that night, because he thought he would have something for me to sign and keep for him. During the conversation, he never even brought up Susan or her kids, or the Golddigger.

Later in the day, I don't remember when, I got a call from Jim reminding me to be back after supper, and I told him I sure would be. He also mentioned to me that I should not bring up Susan or her family, because he thought that might upset James. Of course, right after suppertime, about 6:30 p.m., I went on back down to see James, since I sure wanted to help him with anything I could. As I pushed open the door, Jim looked a little startled at me, and just as I was about to come in, James sat up in bed and looked in my direction and said just as plain as anything, "Is that you, Elizabeth?" Jim put his hands on his shoulders and sort of pushed him back into the bed and asked him to be calm and not worry any more and said a few things like that to him in a very kindly way. James never said anything else I could understand while I was there for the next few minutes, and he just kept staring at Jim and had a little smile on his face. I was only there a few minutes when Jim asked me to come on out in the hall. He handed me a piece of paper and told me that it was the thing James had wanted me to help with. Jim told me it was his dad's will, and he said to me, "Ernest, you should take this and put this in Dad's room, wherever he keeps his papers, and don't ever tell anyone about it, until I give you the go ahead. That's the way Dad would want it."

I took the Will back to my room, and the next morning, I decided to read it. I could see that it was in James' handwriting, and since he had told me that there was something he wanted me to sign, I figured he wanted me to be his witness on his Will. So I wrote down at the bottom of it, "I, Ernest Potter, am a witness to this Will."

That night, on October 31, James passed away, and I lost the best friend a man could have. The next morning, Jim came by my room and picked up the Will from me. Since that time, Jim has been kind enough to stay in touch with me by a few phone calls and visits at the Home. In fact, I hear more often from him than I do my own daughter.

/s/ Ernest Potter
ERNEST POTTER

SUBSCRIBED AND SWORN TO Before me by the said Ernest Potter on this 19th day of January, current year.

/s/ Patricia A. McNulty
NOTARY PUBLIC
My Commission Expires at Death.

Statement of Jim Warren

My name is James Dale Warren, Jr., but I always go by "Jim." I am forty-two years old. I am single and live in New York City where I perform and write with The Acting Company. My father was James Dale Warren, now deceased, and my mother was Elizabeth Warren, who lived in New York City until her death several years ago. Susan Gearhart is my half-sister, born to my father and his second wife, Mary.

When I was two years old, my mother and my father divorced, and my mother eventually told me that the divorce came about due to my father's having developed a relationship with Mary, whom he later married. For the first few years of my childhood, I had little contact with my father, since the divorce was not on a particularly pleasant basis, but I always received a Christmas present and a birthday present from him every year. I don't know what kind of support he might have sent my mother to raise me, but I know that I did not receive anything from my father to help me get through college or drama school, although I was well aware that he could afford to help me if he chose. During my last year in college, I traveled to Happy Valley, Nocona, to renew my relationship with my father. That was when I first met Susan Warren Gearhart, my half-sister.

In advance of my trip, I called to make arrangements with my dad, but I was only able to speak with Susan. She seemed very unhappy about my plan to visit with my dad, but I ignored her. When I arrived in Happy Valley, I was not very warmly received by Susan or her mother, Mary, who was still living at that time. As it turned out, they had not even told my father that I would be arriving, and I suppose they just hoped I might not ever show up due to the way they had discouraged me from coming. My father took some time off from his work to visit with me, and I really enjoyed meeting him.

At the time, I looked pretty much like a bum or a "hippie." I guess my father was a little bit disturbed by my appearance, and he told me I probably wouldn't be able to make very much of a career for myself by being a drama major in college. On the other hand, he was genuinely glad to get to visit with me and encouraged me to come back whenever I could find time in the future. As I was leaving, Susan offered to take me to the bus station. During that ride, Susan told me I should not return to Happy Valley because it upset her mother, Mary, too much, and she explained that Mary was in a very weak physical condition. She told me my father was doing fine and was very happy and that I should not stir up any problems for him or his family. She said if anything ever came up that I should know about that she would certainly keep in contact with me. Then, of all things, when I got out of the car she jammed two $50 bills into my shirt pocket and told me she hoped that would help me out a little. I guess I didn't really hold that against her any, and I certainly did look like a bum, but that was a pretty insulting thing for her to do.

Over the next many years, I was able to speak with my father only a few times, since most of the telephone calls to his home were intercepted by Susan. I never heard back from him when Susan took my calls. I really didn't put too much more effort into getting in touch with my father, because I was working so hard on trying to make it as an actor, or as a playwright. I got mixed up with drugs once and had a hard time pulling myself back together, and I wouldn't doubt but that Susan made sure her father learned about that. Finally, I got some real encouragement by the success of one of my plays at a community theatre, and I took my life and my writing more seriously.

In about April of last year, I finished one of my scripts and took it around to several agents, producers and other people in the business to see whether they thought it might be a Broadway potential. Nearly everyone I spoke with told me it looked like it had the makings of a big success. The only problem was that everyone I spoke with told me I'd have to give up almost all of the profits on the thing to those who would be providing financial backing for the production. The more I checked into it, the more I realized that if I couldn't put up a healthy sum of money of my own, that I'd have to give up all of the control over the production, as well as almost all of the profit in order to get the play produced. It was then that I began considering contacting my dad to see if he would provide me with some financial help.

Sometime mid-May 20, I tried to contact my dad, but Susan received the phone call and was pretty vague about where my father was and whether or not he would call me back. I tried again to call my father sometime in the middle of July, and the same thing happened. Finally, in early October I called the house and Susan's husband, Bill Gearhart, answered, and he told me that my father was in the Happy Valley Nursing Home and gave me the telephone number. I couldn't believe my father was in a nursing home, since Susan had not even told me he was in poor health, much less that she had put him in a home.

On October 12, I called my dad and spoke with him in a long telephone conversation which must have lasted over an hour. It was the best talk we ever had. My dad was very interested in helping me finance my play, and he talked about loaning me some money or working out some way by which he could help me protect my interest in my work. He had a lot of personal things to say to me, which he had never expressed before, about his own feelings about having not been around when I was a kid and not having been responsible for helping me out with anything. I told him that none of that was important and that, of course, I didn't expect him to help me out now just to make up for all the things he had failed to do in the past.

Shortly after that I received a letter from him which again stated his interest in helping me with my play. I was making plans to visit with him as soon as I could get away from New York. Then, out of the blue, came a call from Ernest Potter, who explained that he was my father's roommate at Happy Valley Nursing Home. He told me my father had suffered a stroke and was in pretty bad shape. I thanked him and told him I would be coming to Happy Valley as soon as I could get there and that I would come by his room to see him.

I traveled all night long to get to Happy Valley, Nocona, and when I arrived the next morning at the Happy Valley Nursing Home, I headed to the room number on my dad's letter. A nurse saw me about to enter the room and asked if I knew Mr. Warren, and 1 explained that I was his son. I have since learned that this nurse's name is Pat Duffey. She told me that they had just received a call that Mr. Warren's daughter, Susan, had been involved in a car wreck on the way to the hospital. The nurse said Susan received some injuries to her face and other injuries that were not life threatening. The nurse said Susan could not come to see her father as a result. She explained that it would be best for Mr. Warren, in his condition, not to know about the incident, and she asked me to be certain not to mention it. She further stated she was glad I was going to be there in order that someone from the family would be present during Mr. Warren's recovery period. I went on to my dad's and Ernest Potter's room, and Ernest was there. He seemed really happy to meet me, and I sat down for a few minutes to inquire as to my dad's condition. He said he didn't know very much, and so I went on to the hospital wing to see my father.

When I arrived at his room, I found my father awake and quite alert. He was glad to see me, but he asked why I had bothered to fly out to see him before he returned to feeling a little better. I explained to him that I wanted to be there with him because I thought he might need me for support and comfort while he attempted to get back on his feet. We then began talking generally about just a lot of things, nothing in particular. I guess we must have talked a couple of hours that morning, which was October 29, I believe. I would say that I did most of the talking, since he was still having some speech problems. A few times, he asked me about where Susan was, and I pretty much dodged the question. As soon as they brought in his medication, around noon, I left to go and check into a motel room and came back later in the afternoon for about an hour. Then I came to visit him for a couple of hours in the early evening. His condition stayed about the same all day long, and he was extremely pleased to see me. He asked me to come spend the day with him the next day.

The next day, which was October 30, I brought some of my work to his room to sit there and write some letters to some people I was working with on my new play. Of course, in my father's condition, I couldn't bring up the topic of my need for some financial support from him, but we did talk about my work a little bit, and he seemed very interested in my telling him about some of the things I had written. He also asked me to talk to him about Elizabeth, my mother, and about our life in New York City. I spent most of the day just sitting either in his room or down the hall working on my own things, since I didn't want him to tire out. During the day, Susan called while I was there and I told her he was doing quite well and I'm sure I told her who I was. She showed about as much interest in me as she always had. Also, once when I was down the hall, I saw a man walk in to see my father while my father was sleeping, and I subsequently learned that it was Bill Gearhart. I don't know whether they were able to visit, but I doubt it, since my father was asleep at the time. Just as I was about to leave on the evening of October 30, [last year], my dad asked me to be sure and come back to visit the next day, and then he said to me, "I really doubt that I will ever live to see the outside of this hospital, and there are a few things I haven't taken care of yet."

The next morning when I returned to my father's room, he asked me to get Ernest Potter to come visit him. I did so, and he and Ernest had a nice visit that morning.

I really can't recall any of the details of their conversation, though I think he told Ernest he would like for him to come back and visit him again sometime.

After Ernest left, my dad told me that he wanted to write something, and he asked me to give him a piece of paper and a pen. Later in the day, about 5:30 or so, he started writing on the piece of paper. At the time, I observed him to be normal and mentally alert. He was a little bit tired at the time, and when I suggested that he stop worrying about writing anything, he got very upset and even cried a little bit and pleaded with me to help him get on with what he intended to do. At one point he did ask me to steady his hand a bit because it was shaking. When I did so, I observed only a few of the words he was writing, and I didn't really know what he was doing. When he finished, he folded the piece of paper and placed it on his bedside table. Sometime later, I observed his breathing to become somewhat forced, and I contacted the nurses' station to tell them to come check on him. From that point on, his condition seemed to change for the worse. During that evening, Ernest Potter came by for a few minutes, and he said, "I'm here like your dad asked." When Ernest left, I went outside and handed to him the piece of paper that my dad had been writing out, which I assumed to be either a loan to me or a letter to someone, and I might have even thought at that time that it was a will. I don't really recall telling Ernest that the paper was my dad's will or anything else I may have said to Ernest at the time, since I was so upset.

Shortly after Ernest left, my dad's condition got so much worse that I was forced to leave the room. The nurses and doctors were there for the rest of the evening, and shortly after 11:30 p.m., the same nurse who had spoken with me on the first date of my arrival, Pat Duffey, came outside to tell me that my father had suffered an additional stroke and had passed away as a result.

The next morning I went by to see Ernest Potter to thank him for his friendship and kindness extended to me and my father. It was at that time that Ernest gave me the will my father had written. I then observed that Ernest had written on the will that he was a witness to it, and I asked him why he had done that. Ernest told me that he thought that would make everything legal and that he knew that was what my dad wanted. I think Ernie Potter is a very good man, and I have kept in touch with him since that time.

/s/ James Warren
JAMES WARREN

SUBSCRIBED AND SWORN TO Before me by the said James Warren on this 25th day of January, current year.

/s/ Patricia A. McNulty
NOTARY PUBLIC
My Commission Expires at Death.

EXHIBITS

EXHIBIT 1

HAPPY VALLEY
NURSING HOME HOSPITAL
1500 LAMA LANE
HAPPY VALLEY, NOCONA
CLINICAL SURVEY

PATIENT: Warren, James D.   Room: 101
PHYSICIAN: A. Sandoval, M.D.   Dictated: 10/31/last year
ADMITTED: 10-28-XX
EXPIRED: 10-31-XX

ADMITTING DIAGNOSIS:

1) Hypertension
2) Cerebral Arteriosclerosis
3) RIO CVA

FINAL DIAGNOSIS: Left-sided Cerebrovascular Accident

HISTORY:
This 76-year-old white male was admitted Tuesday, October 28, at 9:45 a.m. with right-sided hemiparesis of one-hour duration. He had a history of transient ischemic attacks × 10 months and of hypertension × 6 years. Previously, he lived in the general population of the Home. This was his first admission to the Hospital since coming to the Home.

PHYSICAL FINDINGS:
Patient was agitated on admission. BLP was 160/112. P-108. R-24. There was marked weakness of the right side. Pupils were equal – left pupil demonstrated sluggish reaction to light. Patient was oriented to time, place, person. Carotid bruits were present – left and right. Blood work was within normal limits, except for a slightly elevated blood sugar of 140.

HOSPITAL COURSE:
Patient was started on Coumadin and Aldomet. Vital signs were stabilized and cerebral angiography was scheduled for November 1. On the evening of October 31, however, the patient began complaining of blurred vision and the staff reported a definite left facial weakness and difficulty with breathing. He became increasingly lethargic and vital signs became increasingly unstable. He expired at 11:35 p.m.

JDW

4250 Riverside Lane
Happy Valley, Nocona

May 26

Last Will and Testament

I, James Dale Warren, do hereby make this my Last Will and Testament. I revoke all prior wills, as it is my intent at this time to write my Last Will and Testament before I go on to my reward. Being of sound mind and sound body, I hereby leave to my devoted and faithful daughter, who has cared for me for many years, the interest and principal of my $100,000 savings account, and our family home at 4250 Riverside Lane. I also leave to Susan all of my other property of any kind, except that I leave to my grandchildren my old beagle, Cassandra, because I know they will continue to care for her.

James Dale Warren
Happy Valley, Nocona

HAPPY VALLEY NURSING HOME

❦

October 13

Dear Son,

Thanks for your phone call last night. It meant a lot to me to hear from you and to learn that you are not bitter about the fact that I could not be a father to you while you were growing up.

Your half-sister, Susan, has remarried recently, to a guy named Bill Gearhart. He is a stockbroker, not very successful, but enough to take care of Susan and the kids. I have been here in this Home since April, and I don't mind it too much, except I really miss watching Kim and James grow up. I love them like they were my own.

I have thought about your problem of needing a grub-stake to produce your new play. I have decided to find a way to help you. It would really make me feel wonderful if I could help you do something great in your life.

I really look forward to your next phone call and especially to your promised visit in the near future.

Dad

1500 Lama Lane

Happy Valley

Nocona

Please write me at:
James Warren
Room 13
1500 Lama Lane
Happy Valley Nursing Home

Oct 31

HAPPY
VALLEY
NURSING
HOME

🍎

This is my last will and I revoke all others. I am of sound mind but I am going to die. I leave all of my estate and property of any to my Dear son, Jim, because he needs $50,000 to start a new life except for Mary's jewelry and family china which I leave to Susan who is traveling with her husband.

James Warren

1500 Lama Lane

Happy Valley

Nocona

I, Ernest Potter, am a witness to this will.

October 31

Charge of the Court

LADIES AND GENTLEMEN OF THE JURY:

This case is submitted to you on special interrogatories consisting of specific questions about the facts, which you must answer from the evidence you have heard in this trial. You are the sole judges of the credibility of the witnesses and the weight to be given their testimony, but in matters of law, you must be governed by the instructions in this charge. I shall now give you additional instructions which you should carefully and strictly follow during your deliberations.

1   Do not let bias, prejudice, or sympathy play any part in your deliberations.
2   Since every answer that is required by the charge is important, no juror should state or consider that any required answer is not important.
3   You must not decide whom you think should win, and then try to answer the questions accordingly.
4   Certain words are used in this charge for which you are given a proper legal definition, and you are bound to accept the Court's definition in place of any other meaning.
5   There is no "Dead Man's Statute" in the state of Nocona, and thus you may consider in your deliberations whatever evidence the Court may have admitted, with any limiting instructions, pertaining to the decedent.
6   Answer with "Yes" or "No" unless otherwise instructed. A "Yes" answer must be based on a preponderance of the evidence. If you do not find that a preponderance of the evidence supports a "Yes" answer, then answer "No."
7   PREPONDERANCE OF THE EVIDENCE means the greater weight and degree of credible testimony or evidence introduced before you and admitted in this case.

INTERROGATORY NO. 1: Do you find from a preponderance of the evidence that at the time James Dale Warren, Deceased, executed the holographic will dated October 31, last year, introduced in evidence in this case, he had testamentary capacity?

> *Definition:* "Testamentary capacity." In connection with the foregoing interrogatory, you are instructed that, for a person to have "testamentary capacity," as that term is used in this charge, such person at the time of the execution of the will must have had sufficient mental ability to understand the business in which he was engaged, the effect of his act in making the *will*, the nature and extent of his property; he must have been able to know his next of kin and the natural objects of his bounty and their claims upon him; he must have memory sufficient to collect in his mind the elements of the business about to be transacted and to hold them long enough to perceive at least their obvious relation to each other and to be able to form a reasonable judgment as to them.

ANSWER TO INTERROGATORY NO. 1: $\overline{\text{Answer "Yes" or "No"}}$

INTERROGATORY NO. 2: Do you find from a preponderance of the evidence that at the time James Dale Warren executed the holographic will dated October 31, last year, introduced in evidence in this case, he was caused to do so under and by reason of the undue influence of Jim Warren?

> *Definition:* "Undue influence." In connection with the foregoing interrogatory, you are instructed that the term "undue influence" means such improper domination, constraint, or control of one person, exercised over the mind of another as to be sufficient to subvert and overthrow such other person's volition, so that the party influenced has been thereby induced to do what he would not have done had he been left to act freely and voluntarily. The influence must be such that the act so done represents a result of the exercise of such domination, constraint or control, rather than the will and expression of the party doing the act. Undue influence may be any fraudulent or designing means employed upon and with the maker of a will by which, under the circumstances and conditions by which such maker was surrounded, he could not well resist and which controlled his volition and induced him to do that which otherwise he would not have done.

ANSWER TO INTERROGATORY NO. 2:   _____
                                   Answer "Yes" or "No"

Glossary of terms and symbols

A. Terms

Throughout this book, we have introduced and used terms that embody concepts in the fields of evidence and logic. Many of the terms regularly used in discourse about the law of evidence are also employed in discourse about logic and the logic of proof, terms such as *relevance, material facts,* and *probative value.* Other terms are primarily used in the study of logic and may not be familiar even to those who have studied the law of evidence, terms such as *catenate inferences, cognitive competence, conjunction,* and *convergence.* Finally, there are terms that relate primarily to the study of proof in an adjudicative setting and have special meanings for those involved in that field, terms such as *theory of a case, story,* and *theme.*

The purpose of this glossary is to provide students with basic definitions of the main terms used in this book that may be unfamiliar. Most of these terms embody concepts that require careful analysis and elucidation. To the extent required, we have developed these concepts in the text. Some of these terms embody controversial concepts, and there may be disagreement about their precise meaning. For these, we have chosen the meaning that facilitates the points developed here and have simply stipulated that to be the meaning of the term as used in this book.

Students should bear in mind that, to serve its intended purpose, the definitions in this glossary must be concise and cannot fully develop the nuances and qualifications necessary to a full understanding of the concepts the terms express. As a reminder and further aid, we have parenthetically identified the pages where the more novel or difficult terms are discussed and developed in the text. Students may also wish to consult standard texts or treatises on the law of evidence for further amplification of some of the terms defined here.

Abductive reasoning.   A creative process of using known data to generate hypotheses to be tested by further investigation.

Accuracy.   Also termed *sensitivity.* An attribute of the credibility of certain kinds of tangible evidence such as those provided by sensing devices and tabled information.

Ancillary evidence. Evidence about other evidence and its probative strength; also termed *indirectly relevant evidence*. Such evidence acts either to increase or to reduce the strength of links in chains of reasoning set up by *directly relevant evidence* (q. v.).

Authenticity. An attribute of the credibility of tangible evidence referring to whether a tangible item is what it is represented to be.

Autoptic proference. Literally, evidence that will be perceived by the tribunal through one of its senses. Wigmore used the term for what is conventionally referred to as "real evidence," a term which he considered ambiguous. In this book it is used to include testimonial assertions the tribunal will hear, as well as other evidence it will perceive with its senses.

Bias. A term commonly used with reference to witnesses who provide testimonial evidence. The term usually refers to the extent to which a *witness's* interests, incentives, or stakes may influence what this witness observed or reported. There are several different kinds of bias that may influence a witness's observations, objectivity, and veracity.

Catenate inferences. A series of inferences forming a chain; inferences upon inferences.

Circumstantial evidence. Circumstantial evidence is evidence that makes the existence of a penultimate probandum more or less probable "indirectly," in that at least one further inferential step is involved. In legal usage sometimes contrasted loosely with testimonial evidence. Circumstantial evidence is the most common kind of evidence in legal proceedings. Subject to the rules of admissibility it can be relevant, valid, and of probative value. It is a common error to treat circumstantial evidence as inferior to testimonial or real evidence.

Cognitive competence. Ability to know and understand information on the basis of the general stock of knowledge in a given society. In the logic of proof, it is generally assumed that nearly all adult members of society are capable of drawing upon a shared common stock of knowledge and applying ordinary principles of practical reasoning.

Cognitive consensus. The idea that there is a generally shared "stock of knowledge" in a given society, commonly reflected by common sense generalizations or generally known facts of which a tribunal will take judicial notice or the like.

Combination. A logical process by which judgments about the probability that individual elements of a compound proposition are true are combined into a judgment about the probability that the compound proposition as a whole is true. Whether and by what process individual judgments may properly be combined is the subject of serious controversy and theoretical debate. Cf. Conjunction, Probability.

Conflicting evidence. Evidence about events that can occur jointly but which favor different probanda or propositions. For example, evidence about one event may favor proposition P while evidence about another event may favor proposition not-P.

Conjunction. The combination of judgments about the probability of individual facts in issue into a single judgment about the case as a whole. "The problem of conjunction" refers to the contested issue whether legal standards of proof apply to the ultimate probandum (a compound proposition) and the case as a whole or to individual penultimate probanda (material facts) separately.

Contradictory evidence. Evidence about two or more events that are mutually exclusive, i.e. they cannot occur jointly. For example, one evidence item says that event E occurred and another evidence item says that event E did not occur.

Convergence. Two inferences converge when they combine together to support or negate an interim or penultimate probandum.

Corroboration. Literally, strengthening, as when two witnesses independently testify to the truth of the same proposition (cf. convergence). The term is used in at least two senses: (1) to signify the production of an additional witness or two, duplicating the assertion of a prior witness; or (2) to signify the auxiliary evidential facts offered by a proponent to *negative the explanations* by which the opponent seeks to weaken the inference from some original evidentiary fact of the proponent. In the latter aspect, "corroboration" involves not a new logical process, but a new stage in the presentation of evidence.

Credential [of evidence]. A term used to describe a property of evidence that needs to be established or justified. Three major credentials of evidence are: relevance, credibility, and probative force.

Credibility. Concerns the extent to which an item of evidence or a source of evidence may be believed. On occasion, this term is wrongly equated with the term reliability [q.v.], which has a more restricted definition. As a credential of evidence, credibility or believability has several different attributes that depend upon the form of evidence, whether it is tangible or testimonial.

Credibility attributes [for tangible evidence]. These attributes are: authenticity, accuracy, and reliability.

Credibility attributes [for testimonial evidence]. These attributes are: veracity, objectivity, and observational sensitivity.

Deductive argument. The form of argument in which a major premise is applied to a minor premise to establish that a conclusion is valid. In evidential reasoning, the major premise may be a proposition of law or, more often, a generalization.

Direct evidence.   In legal usage the term is ambiguous: it is sometimes used in contrast with circumstantial evidence (q.v.) or with hearsay (q.v.) or with ancillary evidence, which is indirectly relevant (q.v.). In a narrow sense it refers to testimony from a witness who states that she actually saw, heard, or otherwise experienced a material fact in issue (e.g., "I saw X cause Y's death").

Directly relevant evidence.   Evidence is said to be directly relevant if a defensible chain of reasoning can be constructed that links this evidence with a major proposition whose proof is at issue.

Discovery.   This term is used in two different ways in applications in law. The first, called investigative discovery, refers to the evidence, hypotheses, and arguments generated by an attorney or other enquirer during fact investigation. The other, called legal discovery, refers to the legally sanctioned process of obtaining evidence from a usually unwilling opponent. In England the latter is now called "disclosure."

Eliminative induction.   A method of proof in which a variety of evidential tests are employed in an effort to eliminate alternative hypotheses being considered. The hypothesis that best resists our attempts to eliminate any hypothesis is the one that can be taken most seriously.

Epistemology.   A branch of philosophy concerning the acquisition of and validity of knowledge.

Evidence.   Any facts considered by the tribunal as data to persuade them to reach a reasoned belief on a probandum. The term is sometimes used to refer to evidential data or autoptic preferences and sometimes to refer to other facts taken as established for purposes of argument.

Evidence and events.   There is an important distinction to be made between evidence of some event and the event itself. Having evidence that an event occurred does not entail that this event did occur. What is at issue is the credibility of the evidence and its source(s).

Evidential data.   See autoptic preference.

Evidentiary fact.   See *factum probans.*

Fact.   Any event or act or condition of things, assumed (for the moment) as having happened or having existed.

Fact of consequence.   An important probandum. The term is slightly wider than material facts in that it refers to probanda undermining or reinforcing the credibility of evidence as well as to ultimate and penultimate probanda.

Facts in issue.   Material facts or facts constituting the elements of an ultimate probandum; *not* necessarily disputed facts, for some elements of an ultimate probandum may not be a matter of contention between the parties. "A fact-in-issue is a fact as to the correctness of which the tribunal, under the law of the case, must be persuaded" (J. Wigmore (1935) 7). Exceptionally, a fact in issue may be one of a set of jointly sufficient conditions rather than a necessary condition for success in a case: for example, one of a series of defenses, any one of which is sufficient to exonerate a defendant in a civil or criminal case (e.g., self-defense or insanity in a criminal case or fair comment or qualified privilege in a defamation action).

Factum probandum.   A proposition to be proved. See *probandum*; compare intermediate *probandum*, penultimate *probandum*, and ultimate *probandum*.

Factum probans.   Evidencing the proposition to be proved: A factual proposition offered as support for a further inferred proposition, i.e. a *factum probandum*.

Generalization.   A general proposition claimed to be true which is used implicitly or explicitly to argue that a conclusion has been established. All or almost all inductive arguments can be translated into syllogistic form by articulating as a universal the assumed generalization which provides the basis for the induction claimed.

Hearsay.   A statement, other than one made by the declarant while testifying at trial or hearing, offered in evidence to prove the truth of the matter asserted. Fed. R. Evid. 801(c).

Hypothesis.   A general proposition put forward as a possible explanation for known facts from which additional investigations can be planned to generate evidential data that will tend to strengthen or weaken the basis for accepting the proposition as the best or strongest explanation of the available data.

Inductive argument.   An argument that one proposition (taken as established), a *factum probans*, makes another proposition in the case, a *factum probandum*, more or less probable than it otherwise would be. The argument is frequently by analogy and almost always rests upon an assumed generalization upon whose acceptance the strength of the argument depends.

Inference.   "The process of thought, by which we reason from evidence toward proof ... " J. Wigmore (1935).

Inference upon inference.   See catenate inferences.

Interim *probandum*.   A proposition to be proved which itself will tend to support or negate, directly or indirectly, an ultimate *probandum* as part of a chain of inferences. Such a proposition is a *factum probandum* in relation to propositions

offered as supporting it and a *factum probans* in relation to propositions for
which it is offered as support.

Judicial notice.   "A judicially noticed fact must be one not subject to reasonable
dispute in that it is either (1) generally known within the territorial jurisdiction
of the trial court or (2) capable of accurate and ready determination by resort
to sources whose accuracy cannot reasonably be questioned." Fed. R. Evid.
201(a).

Marshaling.   Refers to the bringing together of thoughts and evidence during
fact investigation and argument construction. Having useful strategies for
marshaling thus helps advance the processes of fact investigation and of proof.

Marshaling magnets.   New hypotheses or probanda are frequently generated by
considering combinations of existing information. A marshaling "magnet" is a
metaphoric description of evidence marshaling operations that serve to attract
particular combinations of evidence from some collection of data or trifles and
that can assist in generating new hypotheses or probanda or that can open up
new lines of inquiry and evidence.

Material facts.   See ultimate *probandum*, facts in issue, and penultimate *probanda*.

Penultimate *probanda*.   Simple propositions, each of which state one element of
a crime or claim or defense that must be established in order for the proponent
to prevail. The penultimate *probanda* in a case can be derived from the ultimate
probandum or *probanda* for the case and represent the decomposing of a
compound proposition into simple propositions identifying each of its essential
components. For most purposes, each of the penultimate *probanda* is a material
fact or a fact in issue.

Probability.   "The word 'probable' as used in everyday discourse describes a
state of affairs which we do not know for certain to be the case, but which
we are well inclined to believe..." In its more technical usage, the term
"probability" denotes a quantitative measure of the uncertainty associated
with some unknown state of affairs – or, as it is technically called, "event."
(See Dawid, appendix.) Differing conceptions of probability are a matter of
considerable controversy and debate within statistics and the logic of proof.

Probandum.   Literally, a proposition to be proved. An ultimate *probandum* is
a proposition which must be proved to some specified degree by the party
asserting it in order to succeed in the case, i.e., the material facts or facts in
issue. See also *factum probandum*, interim *probandum*, penultimate *probanda*,
and ultimate *probandum*.

Probative force or value.   A term denoting a judgment about (a) the importance
of the fact of consequence to which proffered evidential data is relevant and (b) the

degree to which that data might alter the probability that the fact of consequence was or was not true. Probative value is the term usually employed in assessing the significance of specified evidential data for determining whether it should be admitted notwithstanding otherwise improper prejudicial effects the data may have. In contrast, "weight" is the term ordinarily employed in assessing the extent to which the whole of the evidence in a case establishes the ultimate *probandum* or *probanda* to the degree of certainty required by the applicable standard of proof.

Proof.   "The persuasive operation of the total mass of evidentiary facts, as to *a probandum*." (Wigmore (1937) 9.) See, further, Standard of proof.

Proposition.   A statement that is true or false, that can be affirmed or denied.

Quantitative rules.   Rules that require certain kinds of evidence to be produced in specified quantity (e.g., "corroborated").

Quantum of evidence.   The amount of evidence; see also quantitative rules.

Real evidence.   Typically, physical evidence presented to the fact-finder. See autoptic proference.

Redundancy.   Applied to evidence, this term refers to evidence that either says the same thing over again or does not add anything to what we already have. (In law, the term *cumulative* is often used with reference to redundant evidence.)

Relevance.   "Relevant evidence" means evidence having any tendency to make the existence of any fact that is of consequence to the determination of the action more probable or less probable than it would have been without the evidence. Fed. R. Evid. 401.

Reliability.   A reliable process is one that is repeatable or consistent. The term is usually applied to devices and tests of various kinds. This term is often used incorrectly as a synonym for the term *credibility* or *believability*, which involves other attributes.

Simple proposition.   A proposition that makes only one point: for example, "It was X who murdered Y" as contrasted with "X murdered Y." As a rule of thumb nearly all items on a key-list should be simple propositions.

Standard for decision.   The generic term for the standard that an official or functionary is required or expected to apply in respect of a given decision. For example, the standard that a prosecuting authority has to satisfy with respect to a decision to prosecute. Standards of proof are one species of standards for decision.

Standard of proof.   The degree of persuasion required for the proponent to establish a particular fact in issue (or, possibly, the case as a whole). The standard of proof in civil cases is typically "the preponderance of the evidence" or "the balance of probabilities." In criminal cases the prosecution has to satisfy the standard of "beyond reasonable doubt" in order to succeed. In some non-criminal cases, the standard of proof is said to be "clear and convincing." There is controversy as to whether the standard of proof applies independently to each fact in issue or, by conjunction, to the probability of the facts in issue in respect of the case as a whole (the problem of conjunction).

Story.   "A narrative of particular events arranged in a time sequence and forming a meaningful totality." *Rethinking* 223 (adapted from Ricoeur).

Substance-blind.   A term used to describe a particular way of categorizing forms and combinations of evidence without regard to its substance or content. Such a categorization is based on the inferential properties of evidence and not on its content.

Tangible evidence.   Evidence that can be directly examined by persons drawing conclusions to see what event(s) this evidence reveals. Examples include objects, documents, images, measurements, and charts.

Testimonial evidence.   Evidence provided by a human source to the evaluator of the evidence. Testimonial evidence about some event can be based on direct observations, secondhand reports from another source, or on the basis of opinion or inferences based on information about the occurrence of other events. In law: evidence given by a competent witness under oath or affirmation and in the presence of the tribunal.

Theme.   An element in an argument that is considered sufficiently important by the person presenting the argument to deserve emphasis by repetition.

Theory of a case.   An overall strategic argument concerning the case as a whole, typically used by an advocate or judge to structure the argument and guide choices on particular aspects of it.

Ultimate *probandum.*   The proposition of fact that the proponent (the party with the burden of proof) must establish or negate in order to prevail in the case. Viewing the rule of law that governs the case as a major premise, the ultimate *probandum* is the minor premise that, if all of its elements were proved, would compel the conclusion that its proponent urges. In a case in which the prosecution or a plaintiff alleges separate crimes or claims or in which a defendant alleges an affirmative defense upon which she has the burden of proof, there may be more than one ultimate probandum, i.e. multiple ultimate probanda.

Warrant.   A term used in argument construction to refer to the grounds or license for linking one proposition to another in a chain of reasoning. Warrants and their backing by ancillary evidence are said to form the "glue" holding an argument together. See also Generalization.

Weight.   See Probative force or value.

B. Symbols

The modified Wigmorean charting system or palette presented in this book requires only eight symbols. Five are likely to be required for any chart:

□   (1) the square for depicting testimonial assertions;

○   (2) the circle for depicting circumstantial evidence or inferred propositions;

<   (3) the open angle to identify an argument that provides an alternative explanation for an inference proposed by the other side;

◁   (4) a vertical triangle to identify an argument that corroborates a proposed inference;

→↑   (5) a line to indicate the "direction" of a proposed inferential relationship between or among propositions – vertical line indicates "tends to support"; horizontal lines indicate "tends to negate or weaken." The direction from evidential data to asserted inferences is always up, from bottom to top. Directional arrows are only occasionally necessary where the line standing alone might be misunderstood.

The nature of a judicial trial makes it necessary to have symbols to identify the kinds of evidential data or the source of the propositions the tribunal will be asked to take as the basis for the arguments advanced. Wigmore specified two, and we have found a third useful:

∞   (6) an infinity symbol to identify testimonial assertions that the fact-finders will hear or other autoptic preferences they will perceive with their other senses;

¶   (7) a paragraph symbol to identify facts the tribunal will judicially notice or otherwise accept without evidential support; and

G   (8) the letter "G" to denote a generalization that is likely to play a significant role in an argument in a case, but that is not a proposition that will be supported by evidence or that the tribunal will be formally asked to notice judicially.

References

Abbott, W. F. and J. Ball (eds.) 1999, *A Handbook of Jury Research*, Philadelphia: ALI/ABA.

Abimbola, K. 2002, "Questions and Answers: The Logic of Preliminary Fact Investigation," 29 J. of L. and Society 533.

Abramowitz, Elkan 1986, "Theory and Theme of the Case" in D. L. Rumsey (ed.), *Master Advocates' Handbook*.

Acorn, A. E. 1991, "Similar Fact Evidence and the Principle of Inductive Reasoning: Making Sense," 11 OJLS 63.

Amadiume, I. and A.-N. Abdullahi (eds.) 2000, *The Politics of Memory: Truth, Healing and Social Justice*, London: Zed Books.

Anderson, Terence 1991, "Refocusing the New Evidence Scholarship," 13 Cardozo L. Rev. 783.

Anderson, Terence 1999, "On Generalizations I: A Preliminary Exploration," 40 South Texas L. Rev. 455.

Anderson, Terence 1999, "The Netherlands Criminal Justice System: An Audit Model of Decision-Making" in Malsch and Nijboer (eds.), *Complex Cases*.

Anderson, Terence and Mark Geller 2003, "The Last Wedge," "Wigmore Meets the 'Last Wedge,'" "Wigmorean Analysis and the Survival of Cuneiform" in Twining and Hampsher-Monk (eds.), Chs. 3–5.

Anderson, Terence and William Twining 1998, *Analysis of Evidence*, Evanston: Northwestern University Press.

Bailey, James F. III and Oscar M. Trelles II 1980, *The Federal Rules of Evidence: Legislative Histories and Related Documents*, Buffalo, NY: Hein.

Bambrough, R. (ed.) 1974, *Wisdom: Twelve Essays*, Oxford: Blackwell.

Baring-Gould, William S. 1967, *The Annotated Sherlock Holmes*. New York: Clarkson Potter.

Benet, Stephen Vincent 1961, *John Brown's Body, as staged at the Yale Drama School and Off-Broadway, under the direction of Curtis Canfield*, New York Dramatists Play Service.

Bennett, P. 1986, in D. L. Rumsey (ed.), *Master Advocates' Handbook*.

Bennett, W. Lance and M. Feldman 1981, *Reconstructing Reality in the Courtroom*, New Brunswick, NJ: Rutgers University Press.

Bentham, Jeremy 1825, *A Treatise on Judicial Evidence* (trs. Anon from E. Dumont, *Traité des Preuves Judiciaires*).

Bentham, Jeremy 1827, *Rationale of Judicial Evidence* (J. S. Mill ed.), London: Hunt and Clarke.

Bentham, Jeremy 1837–43, *An Introductory View of the Rationale of the Law of Evidence for Use by Non-lawyers as well as Lawyers* (VI *Works* 1–187), Bowring edition, Originally edited by James Mill circa 1810.

Bienen, L. 1983, "A Question of Credibility: John Henry Wigmore's Use of Scientific Evidence in Section 924A of the Treatise on Evidence," 9 Cal. W. L. Rev. 235.

Binder, David A. and Paul Bergman 1984, *Fact Investigation: from Hypothesis to Proof*, St. Paul, Minn.: West.

Burrill, Alexander M. 1868, *A Treatise on Circumstantial Evidence*, New York.

Carnap, R. 1962, *The Logical Foundations of Probability*, 2nd edn, Chicago: University of Chicago Press.

Cohen, L. Jonathan 1977, *The Probable and the Provable*, Oxford: Oxford University Press.

Cohen, L. Jonathan 1980, "The Logic of Proof," Criminal L. Rev. 91.

Cohen, L. Jonathan 1983, "Freedom of Proof," in W. Twining (ed.), *Facts in Law*, Wiesbaden: Franz Steiner Verlag.

Cross, Sir Rupert 1979, *Cross on Evidence*, 5th edn, London: Butterworths.

Crown Prosecution Service 2003, Code for Prosecutors, <www.cps.gov.uk>.

Damaska, Mirjan R. 1986, *The Faces of Justice and State Authority: A Comparative Approach to the Legal Process*, New Haven: Yale University Press.

Damaska, Mirjan R. 1997, *Evidence Law Adrift*, New Haven: Yale University Press.

Daston, L. 1988, *Classical Probability in the Enlightenment*, Princeton, N.J.: Princeton University Press.

Davis, John W. 1940, "The Argument of an Appeal," reprinted in *Jurisprudence in Action*, 1953, New York: Baker, Voorhis and Co, 181.

Dawid, A. P. 2002, "Bayes's Theorem and Weighing Evidence by Juries," Proceedings of the British Academy 113, 71–90.

Dawid, A. P. 2005, "Statistics and Law," (forthcoming).

Dawid, A. P., J. Mortera, V. L. Pascali, and D. W. van Boxel 2002, "Probabilistic Expert Systems for Forensic Inference from Genetic Markers," Scandinavian Journal of Statistics 29, 577–95.

Dennis, Ian H. 2004, *The Law of Evidence*, 3rd edn, London: Sweet & Maxwell.

Dingley, Astrid 1999, "The Ballpoint Case: A Wigmorean Analysis," in Malsch and Nijboer (eds.), *Complex Cases*, Ch. 9.

Director of the Administrative Office of the United States Courts, Annual Reports (Washington D.C.).

Doyle, Arthur Conan 1888, *A Study in Scarlet*, London: Ward Lock.

Doyle, Arthur Conan 1893, "Silver Blaze," in *The Memoirs of Sherlock Holmes*, London: George Newnes.

Doyle, Arthur Conan 1993, *The Memoirs of Sherlock Holmes*, Oxford: Oxford University Press.

Eco, U and Sebeok, T. 1983, *The Sign of Three: Dupin, Holmes, Peirce*, Bloomington, Ind.: Indiana University Press.

Eggleston, Sir Richard 1983, *Evidence, Proof and Probability*, 2nd edn, London: Weidenfeld and Nicolson.

Ekelof, P. O. 1964, "Free Evaluation of Evidence," 8 Scandinavian Studies in Law 47.

Feteris, Eveline 1999, "What Went Wrong in the Ball-point Case?" in Malsch and Nijboer (eds.), *Complex Cases*, Ch. 8.

Finklestein, Michael O. and William B. Fairley 1970, "A Bayesian Approach to Identification Evidence," 83 Harvard L. Rev. 489.

Fisher, George 2002, *Evidence*, New York: Foundation Press.

Frankfurter, Felix 1927, *The Case of Sacco and Vanzetti*, Boston: Little, Brown.

Friedman, R. 1998, *The New Wigmore: A Treatise on Evidence*, New York: Aspen Law and Business.

Gilbert, Sir Jeffrey 1754, *The Law of Evidence*, Dublin: P. Byrne.

Goldberg, Jeffrey 2003, "The Unknown: The CIA and the Pentagon Take on Al Qaeda and Iraq," The New Yorker, Feb. 10, 40–47.

Graham, Kenneth W. Jr. 1983, "The Practice of Progressive Proceduralism," 61 Texas L. Rev. 829.

Graham, Kenneth W. Jr. 1987, "'There'll Always be an England': the Instrumental Ideology of Evidence," 85 Michigan L. Rev. 1204.

Greenleaf, Simon 1842, *A Treatise on the Law of Evidence*, Boston: Little, Brown.

Haack, Susan 1993, *Evidence and Inquiry: Towards Reconstruction in Epistemology*, Cambridge, Mass.: Blackwell.

Haack, Susan 1996, *Deviant Logic, Fuzzy Logic*, Chicago: University of Chicago Press.

Haack, Susan 1998, *Manifesto of a Passionate Moderate*, Chicago: University of Chicago Press.

Haack, Susan 2003, *Defending Science Within Reason*, New York: Prometheus Books.

Haack, Susan 2004, "Trials and Tribulations: Science in the Courts," 17 Ratio Juris.

Hacking, Ian 1975, *The Emergence of Probability: A Philosophical Study of Early Ideas about Probability, Induction, and Statistical Inference*, Cambridge: Cambridge University Press.

Jacob, Joseph 2001, *Civil Litigation Practice and Procedure in a Shifting Culture*, London: Emis Publishing.

Jesse, F. Tennyson 1934/1979, *A Pin to See the Peepshow*, London: Virago.

Jevons, W. Stanley 1877, *The Principles of Science: A Treatise on Logic and Scientific Method*, 2nd edn, New York: Macmillan.

Joughin, Louis and Edmund Morgan 1948/1978, *The Legacy of Sacco and Vanzetti*, Princeton: Princeton University Press.

Kadane, Joseph B. and David A. Schum 1996, *A Probabilistic Analysis of the Sacco and Vanzetti Evidence*, New York: J. Wiley.

Kafka, Franz 1995, *The Complete Stories* (ed. N. N. Glazer), New York: Schocken Books.

Kainen, Jame L. 1992, "The impeachment exception to the exclusionary rules: policies, principles, and politics", 44 Stanford L. Rev. 1301.

Kaye, David 1979, "The Paradox of the Gate-Crasher and Other Stories," Arizona State L. J. 101.

Kemelman, Harry 1947, "The Nine Mile Walk," *Ellery Queen Mystery Magazine* 41.

Keynes, J. M. 1921, *A Treatise on Probability*, London: Macmillan.

Kolgomorov, A. N. 1933, *Foundations of the Theory of Probability*, New York: Chelsea Publishing (1955 Reprint).

Krog, A. 1999, *Country of My Skull*, London: Vintage.

LaFave, Wayne R., Jerold H. Israel, and Nancy J. King (eds.) 2004, *Criminal Procedure*, 4th edn, St. Paul, Minn.: West.

Leary, Richard 2003, "UK National Intelligence Model and FLINTS," Int. J. Police Science and Management.

Lempert, Richard O. 1977, "Modeling Relevance," 75 Michigan L. Rev. 1021.

Lempert, Richard 2001, "The Economic Analysis of Evidence Law: Common Sense on Stilts," 87 Virginia L. Rev. 1619.

Levin, Leo (ed.) 1956, *Evidence and the Behavioral Sciences*, Mimeo, University of Pennsylvania Law School.

Levin, Leo 1956, "Persuading the Jury with Facts Not in Evidence: The Fiction-Science Spectrum," 105 U. Pennsylvania L. Rev. 139.

Llewellyn, Karl N. 1936, "On Warranty of Quality, and Society," 36 Columbia L. Rev 699.

Llewellyn, Karl N. 1941, "Theory of Legal 'Science,'" 20 N. Carolina L. Rev 1.

Llewellyn, Karl N. 1950, *Law in Our Society* (unpublished, University of Chicago Law School).

Llewellyn, Karl N. 1960, *The Common Law Tradition: Deciding Appeals*, Boston: Little, Brown.

Llewellyn, Karl N. 1962, *Jurisprudence: Realism in Theory and Practice*, Chicago: University of Chicago Press.

Malsch, M. and J. F. Nijboer (eds.) 1999, *Complex Cases: Perspectives on the Netherlands Criminal Justice System*, Amsterdam: Thela Thesis.

Mauet, Thomas A. 2005, *Trials: Strategy, Skills, and the New Powers of Persuasion*, New York: Aspen.

McCormick, Charles T. 1999, *McCormick on Evidence*, 5th edn, John W. Strong et al. (eds.), St Paul, Minn.: West.

McNamara, Philip 1986, "The Canons of Evidence: Rules of Exclusion or Rules of Use?" 10 Adelaide L. Rev. 341.

Michael, Jerome and Herbert Wechsler 1940, *Criminal Law and its Administration*, Chicago: Foundation Press.

Moore, Charles C. 1908, *A Treatise on Facts or the Weight and Value of Evidence*, Northport, NY: Edward Thompson.

Morgan, Elaine, "Preface" in F. Tennyson Jesse, *A Pin to See the Peepshow*, London; Virago.

Murphy, Peter 1999, *Evidence, Proof and Facts: A Book of Sources*, Oxford: Oxford University Press.

Murphy, Peter W. 2001, "Teaching Evidence, Proof, and Facts: Providing a Background in Factual Analysis and Case Evaluation," 51 J. Legal Ed. 568.

Nagler, A. M. 1952, *Sources of Theatrical History*, New York: Theatre Annual.

National Commission on Terrorist Attacks upon the United States 2004, *The 9/11 Commission Report: Final Report of the National Commission on Terrorist Attacks upon the United States*, New York: W. W. Norton.

Nesson, Charles 1979, "Reasonable Doubt and Permissive Inferences: The Value of Complexity," 92 Harv. L. Rev. 1187.

Nicolson, Donald 1994, "Truth, Reason and Justice: Epistemology and Politics in Evidence Discourse," 57 Modern L. Rev. 726.

Nino, C. S. 1996, *Radical Evil on Trial*, New Haven: Yale University Press.

Oldroyd, D. 1986, *The Arch of Knowledge: An Introductory Study of the History and Philosophy and Methodology of Science*, New York: Methuen.

Palmer, Andrew 2003, *Proof and the Preparation of Trials*, Pyrmont, NSW: LawBook Co.

Pardo, Michael S. 2000, "Judicial Proof, Evidence and Pragmatic Meaning: Toward Evidentiary Holism," 95 Northwestern University L. Rev. 399.

Park, Roger C. 2001, "Grand Perspectives on Evidence Law," 87 Virginia L. Rev. 2055.

Peirce, C. S. 1903, "Perceptual Judgments," in J. Buchler (ed.), *Philosophical Writings of Peirce*, New York: Dover 1955.

Pennington, Nancy and Reid Hastie 1993, "The Story Model for Juror Decision Making," in Reid Hastie (ed.), *Inside the Juror: The Psychology of Juror Decision Making*, Cambridge: Cambridge University Press.

Pollock, Sir F. 1899, Review of Thayer (1898) 15 L.Q.R. 86.

Popper, K. 1968, *The Logic of Scientific Discovery*, New York: Harper Torchbooks.

Posner, Richard 1999, "An Economic Approach to the Law of Evidence," 51 Stanford L. Rev. 1477.

Rawls, John 1987, "The Idea of an Overlapping Consensus," 7 Oxford J. Legal Studies 1.

Ricoeur, Paul 1981, *Hermeneutics and the Human Sciences: Essays on Language, Action, and Interpretation*, New York: Cambridge University Press.

Rimmon-Kenan, S. 1983, *Narrative Fiction: Contemporary Poetics*, New York: Methuen.

Roberts, Paul 2002, "Rethinking the Law of Evidence: A Twenty-first Century Agenda for Teaching and Research," 55 Current Legal Problems 297.

Roberts, Paul and Adrian Zuckerman 2004, *Criminal Evidence*, Oxford: Oxford University Press.

Robertson, Bernard 1990, "John Henry Wigmore and Arthur Allan Thomas: an Example of Wigmorian Analysis," 20 Victoria University of Wellington L. Rev. 181.

Rumsey, D. Lake (ed.) 1986, *The Master Advocate's Handbook*, St. Paul, Minn.: NITA.

Schmalleger, Frank 1996, *Trial of the Century: People of the State of California v. Orenthal James Simpson*, Upper Saddle River, NJ: Prentice Hall.

Schum, David 1986, "Probability and the Processes of Discovery, Proof and Choice," 66 Boston U. L. Rev. 830.

Schum, David 1987, *Evidence and Inference for the Intelligence Analyst*, Lanham, Md.: University of America Press.

Schum, David 1992, "Hearsay from a Layperson," 14 Cardozo L. Rev. 1.

Schum, David 1994, *The Evidential Foundations of Probabilistic Reasoning*, New York: J. Wiley.

Schum, David 1999, "Marshaling Thoughts and Evidence during Fact Investigation," 40 S. Texas L. Rev. 401.

Schum, David and Peter Tillers 1990, A Technical Note on Computer-assisted Wigmorean Argument Structuring (Report no 90-1 under NSF Grant SES 87043877).

Shafer, G. 1976, *A Mathematical Theory of Evidence*, Princeton, NJ: Princeton University Press.

Shapiro, Barbara J. 1982, *Probability and Certainty in Seventeenth-Century England*, Princeton, NJ: Princeton University Press.

Shapiro, Barbara J. 1991, *Beyond Reasonable Doubt and Probable Cause: Historical Perspectives on the Anglo-American Law of Evidence*, Berkeley, Cal.: University of California Press.

Sidgwick, Alfred 1884, *Fallacies. A View of Logic from the Practical Side*, New York: D. Appleton.

Siegel, Michael 1994, "A Pragmatic Critique of Modern Evidence Scholarship," 88 Northwestern U. L. Rev. 995.

Skryms, Brian 1986, *Choice and Chance: An Introduction to Inductive Logic*, 3rd edn, Belmont, Cal.: Wadsworth.

Stein, Alex 2005, *Foundations of Evidence* (forthcoming).

Thayer, J. B. 1898, *A Preliminary Treatise on Evidence at the Common Law*, Boston: Little, Brown.

Tillers, Peter 1983, "Modern Theories of Relevancy," from *Wigmore on Evidence*, 1-1A, Tillers Revision, Boston: Little, Brown.

Tillers, Peter (ed.) 1991, "Decision and Inference in Litigation" (Symposium), 13 Cardozo L. Rev. 253–1079.

Tillers, Peter and Eric Green 1986, "Symposium: Probability and Inference in the Law of Evidence," 66 Boston University L. Rev. 377–952.

Tillers, Peter and Eric Green 1988, *Probability and Inference in the Law of Evidence: The Limits and Uses of Bayesianism*, Dordrecht, NL: Kluwer.

Tillers, Peter and David Schum 1988, "Charting New Territory in Judicial Proof: Beyond Wigmore," 9 Cardozo L. Rev. 907.

Tillers, Peter and David Schum 1991, "A Theory of Preliminary Fact Investigation," 24 U. C. Davis L. Rev. 931.

Toulmin, S. 1964, *The Uses of Argument*, Cambridge: Cambridge University Press.

Tribe, Laurence H. 1971, "Trial by Mathematics: Precision and Ritual in the Legal Process," 84 Harvard L. Rev. 1329.

Twining, William 1973, *Karl Llewellyn and the Realist Movement*, London: Weidenfeld and Nicolson.

Twining, William 1980, "Debating Probabilities," U Liverpool L. Rev. 51.

Twining, William (ed.) 1982, *Facts in Law*, Wiesbaden: Franz Steiner Verlag.

Twining, William 1985, *Theories of Evidence: Bentham and Wigmore*, London: Weidenfeld & Nicolson.

Twining, William 1988, "Hot Air in the Redwoods," 86 Michigan L. Rev. 1523.

Twining, William 1994, *Rethinking Evidence: Exploratory Essays*, Evanston, Ill.: Northwestern University Press.

Twining, William 1997, "Civilians Don't Try: A Comment on Mirjan Damaska's 'Rational and Irrational Proof Revisited,'" 5 Cardozo J. of Int. and Comp. L. 69.

Twining, William 1997, "Freedom of Proof and the Reform of Criminal Evidence," 31 Israel L. Rev. 439.

Twining, William 1997, "Recent Trends in Evidence Scholarship," in J. F. Nijboer and J. M. Reijntjes (eds.), *Proceedings of the First World Conference on New Trends in Criminal Investigation and Evidence*, Lelystad: Koninklijke Vermande, 13–22.

Twining, William 1999, "Narrative and Generalizations in Argumentation about Questions of Fact," 40 South Texas L. Rev. 351.

Twining, William 2002, *The Great Juristic Bazaar*, Aldershot: Ashgate/Darmouth.

Twining, William 2002, "The Ratio Decidendi of the Parable of the Prodigal Son" in *The Great Juristic Bazaar*, Ch. 16.

Twining, William 2003, "Evidence as a Multi-disciplinary Subject," 2 Law, Probability and Risk 91.

Twining, William 2005, "Taking Facts Seriously – Again" (forthcoming).

Twining, William and Iain Hampsher-Monk (eds.) 2003, *Evidence and Inference in History and Law: Interdisciplinary Dialogues*, Evanston, Ill.: Northwestern University Press.

Twining, William and David Miers 1999, *How to Do Things with Rules: A Primer of Interpretation*, 4th edn, London: Butterworths.

Wagenaar, W. A., P. J. Van Koppen, and H. F. M. Crombag 1993, *Anchored Narratives: The Psychology of Criminal Evidence*, New York, NY: St. Martin's Press.

Walton, Douglas 1989, *Informal Logic: a Handbook of Critical Argumentation*, New York: Cambridge University Press.

Walton, Douglas 2002, *Legal Argumentation and Evidence*, University Park, Pa.: State University of Pennsylvania Press.

Watson, Eric (ed.) 1915, *The Trial of George Joseph Smith*, London and Edinburgh.

Watson, Thomas J. and Peter Petre 1990, *Father, Son and Co.: My Life at IBM and Beyond*, New York: Bantam Books.

Weis, René 2001, *Criminal Justice: The True Story of Edith Thompson*, London: Penguin.

White, James B. 1985, *Heracles' Bow*, Madison: University of Wisconsin Press.

Whitehead, Alfred North 1939, *An Introduction to Mathematics*, New York: H. Holt.

Wigmore, John Henry 1913, "The Problem of Proof," 8 Illinois L. Rev. 77.

Wigmore, John Henry 1913, 1988, *The Principles of Judicial Proof: As Given by Logic, Psychology, and General Experience, and Illustrated in Judicial Trials*, Littleton, Colorado: F. B. Rothman.

Wigmore, John Henry 1935, *A Students' Textbook of the Law of Evidence*, Chicago: The Foundation Press, Inc.

Wigmore, John Henry 1937, *The Science of Judicial Proof, as Given by Logic, Psychology, and General Experience and Illustrated in Judicial Trials*, 3rd edn, Boston: Little, Brown.

Wigmore, John Henry 1940, *A Treatise on the Anglo-American System of Evidence in Trials at Common Law*, 2nd edn, Boston: Little, Brown.

Williams, Glanville 1979, "The Mathematics of Proof I & II," Crim. L. Rev. 297, 340.

Williams, Glanville 1980, "A Short Rejoinder," Crim. L. Rev. 103.

Wisdom, John 1965, *Other Minds*, 2nd edn, Oxford: Blackwell.

Woolf, Lord H. 1996, *Access to Justice* (Final Report), London: HMSO.

Wright, Charles A. 1998, *Federal Practice and Procedure*, St. Paul, Minn.: West.

Young, Filson 1951, *Trial of Frederick Bywaters and Edith Thompson*, 2nd edn, Edinburgh and London: W. Hodge & Company, Ltd.

Zadeh, L. 1965, "Fuzzy Sets," 8 Information and Control 338.

Zander, Michael 2003, *Cases and Materials on the English Legal System*, 9th edn, London: LexisNexis UK.

Zangwill, Israel 1895, *The Big Bow Mystery*, Chicago: Rand, McNally.

Zuckerman, Adrian A. S. 1986, "Law, Fact or Justice?" 66 Boston U. L. Rev. 487.

Index